Frederick County Virginia

Marriage Bonds 1773-1850

Joan D. Hackett and Rebecca H. Good

HERITAGE BOOKS
2006

HERITAGE BOOKS
AN IMPRINT OF HERITAGE BOOKS, INC.

Books, CDs, and more—Worldwide

For our listing of thousands of titles see our website
at
www.HeritageBooks.com

Published 2006 by
HERITAGE BOOKS, INC.
Publishing Division
65 East Main Street
Westminster, Maryland 21157-5026

Copyright © 1992 Joan D. Hackett and Rebecca H. Good

Other books by the authors:
*Marriage Records of Warren County, Virginia, 1836-1853,
Including Marriage Bonds and Minister's Returns*

Other books by Rebecca H. Good:
Finding Your People in the Shenandoah Valley of Virginia, Fourth Edition
Rebecca H. Good and Rebecca A. Ebert

All rights reserved. No part of this book may be reproduced or transmitted in any form or by any means, electronic or mechanical, including photocopying, recording or by any information storage and retrieval system without written permission from the author, except for the inclusion of brief quotations in a review.

International Standard Book Number: 978-1-55613-674-9

CONTENTS

Preface..v

Frederick County, Virginia,
Marriage Bonds...1

Index..288

PREFACE

The original marriage bonds of Frederick County, Virginia, are in storage at the Frederick County Courthouse at Winchester. Due to their fragile condition, they are not available to the public. A couple of versions of the Frederick County Marriage Register No. 1 have been published, but the bonds in their totality have never been abstracted.

The marriage register, which covers the years 1772 through 1850, does not contain all the intended marriages as reflected by the bonds. In some instances, where no minister's return was present, it is possible that no marriage took place. However, loss of records and hindrances to travel and communication undoubtedly account for the lack of some ministers' returns. Most genealogical authorities accept the bond as proof where no information to the contrary has been presented. The marriage register itself contains a number of bonds for which no minister's return was recorded, so it must be considered that much valid information was not entered into the record.

We present this abstract with the hope that the information contained herein will expand the field of knowledge pertaining to early Frederick County families. It is not our intention to replace the published abstracts of the register, but merely to supplement them. To provide a wider view of family connections, we have included a complete index, naming parents and bondsman as well as the principals in the marriage. In most cases, the parent acted as bondsman.

The original bonds from 1772 through 1850 were photocopied some years ago by the Church of Jesus Christ of Latter Day Saints. These photocopies, consisting of three microfilm rolls, are available on interlibrary loan from the Virginia State Archives. The initial transcript of this work was made by Joan D. Hackett from the microfilm copies. With the kind permission of Mr. George B. Whitacre, Clerk of the Circuit Court of Frederick County, Rebecca H. Good examined the originals and made corrections and additions to the transcript. When the spelling of the name in the body of the bond differed from the signature at the end of the bond, the spelling found in the signature was used. When persons signed in the German script, it is so noted.

The form of the original bond, which was used throughout Virginia in this period, was as follows:

Know all men by these presents, That we

are held and firmly bound unto
    Governor of Virginia, in the just and full sum of one hundred and fifty dollars, to which payment well and truly to be made, to the said Governor or his successors, we bind ourselves, our and each of our heirs, executors and administrators, jointly and severally, firmly by these presents. Sealed with our seals, and dated this
    day of

The condition of the above Obligation is such, that whereas there is a Marriage shortly intended to be solemnized between

now, if there be no lawful cause to obstruct the said Marriage, then the above Obligation to be valid, otherwise to remian in full force and virtue.

Signed, sealed and delivered
    in the presence of

    The name of the Governor and of the groom and his bondsman were entered into the top spaces of the bond, and the name of the groom and the bride were entered into the space provided for them. Finally, both the groom and the bondsman signed at the end of the document. Spellings were often inconsistent throughout the document.

The purpose of the bond was to indemnify the Commonwealth against any trouble or expense that might be incurred should the parties give false information as to their eligibility to marry.

FREDERICK COUNTY, VIRGINIA, MARRIAGE BONDS

Bonds Dated 1773 to 15 Jan 1811

1 Jan 177___ Morgan & Sarah Smith. Bondsman, Edmund Taylor. (Bond fragmented, partly illegible)
19 Jan 1773 Consent Only. "Ples to grant Mr. Morgan Alexander marrig lisans to my Daughter as it is agreabel to me and you will oblig ..." (one word obscured). Addressed to "the Clerk of Frederick Conte" and signed "Humble sarvant Ed Snickers."
7 Sep 1773 Richard Roach & Sarah Lindsey, daughter of Edmond & Mary Lindsey. Bondsman, Jacob Lindsey. Consent in writing by bride's parents, dated 6 Sep 1773, found loose in Bond Book
15 Oct 1773 John Emmett & Mary McDrum. Bondsman, John Nisewanger, witness John Skelding
1 Apr 1774 Robert Wood and Comfort Welsh, infant under 21 of Parish of Frederick. Bondsman, James Wood. Thos Welsh of province of Maryland gave consent 21 Mar 1774 that his daughter Comfort marry Robert Wood. Witness, Rachael Scott, Elizabeth Welsh, Mathew Glen, Allen McDonald
21 Jul 1774 Thomas Reynolds & Mary Smith. Bondsman, William Clancy
13 Aug 1774 Peter Catlett & Mary Bell, daughter of John Bell who cosnents in writing. George Bell, son of John Bell, Bondsman. John Bell asked that his friend Peter Catlett be given license to wed
31 Aug 1776 Jacob Kiger & Mary Overaker, spinster. Bondsman, George Kiger
7 Mar 1777 Philip Clayton & Mildred Dixon, spinster. Bondsman, Thos Moore Jnr
27 Jun 1777 Edward Smith & Elizabeth Bush, daughter of Philip Bush. Bondsman, John Cox
28 Jul 1777 Peter Wolfe & Anne Cornwell. Bondsman, Jeremiah Garner
18 Oct 1777 John Jones & Eleanor Alexander, widow. Bondsman, Robert Boyce

4 Sep 1777 Jonathan Jenkins & Ann Hog, spinster. Bondsman, Trystram Ewing

no date. Ja Ay?? Berry requested that license be granted to John Humphries to wed (name not given) Consent only

2 Sep 1788? (year blotted out) Jesse McFerson & Nancy Ash, spinster. Bondsman, Levin Dorsey

2 Sep 1788 Joseph Caldwell & Mary Griffith. Bondsman, Abraham Taylor

3 Sep 1788 Lewis Barnett & Mary Iles. Bondsman, Joseph Adams

5 Sep 1788 Aron Oglisby & Susannah Emmonds. Bondsman, Isaiah Ogleslbee

20 Sep 1788 John Newland & Mary Waer. Bondsman, Joseph Weer

24 Sep 1788 James Cockran & Mary Hogans. Bondsman, Thomas Eagan

11 Oct 1788 James Barron & Hannah Brown. Bondsman, John Walters

15 Oct 1788 Agus (Agur?) T. Furman & Elennor Stephens, spinster. Bondsman, David Holmes

18 Oct 1788 Benjamin Holzenpeler & Margaret Wax, spinster. Bondsman, Henry Wax. Groom and bondsman sign in German

18 Oct 1788 Michael Mauck & Barbara Kuser, spinster. Bondsman Mathias Mauck

18 Oct 1788 Thomas Cooper & Sarah Livingston. Bondsman, Thomas Bodkin

21 Oct 1788 John Saunders & Charity Cole, spinster. Bondsman, Daniel Cole

23 Oct 1788 Richard Lee & Ann Green, spinster. Bondsman, George Allen

24 Oct 1788 Thomas Haller & Ruth Henderson. Bondsman, Peter Kehoe

7 Jun 1792 William Jacobs & Jemima Millikin. Consent by Eliza Millikin, mother of bride. Bondsman, John Jones; witnesses, Samuel Dixon, Gasper Minick. Repaired with tape

2 Oct 1792 John Wimer & Ann Wharf. Bondsman, Michael Humble

Dec 17?? Joseph Holmes? (Hotmic?) & Elvia ???. Bondsman, Frederick Conrad Jr

20 Mar 1793 John Lyles & Sarah Glass. Bondsman, Robert Glass

21 Mar 1793 Daniel Freestone, "batchelor," & Lydia Decker, spinster. Bondsman, Henry Decker

26 Mar 1793 Elijah Littler & Margaret Williams, daughter of Barnett Williams, who consents in writing. Bondsman, Saml Littler

27 Mar 1793 John Parker, "batchelor," & Hannah Millner, spinster, daughter of John Millner, who consents in writing. Bondsman, John Jackson. John Jackson & John Ball witness John Millner's signature.

2 Apr 1793 Laurence Owen Blakemore & Mary Wilson. Bondsman, James Hickman

9 Apr 1793 Spencer Sharp & Nancy Arnold, of age, who writes her own consent. Bondsman, James Strother

10 Apr 1793 Thomas McClun & Elizabeth Bailey. Bondsman, John Barrow

11 Apr 1793 Peter Cooly & Sarah Adamson. Bondsman, John Reynolds, who signs in German

12 Apr 1793 John Malony & Elizabeth Keys, probably 24 years of age. John Morgan testified as to her age. Bondsman, John Morgan

13 Apr 1793 Baily Bishop & Arianna Spurrier. Bondsman, Elisha Spurrier

20 Apr 1793 James Flaugherty, of age, & Jenny Graham, of age. Bondsman, James Compton

24 Apr 1793 Stephen Way & Mary Richardson, daughter of Samuel Richardson, the bondsman

25 Apr 1793 Allen Rea & Eleanor (Nelley) Fisher. Consent in writing by Susana Fisher. Witnesses to Susana's signature were Luis Fisher, John Rea, & Joseph Rea. Bondsman, John Rea

25 Apr 1793 Fredk Conrad Jr & Frances Thruston. Bondsman, David Holmes

29 Apr 1793 Thomas Brownfield & Elizabeth Fisher. Bondsman, William Adams? & Barak Fisher

29 Apr 1793 Edward Mercer & Mary Dinah Steer, about 25, niece of Joseph Steer & Grace Steer. Bondsman, Thomas Babb

30 Apr 1793 Job Buckley & Susanna Newcomb, over 21, daughter of Susanna Newcomb, who consents in writing. Bondsman, James Simpson

4 May 1793 Jonathan Smith & Lydia Kecheval. Bondsman, Henry Beatty

4 May 1793 Eli Mills & Esther Beaty. Bondsman, David Beaty

7 May 1793 John Brown & Elizabeth Curlett. Bondsman, Peter Helphenstine; consent in writing by Rachel Curlet, witness George Grim

7 May 1793 George Clark, Batchr, & Daicey Farmer, Spinster. Bondsman, Wm Farmer

8 May 1793 Thomas Dunn & Rebecca Wickersham. Bondsman, Willliam Wickersham

11 May 1793 Job Malin & Ann March, daughter of Michael March, the bondsman, who signs in German

11 May 1793 John Madden & Catharine Bonham. Bondsman, Thomas Jones, who consents in writing

13 May 1793 David Devo & Margaret Jewell, daughter of William Jewell. Consent also signed by Margaret Jewell. Seth Strattan & Sarah Devo, witnesses to consent. Bondsman, Seth Stratton

14 May 1793 Michael Groves & Elizabeth Booker. Bondsman, Jacob Booker, who signs in German

16 May 1793 George Rudolph & Christiana Hotsinpillor, daughter of Barbara Jones. Barbara Jones' signature was witnessed by William Marques & Joseph Frye. Bondsman, Joseph Frye

20 May 1793 Valentine Carver & Barbara Hoie. Bondsman, Henry Lewis, who signs in German

20 May 1793 Mathew Rust & Deborah Undrell, living in household of Thos Ward who writes that bride has no father or mother living and no relation in this state (and that) she is far advanced in her twenty first year of age. Bondsman, Dale Carter

21 May 1793 James Lee Martin & Mary Fry. Bondsman, Christopher Fry, who signs in German

28 May 1793 Absalom Banbridge & Elizabeth Taylor, spinster. Bondsman, Gilbert Meem

28 May 1793 William Snickers & Frances Washington. Bondsman, Robert Macky

28 May 1793 Abner Babb & Susanna Robinson, daughter of James & Mary Robinson, who consents in writing. Bondsman, Thomas Babb

30 May 1793 Turner Scoggins & Elizabeth Archey, daughter of Ann Archey. Bondsman, James

Elkins. James Elkins & ? Emmons witnessed the signature of Ann Archey

31 May 1793 Jacob Scot & Eleanor Oglesby, born Jan 1772. Bondsman, Wm Tait. Willm Wood & William Tait witnessed the signature of George Ogelvee, father of bride, who consents

31 May 1793 Zachariah Jones & Mary Jennings, of lawful age, daughter of Edward Jennings. Bondsman, Garey Robinson. Consent of Edward Jennings witnessed by John Hickman & Arthur Smith

3 Jun 1793 John Palmer & Elizabeth Kendall. Bondsman, Thos Biggs

4 Jun 1793 James Smoote & Mary Cahoon, daughter of Daniel Cahoon, the bondsman

4 Jun 1793 Joseph Catterlin Junr & Sarah Brecount, daughter of David Brecount, both under age. Bondsmen, Joseph Catterlin & David Brecount. Parents of both parties gave consent

4 Jun 1793 Thomas Homes & Rachel Reed. Bondsman, John Wilkison. Consent in writing by John Reed. Witnessed by Job Wilkison & James Wilkison

13 Jun 1793 Daniel Dillon & Sarah Fry (Jay?), daughter of David Fry (Jay?). Consent witnessed by Amos Paxson & Daniel Freestone, Bondsman, Amos Paxson

14 Jun 1793 John Morley & Elizabeth Shephard, daughter of Chau..Shepha... Consent witnessed by Richard Shephard & Thomas Paige or Pain?. Bondsman, Richard Shephard

14 Jun 1793 John Garret & Ann Allensworth, who writes her own consent. Her signature witnessed by William Remy & Butler Allensworth. Philip Allensworth makes oath that Ann is 24 or 25 years old, "agreeable to the information of his mother who has known the said Ann from her childhood." Bondsmen, Philip Allensworth & John Jones

15 Jun 1793 David Hickey & Catharine Cohagin. Bondsman, John Noldin

16 Jun 1793 Thomas McFarling & Mary Stump, spinster. Bondsman, James Eddy; consent signed "Thomas McFarland"

17 Jun 1793 Francis Gordon & Mary Barger, orphan of --- Barger, decd. Consent by Robert

Hazelwood & Mary Hazelwood, guardians for Mary Barger. Bondsman, John Gorden

20 Jun 1793 John Cryder, batch., & Mary Johnston, widow. Bondsman, John W. Ginnis (McGinnis?)

22 Jun 1793 Lewis Stump & Hannah Shambaugh, daughter of Philip & Margaret Shambaugh, who consent in writing. Bondsman, John Stump

22 Jun 1793 Abraham Nisewanger & Lydia Nisewanger. Bondsman, John Ginnis

24 Jun 1793 Philip Ammick/Eamigh & Catharine Huffman. Bondsman, Conrad Crebs

25 Jun 1793 Joshua Myers & Tabitha Stephens, daughter of Joseph & Celea Steavens, who consent. Bondsman, John Windsor Driver

25 Jun 1793 Robert Hodge & Ruth Perrill, daughter of Joseph Perrill, the bondsman

6 Jul 1793 Robert Boxell & Elizabeth Oare, daughter of Ann Oare, who consents in writing. Bondsman, Aaron Bonham

10 Jul 1793 Joseph Brown & Mary Smith. Bondsman, John Boxell

20 Jul 1793 Benjamin Overstake & Elizabeth Wenkland. Bondsman, Henry Wenkland

22 Jul 1793 John Funk & Jemima Britain. Bondsman, Joseph Britain

James Snodgrass & Elizabeth Cusick/Cusyck. Consent, Vance Bush. Witness, Capt John Brady. Bondsman, John Brady

22 Jul 1793 Thomas Reed & Jane Bonard, age 27. Bondsman, Joseph Johnston

29 Jul 1793 Samuel Hicks & Agness Latty, daughter of Joseph Latta (Latty), the bondsman

1 Aug 1793 William Taylor & Alsey Kean, daughter of John Kean, the bondsman

1 Aug 1793 Gilbert Meem & Frances Simrell, daughter of James Simrell, who consents in writing. Bondsman, George Beatty

3 Aug 1793 Nimrod Owens & Beady Smith, daughter of Humphry & Elizabeth Grubs, who consent in writing. Bondsman, Daniel Grubbs

3 Aug 1793 George Secrist & Anna Fry, ward of Benjamin Fry, the bondsman

5 Aug 1793 Leonard Weaver & Ingle Slusher, daughter of Fredk Slusher, the bondsman, who signs in German

8 Aug 1793 Elijah Sparks & Elizabeth Weaver, daughter of Frances Weaver (female), the bondsman

9 Aug 1793 Henry Daingerfield & Elizabeth Mynn Thruston, spinster. Bondsman, David Holmes

10 Aug 1793 John Lee & Eleanor Ellis, age 22. Bondsman, Jonas Likans

11 Aug 1793 William Jones & Ann Blakemore, spinster, daughter of Thos Blakemore. Bondsman, Abrm Neill

17 Aug 1793 Joseph Britton & Margaret Martin, parents both agreed, signed, John Radenour & Elizabeth Radenour. Bondsman, Wilson Britton

31 Aug 1793 John Perry & Nancy Anderson. Bondsman, John Hayney

3 Sep 1793 Nimrod Long & Eleanor E Williams. Bondsman Wm C Williams

6 Sep 1793 Eli Grubbs, Batchelor, & Nancy Robinson, daughter of Wm Robenson, who consents in writing. Witnesses, John Robinson & John Romine. Bondsman, George Cooper

3 Sep 1793 Jacob Anderson & June Cochran. Bondsman, George Sommerville

11 Sep 1793 James Barber, widower, & Mary Harper. Bondsman, Thos Harper

13 Sep 1793 Robert McKee & Jane Cather. Bondsman, Jasper Cather

14 Sep 1793 John Barnett & Druscilla Rowlands. Bondsman, Abner Gossett

Abner Gossett "about two years past he was requested by Martha Dawson (George Dawson her Husband being also present) to register the names and ages of her Children in a Common Prayer Book...Druscilla Rowlands Daughter of the said Martha Dawson by a former Husband was born on the 1st day of May 1771. That he was at the House of the said Dawson this day (his home being there) and was looking at the register aforesaid in the presence of the said George & Martha & they then said they conceived their was a mistake in the register aforesaid & that agreeable to the best Calculation they could make the said Druscilla Rowlands was 21 Years Olde the first day of last May Given under my hand this 14th day of Sepr 1793"

14 Sep 1793 Jacob Hotsinbeller & Milly Seagle. Bondsman, George Marker

17 Sep 1793 Edward Kearnes, son of Patrick Kerns (Karns), & Rachel Barnett. Ezekiel & Prudens Marple testified "that Rachel Barnet is of full age and served her tiam with us and she has no parents a live in this country and she is free to marry.." Their signatures were witnessed by Patrick Rams & Liews Norris

25 Sep 1793 Nicholas Hodgson & Elizabeth McAnully. Bondsman, Peter Chrisman

25 Sep 1793 Thos Cunningham & Mary Keller. Bondsman, Charles Helzel

24 Dec 1794 Peter Sperry & Barbara Hummrickhouser. Bondsman, John (bond torn)

25 Dec 1794 David Perry & Rosanna May. Bondsman, Samuel May

27 Dec 1794 Thomas Keenan & Margar.. (bond torn). Bondsman, George Dick

29 Dec 1794 Elisha Emmons & Elizabeth Dewalt. Bondsman, John Romine

30 Dec 1794 John Barney & Catharine B--- (bond torn). Bondsman, John Gray

30 Dec 1794 Beal Dimmett & Belinda Dimmett. Bondsman, Ezekiel Dimmett

31 Dec 1794 Richard Steele & Mary Nicklin. Bondsman, Joseph Nicklin

31 Dec 1794 James Triplet & Nancy Oliver. Bondsman, John Foster

1 Jan 1795 Arthur Gorden & Mary Littlisher. Bondsman, John Littlishr

3 Jan 1795 Benjamin Edmonds & Mary Ducker. Bondsman, Joseph Vanhorn

3 Jan 1795 Francis Baker & Margaret Evans. Bondsman, James Jackson

6 Jan 1795 William Fallert & Jane Mckee. Bondsman, Robert McKee

6 Jan 1795 John Shadley & Docia Oglisvie. Bondsman, Wm Jewell

7 Jan 1795 Joseph Dickay & Elizabeth Fuller. Bondsman, George Chopson

8 Jan 1795 Joseph Craig & Elizabeth Martin. Bondsman, William Martin

10 Jan 1795 George Smith & Frances Curlet. Bondsman, John Taylor

10 Jan 1795 Peter Shinholtzr & Matilina Holt. Bondsman, George Holt

12 Jan 1795 William Mosley & Elizabeth Smith. Bondsman, Robert Smith

13 Jan 1795 Peter Tewault & Margaret Brill. Bondsman, Henry Brill

13 Jan 1795 Benjamin Fenton & Ann Jackson. Bondsman, Peter Babb

14 Jan 1795 William Peyton & Elizabeth Lacy. Bondsman, John Danks

14 Jan 1795 Jeremiah Langley & Mary Anderson. Bondsman, Basel Lecke

16 Jan 1795 William Helphenston & Sarah Cordell. Bondsman, Conrad Kremer

26 Jan 1795 Jacob Edenburgh & Margaret Hunsucker. Bondsman, Daniel Hunsucker

26 Jan 1795 Ellis Pugh & Mary Rees. Bondsman, Jacob Crumpton

28 Jan 1795 Isaac Ridgway & Susannah Simmons. Bondsman, Joseph Chew

29 Jan 1795 Kidd Smith & Cresa Leach. Bondsman, Richard Turner

30 Jan 1795 Daniel Schreklingast & Mary Snyder. Bondsman, Henry Snyder

11 Feb 1795 William Blundell & Peggy Marcus. Bondsman, Henry Schofield

16 Feb 1795 Isaac Marquess & Elizabeth Beavers. Bondsman, Kide Smith

16 Feb 1795 Thomas Butterfield & Lydia White. Bondsman, James Butterfield

26 Feb 1795 Thomas McCracken & Margaret Smith. Bondsman, James Smith

28 Feb 1795 William Morgan & Phebe Ball. Bondsman, Elijah Coate

3 Mar 1795 Rubin Clark & Susanna Suddeth. Bondsman, Joseph White

6 Mar 1795 James McDonald & Mary Cather. Bondsman, Jasper Cather

9 Mar 1795 Jacob Boucher & Margaret Crum. Bondsman, Anthony Crum

9 Mar 1795 Robert Hodgson & Susanna Long. Bondsman, Thomas Long

9 Mar 1795 William Dixon & Mary Cahoon. Bondsman, Robert Cahoon

10 Mar 1795 William Reynolds & Rebecca Harris. Bondsman, Stephen Reynolds

11 Mar 1795 Joseph Passmore & Sarah Fenton. Bondsman, Tabort Ager

25 Mar 1795 William Shaw & Lydia Bonham. Bondsman, Stephen Jones
31 Mar 1795 Barnard Fagan & Ann Warden. Bondsman, Henry Adams
1 Apr 1795 Shelton Kendel & Mary Randle. Bondsman, Thos Burriss
7 Apr 1795 Isaac Lafollet & Mary Kail. Bondsman, Peter Kail, who signs in German
7 Apr 1795 Joseph Miller & Elizabeth Parkins. Bondsman, Samuel Vowell
14 Apr 1795 Barak Fisher & Mary Hage. Bondsman, Wm Hoge jnr
15 Apr 1795 Stephen Bond & Catherine Philips. Bondsman, George Bond
16 Apr 1795 James Beagles & Ann Hess. Bondsman, Peter Spear/Speer
18 Apr 1795 David Grapes & ? (bond torn). Bondsman, Martin Shaver (George Price crossed out)
21 Apr 1795 William Piper & Ann Steele. Bondsman, John Steel
27 Apr 1795 Eli Pugh & Catharine Fisher. Bondsman, Jesse Pugh
28 Apr 1795 Saml Nicholls & Ann Edmondson. Bondsman, Archd Edmonston
6 May 1795 Joseph Alexander & Anne Thomas. Bondsman, John Walters
12 May 1795 Abraham Shull & Hannah Thomas. Bondsman, Benjamin Frye
18 May 1795 William Manoliucks & Margaret Drumm. Bondsman, John Drumm
21 May 1795 James Lang & Peggy Morrow. Bondsman, Almon Sanders
3 Jun 1795 Phineas Swartz & Nancy McCall. Bondsman, Nathan McCall
13 Jun 1795 Jacob Baker & Barbara Hieronimus. Bondsman, Conrad Hieronimus
17 Jun 1795 Jesse McCue & Elizabeth Whitacre. Bondsman, John Beaty
18 Jun 1795 James Jackson & Elizabeth Roland. Bondsman, Thomas Rowland
26 Jun 1795 John Moffett & Ann Howard. Bondsman, John Carswell
30 Jun 1795 James Osbourn & Lydia Anderson. Bondsman, Bazil Leak
4 Jul 1795 William White & Elizabeth Peterson. Bondsman, John Peterson

4 Jul 1795 Corben Coulter & Margt McCabe, widow. Bondsman, William White

4 Jul 1795 Nathaniel Walleas & Charity Jordan. Bondsman, Robert Macky

4 Jul 1795 Casper Seaver, widower, & Rosanna Streit, widow. Bondsman, Lewis Wolfe

7 Jul 1795 William Hoge & Rachel Steel, widow. Bondsman, Benjamin Rutherford

15 Jul 1795 George Redd & Frances Fisher. Bondsman, Hugh Kennedy

18 Jul 1795 Thomas Blaylock & Ann Smith. Bondsman, David Smith

25 Jul 1795 Peter Dick & Mary Garner. Bondsman, Henry Garner

25 Jul 1795 Joseph Engle & Eleanor Perkins. Bondsman, William Hills

27 Jul 1795 William Coffman & Elizabeth Bezant. Bondsman, Moses Henry

1 Aug 1795 Joseph H Jones & Lucy Young. Bondsman, Mathew Clarke

4 Aug 1795 Adam Grove & Eve Shiner. Bondsman, Frederick Carper

8 Aug 1795 James Wine & _____ Settle. Bondsman, William Shumate

10 Aug 1795 Cyrus Gray & Mary Magdalen Bougher. Bondsman, John Keach

11 Aug 1795 Reubin Crafford & Jane Jacobs. Bondsman, Francis Jacobs

17 Aug 1795 George Goose & Florence Steel, widow. Bondsman, Jost Keeler; Keeler and Goose sign in German

19 Aug 1795 Thomas Neill & Phebe LaRue. Bondsman, Thomas Helm

25 Aug 1795 John Anderson & Catharine Haymaker. Bondsman, Adam Haymaker

25 Aug 1795 Gasper Settlemire & Mary Martin. Bondsman, James Purviance

25 Aug 1795 Michael Switzer & Mary Magdalene Klyne. Bondsman, Jacob Klein

25 Aug 1795 Jacob Clevinger & Catharine Thomlin. Bondsman, Samuel Stokes

26 Aug 1795 James Ducker & Charlotte Keyes. Bondsman, Wm Baylis

27 Aug 1795 Benja Burton & Catharine Brown. Bondsman, Vencon Brown

28 Aug 1795 Thomas Fleming & Hannah Marr. Bondsman, John Marcks

4 Sep 1795 William Kennedy & Esther Romine. Bondsman, John Morford

12 Sep 1795 Nicholas Cuningham & Anna Lee. Bondsman, John Cuningham

12 Sep 1795 Isaac Foley & Deborah Holland. Bondsman, Archibald Holland

15 Sep 1795 William Stewart & Hannah Wizer. Bondsman, Isaac Wiear

17 Sep 1795 Anthony Crum & Freny Cyphert. Bondsman, Peter Senseney

19 Sep 1795 James Hathaway & Mary Gibbs Helm. Bondsman, William Boum; bond says "Bourn"

19 Sep 1795 Philip Orndorff & Eleanor Williams. Bondsman, John Orndorff

26 Sep 1795 Henry Groves & Susannah Kline. Bondsman, Adam Kline. Groom & bondsman sign in German

29 Sep 1795 William Wright & Amy Frazier. Bondsman, David Parkins

1 Oct 1795 Edward Drake & Catharine Lawyer. Bondsman, John Lawyer

3 Oct 1795 Will Cronnen & Rachael McCormick. Bondsman, Thos Graham

6 Oct 1795 Samuel Burton & Mary Fulk. Bondsman, Jacob Fulk

7 Oct 1795 John Nisewanger & Sarah Grove. Bondsman, John Groves, who signs in German

8 Oct 1795 Jesse Seybold & Margaret Dotson. Bondsman, George Pullin

12 Oct 1795 James Short & Sarah Bartlett. Bondsman, John Taylor

13 Oct 1795 Jacob Grove & Catharine Lonas. Bondsmen, John Groves (in German) & Daniel Thornberry

14 Oct 1795 James Russell & Ann Throckmorton, spinster. Bondsman, Thomas Throckmorton

19 Oct 1795 Casper Kline & Catharine Somsell. Bondsman, Charles Helzel

22 Oct 1795 John Farmer & Hannah Adams. Bondsman, Samuel Hart

22 Oct 1795 James McPherson & Elizabeth Davis. Bondsman, Gary Davis

22 Oct 1795 John Anderson & Hannah Johnston. Bondsman, John Fulkeson

23 Oct 1795 Jacob Danner & Hannah Senseney. Bondsman, Peter Senseney

26 Oct 1795 John Pickering & Mary Carpenter. Bondsman, George Carpenter
28 Oct 1795 Dedrick Bythenman & Mary Crum. Bondsman, Christian Crum
7 Nov 1795 James Silver & Nancy Hand. Bondsman, Richd Bryarly
10 Nov 1795 John Anderson & Mary Pearce. Bondsman, Joseph Peirce
11 Nov 1795 Hugh Reynolds & Mary Lockridge. Bondsman, George Lockridge
11 Nov 1795 John Doster & Lydia McNease. Bondsman, William Dehaven
14 Nov 1795 John Weaver & Elizabeth Snyder. Bondsman, Henry Snyder
16 Nov 1795 Moses Shepherd & Mary Ross. Bondsman, Martin Garnett
24 Nov 1795 John Thomas & Jean Madden. Bondsman, Mabra Madden
25 Nov 1795 Peter Vanaurt & Mary Griffith. Bondsman, William Hendry
30 Nov 1795 Joseph Langley & Agnes Cochrane. Bondsman, Benja Langley
1 Dec 1795 David Timberlake & Mary Davis. Bondsman, William Davis
2 Dec 1795 George Davis & Sarah McKnight. Bondsman, Charles McCrea; signed "Mica"
3 Dec 1795 Charles Brent & Rachael Moore. No bondsman
4 Dec 1795 John Barker & Afsenesh Allen. Bondsman, John Hoff
5 Dec 1795 Thos Berry & Deborah Porter. Bondsman, Thos Gassaway
5 Dec 1795 Zachariah Murphy & Catha Hoyle, widow. Bondsman, John Cawood
7 Dec 1795 Richard Anderson & Lucresa Howell. Bondsman, George Black
8 Dec 1795 Jacob Thompson & Mary Grady. Bondsman, Nicholas Purtle
8 Dec 1795 Joseph Pugh & Mary Caudy. Bondsman, Richard Lyon
8 Dec 1795 Robert Pugh & Ann McDonald. Bondsman, Jacob Millslagle
8 Dec 1795 Joseph McCarty & Rebecca Curlett. Bondsman, George Grim
17 Dec 1795 Thomas Evans & Hannah Lupton. Bondsman, John Ball

17 Dec 1795 John Buff & Eleanor Vanort. Bondsman, William Hendry

18 Dec 1795 Henry Lonus & Eleanor Romine. Bondsman, Peter Romine

19 Dec 1795 John Townsend & Catharine Davis. Bondsman, Abraham Davis (signed "Dabis")

26 Dec 1795 George Cumings & Sarah Taylor. Bondsman, Daniel Grubs

26 Dec 1795 John Lefevre & Polly Kannan. Bondsman, John Kennan

1 Jan 1796 John Longacre & Sarah Holmes. Bondsman, Will Holmes

2 Jan 1796 Isaac Bond & Sarah Fryar. Bondsman, William Bond

3 Jan 1796 William Miles & Elizabeth Corder. Bondsman, Benjamin Corder

5 Jan 1796 Enoch Talbott & Leannah Fisher. Bondsman, Baldwin Johnson

5 Jan 1796 Benjamin Peck & Deborah Bonham. Bondsman, Jeremiah Barnham

5 Jan 1796 Jeremiah Bonham & Eleanor McDonald. Bondsman, Martin Barnham

7 Jan 1796 Adam Johnston & Margaret Ashenhust. Bondsmen, Oliver Ashenhust & William Ashenhust

14 Jan 1796 William Reveale & Mary Ashby. Bondsman, Thos Ashby

16 Jan 1796 Henry Dudly & Elizabeth Shultz. Bondsman, Henry Clouser

21 Jan 1796 Amos Taylor & Mildred Fenton. Bondsman, Cuthbert Hayhurst

25 Jan 1796 Abraham Chrisman & Mary Fry. Bondsman, Joseph Frye (who signs in German)

30 Jan 1796 Samuel Poston & Jane Slane. Bondsman, Thomas Slane

3 Feb 1796 Aaron Cromley & Jane Atherton. Bondsman, Thomas Gray

8 Feb 1796 Abra Chrisman & Mary Fry. Bondsman, Joseph Frye (bond entered twice)

8 Feb 1796 Elijah Coats & Mary Graves. Bondsman, John Graves

9 Feb 1796 Francis Dutton & Lydia Booth. Bondsman, John Butterfield

12 Feb 1796 Joseph Harsh & Mary Rutter, widow. Bondsman, Thomas Harshe

15 Feb 1796 John Smith & Kitty Scott. Bondsman, Jacob Scott

16 Feb 1796 Isaac Renner & Motalina Brill. Bondsman, Henry Brill
16 Feb 1796 John Congrows & Tasie Goar. Bondsman, James Walter
17 Feb 1796 Abraham Plum & Ann Reed. Bondsman, George Reed
17 Feb 1796 James Willis & Sarah Stricklin, widow. Bondsman, Baldwin Johnson
20 Feb 1796 Jacob Larue & Phebe Hodgen. Bondsman, Jacob Larue Jr
22 Feb 1796 Jacob Reese & Hannah Brannom, daughter of John Brannom, the bondsman
23 Feb 1796 Richard Taylor & Darcus Thomas. Bondsman, John Taylor
24 Feb 1796 John Barrick & Margaret Lawyer. Bondsman, Adam Lawyer
25 Feb 1796 John Weaver & Susanna Sork. Bondsman, Matthias Sork
25 Feb 1796 Patrick Sprint & Susanna Stone. Bondsman, Henry Mark
27 Feb 1796 George Taylor & Ann Peck. Bondsman, John Peck
1 Mar 1796 John Cordell & Rebecca Jennings. Bondsman, Humphrey Grubbs
4 Mar 1796 John Fraker & Elizabeth Purtlebaugh. Bondsman, Michl Fraker, who signs in German
7 Mar 1796 Will Sommerville & Mary Hickmon. Bondsman, Adam Hickman, Jr.
7 Mar 1796 William Bond & Elizabeth McFarland. Bondsman, John McFarland
10 Mar 1796 Edward McGuire Jr & Elizabeth Holmes. Bondsman, Hugh Holmes
10 Mar 1796 Johnston Fletcher & Maria Lautz. Bondsman, Peter Helphinstine
10 Mar 1796 Hugh Holmes & Elizabeth _____ (last name illegible) Bondsman, Frederick Conrad
11 Mar 1796 Thomas Helm & Elizabeth ?Walden. Bondsman, Meredith Helm
14 Mar 1796 James Scott & Hannah Johnston
14 Mar 1796 William Griffis & Milly Sandsberry. Bondsman, William Sandsberry
15 Mar 1796 Jacob Moore & Rebecca Gray. Bondsman, Thoma--- (bond torn)
16 ?? (bond torn) 1796 Adam Kerns & ?. Bondsman, Thomas --- (bond torn)

2 Jan 1797 Henry Bartlett & Elizabeth Davis, daughter of William Davis, the bondsman

9 Sep 1797 Casper Strosnider & Sarah Cyphret. Bondsman, Adam Strosnider

11 Sep 1797 Absalom Gains & Patty Scarff. Bondsman, Samuel Griffen

14 Sep 1797 Enoch Williams & Lydia Felton. Bondsman, Thomas Felton

16 Sep 1797 John Heide & Jane Sterlings. Bondsman, Hutcheson Sterlings

18 Sep 1797 Christian Hoyle & Mary Davis. Bondsman, Zachariah Murphey

18 Sep 1797 Saml Peck & Elizabeth Drake. Bondsman, Gershom Drake

25 Sep 1797 David Trowbridge & Mary Grady. Bondsman, Michael Grady

25 Sep 1797 Jacob Parrell, "batchelor," & Mary Nixon, spinster. Bondsman, John Clutter

29 Sep 1797 William McVicker & Dinah Mercer. Bondsman, Moses Mercer

28 Sep 1797 John Samsell & Anna Groves. Bondsman, Casper Kline

3 Oct 1797 John Cain & Chloe Horton. Bondsman, John Chapman

4 Oct 1797 John McAlester & Elizabeth Joliffe. Bondsmen, Amos Jolliffe, Elizabeth Dailey, & Province McCormick

5 Oct 1797 Francis Neff & Elizabeth Dooley. Bondsman, Peter Cooly

9 Oct 1797 Nicholas Roper (Rosser?) & Mary Horn. Bondsman, James Walker, Esq.

12 Oct 1797 William Middleton & Milly McFerron. Bondsman, John Knister

14 Oct 1797 James Watson & Lettice Burnett. Bondsman, Rachel Carter

16? Oct 1797 Thomas McKewan & Rachel Harry. Bondsman, James McDonald

17 Oct 1797 John Matheny & Martha Brown, widow. Bondsman, William Harper

17 Oct 1797 John Kendall & Verlinda Sandsberry. Bondsman, Peter Spiers

19 Oct 1797 William Taylor & Elizabeth Dunlap. Bondsman, Benjamin Taylor

23 Oct 1797 Geo Clevinger & Rachell Cooper. Bondsman, Vincent Crabb

28 Oct 1797 Jacob Harman & Christinna Mock. Bondsman, Geo Mock

28 Oct 1797 Geo Reiley & Sarah Brown. Bondsman, James Henry
30 Oct 1797 George Seagler & Mary Scell. Bondsman, Jacob Seagler (signed Jacob Zidglur)
2 Nov 1797 Saml Morris & Rebeccah McDonald. Bondsman, Jacob Lindsay, in bond, Samuel Lindsey in sig.
2 Nov 1797 William Williams & Elizabeth Branon. Bondsman, John Brenon (signed James his mark Brinon)
2 Nov 1797 Peter Babb & Jane Bell. Bondsman, William Williams
4 Nov 1797 Thomas Watson & Martha Moffett, spinster. Bondsman, Walter Moffett
4 Nov 1797 William Rowzey, "Batchelor," & Nancy Hoff, spinster. Bondsman, Morgan Hoff
9 Nov 1797 Daniel Murphy & Susanna Daugherty, widow. Bondsman, John Daugherty
9 Nov 1797 Philip Burwell & Elizabeth Page. Bondsman, Nathaniel Burwell
11 Nov 1797 Jacob Lindsey, "batchelor," and Mary Eveins, spinster. Bondsman, William Cotrell
11 Nov 1797 Stephen Johnson & Lydia Clevinger. Bondsman, Jacob Anderson
15 Nov 1797 Nichs Watkins & Mary Freeman. Bondsman, Wm Freeman
15 Nov 1797 Thomas Grimes & Jane Riley. Bondsman, Mark Harper
16 Nov 1797 Nathaniel Cowan & Sarah Rice. Bondsman, Alexander Simerall
16 Nov 1797 Charles Folke & Jane Farmer. Bondsman, Thomas Farmer
20 Nov 1797 Samuel Hogan & Jane Murphy. Bondsman, John Cuningham
28 Nov 1797 William Scroggin & Mary Clark. Bondsman, Hugh Johnston
29 Nov 1797 John Crider & Elizabeth Lemly. Bondsman, Isaac Jennings
2 Dec 1797 Alexander Simrall & Sally Donaldson. Bondsman, Gilbert Meem
7 Dec 1797 John Corbett & Margaret Standford, widow. Bondsman, William Stanford
8 Dec 1797 Abraham Phleager & Margaret Goodekunts. Bondsman, George Phleager
9 Dec 1797 Vincent Vaughan & Mary Shipe. Bondsman, Stephen Hotsenpellar

11 Dec 1797 Charles McDonald & Jumima Carter. Bondsman, John Gilles

12 Dec 1797 James Payne & Elizabeth Overton. Bondsman, Stephen Miller

12 Dec 1797 William Rout & Ann Stage. Bondsman, Isaac Chrisman

19 Dec 1797 Isaac Ramy & Margaret Dearmont. Bondsman, Peter Dearmont

21 Dec 1797 John Milhorn & Elizabeth Cackley. Bondsman, John Cackley

22 Dec 1797 Thomas Chapman & Mary Stone. Bondsman, Walter Watson

23 Dec 1797 Abner Gossett & Mary Mercer. Bondsman, William Gossett

30 Dec 1797 Joseph Baker & Elizabeth Weavor. Bondsman, Jacob Weavor

3 Jan 1798 William Hutton & Catherine Minicks. Bondsman, Henry McCarden

2 Jan 1798 William Jones & Polly Pine (line drawn through her name). Bondsman, Nicholas Hanshaw

9 Mar 1798 Jacob Monmouth & Elizabeth Alexander. Bondsman, Benjamin Rutherford

11 Apr 1798 John Hooper & Polly Bailey. Bondsmen, William Clemmans & W. Fredk Hurst

12 Apr 1798 Joseph Stickley & Peggy Harman. Bondsman, Mathias Harman

12 Apr 1798 Robert Rogers & Marcy Bealle. Bondsman, Jacob Jenkins

12 Apr 1798 Jacob Tarflinger & Barbara Kline. Bondsman, Jacob Kline

14 Apr 1798 Henry Helpenstine & Nancy Holdenby, daughter of William Holdenbary, who consents in writing. Bondsman, Philip Shearer

18 Apr 1798 Henry Mark & Katey Stone, daughter of Lewis Stone, the bondsman, who signs in German

23 Apr 1798 Daniel Pendor & Jane Sill. Bondsman, Aquila Dyson

23 Apr 1798 John Crampton & Sidney Barret, over 21, her father deceased. Bondsman, Jacob Crampton

25 Apr 1798 James McKinsay & Susannah Bruin, upwards of 21. Bondsman, Arthur Carter

25 Apr 1798 George Green & Charlotte Babb, daughter of Blanch Babb. Bondsman, Thomas Babb

9 May 1798 Samuel Rannells & Peggy Gilkeson, upwards of 21 years of age. Bondsman, Jas Vance

9 May 1798 Soloman Groves & Fanny Marquess. Bondsman, Isaac Marquess

11 May 1798 Jesse Grigsby & Betsy Northern. Bondsman Jonathan Northern. Betty Northern, Betsey Northern, & Caty Northern requested the license

19 May 1798 Jesse Glasscock & Dilly Lewis. Bondsman, Reuben Elliott

23 May 1798 Thomas Sprout & Jane Melon. Bondsman, Joseph Carter

31 May 1798 John Richards & Mary Bean. Bondsman, Mordecai Bean

7 Jun 1798 Adam Miller & Nancey Cheek. Bondsman, Richard Wall. Nancey Cheek was daughter of James & Katey Cheek. Parents' consent is dated 7 Jun 1798, Front Royal

14 Jun 1798 Samuel Jewett & Rachael Painter, daughter of Isaac Painter. Bondsman, Seth Stratton

30 Jun 1798 Robert Stigley (Stidley written over) & Mary Simpson, sister of John Simson, the bondsman

30 Jun 1798 Jacob Kuntz & Dolly Boman. Bondsman, Humphrey R Johnston (signed Johnson)

2 Jul 1798 John Noble & Mary Pickslar, daughter of Jacob Pickslar, who consents in writing. Bondsman, Daniel Millar

21 Jul 1798 Richard Wall & Dosie Griggsby. Bondsman, Original Wroe

28 Jul 1798 John Larue & Hanner (Hannah) Jackson, daughter of James Jackson. Bondsman, Jacob Edinborough

1 Aug 1798 John McKay & Elizabeth Sugars. Bondsman, Samuel Licks

4 Aug 1798 Daniel Bowman & Judith Good, daughter of Peter Good, who signs "Gut." Groom & bondsman sign in German

4 Aug 1798 Benjamin Price & Rebecca Fisher, father deceased, sister of Barick Fisher

6 Aug 1798 David Oglevie & Hannah Mckay, upwards of 21 years, daughter of Jobe Mckay & Ann Mckay. Bondsman, Joseph Irwin. Consent in writing by Ann Mckay states "my husband prior to his departure for Canitucky gave his consent"

8 Aug 1798 John Henry & Clarkey Reiley. Bondsman, Hugh Reiley

11 Aug 1798 Michael Funk & Savina Slusher, daughter of Frederick Slusher, the bondsman, who signs in German

16 Aug 1798 George Williamham, son of John Willingham, & Sarah Steward. Bondsman, George Steward. Consent for groom signed John Williamham & Milley Williamham. Witness to consent, John Keys, Lemson Barrett

25 Aug 1798 Thomas Christy & Agnes Rogers, daughter of Catharine Rogers, and step sister of John Rutter, the bondsman, who signs as "Ritter"

22 Aug 1798 Henry Davis, son of Daniel Davis, & Hanah Wilson, daughter of Jeremiah Wilson

1 Sep 1798 Owen Rogers & Eleanor Nelson. Bondsman, Jacob Jenkins

4 Sep 1798 Gilbreath Burton & Elenor Talbott. Bondsman, Hezekiah Young. Consent in writing by William Talbott, bride's father

13 Sep 1798 David Fawcett, upward of 21 years, & Phebe (Phoby) Lupton. Bondsman, John Jamison

15 Sep 1798 Jacob Miller & Lucy Hicks. Bondsman, David Hicks

18 Sep 1798 Daniel Cole & Elizabeth Wilcox (Wilcock), upward of 22 years. Consent in writing: "This is to certify ... that I am free and willing that Danl Cole should obtain licens to marry my daughter Elizabeth Wilcox." Signed Abigail Burk. Bondsman, William Marshall

22 Sep 1798 Obed Noland & Priscilla Bailey, widow. Bondsman, Dillon Bridges

28 Sep 1798 Aaron Henry & Ann Airs, father deceased, upward of 22 years, daughter of Judith Airs. Bondsman, James Henry

29 Sep 1798 Richard Spencer & Mary Melon, daughter of Jacob Melon. Bondsman, William Malin

29 Sep 1798 Thomas Ewing & Ediah Crawford, daughter of John Crawford, who consents in writing. Bondsman, John McGinnis

1 Oct 1798 Evan Lewis & Ann Marple. Bondsman, Enoch Marple

1 Oct 1798 James Vance & Ruth Glass. Bondsman, William T Simrall

8 Oct 1798 James McBride & Catherine Trisler. Bondsman, Simon Rogers

8 Oct 1798 George Purcell & Priscilla Nokes. Bondsman, Baldwin Coppesy

9 Oct 1798 William Langley & Elizabeth Cochran (father & mother deceased). Bondsman, Benjamin Langley

15 Oct 1798 Fairfax Washington & Sarah Armistead. Bondsman, Alexander Balmain

16 Oct 1798 William Kinlin & Lydia Littler. Bondsman, James Bruce

17 Oct 1798 Curtis Langley & Susanah Ridgeway. Bondsman, Jesse Britton

18 Oct 1798 Jacob Crist & Rogina Cartmill, daughter of Nathan Cartmill, the bondsman

24 Oct 1798 Robert Vance & Mazy Beall. Bondsman, Robert White Jr

24 Oct 1798 Reubin Elbon & Mary Gorley. John Gerley & Ann Gerley, consent. Bondsman, Samuel Thompson

26 Oct 1798 Jacob Crysor & Leah Garrett, daughter of Luke & Mary Garrett, who consent in writing. Witness to their consent, Luke Garrett. Bondsman, Luke Garrett

26 Oct 1798 Amanuel Allensworth & Kitty Black. Bondsman, Luke Garrat/Garrett. Consent in writing by Catherine Allensworth. Witness, Simon Allensworth, Butler Allensworth. Kitty Black is upwards of 21 years and daughter of said Catherine

27 Oct 1798 Hugh Craig & Elizabeth Thompson. Bondsman, John Craig

6 Nov 1798 Alex Childs & Ann Maria Grifiths, daughter of David Grifiths

7 Nov 1798 George Larrick & Rebecca Brinker, spinster, daughter of Rebecca (Rebekah) Brinker, who consents in writing. Bondsman, George Brinker

8 Nov 1798 William Simpson Lang & Elizabeth Smith, upwards of 23 years. Consent in writing by Elizabeth Smith, mother of bride. Bondsman, Tobias Walters

10 Nov 1798 Abel Reeder & Elizabeth Marquis. Bondsman, Mary Marquis

10 Nov 1798 George Thomas & Elizabeth Freeman, daughter of William Freeman, the bondsman

27 Nov 1798 Harman Coffman & Margaret Hickman. Bondsman, John Senseney

27 Nov 1798 David Griffiths Jr & Priscilla Griffith. Bondsman, David Griffiths Sr

8 Dec 1798 Joseph McFarland & Hannah Speers. Bondsman, Peter Speers

28 Dec 1798 John Noblar & Jane Campbell, daughter of Elizabeth Campbell, who consents in writing. Bondsman, John McGinnis

2 Jan 1799 Henry Bartlett & Elizabeth Davis, daughter of William Davis, the bondsman. Witness, Fredk Hurst

29 Jan 1799 John Faguson McKee & Jane Marple, daughter of Ezekiel Marple, the bondsman

25 Jun 1799 John Grigsby & Sarah Holmes. Bondsman, Charles Robison

25 Jun 1799 James McNally & Priscilla Brookhaffer. Bondsman, Ezekiel Carter

8 Jul 1799 Samuel Trenary & Mary Archer. Bondsman, Thomas Grubbs

16 Jul 1799 Ollaver Dowell & Chloe Horton. Bondsman, John Chapman

18 Jul 1799 George Gardner & Jane Sharman. Bondsman, John Sharman

18 Jul 1799 Jonathan Ellis & Martha Owgon. Bondsman, Jacob Jenkins

24 Jul 1799 Samuel Graham & Hannah Jenkins, widow of John Jenkins dec. Bondsman, John Newman

30 Jul 1799 John Ryley & Elizabeth Conrad. Bondsman, William Lehew

1 Aug 1799 Daniel Carter & Eleanor Murphy, resides in the said county of Frederick..upwards of twenty one. Bondsman, Benjamin Jones. "the license of Daniel Carter to Eleanor Murphey dated 1 Aug 1799 was neither blotted or scratched. This memo is made as there is a possibility they may be altered..."

2 Aug 1799 William Clevinger & Aminy Powers. Bondsman, Peter Cooley

2 Aug 1799 George Harman & Chloe Clevinger. Bondsman, William Wright

2 Aug 1799 Vance Pangle & Rebaca Longacre. Bondsman, Nicholas Hodgson

7 Aug 1799 Hubbard Jones & Rachel Conway, widow of Jas Conway Decd. Bondsman, George Brown

10 Aug 1799 George Savage & Mary Miers. Bondsman, Jacob Miers
13 Aug 1799 Isaac Painter & Elizabeth Ridd. Bondsman, Peter Lauck
14 Aug 1799 Isaac Woodrow & Elizabeth Blackemore. Bondsman, Edward Slater
17 Aug 1799 Abraham Clevinger & Unus Branson. Bondsman, Robert Branson
19 Aug 1799 Daniel Adams & Elizabeth Day, widow of Jeremiah Day deceased. Bondsman, James Rose
19 Aug 1799 Gabriel Davis & Sarah Fenton. Bondsman, Meredith Darlington
20 Aug 1799 Daniel McDaniel & Jane Grimes. Bondsman, James Cumpton/"Compton" in sig.
21 Aug 1799 Isaac Patch & Polly Anderson, sister of John Anderson, the bondsman
28 Aug 1799 James Harsha & Mary Margarett Taylor. Bondsman, John Grigsby
2 Sep 1799 Jonah Miers & Rebeccah Stephens. Bondsman, Joshua Moyers
2 Sep 1799 Jesse Orndorff & Catharine Strosnider. Bondsman, Philip P Bucher
3 Sep 1799 James Green & Polly Marshall. Bondsman, James Marshall
6 Sep 1799 Moses Jacobs & Leciney Collins. Bondsman, Samuel King
10 Sep 1799 Joshua McCawley & Jane Rush. Bondsman, Adam Haymaker
13 Sep 1799 Joseph Shull & Rebecca Seabert. Bondsman, Adam Seabert
21 Sep 1799 Ambrose Barnett & Frances Mitchell, widow & relict of Carey Mitchell dec. Bondsman, Archibald Brownley
22 Sep 1799 William Elzey & Elizabeth Myers, widow & relict of Stephen Myers dec. Bondsman, Thos Dann
24 Sep 1799 Baylis Davis & Betsy Raynolds. Bondsman, George Raynolds
27 Sep 1799 Vincent Crabb & Sally Jamieson, daughter of John Jameson, the bondsman
28 Sep 1799 Joseph P Clark & Mary Glasscock. Bondsman, Henry Nichols
28 Sep 1799 Fielding Luttrell & Elizabeth Burkheimer, daughter of Philip Burkheimer, the bondsman

1 Oct 1799 John Honnold (Honnol in sig.) & Ruth Clarke. Bondsman, Thomas Cooper

1 Oct 1799 Jacob Honnole & Abigail Shipman. Bondsman, John Honnole

2 Oct 1799 John Randolph & Jenny Owens. Bondsman, Mishael Pugh

2 Oct 1799 John Clarke & Ruth Booth. Bondsman, Abraham Johnson

8 Oct 1799 George Griffin & Nancy Johnston, daughter of Elizabeth Johnston, the bondsman

9 Oct 1799 Joseph Mercer & Nancy Youally. Bondsman, William Mercer

10 Oct 1799 Walters Taylor Junr & Polley Jones. Bondsman, Walters Taylor Snr

12 Oct 1799 Charles Buck Jnr & Polly Price. Bondsman, John Elsey

12 Oct 1799 Peter Seilor & Elizabeth Hauvermale. Bondsman, Adam Hingle. Witness, Rebeccah Hawvermale

15 Oct 1799 Abner Hodgson & Rebecca Johnston. Bondsmen, John Hodgson & Elizabeth Hodgson

17 Oct 1799 Philip Kline & Polly Featherling, daughter of George Featherling, the bondsman

17 Oct 1799 William McCaully & Nancy Templeman, widow & relict of John Templeman. Bondsman, Daniel Miller

19 Oct 1799 Stephen McDonald & Margaret Peacock. Bondsman, William Tyler

19 Oct 1799 Enoch McDaniel & Peggy Evans of Fredk. Bondsman, Abraham McDaniel (McDonald)

23 Oct 1799 Amos Johnson & Mary Grosman, daughter of Simon Grosman, the bondsman

24 Oct 1799 William McCabe & Mary Kelly of Frederick County. Bondsman, William Kelley juner

26 Oct 1799 Samuel Berry & Sarah Kendall of Frederick County. Bondsmen, George Kendall & Reuben Berry

28 Oct 1799 Charles Cain & Mary Hood of Frederick County. Bondsman, Eli Richards

2 Nov 1799 Peter Hatt, son of George Hatt, and Catharine Deal, daughter of Conrad Deal, the bondsman. Groom signs in German

4 Nov 1799 Joseph Longacre & Elizabeth Jackson. Bondsman, Joseph Pool

4 Nov 1799 William Campbell & Mary Johnston, daughter of Rebecca Hodgson. Bondsmen, Rebecca Hodgson & Thomas Mackewan
4 Nov 1799 John Ashenhurst & Nancy Scott. Bondsman, Mary Scott
5 Nov 1799 John Snapp & Mary Lowry. Bondsman, Moses Lawry
5 Nov 1799 George Longerbane & Jane Tellman of Frk County. Bondsman, John Longerbane
6 Nov 1799 Philip Cryder & Nancy McClintuck. Bondsman, Samuel McClintuck
9 Nov 1799 William Carty & Polly Weaver, daughter of Leonard Weaver, the bondsman
11 Nov 1799 Joseph Abriel & Margaret Reed, daughter of Thomas Reed, the bondsman
13 Nov 1799 Moses Lowry & Mary Snapp of Frederick County. Bondsman, John Snapp
19 Nov 1799 Peter Wolfe & Clary Ridgway of Frederick County. Bondsman, John Ridgeway
22 Nov 1799 Henry Grove & Mary Lawyer. Bondsman, John Grove
28 Nov 1799 James Hammond & Margaret Skelling. Bondsman, William Foley
30 Nov 1799 Amos Clayton & Elizabeth Luke. Bondsman, Peter Luke
30 Nov 1799 Joseph Sample & Catharine Pearce, daughter of Joseph Pierce, the bondsman
2 Dec 1799 Joseph Chew & Elizabeth Thomas, daughter of Sampson Thomas, the bondsman
6 Dec 1799 John Hiatt & Sarah Lock, daughter of George Lock, the bondsman
7 Dec 1799 James Rogers & Rhoda Adams, daughter of John Adams, the bondsman
7 Dec 1799 Jacob Shultz & Susan Carson. Bondsman, Jacob Larrick
9 Dec 1799 John Kemp & Tabitha Love. Bondsman, William Kemp
12 Dec 1799 Josiah McCabe & Leana Carter. Bondsman, William Kelley
16 Dec 1799 Jesse Dowell & Jenney Conner. Bondsman, Thomas Conner
16 Dec 1799 Simeon Fryer & Barbara Brown of Frederick County. Bondsman, James Brown
17 Dec 1799 Caleb Seal & Ann Smith. Bondsman, Samuel Smith
18 Dec 1799 Andrew Leckhart & Mary Wall, daughter of William Wall, the bondsman

18 Dec 1799 John Taylor & Ann Wall, daughter of William Wall, the bondsman

19 Dec 1799 Nathan Kerns & Rachael Reed, daughter of Thomas Reed, the bondsman

21 Dec 1799 Nathaniel Hilling & Polly Riley. Bondsman, Benjamin Corder

23 Dec 1799 Thomas Johnston & Hatha McKoy. Bondsman, John McCoy

27 Dec 1799 George Earhart & Polly Marks. Bondsman, James Howe

28 Dec 1799 Robert Hodgson & Lurannah Watson. Bondsman, Henry Watson

24 Dec 1799 Thomas Ireland & Sarah Clevinger. Bondsman, Wm Clevinger

30 Dec 1799 Eliakim Anderson & Jane Anderson, daughter of Eliakim Anderson, the bondsman

31 Dec 1799 Leonard Hurdle & Anna Marsh, daughter of Richard Marsh, the bondsman

31 Dec 1799 Abraham Romine & Hannah Romine, daughter of John Romine, the bondsman

2 Jan 1780 Benjamin Freeman & Catharine Frumm, daughter of William Frumm, the bondsman

5 Jan 1800 Samuel Ferguson & Mildred Garrison, daughter of Ephraim Garrison, the bondsman

6 Jan 1800 Thomas Sumption & Sarah Evans. Bondsman, Joseph Morgan

8 Jan 1800 William Kemp & Sarah Hendly. Bondsman, John Boyd

9 Jan 1800 Michael Albert & Sarah Anderson. Bondsman, Jacob Anderson. "Michael Albert, father of Michael Albert, personally appeared and gave consent..."

10 Jan 1800 Jacob Hickman & Alice Way. Bondsman, Abel Way

10 Jan 1800 Thomas Doughty & Elizabeth Kemp. Bondsman, John Kemp

14 Jan 1800 Jacob Philips & Susannah Henry, widow & relict of John Henry. Bondsman, Casper Smith

20 Jan 1800 Wilson Norman, free Negro, & Charity Jacobs, daughter of Heney (female) Norman, free Negro, upwards of 21. Bondsman, Heney Norman

21 Jan 1800 James Redman & Eve Corder, upwards of 21 years old, daughter of Joseph

Corder of Frederick County. Bondsmen, Isaac Redman & James Corder

22 Jan 1800 John Heafer & Priscilla Ryan. Bondsman, Daniel Miller

24 Jan 1800 Joseph Hite & Catharine Cartmell, daughter of John Cartmell, the bondsman

25 Jan 1800 Thomas Draper & Grace Antrim. Bondsman, Edward Antrim

27 Jan 1800 William Bartlett & Lydia Powell, daughter of Robert Powell, the bondsman

28 Jan 1800 Abraham Ramey & Ann Massie, daughter of William Massie. Bondsman, John Humston

1 Feb 1800 John Ralston & Sarah Cockran, daughter of Edward Holland, the bondsman

4 Feb 1800 Richard Brookover & Mary Cochran. Bondsman, Benjamin Langley

5 Feb 1800 John Cather & Elizabeth McKee, daughter of Robert McKee, the bondsman

10 Feb 1800 Jesse Wright & Sarah Crumley. Bondsman, Thomas Crumly

18 Feb 1800 Jesse Carroll & Ginny Nutt, daughter of Edward Nutt of Frederick County, the bondsman

20 Feb 1800 Elijah Kercheval & Sally Green. Bondsman, James Green

21 Feb 1800 John Vanaurt & Lydia Ramey of Frederick County. Bondsman, John Ramey/"Remey" in signature

21 Feb 1800 Samuel Ramey & Hannah Fetheringale. Bondsman, John Ramy

22 Feb 1800 Robert Smith & Ann Littler, daughter of John Littler, the bondsman

24 Feb 1800 Benjamin Elliott & Jean Humston. Bondsman, John Humston

3 Mar 1800 Marshall Stone & Lydia Minshall, daughter of Edward Minshall, the bondsman

6 Mar 1800 Thomas Wilson & Elizabeth Stephenson. Bondsman, Joseph Sexton

10 Mar 1800 Edward Draper & Lucy Owens of Frederick County. Bondsman, John Rose

15 Mar 1800 Presly Talbott & Mary Brent, daughter of Charles Brent of Frederick County

19 Mar 1800 David Hickey & Ann Richardson, daughter of Saml Wilson, the bondsman

21 Mar 1800 Thomas Blackburn & Sally B. Haynie. Bondsman, John Mustin

22 Mar 1800 Thomas Baker & Sarah Hyland. Bondsman, John Smith

24 Mar 1800 Philip Peer & Lidia Swayne. Bondsman, Abner Swayne

24 Mar 1800 William Albin & Caty Ritenour, daughter of Michael Ritenour, the bondsman

24 Mar 1800 James Rodgers & Auny Short, daughter of James Short. Bondsman, George Short

1 Apr 1800 Isaac Dunovan & Sarah Keeran. Bondsman, Eli Keeran

2 Apr 1800 Joseph Singer (Thomas Singer at top of bond) & Phebe Powell of Frederick County. Bondsman, Job Fallis

5 Apr 1800 John Binnegar & Ann Marles, daughter of Jacob Marles. Bondsman, John Hodgson

7 Apr 1800 Isaac Kackley & Catherine Millhorn. Bondsman, George Lamp

8 Apr 1800 Rezin Mason & Mary Werr. Bondsman, Joseph Weer

15 Apr 1800 Moses Lehew/Lehue & Hannah Branson, daughter of Lionel Branson of Frederick County. Bondsman, Daniel Cloud

15 Apr 1800 James Sullivan & Mary Martin, stepdaughter of Daniel Fry, the bondsman

21 Apr 1800 Robert Cross & Mary Seibert of Fredk County. Bondsman, Gabriel Cross

24 Apr 1800 David Benegar & Elizabeth Wickersham, daughter of William Wickersham. Bondsman, Jonas Chamberlin

5 -------- (day & month blank) John Settle & Margery Forguson Sutor, daughter of John Sutor, Clerk of County of Frederick, who gave consent in person. (Is this a reference to Frederick County, Maryland?). Bondsman, John Sutor

5 May 1800 William Vanlandingham & Elizabeth Featheringall, daughter of John Featheringall of Frederick County. Bondsman, Richard Bryarly

12 May 1800 William Maddin & Jinny Hainey of County of Frederick. Bondsman, Thomas Hunter, who made oath that bride is over 21

12 May 1800 Abraham Cryder & Leah Dailey, widow of Joseph Dailey decd of Frederick County. Bondsman, George Larrick

15 May 1800 John Campbell & Ruth Hodgson, daughter of Robert Hodgson dec of Frederick County. Bondsman, John Hodgson

16 May 1800 Thornly Berry & Betsy W. Kendal. Bondsman, Presley Moor

24 May 1800 Samuel McMeeken & Ann Clark of Frederick County. Bondsman, John Randall

29 May 1800 Anthony Bell & Mary McCoole of Frederick County. Bondsman, William Gosset Jur

6 Jun 1800 Richard Copeland & Uphamy Henderson, daughter of William Henderson, the bondsman

11 Jun 1800 Sampson Garner & Sarah Clendenen of Frederick County. Bondsman, John Bowen

17 Jun 1800 William Grubbs & Rachael Smith of Frederick County upwards of 21. Bondsman, John Fawcett

17 Jun 1800 William Holmes & Mary Bond, a widow. Bondsman, Joseph Longacre

23 Jun 1800 Andrew Newman & Sarah Halbert of Frederick County. Bondsman, Henry Huntsberry, who signs in German

23 Jun 1800 Joseph Norman & Nancy Jennings. Bondsman, John Wall

25 Jun 1800 Alexander Stewart & Polly Gassaway. Bondsman, Cornelius Baldwin

23 Jul 1800 Joseph Hollingsworth & Peggy Beeler. Bondsman, Thos Neill

21 Jul 1800 William Davison & Maria Smith. Bondsman, Thompson McDonald

24 Jul 1800 William Anderson & Lydia Morgan. Bondsman, John Shanon

26 Jul 1800 George Crummy & Winifred Killey, widow of John Kelly, dec. Bondsman, Abner Wickersham

29 Jul 1800 Robert Gray & Ann Vance, widow & relict of William Vance dec. Bondsman, Thomas McKewan

30 Jul 1800 William Irwin & Dolly Young. Bondsman, Griffin Taylor

1 Aug 1800 Asa Hankins & Nancy White of the County of Frederick. Bondsman, Amos Hankins

1 Aug 1800 Amos Hankins & Nancy Chipley of Frederick County. Bondsman, Asa Hankins

14 Aug 1800 Andrew Rice & Rosina Burkharmer, daughter of Henry Burkheimer, the bondsman, who signs in German

19 Aug 1800 James Morrison & Mary Spinder, widow & relict of William Spinder decd. Bondsman, John W. Driver

21 Aug 1800 Eli Smith & Jenny McDonald of Frederick County, daughter of Thomas McDonald. She was upwards of 21 years of age. Bondsman, Gabriel Davis

21 Aug 1800 William Booram & Mary Brooks. Bondsman, French.Hansbrough

22 Aug 1800 John Frederick & Lydia Earheart, daughter of Philip Earheart of Frederick County, the bondsman, who signs in German

23 Aug 1800 Thomas McIntire & Mary Dick, daughter of Peter Dick, the bondsman

26 Aug 1800 John Kackly & Ann Bachlor, ward of Philip P. Bucher of Frederick County. Bondsman, Moses Russell

1 Sep 1800 Rees Baldwin & Lydia Evans of Frederick County. Bondsman, Francis Baker

8 Sep 1800 Nathan Littler Junr & Jane Robinson, daughter of James Robinson of Frederick County. Bondsman, Abner Babb

9 Sep 1800 Basten Dotts & Elizabeth Rice, daughter of Jacob Rice of Frederick County, the bondsman

10 Sep 1800 Solomon Grapes & Elizabeth Switzer, daughter of Jacob Switzer, the bondsman, who signs in German

13 Sep 1800 William Sheehon & Hannah Light, daughter of Frederick Light of Frederick County, the bondsman

19 Sep 1800 Francis Davis & Ann Calvert of Frederick County. Bondsman, Isaac Dowell

22 Sep 1800 James Nutt & Rachel Cartmell, daughter of Thomas Cartmell. Bondsman, Joseph Cartmell

27 Sep 1800 William H. King & Alice Duff, daughter of Peter Duff of Frederick County. Bondsman, Dale Carter

23 Sep 1800 James Thompson & Lettice Beattey of Frederick County. Bondsman, John Beattey

25 Sep 1800 Elisha I. Hall & Catharine Smith Spinster. Bondsman, Adam Douglass

2 Oct 1800 Barnabas McCauley & Anna Doughty of Frederick County, sister of Daniel Doughty, the bondsman

20 Dec 1800 William Vannort Junr & Betsy Maltimore. Bondsman, William Vannort Sr

22 Dec 1800 Joseph Stump & Elizabeth Aid, widow of John Aid. Bondsman, Daniel Stump

30 Jan 1801 John Tuttle & Catharine Farrell, widow & relict of John Ferrell dec. Bondsman, Peter Cooley

31 Jan 1801 Abraham Stallings & Sarah Carr, daughter of Thomas Carr of Frederick County, the bondsman

4 Feb 1801 Benjamin Castleman & Elizabeth Goff. Bondsman, David Castleman

14 Feb 1801 James Mitchel & Susannah Catlet. Bondsman, James Dawson

14 Feb 1801 Philip Taflinger & Elizabeth Barrow, daughter of William Barrow, the bondsman

6 Mar 1801 Nicholas Fitsimons & Isabella Murphy, daughter of Patrick Murphy, the bondsman

7 Mar 1801 Tewalt Hickle & Mary Graves of Frederick County, daughter of Philip Graves. Bondsman, William Hooke

9 Mar 1801 Elijah Hawkes & Eddy McVea. Bondsman, John McFeeley

10 Mar 1801 Adam Hott & Catharine Hott, widow & relict of Peter Hott dec. of Frederick. Bondsman, Henry Hott, who signs in German

10 Mar 1801 David Taylor & Martha Hott, daughter of Henry Hott, the bondsman, who signs in German

10 Mar 1801 Jacob Jones & Elizabeth Bell. Bondsman, Thomas Bell

25 Mar 1801 Israel Jones & Margaret Conner. Bondsman, John Withrow

25 Mar 1801 Philigathus Roberts & Peggy Helm. Bondsman, Meredith Helm

19 Mar 1801 Jacob Adams & Rachel Adams, daughter of William Adams of Frederick County. Bondsman, James McCoole Junr

20 Mar 1801 John Buscart & Catharine Taylor, daughter of George Taylor of Frederick County. Bondsman, Joseph Peck

2 Apr 1801 William Alloway & Mary Wickersham, daughter of William Wickersham, the bondsman

3 Apr 1801 Jacob Rhodes & Martha Shipler. Bondsman, George Linn

4 Apr 1801 Isaac Horbaugh & Mary Garrett. Bondsman, Henry Garret

4 Apr 1801 James Smith & Catherine Taylor, daughter of Abraham Taylor, the bondsman

6 Apr 1801 Wm ?McFate (or Wm. M. Fate) & Mary McLean. Bondsman, Thomas McLean

6 Apr 1801 Hugh McMillan & Mary Love. Bondsman, John Kemp

8 Apr 1801 John Witherrow & Sarah Roland, daughter of Gerold Roland, the bondsman

9 Apr 1801 Frederick Light & Mary Oubry, daughter of Henry Oubry, the bondsman

11 Apr 1801 Snoden Martin & Elizabeth Thornberg, daughter of Danl Thornbrugh (sic)

18 Apr 1801 Henry Snider & Mary Hull. Bondsman, Abraham T. Pflieger

23 Apr 1801 Amos Foreman & Hannah Goff, daughter of John Goff of Frederick County, the bondsman

24 Apr 1801 Morris Ellis & Mary Smith, widow & relict of Jeremiah Smith of Frederick County. Bondsman, William Doster

27 Apr 1801 David Groves & Elizabeth Step, daughter of George Step, the bondsman

27 Apr 1801 Jacob Miller & Martha Miller, widow & relict of Richard Miller decd. Bondsman, Joseph Fawcett

4 May 1801 John McFadden & Susannah McIlwane (widow). Bondsman, Elijah Littler

4 May 1801 Thomas Farris & Margaret Martin of Fredk County. Bondsman, James Boles

4 May 1801 John McFadden & Susannah McIlwane (widow). Bondsman, Elijah Littler

7 May 1801 Thomas Reed & Catherine White. Bondsman, Jonathan White

13 May 1801 John Shackleford & Ann Newman. Bondsman, James Newman

13 May 1801 Patrick ?Hamway & Polly Brown. Bondsman, Tobias Walters

15 May 1801 David Mercer & Mary Hannon of Freerick County. Bondsman, Moses Mercer
16 May 1801 George Huddle & Barbara Wilfong of Frederick County. Bondsman, Tobias Stickley
19 May 1801 Thomas Mulloy & Sary Brown. Bondsman, John Douglass
30 May 1801 Joseph Catterlin & Mary Mercer of Frederick County. Bondsman, Robert Mercer
1 Jun 1801 Simon Allensworth & Elizabeth Elzey, daughter of John Elzey, the bondsman
2 Jun 1801 Jacob File & Sarah Adams of Frederick County. Bondsman, John Farmer
6 Jun 1801 Peter Hummer & Unis Tavender of Frederick County. Bondsman, Thomas Martin
6 Jun 1801 William Stewart & Sarah Cole of Frederick County. Bondsman, Benjamin Van Landingham
13 May 1801 (June written below in pencil) Patrick ?Hamway & Polly Brown. Bondsman, Tobias Walters
17 Jun 1801 Benjamin Barrett & Sarah Ward of Frederick County. Bondsman, Jacob Jenkins
23 Jun 1801 Joseph Thompson & Jane Ewing. Bondsman, Thomas Ewing
24 Jun 1801 Daniel Mytinger & Maria White. Bondsman, John McCoun
29 Jun 1801 John Ashwood & Hester Ashton of Frederick County. Bondsman, William Marshall
6 Jul 1801 William Wilson Jr and Catharine Hotzenpiller of Frederick County. Bondsman, Ralph Selby
14 Jul 1801 Peter Roystone & Ann Anderson, daughter of Joseph Anderson
26 Jul 1801 Mahlon Panter & Hannah Davis. Bondsman, Isaac Painter
3 Aug 1801 Richard Wilson & Mary Concklin, daughter of David Conklyn, the bondsman
5 Aug 1801 Benjamin Sherriff & Elizabeth Dean. Bondsman, George Wisecarver
8 Aug 1801 William Gray & Jane Campbell of Frederick County. Bondsman, William Clemens
10 Aug 1801 John Green & Lydia Davis, daughter of Samuel Davis of Frederick County. Bondsman, George Chamblin
15 Aug 1801 John Harris & Nancy Binegar of Frederick County. Bondsman, Samuel Binegar

18 Aug 1801 Andrew Cyphert & Hannah Marl, daughter of Jacob Marll, the bondsman

19 Aug 1801 Jacob Keller & Elizabeth Cyfret, daughter of George Cyfret of Frederick County, the bondsman

19 Aug 1801 Thomas Cunningham & Jenny Housten of Frederick County. Bondsman, James Brown

20 Aug 1801 Joseph Fawcett & Milly Carpenter of Frederick County. Bondsman, John Pickering

20 Aug 1801 Hugh Fitzsimons & Sarah McMahon, widow & relict of Timothy McMahan decd. Bondsman, William Cronnen

24 Aug 1801 Henry Taylor & Elizabeth Carr of Frederick County. Bondsman, Arthur W. Carter

2 Sep 1801 Jacob Hoffman and Mary Gilham, widow & relict of Peter Gilham decd of Frederick County. Bondsman, Joseph Venable

3 Sep 1801 Archibald Young & Lettice Morgan, widow & relict of Enoch Morgan decd of Frederick County. Bondsman, William Carrell

4 Sep 1801 Francis Barr & Nancy Willington of Frederick County. Bondsman, John Willington

8 Sep 1801 Alexander Homes and Priscilla Roberts of the County of Frederick. Bondsman, John Grigsby

10 Sep 1801 George Morgan & Clara Coates, daughter of Thomas Coats of Frederick County. Bondsman, Noah Morgan

11 Sep 1801 Thomas Lambert & Diana Harkins, widow of Daniel Harkins & daughter of Stephen Bollinger, the bondsman

12 Sep 1801 Adam Clevenger & Sally Beadles of Frederick County. Bondsman, Jacob Clevenger

12 Sep 1801 Henry Kern & Rachel Richard, daughter of Henry Richard of Frederick County, the bondsman, who signs in German

10 Sept 1801 Thomas Garrison & Jean Wittington, daughter of Jonathan Whittington of Frederick County, the bondsman

17 Sep 1801 William Orndorff & Elizabeth Cooper, daughter of John Cooper of Frederick County. Bondsman, William Cooper

19 Sep 1801 Robert Beaty & Theodotia Clevinger, daughter of Mary Robertson late Mary Clevinger. Bondsman, Joseph Shackelford

22 Sep 1801 Lewis Chastain & Alice Shearman spinster. Bondsman, William Timberlake
23 Sep 1801 William Powell Simmons & Jane Cole. Bondsman, William Marshall
28 Sep 1801 Richard Kean & Margaret Ogilvie. Bondsman, John Bond
3 Oct 1801 John Neff & Elizabeth Hickey, daughter of Edward Hickey, the bondsman
5 Oct 1801 William Campbell & Mary Plumb, daughter of Casimer Plumb, the bondsman
6 Oct 1801 George Stipe & Elizabeth Ryan, widow & relict of John Ryan decd of Frederick County. Bondsman, J. Peyton
6 Oct 1801 Elisha Emmons & Polly Perkizer, daughter of Michael Perkizer of Frederick County. Bondsman, Benjamin Kendrick, who signs in German
6 Oct 1801 William Gilham & Mary Goodycuntz of Frederick County. Bondsman, George Goodykuns
7 Oct 1801 William Adams Jr. & Sarah Dawson, daughter of George Dawson of Frederick County, the bondsman
7 Oct 1801 Philip Miller & Sarah Bougher, daughter of John Bougher of Frederick County, the bondsman. Both groom & bondsman sign in German
9 Oct 1801 Daniel Hart & Prudence Blackford, widow & relict of Peter Blackford decd late of Frederick County. Bondsman, Thomas McKewan
10 Oct 1801 Elisha Leach & Margaret Littleton of Frederick County. Bondsman, William Littleton
10 Oct 1801 James Coolbee & Catharine Stonebrook of Frederick County. Bondsman, David Bowland
14 Oct 1801 Martin Cryder & Mary Niswanger of Frederick County, daughter of John Niswanger, the bondsman.
14 Oct 1801 Edward Bollen & Jemima Mitchell of Frederick County. Bondsman, James Compton
17 Oct 1801 James Smallwood & Patty Graham of Frederick County. Bondsman, Isaac Ramey
19 Oct 1801 Mandly Taylor & Catharine Williams, ward of Joseph Pollard, the bondsman

19 Oct 1801 Thomas Buck junr & Amelia Lee Dawson, daughter of Benjamin Dawson, the bondsman

19 Oct 1801 Robert Dunn & Catharine Wickersham of Frederick County. Bondsman, Thomas Dunn

19 Oct 1801 John Steel & Nancy Gardner, daughter of William Gardner of Frederick County. Bondsman, George Gardner

19 Oct 1801 John Littleton & Seniah Leach, daughter of Elijah Leach of Frederick County

20 Oct 1801 Abel Benton & Nancy Lenox. Bondsman, Jacob Kackley

21 Oct 1801 Miller Spencer & Sidney Rogers, daughter of Evan Rogers of Frederick County. Bondsman, James Robinson

21 Oct 1801 Henry Negley & Hannah Tremble of Frederick County. Bondsman, Henry Seever

21 Oct 1801 George Tilman, who is 20 years old last February last, & Mary Denny, daughter of David Denney, the bondsman

23 Oct 1801 Daniel Ox & Catharine Farver of Frederick County of lawful age. Bondsman, Christian Hoppermill

24 Oct 1801 Jacob Foley & Catharine Swatz of Fredk County. Bondsman, Christian Harrel or ?Hamrel, who signs in German

26 Oct 1801 Philip Sonner & Catharine Gantz, widow of ------ Gantz. Bondsman, Isaac Littler

27 Oct 1801 Saml Baker & Lucy Ship, daughter of Ewel Ship of Frederick County. Bondsman, Ebin Taylor

27 Oct 1801 Eben Taylor & Nancy Ship, daughter of Ewill Ship. Bondsman, Saml Baker

28 Oct 1801 Alexr Bradford & Edith Catlett, daughter of James Catlett of Frederick County. Bondsman, Peter McPherson

28 Oct 1801 James Martin & Elizabeth Lee of Frederick County. Bondsman, Asa Hankins

2 Nov 1801 William Tanquary & Elizabeth Saddler, daughter of William Saddler of Fredk County, the bondsman. Groom signs as Abraham Tanquary

2 Nov 1801 Daniel Settle & Jane Wroe, daughter of Benjamin Wroe of Fredk County, the bondsman

4 Nov 1801 Saml Stallings & Elizabeth Poole, daughter of William Poole of Frederick County. Bondsman, John Strickling

5 Nov 1801 Thomas Davis & Ann Mckee. Bondsman, William Hooke

11 Nov 1801 Henry Piper & Elizabeth Samsel. Bondsman, John Samsel

13 Nov 1801 Jacob Williams & Elizabeth GreenLee of Frederick County of lawful age. Bondsman, John Jones

11 Nov 1801 Tenly Murphy & Nancy Richardson. Bondsman, Thos Murphy

13 Nov 1801 Eli McArter & Rebecca Brown, daughter of Abraham Brown, the bondsman

14 Nov 1801 David Wright & Rebecca Milburn, daughter of Andrew Milburn of Frederick County, the bondsman

16 Nov 1801 Alfred H. Powell & Sidney Ann Thruston, daughter of Charles M. Thruston of Frederick County. Bondsman, Thomas Mckewan

21 Nov 1801 Charles Lobb & Sarah Ross of Frederick County of lawful age. Bondsman, Elisha Moore

24 Nov 1801 Edward Smith & Jane Shaver of Frederick County. Bondsman, Martin Smith

25 Nov 1801 Josias Ferguson & Betsy Orier, daughter of Jesse Orier of Frederick County, the bondsman

25 Nov 1801 James Marshall & Susan Orear, daughter of Benjamin Orear of Frederick County. Bondsman, Jesse Orear Jr

30 Nov 1801 John Rutter & Jayne Buckley, daughter of Abraham Buckley of Frederick County, the bondsman

2 Dec 1801 Daniel Holloway & Mary Holloway spinster. Bondsman, Joseph Holloway

3 Dec 1801 Noah Morgan, son of Enoch Morgan, & Sarah Wilson, daughter of Nathl Wilson of Frederick County. Bondsman, Enoch Morgan

4 Dec 1801 Jacob Arterbourn & Levi Williams of Frederick County. Bondsman, John Peyton

7 Dec 1801 George Deal & Catharine Hott, daughter of Henry Hott of Frederick County, who signs in German

7 Dec 1801 Robert Southard & Tiner Riggle, daughter of George Riggle of Frederick County. Bondsman, Sebastian Southard

14 Dec 1801 Isaac Scott & Elizabeth Thompson of Frederick County. Bondsman, John Thompson

14 Dec 1801 Samuel Griffith & Elieanor Rubb, daughter of John Rubb of Frederick County. Bondsman, Elijah Griffith

15 Dec 1801 Philip Phetty & Rachel Carter, widow. Bondsman, Arthur W. Carter

15 Dec 1801 Thomas Turner & Caron Littleton, daughter of Charles Littleton of Frederick County. Bondsman, William Littleton

15 Dec 1801 Edward B. Jones & Frances Harrison of Frederick County. Bondsman, Williamson P. Jones

16 Dec 1801 Jacob Kern & Sarah Ryan, daughter of Darby Ryan, the bondsman

18 Dec 1801 Jacob Vanourt & Edia Lehew, daughter of Spencer Lehew of Frederick County. Bondsman, Spencer Lehew, Junr

21 Dec 1801 Peter Hurst & Ann Rust, daughter of Peter Rust of Frederick County. Bondsman, Machen C. Respess

22 Dec 1801 Andrew Ronimus & Catharine Alemong, stepdaughter of John Rogers of Frederick County, the bondsman

24 Dec 1801 Thomas Halbert & Mary Beavers, daughter of John Beavers of Frederick County. Bondsman, Moses Beavers

25 Dec 1801 William Lupton Junr & Elizabeth Bowers, daughter of Henry Bowers of Frederick County. Bondsman, Jacob Bowers

25 Dec 1801 Stuffle Sluser Jr. & Ann Myers, daughter of William Myers of Frederick County. Bondsman, Samuel Rogers

26 Dec 1801 Samuel Orndorff & Sarah Shull, sister of Joseph Shull, the bondsman

28 Dec 1801 John Nicholas & Mary Rowzey, daughter of Reuben Rowzey of Frederick County, the bondsman

30 Dec 1801 Thomas Johnston & Susannah Hawes, daughter of Charles Hows, the bondsman

2 Jan 1802 Gasper Carver & Nancy Saway. Bondsman, Reubin Clarke

4 Jan 1802 Thomas Baldwin Jr. & Nancy Kurtz, ward of Joseph Hair or Haire, the bondsman

5 Jan 1802 Thomas Short & Nancy Tucker of lawful age of Frederick County. Bondsman, Cornelius Vincent

5 Jan 1802 Jesse Anderson Jr. & Catharine Sands of Frederick County of lawful age. Bondsman, Jonah Iden

8 Jan 1802 William D. Hendren & Sally Allensworth of Frederick County. Bondsman, Reuben Allensworth

9 Jan 1802 William Dean & Martha Dixon, widow of John Dixon decd of Frederick County. Bondsman, John Daugherty

9 Jan 1802 David Anderson & Mary Huff, daughter of Morgan Huff of Frederick County, the bondsman

11 Jan 1802 Philip Burroughs & Susannah John of lawful age of Frederick County. Bondsman, James Standford

20 Jan 1802 David Frieze & Mary Whollian, daughter of John Whollian of Frederick County, the bondsman

23 Jan 1802 Hezekiah Stallings & Lethea Woodward, daughter of Benedict Woodward of Frederick County, the bondsman

23 Jan 1802 Edward Gilpin & Nancy Featheringill, daughter of George Featheringal of Frederick County. Bondsman, James Gilpin

23 Jan 1802 William Bush & Evo Maria Barlay, daughter of John Barlay of Frederick County, the bondsman

25 Jan 1802 Samuel Read & Jane Dowell, daughter of Thomas Dowell of Frederick County. Bondsman, Joseph Smith

26 Jan 1802 Ezekiel White & Rachel Willis, daughter of Nancy Willis of Frederick County. Bondsman, John Ramy

26 Jan 1802 Isaac Redman & Catharine Wheeling of Frederick County. Bondsman, John Spence

27 Jan 1802 John Vanhorn & Elizabeth Butler of Frederick County. Bondsman, John Pierce

4 Feb 1802 William Strupe & Any Nicklin of Frederick County. Bondsman, Joseph Nicklin

9 Feb 1802 John Chapman & Mary Ramsay. Bondsman, Robert Throckmorton

10 Feb 1802 Samuel Forguson & Catharine Jolly, daughter of Benjamin Jolly of Frederick County. Bondsman, Joseph Sexton

17 Feb 1802 George Stipe & Catharine Cyfret, daughter of George Cyfret of Frederick County, the bondsman

18 Feb 1802 Bartholemew Mckee & Nancy Reid of Frederick County. Bondsman, James Reid

20 Feb 1802 Abner Ferguson & Mary Morgan, daughter of Tho. Morgan of Frederick County, the bondsman

23 Feb 1802 George Snyder & Anna Busher, daughter of John Busher of Frederick County, the bondsman, who signs in German

24 Feb 1802 Adam Hill & Ann Likens, daughter of Henry Likens decd late of Frederick County. Bondsman, Collin Carrell

24 Feb 1802 George Probasco & Elizabeth Custer spinster. Bondsman, Saml Custer

26 Feb 1802 James Byland & Sarah Macmillan spinster. Bondsman, John Kirby

27 Feb 1802 George Seevers & Nancy Welsh of Frederick County. Bondsman, Casper Sewers Jr

27 Feb 1802 Ephraim Fenton & Polly Ryan of Frederick County. Bondsman, John Heaper

1 Mar 1802 John Blake & Ann Chamblen spinster. Bondsman, Thomas Chamblin

2 Mar 1802 William Peters & Sophia Lair, daughter of Conrad Lair who appeared and gave consent. Bondsman, George Beemer

13 Mar 1802 Christopher Tarflinger & Elizabeth Heckethorn, daughter of Daniel Heckerthorn, the bondsman, who signs in German

26 Mar 1802 Jesse Britton & Susannah Noland, daughter of Pierce Nolain of Frederick County, the bondsman

6 Mar 1802 Peter Funk & Mary Rinehart of Frederick. Bondsman, John Barrow

9 Mar 1802 William Weaver & Peggy Carson of Frederick County. Bondsman, John Weaver

24 Mar 1802 Stephen Chilton & Susan Turner, daughter of Hezekiah Turner of Fredk County. Bondsman, John A. Smith

5 Apr 1802 William R Buck & Lucy Blakemore. Bondsman, Thomas Neill

9 Apr 1802 William Conrad & Elizabeth Doughty of Frederick County. Bondsman, Daniel Doughty

10 Apr 1802 Thornton Fleming & Grace Dunbar of Frederick County. Bondsman, Geo Reed

15 Apr 1802 James Reed & Nancy Bell, daughter of George Bell of Frederick County. Bondsman, John McMeekin

15 Apr 1802 John Chamblin & Anna Vanbuskirk, daughter of Abraham Vanbuskirk of Frederick County, the bondsman

16 Apr 1802 Jacob Manker & Mary Forsithe of Frederick County. Bondsman, Nicholas Unger

20 Apr 1802 John Green & Winifred Catlett, daughter of John Catlett of Frederick County. Bondsman, Peter Catlett

21 Apr 1802 David Darlinton & Anna McCoole of Frederick County of lawful age. Bondsman, Joel I. Justin

26 Apr 1802 Daniel Doughty & Anna McAuley, daughter of John Mcauly of Frederick County, of lawful age. Bondsman, Henry McAuley

30 Apr 1802 John Groves & Susannah Bougher. Bondsman, John Nighswanger or Nisewanger

1 May 1802 Joseph Majors & Polly Polock of Frederick County of lawful age. Bondsman, John Hurford

3 May 1802 Henry Kain & Winney Jones, ward of Water Slater, the bondsman

4 May 1802 Meredith Darlington & Catharine McCoole, daughter of John McCoole, the bondsman

13 May 1802 Isaac Heiskell & Mary Sowers. Bondsman, John C. Sowers

24 May 1802 John Gibbons & Elizabeth Thompson of Frederick COunty of lawful age. Bondsman, Moses Lowry

24 May 1802 William Orr & Nancy Parkison. Bondsman, Aaron Bonham

27 May 1802 Zephaniah Leisure & Elizabeth Atchison of lawful age. Bondsman, Robert Crockett

27 May 1802 Jacob Piper & Catharine Snapp, daughter of George Snapp of Frederick County, the bondsman

31 May 1802 Henry Richard & Elizabeth Copelin, daughter of Henry Copelin, the bondsman

8 Jun 1802 William Hickman & Fanny Richardson, widow & relict of Edward Richardson decd. Bondsman, Samuel Irwin

8 Jun 1802 Spencer Lahew & Nancy Catlett, daughter of John Catlett of Frederick County. Bondsman, Butler Allensworth

10 Jun 1802 John Ambrose & Betsy Crum, daughter of Christian Crum of Frederick County. Bondsman, Simon Lauch. Groom signs in German

12 Jun 1802 Thomas Bailey & Elizabeth Albert, daughter of William Albert of Frederick County, the bondsman

17 Jun 1802 John Heiskell & Ann Sowers, daughter of Jacob Sowers of Frederick County. Bondsman, John C. Sowers

21 Jun 1802 William Martin and Susannah Lanham, daughter of Henry Lanham of Frederick County. Bondsman, Dennis Lanham

26 Jun 1802 David Baldwin & Margaret Ellis, widow of Thomas Ellis decd late of Frederick County. Bondsman, John Newbrough

14 Jun 1802 Alexander Milton & Sarah Stribling, widow & relict of John Stribling decd. Bondsman, Eben Taylor

3 Jul 1802 Thomas Stewart & Susannah Stuart of Frederick County of lawful age. Bondsman, James Stewart

6 Jul 1802 James H. Davis & Harriet B. Smith of Frederick County of lawful age. Bondsman, Benjamin N. Barnett

17 Jul 1802 John Reynolds & Elizabeth Tharp widow. Bondsman, William Bush

17 Jul 1802 John Myers & Betsy Goodnight, daughter of John Goodnight of Frederick County, the bondsman

27 Jul 1802 George Riggle & Polly Johnston, daughter of John Johnston of Frederick County. Bondsman, Joseph Riggle

30 Jul 1802 Joseph Draper & Jane Kellor, daughter of John Kellor of Frederick County, the bondsman

3 Aug 1802 Joshua Beatty & Edith Clevinger of Frederick County, daughter of Joseph Clevinger decd. Bondsman, John Clevinger

3 Aug 1802 John Ramey & Mary Cordell of Fredk Cty. Bondsman, William Hand

7 Aug 1802 Benjamin Hockman & Elizabeth Purkhiser, spinster of Fredk County. Bondsman, Samuel Purkhiser

12 Aug 1802 Joseph Kenny & Frances Moore, daughter of Anthony Moore of Frederick County, the bondsman

18 Aug 1802 David Smith & Agnes Christie (of lawful age) of Frederick County. Bondsman, Pollard Hardgrove

18 Aug 1802 Gideon Edwards & Mary Dillon, daughter of John Dillon of Frederick County of lawful age. Bondsman, Richard Fallis

21 Aug 1802 Jesse Curtes & Nancy Curtes, daughter of Henry Curtes

24 Aug 1802 William Hogan & Mary Lewis of lawful age of Frederick County. Bondsman, Amos McLaughlin

26 Aug 1802 Eleazer Barrow & Rebecca Wilson of lawful age of Frederick County. Bondsman, Esaias Earle

26 Aug 1802 George Mock & Mary Gaunder, daughter of Peter Gaunder of Frederick County. Bondsman, Jacob Gander

30 Aug 1802 William Southard, son of John Southard, & Ann Darr, daughter of George Darr, the bondsman

8 Sep 1802 James D. Bruler & Nancy Cochran, daughter of Robert Cochran of said County, the bondsman

9 Sep 1802 David Ferguson & Johnnah Clevinger, daughter of Joseph Clevinger of Frederick County. Bondsman, John Romine

9 Sep 1802 Samuel Weldon a free man and not a slave & Nancy Wells of lawful age of Frederick County. Bondsman, Benj. Dawson

11 Sep 1802 Samuel Lewis & Christina Seabert, daughter of Jacob Seabert decd late of Frederick County. Bondsman, Henry Miller. Witness, Margaret Seabert, mother of Christiana

30 Aug 1802 Joseph Smith & Joahnah Aton of Frederick County. Bondsman, William McCormick

30 Aug 1802 William Newby & Elizabeth Ball, ward of James Singleton, the bondsman

4 Sep 1802 Jonathan Lang (the signature is Jona Shank) & Sarah Barnes of Frederick County. Bondsman, Adam Pully

7 Sep 1802 Michael Freize & Rachel Ward of lawful age. Bondsman, Benjamin Barrett

5 .... 1802 Jacob Barrick & Jane Harrison, daughter of George Harrison of Frederick County, the bondsman

6 Oct 1802 Abraham Woodrow & Nancy Kerfott of Frederick County of lawful age. Bondsman, William G. Kerfott

17 Sep 1802 Butler Allensworth & Henrietta Catlett, daughter of John Catlett of Frederick County. Bondsman, Spencer Lehew, Junr

20 Sep 1802 Israel Jenkins & Elizabeth Horseman, daughter of David Horseman of Fredk County, the bondsman

2 Oct 1802 William Campbell & Amey McNelly, widow & relict of William McNelly decd of Frederick County. Bondsman, James Roberts

5 Oct 1802 Samuel Benegar & Judith Smith, daughter of Andrew Smith of Frederick County, the bondsman

9 Oct 1802 James Willis & Polly Holmes, daughter of John Holmes of Fredk, the bondsman

11 Oct 1802 John Cartmell & Anna Pearson, daughter of Alex Pearson, the said Anna being now a resident in Fredk County. Bondsman, Thomas McKowan

26 Oct 1802 John Davis & Elizabeth Marsh, daughter of Richard Marsh, the bondsman

5 Nov 1802 James Elkins & Nancy Sanford of Frederick County of Lawful age. Bondsman, William Franks

29 Oct 1802 William Whittington & Rebecca Mullenecks, daughter of Henry Mullenecks, the bondsman (she of Frederick County)

1 Nov 1802 Mark Harper & Olivia Kidd of Frederick County of lawful age. Bondsman, John Antram

6 Nov 1802 Stephen Mires & Rachel Griffen of Frederick County of lawful age. Bondsman, Edward Griffin

9 Nov 1802 Peter Funk & Hannah Elzey of Frederick County of lawful age. Bondsman, Robert McClenahan

22 Nov 1802 Jeremiah Garner & Elizabeth Hurford of Frederick County both of lawful age. Bondsman, Joseph Hurford

22 Nov 1802 Alexander Carter & Tracy Settle of Frederick County. Bondsman, John Settle

22 Nov 1802 Martin Cooper & Anna Williams of lawfull age (both of Fredk County). Bondsman, William Orndorff

24 Nov 1802 Stephen Chilton & Susan Turner, daughter of Hezekiah Turner of Frederick County. Bondsman, John A. Smith

3 Jan 1803 Nathan Jones & Rosana Binigar of Frederick County of lawful age. Bondsman, John Binnegar

5 Jan 1803 William Beaty & Maryann Ro---- (bond torn) of Frederick County of lawful age. Bondsman, John ---- (bond torn)

8 Jan 1803 Gersham Drake & Phebe Coleman relict of Peter Coleman ded of Frederick County. Bondsman, Francis Drake

11 Jan 1803 John Dawson & Sarah Farmer of Frederick County of lawfull age. Bondsman, Thomas Farmer

20 Jan 1803 George Taylor & Nancy Shannon, ward & stepdaughter of Humphrey Kain; witness, Molly Kain. Groom signs "Walter Taylor"

25 Jan 1803 Isaac Booth & Sarah Hanshaw, daughter of William Hancher of Frederick County, the bondsman

29 Jan 1803 William Havely & Hannah Dehaven, daughter of Isaac Dehaven of Frederick County, the bondsman

11 Jan 1803 Henry Oldacre & Susanah Groves of Frederick County of lawful age. Bondsman, John Groves

18 Jan 1803 Nehemiah Garrison & Rebeccah Kennor, daughter of Thomas Kennor of Fredk County. Bondsman, Griffin Taylor

2 Feb 1803 William F. Simrall & Polly Gilkeson of Frederick County. Bondsman, Robert D. Glass

3 Feb 1803 William Smith & Margaret Knight, daughter of William Knight of said County. Bondsman, James Little

5 Feb 1803 William Haddox & Hannah Hall of Frederick County of lawful age. Bondsman, John Haddox

8 Feb 1803 Charles Bowen & Nancy Howard of Frederick County, of lawful age. Bondsman, Isaac Bowen

12 Feb 1803 Daniel Baker & Mary Castleman, daughter of John Castleman of Frederick County. Bondsman, Elisha Smith

12 Feb 1803 Henry Stiger & Mary Oconner, daughter of Jeremiah Oconner of Fredk County, the bondsman

17 Feb 1803 William Pickering & Mary Wilson, daughter of James Wilson of Frederick County, the bondsman

22 Feb 1803 Edward Wade & Sarah Lewis of Frederick County. Bondsman, Thomas Furr

24 Feb 1803 Jacob Mason and Hannah Cogill, daughter of Adam Cogill of Frederick County, the bondsman

26 Feb 1803 Thomas Emmons & Polly Dasis of Frederick County. Bondsman, Elias Emmons

26 Feb 1803 Henry R. Intch & Mary Ejan of Frederick County. Bondsman, William Gossett

28 Feb 1083 Thomas Long & Hannah Myers of Frederick County. Bondsman, George Reid

28 Feb 1803 George Lafollett & Hannah Moore, a bound girl of Joseph Gordon of Frederick County, the bondsman

4 (Feb crossed out & Mar written below) 1803 Joseph Perry & Hannah Longacre, daughter of Joseph Longacre of Frederick County, the bondsman

8 Mar 1803 John Campbell & Dolitha Catlett of Frederick County. Bondsman, David Catlett

10 Mar 1803 Peter Myers & Hannah Hooker of Frederick County. Bondsman, William Jones

15 Mar 1803 George Jones & Mary Trotter of Frederick County. Bondsman, William Trotter

17 Mar 1803 John Giffin & Sally Mckee of Frederick County of lawful age. Bondsman, Bartholomew McKee

21 Mar 1803 William Brooks & Susanah Congroves. Bondsman, Isaac Bull

22 Mar 1803 Michael Doran & Mary White of Frederick County. Bondsman, Henry Bartlett

21 Mar 1803 James Hammick & Catherine Stigler of Frederick County. Bondsman, John Stigler

23 Mar 1803 William Chew & Lydia Hancher of lawful age of Fredk County. Bondsman, William Huggins

4 Apr 1803 Thomas F. Knox & Mary Riely, daughter of James Riely, the bondsman

9 Apr 1803 Benjamin Frye Jr. & Mary Frye, daughter of Benjamin Frye of Frederick County. Bondsman, Thomas Frye

9 Apr 1803 Daniel Kerns & Hannah Audedell, daughter of Elias Audedell, the bondsman

11 Apr 1803 John Swearingen & Elizabeth A. Bond of Frederick County. Bondsman, William Bond

12 Apr 1803 David Williams & Anna Grubs of Frederick County. Bondsman, Daniel Grubs

20 Apr 1803 Joseph Mitchell & Winnyfred Jones of Frederick County. Bondsman, Adam Kiger

20 Apr 1803 Michael Phliegar & Catherine Steel of Frederick County of full age. Bondsman, Benjamin Langley

23 Apr 1803 William Lines & Atheliah Doster of Frederick County. Bondsman, William Doster

2 May 1803 John Redd & Sarah Bligh of Frederick County of full age. Bondsman, Jacob Gander

8 May 1803 Edward Jenkins & Sarah Striger of full age. Bondsman, Edward Jenkins Senr

17 May 1803 Patrick Duncan & Agnus White of full age. Bondsman, James Graham

18 May n.d. George Borden & Rebecca Fred, upward of 21 years of age of Frederick County. Bondsman, John Poe

23 May 1803 Abraham Wisecarver & Catharine Armstrong, both of Frederick County. Bondsman, Joseph Wisecarver

25 May 1803 William Housman & Abigail Britton of Fredk County. Bondsman, Jesse Britton

25 May 1803 James Riley & Capanara Chappelear. Bondsman, Richard Chappellear

29 May 1803 John Russell & Elizabeth Touchstone of Frederick County. Bondsman, William Touchstone

30 May 1803 Conrod Cyder & Margaret Thompson of Frederick County & upwards of 21 years of age. Bondsman, James Thompson

1 Jun 1803 Thomas Riley & Sarah Savage of Frederick County. Bondsman, George Savage

6 Jun 1803 Isaac Clutz & Elizabeth Dunn. Bondsman, Isaac Klatz Snr

8 Jun 1803 James Tanquary & Rachel Roger. Bondsman, Daniel Roger

17 Jun 1803 Solomon Silkwood & Hannah Reid. Bondsman, George Reed

25 Jun 1803 Maholan Clevender & Betsey Clarke. Bondsman, William Scrovins

5 Jul 1803 Alexander McWhorter & Jane Alban of the County of Frederick. Bondsman, Robert Alban

27 Jun 1803 Cyrus Farr & Elizabeth Gibson. Bondsman, Jesse Britton

29 Jul 1803 Moses Newbank & Hanah Froman, widow of Amos Forman ded (sic) of Frederick County. Bondsman, William Gough

20 Jul 1803 Hezekiah Conn & Isabella Buck, daughter of Thomas Buck Esq. of Frederick County, the bondsman

23 Jul 1803 Frederick Kyle & Ann Mauck, widow & relict of Matthias Mauck, decd. late of Frederick County. Bondsman, Jacob Farrow

25 Jul 1803 James Shambling & Deborah Reed of Frederick County. Bondsman, Thomas Shore

1 Aug 1803 Thomas Amis & Susanah Brookhover of Frederick County. Bondsman, Benjamin Langley

6 Aug 1803 John McBride & Ann Maley of full age of the County of Frederick. Bondsman, James Carter

16 Aug 1803 William Wingfield & Sarah Myers of full age of Frederick County. Bondsman, John Myers

16 Aug 1803 William Ensley & Sarah Hoffman of Frederick. Bondsman, Henry Huffman

22 Aug 1803 Hugh Halvey & Sarah Davis. Bondsman, James Babb

24 Aug 1803 Samuel Crawford & Sarah Anderson, daughter of Joseph Anderson of Frederick County, the bondsman

24 Aug 1803 John Smith & Rebecca Jones. Bondsman, John Jones

27 Aug 1803 Tobias Walters & Sally Walker. Bondsman, William Walker

3 Sep 1803 Vincent Pendergass & Mary Scarff, daughter of John Scarff of Frederick County. Bondsman, Lewis Amiss

12 Sep 1803 Abraham Nelson & Mary Conner. Bondsman, Peter McMurray

13 Sep 1803 William Lemon & Mary Donaldson, ward of George Bruce of Frederick County, the bondsman

13 Sep 1803 Daniel Davison & Margaret Anderson of lawful age. Bondsman, James Davison

14 Sep 1803 Thomas Carr & Maria Cotes, daughter of Edward Cotes, the bondsman

17 Sep 1803 John W. Millar & Polly Headly. Bondsman, William Headly Jun

19 Sep 1803 Asa Ramey & Darcas Elzey. Bondsman, John Elzey

21 Sep 1803 Stephen Davis & Kitty T. Pollard of Frederick County. Bondsman, Mandly Taylor

21 Sep 1803 Christian Stipe & Catharine Goodykuntz of Frederick County. Bondsman, Daniel Goodykuntz

22 Sep 1803 William Badger & Polly Emmory of lawful age. Bondsman, Richard Fallis

22 Sep 1803 Job Smith & Fanny Rogers, daughter of William Rogers of Frederick County. Bondsman, Noah Haines

24 Sep 1803 William Witheroe & Elizabeth Nelson. Bondsman, John Nelson

27 Sep 1803 Abraham Williamson & Barbary Knipe, daughter of Henry Knipe, the bondsman

29 Sep 1803 Jacob Hilliard & Elizabth Taylor, daughter of George Taylor of Frederick County, the bondsman

4 Oct 1803 Henry Miller & Catharine Barr of full age of Frederick County. Bondsman, Frederick Barr

5 Oct 1803 Jacob Jenkins & Rebekah Lockhart, daughter of Robert Lockhart of Frederick County, the bondsman

6 Oct 1803 James Hurry & Rebekah Elzey of Frederick County of lawful age. Bondsman, Isaac Elzey

13 Oct 1803 Henny Whiteman Jr. & Elizabeth Clarke, daughter of George Clarke of Frederick County, the bondsman

13 Oct 1803 Nathaniel Potts & Mary Hamson of lawful age of Frederick County. Bondsman, James Hamson

22 Oct 1803 David Hayes & Mary Horseman, daughter of David Horseman of Frederick County, the bondsman

24 Oct 1803 Joseph Cope & Hanah Davis of Frederick County of lawful age (widow of Jas Davis). Bondsman, John Cope

24 Oct 1803 Jno Booling & Jane Hooe of Frederick County of lawful age. Bondsman, Charles Kain

29 Oct 1803 John Bailey & Sarah Marsh, daughter of Richard Marsh of Frederick County, the bondsman

29 Oct 1803 Thomas Jenkins & Elizabeth Vanbuskirk, daughter of Abraham Vanbuskirk of Frederick County, the bondsman

31 Oct 1803 John McNeale & Polly Deale. Bondsman, John Haddock

7 Nov 1803 Joseph Barrett & Unity Fulcamore of Frederick. Bondsman, Arthur Barrett

10 Nov 1803 John Cole & Elizabeth Persley, widow & relict of John Persley deceased. Bondsman, Benjamin Taylor

12 Nov 1803 Lloyd Bishop & Elizabeth Bishop of lawful age of Frederick County. Bondsman, Brice Bishop

15 Nov 1803 John Young of Jefferson County & Hester Hollingsworth of lawful age of Frederick County. Bondsman, Robert Hollingsworth

17 Nov 1803 Moses Beavers & Hannah Holbert. Bondsman, Thomas Halbert

18 Nov 1803 Joseph Whissen & Soloma Snapp. Bondsman, Joseph Snapp

22 Nov 1803 Richard Riley & Sarah Henderson. Bondsman, William Henderson

28 Nov 1803 Charles Ware & Frances Whiting of lawful age of Fredk County. Bondsman, Benjamin N. Barnet

29 Nov 1803 Samuel Sadler & Mary Heronimus. Bondsman, Jacob Myers

30 Nov 1803 William Catlett & Lucy Ashby of lawful age and of Frederick County. Bondsman, William Ashby

3 Dec 1803 James Watson & Elizabeth Bougher of lawful age and of Frederick County. Bondsman, Walter Watson

5 Dec n. d. William Lytleton & Mary Turner. Bondsman, Richard Turner

5 Dec 1803 Henry Fridley & Sarah Dier. Bondsman, John Morgan

5 Dec 1803 John Fleming & Hannah Barnes. Bondsman, Philip Smith

13 Dec 1803 Andrew Correll & Barbara Grapes, widow & relict of Abraham Grapes decd. Bondsman, Nicholas Kern

19 Dec 1803 John Chishire & Pailey Grubbs of lawful age of Frederick County. Bondsman, Stephen Vaughan

19 Dec 1803 Thomas McDonald & Susannah Corder, daughter of Joseph Corder of Frederick County. Bondsman, John McDonald

19 Dec 1803 Samuel Sydnor & Isabella Hening of Frederick County. Bondsman, Robt Hening

21 Dec 1803 George Michel Fry & Mary Wolfe, daughter of Stofel Wolfe of Frederick County. Bondsman, George Wolfe

21 Dec 1803 Samuel Johnson & Lucretia Hutchins. Bondsman, Zacharia Sanks

21 Dec 1803 Benjamin Leach & Mary Hooper (father present). Bondsman, Samuel Hooper. (Groom's name is Samuel Hooper at top of bond but Benjamin Leach in signature)

26 Dec 1803 Robert Grimes & Polley French. Bondsman, James Hogland

28 Dec 1803 William Pool & Sarah Marple, daughter of Ezekiel Marple of Frederick County, the bondsman

28 Dec 1803 Jeremiah Riddle & Mary Berry, daughter of F.? Berry of Frederick County. Bondsman, Benjamin Berry

28 Dec 1803 Henry Templeman & Catharine Lair. Bondsman, Frederick Carper

30 Dec 1803 Jacob Allender & Hannah Shepherd, widow & relict of Presley Shepherd. Bondsman, John Morgan

31 Dec 1803 Joseph Gallennoe & Catharine Stone of lawful age of Frederick. Bondsman, Alexander Mahew

31 Dec 1803 John Humpston & Matilda Settle. Bondsman, Larken Settle

2 Jan 1804 John Haddox & Mary Conrod. Bondsman, Enoch Haddox

4 Jan 1803 (sic) Peter McArty, son of Andrew McArty, & Nancy Jones, ?daughter of John Jones. Bondsmen, Andrew McCarty & John Jones (with 1804 bonds)

5 Jan 1804 William Warren & ?Aner Nichols, widow & relict of Henry Nichols decd. Bondsman, Amasa Lanham

6 Jan 1803 (1804 written below) Jacob Hotspiller & Mary Spur. Bondsman, John Spurr

19 Jan 1804 Thomas Hansecker & Ruth Rusk. Bondsman, Robert Rush

21 Jan 1804 John Rutter & Sarah Featheringall. Bondsman, John Ramy

23 Jan 1804 Whiting Washington & Rebecca Smith, daughter of Major Charles Smith of said county. Bondsman, Bushrod Taylor

28 Jan 1804 Zedeck Rogers & Mary Joice Bondsman, Peter Stephens

28 Jan 1804 Elias Milburn & Elizabeth Sheetz, daughter of George Sheetz of Frederick County, the bondsman

7 Feb 1804 William Boxell & Sarah Wasson, daughter of James Wason, the bondsman

7 Feb 1804 Elijah Pollard & Nancy Ireland. Bondsman, James Ireland

8 Feb 1804 Anthony Mawk & Sarah Price, ward of Michael Printz, the bondsman

8 Feb 1804 William Reed & Mary Davis. Bondsman, Francis Langham

14 Feb 1804 Lewis Largent & Eleanor Hull. Bondsman, John Largent

14 Feb 1804 William Wroe & Sally ?S.C. Wroe, daughter of Benjamin Wroe, the bondsman

14 Feb 1804 Samuel Kackley & Eliza Kackley of full age. Bondsman, Jacob Kackley

15 Feb 1804 Henry Gimlich Cartwright & Susannah Walters, daughter of Samuel Waller. Bondsman, John Walter. Note: "Cartwright" may denote occupation

18 Feb 1804 William Cornwell & Margaret Haynie of Frederick County. Bondsman, John Haynie

18 Feb 1804 Joel Morehead & Kitty Ashby, daughter of Lewis Ashby of Frederick County. Bondsman, Joseph D. Smith

21 Feb 1804 Elijah Prichard & Mary Norris, daughter of Joseph Norris of Frederick County, the bondsman

22 Feb 1804 John Ball & Susanah Parkins, widow of Joseph Parkins of Frederick County. Bondsman, John Clark

6 Mar 1804 Harrison Scofiald & Elizabeth Long. Bondsman, Samuel Rogers

7 Mar 1804 Thomas Duff & Sally Conklin, daughter of David Conklin

10 Mar 1804 Saml Corbett & Betsy Maxwell, daughter of Wm Maxwell of Fredk County

16 Mar 1804 Ranson Kendall & Lucy King of Frederick County of Lawfull age. Bondsman, Elias King

17 Mar 1804 Redmond Grigsby & Catharine Weakley. Bondsman, William Weakley

19 Mar 1804 James Carter & Margaret Picken. Bondsman, Samuel Picken

19 Mar 1804 David Marple & Margaret Purgelbaugh, daughter of George Purgelbaugh of this county. Bondsman, Enoch Marple

20 Mar 1804 David Brown & Jenny Hancher of lawful age. Bondsman, Isaac Booth

24 Mar 1804 Nicholas Clabaugh & Ann Sperry spinster. Bondsman, John Clabaugh

24 Mar 1804 Samuel Sample & Nancy Ridenour. Bondsman, Michl Ridenour

28 Mar 1804 Daniel Wilkins & Sarah Ellis, daughter of Morris Ellis. Bondsman, Joseph Carter

31 Mar 1804 William Gosson & Liddy Ellis. Bondsman, Joseph Sonanstone

2 Apr 1804 John Pugh & Deborah Day, widow & relict of David Day of Frederick County. Bondsman, Elijah Littler

2 Apr 1804 William Green & Elizabeth Brent, daughter of Charles Brent of Frederick County. Bondsman, Elijah Kercheval

3 Apr 1804 William Daley & Elizabeth Kingore, daughter of Wm Kingore of Frederick County, the bondsman

5 Apr 1804 Ignatius Edwards & Nancy Collins of lawful age of Frederick County. Bondsman, ?Brian Collins

5 Apr 1804 John Crook & Rachel Murray, widow & relict of John Murray decd. Bondsman, Christopher Beard

5 Apr 1804 Caspar Sevier Junr & Ann Moffitt, daughter of Robert Moffitt of this county. Bondsman, John Moffett

7 Apr 1804 Willis Lake & Nancy Grigsby, daughter of William Grigsby. Bondsman, Robert Foster

10 Apr 1804 Michael Reager & Nancy Rosser, daughter of Thos Rosser of Frederick County. Bondsman, Ezer Ellis

10 Apr 1804 Michael Price & Susannah Burke, daughter of Cornelius Burke. Bondsman, David Hancher

13 Apr 1804 Robert Warrick & Mary Shivers. Bondsman, Scarlett Owens

14 Apr 1804 Joseph Whitacre & Lettice Harrell of Frederick County of lawful age. Bondsman, Nathan Harrell

14 Apr 1804 Jacob Dick & Sarah McIntire of Frederick County of lawful age. Bondsman, Charles McIntire

16 Apr 1804 Henry Borders & Delilah Awbrey, daughter of Samuel Awbrey. Bondsman, Kid Marquess

30 Apr 1804 John Cope & Mary McCabe. Bondsman, Joseph Cope

2 May 1804 John Hickerton, son of Daniel Hickerton, & Doratha Shambough, daughter of Philip Shambough

5 May 1804 James Wilson & Mary Thomas, daughter of James Thomas of Frederick County, the bondsman

15 May 1804 John R. Lemon & Rebecca Donaldson, ward of George Bruce, the bondsman

23 May 1804 Samuel Beavers & Sarah Turner, daughter of Richard Turner of Frederick County. Bondsman, William Littleton

24 May 1804 Thomas Campill & Prudence Ford, daughter of John Ford of this county, the bondsman

26 May 1804 Jacob Gibbins & ?Peggy Groves, daughter of John Groves of this county, the bondsman

4 Jun 1804 John Tedford & Susannah Brown. Bondsman, Alexander Mark

4 Jun 1804 William Nosset & Delilah Hickle, daughter of Samuel Hickle. Bondsman, Joseph Nosset

9 Jun 1804 Samuel Craig & Liddy Taylor. Bondsman, Abraham Taylor

13 Jun 1804 Robert Mattex & Jane Colvill. Bondsman, Daniel McCaully

14 Jun 1804 Moses Hoge Jun & Salley B. Chipley. Bondsman, John Peyton

28 Jun 1804 James Macoughtry & Sarah Likens, widow & relict of Henry Likens decd of Frederick County. Bondsman, Moses Smith

30 Jun 1804 Isaac Elzey & Matilda Burges, daughter of John West Burgess, the bondsman

30 Jun 1804 Philip Thomas & Mary Swope, widow of John Swope deceased. Bondsman, Alexander Mahew

4 Jul 1804 Christian Heckathorn & Mary Deal, ward of Anna Deal, the bondsman

6 Jul 1804 John Watson & Ann B. Hove, daughter of Edward Hove of Frederick County, the bondsman

23 Jul 1804 Henry McLeod & Berthamia Shackleford, daughter of Joseph Shackleford of Frederick County, the bondsman

23 Jul 1804 Thomas Babb Jr. & Lydia Dillon, daughter of John Dillon of Frederick County. Bondsman, John Bowen

25 Jul 1804 William Dooley & Nancy Martin, ward of James Bennett, the bondsman

28 Jul 1804 Philip Deadrick & Christiana Myers, daughter of John Myers of said County, the bondsman

30 Jul 1804 James Green & Elizabeth Stage of Frederick County. Bondsman, James Stanford

4 Aug 1804 John Howell & Elizabeth Bonham of full age. Bondsman, David Bonham

4 Aug 1804 John Welsh & Ruth Metcath. Bondsman, Charles Martin

7 Aug 1804 William Kendle & Elizabeth Lawflin. Bondsman, Zebedee Kindle

11 Aug 1804 Samuel Cahoon & Polly Anderson, daughter of Jno. Anderson, the bondsman

13 Aug 1804 Charles Streit & Catherine Freeze, daughter of Martin Freeze, the bondsman

18 Aug 1804 William Bean & Polly Mauck, daughter of Michael Mauck of Frederick, the bondsman

18 Aug 1804 Jacob Sager & Susannah Garmong, daughter of Christian Garmong, the bondsman

22 Aug 1804 Thomas Featheringale & Elizabeth Settlemyre of Frederick County. Bondsman, Abraham Niswander

24 Aug 1804 John Murray & Synthia Johnsten of full age of Frederick County. Bondsman, James Boles

25 Aug 1804 Hugh Christy & Catharine Rogers of Frederick County. Bondsman, John Rutter

28 Aug 1804 Jacob Larrick & Catharine Snapp, daughter of Jacob Snapp of Frederick County, the bondsman

30 Aug 1804 William Payne & Frances Powers (widow & relict of Jack Powers decd of Frederick County)

1 Sep 1804 Jacob Clyne & Margaret Williamson, daughter of Ralph Williamson of Frederick County, the bondsman

5 Sep 1804 Stephen Vaughan & Nancy Cain of Frederick County. Bondsman, Thomas Vaughan

5 Sep 1804 John Hogain & Ann Berry, widow & relict of Enoch Berry decd. Bondsman, Isaac Littler

n.d. Jacob Burner Jr. & Elizabeth Hannan, daughter of Mathias Hannan of this county. Bondsman, John Hannan

2 Oct 1804 Hezekiah Edwards & Elizabeth Houseman, daughter of Martin Houseman, the bondsman

13 Oct 1804 Abel Thompson & Elizabeth Scarff, daughter of James Scarff, the bondsman

15 Oct 1804 John H. Hendren & Rebekah Baker, daughter of Jacob Baker of this county. Bondsman, Daniel Baker

18 Oct 1804 John Gaunt & Tabitha Mott, widow & relict of Joseph Mott decd. Bondsman, Frederick Dobyns

24 Oct 1804 John Bucher & Polly Schnider of lawful age of Fredk County. Bondsman, Bondsman, George Schneider, who signs in German

25 Oct 1804 Laurence Snapp & Mary Blackmore, daughter of Rachel Blackmore of this county. Bondsman, Nathl Blackmore

31 Oct 1804 John Bell & Sarah Edwards of lawful age of said county. Bondsman, Thomas McKewan

31 Oct 1804 Conrad Huntsberry & Margaret Holden of lawful age of Frederick County. Bondsman, John Reed

8 Nov 1804 Moses Largent & Nancy Leavael, daughter of Thomas Leavael, the bondsman

9 Nov 1804 George Horten Norris & Jane Bowles Wormley, daughter of James Wormley Esquire. Bondsman, John Cruges Wormley

15 Nov 1804 Addison B. Armstead & Mary Howe Peyton. Bondsman, Alfred H. Powell

17 Nov 1804 Peter Keller & Elizabeth Beatty of County of Frederick of lawful age. Bondsman, James Simpson

20 Nov 1804 William Dutton & Ann Garnett, daughter of Martin Garnett of County of Frederick, the bondsman

26 Nov 1804 John Poe & Catharine Borders, daughter of George Borders, the bondsman

27 Nov 1804 John Pitcock & Maudeline Renner of lawful age of County of Frederick. Bondsman, Mathias Nelson

1 Dec 1804 James Lake & Susannah Redding of Frederick County. Bondsman, Thomas Foster in bond, Robert Foster in signature

5 Dec 1804 George Snapp & Anna Myers, daughter of Joseph Myers, the bondsman

11 Dec 1804 John Hott, son of George Hott, & Margaret Frees of Frederick County. Bondsman, Martin Frees

13 Dec 1804 John Cochran & Jane Treige of Frederick County. Bondsman, Sarah Bradford

18 Dec 1804 John Stephens & Martha Brown of Frederick County. Bondsman, Peter Stephens, who signs in German

19 Dec 1804 Travis Glasscock & Elizabeth Garnet. Bondsman, Martin Garnet

21 Dec 1804 John S. Ball & Ann Sydnor, widow & relict of John Sydnor decd of Frederick County. Bondsman, Augustine Green

22 Dec 1804 Hannaniah Pugh & Sarah Darlington of Frederick County. Bondsman, John Darlington

22 Dec 1804 Michael McCartney & Ann Audiddle of Frederick County. Bondsman, Elias Adiddell

24 Dec 1804 John Shambough & Rebeccah Kendrick of Frederick County, ward of John Boyles

24 Dec 1804 John Morgan & Elizabeth Gaunt of Frederick County. Bondsman, John Gaunt

24 Dec 1804 Israel Ewing & Polly Anderson of lawful age of Fredk County. Bondsman, James Anderson

24 Dec 1804 Abraham Vaughan & Ezalpha Moore of Frederick County of lawful age. Bondsman, Vincent Vaughan

28 Dec 1804 Conrad Martin & Eve Yander or Gander of Frederick County. Bondsman, Henry Martin

28 Dec 1804 William Denny & Elizabeth Mytinger of Frederick County. Bondsman, Daniel Mytinger

29 Dec 1804 Bartleman Burris & Sarah Pace or Race of Frederick County. Bondsman, William Burris (ink very dim)

31 Dec 1804 James Simrall & Rebecca Graham of Frederick County. Bondsman, Gilbert Meem

1 Jan 1805 John Wingfield & Elizabeth Good, daughter of Felix Good (she now an inhabitant of Frederick County. Bondsman, John Delong

1 Jan 1805 Thomas Wroe & Elizabeth Newman of Frederick County. Bondsman, Edmund Newman

2 Jan 1805 John Fitzpatrick & Phebe Largent of the County of Frederick. Bondsman, Aaron Largent

7 Jan 1805 Zebidee Kindall & Susanah McKoy both of Frederick County. Bondsman, Thomas Johnston

9 Jan 1805 David Babb & Mary Hensell of Frederick County. Bondsman, Henry Babb

14 Jan 1805 Robert Bryarly & Sarah Rust, orphan of Jeremiah Rust decd. Bondsman, John Brady

14 Jan 1805 John Buckley & Catharine Relph of Frederick County. Bondsman, Thomas Relph

21 Jan 1805 Jacob Bruner & Alley Capper of Frederick County. Bondsman, Jesse John

5 Feb 1805 William Price & Mary Peters of Frederick County. Bondsman, Benjamin Beemer

7 Feb 1804 Robert Williams & Sarah Ellis, widow of Elisha Ellis of Frederick County. Bondsman, William Doster

12 Feb 1805 Jacob Willey & Lydy Gibbons of Frederick County. Bondsman, Jacob Gibbins

17 Feb 1805 Lewis Amiss & Elizabeth Martin or Mastin. Bondsman, Francis T. ?Martin

20 Feb 1805 John Brown & Polly Taite of Frederick County. Bondsman, Joseph Hampton

21 Feb 1805 Isaac Philips & Cassandra Wynn of Frederick. Bondsman, J.? Bearen

15 Mar 1805 William Duke & Elsae Lewis of Fredk County. Bondsman, Thos Lewis

20 Mar 1805 Joel Martin & Rachel Elles. Bondsman, James Bennett

22 Mar 1815 Henry Printz & Elizabeth Barr, widow & Relict of Peter Barr Decd. Bondsman, Thomas McKewan

23 Mar 1805 Richard Dougherty & Elizabeth Allensworth of Frederick County. Bondsman, Jacob Crizzor

23 Mar 1805 William Garner & Mishael Self of Frederick County. Bondsman, John Brown

25 Mar 1805 Michael Smith & Nancy McCloud of Frederick County. Bondsman, Andrew Pitman

26 Mar 1805 George Johnston & Margaret Davis, daughter of Benja. Davis, the bondsman

27 Mar 1805 Clement Spikenall, son of Basil Spikenall, & Hannah Frazier, daughter of Hannah Frazier. Parents are bondsmen

28 Mar 1805 Washington Drew & Dilly Smith, daughter of Jonathan Smith, the bondsman

28 Mar 1805 Robert Bennet & Lidy Anderson, widow of William Anderson. Bondsman, Abel Morgan

30 Mar 1805 Mordecai Gill & Jane Farquson. Bondsman, Edward Pendle

1 Apr 1805 James Taylor & Willey Ann Gray, daughter of Thomas Gray, the bondsman

2 Apr 1805 George Beddow & Eley Lewis of Frederick. Bondsman, Adam Brown

4 Apr 1805 Timothy Wilcox & Winney Allen of lawful age of Frederick County. Bondsman, David Hancher

6 Apr 1805 Thomas Rose & Polly Murphey. Bondsman, Benjamin Jones

9 Apr 1805 George Ruble & Jane Gobin, widow & relict of Hugh Gobin decd of Frederick County. Bondsman, Eli Pugh

9 Apr 1805 Conrad Hott & Mary Stipe of lawful age of Frederick County. Bondsman, George Hott

10 Apr 1805 Jacob Boyers & Elizabeth Lauck. Bondsman, Simon Lauck

11 Apr 1805 Joseph Carter & Ann Simpson, widow & relict of William Simpson decd of Frederick County. Bondsman, Thomas McKewan

16 Apr 1805 Samuel Cooper, free Negro, & Rachael ?Colum (a free woman). Bondsman, James Stear

18 Apr 1805 Henry Bennett & Eusy Morgan. Bondsman, Enock Morgan

18 Apr 1805 Samuel Rowland & Elizabeth Spicknall, daughter of Leonard Spicknall, the bondsman

22 Feb 1805 Joseph Marple & Mary Bucklebough, daughter of George Bucklebough, the bondsman. No signature for groom. See 14 Sep 1805

30 Apr 1805 Benjamin McFeely & Mary ?Jacobs. Bondsman, Reuben Crofford

27 May 1805 Joseph Eaton & Susanah Fisher. Bondsman, Jacob Hockstain

28 May 1805 Justinian Grubbs & Clara Wallers. Bondsman, William Waller

28 May 1805 William B. Randolph & Ludia Lupton. Bondsman, David Fawcett

29 May 1805 Edward Marsh & Anna Maria Linn. Bondsman, John Linn

1 Jun 1805 Daniel Crabb & Rachel Cassandra Harvey, daughter of William Harvey, the bondsman

1 Jun 1805 Joseph Bonsell & Phebe Adams, daughter of Joseph Adams of Frederick County, the bondsman

3 Jun 1805 John Darr & Rebecca Shepherd, daughter of Thomas Shepherd, the bondsman

8 Jun 1805 James Williams & Sarah Grubbs, daughter of Thomas Grubbs of Frederick County. Bondsman, Joel Emmons

5 Jun 1805 Isaac Bowen & Jane Sowers, daughter of John Sowers. Bondsman, James Howard. (Bond says Isaac in one place & Phineas in another. Signed "Isaac")

8 Jun 1805 Alexander Jamison & Polly Jones, daughter of James Jones of Frederick County. Bondsman, William Jones

8 Jun 1805 Thomas Lewis & Mariann Hannings both of Frederick. Bondsman, John Nutt

12 Jun 1805 George Reed & Martha Tildon, daughter of John B. Tiddon both of Frederick County. Bondsman, James Newham

12 Jun 1805 Philip Grove & Anne Maria Shull, widow & relict of Henry Shull decd. Bondsman, Malin Pugh

12 Jun 1805 Peter Spoon & Peggy Hickman of Frederick County. Bondsman, Hamon Brill

15 Jun 1805 James John Gardner & Susanah Earhart of Frederick County. Bondsman, Anthony Moore

18 Jun 1805 Fewell Cox & Elizabeth Hooper of Frederick County. Bondsman, Abraham Hooper

19 Jun 1805 Youel Gilbert & Sarah Southward, daughter of John Southward, the bondsman

19 Jun 1805 David Rees & Sarah Chew of Frederick County. Bondsman, James Daniel

24 Jun 1805 William Compton & Catharine Longerbone of Frederick County. Bondsman, George Tilman & Abraham Longerbone

29 Jun 1805 Abner Clarke & Isabella Weer, daughter of Joseph Weer, the bondsman

2 Jul 1805 John Jones & Dorothy Helpbringer. Bondsman, Michael Helpbringer

13 Jul n. d. Henry Haymaker & Mary Johnston, daughter of Charles Johnson of Frederick County, the bondsman

17 Jul 1805 Lewis Arniss & Elizabeth Martin. Bondsman, Francis F. Martin

22 Jul 1805 Reed Wright & Sarah T. Mastin, daughter of Mrs Charlotte Marstin of Frederick County. Bondsman, John Mastin

30 Jul 1805 Johnston Lacey & Ruth Clevinger, daughter of Asa Clevinger. Bondsman, Jacob Clevinger

31 Jul 1805 Gary Davis & Elizabeth Tambelin. Bondsman, Thomas Murphy

3 Aug 1805 William Mayhugh & Kitty Winn, daughter of Rachel? Winn. Bondsman, Bryan Mayhugh

14 Aug 1805 William Anderson & Esther Romine, daughter of John Romine of Frederick County, the bondsman

19 Aug 1805 John Smith & Nancy Archer of Frederick County. Bondsman, Barzillai Bates

19 Aug 1805 John Stipp & Mary Ann Thompson, ward of Thomas Lloyd of Frederick County, the bondsman

26 Aug 1805 Daniel Duly & Mary Ann Helm, ward of Thomas Littleton, the bondsman

29 Aug 1805 Joseph Swope & Sally Redman, daughter of Mary Redman. Bondsman, Joseph Redman

31 Aug 1805 Henry Stricker & Eleanor Rogers, daughter & ward of Catharine Rogers, the bondsman

31 Aug 1805 Henry Lantz & Mary Jesper, widow & relict of Abraham Jesper decd of Frederick County. Bondsman, Andrew Secrist

2 Sep 1805 James Wilson & Elizabeth Rakestraw, daughter of John Rakestraw of Frederick County. Bondsman, William Bonifield

6 Aug 1805 Andrew Vance & Margaret Batchellor. Bondsman, George Brill

9 Sep 1805 Moses Scott & Tacey Gray, daughter of Susanna Gray, the bondsman

14 Sep 1805 Joseph Marple, son of Enoch Marple, & Mary Purtlbaugh, daughter of George Burtlebaugh of the County of Frederick. Bondsman, Enoch Marple

17 Sep 1805 Robert Beard & Rachall Wright of lawful age of Frederick County. Bondsman, David Osburne

23 Sep 1805 Robert Dunbar & Hannah Cox Briarly. Bondsman, Thomas McKawan

6 Nov 1805 Thomas Bail & Jane Graves, daughter of Charles Graves, the bondsman

9 Nov 1805 Adam Pully & Nancy Lenox, widow & relict of John Lenox dec (she of Frederick County). Bondsman, Jonathan Shull

29 Apr 1806 Peter Miller & Priscilla Watson. Bondsman, Moses Watson

30 Apr 1806 Charles Magill & Catharine Grove. Bondsman, Abraham Grove

5 May 1806 Lewis Largin & Betsy Hull of Frederick County of lawful age. Bondsman, Aaron Largen

5 May 1806 Reuben Allensworth & Elizabeth Cordell, of lawful age. Bondsman, John Ramey

6 May 1806 Ezekiel McFarland of lawful age & Sarah Rezin, daughter of Robert Rezin of Frederick County, the bondsman

7 May 1806 Joseph Berry & Hannah McFarlin, daughter of John McFarlin of Frederick County, the bondsman

12 May 1806 John Shiner & Margaret Rutter, daughter of Henry Rutter, the bondsman

13 May 1806 William Poyles & Mary Ann ---- (middle name illegible) McMahon, ward of Sarah Simmons, formerly Sarah McMahon, the bondsman

14 May 1806 Abraham Shank & Polly Cochran, daughter of Robert Cochran of Frederick, the bondsman

21 May 1806 Henry Tipple & Elizabeth Stump of Frederick County. Bondsman, William Haddox

21 May 1806 David Bryarly/Brierly & Jane Murry, ward of John S. Woodcock Esq. Bondsman, Samuel Brierly (Bryarily)

22 May 1806 Jesse Jury & Martha Job, daughter of Charity Job of Frederick County. Bondsman, Baltzer Sellers

26 May 1806 James Stewart & Elizabeth Pierpoint, daughter of Joseph Pierpoint of Frederick County, the bondsman

7 Jun 1806 Samuel Hoover & Nancy Weaver. Bondsman, Abraham Weaver

9 Jun 1806 Daniel Wade & Isabella Gawthrop of Frederick County of lawful age. Bondsman, Jacob Taylor

10 Jun 1806 John Jones & Sarah Nevitt of lawful age. Bondsman, Jabez Smith

10 Jun 1806 Jacob Snyder & Eve Klyne, daughter of Jacob Klyne of this county, the bondsman

13 Jun 1806 James Hart & Peggy Poyles, daughter of Ann Poyles of Frederick County. Bondsman, Thomas Jackson

16 Jun 1806 Samuel O. Hendren & Jane Ireland, daughter of James Ireland decd of this county. Bondsman, Isaac Chrisman

16 Jun 1806 James Hackney & Jane Boyd, daughter of Robert Boyd of Frederick County, the bondsman

16 Jun 1806 John L. Stubblefield & Frances Jones. Bondsman, Edward B. Jones

21 Jun 1806 Arthur Graham & Martha Withero of lawful age. Bondsman, Thomas Keenan

5 Jul 1806 Peter Timmens & Elizabeth Dyer, daughter of John Dyer of Frederick County. Bondsman, John Morgen

7 ?Jul 1806 Levi Hicks & Emalia McKay. Bondsman, John McCoy

16 Jul 1806 Septimus Clark & Jane Olvie. Bondsman, John Redman

18 Jul 1806 Henry Bradford & Betsy Plumb of Frederick County of lawful age. Bondsman, John Pitman

19 Jul 1806 Absalem Gardner & Rosanna Crum, daughter of Christian Crum of Frederick County, the bondsman

31 Jul 1806 Samuel McCallum & Nancy Spears, widow & relict of Robert Spears deceased. Bondsman, David Hancher

5 Aug 1806 Daniel Freeze & Catharine Tarflinger, daughter of Jacob Tarflinger of Frederick County, who signs in German

11 Aug 1806 Joseph White & Elizabeth Brill. Bondsman, Henry Briel Snr

13 Aug 1806 Elijah Hansbrough & Fanny Sampson. Bondsman, Joseph Sampson (Samson)

13 Aug 1806 John Walter & Dorothy Ashby, daughter of Enoch Ashby, the bondsman

19 Aug 1806 William Bolin & Susanah Hood. Bondsman, Jno Bolin

20 Aug 1806 David T. Davis & Elizabeth Hedges, daughter of Joseph Hedges of Frederick County. Bondsman, John Hedges

21 Aug 1806 John F. Price & Elizabeth Cowdery, widow & relict of Jonathan Cowdery deceased. Bondsman, John Fry, who signs in German

21 Aug 1806 Thomas Holleway & Mary Gardiner of lawfull age. Bondsman, John Steele

22 Aug 1806 Samuel Mooney & Nancy Banks, ward of Edward Banks, the bondsman

23 Aug 1806 Enoch Wickersham & Elizabeth Williams of lawfull age. Bondsman, Joseph Barrett

1 Sep 1806 George Noland & Nancy Harding, both of lawfull age. Bondsman, John Spurr

1 Sep 1806 Clemon White & Ann Payne, both of lawfull age & inhabitants of this County. Bondsman, Saml Berson/Bryson

10 Sep 1806 John Conner & Elizabeth Ballinger, daughter of Samuel Ballinger of Frederick County. Bondsman, Enoch Haddox

12 Sep 1806 Thomas Hanshaw & Eleanor Brown, daughter of John Brown of Frederick County, the bondsman

15 Sep 1806 Joseph Coreson & Grisel Campbell. Bondsman, John S. Campbell

19 Sep 1806 Frederick Howser & Mary Myers, ward of Daniel Mytinger, the bondsman

20 Sep 1806 Joseph Browning & Winneford Headley, daughter of William Headley Senr. of Frederick County. Bondsman, William Headley Jr.

25 Sep 1806 Hezekiah Guy & Mary Sigler, daughter of Jacob Ziagler, the bondsman

29 Sep 1806 Thomas Lindsay Jr. & Keziah Jones, daughter of Stephen Jones of Frederick County, the bondsman

1 Oct 1806 Elisha Whitacre & Elizabeth Mckee, widow of Jesse Mckee. Bondsman, Peter Preist

2 Oct 1806 John Davis & Ann B. Scarff, daughter of John Scarff of Frederick County, the bondsman

6 Oct 1806 William Collin & Nancy Long, daughter of James Long of Frederick County. Bondsman, Jas. Long

8 Oct 1806 Peter Priest & Rebeckah Rout, daughter of Sarah Smith of Frederick County. Bondsman, James Kirby

8 Oct 1806 James Kerby & Fannah Smith, daughter of Sarah Smith of Frederick County. Bondsman, Peter Priest

11 Oct 1806 James Wiley & Glinda Poole, daughter of Peter Poole, the bondsman

15 Oct 1806 David Cusick & Elizabeth Keeler. Bondsman, Vance Bush

15 Oct 1806 Samuel Parent & Jane Lynn of lawful age. Bondsman, Robert Beatty

17 Oct 1806 Lewis Hoff & Margaret Sowers, daughter of Jacob Sowers of Frederick County. Bondsman, John Heiskell

17 Oct 1806 John Marney & Jane Vance widow & relict of Saml Vance dec late of Frederick County. Bondsman, Andrew Vance

17 Oct 1806 John Dehaven & Rody Doster of this County. Bondsman, Isaac Dehaven

22 Oct 1806 John Heberling & Mary Crumley of lawful age. Bondsman, Stephen Crumly

22 Oct 1806 Lewis Crane & Asy Smith of Frederick County and of lawful age. Bondsman, Joseph Sidebottom

28 Oct 1806 John Lipscomb & Sarah Smith, daughter of Daniel Smith of Frederick County, the bondsman

28 Oct 1806 Samuel McCormick & Margaret Hampton. Bondsman, Samuel Vance

29 Oct 1806 Moses McDonald & Catharine Light. Bondsman, Peter Light

29 Oct 1806 Henry Bradford, son of Henry Bradford Sr, & Rebecca Christy, daughter & ward of Phebe Christy. Parents are bondsmen

3 Nov 1806 John Augustine Vandel & Elizabeth Blany, Widow of William Blany. Bondsman, Nicholas Fitzsimmons

3 Nov 1806 Isaac Fry & Hannah Cowgill of lawful age and an inhabitant of Frederick County. Bondsman, John Halley/Hatley

3 Nov 1806 Robert Butter & Nancy Hall, widow of Joseph Hall late of Frederick County. Bondsman, William McCormick

4 Nov 1806 Jeremiah Bowlding & Sarah Venable, daughter of Joseph Venable. Bondsman, John Martin

5 Nov 1806 William Clarke & Margaret Lewis, daughter of John Lewis of Frederick County, the bondsman

11 Nov 1806 Joseph Peirce & Mary Shuter (Suter written below). Bondsmen, Catharine Pierce & William Suter

17 Nov 1806 Joshua Bishop Jr. & Margaret Simes or Simms of Frederick County. Bondsman, Ephraim Fenton

1 Dec 1806 John Long & Henrietta Chrisman, daughter of Jane E. Williams of Frederick County. Bondsmen, John Pitman & Jane E. Williams

8 Dec 1806 Benjamin Hardacre & Nancy McFaddin, daughter of John McFaddin

8 Dec 1806 Jesse Kemp & Charlotte Leach, daughter of Valentine Leach of Frederick County. Bondsman, Leroy Leach

13 Dec 1806 Nathan Young & Amelia Noland, daughter of Pierce Noland of Frederick County. Bondsman, William Doster

17 Dec 1806 Samuel Allen & Sarah Smith, daughter of Mary Ellis of Frederick County. Bondsman, Caleb Seal

17 Dec 1806 Frederick Larrick & Elizabeth Secrist of Frederick County. Bondsman, George Secrist

20 Dec 1806 Frederick Tole & Margaret Good, daughter of Felix Good of Frederick County. Bondsman, Benjamin Williams

20 Dec 1806 Adam Hurbough & Nancy Wolfe widow & relict of George Wolfe of Frederick County. Bondsman, Andrew Vance

22 Dec 1806 James Barden & Winney Hankins of Frederick County of lawful age. Bondsman, Jesse McKay

23 Dec 1806 John Marple & Jane Wright, daughter of George Wright of Frederick County, the bondsman

24 Dec 1806 Michael Hale & Rosamond Relph, daughter of Thomas Relph of Frederick County, the bondsman

25 Dec 1806 Jacob Newland & Martha Malony, daughter of Sarah Malony now Sarah Crocket of Frederick County. Bondsman, Joseph Kerns

27 Dec 1806 John Smith & Edy Wood of lawful age. Bondsman, Lewis Wood

27 Dec 1806 Lewis Wood & Hannah Leach of lawful age. Bondsman, John Smith

27 Dec 1806 John Carter & Rebecca Rowland, daughter & ward of Elizabeth Rowland of Frederick County. Bondsman, Samuel Rowland

27 Dec 1806 George Grice & Mary Farmer, daughter of John Farmer of Frederick County, the bondsman

27 Dec 1806 Francis T. Mastin & Arabella Hoge, daughter of Solomon Hoge of Frederick County. Bondsman, Lewis Amiss

31 Dec 1806 George Bonecutter & Phebe Wright, daughter of John Wright of Frederick County. Bondsman, James W. Holliday

27 Dec 1806 Samuel Young & Mary Britton, daughter of Jesse Britton of Frederick County, the bondsman

1 Jan 1807 John Lang & Mary Beale, daughter of Margaret Beale of Frederick County. Bondsman, John Sutherland

2 Jan 1807 Amos Adams & Nancy Miles, daughter of Josias Miles of Frederick Co. Bondsman, John Miles

5 Jan 1807 William Watkins & Lucretia Philips, daughter of Isaac Philips. Bondsman, Henson Barret

6 Jan 1807 Joseph Smith & Jane Davis, daughter of Benjamin Davis of Frederick County, the bondsman

12 Jan 1807 Nimrod Catlett & Sarah Poyles, daughter of Ann Poyles of Frederick County. Bondsman, Alexander Hart

12 Jan 1806 Charles McCrea Jr. & Phebe Lindsey, daughter of John Lindsey of Frederick County, the bondsman

13 Jan 1807 John Wright Junr & Elizabeth Stephens, daughter of Peter Stephens of Frederick County, the bondsman

13 Jan 1807 Stephen Barns & Eleanor Scarff, daughter of John Scarff of Frederick County. Bondsman, Jesse Scarf

13 Jan 1807 George Cowgill & Francis Jackson, daughter of Francis Jackson of Frederick County, the bondsman

13 Jan 1807 Barnet Croson & Dorcas Croson, daughter of Zeheniah Croson of Frederick County

20 Jan 1807 Isaac Larrick & Mary Hodgson, daughter of John Hodgson of Frederick County

21 Jan 1807 George Berry & Lucinda Settle, daughter of Strother Settle of Frederick County. Bondsman, Geo Cooper

23 Jan 1807 Elijah Milton & Elizabeth Reynolds of Frederick County of lawful age. Bondsman, Alexander Milton

27 Jan 1807 James Lindsey & Sarah Berry, daughter of Joseph Berry late of Frederick County. Bondsman, Thos. Neill

2 Feb 1807 John Chenowith & Susanna Seal, daughter of Caleb Seal of Frederick County, the bondsman

2 Feb 1807 Richard Russell & Sarah Grapes, daughter of Jacob Graves of Frederick County, the bondsman

3 Feb 1807 Joshua Cope & Isabella McCrea, daughter of Charles McCrea. Bondsman, William Hill

7 Feb 1807 James Brown & Elizabeth Cunningham of this county. Bondsman, John Cunningham

10 Feb 1807 John Simpson & Anna Anderson of this county. Bondsman, George McCormick

17 Feb 1807 John Settles & Elizabeth Reddon of said County of lawful age. Bondsman, Robert Foster

17 Feb 1807 David Barrett Junr. & Winneford Kirby, daughter of John Kirby of Frederick County. Bondsman, David Barrett Senr.

19 Feb 1807 John McFarling & Judith Snyder, daughter of Conrad Snyder of Frederick County of lawful age. Bondsman, Nicholas Taylor

21 Feb 1807 Benjamin Davenport & Margaret Shannon Cramer, daughter of Ambrose Cramer, the bondsman

23 Feb 1807 Edward Hall & Elizabeth Brient, daughter of Robert Brient. Bondsman, Samuel Rogers

24 Feb 1807 Thomas Castleman & Ms. Hannah B. Frost, daughter of Amos Frost of Frederick County. Bondsman, William Taylor Jr.

25 Feb 1807 Jeremiah Reed & Elizabeth Hickle, daughter of Tewalt Hickle of Frederick County. Bondsman, George Hickle

2 Mar (date not given) George Stringfellow & Sussanah Gray, widow of Joseph Gray, dec. Bondsman, Joseph Allen

2 Mar 1807 Elias Williams & Honor Tranary, daughter of Samuel Trenary, the bondsman

3 Mar 1807 John Piper & Margaret Snapp, daughter of George Snapp, the bondsman

3 Mar 1807 Henry Bridine & Jane Kidd, daughter of Jane Kidd of Frederick County. Bondsman, Mark Harper

7 Mar 1807 Peter Dick & Jane McWhorter, daughter of Robert McWhorter of Frederick County. Bondsman, Meredith Darlington

9 Mar 1807 Abraham Bixler & Sarah Rhodes of Frederick County. Bondsman, Jacob Rhodes

17 Mar 1807 John Joliffe & Ms. Frances Helm of Frederick County. Bondsman, Isaac Swearingen

18 Mar 1807 Edward ?Hessey & Catharine Venable, daughter of Joseph Venable of Frederick County, the bondsman

21 Mar 1807 John Milbourn & Rebeca Likens, daughter of Mary Likens of Frederick County, the bondsman

26 Mar 1807 John Marker & Catharine Whissen. Bondsman, Joseph Whissen

28 Mar 1807 William Minor & Hannah Rust, daughter of Peter Rust of Frederick County. Bondsman, Lewis Stevens

1 Apr 1807 James Nelson & Susannah Keiter, daughter of George Keiter of Frederick County. Bondsman, John Keiter

3 Apr 1807 Gerrard Sexton & Letticia Williams, daughter of Jane E. Williams of Frederick County, the bondsman

6 Apr 1807 John Cougil & Margaret Steel. Bondsman, Thomas Steel

6 Apr 1807 John Gard & Margaret Giffin, daughter of William Giffin, the bondsman

8 Apr 1807 Redman Lake & Lydia Drum. Bondsman, Robert Foster

15 Apr 1807 John Anderson & Sarah Fawson of lawful age. Bondsman, Robert McCleve

15 Apr 1807 Henry Wisecarver & Leah Snapp, daughter of Jacob Snapp of Frederick County, the bondsman

16 Apr 1807 William Grimes & Nancy Johnston. Bondsman, Henry Haymaker

18 Apr 1807 Jesse White & Catherine Hutsler, daughter of Jacob Hutsler, the bondsman, who signs in German

18 Apr 1807 Abraham Creswell & Mary Chenoweth, daughter of William Chennoweth of Frederick County, the bondsman

18 Apr 1807 Jesse White & Catherine Hutsler, daughter of Jacob Hutsler of Frederick County, the bondsman, who signs in German

22 Apr 1807 Nathaniel Cartmell & Sarah Bean of Frederick County. Bondsman, James Bean

22 Apr 1807 Thomas Marple, son of Ezekiel Marple, the bondsman, & Ann Fuller of Frederick County of lawful age

30 Apr 1807 Robert Wilson & Ann Griggs, daughter of Susanna Griggs of Frederick County, the bondsman

30 Apr 1807 Jacob Gardner & Elizabeth McGoohen of Frederick County of lawful age. Bondsman, Peter Ham

8 May 1807 Smith Bonham & Ann Cleavinger of lawful age of Frederick County. Bondsman, John Howell

8 May 1807 Adam Bailey & Lydia Mercer of Frederick County of lawful age. Bondsman, Joseph Mercer

8 May 1807 Adam Kern & Margaret Redman, daughter of Michael Redman of Frederick County, the bondsman

9 May 1807 John Holliday & Catharine Hart of Frederick County. Bondsman, William Silvers

13 May 1807 Isaac Denton & Mary Settlemire, daughter of Casper Settlemire of Frederick County, the bondsman

23 May 1807 George Marple, son of Ezekial Marple, & Mary G. McFarlin, ward of James Leach. Bondsmen, Ezekiel Marple & James Leach

26 May 1807 Jacob Roads & Rhoda Niswander of Frederick County of lawful age. Bondsman, Abraham Niswanger. Groom signs in German

27 May 1807 James Smallwood & Sarah Loyd, widow of Stephen Loyd, dec. of Frederick County. Bondsman, Nimian Magruder

1 Jun 1807 John Maxwell & Parthemia Cartmell, widow & relict of Edward Cartmell, decd of Frederick County. Bondsman, Jacob Delong

8 Jun 1807 John Fisher & Elizabeth Deal, daughter of Ann Deal, widow & relict of Conrad Deal deceased of Frederick County. Bondsman, Ann Deal

8 Jun 1807 Robert Smith & Mary Davidson, daughter of James Davidson of Frederick County, the bondsman

10 Jun 1807 Joseph Glascock & Mary Strother, daughter of James Strother. Bondsman, George Farrow

13 Jun 1807 Peter Yoe & Mary Secrist of Frederick County of lawful age. Bondsman, George Secrist

13 Jun 1807 Edward Banks & Barbara Hott of Frederick County (daughter of George Hott deceased). Bondsman, Conrad Hott

1 Jul 1807 Thomas Burke & Elizabeth Eddy of Frederick County of lawful age. Bondsman, John Eddy

6 Jul 1807 Samuel Lanham, son of Henry Lanham, & Ann Smallwood, daughter of Hebron Smallwood of Frederick County, the bondsman

8 Jul 1807 Isaac Thacker & Elizabeth Lock, daughter of George Locke, the bondsman

14 Jul 1807 Isaac Mylinger & Elizabeth Pitman, daughter of Andrew Pitman of Frederick County, the bondsman

20 Jul 1807 William Corbett & Margaret Waxwell of Frederick County of lawful age. Bondsman, William George

21 Jul 1807 Jesse Trowbreidge & Sarah Pugh, daughter of Malin Pugh of Frederick County, the bondsman

22 Jul 1807 Moses Barker & Margaret Brison, daughter of Samuel Brison of Frederick County, the bondsman

24 Jul 1807 James Seile & Nancy Alseep, ward of John Matthias of Frederick County, the bondsman

6 Aug 1807 Philip Stone & Christiana Crum, daughter of Christian Crum of Frederick County, the bondsman

17 Aug 1807 Job Messer & Mary Shrade of lawful age of said county. Bondsman, Mark Kerr

27 Jul 1807 Ralph Williams & Catharine McConnell of lawful age of Frederick County. Bondsman, James Lucky

19 Aug 1807 John Cadwallader & Elizabeth Cornelius. Bondsman, Dennis McConnell

22 Aug 1807 Abraham Painter & Sarah Branson. Bondsman, John Humston

26 Aug 1807 John Tewalt & Catharine Brill, daughter of Henry Brill of Frederick County, the bondsman

29 Aug 1807 Daniel McConnell & Mary Courtney of Frederick County. Bondsman, Barnabas Courtney

31 Aug 1807 Jacob Berlin & Sarah Handle, widow & relict of Nicholas Handle deceased. Bondsman, Edward Marsh

31 Aug 1807 Horatio Murphy & Mary Cole, daughter of John Cole of Frederick County. Bondsman, William Marshall

1 Sep 1807 John Newland & ELizabeth Gaunt, daughter of Martin Gaunt of Frederick County, the bondsman

4 Sep 1807 Peter Loy & Elizabeth Lewis, daughter of Samuel Lewis. Bondsman, Conrad Loy

(day not legible) Sep 1807 John Hamrick & Elizabeth Stigler of Frederick County of lawful age. Bondsman, John Stigler

5 Sep 1807 William Trussel & Rehbecca Rhodes, daughter of John Rhodes, the bondsman

8 Sep 1807 Joseph Baker & Sarah Lockhart, daughter of Robert Lockhart of Frederick County. Bondsman, Isaac Baker

12 Sep 1807 Jacob Borer & Elizabeth Marple, daughter of Enoch Marple of Frederick County, the bondsman

16 Sep 1807 David Clevinger & Polly Trenary, daughter of Samuel Trenary of Frederick County, the bondsman

5 Oct 1807 Joseph Parish, son of William Parish, & Mary Slonnaker of Frederick County, daughter of Christian Slonnaker. Bondsmen, William Parrish & Jacob Oats

3 Oct 1807 William Mansfield Jones & Ann H. Jones, daughter of William Jones of Frederick County, the bondsman

13 Oct 1807 Thomas Booth & Susanna ?Saveley. Bondsman, Isaac Booth

22 Oct 1807 John Lupton & Susannah Williams, daughter of Daniel Williams of Frederick County, the bondsman

22 Oct 1807 Henry Spore & Elizabeth Ramey. Bondsman, John Spore

23 Oct 1807 Isaac Romine & Mary Shusher of lawful age. Bondsman, Acquilla Osbourne

28 Oct 1807 William Morris & Sarah Cartmell, daughter of Thomas Cartmell of Frederick County. Bondsman, Joseph Cartmell

28 Oct 1807 David Belford & Peggy Anderson of lawful age of Frederick County. Bondsman, John Anderson

29 Oct 1807 John Alexander & Mary Nutt, daughter of Edward Nutt of Frederick County, the bondsman

2 Nov 1807 Posey Askins & Nancy Barns, daughter of James Barns of Frederick County, the bondsman

10 Nov 1807 Jacob Patch Jnr & Rachael Brelsford, daughter of Barnard Brelsford of Frederick County, the bondsman

2 Nov 1807 Richard Murray & Hannah Parent of Frederick County. Bondsman, Ferguson Bell

11 Nov 1807 William H. Dulany & Elizabeth Shackleford, daughter of James Shackleford of this county. Bondsman, Samuel Shackleford

14 Nov 1807 James Thompson & Susanna Scott. Bondsman, William Vanhorn

18 Nov 1807 Tilbury Jones & Margaret Goff, daughter of John Goff of Frederick County. Bondsman, Thomas Lloyd

17 Nov 1807 Robert Craig, son of Susannah Craig, & Nancy Kelly. Bondsman, Jemimah Bowling (female)

23 Nov 1807 John Lock & Mary Smith, daughter of Bartholomew Smith of Frederick County, the bondsman

25 Nov 1807 Francis Hutchins & Susanna Hall, widow of Joseph Hall decd late of Frederick County. Bondsman, Jacob Shively

25 Nov 1807 Jacob Vandiver & Elizabeth Myers. Bondsman, Warner Throckmorton

26 Nov 1807 Wiliam Potts & Isabella Dowlins of lawful age. Bondsman, Isaac Phillips

1 Dec 1807 Henry Strickling & Rachel McDonald, daughter of Abraham McDonald of Frederick County, the bondsman

1 Dec 1807 John Kinsler & Ann Rogers of Frederick County of lawful age. Bondsman, Thomas Rogers

1 Dec 1807 James Rains & Molly Smith, daughter of Kirby Smith of Frederick County. Bondsman, William Garner

3 Dec 1807 Jonathan McLurr & Sarah Cryder, daughter of Jacob Cryder of Frederick County. Bondsman, John Cryder

8 Dec 1807 Lewis Switzer & Eliza Bell, stepdaughter of Edward Mercer of Frederick County, the bondsman

9 Dec 1807 John Neel & Polly Frank of Frederick County of lawful age. Bondsman, John Rosenberger, who signs in German

10 Dec 1807 Edward Rice & Elizabeth Files of Frederick County of lawful age. Bondsman, Henry Ullery

11 Dec 1807 Martin Suverby & Mary Havey of lawful age. Bondsman, William Cain

15 Dec 1807 George Keyes & Anna Sands of Frederick County of lawful age. Bondsman, John Spaid

16 Dec 1807 Charles Johnston & Mary Dowall, widow & relict of William Dowell decd of Frederick County. Bondsman, Elijah Dowall

12 Dec 1807 James Hurt & Mary Newham, daughter of James Newham of Frederick County. Bondsman, Beatty Carson

19 Dec 1807 Jacob McKay & Elizabeth Antram, ward of Joshua Antram, the bondsman

?25 Dec 1807 Thomas Rogers & Regina Cartmill, daughter of Parthenia Maxwell formerly Parthenia Cartmill of Frederick County. Bondsman, Reuben Kiles

20 Dec 1807 Joseph Shepherd & Amelia Burchill, daughter of John Burchill of Frederick County, the bondsman

23 Dec 1807 Robert Cornwell & Sibey Ashby of lawful age. Bondsman, William Reveil

23 Dec 1807 Marquis Kean & Hester Emmons, daughter of Joel Emmons, the bondsman

24 Dec 1807 Lewis Jones & Arabella Pepper, widow & relict of James Prepers decd of Frederick County. Bondsman, James McCrackin

1 Jan 1808 Joseph Fry & Sarah Richards, daughter of Henry Richards of Frederick County, who signs in German

24 Dec 1807 Robert Benn & Franky Riley. Bondsman, James Sowers

4 Jan 1808 Philip Louck & Ruth Groves, daughter of Ezra Grover (sic), the bondsman

8 Jan 1808 Philip Lamp (in bond, "Lap" in signature) & Elizabeth Whiteman, daughter of Jacob Whiteman, the bondsman

9 Jan 1808 Thomas Wilson & Jane McPherson of Frederick County of lawful age. Bondsman, Peter Cooley

13 Jan 1808 John Moore & Kitty Siders of lawful age. Bondsman, Conrad Siders

18 Jan 1808 Daniel Tucker & Ester McMullen, daughter of Alexander McMullen of Frederick County, the bondsman

19 Jan 1808 Thomas Catlett & Polly Poyles, daughter & ward of Ann Poyles of Frederick County. Bondsman, Nimrod Catlett

26 Jan 1808 John Rosinberger & Nancy Highby of Frederick County of lawful age. Bondsman, John Highby

30 Jan 1808 John McFarland & Catharine Maury, daughter of Frederick Maury of Frederick County, the bondsman

1 Feb 1808 William Fisher, son of Lewis Fisher, & Fanny Gaunt, daughter of Martin Gaunt of Frederick County. Fathers are bondsmen

2 Feb 1808 John Williams & Mary Thompson, ward of Jobn Lowry decd. Bondsman, John Lowry, guardian of bride (sic)

2 Feb 1808 Thomas Brown & Martha Myers, daughter of John Myers of Frederick County, the bondsman

24 Feb 1808 Thomas Day & Mary Allen, daughter of George Allen of Frederick County, the bondsman

29 Feb 1808 William Franks & Nancy ORear, daughter of Benja ORear Esq. of Frederick County. Bondsman, John ORear

29 Feb 1808 Edward Bulger & Catharine Snapp, daughter of Joseph Snapp of Frederick County. Bondsman, Joseph Whisson

29 Feb 1808 John Crow & Martha Shepherd, widow & relict of Thomas Shepherd decd. Bondsman, William Castleman

29 Feb 1808 James Whaley & Elizabeth Hall, widow of Benjamin Hall. Bondsman, William Castleman

2 Mar 1808 John Fry & Sarah Mitchell, daughter of Thomas Mitchell of Frederick County, the bondsman

3 Mar 1808 Fielding Cornwell & Milley Ashby. Bondsman, Isaac Romine

3 Mar 1808 Joseph Nosset & Eve Myers of lawful age of Frederick County. Bondsman, John Miers

15 Mar 1808 William Trotter & Barbara Dick of lawful age. Bondsman, Peter Dick

20 Mar 1808 John Myers & Sarah Love. Bondsman, Joseph Nosset

26 Mar 1808 Colin Leach & Dorcas Grosman. Bondsman, William Vanhorn. Bride's name possibly "Crosen")

29 Mar 1808 Jacob Martin & Hannah Hanshaw. Bondsman, Thomas Hanshaw

29 Mar 1808 John Ross & Mary Stallings. Bondsman, Thomas Neill

31 Mar 1808 Michael Helpbringer & Sarah Willington. Bondsman, Jacob Williams, who signs in German

4 Apr 1808 William Allemong & Charity Lewis of Frederick County of lawful age. Bondsman, Lewis McCoole

4 Apr 1808 William P. Ball & Elizabeth Singleton. Bondsman, Thomas A. Tidball

13 Apr 1808 Thomas Jackson & Mary Bastian, daughter of Adam Bostyan of Frederick County, the bondsman

14 Apr 1808 Samuel Thornaberry & Sarah Chapman, daughter of William Chapman of Frederick County, the bondsman

16 Apr 1808 Negro William & Negro Lucy. Bondsman, William Doster

16 Apr 1808 Jacob Cable & Phebe Crupper, daughter of John Crupper, the bondsman of Frederick County

16 Apr 1808 Michael Housman & Sarah Kile, widow & relict of James Kile decd. Bondsman, Enoch Marple

18 Apr 1808 Isaac Payne & Elizabeth Bruce, daughter of James Bruce of Frederick County. Bondsman, John Jolliffe Esq.

20 Apr 1808 Leonard Ellis & Mary Babb of lawful age. Bondsman, John Strider

26 Apr 1808 Samuel Hale & Mary Johnston of Frederick County of lawful age. Bondsman, John Johnston

2 May 1808 James McConnel & Elizabeth Luckey, daughter of Joseph Luckey Esq of Frederick County. Bondsman, James Luckey

19 May 1808 David Hening & Letticia Rust, daughter of Benedict Rust of Frederick County. Bondsman, Matthew Rust

25 May 1808 John Painter & Rachel Redd, daughter of George Redd of Frederick County, the bondsman

28 May 1808 Caleb Brady & Agnes Gray, daughter of James Gray of Frederick County, the bondsman

28 May 1808 Adam Bauer & Elizabeth Wetzel, daughter of John Wetzel, the bondsman

30 May 1808 William Barrow & Catherine Mesmore. Bondsman, John Crider Senr

6 Jun 1808 Henry Richards & Hannah Riley. Bondsman, George Riley

6 Jun 1808 George Kackley & Elizabeth Johnston. Bondsman, Elias Kackley

7 Jun 1808 Smith Wilson & Jane Letitia Corbett, daughter of James Corbett of Frederick County, the bondsman

11 Jun 1808 Jeremiah Oconner & Elizabeth Tinchman of Frederick County of lawful age. Bondsman, Conrad Kramer

11 Jun 1808 Abraham Simon & Charity Stone, daughter of Margaret Stone of Frederick County. Bondsman, Lewis Stone

13 Jun 1808 Daniel Stump, son of Joseph Stump, & Catherine Aid, ward of Joseph Stump of Frederick County, the bondsman

13 Jun 1808 William Racey & Mary Myers, daughter of John Myers of Frederick County. Bondsman, George Cale

16 Jun 1808 Elias Holsclaw & Anna Windsor, daughter of Thomas Windsor of Frederick County, the bondsman

20 Jun 1808 Thomas Curry & Mary Settlemire, daughter of (illegible) of Frederick County. Bondsman, David McCleland

20 Jun 1808 Nicholas Taylor & Catharine Myers, daughter of John Myers of Frederick County. Bondsman, Conrad Loy

21 Jun 1808 John Racy & Rebecca Orndorff, daughter & ward of Hannah Orndorff of Frederick County. Bondsman, Samuel Orndorff

9 Jul 1808 Martin Cartmill & Ann Ball. Bondsman, Thomas A. Tidball

30 Jul 1808 Luke Blacker & Rebecca Albin, daughter of Robert Albin of Frederick County, the bondsman

1 Aug 1808 John Smith & Elenor Cole. Bondsman, John Cole

10 Aug 1808 Walter Watson & Nancy Lucas, daughter of Thomas Lucas, the bondsman

13 Aug 1808 Jesse Vincent & Elizabeth Smith, granddaughter & ward of Joseph Smith Senr. of Frederick County. Bondsman, Thomas Smith Jr.

22 Aug 1808 John Day & Polly Corder, daughter of Benjamin Corder, the bondsman

23 Aug 1808 James Monsy & Mary Hutchins, daughter of Francis Hutchins of Frederick County. Bondsman, Nicholas Monsy

24 Aug 1808 Peter Shade & Mary Miller, daughter of Casper Miller, the bondsman

27 Aug 1808 John Suter & Margaret Settle, daughter & ward of Elizabeth Settle. Bondsman, John Settle

29 Aug 1808 Adam Settle & Martha Patton of lawful age. Bondsman, John Patton

31 Aug 1808 Jacob Sigafuse & Elizabeth Brill, daughter of Henry Brill, the bondsman

3 Sep 1808 John Beavers & Margaret Buskirk, daughter of Abraham Van Buskirk

3 Sep 1808 Bernard Brelsford & Anne Simpson. Bondsman, William VanHorn

3 Sep 1808 William Cole & Mary McNally of lawful age. Bondsmen, Mary Taylor & Benjamin Richards

9 Sep 1808 Henry Kline & Eady Ramey, daughter of William Ramey of Frederick County, the bondsman

10 Sep 1808 Edward Gray, son of Sarah Gray, & Polly Scott, daughter of Isaac Scott. Parents are bondsmen

14 Sep 1808 John Powers & Catherine Carnagy. Bondsman, James Powers

21 Sep 1808 Lewis McCoole & Nancy Weaver, daughter of Jacob Weaver of Frederick County, the bondsman, who signs in German

22 Sep 1808 David Allen & Sarah Taylor, daughter of Griffin Taylor. Bondsman, Thomas Tidball

24 Sep 1808 Joshua Pilcher & Mary Ann Dawson, daughter of George Dawson, the bondsman

3 Oct 1808 Michael Hoeman & Mary Crumm of Frederick Country. Bondsman, Christian Crum

3 Oct 1808 John Handle & Sarah Bowers, daughter of George Bowers of Frederick County, the bondsman

10 Oct 1808 John Wade & Mary Butterfield, daughter & ward of Ann Butterfield of Frederick County, the bondsman

10 Oct 1808 John Butterfield, son & ward of Ann Butterfield of Frederick County, & Edith Cloud of same place. Bondsman, Ann Butterfield

15 Oct 1808 Walter Tanquery & Abagail Painter. Bondsman, Alexander Compton

15 Oct 1808 Robert Mills & Eliza B. Smith. Bondsman, William Davison

17 Oct 1808 Lewis Preist & Mary Baker, daughter of Jacob Baker of Frederick County. Bondsman, Isaac Baker

17 Oct 1808 John Siders & Isabella Kline, daughter of William Kline, the bondsman

19 Oct 1808 Jacob Heironimus & Elizabeth Brown, daughter of Joel Brown, the bondsman

20 Oct 1808 Georges Dingas & Jane Temple of lawful age of Frederick County. Bondsman, George Cowgill

24 Oct 1808 Andrew Robinson & Peggy Jackson, daughter of Ruth Jackson. Bondsman, Benjamin Fenton

27 Oct 1808 William Tomblin & Rebecca Ashby. Bondsman, Acquilla Osborn

27 Oct 1808 Joseph Underwood & Ann McNelly, daughter of Amy Campbell of Frederick County. Bondsman, Thomas Bell

9 Nov 1808 John Keneaster & Catherine Philips, daughter of Philip Philips, the bondsman

11 Nov 1808 James Neff & Catherine Singhase, daughter of Christian Singhase, the bondsman

15 Nov 1808 Abraham Elliott & Catharine Dugan of Frederick County, both of lawful age. Bondsman, William Hilling

15 Nov 1808 John Carter & Mary Byrd, daughter of Francis Byrd of Frederick County, the bondsman

15 Nov 1808 Peter Senseney & Louisa Catlett, daughter of John Catlett. Bondsman, Robert Turner

16 Nov 1808 James Dewaney & Sarah Campbell, daughter of John Campbell, the bondsman

23 Nov 1808 John Reed & Martha Kearns, daughter of Jacob Kearns. Bondsman, Nathan Kearns

30 Nov 1808 Philip Cyphert & Mima Johnston of Frederick County of lawful age. Bondsman, Jacob Weaver, who signs in German

5 Dec 1808 David Shepherd & Phebe Hooper. Bondsman, Dolphin Drew

5 Dec 1808 Enos Matson & Elizabeth Mercer, daughter of William Mercer of Frederick County, the bondsman

6 Dec 1808 William Jenkins & Mary Wilson, widow and relict of Richard Wilson dec. Bondsman, David Camblyn

7 Dec 1808 Alexander Duke & Rachel Lewis, daughter of Abraham Lewis of Frederick County, the bondsman

10 Dec 1808 Michael Lay & Elizabeth Martin, widow of Thomas Martin, dec. Bondsman, Samuel Craig

17 Dec 1808 Philip Hoover & Lavina Bedingar. Bondsman, Joseph Parker

21 Dec 1808 Henry Hoover & Nancy Rutter, daughter of Henry Rutter, the bondsman

20 Dec 1808 James Hawley(signature) Halley(in bond) & Lucy Williams, daughter of Sarah Williams. Bondsman, Andrew Turner

20 Dec 1808 Willis Gaunt, son of Martin Gaunt, & Nancy Dickson, daughter of John Dickison, the bondsman

21 Dec 1808 Jacob Little & Polly Ritenour, daughter of Michael Ritenour, the bondsman

24 Dec 1808 John McCaully & Jane Gray, daughter of James Gray, the bondsman

26 Dec 1808 Isaac Grant & Rhoda Leach. Bondsman, John Leach

27 Dec 1808 Stephen Davis & Nancy Gilkeson, daughter of Sarah Gilkeson, the bondsman

27 Dec 1808 Moses Watson & Polly Kello, daughter of John Kello, the bondsman

27 Dec 1808 David Capper & Hannah Hangfield of Frederick County both of lawful age. Bondsman, John Wingfield Capper

28 Dec 1808 Peter Stephens, Jr & Sarah Parlett, daughter of Joshua Parlett, the bondsman

29 Dec 1808 Thomas Norfolk & Leah Patch. Bondsman, Jacob Patch

2 Jan 1809 James Smith & Mary Winn, daughter of Robert Wynn of Frederick County, the bondsman

3 Jan 1809 George W. Kiger & Rebecca Reis of Frederick County. Bondsman, David Castleman, Jr.

3 Jan 1809 Reuben Kiles & Katy Earhart, daughter of Mary Earhart of Frederick County. Bondsman, Ezer Ellis

4 Jan 1809 Benjamin Lett, a free man & not a slave, & Mary Calaman, a free mulatto, daughter of Moses Calaman, the bondsman

6 Jan 1809 James Albin & Ann Ellis, daughter of Morris Ellis, the bondsman

7 Jan 1809 Thomas Hollingsworth & Rachel Jones of Frederick County. Bondsman, William Wilson

16 Jan 1809 John Elzey & Nancy Self, daughter of John Self of Frederick County. Bondsman, William Self

20 Jan 1809 Charles Grubbs & Rebecca Walters, daughter of John T. Walters. Bondsman, Samuel Simpson

24 Jan 1809 James Archer & Achrah Clevinger of lawful age. Bondsman, Peter Tomlin

24 Jan 1809 Alexander McDonald & Elizabeth Beckner. Bondsman, Archibald McDonald

3 Feb 1809 Isaac Baker & Leticia Ireland of Frederick County. Bondsman, Elijah Pollard

6 Feb 1809 Lewis Stump & Elizabeth Wright, widow & relict of William Wright, dec. of Frederick County. Bondsman, Joseph Heck

6 Feb 1809 Atwell Johnston & Rhoda Fry, ward of Joseph Whissen of Frederick County, the bondsman

11 Feb 1809 Elias Kackley & Jane B. Dyson, daughter of Aquilla Dyson, the bondsman

13 Feb 1809 William Alexander & Mary Green of Frederick County. Bondsman, Austin Green

16 Feb 1809 James Harris & Hannah Lowry. Bondsman, Moses Lowry

16 Feb 1809 James Brent & Rachel Touchstone, daughter of William Touchstone, the bondsman

22 Feb 1809 John Hughes & Mary Gaunt, daughter of Martin Gaunt, the bondsman

1 Mar 1809 Vincent Foster & Naomi Hickman of Frederick County of lawful age. Bondsman, Charles Carter

9 Mar 1809 Conrad Swatz & Olivia Mercer, daughter of Job Mercer, the bondsman

15 Mar 1809 Jacob Hutsler Jr. & Nelly Davis, daughter of Phebe Davis, the bondsman

15 Mar 1809 Daniel Webb Williams & Jemima Lewis, daughter of Abraham Lewis, the bondsman

17 Mar 1809 Alexander Compton & Lucinda Ireland. Bondsman, Elijah Pollard

20 Mar 1809 Aaron Matson & Polly Hollingshedd of Frederick County of lawful age. Bondsman, John Dowell

20 Mar 1809 Henry Hott & Mary Ley of Frederick County. Bondsman, Conrad Lay

27 Mar 1809 Jacob Shambough & Mary Barrow, daughter of William Barrow, the bondsman

3 Apr 1809 Thomas Henson & Nancy Dick, daughter of Thomas Dick, the bondsman

3 Apr 1809 Joseph B. Littler & Mary E. Savage, daughter of Joseph Savage of Frederick County, the bondsman

4 Apr 1809 Jacob Jones & Marianne Shepherd of Frederick County. Bondsman, Jacob Lewis

8 Apr 1809 James Taylor & Sarah Pickering, daughter of John Pickering, dec. late of Frederick County. Bondsman, William Doster

11 Apr 1809 Wm Moore Fauntleroy & Frances W. Ball, daughter & ward of Druscilla Ball of Frederick County. Bondsman, Lawrence Butler

13 Apr 1809 Thomas Weaver & Elenor Hughes. Bondsman, Thomas Hughes

24 Apr 1809 Nathan Kerns & Sarah Whitaker, daughter of Joshua Whitaker of Frederick County, the bondsman

24 Apr 1809 Hosea Danley & Sarah Taylor, daughter of James Taylor, the bondsman

24 Apr 1809 William Newell & Rebecca Cooper of Frederick County. Bondsman, Jacob Cooper

25 Apr 1809 John Guard & Isabella Cornelius. Bondsman, John C. Poole

3 May 1809 William Crafford & Elizabeth Stoner, ward of Alexander Smith, the bondsman

11 May 1809 John Woodford & Sarah Mann. Bondsman, James Willis

13 May 1809 John Bailes & Elizabeth Lawyer of Frederick County of lawful age. Bondsman, Jacob Lawyer

15 May 1809 Thomas Knight & Nancy Stiggers, ward of Mary Stiggers of Frederick County. Bondsman, James Smith

16 May 1809 Armistead Thompson Mason & Eliza Parker. Bondsman, Thomas Parker. (Surname may be Thompson and Mason his occupation)

20 May 1809 Jacob Frederick & Susannah Earhart. Bondsman, Rachal Frederick

27 May 1809 Jacob Ware & Mary Stidley of Frederick County. Bondsman, David Devo

3 Sep 1810 James H. Sowur & Sarah G. Sherrard of Frederick County. Bondsman, Robert D. Glass

4 Sep 1810 Daniel McCarty & Elizabeth Richards of Frederick County of lawful age. Bondsman, Peter Hunsicker

11 Sep 1810 James Pickrell & Mary Smedly, daughter of William Smedly of Frederick County. Bondsman, Joseph Neal

12 Sep 1810 Robert C. Tilden & Elizabeth Vance of Frederick County. Bondsman, Peter Myers

15 Sep 1810 Joseph Nesmith & Sarah Barr. Bondsman, Francis Watson

19 Sep 1810 Alexander Smilie & Katy Robinson, daughter of Braxton Robinson, the bondsman

21 Sep 1810 James Dillon, son of John Dillon, & Sarah Ward of lawfull age of Frederick County. Bondsman, Gideon Edwards

22 Sep 1810 John B. Dyson & Nancy Garrett. Bondsman, George Garrett

22 Sep 1810 John Hicks & Sarah Shores. Bondsman, Lewis Smoot

22 Sep 1810 Jacob Patch & Nancy Garrett. Bondsman, George Albert

27 Sep 1810 John Crouse & Jane Smith (widow of Charles Smith) of Frederick County. Bondsman, John Fleming

29 Sep 1810 David Garrett & Mary Martin (of lawful age) of Fredk County. Bondsman, Luke Garret

6 Oct 1810 Henry Baroff & Elizabeth McCarty, ward of John McCarty of Frederick County

10 Oct 1810 James Watson & Rebekah Kendrick, daughter of Hannah Kendrick, the bondsman.

12 Oct 1810 William Elliot & Nancy Wright, daughter of George Wright of Frederick County, the bondsman

13 Oct 1810 Samuel Lewis & Betsy Muma of Frederick County of lawful age. Bondsman, George Muma

24 Oct 1810 George Brinker & Elizabeth Haney of Frederick County of lawful age. Bondsman, Jacob Kendrick

25 Oct 1810 Stacy M. Wilson & Frances Glenn of Frederick County of lawful age. Bondsman, John Withrow

19 Dec 1810 Fielding Sowers and Sally Brownley of Frederick County. Bondsman, William Cook

19 Dec 1810 William Payne & Catharine Bolton of Frederick County. Bondsman, Charles Beckley

20 Dec 1810 Nicholas Cross & Polly Tennor, ward of Jacob Lanham of Frederick County, the bondsman

20 Dec 1810 Elisha Smallwood & Delilah Dowell, daughter of Mary Johnston of Frederick County, the bondsman

21 Dec 1810 Henry Hamilton & Catharine Kackley of Frederick County. Bondsman, Samuel Kackley

27 Dec 1810 Ellis Minshall & Anna Harrel, ward of Mary Harrel of Frederick County. Bondsman, Jacob Gander

28 Dec 1810 David Pinkly & Rachael Frye of Frederick County, daughter and ward of Elizabeth Frye. Bondsman, Joseph Whisson

31 Dec 1810 William Westbrook & Darcus Moffott, daughter of John Moffitt, the bondsman

4 Jan 1811 John Corder & ..... (first name illegible) McDonald, daughter of John McDonald of Frederick County, the bondsman

6 Jan 1810 Lewis Stone & Eve Slagle of Frederick County of lawful age. Bondsman, John Slagle. Although this bond was dated 1810, it was located with other January 1811 bonds on the film.

7 Jan 1811 Stephen Retter & Polly Bolton, daughter of Henry Ritter of Frederick County, the bondsman

8 Jan 1811 James Sherran & Fanny Moore, ward of Casper Seevers, the bondsman

10 Jan 1811 William Bradford & Elizabeth White, daughter of Michael White of Frederick County. Bondsman, George A. Magruder

10 Jan 1811 Abraham Piper & Polley Young, daughter of Anthony Young, the bondsman

15 Jan 1811 Charles Fussell & Sarah Flemings, daughter of Archibald Flemings of Frederick County. Bondsman, Colmor Lanham

15 Jan 1811 Jacob Weaver Jr. & Alivia McCoole, daughter of John McCoole of Frederick County, the bondsman

Marriage Bonds No. 10, 1811-1815 Frederick County, Virginia

17 Dec 1811 William Rogers & Mary Leonard, daughter of Jeremiah Leonard, the bondsman

17 Dec 1811 Jacob Williams & Ruth Wilson, daughter of Jacob Wilson. Bondsman, Thomas Wilson

18 Dec 1811 Samuel Craig & Elizabeth Tilly of Frederick County. Bondsman, George Tilly

20 Dec 1811 Charles Howard & Sarah Drake, daughter of Samuel Drake, the bondsman

20 Dec 1811 Michael Singhass & Charlotte Barly, daughter of John Barley, the bondsman

21 Dec 1811 Benjamin ?Drowning & Catharine Chamblin. Bondsman, Shadric Laws

21 Dec 1811 Samuel Hollingsworth & Susan Richardson, daughter of William Richardson, the bondsman

23 Dec 1811 John Latham & Elizabeth Monroe, widow of John Monroe, dec. of Frederick County. Bondsman, George Reynolds

25 Dec 1811 James Rogers & Mary Dingas. Bondsman, Jacob Lemley

27 Dec 1811 Benjamin Hancher & Susannah Simpson, daughter of James Sympson (sic) of Frederick County, the bondsman

28 Dec 1811 William King & Mary Conner, of lawful age, daughter of James Conner of Frederick County. Bondsman, James Read

28 Dec 1811 William Gloyd & Sarah Scaggs. Bondsman, George Larrick

30 Dec 1811 Isaac Strosnider & Leah Tewalt, of lawful age of Frederick County. Bondsman, Abraham Tewalt

1 Jan 1812 Jacob Nicklin & Clarissa Marsh, daughter of Richard Marsh, the bondsman

1 Jan 1812 James Hathaway & Henrietta Baylis, dau of Capt William Baylis of Frederick County, the bondsman

2 Jan 1812 Joseph Tate & Margaret Riley of Frederick County. Bondsman, William Roach

4 Jan 1812 Valentine Peyton & Mary Morgan, daughter of Martha Morgan of Frederick County. Bondsman, Abraham Chapman

9 Jan 1812 Richard Sutton & Martha Kidd, daughter of Richard Kidd, the bondsman

16 Jan 1812 John Miller & Juliann Shaver of lawful age, of Frederick County. Bondsman, Ezekiel Carter

19 Jan 1812 William Wilkin & Isabella I Steele. Bondsman, Samuel Steele

20 Jan 1812 John Crumly & Elizabeth Hancher, daughter of William Hancher, the bondsman

27 Jan 1812 Adam Shades & Betsy Hingle, daughter of Adam Hingle

31 Jan 1812 John Cave & Elizabeth White. Bondsman, Samuel Cave

31 Jan 1812 John Jones & Ann Redman Jackson, daughter of Nathaniel Jackson of Frederick County. Bondsman, Dennis O'Conner

30 Jan 1812 William Agre & Elizabeth McFadden of Frederick County. Bondsman, Robert McFaddin

1 Feb 1812 William Davis & Rachel Gawthrop. Bondsman, Daniel Wade

3 Feb 1812 George Hill & Susan Bails, daughter of Thomas Bails of Frederick Co. Bondsman, Moses Bails

6 Feb 1812 David Fisher & Susannah Wright. Bondsman, Ann Deal

7 Feb 1812 Joseph Bryant & Ann Carter, daughter of Ezekiel Carter, the bondsman

7 Feb 1812 Joseph ?Whissent & Elizabeth Carr, daughter of Thomas Carr, the bondsman

11 Feb 1812 Henry Millhorn & Sarah Wetzell, daughter of John Wetzel, the bondsman

18 Feb 1812 William Jackson & Hannah Shepperd, daughter of Thomas Shepherd, decd, of Frederick County. Bondsman, Jacob Shively, who signs "Shivy"

20 Feb 1812 Daniel Fuller & Mary Oferrell of Frederick County. Bondsman, Isaac Scott

22 Feb 1812 Christian Hull & Mary Wever, daughter of John Wever. Bondsman, Geo. A. Eberman

24 Feb 1812 Nathan Evans & Mary Ann Haburn, of lawful age, of Frederick County. Bondsman, Matthew Habron. Bondsman's name also give as Mandly Haburn.

26 Feb 1812 William Mahew/Mayhugh & Mary Ducker, daughter of William Ducker of Frederick County. Bondsman, Samuel Clemmens

27 Feb 1812 Samuel Cook & Mary Hotzenspillar, ward of Thomas Dann, the bondsman

20 Feb 1812 Abraham Dawalt/Tewalt & Rebecca Bly. Bondsman, John Ohaver

29 Feb 1812 Abraham Bauker & Margarett Kackley. Bondsman, John Drake

9 Mar 1812 Joseph Everett Milburn & Rachael Clark. Bondsman, John Harrison

13 Mar 1812 John Orndorf Junr & Elizabeth Pitcock, daughter of Stephen Pitcock of Frederick County. Bondsmen, John Orndorf Sr & Stephen Pitcock

16 Mar 1812 George Harbert & Charity McCool. Bondsman, Thomas Mitchell

17 Mar 1812 Robert P Randall & Nancy Shackelford, daughter of Joseph Shackelford of Frederick County, the bondsman

24 Mar 1812 John Dick & Catharine Trotter of Frederick County. Bondsman, Matthew Trotter

28 Mar 1812 James Pelter & Nancy Syphret, daughter of George Syphret of Frederick County, the bondsman

28 Mar 1812 Joseph Thomas & Christiana Ridenour, daughter of Michael Ridenour. Bondsman, Jonathan Foster

30 Mar 1812 John Snapp & Sally Davis, daughter of James Davis, the bondsman

30 Mar 1812 John Lauck & Elizabeth Crum, daughter of Henry Crum of Frederick County, the bondsman

31 Mar 1812 Joseph Galleno & Nancy Harry of Frederick County of lawful age. Bondsman, David Harry

2 Apr 1812 Thomas Rust & Hannah M Lamkin. Bondsman, Samuel Crabb

9 Apr 1812 John Wiley & Ann Hart, daughter of Samuel Hart, the bondsman

13 Apr 1812 Hiram Cline & Elizabeth Green. Bondsman, John Green Jr

14 Apr 1812 George Castleman & Jane Burchell. Bondsman, John Burchell

21 Apr 1812 Abraham Stump & Margaret Shambaugh, daughter of Philip Shambaugh, the bondsman

21 Apr 1812 John Monroe & Lucy Louthan, widow of George Lowthan, decd, of Frederick County. Bondsman, Michael Pierce

22 Apr 1812 William Leach & Sarah Davis, daughter of Phebe Saunders, formerly Phebe Davis of Frederick County. Bondsman, Benjamin Goldsberry

9 May 1812 John P Sanford & Ann Meredith Helm of Frederick County. Bondsman, John Jolliffe

25 May 1812 John Weaver Junr(?) and Martha McCool. Bondsman, John McCool

28 May 1812 Christian Stipe & Polly Williams of lawful age of Frederick County. Bondsman, William Harrell

29 May 1812 George Moulden & Sarah Davis. Bondsman, Thomas Chamlyn

1 Jun 1812 Lewis A. Smith & Mildred Ashby. Bondsman, William Catlett

4 Jun 1812 Henry Peake & Isabella Snyder, widow of Samuel G. Snyder. Bondsman, John Hening

4 Jun 1812 John Withrow & Minty Johnston of Frederick County. Bondsman, Thomas Hamilton

12 Jun 1812 Littleton Ash & Nancy Corder, daughter of Benjamin Corder, the bondsman

12 Jun 1812 David Pangle & Nancy Johnston, daughter of Nimrod Johnston of Frederick County, the bondsman

12 Jun 1812 Edward Hendren & Sarah Hess, daughter of Abraham Hess of Frederick County. Bondsman, James Davis

15 Jun 1812 Henry Young & Peggy Noel, daughter of John Noel, the bondsman

15 Jun 1812 John Harfeldt & Elizabeth Kennan, daughter of Thomas Kennan of Frederick County. Bondsman, Alexander Kennan

23 Jun 1812 William McGuin & Ann Molding, daughter of Baptist Molding of Frederick County. Bondsman, William Martin

30 Jun 1812 Dennis OConner & Elizabeth Hesser, daughter of George Hesser, the bondsman

20 Jul 1812 Richard Lee & Susan Abernathy, daughter of Samuel Abernathy. Bondsman, John Abernathy

30 Jul 1812 Frederick Mauck & Eve Snyder, widow of Jacob Snyder, decd. Bondsman, Abraham Barrow

31 Jul 1812 Joshua Leach (signed Joshua Leitch) & Margaret Gobins. Bondsman, Malin Pugh

1 Aug 1812 Frederick Denis & Elizabeth Myers. Bondsman, Elizabeth Elzey

1 Aug 1812 John Jones & Susan Usher of Frederick County. Bondsman, David Fries

5 Aug 1812 Jacob Arisman & Elizabeth Babb, daughter of James Babb, the bondsman

14 Aug 1812 James Jackson & Mary Hastings of lawful age of Frederick County, daughter of William Hastings. Bondsman, James Noble

15 Aug 1812 George Good & Judith Garrett, daughter of Laurence Garrett of Frederick County. Bondsman, Henry Garrett

28 Aug 1812 Benjamin O'Rear & Catherine Jones. Bondsman, Jesse ORear

31 Aug 1812 Edward White & Elizabeth Wisson, daughter of John Wisson, the bondsman

31 Aug 1812 James Martin & Elizabeth Campbell of lawful age. Bondsman, Zadok Rodgers

2 Sep 1812 James Franklin & Mary Smart, daughter of Thomas Smart, the bondsman

5 Sep 1812 John Barnett & Mary Severns, daughter of Edmund Severns, the bondsman

8 Sep 1812 James Rogers & Elizabeth Carper, daughter of Philip Carper, the bondsman

8 Sep 1812 William Thornburg & Hannah Lloyd, relict of Thomas Lloyd, decd. Bondsman, Conrad Huntsberry

10 Sep 1812 John Smith & Hannah Hoge, daughter of William Hoge. Bondsman, David Cather

12 Sep 1812 William Chapman & Sarah Rawyer. Bondsman, James Tanquary

14 Sep 1812 Christopher Bonecutter & Elizabeth Loy, daughter of Conrad Loy. Bondsmen, Harmon Bonecutter and Conrad Loy

17 Sep 1812 Archibald Holland & Mary McGuire. Bondsman, George Phillips, who signs in German

22 Sep 1812 Philip Wright & Barbara Dean, daughter of Ann Dean, the bondsman

22 Sep 1812 John Crampton & Ann Hammock of lawful age of Frederick County. Bondsman, Jacob Shambeck

24 Sep 1812 John D. Carlile & Sarah Holliday. Bondsman, Richard Holliday Jr

24 Sep 1812 James Anderson & Sarah Wiley, daughter of William Wiley, the bondsman

30 Sep 1812 Elijah Albin & Susannah Dalbay. Bondsman, Joseph Dalbey

3 Oct 1812 George Washington Carter & Mary B. Wormley, daughter of Mary Wormley, the bondsman

3 Oct 1812 Abraham Rhodes & Mary Shipler, daughter of George Shipler. Bondsman, Lewis Fulkerson

6 Oct 1812 John Flower & Elizabeth Gordon. Bondsman, Patrick Gordon

14 Oct 1812 Robert Haynie & Catharine Kline, daughter of Michael Kline, the bondsman

15 Oct 1812 William Fegins & Melinda Vickers of Frederick County. Bondsmen, Thomas Vickers & Joseph Lloyd

27 Oct 1812 Thomas Steel & Jane Curry, daughter of Thomas Curry, the bondsman

27 Oct 1812 John Crum & Barbara Crum, daughter of Henry Crum, the bondsman

2 Nov 1812 Elijah Dowell & Dolly Shepherd Bondsman, Elijah Smallwood

7 Nov 1812 William Taylor Junr & Harriet McElaney. Bondsman, T. Allen Tidball

9 Nov 1812 James Wright & Charlotte Madden, widow of Jacob Madden. Bondsman, Mabra Madden

18 Nov 1812 Thomas Campbell & Sally Kitchen, widow of Joel Kitchen. Bondsman, John Campbell

18 Nov 1812 George Tilli & Rhodie Saunders, daughter of John Saunders. Bondsman, David Davis

18 Nov 1812 James McFarlin & Elen Downing, daughter of James Downing, the bondsman

19 Nov 1812 David Davis & Betsy Young, daughter of Samuel Young. Bondsman, John Saunders.

19 Nov 1812 Thomas Bowan & Ruth Vance, daughter of James D. Vance. Bondsman, Joseph Berry

20 Nov 1812 Abner Osburn & Mary Welden, daughter of James Welden, the bondsman

21 Nov 1812 William Noble & Rachel Spencer. Bondsman, James Noble

21 Nov 1812 John Taylor & Catharine Fleet Bondsman, John McFarling

21 Nov 1812 William McCormick & Mary McDonald, widow and relict of James McDonald, decd. Bondsman, George Rice

23 Nov 1812 William Archer & Priscella Sterrett. Bondsman, Samuel Trenary

25 Nov 1812 Isaac Berlin & Rosanna Handle of lawful age. Bondsman, Nicholas Handle

27 Nov 1812 Moses T. Hunter & Mary Snickers. Bondsman, Geo Murray

2 (or 3) Dec 1812 Thomas Brown, (?Jr) & Ann Carter. Bondsman, Joshua Newbrough

3 Nov 1812 Philip Orndorf & Catharine Eo. Bondsman, William Williams

7 Dec 1812 Josiah Swayne & Elizabeth Jenkins, daughter of Abraham Jenkins. Bondsman, Robert Haney

20 Dec 1812 James Lindsey & Priscilla Stubblefield, widow and relict of ?Beverely Stubblefield. Bondsman, William ?Vanhorne

18 Dec 1812 James Cochran Jr & Margaret Millhorn. Bondsman, James Cochran Sr

23 Dec 1812 John Mercer & Rebecca Dolby. Bondsman, Joseph Dolby

24 Dec 1812 William Lane & Catharine Vanmeter. Bondsman, Henry Vanmeter

24 Dec 1812 Stephen Woodward & Mary Allensworth. Bondsman, Philip Allensworth

24 Dec 1812 William Hood & Elizabeth Cochran, daughter of James Cochran

24 Dec 1812 David Harry & Margaret Wholihan, orphan of John Wholihan of Frederick County. Bondsman, David Fries

26 Dec 1812 William Hood & Elizabeth Cochran, daughter of James Cochran, the bondsman

28 Dec 1812 John W. Grove & Jane Young. Bondsman, Anthony Young

28 Dec 1812 Samuel ?Maln/Mallen & Margaret Dick. Bondsman, Peter Dick

31 Dec 1812 George Kendrick & Nancy White, daughter of Mary Doran. Bondsman, John B. Bowie

2 Jan 1813 Jacob Gantz & Eliza Fleming, daughter of John Fleming, the bondsman

2 Dec 1812 Thomas Brown Jnr & Ann Carter. Bondsman, Joshua Newbrough

5 Jan 1813 John Parlett & Elizabeth Yakely, daughter of John Yakely of Frederick County, who signs in German

6 Jan 1813 George Beddow & Hester Tucker, widow of Frederick County. Bondsman, William Neill

6 Jan 1813 James Howard & Mary Mires. Bondsman, William Vance

7 Feb 1813 Baylor Jacobs & Mary Kendrick, daughter of Benjamin Kendrick of Frederick County. Bondsman, John Kendrick

13 Jan 1813 James Crawford & Mary Stribling. Bondsman, Francis Stribling

13 Jan 1813 Carter Neff & Mary Eddy, daughter of John Eddy, the bondsman

20 Jan 1813 John E. Baylis & Madlin Snapp, daughter of Joseph Snapp of lawful age. Bondsman, William Jackson

26 Jan 1813 James W. Babb & Rebecca Scarff, daughter of John Scarff of Frederick County. Bondsman, Henry M. Babb

30 Jan 1813. Thomas Hollandshead & Eve Deal, daughter of Ann Deal, the bondsman

30 Jan 1813 John Frazier & Rebecca Jenkins of lawful age of the County of Frederick. Bondsman, Abner Jury

1 Feb 1813 Aquilla King & Mary Williams of Frederick County. Bondsman, John Allen

3 Feb 1813 George Hansel & Nancy Lee, daughter of George Lee, the bondsman

3 Feb 1813 Adam Hambaugh & Matilda Catlett, daughter of John Catlett of Frederick County. Bondsman, Peter Catlett

5 Feb 1813 John Reed & Eliza Ann Babb, daughter of Henry Mercer Babb of Frederick County

8 Feb 1813 John Lamp & Sarah Morrison, daughter of William Morrison, the bondsman

13 Feb 1813 Adam Strodner & Elizabeth Cooper, daughter of John Cooper, the bondsman

13 Feb 1813 John W. Page & Jane Byrd Page, daughter of Robert Page Esq of Frederick County, the bondsman

15 Feb 1813 Thomas C. Lupton & Sarah Hamilton, daughter of John Hamilton, the bondsman

15 Feb 1813 Alexander Nash & Fanny Albert, daughter of William Albert, the bondsman

27 Feb 1813 Jacob Oller & Susannah Hansel, daughter of George Hansel, the bondsman, who signs in German

27 Feb 1813 Nathan Haines & Rachel McKoy, daughter of Moses McKoy. Bondsman, James McKoy Jr (McKay?)

27 Feb 1813 William Collins & Catharine Wall, daughter of George Wall. Bondsman, James ?Femster

1 Mar 1813 William Neilson & Arianna I. Wormeley of Frederick County. Bondsman, George H. Norris

1 Mar 1813 Nicholas Anderson & Ann Serrit of Frederick County. Bondsman, John Beaver

6 Mar 1813 David Stump & Vina Stoker of Frederick County. Bondsman, Charles Breedlove

8 Mar 1813 Elijah Romine & Lewranny Riley, daughter of George Riley of the County of Frederick. Bondsmen, Reuben Romine & William Riley

12 Mar 1813 Henry Samp & Sarah Ridgeway. Bondsman, John Ridgeway

13 Mar 1813 Marquis Q. Blakemore & Rebecca Winston Chandler, daughter of Carter B. Chandler of Frederick County. Bondsman, George Barnett

16 Mar 1813 Benedict Raynolds & Lucretia Hickman of lawful age of Frederick County. Bondsman, Joseph Moore

20 Mar 1813 William Baldwin & Margaret Mahamn. Bondsman, Peter Ebler

22 Mar 1813 Abraham Barrow & Rebecca Mauck, daughter of Michael Mauck of Frederick County, the bondsman

22 Mar 1813 French F. Glasscock & Mary Graves, daughter of Charles Graves of Frederick County. Bondsman, Charles Graves

23 Mar 1813 Thomas Morris & Elizabeth Hall, daughter of Bennet Hall, the bondsman

25 Mar 1813 Harmon Sines & Mary McKee. Bondsman, Jabez Smith

26 Mar 1813 James Spence & Jane Coe of lawful age of Frederick County. Bondsman, Thomas Coe

27 Mar 1813 George Reed Johnson & Hanah Keckley, daughter of John Keckley, the bondsman

30 Mar 1813 Martin Crawford & Rebeccah Shipe of Frederick County. Bondsman, Thomas Ewing

7 Apr 1813 Robert Cather & Rosanna Johnson of lawful age. Bondsman, William Johnson

12 Apr 1813 Jacob Pangle & Anna Pugh. Bondsman, Azariah Pugh

13 Apr 1813 William Johnston & Elizabeth Miller. Bondsman, Stephen Jonson

13 Apr 1813 Moses Scott & Charity Ridgeway of lawful age of Frederick County. Bondsman, Richard Ridgway

15 Apr 1813 John Farmer & Ann Hannun, daughter of Thomas Hannun, the bondsman

17 Apr 1813 Jacob Pennybaker & Hetty Severns, daughter of Edmund Severns, the bondsman

17 Apr 1813 John Elliott & Hannah Cather, orphan & sister of David Cather, the bondsman

17 Apr 1813 John Haas & Catharine Mummaw of lawful age of Frederick County. Bondsman, George Mummaw

19 Apr 1813 Thomas S. Summers & Sarah Glasscock. Bondsman, Gregory Glasscock

24 Apr 1813 Henry Stephens & Catharine Cooper of lawful age. Bondsman, Leonard Cooper

4 May 1813 John Hawkins & Eliza Talbott, daughter of Edward Talbott, the bondsman

5 May 1813 John Wizer & Priscilla Hall, widow of Thomas Hall, and daughter of John Mahue, the bondsman

7 May 1813 Thomas Monroe & Mary W. Thomas of lawful age of the County of Frederick. Bondsman, John Newman

20 May 1813 Cornelius Baldwin & Amelia Throckmorton. Bondsman, Cyrus B. Baldwin

22 May 1813 John Fitzsimmons & Anne Shipe of Frederick County. Bondsman, James G. Harden

26 Aug 1813 William Keeler & Catharine Sowers, daughter of John Sowers, the bondsman, who signs in German

31 May 1813 Augustus Moreland & Elizabeth Elkins of lawfull age. Bondsman, Vincent Haines

2 Jun 1813 Henry Kenester & Elizabeth Moulding of lawfull age. Bondsman, John Harbert

2 Jun 1813 Charles Smith Jr & Maria Berry. Bondsman, George S. Lane

3 Jun 1813 Robert Ashby & Barbara Lanham. Bondsman, Henry Reynolds

9 Jun 1813 Henry Starr & Catharine Taylor. Bondsman, John Talor

10 Jun 1813 George Habron & Rebecca Armstrong. Bondsman, James Armstrong

11 Jun 1813 Samuel Drake Jnr & Elizabeth Swallom, daughter of Joseph Swallom, the bondsman

14 Jun 1813 Samuel Hardy & Juliana Brown upwards of 21 years of age. Bondsman, John Littleton

9 Jul 1813 Jonathan Gibson & Elizabeth Conrad. Bondsman, John Yoe

10 Jul 1813 Danel Denver & Elizabeth Howard, daughter of Anthony Howard, the bondsman

20 Jul 1813 David Barton & Elizabeth Denn. Bondsman, Henry McNeely

8 Aug 1813 Jacob Garman & Jane Giffin, daughter of William Giffin

6 Aug 1813 Willis Day & Mary Anderson of lawfull age. Bondsman, Thomas Steward

9 Aug 1813 Richard Jackson & Elizabeth Spencer, daughter of Sarah Foley, the bondsman

11 Aug 1813 Richard Henry & Nancy Single of lawfull age. Bondsman, William Chapman

19 Aug 1813 James Grice & Sarah Thompson of lawfull age. Bondsman, Conrad Loy

13 Aug 1813 Philip Setzer & Susanna Muck of lawfull age. Bondsman, Abraham Stickler

21 Aug 1813 William Thompson & Sarah Morris. Bondsman, John McNeal

21 Aug 1813 Alexander Catlett Jr. & Patsy D. Catlett, daughter of John Catlett of Frederick County. Bondsman, William Prince

31 Aug 1813 Charles Capper & Catharine McVicker, daughter of Duncan McVicker, the bondsman

2 Sep 1813 David Muckelwee & Jane Hodgson, daughter of John Hodgson, the bondsman

6 Sep 1813 Thomas Deadrick & Elizabeth Frances Daingerfield. Bondsman, Nathan Anderson

6 Sep 1813 John Horn & Elizabeth Danner. Bondsman, James Sinclair

21 Sep 1813 Samuel Devoe & Meriam Redd, daughter of George Redd, the bondsman

21 Sep 1813 Ezekiel Gilham & Isabelle McMullan, daughter of Robert McMullan, the bondsman

22 Sep 1813 Elijah Fletcher & Anna Giffin, daughter of William Giffin, the bondsman

28 Sep 1813 Edward S. Branham & Mariam Moore of lawfull age. Bondsman, Joseph Moore

30 Sep 1813 George B____(?Bruce, Jr.) & Jane McPhereson. Bondsman, Jas Bruce

1 Oct 1813 James Harry & Lydia Brown. Bondsman, James Harry

11 Oct 1813 Robert Loury (Laury?) & Rachel Crum. Bondsman, Christian Crum

16 Oct 1813 John Spencer & Sarah Butt, daughter of William Butt. Bondsman, William Dehaven

21 Oct 1813 Jacob Pine & Catharine Williams of lawful age. Bondsman, Jackson Williams

25 Oct 1813 George Miller & Mary Becham. Bondsman, William Morgan

26 Oct 1813 Adam Steel & Elizabeth Nicholls of lawful age. Bondsman, Aaron Gibson

26 Oct 1813 Nathaniel Hurst & Catharine Berlin, daughter of Jacob Berlin of Frederick County. Bondsman, Philip Berlin

2 Nov 1813 John S. Spicknall & Elizabeth Ridgway. Bondsman, Bazil Spicknall

4 Nov 1813 Jonathan Smith & Jane Hollingsworth. Bondsman, Isaac Hollingsworth

4 Nov 1813 Timothy Smith & Hannah Green, daughter of John Green. Bondsman, Hiram Cline

8 Nov 1813 Henry Waln & Elizabeth McKee, daughter of John McKee. Bondsman, Samuel Waln

10 Nov 1813 Evan Lewis & Margaret Fleet, widow of Littleton Fleet, deceased. Bondsman, Enoch Marple

15 Nov 1813 Samuel Elzea & Fanny Self, daughter of John Self of Frederick County. Bondsman, John Self

15 Nov 1813 Samuel Smith & Patty Payne. Bondsman, Jonathan Payne

16 Nov 1813 Zadok Hutzlar & Sarah Griffy, daughter of John Griffy

19 Nov 1813 William Bageant & Elizabeth Dick. Bondsman, Hieronimus Dick

22 Nov 1813 John Bowie & Winifred Jackson, daughter of Nathaniel Jackson. Bondsman, Gersham Drake Jnr

4 Dec 1813 Abel Wilkinson & Mary Dowell, daughter of John Dowell, the bondsman

8 Dec 1813 West Burgess & Hanah Senseny. Bondsman, Peter Senseny

20 Dec 1813 William Briscoe Slave to Hannah Fenton & Nancy a free blackwoman. Bondsman, David Fries

22 Dec 1813 Vincent Martin a free black man to Negro Phillis. Bondsman, David Fries

13 Dec 1813 Adam Kurtz & Elizabeth Bennett, daughter of James Bennett, the bondsman

13 Dec 1813 Joseph Cales Jr & Sarah Julinna Maria Lee, daughter of Theodorick Lee, the bondsman

21 Dec 1813 John Kanester & Rebecca ?Boucher. Bondsman, William Vance

22 Dec 1813 Dennis Welch & Margaret Dyer, daughter of John Dyer of Frederick County. Bondsman, Henry Faidley

23 Dec 1813 Jacob Snyder & Rebecca Hickle, daughter of Jacob Hickle, the bondsman. All sign in German

29 Dec 1813 John Jobe & Hanah Cooper, daughter of Thomas Cooper. Bondsman, Elijah Dowell

29 Dec 1813 John Victor & Mary Ann Jane ?Tilden. Bondsman, Geo Reed
1 Jan 1814 Abraham Watson & Ruth Cloud. Bondsman, Henry Watson
3 Jan 1814 William Campbell & Elizabeth Day, daughter of Mary Day. Bondsman, James Day
3 Jan 1814 Henry Lewis & Nancy Hooker. Bondsman, William Hooker (Hoober?)
12 Jan 1814 John Koeler & Elizabeth Mathias widow of John Mathias dec. Bondsman, John Cloud
12 Jan 1814 William Graves & Charlotte Townsend. Bondsman, Ninian Magruder
22 Jan 1814 William Whitelock & Nancy Montgomery. Bondsman, James Likins
28 Jan 1814 George Arrisman & Elizabeth Swatt, daughter of John Swatt, the bondsman
31 Jan 1814 James Cougill & Margaret Anderson. Bondsman, Jesse Anderson
31 Jan 1814 David Weaver & Elizabeth Keeding, daughter of Peter Keeding, the bondsman
31 Jan 1814 Isaac Kiger & Lydia Rutter of lawful age. Bondsman, John Vanhorn
2 Feb 1814 Levi McCormick & Phebe Stewart, daughter of Thomas Stewart, the bondsman
4 Feb 1814 William Jinkins & Ruth Hays. Bondsman, George Albert
14 Feb 1814 Jacob Sperry & Rebecca Smith. Bondsman, John Shambaugh
15 Feb 1814 James Simpson & Maria Olever. Bondsman, Benjamin Helm
16 Feb 1814 Enos Lanham & Hannah Furr. Bondsman, John Cummings
23 Feb 1814 Joseph Anderson & Sarah Davis. Bondsman, John Davis
26 Feb 1814 George Bennett & Margaret Parrell, daughter of John Parrell, the bondsman
28 Feb 1814 Jacob Moyers, son of Michael Moyers, & Lydia Snyder, daughter of Jacob Snyder, the bondsman
28 Feb 1814 John Grubs & Frances Rowzer, daughter of Edward Rowzer
4 Mar 1814 George Wissinger & Elizabeth Watson. Bondsman, Joshua Watson
4 Mar 1814 Joshua Yoe & Alley Duffey, orphan of Bernard Duffey. Bondsman, Levi Duffey
7 Mar 1814 John Simpson, son of James Simpson, & Betsy Patton

8 Mar 1814 Jacob Frear & Jane Davison, daughter of Susanah Davison

12 Mar 1814 Daniel Collis & Lydia Ducker, widow of John Ducker. Bondsman, William Shepherd

19 Mar 1814 George Stump & Elizabeth Ewan, daughter of Thomas Ewan of Frederick County, the bondsman

23 Mar 1814 Aquila Wilson and Stacy Wilson, daughter of Jacob Wilson, the bondsman

26 Mar 1814 Abner Redd & Elizabeth Laurence. Bondsman, Moses Newbanks

29 Mar 1814 Andrew A. Shannon & Martha Gilkison. Bondsman, Joseph Glass

2 Apr 1814 James Higgins & Elizabeth Welsh. Bondsman, Thomas Higgins

2 Apr 1814 John Oats & Mary Oats, daughter of the above bound John Oats. Bondsman, George Karinge

5 Apr 1814 William Rinker & Catharine Yakely, daughter of John Yakely of Frederick County, the bondsman

9 Apr 1814 Robert Craig & Mary McGoughen. Bondsman, George Wilson

14 Apr 1814 George Williams & Nancy Kelly. Bondsman, John Ross

14 Apr 1814 William Taylor & Emily Shepherd. Bondsman, Martha Crow, widow & relict of John Crow, formerly Martha Shepherd

16 Apr 1814 James Barr & Sarah Price. Bondsman, Benjamin Matson

21 Apr 1814 George Smith & Margaret McDonald. Bondsman, Thomas Allen Tidball

22 Apr 1814 William Braithwaite & Alena King. Bondsman, Mingly Mason

25 Apr 1814 Greenberry Chapman & Susanna Craig, daughter of Susanna Craig, the bondsman

28 Apr 1814 William Strother & Margaret Kerns, daughter of Nicholas Kerns. Bondsman, Nicholas Kerns

29 Apr 1814 Bennett Wood & Polly Moore. Bondsman, William Harrell

30 Apr 1814 Robert Allen & Nancy Rowland. Bondsman, Martin Rowland

4 May 1814 Joseph Pasmore & Eleanor Edmondson, older daughter of Ann Edmondson, the bondsman

17 May 1814 Daniel Grove Junr & Catharine Snipe. Bondsman, Michael Kline

5 May 1814 William Mercer, son of Joshua Mercer, and Sidney Wright. Bondsman, Joshua Mercer, the father

24 May 1814 John W. Belfield & Mary B. Daingerfield. Bondsman, William Daingerfield

26 May 1814 Anthony Huffman & Elizabeth Mylinger, widow of Isaac Mylinger dec. Bondsman, John Pitman

30 May 1814 Stephen Prichard & Mary Cartmill. Bondsman, Martin Cartmill

31 May 1814 John W. Gordon & Sarah Bryarly, daughter of Robert Bryarly. Bondsman, David Bryarly

3 Jun 1814 John M. Hickerson & Mary Ann Chrisman. Bondsman, John Miller

11 Jun 1814 Jonas Likins & Catharine Weaver, daughter of Jacob Weaver. Bondsman, Jacob Weaver

15 Jun 1814 David Briarly & Matilda Ann Gordon. Bondsman, David Bryarly

25 Jun 1814 John Hansbrough & Sarah Grubbs. Bondsman, John Grubbs

4 Jul 1814 Matthew Montgomery & Catharine Taylor, widow of Nicholas Taylor dec. Bondsman, Eli Pugh

14 Jul 1814 John Gibson & Catharine Connor, daughter of Christian Conner, the bondsman

14 Jul 1814 Thomas Henshaw & Margaret Baldwin, widow & relict of William Baldwin dec. Bondsman, Jacob Martin

28 Jul 1814 John Yeo & Catharine Shambough, daughter of Daniel Shambough. Bondsman, Joseph Shambough

1 Aug 1814 Peter Groves & Mary Messer, daughter of Joshua Mercer, the bondsman

3 Aug 1814 Thomas Bartlett & Sarah Shores, daughter of John Shores, the bondsman

9 Aug 1814 Hugh Settle & Delilah Redding. Bondsman, Robert Foster

15 Aug 1814 Joshua Wood & Letitia Curl, daughter of James Curl, the bondsman

20 Aug 1814 John Howe & Sarah Mathany, daughter of Thomas Mathany of Fredk County, the bondsman

24 Aug 1814 John Painter & Lucy Elkins, daughter of Elizabeth Elkins of Frederick County. Bondsman, Robert Painter

25 Aug 1814 John Cryder & Ann Gerely, daughter of John Gerely

30 Aug 1814 Jesse Hutchison & Elizabeth Everett. Bondsman, Andrew Mason

31 Aug 1814 David Little & Nancy Riggle. Bondsman, James Riggle

6 Sep 1814 John Curl & Sarah Gibson. Bondsman, Harrison Allen

8 Sep 1814 Moses Bailes & Mary Fish, daughter of Robert Fish, the bondsman

13 Sep 1814 Harris Self & Eliza Grubbs. Bondsman, Thomas Grubbs

19 Sep 1814 Charles U. Lovell & Mary E. Long, daughter of Nimrod Long. Bondman, Robert Turner

23 Sep 1814 George Gander & Catharine Smith. Bondsman, John Shambough

22 Sep 1814 Elijah Ellis & Sarah Yates. Bondsman, Joshua Buffington

22 Sep 1814 William Fulkerson & Amelia James, daughter of Henry James, the bondsman

1 Oct 1814 Godfrey Warner & Nancy Clevenger. Bondsman, John Clevenger

7 Oct 1814 John Wright & Mary Windsor. Bondsman, George Windsor

8 Oct 1814 George Branham & Mary R. Murray. Bondsman, Reuben Moore

11 Oct 1814 William J. Dores & Mary Spillman. Bondsman, James Spillman

19 Oct 1814 Henry Rodes & Lydia Winfield. Bondsman, Elijah Winfield

17 Oct 1814 James Scarf & Polly Foley. Bondsman, Sarah Foley

23 Oct 1814 William Garmong & Mary Davis. Bondsman, Thomas A. Tidball

24 Oct 1814 George Blakemore Jr & Elizabeth Buck. Bondsman, Hezekiah Conn

29 Oct 1814 Henry March & Sarah Phillips, daughter of William Phillips, the bondsman

31 Oct 1814 Ninian Magruder & Elizabeth Lyons, daughter of James Lyons, the bondsman

14 Nov 1814 David Meade & Louisa Nelson. Bondsman, John Page

15 Nov 1814 Charles Higgins, son of William Higgins, & Elizabeth Weaver, daughter of Jacob Weaver. Fathers are bondsmen.
16 Nov 1814 William Ball & Susan Gregory - a free negro woman. Bondsman, James Carter
21 Nov 1814 Matthias Rutter & Eleanor Mackey. Bondsman, John Mackey
22 Nov 1814 Christopher Probasco & Hannah Wood. Bondsman, William Vanhorn
3 Dec 1814 Thomas Adams & Laney Quick, daughter of Martin Quick, the bondsman
8 Dec 1814 John Gregory & Sarah Wheately, daughter of John Wheately, the bondsman
12 Dec 1814 Jacob Butter (Butler?) & Rebecca Hott. Bondsman, John Hott
10 Dec 1814 James Carr & Catharine Boucher. Bondsman, Elias Boucher
10 Dec 1814 Levy Kerr Gilham & Elizabeth Boucher. Bondsman, Elias Boucher
11 Dec 1814 John Dick & Elizabeth Cawood, daughter of John Cawood of Frederick County. Bondsman, Stephen Cawood
20 Dec 1814 George Mummau & Nancy Garmong. Bondsman, Christian Gannang
20 Dec 1814 Benjamin Manor & Catharine Marsh. Bondsman, Richard Marsh
20 Dec 1814 John Marsh & Mary Malony. Bondsman, Richard Marsh
20 Dec 1814 Michael Capper & Elizabeth Follet, daughter of William Follet, the bondsman
22 Dec 1814 Elijah Winkfield & Sarah Good. Bondsman, George Reed
24 Dec 1814 John Stokes & Rachel Foley. Bondsman, Jesse Haines
24 Dec 1814 James Crumley & Elizabeth Dewnie, widow of ----Downie. Bondsman, Joseph Sexton
26 Dec 1814 George Lowry & Nancy Boyce. Bondsman, John Boyce
29 Dec 1814 Moses Russell & Christena Kackley. Bondsman, Benjamin Kackley
29 Dec 1814 William Goff & Christena Wisecarver. Bondsman, Henry Wisecarver
29 Dec 1814 Gregory Hydenrich & Jane Chapman. Bondsman, Joshua Chapman
30 Dec 1814 James Newham & Susan Shipler. Bondsman, Lewis Fulkeson

2 Jan 1815 William Kerfoot & Nancy Timberlake. Bondsman, Richard Holliday

4 Jan 1815 Henry Groves, son of Henry Groves, Sr. & Ann Reed, daughter of Casper Reed. Fathers are bondsmen.

5 Jan 1815 Thomas Reynolds & Rosa Denvers. Bondsman, Patrick Denvers Junr

5 Jan 1815 James Carter & Fanny Gains, daughter of James Gains. Bondsman, Lewis Crigler

6 Jan 1815 Daniel Murphy & Mary Mackey. Bondsman, Nicholas Fitzimmons

11 Jan 1815 William Alexander & Elizabeth Powers. Bondsman, William Carnegy

14 Jan 1815 John Boyce & Catharine Lowry, daughter of Danl Lowry, the bondsman

14 Jan 1815 Tredwell Smith & Elizabeth Lowery. Bondsman, William T. Stubblefield

16 Jan 1815 Thomas Metcalfe & Rachel Harper. Bondsman, John Dews

16 Jan 1815 Charles Negrier & Rebecca Duval. Bondsman, John A. ?Kaufrey

24 Jan 1815 John McMurray & Elizabeth Kerfoot. Bondsman, Thomas Allen Tidball

25 Jan 1815 John Gumby & Elizabeth Albin. Bondsman, James Albin

27 Jan 1815 Henry Louthan & Elizabeth Boles, daughter of John Boles, the bondsman

6 Feb 1815 Amos Kingore & Hannah Buckley. Bondsman, John Rutter

6 Feb 1815 Thomas Dial & Catharine Weaver. Bondsman, Thomas Shepherd

14 Feb 1815 Thomas Haley & Mary Lanham. Bondsman, Jeremiah Lanham

15 Feb 1815 William Giffin & Margaretta Garman. Bondsman, Jacob Garman

18 Feb 1815 Abraham Shambaugh & Rebecah Carter. Bondsman, Richard Carter

11 Mar 1815 Timothy Ohaver & Eleanor Devalt. Bondsman, Abraham Devalt

15 Mar 1815 Morgan Corder & Louisa King. Bondsman, Elisha Mellon

16 Mar 1815 Isaac Frye & Sarah Frye, daughter of Elizabeth Frye. Bondsman, Benjamin Frye Junr

18 Mar 1815 Samuel Eddy & Delilah Evans, daughter of William Evans, the bondsman

23 Mar 1815 Isaac Dehaven & Mary Carlile, stepdaughter of Henry Light. Bondsman, Henry Light

27 Mar 1815 Jacob Null & Peggy Shutts, daughter of George Shutts, the bondsman of Frederick County

27 Mar 1815 Henry Shutts, son of George Shutts, & Sarah Phillips. Bondsman, father of groom

8 Apr 1815 James Gray & Grace Cahill. Bondsman, William Cahill

9 Apr 1815 Henry Noland & Milly Thompson, over 21. Bondsman, John S. Campbell

9 Apr 1815 Joseph Clutter & Margaret Reed. Bondsman, George Reed

11 Apr 1815 Jonathan Piper & Christena Snapp. Bondsman, Samuel Snapp

11 Apr 1815 Joseph Strickling & Nancy Whitacre. Bondsman, Nathan Kerns

Marriage Bonds No. 11 1815-1817 Frederick County, Virginia

24 Apr 1815 Joseph Butter & Lydia Rees. Bondsman, Jacob Rees

24 Apr 1815 David Peasmaker & Mary Smith, daughter of Conrad Smith. Bondsman, Jacob Peasmaker

24 Apr 1815 Casper Rodgers & Susanna Ellis, daughter of Morris Ellis, the bondsman

27 Apr 1815 Alexander Vance & Sarah Peters. Bondsman, Isaac Peters

2 May 1815 Humphrey Davis & Hannah Anderson. Bondsman, George Chamblin

2 May 1815 Henry Washington & Louisa Whiting. Bondsman, Thomas Allen Tidball

3 May 1815 Alexander Cook & Rebecca Rowe, daughter of Benjamin Wroe, the bondsman

5 May 1815 Adam Rutter & Elizabeth Albin. Bondsman, Andrew Albin

15 May 1815 Casper Larrick & Tenah Cooper, daughter of John Cooper, the bondsman

16 May 1815 Henry G. Spayth & Mary Nisewander, daughter of Abraham Nisewander, the bondsman

18 May 1815 William Gilkeson & Sarah Gilkison. Bondsman, John Gilkeson

19 May 1815 Charles Cunningham & Lucy Lloyd. Bondsman, George Trisler

22 May 1815 Henry Secrest, son of George Secrest, & Catharine Clauser. Bondsman, father of groom

23 May 1815 Richard Allen & Lucy Corder, daughter of Mary Corder. Bondsman, John Day

29 May 1815 Robert Cooper & Elizabeth Job, daughter of Jacob Job of Frederick County, the bondsman

31 May 1815 William Lowry, son of Frederick Lowry, decd & Margaret Beller. Bondsman, Hetty Lowry, widow of Frederick Lowry, decd

5 Jun 1815 Daniel Kline & Sarah Grim, daughter of John Grim, the bondsman

15 Jun 1815 William Beaver & Sarah Davis, over 21. Bondsman, Thomas Chamblyn

15 Jun 1815 John M. Crabb & Ann Fleming, daughter of William Fleming, the bondsman

19 Jun 1815 Richard Carter & Esther B. Rogers. Bondsman, Thomas Rogers, jnr.

21 Jun 1815 Hugh Barr & Mary Ladley. Bondsman, Hannoms Gray

23 Jun 1815 Abner Gray & Delilah Middleton, daughter of William Middleton, the bondsman

26 Jun 1815 John Lee & Christina Strodurman. Bondsman, Charles Grim

28 Jun 1815 Thomas Lee & Margaret Hutchinson. Bondsman, John Richardson

3 Jul 1815 Charles Flanigan & Hanah Marpole, daughter of Ezekiel Marpole, dece. Bondsman, Prodence Maypole, widow of Ezekial

10 Jul 1815 William C. Sexton & Mary Williams. Bondsman, Jane E. Williams (widow crossed out)

15 Jul 1815 George Poffenburger & Catharine Null, daughter of Jacob Null, the bondsman

20 Aug 1815 Asher M. Glover & Nancy McFarland. Bondsman, John McFarland

22 Jul 1815 William Pickering & Ruth Fenton, daughter of John Fenton of Frederick County. Bondsman, Gabriel H. Davis

25 Jul 1815 John Carter & Ann Carter. Bondsman, Elam Carter

25 Jul 1815 Charles Constable & Sarah Sanks, widow of John Sanks dec. Bondsman, William Huggins

27 Jul 1815 Samuel McPherson & Sally Douglass of Frederick County. Bondsman, Jesse Dobbyns

29 Jul 1815 James Stewart (Stuard) & Sophia Chew, daughter of Coleby Chew, the bondsman

31 Jul 1815 James Hamrick & Charlotte Shull, daughter of Joshua Shull, the bondsman

7 Aug 1815 William Grubbs & Elizabeth Walters, daughter of John Walters of Frederick County. Bondsman, Watt Walters

8 Aug 1815 John Abbott & Elizabeth Craig, daughter of John Craig, decd. Bondsman, Susanna Craig, widow of John Craig, decd

7 Aug 1815 Francis Neff & Elizabeth Hollandshead, widow of John Hollandshead decd. Bondsman, Abel Thompson

14 Aug 1815 George Rust, over 21, and Martha Marshall, over 21. Bondsman, William Marshall

24 Aug 1815 Henry Brill & Mary Ann Hoffman. Bondsman, David Russall

28 Aug 1815 Nicholas Dick & Mary Johnston. Bondsman, Peter Dick

4 Sep 1815 James Frigger & Jane Chandler, widow of --- Chandler, decd. Bondsman, A. Skinner

5 Sep 1815 William Fagan & Elizabeth Dowell Bondsman, Abel Wilkinson

7 Sep 1815 Jacob Everheart & Ruth Welsh. Bondsman, James Higgins

12 Sep 1815 John Light & Catharine Shutt. Bondsman, George Shutt

5 Sep 1815 Cornelius Paskell & Mary Trenary. Bondsman, Thomas Grubbs

13 Sep 1815 Andrew Bush & Mary Correll. Bondsman, George Trisler

13 Sep 1815 Benjamin Smith & Emelia Hotzenpillar, over 21. Bondsman, James Jones

14 Sep 1815 George Pulse & Elizabeth Harper. Bondsman, Jacob Mullinix

18 Sep 1815 Samuel McCune & Rachel Sexton, daughter of Joseph Sexton, the bondsman

19 Sep 1815 Lewis Neill & Ann Stribling. Bondsman, Francis Stribling

19 Sep 1815 Samuel Cooly & Fanny Barns, over 21. Bondsman, Samuel W. Perry

21 Sep 1815 Isaac R. Gardner & Comfort M. Rust, daughter of John Rust, the bondsman

23 Sep 1815 Joseph Whittingham & Susannah Gibbons. Bondsman, Jacob Gibbons

25 Sep 1815 Belfield Jinkins & Elizabeth Stokes. Bondsman, Thomas Grubbs

5 Oct 1815 William Lauck & July Ann Cochran, daughter of Robert Cochran of Frederick County, the bondsman

6 Oct 1815 Thomas Nelson & Sarah W. Page. Bondsman, William B. Page

10 Oct 1815 Ignatius Windsor & Elizabeth Mason, dau of Bingledy Myson, the bondsman

16 Oct 1815 Barrick Fisher & Rhoda Rogers. Bondsman, John McCoole

18 Oct 1815 William Cather & Sarah Seecrist. Bondsman, George Seecrist

20 Oct 1815 Anthony Howard & Catherine Blackord. Bondsman, Henry Blackord

3 Nov 1815 Andrew Loy & Hannah Smith. Bondsman, George Smith

3 Nov 1815 Henry Weaver & Peggy Stone, both upward of 21. Bondsman, George Schrack

4 Nov 1815 Richard Flower & Mary Fenton. Bondsman, William Pickering

6 Nov 1815 William Marshall & Nancy Rust of Frederick County. Bondsman, Matthew Rust

7 Nov 1815 George W. Murdock & Jaquelina H. Smith. Bondsman, William Morris

7 Nov 1815 Isham L. Watkins & Winifred Berry. Bondsman, Thomas H. Stark

13 Nov 1815 Isaac Hurford & Penelope Johnston. Bondsman, Jesse Hurford

13 Nov 1815 George Sheets & Cetrin Grim. Bondsman, John Grim. Groom signs in German

14 Nov 1815 Robt Ashby & Elizabeth Ash, daughter of Frank Ash of Frederick County, the bondsman

18 Nov 1815 John Adams & Catherine Dick. Bondsman, John Hansell

18 Nov 1815 Henry Parr & Polly Perry of Frederick County. Bondsman, Jas Clare

22 Nov 1815 John Pierce & Nancy Louthen, both over 21. Bondsman, William Kearfoot (Kerfoot)

22 Nov 1815 Sebastian Graff & Hannah Whiting. Bondsman, Richard Milton

27 Nov 1815 William Gibbins & Elizabeth Whittington, daughter of Joseph Whittington, the bondsman

28 Nov 1815 Adam Frank & Sarah Pugh of Frederick County. Bondsman, Azariah Pugh

30 Nov 1815 John Lawrence & Elizabeth Davis, daughter of Jas Davis, the bondsman

1 Dec 1815 William McGuinn & Elizabeth Hall. Bondsman, Benjamin Richards

4 Dec 1815 Robert McFadden & Sarah Buckley. Bondsman, Abraham Buckley

4 Dec 1815 John Smith & Susan Crouse. Bondsman, Lewis A. Smith

8 Dec 1815 Jacob Rutter & Kitty White, both parties over 21. Bondsman, Michael White

8 Dec 1815 Jacob Clevenger & Elizabeth Crouse. Bondsman, John Keller

8 Dec 1815 William Timberlake & Nancy Pollard. Bondsman, Robert W. Hamilton

11 Dec 1815 James Baker & Ann H. Murphy. Bondsman, James Bowen

12 Dec 1815 John Risler & Kitty Madden, daughter of Mabray Madden, the bondsman

12 Dec 1815 William Sommers & Rebeccah Glasscock. Bondsman, Williamm Glasscock

19 Mar 1817 Even Rogers & Hannah Dalby. Bondsman, John Dalby

11 Dec 1815 Jeremiah Reed & Nancy Cougill. Bondsman, James Cougill

12 Dec 1815 John P. Smith & Mary G. Barton. Bondsman, Jas G. Barton

12 Dec 1815 George Shell & Polly Scroghins, stepdaughter of John Carter, the bondsman

13 Dec 1815 Benjamin Daniel & Sydny Fenton. Bondsman, Benjamin Fenton

15 Dec 1815 Thomas M. Wilson & Mary Ann Wilson. Bondsman, Aquilla Wilson

14 Dec 1815 James Dailey & Comfort Wood. Bondsman, William Wood

16 Dec 1815 Joel Goodrich & Margaret Edmonds. Bondsman, James Wines

18 Dec 1815 Robert Fisher & Barbarah Hansell, daughter of George Hansell, the bondsman, who signs in German

20 Dec 1815 James Robinson & Ann Dehaven. Bondsman, John McCoole

20 Dec 1815 Leonard Spicknell & Elizabeth Rowland. Bondsman, Samuel Rowland

21 Dec 1815 Benjamin Barr & Minna Williams. Bondsman Thomas Night

25 Dec 1815 John Kendrick & Lucinda Headly. Bondsman, Newton Headly

27 Dec 1815 Robert Anderson & Margaret Bean, daughter of Sarah Bean, the bondsman

27 Dec 1815 Landon Jolly & Letty Masefield. Bondsman, William Smith

28 Dec 1815 Benjamin Robinson & Catherine Peacemaker. Bondsman, Jacob Peasmaker

29 Dec 1815 Eli Davis & Elizabeth Scaff. Bondsman, James Scaff

1 Jan 1816 John Denny & Mary Jones. Bondsman, John Gant

2 Jan 1816 Isaac Payne & Margaret Evans. Bondsman, Levi Tarr

3 Jan 1816 Jacob Knipe & Margaret Leonard. Bondsman, Jeremiah Leonard

3 Jan 1816 Benjamin Harrison & Mary W. Page. Bondsman, William Byrd Page

3 Jan 1816 David Lupton & Leith (Luth?) Adams. Bondsman, John Adams

6 Jan 1816 Jonathan Kackley & Mary Dyson, daughter of Aquilla Dyson of the County of Frederick. Bondsman, Joseph Dyson

6 Jan 1816 Peter Rust & Elizabeth Rust. Bondsman, Matthew Rust

8 Jan 1816 William Madden & Sarah Risler. Bondsman, John Risler

8 Jan 1816 George F.A. Townsend & Sarah Graves. Bondsman, Joseph Graves

9 Jan 1816 Even Grant & Mary Mecashland. Bondsman, Robert Foster

9 Jan 1816 Edwin Bales & Sarah Smoots. Bondsman, Elezor Barrow

12 Jan 1816 Robert Meldrume & Elizabeth Belt (Bell?). Bondsman, George Syphers

13 Jan 1816 Henry Stephenson & Polly Nelson, a Negro woman of this County. Bondsman, Thomas Robinson

16 Jan 1816 Nathl B. Triplett & Mary Henry. Bondsman, Thomas Lee

16 Jan 1816 Solomon R. Jackson & Nancy Cleveland, daughter of Elijah Cleveland, the bondsman

18 Jan 1816 Samuel C. Peck and Mary Craig. Bondsman, Samuel Craig

22 Jan 1816 Noah Williams & Harriet Watters. Bondsman, Walter Waters

22 Jan 1816 John Stephens & Nancy White, daughter of John White, the bondsman

23 Jan 1816 Jesse Waln & Nancy Hubbard. Bondsman, Ezekial Neff

25 Jan 1816 Obediah Newman & Sarah Monroe. Bondsman, John Newman

25 Jan 1816 Thomas Dews & Elizabeth Stonestreet. Bondsman, James Taylor

27 Jan 1816 Francis Neale & Mary Ferguson. Bondsman, Joshua Ferguson

1 Feb 1816 Gabriel McDonald & Catherine Kackley, daughter of Abraham Kackley, the bondsman

1 Feb 1816 Philip McDamith & Ann Hart (both upwards of 21 years of age). Bondsman, Vance Hart

2 Feb 1816 William Mathew & Pheba Yeats, daughter of John Yeats, the bondsman

2 Feb 1816 Elijah Catlett & Peggy Sperry, daughter of Peter Sperry, the bondsman

8 Feb 1816 John Henson Pickerell & Catherine Yeo. Bondsman, Mary Yoe

10 Feb 1816 Alexander Fitzhugh & Eliza Clare. Bondsman, James Clare

10 Feb 1816 Lewis Brumley & Mary Swartz, daughter of John ?Swartz, the bondsman. Last name of bondsman in German script

15 Feb 1816 Nathan Parkins & Sydney Sowers. Bondsman, John Heiskell

15 Feb 1816 John Paricale (probably Purcell) & Elizabeth Crupper, daughter of John Crupper, the bondsman

16 Feb 1816 James Miller & Kitty Allensworth. Bondsman, William Allensworth

19 Feb 1816 Robert McKay & Elizabeth McMorris, daughter of David McMorris, the bondsman

19 Feb 1816 Thomas Day & Flora Jenkins, daughter of Edward Jenkins, the bondsman
24 Feb 1816 James Davison & Milly Wilson (a widow). Bondsman, Thomas Allen Tidball
24 Feb 1816 Thomas Steel & Sarah Carter, daughter of Samuel Carter, the bondsman
24 Feb 1816 Jacob Larrick & Catherine Spilman, daughter of Jacob Spilman, the bondsman
26 Feb 1816 William Wood & Margaret Ridgway. Bondsman, Amos I. Bruce
26 Feb 1816 Wm Stephenson & Lucy Catlett, daughter of Henry Catlett. Bondsman, Calmes Catlett
28 Feb 1816 Vincent Settle & Kitty Shull, daughter of Joshua Shull, the bondsman
28 Feb 1816 Jacob Miller & Mary Bagent, daughter of John Bagaent, the bondsman
28 Feb 1816 Jacob White & Elizabeth Duncan, daughter of Patrick Duncan, the bondsman
28 Feb 1816 Simon Harrell & Lydy Harrison widow of Saml Harrison. Bondsman, Isaac Harrison
1 Mar 1816 Abel Wilkinson & Sarah Scarf. Bondsman, John Dowell
2 Feb (March written below Feb) 1816 George Silvers & Barbara Myers, daughter of John Myers, the bondsman
4 Mar 1816 Joseph G. Smart & Rebecca Shipe. Bondsman, James D. Gardner
4 Mar 1816 Samuel Kackley & Elizabeth Dyson. Bondsman, Joseph Dyson
5 Mar 1816 Martin Goss & Lydy Simpson. Bondsman, Henry Swallom
6 Mar 1816 Isaac Conrad & Mary Nowland, daughter of William Nowland, the bondsman
6 Mar 1816 Charles Whetzell & Scinty Gregorey, daughter of Presley Gregorey, the bondsman
7 Feb (March written below February) 1816 William Parish & Sarah Rineheart. Bondsman, John Foreman
12 Mar 1816 John Carper & Christena Lawyer. Bondsman, Henry Nevell
13 Mar 1816 Saml Lauck & Milly Lindsey. Bondsman, Peter Lauck
13 Mar 1816 Asa Lee & Elizabeth Higgins, daughter of Wm Higgins, the bondsman

17 Mar 1816 Henry Clines & Catherine Ramey. Bondsman, Danl Smallwood

18 Mar 1816 Barak Fisher & Sarah Long. Bondsman, Conrad Long

18 Mar 1816 Jacob Neff & Elizabeth Ane Nutt. Bondsman, Edward Nutt

19 Mar 1816 Richd Jones & Polly Lowry, daughter of Nancy Lowry, the bondsman

23 Mar 1816 Richard Hollingshead & Polly Babb. Bondsman, James Babb

26 Mar 1816 Thomas F. Webster & Elizabeth Pulse. Bondsman, George Pulse

28 Mar 1816 Zachariah Marques & ?Hetty Lou Lowry. Bondsman, James Taylor

30 Mar 1816 Joseph Larrick & Nancy Mauck. Bondsman, Michael Mauck

31 Mar 1816 Elias King & Mary King widow & relict of Aquilla King decd. Bondsman, Ransam ?Kinlin (probably Kindall)

30 Mar 1816 Charles Beckley & Elizabeth Tapp, daughter of Lewis Tapp

1 Apr 1816 Edrian Davenport & Olevia Clark. Bondsman, John Davenport

1 Mar 1816 Jonathan Wickersham & Mary Scarff. Bondsman, William Scarff

2 Apr 1816 Joseph Spangler & Margaret Kremble. Bondsman, Jacob High

4 Apr 1816 John Larick & Rebecoah Rigway. Bondsman, William Lock

6 Apr 1816 Jeremiah C. Butcher & Hannah Thomson. Bondsman, John McCoole

8 Apr 1816 Samuel Snapp & Rachel Davis. Bondsman, James Davis

10 Apr 1816 Isaac Pigeon & Mary Sanders. Bondsman, James Cullen

10 Apr 1816 Benjamin Roe & Elizabeth Paget, daughter of Edmund Paget, the bondsman

15 Apr 1816 Thomas Risler & Louisa Clark. Bondsman, John Davenport

15 Apr 1816 George Slownaker & Nancy Merchant. Bondsman, Dustus Merchant

?13 Apr 1816 David Denny & Rebecca Nesmith. Bondsman, Thomas Nesmith

27 Apr 1816 William Scrivner & Elizabeth Coe of Fredk County Bondsman, Westly Coe

4 May 1816 Stephen Dicks & Sarah Rolston, widow of John Rolston decd. Bondsman, Peter Cooley

9 May 1816 Nathl Offutt & Rebeccah Orear, both parties over 21. Bondsman, Jesse Orear

16 May 1816 Alfred H. Powell & Ann Kean. Bondsman, David Holmes

19 May 1816 David Grant & Easter Peterson. Bondsman, Lewis Dansey

28 May 1816 John Henry & Sally Loyd. Bondsman, John Funcke

10 Jun 1816 Richd Hardesty & Sarah Pierce. Bondsman, John Pierce

10 Jun 1816 Thomas Jordan & Elizabeth Frost of Frederick County. Bondsman, William Taylor

14 Jun 1816 Nathan Mullennix & Catherine Pulse. Bondsman, Philip Stone

19 Jun 1816 Thomas Anderson & Margaret Burner. Bondsman, Joseph Johnson

20 Jun 1816 Thomas Wharton & Rebecca B. Harris. Bondsman, Benjamin Harris

24 Jun 1816 George Ashby & Martha Riely. Bondsman, George Riely

24 Jun 1816 Edwd Gilbert & Elizabeth Daley daughter of Samuel Dailey

1 Jul 1816 Craven Shaw & Mary Carper. Bondsman, Philip Carper

4 Jul 1816 Daniel McEntire & Lydia Hittle. Bondsman, Jacob Snyder, who signs in German

16 Jul 1816 Joseph Myers & Mary Maumaugh. Bondsman, George Maumau

8 Aug 1816 James Rigden & Ann Jones, daughter of Zachariah Jones. Bondsman, Z. Jones

17 Mar 1817 William Johnston & Catharine Laing. Bondsman, James Laing

18 Mar 1817 William Lloyd & Betsy Blake. Bondsman, Philip McGuire

8 Aug 1816 Thomas Landrom & Margaret Ann Crider. Bondsman, John Crider

19 Aug 1816 James Davis & Nancy Hess. Bondsman, Joseph Pannill

20 Aug 1816 William Jackson & Elizabeth Carter, daughter of Arthur W. Carter of Frederick County, the bondsman

21 Aug 1816 George Dutts & Susan Whitzlar daughter of Barbara Whitzlar, the bondsman

23 Aug 1816 Thomas C. Wyndham & Elizabeth Everhart. Bondsman, Leml Bent

23 Aug 1816 Elisha Gray & Catharine Parrott, daughter of Joshua Parrott, the bondsman

26 Aug 1816 James P. Miller & Hannah Smith of the County of Frederick. Bondsman, Robert Smith

31 Aug 1816 George Johnston & Susanah? Johnston widow of William Johnston decd

12 Sep 1816 Isaac Shambaugh & Nancy Barrow, daughter of William Barrow, the bondsman

12 Sep 1816 John Haynes & Jane Fleming, daughter of William Fleming, the bondsman

14 Sep 1816 Mahlon Morris & Fanny Brown. Bondsman, Frisby Morris

14 Sep 1816 Joseph Adams & Edah Lupton of Frederick County. Bondsman, John Hansell

15 Sep 1816 Joshua Watson & Luca Dowdan. Bondsman, Bazel Spicknall

17 Sep 1816 William Chambers & Sarah Montgomery. Bondsman, Thomas Montgomery

20 Sep 1816 John Kingore & Margaret Carper. Bondsman, Frederick Carper

21 Sep 1816 Robert Hubbard & Tacy Waln, daughter of William Waln, the bondsman

25 Sep 1816 Elisha Newcomb & Eve Loyer (both upwards of 21 years of age). Bondsman, Henry Navell

25 Sep 1816 John Foster & Maria Campbell. Bondsman, John B. Campbell

28 Sep 1816 Westley Dehaven & Louisa Fisher of Frederick County. Bondsman, Barak Fisher Jr

30 Sep 1816 John R. T. Corbin & Harriet S. Helm. Bondsman, George Murray

2 Oct 1816 William Patten & Catherine Rutter, daughter of Henry Rutter, the bondsman

3 Oct 1816 Samuel Turner & Matilda Beckley, daughter of Charles Beckley, the bondsman

9 Oct 1816 Jacob Carr & Mary Martin of Frederick County. Bondsman, John Pickering

10 Oct 1816 Michael White & Malinda Crupper, daughter of John Crupper, the bondsman

15 Oct 1816 Francis B. Whiting & Mary Burwell. Bondsman, William Burrell

15 Oct 1816 Andrew Chunn & Sarah Sowers. Bondsman, Baalis Davis

26 Oct 1816 John Kiter & Sarah Beall of lawfull age. Bondsman, John Weaver
28 Oct 1816 Abraham Hickman & Mary Nelson. Bondsman, Peter Renner
5 Nov 1816 Joseph Carter & Betsy Carter. Bondsman, John Carter
6 Nov 1816 Isaac Skelton & Rebeccah Lehew. Bondsman, Spencer Lehew
12 Nov 1816 George Lewis Ball & Catharine Kerfoot. Bondsman, Andrew Chunn
13 Nov 1816 William G. Whitloe & Elizabeth Simpson. Bondsman, Peter McCarty
15 Nov 1816 Thos Bragg & Edy Cockrell. Bondsman, Thomas Beall
14 Nov 1816 Adam Gruber & Barbara Boughman. Bondsman, John Umbenhower
20 Nov 1816 Jonathan Orndorff & Mary Scantz. Bondsman, Michael White
21 Nov 1816 John Lee & Leucinda Flinn. Bondsman, Volentine Flinn
21 Nov 1816 Thomas Anderson & Elizabeth Stephens. Bondsman, Daniel Anderson
25 Nov 1816 Jacob Kendrick & Rebecca Headley. Bondsman, John Kendrick
25 Nov 1816 David Grubbs & Hannah Rogers. Bondsman, Henry Groves
25 Nov 1816 Theophiles Lawson & Sarah Wood (Word?). Bondsman, Robert Foster
27 Nov 1816 William Karns & Nancy Kerns. Bondsman, Barry Kerns
2 Dec 1816 William Norman & Sally Jones a free negro woman. Bondsman, Simon Hawkins
2 Dec 1816 William Hamilton & Mary Earl. Bondsman, Ezias Earle
5 Dec 1816 Evan Pearpoint & Mary Bickley. Bondsman, Isaac Groves
6 Dec 1816 William Rowles Jnr. & Dolly Leach. Bondsman, Jesse Kemp
8 Dec 1816 John McCune & Elizabeth Spignall, widow of John Spignall. Bondsman, George Hansell
11 Dec 1816 David Briarly & Eliza Brent. Bondsman, Samuel B. Sydnor
12 Dec 1816 John Stip & Maria Mauck, daughter of Michael Mauck, the bondsman, who signs in German

14 Dec 1816 Joseph Shambaugh & Anna Duffey, daughter of Ann Bailey. Bondsman, Jacob McKay Jr

14 Dec 1816 George Syphers & Rachel Hailton. Bondsman, Martha B. Angier

18 Dec 1816 Thomas Smith & Elizabeth Scrogans, upwards of 20 years of age. Bondsman, Jesse Haines. Jesse Haines "made solemn affirmation"

19 Dec 1816 Joseph Secrist & Elizabeth Hannum, daughter of Thomas Hannum, the bondsman

25 Dec 1816 Edward Jinkins Murray & Catherine Jinkins, daughter of Edward Jinkins, the bondsman

23 Dec 1816 Lewis Ellis & Mildred Ball. Bondsman, John Piper

30 Dec 1816 Patrick Denver & Jane Campbell, daughter of William Campbell

31 Dec 1816 Jacob Kiter & Mary Lewis, daughter of Jacob Lewis, the bondsman

1 Jan 1817 James Smith & Mary Thompson. Bondsman, Jacob Cryder

2 Jan 1817 Thomas Lee & Anna Good. Bondsman, Felix Good

2 Jan 1817 Joseph Carter & Elizabeth Lupton. Bondsman, Christopher Probasco

2 Jan 1817 William Groves & Susannah Buzzard, over 21. Bondsman, Adam Groves

3 Jan 1817 Thomas Raynolds & Elizabeth P. Wigginton. Bondsman, William Wigginton

10 Jan 1817 John Riley & Tereza Benn. Bondsman, Robert Benn

10 Jan 1817 John B. Reid & Maria Benn. Bondsman, Robert Benn

13 Jan 1817 Robert Simpson & Mary Hampton. Bondsman, Joseph Hampton

14 Jan 1817 William Beatty & Elizabeth Lawer, daughter of John Lawer. Bondsman, Henry Naple

16 Jan 1817 Edward Wiatt & Dalconame? (bride's name not legible) Brayerly, daughter of Robert Brayerly. Bondsman, Bushrod Taylor

21 Jan 1817 John Thornburgh & Lydia Carter, daughter of Joseph Carter, the bondsman

24 Jan 1817 Jacob Mauck & Rebecca Weaver, daughter of Christian Weaver, the bondsman

27 Jan 1817 Thomas Figg & Anny Oland. Bondsman, John Rosenberger

28 Jan 1817 Henry Baker & Susan Singhass daughter of Christian Singhass, the bondsman, who signs in German

28 Jan 1817 Hansford Pursell & Rebeccah Wood, daughter of Alexander Wood, the bondsman

31 Jan 1817 John Carson & Sarah Stephens, daughter of Bryan M. Stephens, the bondsman

4 Feb 1817 George Lay & Ura (?Una) Martin. Bondsman, Michel Ley

5 Feb 1817 James D. Gilkeson & Sally D. Bell, daughter of John Bell, the bondsman

7 Feb 1817 Tailiaferro Vickers & Henretta Romine. Bondsman, Thomas Vickers

7 Feb 1817 Thomas Lang & Elizabeth Ellet, daughter of William Elliott, the bondsman

10 Feb 1817 Michael Albert & Sarah Kile. Bondsman, Francis Kile

10 Feb 1817 John L. Smith & Mary Ash, daughter of Francis Ash. Bondsman, Buckner Ash

12 Feb 1817 James Jones & Elenor Marquis. Bondsman, John McCauley

13 Feb 1817 Andrew Allen & Mary Self. Bondsman, Daniel James

13 Feb 1817 Francis Kile & Nancy Marpole, widow of Ezekiel Marpole dec. Bondsman, Michael Albert

13 Feb 1817 Thomas Raines & Mary Brown, daughter of --- Brown, decd
Bondsman, James Philips

19 Feb 1817 Isaac Wood & Maria Littler. Bondsman, Charles Littler

24 Feb 1817 William Snyder & Catherine Yeager. Bondsman, Solomon Hester

25 Feb 1817 Mathew Carpenter & Harriet Benson, daughter of Isabella Benson. Bondsman, William Benson

25 Feb 1817 Joseph Dalbey & Nancy Scrivener, daughter of Vincent Scrivener, the bondsman

-- Feb 1817 Jacob Vandiver & Fanny Kennon. Bondsman, Francis Neal

1 Mar 1817 William Bowre & Hannah Hancher, daughter of Nicholas Hancher, the bondsman

14 Mar 1817 Elie Hicks & Charity Anderson. Bondsman, Elie Anderson

24 Mar 1817 William Craig & Mary Sperry, daughter of Jacob Sperry, the bondsman

24 Mar 1817 Jacob Mauck & Abigal Shambaugh, daughter of Daniel Shambaugh. Bondsman, Marcus Baker

24 Mar 1817 Adam Pearse & Martha McMurray. Bondsman, Peter McMurray, Jr.

27 Mar 1817 Samuel Murphey & Polly Thruston. Bondsman, Edward Burns

Marriage Bonds No. 12 1817-1820

3 Mar 1817 Joseph Ralph & Sarah Biddenger daughter of Christopher Biddenger. Bondsman, John Ralph

11 Mar 1817 Thomas Lewis & Di-- Neff daughter of Francis Neff, the bondsman

11 Mar 1817 Samuel Davison & Lydia Sepenger. Bondsman, Jacob Larrick

31 Mar 1817 John Shafer & Winny Lloyd. Bondsman, John Morgan

31 Mar 1817 William R. Ashby & Rebecca Buck, daughter of Thomas Buck, the bondsman

1 Apr 1817 Alexander Smith & Betsey Miller. Bondsman, William Evans

14 Apr 1817 Benjamin Lang & Metilda Lloyd. Bondsman, George Black

16 Apr 1817 John Hodges & Mary Vance, over 21. Bondsman, Frederick Bell

19 Apr 1817 Matthias Smith & Sinah Watson, daughter of William Watson, the bondsman

21 Apr 1817 James Conner & Peggy Huddle. Bondsman, Benjamin Richard

22 Apr 1817 Oliver McKenney & Catharine Barton. Bondsman, Samuel Barton

24 Apr 1817 John Rogers & Margaret Harbert. Bondsman, Evan Rogers

28 Apr 1817 Benjamin G. Yates & Catharine Price. Bondsman, Peter Price

29 Apr 1817 William Clevinger & Martha Gilham. Bondsman, James Watson

5 May 1817 George Showalters & Elizabeth Venible. Bondsman, Jeremiah Bowling

5 May 1817 John Brown & Harriet Johnson, daughter of Minty Wittmore. Bondsman, Thomas H. Duke

5 May 1817 Edward Lawrence & Sarah Nesmith. Bondsman, Lewis Neill

5 May 1817 Alexander L. Jones & Marian Cannavan. Bondsman, James Moore
5 May 1817 Elie Oliver & Lucy Corder. Bondsman, Benjamin Helm
6 May 1817 George Risler & Mary Rowland. Bondsman, John Carter
9 May 1817 Jacob Keckley & Leah Clowser. Bondsman, John Clowser
10 May 1817 John Thomas Hickman & Rebecca Trout. Bondsman, Jacob Trout
12 May 1817 Abraham Rinehart & Mary Johnston. Bondsman, Joseph Johnson/Johnston
17 May 1817 Winder H. Kenner & Rachel McKay. Bondsman, Levi Duffey
20 May 1817 George House & Polly Dean, daughter of William Deane, the bondsman
21 May 1817 George Parrell & Henny ?Callin. Bondsman, Moses Calin
21 May 1817 Simon Carson junr & Jane Anderson. Bondsman, Benedick Rust
28 May 1817 Jacob Isler & Martha Richards, daughter of Daniel Richard, the bondsman
28 May 1817 Samuel Few & Mary Ann Pritchard. Bondsman, Howson Pritchard
31 May 1817 Edward Tigner & Elizabeth Swatz, daughter of John Swartz/Swatz, the bondsman
2 Jun 1817 Wilford P. Massie & Patsy D. Kiger (both upwards of 21 years of age). Bondsman, Joseph W. Kiger
2 Jun 1817 James Hay & Eliza G. Burwell. Bondsman, William Burwell
10 Jun 1817 Reuben Salyers & Margaret Delong. Bondsman, David Smith
1 Jul 1817 James Ryan & Elizabeth Crissmore, daughter of Anthony Crissmore, the bondsman, who signs in German
8 Jul 1817 Joseph McIntosh & Rachel Bruce. Bondsman, Daniel Gold
31 Jul 1817 Elias Jones & Elizabeth Kline of Frederick County. Bondsman, Michael Kline
5 Aug 1817 Thomas Duke & Sydny Johnston, daughter of Susannah Muse, late Susannah Johnston. Bondsman, Thomas Shepheard
11 Aug 1817 Samuel Leach & Polly Wood, widow of Bennett Wood, dec. Bondsman, John Suter

24 Mar 1817 Jacob Mauck & Abigal Shambaugh, daughter of Daniel Shambaugh. Bondsman, Marcus Baker
24 Mar 1817 Adam Pearse & Martha McMurray. Bondsman, Peter McMurray, Jr.
27 Mar 1817 Samuel Murphey & Polly Thruston. Bondsman, Edward Burns

Marriage Bonds No. 12   1817-1820

3 Mar 1817 Joseph Ralph & Sarah Biddenger daughter of Christopher Biddenger. Bondsman, John Ralph
11 Mar 1817 Thomas Lewis & Di-- Neff daughter of Francis Neff, the bondsman
11 Mar 1817 Samuel Davison & Lydia Sepenger. Bondsman, Jacob Larrick
31 Mar 1817 John Shafer & Winny Lloyd. Bondsman, John Morgan
31 Mar 1817 William R. Ashby & Rebecca Buck, daughter of Thomas Buck, the bondsman
1 Apr 1817 Alexander Smith & Betsey Miller. Bondsman, William Evans
14 Apr 1817 Benjamin Lang & Metilda Lloyd. Bondsman, George Black
16 Apr 1817 John Hodges & Mary Vance, over 21. Bondsman, Frederick Bell
19 Apr 1817 Matthias Smith & Sinah Watson, daughter of William Watson, the bondsman
21 Apr 1817 James Conner & Peggy Huddle. Bondsman, Benjamin Richard
22 Apr 1817 Oliver McKenney & Catharine Barton. Bondsman, Samuel Barton
24 Apr 1817 John Rogers & Margaret Harbert. Bondsman, Evan Rogers
28 Apr 1817 Benjamin G. Yates & Catharine Price. Bondsman, Peter Price
29 Apr 1817 William Clevinger & Martha Gilham. Bondsman, James Watson
5 May 1817 George Showalters & Elizabeth Venible. Bondsman, Jeremiah Bowling
5 May 1817 John Brown & Harriet Johnson, daughter of Minty Wittmore. Bondsman, Thomas H. Duke
5 May 1817 Edward Lawrence & Sarah Nesmith. Bondsman, Lewis Neill

5 May 1817 Alexander L. Jones & Marian Cannavan. Bondsman, James Moore
5 May 1817 Elie Oliver & Lucy Corder. Bondsman, Benjamin Helm
6 May 1817 George Risler & Mary Rowland. Bondsman, John Carter
9 May 1817 Jacob Keckley & Leah Clowser. Bondsman, John Clowser
10 May 1817 John Thomas Hickman & Rebecca Trout. Bondsman, Jacob Trout
12 May 1817 Abraham Rinehart & Mary Johnston. Bondsman, Joseph Johnson/Johnston
17 May 1817 Winder H. Kenner & Rachel McKay. Bondsman, Levi Duffey
20 May 1817 George House & Polly Dean, daughter of William Deane, the bondsman
21 May 1817 George Parrell & Henny ?Callin. Bondsman, Moses Calin
21 May 1817 Simon Carson junr & Jane Anderson. Bondsman, Benedick Rust
28 May 1817 Jacob Isler & Martha Richards, daughter of Daniel Richard, the bondsman
28 May 1817 Samuel Few & Mary Ann Pritchard. Bondsman, Howson Pritchard
31 May 1817 Edward Tigner & Elizabeth Swatz, daughter of John Swartz/Swatz, the bondsman
2 Jun 1817 Wilford P. Massie & Patsy D. Kiger (both upwards of 21 years of age). Bondsman, Joseph W. Kiger
2 Jun 1817 James Hay & Eliza G. Burwell. Bondsman, William Burwell
10 Jun 1817 Reuben Salyers & Margaret Delong. Bondsman, David Smith
1 Jul 1817 James Ryan & Elizabeth Crissmore, daughter of Anthony Crissmore, the bondsman, who signs in German
8 Jul 1817 Joseph McIntosh & Rachel Bruce. Bondsman, Daniel Gold
31 Jul 1817 Elias Jones & Elizabeth Kline of Frederick County. Bondsman, Michael Kline
5 Aug 1817 Thomas Duke & Sydny Johnston, daughter of Susannah Muse, late Susannah Johnston. Bondsman, Thomas Shepheard
11 Aug 1817 Samuel Leach & Polly Wood, widow of Bennett Wood, dec. Bondsman, John Suter

11 Aug 1817 John C. Howe & Hannah Minoin. Bondsman, Jacob Rees

26 Aug 1817 Samuel Singhass & Peggy Collins, stepdaughter of Andrew Baker, the bondsman

28 Aug 1817 Samuel Mendenhall & Martha Reed, daughter of William Reed of Frederick County, the bondsman

29 Aug 1817 Elias Oglesby & Mary Stump of the County of Frederick. Bondsman, John Oglesby

2 Sep 1817 John Culver & Mary McCormick. Bondsman, Dawson McCormick

12 Sep 1817 William T. Stubblefield & Susan Kannon, daughter of Sarah Kannon. Bondsman, Bushrod T. Stribling

12 Sep 1817 Isaiah Oglesbee & Sarah Devoe, daughter of David Devoe. Bondsmen, John Oglesbee & David Devoe

17 Sep 1817 James Deshon & Peggy Craig, daughter of Susannah Craig, the bondsman, widow of John Craig dec of this county

12 Oct 1817 Isaiah Oglesby & Sarah Devoe, daughter of David Devoe. Bondsmen, John Devoe & David Devoe

17 Oct 1817 David Ferril & Mary Smith. Bondsman, David Fries

20 Oct 1817 Peter Cooly & Sarah Chapman, widow of Elie Chapman dec. Bondsman, George Trisler

23 Oct 1817 David Watson & Sarah Saunders of Frederick County. Bondsman, James Walls

2 Nov 1817 Nathan Jones & Stena Myers, daughter of John Myers of Frederick County, the bondsman

25 Oct 1817 Joseph Parmer & Elizabeth Puller, daughter of Lester Puller of Frederick County, the bondsman

29 Oct 1817 Stephen Johnson & Elizabeth White. Bondsman, Samuel Cooley

29 Oct 1817 William Cloud & Mary Smith, daughter of Levi Smith. Bondsman, George Albert

4 Nov 1817 Bushrod Taylor & Elizabeth S. Milton. Bondsman, Thomas Allen Tidball

3 Nov 1817 John Grim & Jane Christy, daughter of Robert Christy of this county, the bondsman

8 Nov 1817 George Cartmell & Lydia Glasscock, daughter of William Goasscock of Frederick County. Bondsman, Absalum B. McClun

11 Nov 1817 Abinago Page & Elizabeth Shehen, daughter of Hannah Shehan, widow of William Shehen dec. Bondsman, Rezin Mason

12 Nov 1817 William Branor & Suzannah Smith of lawfull age and of Frederick County. Bondsman, John G. Lipscomb

13 Nov 1817 James Brewer & Mary Hinkle, daughter of Adam Hinkle of Frederick County, the bondsman

19 Nov 1817 Henry Hall & Hannah Messer. Bondsman, William Brown

19 Nov 1817 John Dailey & Susannah Braithwait, daughter of William Braithwait, the bondsman

19 Nov 1817 Christopher Winfree & Cornelia Tilden, daughter of John B. Tilden of Frederick County. Bondsman, John Victor

25 Nov 1817 John Keeler & Margaret Thompson of Frederick County. Bondsman, Henry Bradford

26 Nov 1817 William Martin & Mary Johnston, daughter of Susannah Muse, late Susannah Johnston. Bondsman, Thomas Duke

29 Nov 1817 Robinson Babb & Rachel Bayly, daughter of William Bailey, the bondsman

6 Dec 1817 Joseph Gamble Jr & Eliza Cook. Bondsman, Joseph Gamble

8 Dec 1817 Wm Crow & Mary McCarty, daughter of Joseph McCarty, the bondsman

17 Dec 1817 James Pine & Mary Sivyers, daughter of George Sivyers, the bondsman

17 Dec 1817 John Evert & Susannah Null, daughter of Jacob Null of Frederick County, the bondsman

17 Dec 1817 Jacob Null & Susannah Poffenburger, daughter of John Poffenburger of Frederick County, the bondsman

17 Dec 1817 Jesse Hurford & Eve Ann Hass, daughter of Conrad Hass of Frederick County. Bondsman, John Haas

20 Dec 1817 Bushrod Stribling & Penelope Gatewood. Bondsman, James Ship

19 Dec 1817 Charles Hainy & Sarah Kanara of Frederick County. Bondsman, Thomas Grubbs

19 Dec 1817 William Board & Matilda Oliver, daughter of James Oliver of Frederick County. Bondsman, Mason Oliver

22 Dec 1817 George Cornwall & Sarah Fleming, daughter of Archibald Fleming, the bondsman

23 Dec 1817 Joel Hastings & Nancy Randolph of Frederick County. Bondsman, Jacob Shofner, who signs in German

3 Jan 1818 Alexander Roe & Catharine Hansel, daughter of George Hansel, the bondsman, who signs in German

5 Jan 1818 William Scarff & Elizabeth Likins, daughter of Mary Likins, the bondsman

5 Jan 1818 David Groves & Catherine Seevers, daughter of Casper Seevers. Bondsman, Cyrus W. Murray

6 Dec (Jan written later) 1818 Amos Puller & Rebeccah Romine, daughter of Ellener Romine. Bondsman, Michael Dearmont

8 Jan 1818 Westley Grubbs & Susannah White, daughter of Mary White. Bondsman, Joseph White

13 Jan 1818 Abraham Isler & Susan Cloud. Bondsman, Daniel Richard

13 Jan 1818 Jesse Haines & Rebeccah Silver, daughter of James Silver of Frederick County. Bondsman, Gershom Silver

15 Jan 1818 Jacob Kline & Catherine Brill, daughter of Henry Brill, the bondsman

16 Jan 1818 Elisha Piper & Elizabeth Snapp, daughter of Jacob Snapp, the bondsman

16 Jan 1818 Richard M. L. Timberlake & Sarah Timberlake, daughter of David Timberlake, the bondsman

18 Jan 1818 Henry Lloyd & Mary Miller. Bondsman, Cornelius Gibbens & Bennett Hall

18 Jan 1818 Isaac Oldacre & Catherine Little. Bondsman, John Barrow

20 Jan 1818 John Rutherford & Mary Carter of Frederick County. Bondsman, George Albert

21 Jan 1818 Casper Allamong & Christena Dick of Frederick County. Bondsman, John Dick

Jan 1818 John Hite & Rachel Grubbs. Bondsman, David Grubbs

26 Jan 1818 John B. Earle & Maria B. Miller, daughter of Alexander Miller, the bondsman

27 Jan 1818 Jacob Anderson & Margaret Carper, daughter of Frederick Carper, the bondsman

28 Jan 1818 Elias Cooksey & Martha Ann Morgan, daughter of William Morgan, the bondsman

28 Jan 1818 William Sowers & Catherine Jinkins, daughter of Wm Jinkins. Bondsman, Thomas Jinkins

2 Feb 1818 Charles Butler & Peggy Monroe. Bondsman, John Latham

2 Feb 1818 Morgan H. Marpole & Elizabeth Bohan. Bondsman, Moses Newbanks

7 Feb 1818 William Adams Junr. & Rachel Quick, daughter of Martin Quick, the bondsman

9 Feb 1818 John Brobeck & Mary Ann Snapp, daughter of Adam Snapp, the bondsman

10 Feb 1818 John Vance & Eliza Hoge of Frederick County. Bondsman, Robt. C. Tilden

11 Feb 1818 Daniel White & Harriet White of Frederick County. Bondsman, George White

12 Feb 1818 James Wigginton & Christena Whetsel, daughter of John Whetsel, the bondsman

17 Feb 1818 Ephraim Miller & Esther Kiter, daughter of George Kiter of County of Frederick. Bondsman, John Kiter

23 Feb John Louthan & Margaret Carter, daughter of Arthur W. Carter. Bondsman, Arthur W. Carter

16 Feb 1818 Elisha Smallwood & Sarah Dowell. Bondsman, John Dowell

24 Feb 1818 Mark Duke & Margaret McCarty, daughter of Andrew McCarty, the bondsman

25 Feb 1818 John Anderson & Nancy Turner. Bondsman, Daniel Murphy

28 Feb 1818 Daniel Ritenour & Elizabeth Drake of Frederick County. Bondsman, Henry Navel

3 Mar 1818 Robert Rodgers & Margaret Venable. Bondsman, David S. Danner

9 Mar 1818 George Chrisman & Dorotha Saunders. Bondsman, John Payne

11 Mar 1818 Benjamin Frye & Juliett Bean, daughter of James Bean, the bondsman

17 Mar 1818 Nicholas Perry & Margaret Hodson, daughter of Rob Hodgson, the bondsman

17 Mar 1818 John Beemer & Elizabeth Kean, daughter of Nicholas Kean, the bondsman

17 Mar 1818 Rezin Mason & Hannah Shehin, widow of Wm Shehen, decd. Bondsman, Andrew Mason

4 Apr 1818 James Sargeant & Polly Williams of Frederick County. Bondsman, George Hansall

11 Apr 1818 Abraham Hiskett & Phebe Hicks, daughter of John Hicks decd. Bondsman, John Lay

11 Apr 1818 Jacob Reed & Nancy Stipe, daughter of Henry Stipe, the bondsman

21 Apr 1818 Jonas Whitacre & Mary Kerns, daughter of Nathan Kerns, the bondsman

24 Apr 1818 Thomas F. Railsback & Louiza V. Allensworth, daughter of Philip Allensworth, the bondsman

27 Apr 1818 George Swatz & Phoeby Messer of Frederick County. Bondsman, Calip Messer

28 Apr 1818 John Crawford & Martha Shepherd of Frederick County. Bondsman, Joel Hastings

29 Apr 1818 Henry Rutter Junr & Mary Beatty of County of Frederick. Bondsman, Peter Keller & Henry Rutter Sen

4 May 1818 Robert McWhorter & Mary Linn of Frederick County. Bondsman, John McCoole

7 May 1818 George Whitacre & Elizabeth Mckee of Frederick County. Bondsman, Joseph Strickling

12 May 1818 John Strother & Elizabeth W. Clopton. Bondsman, Thomas Allen Tidball

18 May 1818 John S. Clark & Catherine Evens, daughter of Samuel Evens of Frederick County. Bondsman, Reuben Clark

19 May 1818 John Frost & Catherine Crum, daughter of Henry Crum of Frederick County. Bondsman, John Crum

18 Jun (sic) 1818 Anthony Buckwalter & Mary Buzzard of Frederick County. Bondsman, William Groves

24 May 1818 Jessee Baily & Margaret Penabaker, daughter of William Penabaker of Frederick County, the bondsman

3 Jun 1818 William Bean & Hannah Hall, daughter of Bennett Hall, the bondsman

4 Jun 1818 David Funk, upward of 21 years of age, & Mary Place, daughter of Abraham Place, the bondsman

8 Jun 1818 James B. Simmons & Elizabeth Weaver, daughter of John Weaver of Frederick County. Bondsman, Jacob Weaver

10 Jun 1818 Solomon Moore & Rebeccah Barrow. Bondsman, Michael Mauck

12 Jun 1818 Benjamin Stine & Rachel Barchelbaugh, daughter of George Barchelbaugh of Frederick County. Bondsman, Henry Bantelbaugh (Bartelbaugh?)

15 Jun 1818 Isaac Harrison & Mary Hughes, daughter of William Hughes, the bondsman

15 Jun 1818 John Snyder & Sarah Lyons, daughter of James Lyons. Bondsman, James Lyons

15 Jun 1818 Armistead Wilson & Sarah Gaugh, upward of 21. Bondsman, James Davison

22 Jun 1818 Peter Adams & Eliza Fisher, daughter of Barrach Fisher. Bondsman, William Campbell

25 Jun 1818 John McAllister & Alice Wilson. Bondsman, Walter Tanquary

27 Jun 1818 Jesse Ramey & Hannah Kendrick. Bondsman, John S. Mackey

3 Jul 1818 Benjamin Keckley & Mary Orndorf, daughter of John Orndorf, the bondsman

10 Jul 1818 Ebenezer Roe & Eleanor Marshall, daughter of John Marshall, the bondsman

10 Jul 1818 Sidney Smith & Elizabeth Strother. Bondsman, Enoch Strother

10 Jul 1818 Thomas Edwards & Eleanor Scott, daughter of Samuel Scott, the bondsman

22 Jul 1818 Hiram Neville & Harriet Babb, daughter of Henry M. Babb, the bondsman

27 Jul 1818 Reuben L. Berkley & Nancy D. Hancock, daughter of George Hancock. Bondsman, John H. Hancock

1 Aug 1818 John Carter & Elliner Courtney of Frederick County. Bondsman, Samuel Wirel

10 Aug 1818 Jonah Shepherd & Catherine Ferguson, daughter of James S. Ferguson. Bondsman, Joshua Ferguson

10 Aug 1818 James Evans & Peggy Wilkin of Frederick County. Bondsman, Richard Barrett

16 Aug 1818 WIlliam Henning & Mary Irvin Beatty, daughter of Henry Beatty, the bondsman

17 Aug 1818 John Romine & Maria Romine, daughter of Reuben Romine, the bondsman

17 Aug 1818 James Wright & Elizabeth Elliott, daughter of Reuben Elliott of Frederick County, the bondsman

19 Aug 1818 Henry Printz & Elizabeth Marquis, widow of William Marquis decd. Bondsman, Conrad Kreamer
20 Aug 1818 Benjamin Williams & Peggy Foley, daughter of Selly Foley. Bondsman, Joel Williams
29 Aug 1818 Joseph Fenton & Elliner Duncan, daughter of John Duncan of Frederick County, the bondsman
29 Aug 1818 Thornton Newland & Sarah Lewis of Frederick County. Bondsman, William Clark
31 Aug 1818 Griffin Smallwood & Delilah Moore of Frederick County. Bondsman, Philip McGwinn
31 Aug 1818 John C. Bazell & Mary B. Pettet of Frederick County. Bondsman, George W. Pettit
8 Aug 1818 John Rogers & Elizabeth Hancock of Frederick County. Bondsman, Samuel Rogers
9 Sep 1818 Charles Strother & Belinda Tuley, daughter of Joseph Tuley. Bondsman, Thomas Tuley
11 Sep 1818 Samuel Perry & Laura Ryan of Frederick County. Bondsman, James Ball
11 Sep 1818 Archibald G. Robinson & Drusilla Dehaven of the County of Frederick. Bondsman, Henry D. Dehaven
16 Sep 1818 John Bowman & Jane Ann Matilda Williams, daughter of Jared Williams, the bondsman
18 Sep 1818 Daniel Morris & Alecy Barr of Frederick County. Bondsman, Benjamin Barr
30 Sep 1818 John Walton & Mary Ann Rowzy, daughter of Edward Rowzy of Frederick County, the bondsman
5 Oct 1818 William Huggins & Hannah Rodgers. Bondsman, Robert Rogers
6 Oct 1818 William Langley & Elizabeth Hotsinpiller, daughter of Joseph Hotsinpiller, the bondsman
6 Oct 1818 Gilbert Atwood & Catherine Harrell of the County of Frederick. Bondsman, Jeremiah McNeily (signed Jeremiah mc nealy)
7 Oct 1818 Nicholas Handle & Sarah Earheart, daughter of John Earheart
7 Oct 1818 Richard Caywood & Mima Everheart, daughter of Michael Everheart, the bondsman

12 Oct 1818 James Deal & Nancy Conrad of the County aforesaid. Bondsman, Levi Conrad

21 Oct 1818 John Bruner & Mary Cole of the County aforesaid. Bondsman, Westley Coe

27 Oct 1818 Nathan Chapman & Margaret Hansell, daughter of George Hansell, the bondsman, who signs in German

28 Oct 1818 Augustine Kigar & Susanna Brown, daughter of Joseph Brown. Bondsmen, Jacob Kigar & John Nulton & Joseph Brown (father)

3 Nov 1818 James Hesket & Sarah Hicks of Frederick County. Bondsman, Dolphin Drew

5 Nov 1818 Joshua Barthlow & Sarah Watter of County of Fredcerick. Bondsman, Laurence Walter

11 Nov 1818 Michael Crouse & Elizabeth Sherf of Frederick County. Bondsman, Jacob Shade

16 Nov 1818 Becknell Alverson & Lucy Powell. Bondsman, Benjamin Orear

19 Nov 1818 Israel Dyer & Emely Hope, daughter of Christian Hope of Frederick County, the bondsman

20 Nov 1818 John Stevens & Sarah Ramey, daughter of Caleb Ramey of Frederick County. Bondsman, Jesse Ramey

20 Nov 1818 Roger Jones & Mary Ann Mason Page. Bondsman, William B. Page

30 Nov 1818 Isaac White & Mary Ann Hite, daughter of Mathias Hite, the bondsman

1 Dec 1818 William Garrison & Nancy Littleton, daughter of Thomas Littleton, the bondsman

1 Dec 1818 Thompson Richards & Jane Fleming of Frederick County. Bondsman, Andrew Fleming

16 Dec 1818 Thomas Lefever & Margaret Kearfoot. Bondsman, Ferguson Bell

16 Dec 1818 Samuel Myers & Mary Trout of the County of Frederick. Bondsman, David Trout & James Howard

17 Dec 1818 Richard Raines & Jane Puller, daughter of Lester Pullin, the bondsman

18 Dec 1818 Christopher Kendrick & Mary Way of the County aforesaid. Bondsman, James Way

19 Dec 1818 Jacob Peasemaker & Margaret Smith of the County aforesaid. Bondsman, Adam Peasmaker

20 Dec 1818 Thomas McAtee & Sarah White of the County of Frederick. Bondsman, John Canter

20 Dec 1818 William Barr & Elizabeth Yoe, daughter of Mary Yoe of the County of Frederick, the bondsman

20 Dec 1818 Jacob Lemley & Elizabeth Hotsenpillar of the County of Frederick. Bondsman, John Pitman

22 Dec 1818 William Allen & Nancy Barnett of the County of Frederick. Bondsman, Marquis Blakemore

23 Dec 1818 John Carter & Ales Butler, upwards of 21. Bondsman, John Minser

30 Dec 1818 John Newcomor & Mary Henning of the County aforesaid. Bondsman, David Hening

30 Dec 1818 Robert Long & Nancy Johnston. Bondsman, Philip Syfert

30 Dec 1818 Benjamin Glass & Susan Wood of the County of Frederick. Bondsman, Christopher Probasco

2 Jan 1819 William Eddy & Mary Nesmith. Bondsman, Charles Cunningham

5 Jan 1819 Samuel Foster & Mary Craig, daughter of Josiah Craig, the bondsman

7 Jan 1819 John Denny & Margaret Swatz, daughter of John Swatz, the bondsman

9 Jan 1818 Joseph Steel & Mary Marsh, daughter of Richard Marsh, the bondsman

11 Jan 1819 John Dick & Elizabeth Allemong of the County of Frederick. Bondsman, Casper Allemong

11 Jan 1819 Matthew Curry & Lucy Henning of the County of Frederick. Bondsman, William Ervine

12 Jan 1819 John White & Elizabeth Silver, daughter of James Silver of Frederick County. Bondsman, Gershom Silver

12 Jan 1819 Jacob Keller & Cathrene Groves, daughter of Jacob Groves, the bondsman

12 Jan 1819 Thomas Brown Junr & Lydia Fawcett of Frederick County. Bondsman, John Fawcett

14 Jan 1819 John Saunders Jr & Susannah Taylor, daughter of Jesse Taylor of Frederick County, the bondsman

13 Jan 1819 Henry Brill & Rachel Cooper. Bondsman, Henry Cooper

20 Jan 1819 Joseph Dyson & Sarah Campbell of the County of Frederick. Bondsman, Moses Russell

24 Jan 1819 Henry Tewalt & Rachel Wiscent, daughter of John Wiscent. Bondsman, Henry Wiscent (sic)

24 Jan 1819 James Cather & Nancy Howard, daughter of Anthony Howard, the bondsman

24 Jan 1819 Rudolph T. C. Boude & Elizabeth Ewing, daughter of Thomas Ewing, the bondsman

25 Jan 1819 John Riley & Fanny Puller, daughter of Lester Puller of Frederick County. Bondsman, Elijah Romine

30 Jan 1819 Daniel Anderson & Mary Arnold, daughter of Andrew Arnold of the County of Frederick, the bondsman

1 Feb 1819 Benjamin Wilson & Mary Butler of the County of Frederick. Bondsman, Elijah Cleveland

1 Feb 1819 Augustine Smith & Elizabeth Vanlangdinham, daughter of George Vanlangdinham of the County of Frederick. Bondsman, Thomas W. Raynolds

2 Feb 1819 John Williams & Elizabeth McCleave of the County of Frederick. Bondsman, Jared Williams

3 Feb 1819 George Longerbeen & Elizabeth Smith of the County of Frederick. Bondsman, Evrit Tracy

3 Feb 1819 Joseph V. Gray & Peggy Paton of Frederick County. Bondsman, John Allan

8 Feb 1819 Samuel Mastin & Anna Smith of Frederick County. Bondsman, John Wright

11 Feb 1819 James Pearce & Levina Carter, daughter of Joseph Carter, the bondsman

23 Feb 1819 Joseph Keckley & Elizabeth Turner, daughter of John Turner, the bondsman

23 Feb 1819 Isaac Wolfe & Susannah Dehaven of Frederick County. Bondsman, William Dehaven

23 Feb 1819 John Shipler & Henrietta Scrogan. Bondsman, John Scrogin

24 Feb 1819 George ORear & Kitty Franks, daughter of Henry Franks, the bondsman

1 Mar 1819 John Orndorf & Elizabeth Beeks of the County of Frederick. Bondsman, William Orndorf

2 Mar 1819 Solomin Wolfe & Elizabeth Snapp of the County of Frederick. Bondsman, Elijah Snapp

3 Mar 1819 John Trussell & Matilda Janes (Jones?) of Frederick County. Bondsman, Ninian Magruder

4 Mar 1819 Patrick Dunken & Martha Hotzenpillar of Frederick County. Bondsman, William Langley

8 Mar 1819 Joseph T. Lukins & Eliza Fawcett. Bondsman, Elijah Fawcett

18 Mar 1819 Edward Hedges & Mary Dalley. Bondsman, John Dalley

21 Mar 1819 Robert Crupper & Sarah Bosteyon of Frederick County. Bondsman, John Drake

22 Mar 1819 Eli McCormick & Jane Craig, daughter of Josiah Craig, the bondsman

22 Mar 1819 Thomas Marshall & Catharine G. Taylor. Bondsman, James Ware

23 Mar 1819 Jacob Copenhaver & Nancy Pelter of Frederick County. Bondsman, George Pelter

29 Mar 1819 Peter Babb & Jane Scarff of Frederick County. Bondsman, William Scarff

29 Mar 1819 Gideon Harvey & Catherine Vincent, daughter of Cornelius Vincent, the bondsman

30 Mar 1819 Thomas L. Ogden & Anna Robinson, daughter of John C. Robinson of Frederick County, the bondsman

30 Mar 1819 Benjamin Lockhart & Mary Eavenson. Bondsman, James Russell

7 Apr 1819 Elijah Grove & Lucinda Kercheval of Frederick County. Bondsman, Lewis C. Kercheval

8 Apr 1819 George Simpson & Nancy Farrow of Frederick County. Bondsman, Elias Holtsclaw

13 Apr 1819 Peter Ashton & Mary Ann Shut, daughter of George Shut

17 Apr 1819 Alexander Marks & Sarah Mytinger. Bondsman, William Denny

19 Apr 1819 Alexander Ross Milton & Harriet McCormick. Bondsman, Thomas Allen Tidball

21 Apr 1819 Harry McCarty & Sarah Rolf of the County of Frederick, daughter of Eve Relf. Bondsman, Jonathan Dean

26 Apr 1819 Presley Davis & Ann Milton. Bondsman, Daniel Taggart

28 Apr 1819 Jacob Mesmer & Nancy Jackson, daughter of Thomas Jackson, the bondsman

29 Apr 1819 Jesse Mercer & Margaret Willy, daughter of William Willy of the County of Frederick. Bondsman, John Anderson

6 May 1819 Tilman Mayhew & Ruth Parcel of the County of Frederick. Bondsman, Samuel Rogers

11 May 1819 William Simington & Margaret Brookes of Frederick County. Bondsman, Jothmam Wright

14 May 1819 John Venable & Nancy Day, daughter of James Day of Frederick County, the bondsman

17 May 1819 Joshua Scott & Sarah Holland, daughter of John Holland. Bondsman, Isaac Scott

18 May 1819 Charles Peters & Courtney Robinson, free negroes. Bondsman, Lewis Dansey

18 May 1819 William Hancher & Mary Howe of the County of Frederick. Bondsman, William Huggins

19 May 1819 John Wilson & Mary Ann Wilkey of Frederick County. Bondsman, William Thomas

19 May 1819 William Tinson & Jane Triplett. Bondsman, William Triplett

24 May 1819 Moses W. Brown & Mary Shipe, daughter of Adam Shipe. Bondsman, Elijah Waller

24 May 1819 Meredith Bowen & Catharine Carper, daughter of Philip Carper, the bondsman

15 Jun 1819 Enoch Marple & Elizabeth Johnston, daughter of Amos Johnston, the bondsman

15 Jun 1819 William Cooper & Lucinda Robinson, daughter of Gary Robinson, the bondsman

17 Jun 1819 William Jinkins & Jane Patton of Frederick County. Bondsman, Edward Jinkins

17 Jun 1819 Abraham Forsythe & Jane Wright, daughter of Elizabeth Wright widow of John Wright decd. Bondsman, Elizabeth Wright

25 Jun 1819 Grandison Thomas & Sarah Frost of Frederick County. Bondsman, Thomas Jordan

3 Jul 1819 John Murphy & Elizabeth Corsgill? Bondsman, Isaac Scott

19 Jul 1819 George Clipart & Elizabeth Stump of Frederick County. Bondsman, Isaac Heck

20 Jul 1819 William Davison & Mary Frieze, daughter of Michael Fries, the bondsman

22 Jul 1819 Nathaniel Mercer & Mary Adams of Frederick County. Bondsman, Joseph Thomas

26 Jul 1819 Reuben Stax & Margaret Ann Pickerell, daughter of Jonathan Pickerell, the bondsman

31 Jul 1819 John McMorris & Elizabeth Keckley, daughter of Abraham Keckley. Bondsman, Ann McMorris

2 Aug 1819 Valentine Flin & Matilda Cordell. Bondsman, John Lee

2 Aug 1819 William Utter & Deseriah Tibbs. Bondsman, John Triplett

2 Aug 1819 George Coburn & Mary Jones, daughter of Charles Jones of Frederick County, the bondsman

7 Aug 1819 Leroy Newcomb & Sarah Epler, daughter of Peter Epler, the bondsman, who signs in German

9 Aug 1819 James Gold & Alice Corder. Bondsman, Charles Hughes

14 Aug 1819 James Brison & Sarah Ewans, daughter of Thos Ewins. Bondsman, Westley T. Newham

31 Aug 1819 Cornelius Baldwin & Susan Pritchard. Bondsman, Job S. Hendricks

31 Aug 1819 Abraham Breedlove & Hannah Stokes, daughter of Samuel Stokes of Frederick County. Bondsman, John Yeo

2 Sep 1819 William Grear & Matilda Thompson of Frederick County. Bondsman, John S. Campbell

4 Sep 1819 William Dodd & Mary Stump of Frederick County. Bondsman, Isaac Heck

6 Sep 1819 Martin Little & Sarah Ritenour, daughter of Michael Ritenour, the bondsman

6 Sep 1819 David Rodes & Elizabeth Kline of Frederick County. Bondsman, Daniel Kline

7 Sep 1819 Amos Sergeant & Henrietta M. Clark of Frederick County. Bondsman, David T. Davis

11 Sep 1819 William McKee Jun & Ann Follett, daughter of William Follett. Bondsman, William McKee Sr.

20 Sep 1819 John Hackley & Elizabeth Vaughn, daughter of Vincent Vaughn, the bondsman

20 Sep 1819 Thomas Clow & Fanny Hackley. Bondsman, Vincent Vaughan

20 Sep 1819 Stofly Wood & Eleanor Simonds. Bondsman, Barnett Simonds

25 Sep 1819 Philip Snyder & Ury Lyons, daughter of James Lyons of Frederick County, the bondsman

25 Sep 1819 Abraham Grove & Sidney Messen (Messer?) of Frederick County. Bondsman, James Coe

27 Sep 1819 John Nolan & Elizabeth Grove, daughter of John Grove, Senr. of Frederick County. Bondsman, John Nisewanger

29 Sep 1819 David Mauck & Polly Tigner, daughter of William Tigner of Frederick County, the bondsman

30 Sep 1819 Nicholas Spencer & Mehely Butter (a free negro woman). Bondsman, Thomas Robinson

30 Sep 1819 Edmund Smith & Elizabeth Davison, widow of Thomas P. Davison of Frederick County. Bondsman, Thomas M. Rusk

8 Oct 1819 Isaac R. Elsa, son of John Elsa, & Frances Ramey, daughter of John Ramey of Frederick County. Bondsmen, John Elsea & John Ramey

9 Oct 1819 Joseph Waln & Elinor Dick, daugter of Peter Dick of Frederick County, the bondsman

14 Oct 1819 Nathan Wright & Maria Herford of Frederick County. Bondsman, Jonathan Smith

18 Oct 1819 Joseph Smith & Mary May, daughter of John May of Frederick County, the bondsman, who signs in German

18 Oct 1819 Lemuel Carroll & Sophia Garman of Frederick County. Bondsman, George Smith

26 Oct 1819 John Ashford & Lydia Clevenger, daughter of George Clevenger, the bondsman

1 Nov 1819 George Myers & Polly Showalter, daughter of Jacob Showalter. Bondsman, John Snyder

6 Nov 1819 John Stricker & Polly Taylor of Frederick County. Bondsman, John Reiley & Conrad Taylor

9 Nov 1819 Jonathan Jones junor & Elizabeth Fleming, daughter of William Fleming of Frederick County. Bondsman, Jonathan Jones Snr

11 Nov 1819 Daniel Eagle & Maria Albert, daughter of William Albert of Frederick County

13 Nov 1819 Isaac Smith & Julia Ann Grim, daughter of John Grim of Frederick County, the bondsman, who signs in German

16 Nov 1819 Leonard Likins & Ruth Carter, daughter of James Carter of Frederick County. Bondsman, Jacob Smith

16 Nov 1819 Noah Noble & Catharine S. Swearingen, daughter of Elie Swearingen of Frederick County, the bondsman

16 Nov 1819 John Hancher & Sally Cooper of Frederick County. Bondsman, Thomas Hancher & Julius Godman

17 Nov 1819 William F. Gill, son of Nathaniel Gill, & Mary Young of Frederick County. Bondsman, Nathaniel Gill

20 Nov 1819 William Campbell & Esther Fisher of Frederick County. Bondsman, John McCoole

23 Nov 1819 Horace Luckett & Louisa A. Clopton of Frederick County. Bondsman, Joseph Tuley jr

25 Nov 1819 David Nisewander & Mary J. Danner of Frederick County. Bondsman, David S. Danner

29 Nov 1819 Hugh C. Dyer & Elizabeth Ramey, daughter of Isaac Ramey, the bondsman

29 Nov 1819 William Denny & Margaret Hotzenpiller. Bondsman, George Ritenour

6 Dec 1819 Phinehas Thomas & Francis Keen. Bondsman, Thomas Littleton & Jacob Thomas

7 Dec 1819 Richard Beeson & Elizabeth Crumley, widow of John Crumley decd. Bondsman, Thomas Hancher

8 Dec 1819 George Everhart & Mary Welch of Frederick County. Bondsman, Jacob Everhart

13 Dec 1819 John Grammer & Juliana S. P. Barton of Frederick County. Bondsman, Robert R. Barton

14 Dec 1819 Henry Paul & Sarah Ann Taylor, daughter of Jesse Taylor of Frederick County, the bondsman

15 Dec 1819 Morten Bowen & Elizabeth Greeny, daughter of David Greenlee of Frederick County, the bondsman

15 Dec 1819 John Fry and Magdalene Snap. Bondsman, Elijah Snapp

15 Dec 1819 Joseph Tewalt & Rachel Snap. Bondsman, Elijah Snap

18 Dec 1819 Robert McKay & Virginia Grubs of Frederick County. Bondsman, Jacob McKay

18 Dec 1819 Watson Carter & Rebecca Mullen. Bondsman, William Barber

22 Dec 1819 Thomas Ellsea & Elizabeth Johnson of Frederick County. Bondsman, Lewis Johnson

24 Dec 1819 George Smith & Ann Albin. Bondsman, Thomas Allen Tidball

24 Dec 1819 Marcus Richardson & Elizabeth H. Chrisman. Bondsman, Abraham Miller

29 Dec 1819 Hieronimus Dick & Mary Ann Bruner, daughter of Henry Bruner of Frederick County, the bondsman

3 Jan 1820 Robert Jones & Celia Ann Myers, daughter of Joshua Mays of Frederick County, the bondsman

13 Jan 1820 Jesse Green & Sarah Dower (Dyer?) of Frederick County. Bondsman, Lewis Wood

17 Jan 1820 Isaac Huntsberry & Alsy Wright of Frederick County. Bondsman, Jacob Nickols

18 Jan 1820 John Ransdell & Amy Barton (a free negro woman). Bondsman, Reubin Malvin (free negroe man)

22 Jan 1820 James Tanquary & Hannah McClure. Bondsman, John McClure 25 Jan 1820 Valentine Showalter, son of Jacob Showalter, & Rachel Carson of Frederick County. Bondsmen, Jacob Showalter, who signs in German, & John Snyder

31 Jan 1820 Dennis Daily & Elizabeth Whittaker of Frederick County. Bondsman, John Stewart

5 Feb 1820 Robert Nelson & Mary Oats, daughter of Jacob Oats, the bondsman, who signs in German

7 Feb 1820 William Cox & Nancy McDaniel of Frederick County. Bondsman, William McDaniel

7 Feb 1820 Joseph Snapp & Harriet Wilson, daughter of William Wilson, the bondsman

7 Feb 1820 Michael Musselman & Sophia Grier. Bondsman, John Latham

8 Feb 1820 Ebin Milton & Emily B. Taylor. Bondsman, Alexander Tidball

14 Feb 1820 Cornelius Wiley & Catharine Anderson of Frederick County. Bondsman, Jesse Mercer

14 Feb 1820 Gideon Landacre & Hannah Garrett of Frederick County. Bondsman, John Landakre

15 Feb 1820 Scipio Thompson & Betsy Briscoe a free black woman. Bondsman, Danl Schaeffer

17 Feb 1820 Abraham Myers & Mary Myers of Frederick County. Bondsman, Jacob Hammack

21 Feb 1820 John Peters & Anna Kern, daughter of Nicholas Kern, the bondsman

22 Feb 1820 James Dailey & Sarah Carell. Bondsman, Joshua Littler

4 Mar 1820 James Antram & Ann Pratt, upwards of 21 years of age. Bondsman, John McKay

6 Mar 1820 Samuel Hook & Anna McMorris of Frederick County. Bondsman, George Smith

6 Mar 1820 John Slighty & Sarah White of Frederick County. Bondsman, David White

6 Mar 1820 Jacob Amick & Jane Lowan of Frederick County. Bondsman, William Bush

14 Mar 1820 Alfred Parkins & Eliza Hollingsworth of Frederick County. Bondsman, Isaac Hollingsworth

16 Mar 1820 Jacob Hunsicker & Alce Cooper, daughter of Thomas Cooper, the bondsman

17 Mar 1820 Hanijah Smallwood & Polly Trussel of Frederick County. Bondsman, John Dowell

18 Mar 1820 Henry D. Dehaven & Elizabeth Light, daughter of Frederick Light, the bondsman

20 Mar 1820 George Ash & Helen Bayliss. Bondsman, Henry Bayliss

20 Mar 1820 Thompson Adams & Elizabeth Green. Bondsman, Richard Green

20 Mar 1820 William K. Wood & Mary Campbell. Bondsman, William Campbell

21 Mar 1820 Henry Smoke & Hannah Williams. Bondsman, Willis Day

22 Mar 1820 Henry S. Turner & Lucy Lyons Hopkins. Bondsman, Joseph Lewis (Jnr?)

22 Mar 1820 Henry Glaize & Ann Yeakley. Bondsman, John Yeakley, who signs in German

23 Mar 1820 Jacob Mullenix & Elizabeth Hays. Bondsman, William Jinkins

27 Mar 1820 John Hopkins Jnr & Abby Byrd Nelson Page. Bondsman, George Murray

27 Mar 1820 Sampson Touchstone & Peggy Bowles, daughter of John Bowles of Frederick County, the bondsman

28 Mar 1820 Abraham Garrett & Phebe Bly of Frederick County. Bondsman, Abraham Teawalt

29 Mar 1820 Turner Scrogins & Mary Vaughn, daughter of Vincent Vaughn, the bondsman

Marriage Bonds No. 13 1820-23

4 Apr 1820 Daniel Oliver & Elizabeth Self, daughter of John Self Senr of Frederick County. Bondsman, John Self Junr

5 Apr 1820 Lewis Switz & Elizabeth Jones of Frederick County. Bondsman, John Denny

5 Apr 1820 Valentine Flynn & Catherine Wroe of Frederick County. Bondsman, Benjamin Wroe

6 Apr 1820 John Bruce & Sidney Smith of Frederick County. Bondsman, Philip Smith

14 Apr 1820 Joseph George & Rebecca Seevers. Bondsman, Frederick Lewis

17 Apr 1820 James Callen & Elizabeth Montgomery, daughter of Robert Montgomery, the bondsman

17 Apr 1820 Reuben Bulger & Sarah Tilman, daughter of George Tilman, the bondsman

17 Apr 1820 Mordecai Cloud & Rebecca B. Hickman of Frederick County. Bondsman, Samuel Gardner

20 Apr 1820 Henry Dudley & Magdalen Spilman of Frederick County. Bondsman, Jacob Spilman

3 May 1820 John Hiett & Elizabeth Rinker of Frederick County. Bondsman, William Clark

11 May 1820 Rezin Ashby & Maria Davis. Bondsman, James Downing

16 May 1820 Joseph Brabham & Nancy Wiley, widow of John Wiley deceased. Bondsman, Kid (Kidd) Marquiss

19 May 1820 Zedekiah Heskett & Jane Yates of Frederick County. Bondsman, John Hicks

19 May 1820 Henry Swatz & Elizabeth Day. Bondsman, Samuel Day

20 May 1820 William Denny & Elizabeth Smith, daughter of Mary Knip of Frederick County. Bondsman, Samuel S. Kline

22 May 1820 Lewis Fleet & Juliet Lowry. Bondsman, Evan Lewis

5 Jun 1820 Henry Clouser & Ragena Rozenburger of Frederick County. Bondsman, Isaac Bean

7 Jun 1820 John Rogers & Mary Allemong, widow of Daniel Allemong deceased of Frederick COunty. Bondsman, Joseph Sexton

8 Jun 1820 Jacob Spots & Margaret Scott of Frederick County. Bondsman, Daniel Crum

8 Jun 1820 John Raynolds & Sarah Rogers of Frederick County. Bondsman, Robert B. Rogers

8 Jun 1820 John Craps (Kreps) & Hannah Wright of Frederick County. Bondsman, Nathan Wright

17 Jun 1820 William M. Jones & Sarah Barnes of Frederick County. Bondsman, Austin Flynn

26 Jun 1820 John Stanford & Susan Graves of Frederick County. Bondsman, John Graves

27 Jun 1820 Willis Day & Rebecca Miller of Frederick County. Bondsman, James Dooly

27 Jun 1820 Benjamin Scriviner & Barbara Bruner. Bondsman, David Johnson (Johnston)

29 Jun 1820 Adam Jinkins & Mary Ann Dick, daughter of Henry Dick of Frederick County, the bondsman

3 Jul 1820 Isaac Hickman & Mary Ann Allensworth. Bondsman, John Jacob

8 Jul 1820 Elie Dean & Mary Murphy, widow of Samuel Murphy decd of Frederick County. Bondsman, Thomas Mahany

8 Jul 1820 John Kile & Elizabeth Berrll of Frederick County. Bondsman, Thomas Kile

20 Jul 1820 John Adams & Nancy Wiley of Frederick County. Bondsman, Adam Hart

-- Jul 1820 Hiram Gray & Sarah Poffenburger, daughter of John Poffenburger, the bondsman

25 Jul 1820 David Anderson & Polly Kackley, daughter of Abraham Kackley of Frederick County, the bondsman

27 Jul 1820 James Seevers & Rebecca Wilkin of Frederick County. Bondsman, James Hodge

31 Jul 1820 John M. Blakemore & Leticia A. Buck, daughter of Thomas Buck of Frederick County. Bondsman, Joel T. Harper

2 Aug 1820 Samuel Beatty & Mary Steel of Frederick County. Bondsman, Samuel Grubs

7 Aug 1820 Adam Kline & Catharine Jones, widow of John Jones dec. Bondsman, Jacob Bowers

15 Aug 1820 Elisha Riley & Sarah Smith of Frederick County. Bondsman, William Bailey

16 Aug 1820 Benjamin McCashland & Elizabeth Wheatly. Bondsman, John Beaty

19 Aug 1820 William Hall & Nancy Shalock. Bondsman, James Hall

24 Aug 1820 Andrew Loy & Mary Smith. Bondsman, George Smith

26 Aug 1820 Benjamin Brison & Mary Stephens, daughter of Brian M. Stephens, the bondsman

26 Aug 1820 Samuel Atwell & Nancy Ferguson. Bondsman, James Cowles

31 Aug 1820 Joel Dillon & Jane Butter of Frederick County. Bondsman, Trimble Butter

2 Aug 1820 Samuel Ryan & Ann Collings of Frederick County. Bondsman, George Ryan

4 Sep 1820 James Day & Mary Cline of Frederick County. Bondsman, John Snyder

5 Sep 1820 Walker Louthan & Eliza Carter, daughter of Arthur W. Carter, the bondsman

8 Sep 1820 Francis Thornton & Susan B. Wormeley. Bondsman, Thomas Allen Tidball

11 Sep 1820 Jonathan Dean & Sidney Steel of Frederick County. Bondsman, James Castleman

12 Sep 1820 Benjamin Burton & Eliza H. G. Ship of Frederick County. Bondsman, Edward G. Ship

16 Sep 1820 Joseph Milburn & Mary Long of Frederick County. Bondsman, Conrad Long

18 Sep 1820 Baylis Lake & Eliza Glasscock, daughter of Silas Glasscock of Frederick County, the bondsman

18 Sep 1820 James Hall & Judith Taylor, daughter of Rawleigh Taylor of Frederick County, the bondsman

20 Sep 1820 Joseph Orndorff & Elizabeth Brill. Bondsman, Henry Brill

23 Sep 1820 Hilarius Baker & Mary Allemong. Bondsman, Casper Allemong

26 Sep 1820 Leonard Robertson & Mary Ann Foley of Frederick County. Bondsman, Moses Allen

9 Oct 1820 John Bell & Sarah E. Riding. Bondsman, Edwin B. Ridings

12 Oct 1820 Chrisjohn Corder & Mary Walls of Frederick County. Bondsman, James Groves

14 Oct 1820 Nicholas Hooper & Jane I. Harris, daughter of Benjamin Harris of Frederick County, the bondsman

14 Oct 1820 Joseph Dudley & Margaret Hannum, daughter of Thomas Hannum, the bondsman

16 Oct 1820 John Senseney & Margaret Young, daughter of Anthony Young, the bondsman

17 Oct 1820 Thomas Chapman & Catharine Lemly of Frederick County. Bondsman, John Lemley

17 Oct 1820 Samuel Simpson & Mary Carson Williams of Frederick County. Bondsman, Elisha W. Carson

18 Oct 1820 William Rozenburger & Elizabeth Larrick, daughter of Henry Larrick of Frederick County, the bondsman

21 Oct 1820 William Welch & Nancy Bishop of Frederick County. Bondsman, Henry Everhart

2 Nov 1820 Russell Wilson & Alsey Timberlake. Bondsman, Richard M. S. Timberlake (added later "Alice C" above Alsey and "Brother of Alice" above Richard

6 Nov 1820 George Brown & Ann Baker, daughter of James Baker, the bondsman

6 Nov 1820 James S. Brown & Eliza Bartlett of Frederick County. Bondsman, William D. Bartlett

7 Nov 1820 Sigismund Stribling & Sarah E. T. Ware, daughter of James Ware of Frederick County. Bondsman, Alexander S. Tidball

11 Nov 1820 George Stipe & Kitty Giffen of Frederick County. Bondsman, William Giffin

13 Nov 1820 Robert Anderson & Elizabeth Cryder of Frederick County. Bondsman, John Cryder, blacksmith

13 Nov 1820 Thomas Dunn & Jane Moore. Bondsman, George R. Moore

15 Nov 1820 John Payne & Nancy C. Miller, daughter of Alexander Miller of Frederick County. Bondsman, Henry Holtzclaw

20 Nov 1820 Moses Elsey & Rachel Ellsea. Bondsman, Benjamin Langley

27 Nov 1820 John Throckmorton & Maria Lauck, daughter of William Lock, the bondsman

29 Nov 1820 Daniel Williams & Milly Ann Nolen, widow of Henry Nolen decd. of Frederick County. Bondsman, Joseph Carson

4 Dec 1820 George Shiner & Rachel Pierce. Bondsman, Jacob Gibbons

6 Dec 1820 Joseph M. Longacre & Elizabeth Sexsmith, daughter of Matthew Sexsmith of Frederick County, the bondsman

7 Dec 1820 Elisha Kearns & Rachael Whitacre. Bondsman, Nathaniel Kearns

9 Dec 1820 William Smith & Lucy Bywaters, daughter of William Bywaters, the bondsman

14 Dec 1820 Felix Good & Rachel Orndorff, daughter of John Orndorff of Frederick County

18 Dec 1820 Oliver McCasland & Frances Foster. Bondsman, Elijah Weekley

18 Dec 1820 Joseph Rees (Reace) & Maria Stillions, daughter of Newman Stillions of Frederick County. Bondsman, George Stickle

22 Dec 1820 Richard Hardin & Abegail Ruble. Bondsman, William Adams

23 Dec 1820 Henry Purtlebaugh & Margaret Howard, daughter of Anthony Howard, the bondsman

29 Dec 1820 Christopher Goodnight & Jane Mason, daughter of Andrew Mason, the bondsman

30 Dec 1820 Jonah Britten & Patsy Lock of Frederick County. Bondsman, John Lock

1 Jan 1821 William Leach & Mary Monroe. Bondsman, George Monroe

2 Jan 1821 Samuel Christy & Elizabeth Light. Bondsman, John Light

12 Jan 1821 Samuel Cox & Eleanor McDonald. Bondsman, William Cox

13 Jan 1821 William Headley & Polly Shull. Bondsman, Abraham Shull

15 Jan 1821 Joshua Phillips & Susanna Harden, daughter of George Harden, the bondsman

17 Jan 1821 Andrew Heinzman & Matilda Kern, daughter of Adam Kern of Frederick County, the bondsman

18 Jan 1821 John McClure & Sarah Burke of Frederick County. Bondsman, James G. Fricklen

20 Jan 1821 John Calvert & Ann Parrell of Frederick Country. Bondsman, James Hodge

20 Jan 1821 Thomas Gourly & Nancy Hughs, daughter of Abraham Hughs of Frederick County, the bondsman

22 Jan 1821 Joseph Files & Sarah Hansell, daughter of George Hansell of Frederick County, the bondsman, who signs in German

26 Jan 1821 George Monroe & Jane Monroe. Bondsman, John Latham

29 Jan 1821 John Halbert & Susan Butler (free negros). Bondsman, Anthony Strother (free negro)

2 Feb 1821 Alfred Turner Foster & Mary Garrett, daughter of Jacob Garrett of Frederick County, the bondsman

-- Feb 1821 Uriah Marpole & Rachel Wright, daughter of George Wright of Frederick County. William Elliott, guardian of said Uriah, & George Wright, bondsmen

3 Feb 1821 Joseph W. Kiger & Sally Townsend, widow & relict of George F. A. Townsend decd of Frederick County. Bondsman, Squire Bell

6 Feb 1821 Thomas W. Newell & Mary E. Ashby. Bondsman, Enoc R. Ashby

6 Feb 1821 James Jones & Sally Roberts of Frederick County. Bondsman, William Lane

7 Feb 1821 Marquis D. F. Hall & Sarah Silver. Bondsman, Isaac R. Gardner

8 Feb 1821 Gabriel Harris & Susanna Cooper of Frederick County. Bondsman, Thomas Cooper

16 Feb 1821 John Himelright & Catherine Strowderman. Bondsman, Jonathan Kackley

19 Feb 1821 John Pumphrey & Mary Hamilton. Bondsman, Thomas Hamilton

20 Feb 1821 Charles Mylinger & Eliza Newham of Frederick County. Bondsman, Beatty Carson

20 Feb 1821 John Griffith & Margaret Clendening. Bondsman, Andrew Clendening

20 Feb 1821 Alexander Finnell & Catharine Mitchell widow & relict of John Mitchell deceased of Frederick County Bondsman, Reuben Finnell jr

24 Feb 1821 John McDaniel & Margaret Young. Bondsman, Henry Christie

3 Mar 1821 Robert Luttrell & Fanny Grove, daughter of Jacob Grove, the bondsman

3 Mar 1821 John Middleton & Elizabeth Fleming, daughter of Archibald Fleming. Bondsman, John W. Fleming

5 Mar 1821 James Crabb & Rhoda Garner. Bondsman, Peter Dick

5 Mar 1821 Jacob Hoffman & Elizabeth Sperry. Bondsman, Elia Snyder

5 Mar 1821 Jabez Carter & Elizabeth Smith, ward of Jacob Smith, the bondsman

7 Mar 1821 William Swann & Eliza Kiger. Bondsman, Joseph W. Kiger

13 Mar 1821 William Williams & Sarah Clyne, daughter of Michael Clyne of Frederick County, the bondsman

13 Mar 1813 George Kerns & Elizabeth Griffin. Bondsman, Samuel Giffin

15 Mar 1821 Thomas Lipscomb & Susanna White of Frederick County. Bondsman, George Wolfe

19 Mar 1821 John Orenduph (sic) & Margaret Cochran of Frederick COunty. Bondsman, William Cochran

-- Mar 1821 Joseph Sole & Lucinda Griggsby, daughter of Redmon Griggsby of Frederick County, the bondsman

19 Mar 1821 John Dalby & Jane Wigginton, daughter of Joseph Wigginton of Frederick County, the bondsman

21 Mar 1821 Jacob Ridgway & Ann Royer. Bondsman, William Chapman

21 Mar 1821 Andrew Showalter & Polly McFarland of Frederick County. Bondsman, John Snyder

21 Mar 1821 George Shut & Catharine Light, daughter of Elizabeth Light of Frederick County, the bondsman

24 Mar 1821 John Games & Hester French. Bondsman, Walter French

28 Mar 1821 John Gardner & Lucinda Thompson. Bondsman, Robert Sharman

29 Mar 1821 Thomas Taylor & Clarissa Verta (free negroes). Bondsman, William McPherson (free negro)

31 Mar 1821 Nathaniel Templeman & Delia Strother. Bondsman, Enoch Strother

2 Apr 1821 George Mauch & Elizabeth Christy. Bondsman, James Christie

2 Apr 1821 David S. Danner & Polly Oysler. Bondsman, James Anderson

9 Apr 1821 James Tait & Jane Sutherland, daughter of John Sutherland of Frederick County, the bondsman

9 Apr 1821 John Johnston & Catherine Day, daughter of Samuel Day of Frederick County, the bondsman

11 Apr 1821 James Stackhouse & Elizabeth Pritchard of Frederick County. Bondsman, Job S. Hendrick

16 Apr 1821 William Pennabaker & Elizabeth Howe. Bondsman, John Howe

23 Apr 1821 John Wade & Martha Brabham. Bondsman, McCarty D. Roy

24 Apr 1821 James Dooley & Catherine Miller. Bondsman, Jacob Crizer

25 Apr 1821 Joel Ward junr & Rachel B. Donaldson of Frederick County. Bondsman, Robert Montgomery

30 Apr 1821 John Morrow & Jane L. Kennon of Frederick County. Bondsman, John Lefevre

8 May 1821 Thomas Veach & Lydia Myers, widow & relict of Jacob Myers decd of Frederick County. Bondsman, John Snyder

24 May 1821 David Markwood & Elizabeth Ensley, daughter of William Ensley, the bondsman

2 Jun 1821 Henry Lloyd & Nelly Warren. Bondsman, John Shafer

2 Jun 1821 Peter McMurray & Rebecca Reed. Bondsman, William Reed

2 Jun 1821 Stephen Bell & Martha Lynn of Frederick County. Bondsman, James McCleary

7 Jun 1821 William M. Robertson & Elizabeth Henry. Bondsman, William Vanmetre

7 Jun 1821 Gabriel Benn & Jane Brown. Bondsman, Edward Turner

9 Jun 1821 Uriah Parke & Susan Sample, daughter of Joseph Sample of Frederick County, the bondsman

19 Jun 1821 Zachariah Garner & Sarah McCarty, daughter of Joseph McCarty of Frederick County, the bondsman

26 Jun 1821 Barnett Smith & Mary Orr of Frederick County. Bondsman, Henry Rush

27 Jun 1821 Peyton Southard & Rhoda Rhodes. Bondsman, John Rhodes

5 Jul 1821 Severn Conner & Hannah Hall, daughter of Thomas Hall of Frederick County, the bondsman

19 Jul 1821 Benjamin Elliott & Maria R. Brown of Frederick County. Bondsman, John Baker

21 Jul 1821 Rice Parker & Mary Campbell, widow of -- Campbell deceased of Frederick County. Bondsman, Stephen Johnson

21 Jul 1821 Henry Stickle & Phebe Swick. Bondsman, George Stickle

27 Jul 1821 Benjamin Shambaugh & Isabella Vannort, daughter of Jacob Vannort, the bondsman

1 Aug 1821 John Lewis & Elizabeth Trowbridge of Frederick County. Bondsman, James Carpenter

6 Aug 1820 James Hoover & Leah Cooper. Bondsman, Peter Reynard

6 Aug 1821 William S. Burgess & Catherine I. Wykoff, daughter of Cornelius Wykoff of Frederick County, the bondsman

6 AUg 1821 John B. McLeod & Ann S. Carson, daughter of Simon Carson of Frederick County, the bondsman

7 Aug 1821 Joseph Smith & Eliza Bell, daughter of John Bell of Frederick County, the bondsman

10 Aug 1821 William Trussell & Nancy Reed of Frederick County. Bondsman, John Cockran

18 Aug 1821 Samuel Rogers & Catherine Fisher of Frederick County. Bondsman, William Smith

21 Aug 1821 Jacob Hite & Mary Tapp, daughter of Samuel Tapp, the bondsman

25 Aug 1821 Austin Flynn & Elizabeth Barnes of Frederick County. Bondsman, Edward Barnes

27 Aug 1821 Washington Jarvis & Louisa Wright, daughter of Jothan Wright, the bondsman

22 Aug 1821 Aaron Emmons & Rebecca Rogers of Frederick County. Bondsman, William Rogers

28 Aug 1821 William Gray & Nancy Leizure, daughter of Zepheniah Leizure. Bondsman, Hammans (Hannans?) Gray

31 Aug 1821 Dabney Cauthen & Catharine Loy. Bondsman, John Shaver

3 Sep 1821 Joseph Sperry & Elizabeth Leonard. Bondsman, William Rogers

4 Sep 1821 John I. Johnston & Emily Brownley of Frederick County. Bondsman, James Castleman

7 Sep 1821 Ishmael Vanhorn & Evalina Morgan of Frederick County. Bondsman, John O Conner

8 Sep 1821 Benjamin Tanquary & Lydia Hackney. Bondsman, Walter Tanquary

15 Sep 1821 Henry Guard & Juliet Hotzenpiller of Frederick County. Bondsman, Isaac Conrad

15 Sep 1821 John Williams & Martha Chrismell of Frederick County. Bondsman, Peter Chrisman

17 Sep 1821 John Loye & Mary Marpole. Bondsmen, Benjamin Marpole & Conrad Loye

27 Sep 1821 George H. Raynolds Jr. & Frances C. Williams. Bondsman, George Raynolds Sen

1 Oct 1821 Thomas B. Harvy & Jane S. Tupler of Frederick County. Bondsman, George Fyst

4 Oct 1821 Joseph Smith & Sarah Vincent, daughter of Cornelius Vincent, the bondsman

4 Oct 1821 Edmund N. Grigsby & Lucinda B. Harris of Frederick County. Bondsman, Henry Harris

5 Oct 1821 James Ridings & Ann Newman. Bondsman, Thos Newman

6 Oct 1821 William Thompson & Ann Louisa Sharpless of Frederick County. Bondsman, Augustine Smith

9 Oct 1821 Joseph Lang & Eliza Wilson. Bondsman, Peter Keeding

15 Oct 1821 Henry S. Rodes & Ann Senseney. Bondsman, John Senseney

26 Oct 1821 Joseph Spilman & Margaret Whissent, daughter of John Whissent, the bondsman

27 Oct 1821 Evan Peyton & Mary Ann Jenkins, daughter of Edward Jenkins, the bondsman

30 Oct 1821 Griffin Chiles & Mary Ann Cole, daughter of Isaac Cole of Frederick County, the bondsman

30 Oct 1821 William Fraley & Mary Snyder, daughter of Jacob Snyder, the bondsman, who signs in German

30 Oct 1821 William Foushee & Mildred I. Thatcher of Frederick COunty. Bondsman, Gabriel S. Jones

31 Oct 1821 John Smith, son of Christian Smith, & Eliza Pickerel, daughter of Jonathan Pickerel of Frederick County. Fathers are bondsmen

1 Nov 1821 Isaac White, upward of 21, & Mary Patty, daughter of George Patty of Frederick County, the bondsman

2 Nov 1821 John Krim & Phoebe Drake, widow of Gersham Drake of Frederick County. Bondsman, Robert B. White

14 Nov 1821 Reson Mason & Mary Dick, daughter of Peter Dick of Frederick County, the bondsman

20 Nov 1821 Richard D. Lee & Hannah Briarly. Bondsman, James Briarly

28 Nov 1821 Henry F. Baker, son of John Baker, & Sidney Carter, ward of Joseph W. Carter of Frederick County. Bondsmen, (?Jno) Baker & Joseph W. Carter

30 Nov 1821 Jesse White & Catherine Stipe, daughter of Henry Stipe

4 Dec 1821 James Lessenger & Julian J. Wilson of Frederick County. Bondsman, Thomas Allen Tidball

8 Dec 1821 John White & Sarah McIlwee of Frederick County. Bondsman, John McIlwee

8 Dec 1821 John Shane & Catharine Mason, daughter of Bingley Mason of Frederick County, the bondsman

10 Dec 1821 John Foster & Mary Kingore, daughter of William Kingore of Frederick County, the bondsman

11 Dec 1821 William Rhodes & Eliza Baldwin. Bondsman, Joshua Baldwin

12 Dec 1821 John Jacob & Mary Thatcher, daughter of Thomas Thatcher. Bondsman, Jacob Crizer

17 Dec 1821 George Shaffner & Susannah Curtis. Bondsman, Leonard Hiett

18 Dec 1821 Leroy W. Swift & Delilah Dent, daughter of Thomas Dent of Frederick County, the bondsman

19 Dec 1821 James Alexander & Jane Peyton, daughter of William Peyton, the bondsman

19 Dec 1821 Daniel Ramey, son of Isaac Ramey, & Catharine Grases (Graves?). Bondsman, Isaac Ramey

22 Dec 1821 Wilson Whitacre & Rachel Kerns of Frederick County. Bondsman, Jonas Whitacre

24 Dec 1821 Robert Albin, son of Andrew Albin, & Elizabeth Carter, daughter of Edmund Carter of Frederick County. Fathers are bondsmen

24 Dec 1821 Daniel Fagle & Harriet Bean. Bondsman, Robert Anderson

24 Dec 1821 John Gander & Catharine Shull. Bondsman, Abraham Shull

26 Dec 1821 George Pearson & Elizabeth Britton. Bondsman, James Lynn

31 Dec 1821 John Harper & Hannah Gilham of Frederick County, ward of William Clevenger, the bondsman

31 Dec 1821 James Ritter & Mary Likens. Bondsman, David Likens

2 Jan 1822 Dempsey Carroll & Jane Arnold, daughter of William Arnold of Frederick County, the bondsman

10 Jan 1822 John Pritchett & Rebecca Phalen. Bondsman, Solemon Bishop

14 Jan 1822 John Taylor & Mary C. Kercheval, daughter of Samuel Kercheval, the bondsman

29 Jan 1822 Caspar Rinker & Isabella Copeland, daughter of William Copeland of Frederick County, the bondsman

29 Jan 1822 John Gough & Leah Spillman. Bondsman, Joseph Spilman

2 Feb 1822 Samuel Coe & Catharine Bagent. Bondsman, John Beagant

4 Feb 1822 John Murray & Mary Cahill, daughter of William Cahill of Frederick County, the bondsman

4 Feb 1822 Enoch Marple, ward of Benjamin Marple, & Deborah Davis, daughter of James Davis of Frederick County, the bondsman

6 Feb 1822 Thomas Carr & Mary Blue of Frederick County. Bondsman Andrew McGarrety

7 Feb 1822 John B. Kerfoot & Elizabeth Taylor, daughter of Manly Taylor of Frederick County, the bondsman

9 Feb 1822 Jacob Snyder & Margaret Hughs, daughter of William Hughs of Frederick County, the bondsman

11 Feb 1822 Humphrey Shepherd & Catherine Crigler of Frederick County. Bondsman, Benjamin Crigler

12 Feb 1822 Alexander Simpson & Elizabeth Churchill. Bondsman, Armistead Churchill

13 Feb 1822 Robert Finley & Mary Hastings, daughter of John Hastings of Frederick County

13 Feb 1822 David Farrell, a widower & Elizabeth Whollihan, ward of David Fries of Frederick County

16 Feb 1822 William Hamilton & Nancy Demoff, widow & relict of Throckmorton Demoff

18 Feb 1822 David Buzzard & Louisa Baker, daughter of Jacob Baker

18 Feb 1822 James Bennett & Emalina Kiger, daughter of George Kiger

19 Feb 1822 James Redd & Elizabeth Myers. Bondsman, John Stephens

20 Feb 1822 Levy Griffin & Elizabeth Bedinger. Bondsman, George Griffin

20 Feb 1822 Mason Chiles & Elizabeth Cain. Bondsman, Levi Cain

20 Feb 1822 William Henry Foote & Eliza W. Glass. Bondsman, Robert Gray

21 Feb 1822 Samuel Wilson & Eliza W. Littler. Bondsman, Charles W. Littler

25 Feb 1822 Jonah Lupton & Mary Smith. Bondsman, Patrick Smith

26 Feb 1822 John B. Weldon & Sarah Flore. Bondsman, John Flore

4 Mar 1822 John Monroe & Malinda Wilkerson. Bondsman, George Monroe

4 Mar 1822 Joseph Stephens & Eliza Clayton. Bondsman, James Redd

4 Mar 1822 Elisha Smallwood & Mary Kern, daughter of Nicholas Kern

6 Mar 1822 Daniel Purtlebaugh & Eliza Mayhugh. Bondsman, Nathaniel Mayhugh

7 Mar 1822 Jesse Wood & Hannah Hollingsworth. Bondsman, Thomas Allen Tidball

8 Mar 1822 Thomas Stallions & Preny Warren. Bondsman, Henry Lloyd

9 Mar 1822 Smith Hancher & Mary Stewart, daughter of Samuel Stewart

11 Mar 1822 Abraham Miller & Anna Stickley, daughter of Abraham Stickley of Frederick County

11 Mar 1822 Nathaniel C. Lupton & Elizabeth Hodgson, daughter of Abner Hodgson of Frederick County

12 Mar 1822 Martin Rowland & Margaret Campbell. Bondsman, Harrison Wade

12 Mar 1822 John Bowman & Mary Ann Grim of Frederick County. Bondsman, John Grim, who signs in German

15 Mar 1822 John Muckay & Catharine Pangle of Frederick County. Bondsman, Jacob Pangle. Ages sworn to by Jacob Pangle

16 Mar 1822 Robert Evans & Catharine Richards of Frederick County. Bondsman, Michael White

18 Mar 1822 Jonathan Mason & Helen Braithwaite. Bondsman, William Braithwaite

18 Mar 1822 Lewis Sullivan & Sarah Clark. Bondsman, William Clark

19 Mar 1822 Abraham Ramsey & Susanna Thompson, widow & relict of James Thompson decd of Frederick County. Bondsman, Jacob Spotts

28 Mar 1822 John Sappington & Sarah Carter, daughter of Arthur W. Carter, the bondsman

28 Mar 1822 John Mumma & Peggy Hass. Bondsman, Conrad Hass, who made oath that Peggy is upwards of 21

29 Mar 1822 John Stephenson & Catherine Kindrick. Bondsman, Samuel Kindrick

1 Apr 1822 Joseph Brill & Rebecca Orndorff, daughter of Samuel Orndorff, the bondsman

1 Apr 1822 William T. Helm & Mary Page Brooke. Bondsman, Thomas Blakemore

2 Apr 1822 Peter Lauck & Sarah Frigg, daughter of Thomas Frigg, the bondsman

9 Apr 1822 Oscar Peake & Mary Ellen Sydnor. Bondsman, John Hening

10 Apr 1822 Daniel Shats & Sarah Lay, daughter of Michael Lay, the bondsman

11 Apr 1822 John B. Moreland & Salazy Lloyd, daughter of Samuel Lloye, the bondsman

22 Apr 1822 James Briscoe & Catharine Bazle, daughter of John Bazzle, the bondsman

22 Apr 1822 George Johnson & Mary Day, daughter of Samuel Day of Frederick County, the bondsman

22 Apr 1822 Samuel Griffith & Rebecca Myers, daughter of John Myers of Frederick County, the bondsman

23 Apr 1822 Peter Pendergast & Frances Cordell. Bondsman, John Heel

25 Apr 1822 Peter E. Sperry & Regina Austin. Bondsman, Lewis Lindsey

29 Apr 1822 Abraham Berkeley & Sally Peters. Bondsman, Abner Peters

30 Apr 1822 Daniel Miller & Susan Strother. Bondsman, Enoch Strother

1 May 1822 John Gordon & Sarah Williams. Bondsman, David Cather

1 May 1822 James Douglass & Elizabeth Helpbringer. Bondsman, Cornelius Vincent

6 May 1822 Joseph Jennings & Evalina Withers, ward of Joseph Jennings. Bondsman, Daniel Jennings

6 May 1822 Alexander Brenton & Rebecca Shull. Bondsman, Moses Russell

6 May 1822 Aquilla I. Haines & Elizabeth Taylor. Bondsman, Joseph Hackney

7 May 1822 Jasper McKee & Malinda Anderson, daughter of Thomas Anderson, the bondsman

7 May 1822 Providence Mounts & Emily L. I. W. Noble. Bondsman, William Taylor

7 May 1822 Daniel Grim, son of John Grim, & Rebecca Miller. Bondsmen, Daniel Klyne & John Grim; latter signs in German

7 May 1822 John Hopper & Elizabeth B. Timberlake, daughter of William Timberlake, the bondsman

11 May 1822 George Smith & Mary Crum. Bondsman, Abraham Crum

11 May 1822 James Grantham & Elizabeth Claspill, daughter of Robert R. Claspill (Glaspill?), the bondsman

15 May 1822 Abraham Shull & Rachel Lukins. Bondsman, Joseph F. Lukens

20 May 1822 Chapline E. McCormick & Lydia Gordon. Bondsman, William Dillon

20 May 1822 John Brill & Rachel Cooper. Bondsman, John Cooper

23 May 1822 Peter H. Doyle, upward of 21, & Betsy Marpole. Bondsman, David Marpole. Henry Doyle made oath as to age of groom

24 May 1822 Richard Swift & Mary McGrogan, upward of 21. Bondsman, Thomas Duke
27 May 1822 Richard Osborn & Patsy Shepherd. Bondsman, Humphrey Shepherd
29 May 1822 Thomas Kennerley & Ann Susan Carnegy. Bondsman, Ely Beall
1 Jun 1822 Jesse Furr & Margaret Waggoner. Bondsman, Daniel Stickles
4 Jun 1822 James Smith, son of Christian Smith, & Elizabeth Teawalt, daughter of Peter Teawalt. Fathers are bondsmen
8 Jun 1822 George Unbemhower & Mary Umpenour, daughter of Abraham Umbehouer, the bondsman
8 Jun 1822 John C. Ford & Margaret Leach, upwards of 21. Bondsman, William Leach
10 Jun 1822 George Stephens & Mary Ann Clark, daughter of Reuben Clark, the bondsman
12 Jun 1822 John W. Cooper & Rhoda OBoyle, widow & relict of James OBoyle deceased. Bondsman, John McCoole
24 Jun 1822 Isaac Shipe & Clarissa Turner. Bondsman, Joseph Barns
24 Jun 1822 Samuel McDonald & Elizabeth Graves. Bondsman, John Standford
6 Jul 1822 Francis C. Brown & Mary Ann Newman. Bondsman, Buckner Ashby
8 Jul 1822 Samuel Davis & Nancy McGuinn, widow & relict of Philip McGuinn decd late of Frederick County. Bondsman, William Northern
15 Jul 1822 William Hopewell & Catharine C. Pagett, daughter of Edmund Pagett
22 Jul 1822 William Turner & Charlotte Ashby. Bondsman, Robert Ashby
22 Jul 1822 John Carroll & Philadelphia Ashby. Bondsman, Robert Ashby
31 Jul 1822 Aquilla Allen & Sarah Ann Trenary. Bondsman, Isaac R. Gardner
31 Jul 1822 Thornburgh Grubbs & Mary Beaty. Bondsman, Robert Beaty junr
1 Aug 1822 Shelton McDaniel & Mary Lyons. Bondsman, James Lyons
2 Aug 1822 Conrad Hess & Elizabeth Barton. Bondsman, David Devoe
3 Aug 1822 Isaac H. Pettit & Malinda Walter, daughter of William Walter. Bondsman, Zepheniah K. Walter

6 Aug 1822 Timothy McMan & Mary Gold. Bondsman, James Riely

7 Aug 1822 James Hodge & Elizabeth Cooper, daughter of Thomas Cooper, the bondsman

7 Aug 1822 James B. Hall & Margaret Rozenburger, ward of William Bean, the bondsman

14 Aug 1822 Matthew Rust & Margaret Rust, daughter of Peter Rust, the bondsman

16 Aug 1822 Elisha Carver & Elizabeth Ryan. Bondsman, Samuel W. Perry

26 Aug 1822 Henry Eaton & Catharine Butter. Bondsman, Jacob Oats Jnr

26 Aug 1822 William Mann & Sarah Rinker, daughter of Jacob Rinker, the bondsman

27 Aug 1822 WIlliam D. Holliday & Arianne A. Smith. Bondsman, John Bruce

28 Aug 1822 William S. Newton & Mary McCandless. Bondsman, John Macky

3 Sep 1822 Arthur W. Carter & Ruth M. Noble, widow of John Noble. Bondsman, Thomas Allen Tidball

3 Sep 1822 George W. Kiger & Ann Jane Richards. Bondsman, Thomas Allen Tidball. Henry Richards listed at top of bond

4 Sep 1822 Joseph Scott & Jane Collins, upwards of 21. Bondsman, Moses Collins

11 Sep 1822 William Miller & Sarah Lutteral, daughter of Fielding Lutterell

11 Sep 1822 George Bowling & Mary Stewart, both upwards of 21. Bondsman, William Stewart

11 Sep 1822 Walter Watson & Cassandra Gill, daughter of John Gill, the bondsman

14 Sep 1822 Richard Spurr & Nancy Scarff. Bondsman, William Scarff

17 Jul 1822 Thomas Williamson & Elizabeth Fisher. Bondsman, John McCoole

19 Sep 1822 Eli A. Snyder, son of John Snyder, & Elizabeth McFarlene, daughter of John McFarlene, the bondsman

21 Sep 1822 James Williams & Catherine Myers, daughter of John Myers, the bondsman

23 Sep 1822 Joseph Hansel, son of George Hansel, & Sarah Lemly. Bondsman, George Hansel, who signs in German

23 Sep 1822 John Smoke & Mary Sample. Bondsman, Joseph Sample

24 Sep 1822 John L. Buck & Annie C. Buck, daughter of Thomas Buck junr, the bondsman
25 Sep 1822 Jacob Switzick & Sarah Camerer. Bondsman, William Coffee. Groom signs in German
28 Sep 1822 Peter Gilham & Eliza Jackson, ward of Isaac Bean, the bondsman
30 Sep 1822 Isaac Rogers & Maria Jane Pugh, ward of said Isaac Rogers. Bondsman, James Colville
30 Sep 1822 John McCoole & Cassandra A. Dent, daughter of Thomas Dent, the bondsman
9 Oct 1822 Robert Harrison & Eliza Bruce. Bondsman, Joseph McIntosh
12 Oct 1822 Hiram Taylor & Phebe Lee. Bondsman, George Hensel
14 Oct 1822 Israel Smallwood & Elizabeth Hargrave, daughter of WIlliam Hargrave, the bondsman
19 Oct 1822 Eli Crupper & Fanny Bostyon, daughter of Adam Bostyon, the bondsman
19 Oct 1822 Fielding Luttrell & Elizabeth Miller. Bondsman, Casper Miller
21 Oct 1822 Simpson Glaze & Elizabeth Renner, daughter of Isaac Renner, the bondsman
22 Oct 1822 William P. Branson & Elizabeth Frances Hale. Bondsman, George Hale
24 Oct 1822 John Harkins & Nancy Osborn. Bondsman, James Osborn
26 Oct 1822 Townsend W. Thomas & Evelina O. Shackelford, daughter of Samuel T. Shackelford
28 Oct 1822 John Harris & Elizabeth Northern. Bondsman, Edmond N. Griggsby
28 Oct 1822 William Vincent & Mary Smith. Bondsman, Jacob Weaver
30 Oct 1822 Asbury Jarrett & Eliza S. Lefevre, daughter of John Lefevre, the bondsman
2 Nov 1822 Abner Peters & Mary Stephens, daughter of Henry Stephens, the bondsman
5 Nov 1822 James R. Kain & Susannah Kline. Bondsmen, James Stiele & Eleaser Barrow
9 Nov 1822 Adam Carter & Barbara Shaffner. Bondsman, George Shaffner
11 Nov 1822 Jacob Shinholtzer & Hannah Loy, daughter of Conrad Loy, the bondsman
15 Nov 1822 Jacob Berlin & Polly Krouse. Bondsman, John Smith

16 Nov 1822 Thomas Eaton & Mary Dawson. Bondmsan, Jacob Kerns
20 Nov 1822 John Aliff & Catharine Allison. Bondsman, Martin Allison
20 Nov 1822 James White & Polly Spotts. Bondsman, Lewis A. Smith
23 Nov 1822 Eli Beck & Sarah Hall. Bondsman, James B. Hall
28 Nov 1822 Jacob Carper & Eley Keller, daughter of Jacob Keller, the bondsman
2 Dec 1822 Isaac Kile & Marine Huntsberry, daughter of Conrad Huntsberry, the bondsman
2 Dec 1822 James Withers & Frances Funston, daughter of Oliver Funston, the bondsman
16 Dec 1822 Richard Luttrell & Mary Grove. Bondsman, Jacob Grove
17 Dec 1822 Marshall Rust & Augusta Redman. Bondsman, John Rust
21 Dec 1822 Charles Carlyle, son of William Carlyle, & Ann Crampton. Bondsman, father of groom
23 Dec 1822 Abraham McKay & Harriet Stephens, daughter of Bryan M. Stephens, the bondsman
24 Dec 1822 David Gander & Rachel Shull. Bondsman, Abraham Shull
25 Dec 1822 Moses Bales & Rebecca Stanford. Bondsman, John Stanford
26 Dec 1822 James Abrell & Mary Foy. Bondsman, Joseph Abrell
30 Dec 1822 Enos Osburn & Sarah Castleman. Bondsman, Stephen Castleman
31 Dec 1822 James Affleck & Catharine Hotzenpiller. Bondsman, James Jones
1 Jan 1823 Gersham Silver & Mary Elkins. Bondsman, John Painter
3 Jan 1823 Samuel Thompson & Hannah Noland, daughter of Obed Noland, the bondsman
7 Jan 1823 John Lupton & Rebecca Campbell daughter of William Campbell, the bondsman
7 Jan 1823 Daniel Sowers & Martha E. Rust daughter of John Rust, the bondsman
7 Jan 1823 Allen Williams & Helen M. Helm Bondsman, John Jolliffe

Marriage Bonds No. 14   1823-1828
Frederick County, Virginia

11 Jan 1823 Michael H. Reed & Delilah Ann Hodgson. Bondsman, William Campbell

15 Jan 1823 Benjamin Mainer Sr & Catharine Roach. Bondsman, Henderson Lucas

15 Jan 1823 William Bartlett & Eleanor Grubbs. Bondsman, David Timberlake

17 Jan 1823 Martin B. Clevenger & Elizabeth Chinn (Chism?). Bondsman, James Chinn (Chism?)

21 Jan 1823 John Milhorn & Mary Shull. Bondsman, Lewis Shull

31 Jan 1823 Peter Dick junior & Massy McKnut. Bondsman, John McCoole

1 Feb 1823 Jacob Ritter & Sarah Dailey, daughter of Samuel Dailey, the bondsman

3 Feb 1823 Henry Buzzard & Mary Grove, daughter of Adam Grove, the bondsman

3 Feb 1823 Duncan T. Massie, son of Thomas Massie, & Louzetta Tuley, ward of Henry Mitchell, the bondsman

4 Feb 1823 George McKay & Mary Ferguson. Bondsman, Jacob McKay

6 Feb 1823 John Simpson & Nancy Lang. Bondsman, John Lang Junior

7 Feb 1823 William H. Vanacka & Sarah Sullivan, daughter of Henry Sullivan, the bondsman

10 Feb 1823 James Fry & Martha Gilham. Bondsman, Henry Brill

10 Feb 1823 William Grimes & Lydia Minser. Bondsman, David Rees

10 Feb 1823 Samuel Grubbs & Margarite Windsor, daughter of Jonathan Windsor. Bondsman, John Laws

12 Feb 1823 Alfred Garrett & Eliza Gilham. Bondsman, Benjamin King

12 Feb 1823 Abraham Supinger & Barbara Mauck, daughter of Michael Mauck, the bondsman

17 Feb 1823 Joseph Keeler & Elizabeth Pangle, daughter of Joseph Pangle, the bondsman

17 Feb 1823 Isaac Watson & Evelina Longacre. Bondsman, Watson Carr

21 Feb 1823 Thomas Carson & Catharine Showalter. Bondsman, Andrew Showalter, who signs in German

21 Feb 1823 Daniel Heflebower & Nancy Noland. Bondsman, Jacob Keller

26 Feb 1823 Alfred Carter & Mary Triplett. Bondsman, Samuel Ellsea

26 Feb 1823 Joshua Baldwin & Elizabeth B. George, daughter of William George, the bondsman

8 Mar 1823 George Bartlebaugh & Delbora Babb, ward of Joseph Babb

12 Mar 1823 William Bulger & Catharine Castleman, daughter of John Castleman, the bondsman

17 Mar 1823 Enoch Lewis, son of Evin Lewis, and Joanna Jennings, daughter of Daniel Jennings, the bondsman

17 Mar 1823 Zebedee Gray & Nancy Dowell. Bondsman, Jacob Snyder, who signs in German

21 Mar 1823 Henry Samsell & Susanna Williams, daughter of John Williams, the bondsman

24 Mar 1823 William McDonald & Lucinda Ferguson. Bondsman, William Castleman Junior

25 Mar 1823 Richard Franklin & Elizabeth Stone. Bondsman, Thomas Stone

3 Apr 1823 Charles M. Thorp & Maria L. Darlington. Bondsman, George Hansell

5 Apr 1823 Thomas Turner & Hannah Anderson. Bondsman, George Simpson

7 Apr 1823 John Crum & Rachel McCartney, daughter of Joseph McCartney, the bondsman

8 Apr 1823 John Law & Sarah Windsor. Bondsman, Samuel Grubs

14 Apr 1823 Thomas Fletcher & Barbara Wolery. Bondsman, Jacob Wolery

15 Apr 1823 Washington G. Singleton & Maria A. Waite, daughter of Obed Waite, the bondsman

15 Apr 1823 Abraham Crum & Rebecca McCord, daughter of George McCord senior, the bondsman

19 Apr 1823 Isaac Sidebottom & Mary Ann Ryan. Bondsman, Samuel Ryan

19 Apr 1823 Thomas Linkheart, son of Barney Linkheart, & Ellen Fisher. Bondsman, Barney Linkheart

19 Apr 1823 John Brotherton & Mary Brotherton (Brotherton crossed out & Hodge written above), daughter of Robert Hodge, the bondsman

21 Apr 1823 Peter Shierly & Elizabeth Zeiler, daughter of Peter Zeiler, the bondsman

23 Apr 1823 Gershum Richards & Harriet Malcolm, daughter of Walter Malcolm, the bondsman

30 Apr 1823 Richard John McKim Holliday & Mary Catherine Taylor. Bondsman, Robert T. Baldwin

7 May 1823 Andrew L. Hieronimus & Mary M. Burkhammer. Bondsman, Hieronimus Dicks

12 May 1823 John Nevill, son of Henry Nevill, & Elizabeth Carper, daughter of Frederick Carper. Fathers are bondsmen

13 May 1823 John Ricketts & Eliza Robinson, daughter of Gary Robinson, the bondsman

14 May 1823 Samuel Giffin & Ann Mckee, daughter of William Mckee. Bondsman, William Giffin

14 May 1823 Benjamin Dixon & Ann Mercer. Bondsman, Henry Moon

17 May 1823 David S. Carr & Eleanor Pope. Bondsman, Edmond Pope

26 May 1823 Newton Headley & Mary E. Northern. Bondsman, William Northern

28 May 1823 Joel Pennybaker & Margaret Perry Stribling. Bondsman, Thomas Stribling

30 May 1823 William Niswanger & Mary Wood, daughter of Isaac Wood. Bondsman, Alexander Wood

16 Jun 1823 Francis Stribling Jr & Rebecca Littler. Bondsman, Charles N. Littler

16 Jun 1823 Thomas Stribling & Rachel Ann Littler. Bondsman, Charles N. Littler

16 Jun 1823 Henry Seevers Jnr & Elizabeth Shumate. Bondsman, Tilman Shumate

16 Jun 1823 James H. Smith & Sidney T. Williams. Bondsman, Otho L. Williams

23 Jun 1823 Samuel Lewin & Anne Brown, daughter of George Brown of Frederick County. Bondsman, Moses N. Brown

12 Jul 1823 Hezekiah Trenary & Elizabeth Handle. Bondsman, Nicholas Handle

17 Jul 1823 James B. Simons & Elizabeth Rodes. Bondsman, David Bryarly

26 Jul 1823 Hiram Bishop & Eleanor Holland, daughter of John Holland, the bondsman

30 Jul 1823 James Hanum & Sarah Clouser. Bondsman, Benjamin Clouser

31 Jul 1823 Lewis Leepold & Sarah Cooley, daughter of Peter Cooley, the bondsman

5 Aug 1823 Jacob Kearns & Mary Rosebrough, ward of Jacob Kerns. Bondsman, John Rosebrough, who signs in German

13 Aug 1823 John Lanham & Matilda Fish. Bondsman, Robert Fish

18 Aug 1823 Michael Smith & Rebecca Umbenhuer. Bondsman, Samuel M. Marquis

20 Aug 1823 Harvey Evans & Emely Hesser. Bondsman, John OConner

25 Aug 1823 Richard Wells & Jane Reddice Carson, daughter of Simon Carson, the bondsman

30 Aug 1823 David Vanskivers & Catherine Bales. Bondsman, Moses Beals

30 Aug 1823 John Beagant & Mary Clark, daughter of Abner Clark, the bondsman

1 Sep 1823 John Corder & his ward Sarah Ramey. Bondsman, Isaac R. Elsea

1 Sep 1823 Thornton Haines & Sarah Barr, orphan of John Barr dec & ward of Peter Royston, the bondsman

4 Sep 1823 John Baughman & Elizabeth Hewitt, widow of Daniel Hewitt decd. Bondsman, John Gruber

15 Sep 1823 Thomas Hamilton & Elizabth Windsor. Bondsman, Jonathan Windsor

22 Sep 1823 Thomas McLeod & Elizabeth Ritenour. Bondsman, George Ritenour

27 Sep 1823 Lewis George & Rebecca Barrett. Bondsman, Benjamin Barrett

2 Oct 1823 Isaac D. Mills & Charlotte Sumption. Bondsman, Nelson Foster

6 Oct 1823 Joseph Russell & Jane Richards. Bondsman, George N. Kiger

8 Oct 1823 John Leizure & Nancy Hardin. Bondsman, George Hardin

22 Oct 1823 John Faughanden & Huldah Settlemyers. Bondsman, Frederick Ayrison

29 Oct 1823 Charles McBean & Sarah Harrison of said county. Bondsman, Isaac Harrison

3 Nov 1823 Thomas Chew & Julia Minser. Bondsman, William Huggins

5 Nov 1823 Jacob Weaver & Allianor Beall. Bondsman, John Weaver

7 Nov 1823 Uriah McKnight & Fanny Anderson. Bondsman, John Bruner

12 Nov 1823 Thomas Hiett & Isabella Jane Wilkin, widow & relict of William Wilkin deceased. Bondsman, William Thomas

13 Nov 1823 Joseph Kenny & Ann Windle, widow & relict of Samuel Wildle deceased. Bondsman, John Reed

18 Nov 1823 James H. Bowen & Lucinda Wilkeson. Bondsman, John W. Wilkinson

22 Nov 1823 James McPherson & Jemimah Pearson, widow of James Pearson dec. Bondsman, Jacob Rees

22 Nov 1823 Edward Williams & Rebecca Rees. Bondsman, Jacob Rees

27 Nov 1823 William Shannon & Frances Wilkey. Bondsman, Frances (her mark) Tapp, who made oath that bride is over 21

1 Dec 1823 Thomas Shepherd & Elizabeth Buff. Bondsman, James S. Brown

2 Dec 1823 Elijah Snap & Mary Ann Orndorf. Bondsman, Samuel Orndorf

3 Dec 1823 Jacob Swimley Jr & Sarah Cochran. Bondsman, William Cochran

3 Dec 1823 George Mason & Nancy Lawyer. Bondsman, Abner Clark

3 Dec 1823 John OConner & Elizabeth Wood. Bondsman, Alexander Wood

9 Dec 1823 William Shutz & Fanny Strickling. Bondsman, Joseph Strickling

9 Dec 1823 William B. Hodgkins & Frances Way. Bondsman, James H. Smith

10 Dec 1823 James Coe & Sophia Grove, daughter of Henry Grove, the bondsman

13 Dec 1823 Isaac McCormick & Margaret McCormick, widow of Samuel McCormick. Bondsman, George McCormick

15 Dec 1823 James Drake & Ann Young. Bondsman, Anthony Young

15 Dec 1823 James Whittington & Orrato Mitchell. Bondsman, William Whittington

18 Dec 1823 Benjamin Clowser & Eliza Shrook. Bondsman, Peter Printz

19 Dec 1823 Strother Moore & Maria Haynie, ward of Jacob Kendrick, the bondsman

20 Dec 1823 Jefferson Hackley & Lucy M. Berry. Bondsman, Thornton Haines

22 Dec 1823 Richard Ridgway & Hannah Chenowith. Bondsman, John Chenowith

27 Dec 1823 William Swart & Frances Beaty. Bondsman, William Beaty

29 Dec 1823 John Burchell & Sarah Forster. Bondsman, James Forster

31 Dec 1823 Griffin Taylor & Rhoda Kingore, daughter of William Kingore

31 Dec 1823 Joseph B. Edwards & Mary D. Dick, daughter of Henry Dick, the bondsman

7 Jan 1824 Dawson McCormick & Florinda L. Milton. Bondsman, Province McCormick Jr

9 Jan 1824 John B. Righter & Maria Newbanks. Bondsman, Moses Newbanks

10 Jan 1824 Isaac Cooper & Elizabeth Hastings. Bondsman, John Hastings

15 Jan 1824 John Lang & Susan McMannus widow & relict of Samuel McMannus dec. Bondsman, Thomas Lang

19 Jan 1824 Thomas Phillips & Elizabeth F. Lockheart. Bondsman, Jacob Senseny

19 Jan 1824 Lemuel James & Eliza Lloyd. Bondsman, Jabez Carter

22 Jan 1824 Israel Phillips & Abigail Dehaven. Bondsman, Job Dehaven

24 Jan 1824 John Reed & Mary Brunar. Bondsman, George Brunar

3 Feb 1824 Thomas Fetty & Juliet Dyer. Bondsman, Hugh C. Dyer

10 Feb 1824 Edwin Ridings & Lydia Rodes. Bondsman, John Rodes

10 Feb 1824 John M. Elliott & Lucy H. Bryarly, daughter of Samuel Bryarly, the bondsman

10 Feb 1824 George Miller & Catharine Snyder, daughter of George Snyder, the bondsman, who signs in German

12 Feb 1824 Peter Oats & Sarah Kerns, daughter of Nathan Kerns, the bondsman

16 Feb 1824 Jacob Boyer & Susan Ritenour. Bondsman, Daniel Ritenour

17 Feb 1824 Wright Gatewood & Louisiana Williams. Bondsman, John H. Bowman

26 Feb 1824 Daniel Coontzman & Sarah E. Burton. Bondsman, Levi Burton

26 Feb 1824 Elisha Slusser & Matilda Riley. Bondsman, Charles Vickers

28 Feb 1824 Philip Peaznaker & Mary Slonecker. Bondsman, Michael Slonacker

1 Mar 1824 Henry Swallom & Susan Albin, daughter of Andrew Albin, the bondsman

2 Mar 1824 Nimrod McEndree & Mary Flore, ward of Treadwell Smith. Bondsmen, Treadwell Smith & John Flore

3 Mar 1824 John Tewault & Mary Baker, daughter of Thomas Baker, the bondsman

9 Mar 1824 Samuel Bryan & Susan Jackson, widow & relict of George Jackson dec. Bondsman, David Farrell

9 Mar 1824 John Richards Jnr & Elizabeth Garrett. Bondsman, Giden Landacre

11 Mar 1824 John Smith & Christiana Crouse. Bondsman, John S. Smith

20 Mar 1824 James S. Roach & Mary Hoover. Bondsman, John Hoover

13 Mar 1824 John Heiskell & Sarah White. No Bondsman

16 Mar 1824 John Boice & Margaret Lawyer. Bondsman, Frederick Loury

18 Mar 1824 Isaac Postlethwait & Lucinda Lott. Bondsman, James Carpenter

19 Mar 1824 James Franks & Malinda ORear. Bondsman, Enoch ORear. "James Franks being disabled in his right hand made his mark..."

20 Mar 1824 Michael Hansell & Rachel Adams. Bondsman, John Hansell

22 Mar 1824 Josiah Murphy & Mary Ramey, daughter of Isaac Ramey, the bondsman

22 Mar 1824 George M. Crockwell & Mary Hurr, daughter of John Herr, the bondsman

23 Mar 1824 James I. Hollis & Sarah Lupton, widow & relict of Thomas C. Lupton deceased, daughter of John Hamilton, the bondsman

23 Mar 1824 John Griffith & Ann Hamilton, daughter of John Hamilton, the bondsman

27 Mar 1824 Peter Duff & Sarah Tanquary, daughter of James Tanquary, the bondsman

27 Mar 1824 John White & Hannah Redd. Bondsman, James Redd

27 Mar 1824 Alexander F. Carter & Mary Shull. Bondsman, Thomas Shull

30 Mar 1824 Joshua Johnston & Harriet Lock, daughter of William Lock, the bondsman

31 Mar 1824 David Farrell & Lucretia Jane Goldsborough, daughter of Robert Goldsborough, the bondsman

1 Apr 1824 Aaron B. Glasscock & Emily June Shepherd. Bondsman, James Castleman

2 Apr 1824 John Hieronimus & Elizabeth Coe, daughter of William Coe, the bondsman

5 Apr 1824 John McKee & Ruth Whitacre, daughter of Rachel Whitacre. Bondsman, George Smith

5 Apr 1824 James Fowler & Elizabeth Drish. Bondsman, Horation Drish

7 Apr 1824 Squire Bell & Elizabeth Bazzell, daughter of John Bazzell, the bondsman

8 Apr 1824 James Brooks & Sarah Silvers. Bondsman, Michael Haymaker

12 Apr 1824 Peter Peters & Susan Woodard, daughter of James Woodard, the bondsman

19 Apr 1824 William Windle & Margaret Gaines. Bondsman, Elias March

19 Apr 1824 David Cather & Delilah Williams, daughter of Isaac Williams, the bondsman

20 Apr 1824 James Riley & Martha Lane. Bondsman, George Riley

24 Apr 1824 William Everheart & Mary Russell. Bondsman, Gersham Drake

26 Apr 1823 James Giffin & Selina Stipe, daughter of John Stipe, the bondsman

28 Apr 1824 Solomon Bishop & Nancy Loury. Bondsman, George Lowrey

30 Apr 1824 John Catlett Jnr & Phebe Finch. Bondsman, John Cattlett Snr

4 May 1824 William Smith & Nancy Ivins. Bondsman, Augustine Smith

6 May 1824 John Russell & Uris Darkey. Bondsman, Rezin Ashby

8 May 1824 Robert Monroe & Sidney Grubs. Bondsman, Alexander R. Newman

8 May 1824 Samuel Jennings, son of Daniel Jennings, & Mary Sidebottom. Bondsman, Daniel Jennings

15 May 1824 Manuel Trenary & Hannah Drake, daughter of Francis Drake, the bondsman

25 May 1824 Richard B. Homes & Mary B. Little. Bondsman, Leroy P. Williams

28 May 1824 James Dyer & Nancy Earheart, daughter of John Earheart, the bondsman

29 May 1824 Philip Carper & Polly Syphart. Bondsman, Henry Swallom

31 May 1824 Abraham Haines & Rachel Haines. Bondsman, Thornton Haines. Bond says Ellis Haines

31 May 1824 Matthew Page & Mary C. Randolph, ward of Philip G. Randolph, the bondsman

2 Jun 1824 Robert F. Miller & Martha W. Williams. Bondsman, Jared J. Williams

13 Jun 1824 George W. B. Chapman & Hannah C. Brady. Bondsman, John W. Brady

26 Jun 1824 Rezin Duvall & Eliza Hughs, daughter of Charles Hughs

26 Jun 1824 Bennet Russell & Mary Blue. Bondsman, William Everhart

30 Jun 1824 Levi Rogers & Margaret McCleave. Bondsman, William Rogers

30 Jun 1824 Thomas McLaughlin & Frances A. Taylor, daughter of Jesse Tailor, the bondsman

12 Jul 1824 David Kime & Rachell Weavers. Bondsman, Thomas Jordan

15 Jul 1824 Thomas J. Dorsey & Lucy Esthen Cooke. Bondsman, John L. Gibbons

30 Jul 1824 John Louthan & Lydia Carter. Bondsman, John Monroe

30 Jul 1824 Robert Johnston & Jane Pugh. Bondsman, David Pugh

4 Aug 1824 John Vincent & Julia Ann McDonald, daughter of James McDonald, the bondsman

4 Aug 1824 Daniel Meyers & Ann French his ward. Bondsman, John Shambaugh

16 Aug 1824 William Parker & Mary Bedingr. Bondsman, Robert Hainey

18 Aug 1824 Jacob Reigle & Ruth Anderson. Bondsman, John Beamer

24 Aug 1824 George Sickfort & Elizabet Williams, widow & relict of John William deceased. Bondsman, John Macintire

31 Aug 1824 Thomas Day & Hannah Johnston daughter of John Johnston, the bondsman

31 Aug 1824 Jeremiah G. Walker & Evelin Bedinger. Bondsman, James Colville

4 Sep 1824 John Cornwall, son of Willi Cornwall, & Fanny Kline, daughter of Micha Kline. Fathers are bondsmen

8 Sep 1824 Jonathan H. Regan, son of John Regan, & Selonary W. Jacobs, daughter of Thomas Jacobs. Fathers are bondsmen

13 Sep 1824 Charles D. Browning & Rebecca Moore. Bondsman, Lewis F. Moore

21 Sep 1824 Thomas Marpole & Susan Albert, daughter of Michael Albert, the bondsman

24 Sep 1824 Hiram Mowry, son of Frederick Mowry, & Rebecca Fry, daughter of Elizabeth Fry. Bondsmen, Frid Marrey & Elizabeth Fry

29 Sep 1824 Levi Cain & Mary Ann Kinlin. Bondsman, Sutton I. Harris

1 Oct 1824 William Dunn & Catharine Payne. No bondsman

4 Oct 1824 Robert Shepherd & Catherine Earhart. Bondsman, James Dyer

4 Oct 1824 James Breeze & Amanda F. Shepherd, ward of John S. Peyton, the bondsman

1 Nov 1824 Henry Rush & Nancy Bell. Bondsman, Asa Godman

2 Nov 1824 John Taylor, ward of Jesse Waln, & Nancy Moling. Bondsman, Jesse Waln

3 Nov 1824 Joseph Nolen & Mary Hayes. Bondsman, Samuel Hays

3 Nov 1824 William H. Foster & Margaret Kingore. Bondsman, John W. Wilkinson

5 Nov 1824 Benjamin Braithwaite & Maria Hoffman. Bondsman, William Ensley

10 Nov 1824 Samuel Spengler & Fanny Way. Bondsman, James Way

12 Nov 1824 Benjamin Shultz & Nancy Perrill. Bondsman, Peter Renner

13 Nov 1824 Samuel Jackson & Cinthery McVeigh. Bondsman, Andrew McGarrity

16 Nov 1824 John Smith & Anna Jolley. Bondsman, Landen Jolly

22 Nov 1824 Samuel S. Hammack & Louisa Mauk. Bondsman, Michael Mauk Jr.

23 Nov 1824 Henry Himelright & Elizabeth Fisher. Bondsman, John McColle

25 Nov 1824 Lewis Neill & Frances Ann Hughs. Bondsman, Benjamin Tanquary

2 Dec 1824 Joseph Kilders & Nancy Williams, daughter of William Williams, the bondsman

2 Dec 1824 David Pitcock & Lucy Gilham, ward of William Clevinger, the bondsman

6 Dec 1824 George L. Kerfoot & Catharine D. Sowers. Bondsman, John Kerfoot
9 Dec 1824 Samuel Day & Eliza Daniel. Bondsman, John Hover (Horn?)
10 Dec 1824 Charles McFarling & Euphamia Cloud. Bondsman, George Randall
15 Dec 1824 Benjamin J. E. Dick & Catharine Ann Cornwell, daughter of William Cornwell, the bondsman
13 Dec 1824 Charles Vickers & Partheany Riley. Bondsman, Elijah Romine
15 Dec 1824 Abraham Hess & Nancy Puller. Bondsman, David Bryarley
18 Dec 1824 Nelson Foster & Mary Roberts. Bondsman, Abraham Roberts
20 Dec 1824 Thomas Watson & Susannah Thomas. Bondsman, William Thomas
22 Dec 1824 George Lanham & Nancy Witon. Bondsman, Henry White
27 Dec 1824 Levi Marquis & Sarah Davis. Bondsman, Daniel Murphy
27 Dec 1824 Mahlon S. Grigg & Emily Anderson. Bondsman, Thomas Winkoop
29 Dec 1824 John D. Snyder & Caroline Kline, daughter of Ingleheart Kline, the bondsman
3 Jan 1825 James Grantham & Phoebe F. Larue. Bondsman, John B. Larue
4 Jan 1825 Newton Trenary & Sarah Clawson, daughter of Cornelius Clawson
10 Jan 1825 William Newbrough & Ann Ridgway. Bondsman, Thomas M. Rusk
11 Jan 1825 William Briley & Jane Atwood. Bondsman, Moses Stewart
12 Jan 1825 James T. Hope & Phoebe White. Bondsman, John Louthan
12 Jan 1825 William Catlett & Nancy Miller. Bondsman, William Miller
12 Jan 1825 Walter Franck & Levina Bailey. Bondsman, William Pennybaker
13 Jan 1825 James Swattz & Mahala McDonald, daughter of James McDonald. Bondsman, Isaac Wood
19 Jan 1825 Daniel Powers & Mary Ann Carnegy. Bondsman, Thomas Kennerly

19 Jan 1825 Jared McDonald & Elizabeth McDonald. Bondsman, William McDonald

19 Jan 1825 Nathan Mahew & Betsy Ruble, daughter of John Ruble. Bondsmen, Lloyd Mahew & John Ruble

19 Jan 1825 Lloyd Mahew & Sarah Thompson. Bondsman, Thomas Adams

19 Jan 1825 David Miller & Nancy Luttrell, daughter of Fielding Luttrell

22 Jan 1825 Richard Wells & Rebecca William, daughter of William Williams, the bondsman

26 Jan 1825 William Graham & Nancy Bartlett, daughter of William Bartlett, the bondsman

31 Jan 1825 Elijah M. Long & Jane Randall. Bondsmen, Conrad Long & George Randall

1 Feb 1825 John Taylor & Mary Snider. Bondsman, James Day

2 Feb 1825 Thomas B. Baylis & Mary K. Wilson, daughter of William Wilson, the bondsman

7 Feb 1825 John Reed & Lamarian Rinker, daughter of Jacob Rinker, the bondsman

7 Feb 1825 Daniel Palmer & Sarah Lloyd. Bondsman, Henderson Lloyd

14 Feb 1825 Thornton W. Bowen & Maria E. Cleveland. Bondsman, Solomon R. Jackson

16 Feb 1825 Jesse Corder & Phoebe Corder, daughter of James Corder, the bondsman

16 Feb 1825 Enos Brown & Betsy Walker. Bondsman, Benjamin King

17 Feb 1825 Joseph Hymes & Hannah Herbough. Bondsman, Isaac Richards

18 Feb 1825 George Wolfe, ward of Alexander Vance, & Sarah Keckley. Bondsman, Alexander Vance

19 Feb 1825 John Yeo & Elizabeth Balthis, daughter of William Balthis, the bondsman

19 Feb 1825 Samuel Walker & Catharine Reynolds. Bondsman, Hugh Reynolds

19 Feb 1825 Amos Johnston & Rachael Williams, widow of Ebenezer Williams. Bondsman, William Smith

29 Feb 1825 Henry Crum & Margaret Hotsenpillar. Bondsman, William A. Wilson

1 Mar 1825 John Scott & Lydia Mercer, ward of John Mercer, the bondsman

1 Mar 1825 George Welsh & Margery Curl. Bondsman, David Curl

5 May 1825 John Kendrick & Elizabeth Collins. Bondsman, Robert Hodgson

7 Mar 1825 Martin Snurr & Mary Ann Imswiler. Bondsman, Peter Printz

8 Mar 1825 James Forster & Jane Helm Barnett. Bondsman, Neill Barnett

8 Mar 1825 George Bell & Elizabeth Weaver, widow & relict of John Weaver deceased. Bondsmn, George Reed

9 Mar 1825 Ira Tatum & Mariam McKay. Bondsman, Joshua Hopper

12 Mar 1825 John Grove, son of Jacob Grove, & Nancy Waln. Bondsman, Jacob Grove

19 Mar 1825 Bartholomew Smith & Rebecca Martin. Bondsman, Michael Loy

22 Mar 1825 Joseph Sample & Mary Bartlett, widow & relict of Sanford Bartlett deceased. Bondsman, William Lauck

22 Mar 1825 Joseph Mckee & Sidney Capper. Bondsman, Robert Mckee

23 Mar 1825 Abner Peters & Elizabeth Stephens, daughter of Henry Stephens, the bondsman

24 Mar 1825 Isaac Gray & Charlotte Ransome. Bondsman, Thomas Robinson (free man of color). Grey is also a free man of color.

26 Mar 1825 John Rinehart & Sarah Fagan. Bondsman, John Littler

29 Mar 1825 Peter Sperry & Polly Kremer. Bondsman, Elia Snyder

31 Mar 1825 Bazell Goings & Louisa Gregory. Bondsman, William Ball

1 Apr 1825 Richard Dowell & Sarah Figgins. Bondsman, Wiliam Windsor

4 Apr 1825 Thomas Wilson & Catharine Smith. Bondsman, William Headley

5 Apr 1825 Lewis Lindsey & Nancy Harrison. Bondsman, Isaac Harrison

12 Apr 1825 Reuben Ziler & Betsy Jolly. Bondsman, John Smith

13 Apr 1825 Joseph Coulter & Mary Gainer. Bondsman, John Griffith 3d

15 Apr 1825 William Orem & Mary Ann Martin. Bondsman, Samuel C. Pack

18 Apr 1825 Edmund Tyler & Alice Jane Richards. Bondsman, Daniel P. Conrad

19 Apr 1825 Abraham Paskell & Delilah Smallwood, daughter of Vance Smallwood. Bondsman, John Lanham

20 Apr 1825 Solomon Glaze & Elizabeth Street. Bondsman, George Swiers

21 Apr 1825 Henry Stephens & Susan Murphey. Bondsman, Harrison Murphey

23 Apr 1825 Robert Hodgson & Sarah Renner, daughter of Isaac Renner, the bondsman

28 Apr 1825 Jacob Amick & Tacy Anderson. Bondsman, Thomas Anderson senior

3 May 1825 Jacob Tipton & Harriet Perry. Bondsman, Arnold Bonifield

7 May 1825 Greenberry Thompson & Elizabeth Bostyon. Bondsman, Robert Crupper

16 May 1825 Thomas B. Massie & Sidney Ashby. Bondsman, William Catlett

16 May 1825 William Dillon & Elizabeth Haines, widow & relict of John Haines deceased. Bondsman, Aquilla Haines

27 May 1826 Peter Hannum & Polly Lewis, daughter of Evin Lewis, the bondsman

31 May 1825 William Whittington & Susan Drake. Bondsman, Gershom Drake

31 May 1825 John Jacobs & Rachel Cypher, widow & relict of George Cypher deceased. Bondsman, James Rogers

6 Jun 1825 William McVicker, son of Diana McVicker, & Betsy Shuler. Bondsman, Robert Smith

9 Jun 1825 George Jenkins & Elizabeth Bean. Bondsman, Jacob Anderson

9 Jun 1825 Peter Hartman & Louisa ORear. Bondsman, Enoch ORear

14 Jun 1825 David Ogden & Rebecca Shull, widow & relict of Joseph Shull deceased. Bondsman, Henry Beatty

23 Jun 1825 William Lowery & Rachel Bell. Bondsman, Israel Ewing

9 Jul 1825 John Smoke & Lucy Crebs, daughter of Conrad Crebs

21 Jul 1825 Andrew Collins & Margaret Mastin. Bondsman, John Smith

23 Jul 1825 John Woolford & Catharine Shrode. Bondsman, Christopher Smith

26 Jul 1825 William Sanders & Sarah Snap. Bondsman, Elisha Piper

4 Aug 1825 Ralph Williamson & Margaret Ann Kackley, daughter of Jacob Kackley, the bondsman

4 Aug 1825 Peter Bover & Elizabeth Shade. Bondsman, Jacob Shade

8 Aug 1825 John C. Ewing & Margaret Ritter. Bondsman, Simon Harmon

16 Aug 1825 James G. Hurst & Catharine A. Gunnell. Bondsman, Jacob Baker Junior

22 Aug 1825 John Jacobs & Elizabeth Tayler. Bondsman, Jesse Tayler

27 Aug 1825 Edward Franks & Nancy Franks. Bondsman, Henry Franks

27 Aug 1825 James Kidd & Hester Boyd. Bondsman, John Boyd

29 AUg 1825 Thomas Blakemore & Elizabeth W. Brooke. Bondsman, William T. Helm

1 Sep 1825 Joseph Dalby junior & Emeline Bennett, widow & relict of James Bennett deceased. Bondsman, George W. Kiger

5 Sep 1825 Edward S. Beeson & Julia Ann Ridgway. Bondsman, William Stephenson

19 Sep 1826 Alfred Castleman & Margaret Milton. Bondsman, Ebin Milton

3 Oct 1826 Elijah Moore & Frances Weeden. Bondsman, James G. Moore

7 Oct 1826 Henry L. Grove & Catharine Berkheimer. Bondsman, Andrew Heironimus

12 Oct 1825 Abram Coffee & Eliza Dunn, daughter of Robert Dunn, the bondsman

13 Oct 1825 Richard Keenan, son of Thomas Keenan, & Eve Carper. Bondsman, Thomas Keenan

18 Oct 1825 William D. Henshaw & Charlotte Cooper, daughter of Thomas Cooper, the bondsman

21 Oct 1825 Thomas Plater & Evelina H. Buchanan. No bondsman

27 Oct 1825 Jesse Lukens & Beula Painter, daughter of Robert Painter, the bondsman

29 Oct 1825 John E. Deneal & Matilda B. Earle, daughter of Esaias Earle, the bondsman

3 Nov 1825 Samuel Smith & Julia Maria Tidings. Bondsman, George Smith

8 Nov 1825 Leroy Newcomb & Rebecca Klyne. Bondsman, Elias Jones

9 Nov 1825 John Peirce & Mary Louthan. Bondsman, John Louthan

12 Nov 1825 Isaac Rozenberger & Eliza McClunn. Bondsman, John Lemley

14 Nov 1825 David Evans & Susannah May, daughter of John May, the bondsman, who signs in German

14 Nov 1825 Jacob Garrecht & Elizabeth Shaffner. Bondsman, Adam Carper

16 Nov 1825 John Gibson & Mary Ann Taylor. Bondsman, William Dillon

22 Nov 1825 Joseph Mckay & Salley E. Garrison. Bondsman, Jacob McKay

22 Nov 1825 Milton Smith & Leah Jones, daughter of Nathan Jones, the bondsman

22 Nov 1825 Mason Anderson & Jane Baylis. Bondsman, Thomas Anderson Senior

23 Nov 1825 John Kerfoot, son of William Kerfoot, & Cynthia Bowles, daughter of John Bowles. Fathers are bondsmen

26 Nov 1825 Christopher Slonaker & Polly Stephens. Bondsman, Archibald Stephens

26 Nov 1825 Martin Bimple & Mary Sherideen. Bondsman, Peter Nisewander, who signs in German

26 Nov 1825 William Reed & Jane Dolby, widow & relict of John Dolby deceased. Bondsman, Elijah Scrivener

17 Dec 1825 William Ritenour & Arianna Grove, daughter of John Grove Junior, the bondsman

19 Dec 1825 Alexander R. Newman & Ellen Ash, widow & relict of George Ash deceased. Bondsman, Richard M. Sydnor

19 Dec 1825 James Dailey & Rachel Dailey. Bondsman, John Parlett

22 Dec 1825 Oliver A. Shaw & Ann A. Brooke. Bondsman, Thomas Blakemore

27 Dec 1825 James Beck & Nancy Jones Mustin. Bondsman, James Mustin

27 Dec 1825 Thomas Stone & Mary Ann Haire. Bondsman, Joseph Haire

27 Dec 1825 Otho McKay & Nancy Rockingbaugh, daughter of Jacob Rockingbaugh, the bondsman

28 Dec 1825 William L. Walter & Henrietta Shull. Bondsman, Philip Shell

31 Dec 1825 William Wright & Maria Churchwill. Bondsman, John Wright

2 Jan 1826 Issac B. Cloud & Lettitia Buck. Bondsman, Daniel Cloud
3 Jan 1826 John Grove & Isabella Mason. Bondsman, Abner Clarke
4 Jan 1826 Thomas Jones & Mary Morrison. Bondsman, James Morrison
9 Jan 1826 William Garrison & Sally McDonald, daughter of Jarred McDonald, the bondsman
10 Jan 1826 Jesse Turner & Pamillia Middleton, daughter of William Middleton, the bondsman
14 Jan 1826 Walter Carr & Susanna Johnson, daughter of Amos Johnson, the bondsman
23 Jan 1826 John Huntsberry & Mary Marks, daughter of Henry Marks, the bondsman
24 Jan 1826 William Taylor & Hannah McCormick. Bondsman, Francis McCormick
26 Jan 1826 Robert Compton & Elizabeth Smith, daughter of John Smith. Bondsman, Adam Grove
1 Feb 1826 Conrad Hieronimus & Nancy Garrison. Bondsman, Adam Grove
2 Feb 1826 Isaac F. Rhodes & Mary C. Stone, daughter of Philip Stone, the bondsman
2 Feb 1826 Jacob Sweitzer & Elizabeth Lutterell, daughter of Fielding Luttrell, the bondoman
6 Feb 1826 Philip Williams Jr & Ann M. Hite. Bondsman, John S. Davison
9 Feb 1826 Leonard Myers & Emily C. Poland, widow & relict of John Poland deceased. Bondsman, John W. Grove
13 Feb 1826 Joshua Johnston & Elizabeth Rinehart, daughter of David Rinehart, the bondsman
15 Feb 1826 William C. Langley & Hannah Haymaker, daughter of Michael Haymaker, the bondsman
15 Feb 1826 Hiram Adams & Elizabeth Williams. Bondsman, John Gordon
18 Feb 1826 Jonathan Lovett & Nancy Muse. Bondsman, Edward R. Muse
21 Feb 1826 George Rizer & Sarah Hinkle, daughter of Adam Hinkle, the bondsman
25 Feb 1826 George Cryder & Elizabeth Chapman. Bondsman, Henry Guard

1 Mar 1826 John Clink & Margaret Linar. Bondsman, William Dooley

4 Mar 1826 Alexander Ford & Elizabeth Fegans. Bondsman, John Humston

6 Mar 1826 Benjamin White & Mary Duncan. Bondsman, Jacob White

6 Mar 1826 George K. Sowers & Frances E. Mitchell, daughter of William Mitchell, the bondsman

6 Mar 1826 David Weaver & Ann Beall. Bondsman, Henry Rush

10 Mar 1826 Jonas Shambaugh & Rebecca H. Stephens, daughter of Brian M. Stephens

10 Mar 1826 Alexander W. Bowling & Elizabeth Canavan. Bondsman, John L. Fant

11 Mar 1826 James Lyons & Cecelia Matthews. Bondsman, Squire Matthews

11 Mar 1826 William Lee & Matilda Ryan, stepdaughter of Elisha Carver, the bondsman

13 Mar 1826 George Yakeley & Mary Babb. Bondsman, Robinson Babb

17 Mar 1826 John Saunders & Winnifred Kingore. Bondsman, William H. Foster

20 Mar 1826 Thomas Calvin & Rachel Taylor. Bondsman, Aquilla Haines

21 Mar 1826 Robert Beevers & Mary Marquis. Bondsman, Squire Lee

22 Mar 1826 Peter Oller & Elizabeth Noel. Bondsman, John Noel

23 Mar 1825 Henry Naville & Rachel Brent, widow & relict of Enos Brent deceased. Bondsman, Benjamin Langley

27 Mar 1826 John Kern Jr. & Rebecca T. Mason. Bondsman, Samuel H. Davis

29 Mar 1826 Thomas McKee & Emily Anderson, daughter of Ely Anderson, the bondsman

29 Mar 1826 James McMorris & Maria Anderson, daughter of Ely Anderson, the bondsman

29 Mar 1826 James Wright & Elizabeth Mason. Bondsman, William Elliott

4 Apr 1826 Joseph Chrisman & Jane Chrisman, daughter of Isaac Chrisman, the bondsman

7 Apr 1826 Joshua H. Thomas & Lucy L. C. Colston. Bondsman, James Wigginton

8 Apr 1826 Abraham Grove & Elizabeth Reed. Bondsman, Jacob Grove

11 Apr 1826 James Boyd & Margaret Sullivan, daughter of Henry Sullivan, the bondsman

11 Apr 1826 John Copenhaver & Sally Boles, daughter of John Boles, the bondsman

11 Apr 1826 Isaac Hoff & Juliet A. Von Riesen, widow & relict of John Von Riesen decd. Bondsman, Daniel Linn

12 Apr 1826 Nicholas Handle & Sydney Ann Crawford, daughter of Samuel Crawford, the bondsman

12 Apr 1826 Aquilla P. Moore & Apphia Bryarly. Bondsman, James Bryarly

13 Apr 1826 Jacob Whetzel & Mary McFarlin. Bondsman, Levin McFarlin

17 Apr 1826 George Hamilton & Eunice Bedinger. Bondsman, Jeremiah G. Walker

19 Apr 1826 John Johnston & Isabella Day, daughter of Samuel Day, the bondsman

27 Apr 1826 Joseph W. Carter & Elizabeth N. Barnett. Bondsman, Alexander S. Tidball

29 Apr 1826 Robert C. Miller & Elizabeth Carver. Bondsman, Alexander Marks

6 May 1826 William Lang & Frances Rowzee. Bondsman, Frederick Howser

11 May 1826 Samuel Johnston & Jane Hoye. Bondsman, Isaac Russell

17 May 1826 James Mason & Elizabeth Light, daughter of Henry Light, the bondsman

18 May 1826 Bernard Smith & Mary Butter. Bondsman, John Carter

18 May 1826 John Sumption & Susan Lewis. Bondsman, Enoch Lewis

24 May 1826 John Chrismore & Rachel Marpole, widow & relict of Uriah Marpole. Bondsman, George Randall

1 Jun 1826 Joseph Spots & Lucinda Vanlandingham. Bondsman, James White

5 Jun 1826 James Murphy & Therissa Moore, his ward. Bondsman, Alfred Moore

8 Jun 1826 Daniel Morgan & Elizabeth Earhart. Bondsman, Addison Romine

19 Jun 1826 Thomas Crawford & Dorcas Anderson, widow & relict of Jacob Anderson deceased. Bondsman, James Coats

20 Jun 1826 Samuel Taylor & Elizabeth White, daughter of John White, the bondsman

20 Jun 1826 Lawrence Lewis Daingerfield & Elieanor Chenowith. Bondsman, Richard Ridgeway

10 Jul 1826 George Blakemore & Penelope Johnston Polk, widow & relict of --- Polk. Bondsman, William Eskridge

19 Jul 1826 James Lloyd & Sally Stonesypher. Bondsman, Thomas B. Harvy

19 Jul 1826 Uriah Royston & Hannah White. Bondsman, James Castleman

22 Jul 1826 William McKee & Anna Marple. Bondsman, Enoc Marple

28 Jul 1826 George Ashby & Martha Churchwell, daughter of Charles Churchill, the bondsman

31 Jul 1826 Simon Grim & Sarah Drake, stepdaughter of John Grim, the bondsman

3 Aug 1826 Jesse Calbert & Sarah Mckee. Bondsman, James McMorris

5 Aug 1826 Elias Kackley & Mary Anderson, daughter of Eli Anderson, the bondsman

12 Aug 1826 William Boling & Margaret Moore. Bondsman, Alfred Moore

15 Aug 1826 Carr Bailey Nolls & Sarah Ann Vanhorn. Bondsman, Jonathan Farnsworth

17 Aug 1826 Samuel Taylor & Eliza Smith, daughter of Edward Smith esq. Bondsman, William D. Holliday

21 Aug 1826 James Catlett & Catherine Miller, daughter of Christian Miller, the bondsman

24 Aug 1826 Abner Kerns & Sarah Davis. Bondsman, Nathan Kerns

4 Sep 1826 Simeon Ward & Sarah Johnston. Bondsmen, Joseph Johnston & Thomas Anderson senr

5 Sep 1826 Squire Lee & Alcinda Alexander. Bondsman, Robert Beavers

6 Sep 1826 Mann P. Nelson & Amelia Stith Washington, ward of Edwin B. Burwell, the bondsman

7 Sep 1826 John Milton & Louisa F. Taylor. Bondsman, Ebin Milton

22 Sep 1826 Daniel S. Hammack & Elizabeth Ann Taylor, daughter of Jesse Taylor

23 Sep 1826 John Markwood & Margaret Sproute. Bondsman, John D. Crouch

30 Sep 1826 Michael Dearmont & Lucinda Ferguson of Frederick County. Bondsmen, Hugh C. Dyer (also listed as Carter Dyer) & James Bell

2 Oct 1826 Michael Price & Mary Cochran. Bondsman, Jacob Swimley

5 Oct 1826 William O. Bond & Rachel Tanquary, daughter of Walter Tanquary, the bondsman

5 Oct 1826 Andrew Hanagan & Catharine Peters. Bondsman, John McCaulley

7 Oct 1826 John Myers & Rachel Lewis, daughter of Evin Lewis, the bondsman

10 Oct 1826 John Noel & Letitia Whitacre, stepdaughter of Nathan Kerns, the bondsman

24 Oct 1826 George Everhart & Pernina Snyder. Bondsman, Joshua H. Thomas

25 Oct 1826 Nimrod Adams & Susan Linkheart. Bondsmen, George Dawson & Thomas Linkheart

27 Oct 1826 James Griggs & Francis H. Timberlake. Bondsman, Thomas Timberlake

10 Nov 1826 Thornton Good & Elizabeth Moore. Bondsman, Thomas Moore

13 Nov 1826 Henson Marlow & Peggy Holmes, daughter of John Homes, the bondsman

15 Nov 1826 Henry P. Ward & Elizabeth Ann Riely. Bondsman, James P. Riely

21 Nov 1826 Henry Franks & Ann Douglas. Bondsman, Squire Bell

22 Nov 1826 William H. Vanhorn & Nancy Carter, daughter of John Carter, the bondsman

25 Nov 1826 John William Bucher & Mazy Barrow. Bondsman, Jacob Shambaugh

25 Nov 1826 Notley Swart & Sarah Beaty. Bondsman, William Swart

2 Dec 1826 John Henry & Mary Swart. Bondsman, William Swart

5 Dec 1826 Benjamin Smith & Elizabeth Hall. Bondsman, Samuel Bonham

6 Dec 1826 John Smith Davison & Mary Eltinge Hite. Bondsman, Philip WIlliams Jnr

6 Dec 1826 Christopher Smith & Martha Albin, daughter of Andrew Albin, the bondsman

6 Dec 1826 James E. Robertson & Eveline Allensworth. Bondsman, James Way

7 Dec 1826 Charles R. Burringer & Margaret McCormick. Bondsman, William McCormick

7 Dec 1826 William A. Bell Jr. & Frances Ship, daughter of John Ship, the bondsman

8 Dec 1826 Hatch Dent Gardner & Mrs. Rebecca Allen, widow & relict of Robert Allen deceased. Bondsman, William V. Henry

9 Dec 1826 Catesby Newman & Elizabeth Ann Reed, daughter of George Reed, the bondsman

12 Dec 1826 Clement Spicknall & Elizabeth Huntsberry, daughter of Conrad Huntsberry, the bondsman

16 Dec 1826 James Kean & Ana Fish. Bondsman, Robert Fish

18 Dec 1826 Thomas McDonald & Mary Magruder. Bondsman, William Cox

18 Dec 1826 James Knight & Martha Orr. BOndsman, Ezekiel Bazzell

20 Dec 1826 John Foster & Martha Crow, widow & relict of John Crow deceased. No bondsman

20 Dec 1826 Joseph Snapp & Elizabeth Morrison. Bondsman, John E. Baylis

23 Dec 1826 John Luttrell & Anna Shockey. Bondsman, Robert Lutterell

26 Dec 1826 Peter Cain & Hannah Huntsberry, daughter of Conrad Huntsberry, the bondsman

29 Dec 1826 Elias Fisher & Margaret Messer. Bondsman, Henry Crumley

30 Dec 1826 William Brown & Mary Marple. Bondsmen, John Yakely, who signs in German, & Conrad Long

6 Jan 1827 Isaac Hite & Mary Ann Turner. Bondsman, James Turner

6 Jan 1827 Randal Lockhart & Elizabeth Waln. Bondsman, John Grove

8 Jan 1827 David Parlett & Elizabeth Clark, daughter of William Clark, the bondsman

9 Jan 1827 Daniel Gold & Phebe Scott, widow & Relict of James Scott decd. Bondsman, Josiah Wm. Ware

10 Jan 1827 James V. Glass & Isabella Catlett. Bondsman, Henry Catlett. No signature for bondsman

15 Jan 1827 John McCormick & Margaret Butt, widow & relict of James Butt deceased. Bondsman, James Carter

27 Jan 1827 William Clark & Evelina Devoe, daughter of David Devoe, the bondsman
27 Jan 1827 John Albin & Catharine Butler. Bondsman, Jesse Taylor
29 Jan 1827 George Young & Terissa Watson, daughter of James Watson, the bondsman
29 Jan 1827 James R. Clyne & Mary Ann Hammock. Bondsman, Daniel S. Hammack
1 Feb 1827 Peter Crum & Catharine Duty. Bondsman, Thomas Stone
5 Feb 1827 Manley Oliver & Mildred Catlett. Bondsman, George Simpson
6 Feb 1827 Frederick Lowery & Caroline Fisher, step daughter of David Fisher, the bondsman
6 Feb 1827 Edward Newcomb & Betsey Striker, daughter of Henry Striker, the bondsman
7 Feb 1827 Joseph Clowser & Sarah Orendorff. Bondsman, Isaac Orndorff
10 Feb 1827 John Ramey, son of Isaac Ramey, & Elizabeth Crow. Bondsman, Isaac Ramey
12 Feb 1827 Michael Pierce & Clarissa Painter, widow & relict of Mahlon Painter deceased. Bondsman, Walter Tauquary
20 Feb 1827 William Hawley Jr & Ann Debell. Bondsman, Jeremiah Hawley
21 Feb 1827 Samuel & Mary Ann Bains. Bondsman, Abram S. Burgess
21 Feb 1827 Charles Shortness, son of Thomas Shortness, & Ann Slack. Bondsman, Thomas Shortness
27 Feb 1827 Roden Huffman & Mary Beck. Bondsman, James W. Beck
27 Feb 1827 John Delong & Susan Funk. Bondsman, Isaac Heck
27 Feb 1827 Richard Randols & Catharine Frieze, daughter of Michael Fries
28 Feb 1827 John R. Morgan & Lucidney Debell, daughter of Jeremiah Debell
28 Feb 1827 Robert Morris & Elizabeth Ann Dooley, daughter of William Dooley
3 Mar 1827 William McNelly & Mary Light. Bondsman, Wm Dehaven
5 Mar 1827 John Frederick & Nancy Frye, daughter of Peter Frye
8 Mar 1827 Robert Thompson & Polly Guard. Bondsman, Alexander Marks

12 Mar 1827 James Bryarly & Louisa M. Bryarly, daughter of Samuel Bryarly, the bondsman

24 Mar 1827 James Lloyd & Anna Marple, daughter of Joseph Marple. Bondsman, Conrad Lloyd

28 Mar 1827 William Williams & Mary Chrisman, daughter of Peter Chrisman, the bondsman

29 Mar 1827 William Hewett & Ann Crider. Bondsman, John P. Ridings

30 Mar 1827 James Kean & Bertheny Emmons. Bondsman, Marcus Kean

31 Mar 1827 Mordecai B. Cartmell & Eliza Campbell, daughter of William Campbell, the bondsman

10 Apr 1827 William Reed & Tabitha Myers. Bondsman, John Reed

21 Apr 1827 John E. Bayliss & Catharine M. Davis. Bondsman, Mason Anderson

30 Apr 1827 Asa Glasscock & Kitty Glasscock. Bondsman, Travis Glasscock

2 May 1827 David Stidman & Eliza Jackson, stepdaughter of Samuel Bryan, the bondsman

8 May 1827 William B. Walter & Margaret Ewing. Bondsman, Robert Ewing

9 May 1827 Thornton D. McDonald & Elizabeth Hollingshead. Bondsman, Zadock Rogers

23 May 1827 John W. Pope & Tacy B. Ridgeway. Bondsmen, John Jolliffe & William Wood

25 May 1827 John Pangle & Eleanor Day. Bondsman, David Pangle

31 May 1827 Daniel Steel & Matilda Barrow, daughter of Eleazer Barrow, the bondsman

2 Jun 1827 John Broy & Elizabeth Griggsby. Bondsman, Danl M. Triplett

5 Jun 1827 Isaac N. Buck & Susan Taylor, daughter of Mandly Taylor, the bondsman

7 Jun 1827 John Umpenour & Debby Ewing. Bondsman, Henry Guard

8 Jun 1827 John Garrett & Maria Gilham. Bondsman, William Withers

11 Jun 1827 Richard Perry & Elizabeth Hiett, daughter of Thomas Hiett, the bondsman

11 Jun 1827 William Hoffman & Rachel Bucher. Bondsman, John Marker & Elias Bucher

21 Jun 1827 Richard Crim & Elizabeth Saunders. Bondsman, Michael Hawk
23 Jun 1827 William McElwain & Margaret Brannon? (Branner?) Bondsman, Edward L. Beeson
16 Jul 1827 George W. Stonestreet & Elizabeth Triplett. Bondsman, Walter B. Smoot
16 Jul 1827 Marcus McCormick & Lourenna D. McCormick. Bondsman, Bushrod Taylor
25 Jul 1827 Josiah Kaler & Mary Shade, daughter of Jacob Shade Senr, the bondsman
23 Aug 1827 George Randell & Barbara Rinker, daughter of Jacob Rinker, the bondsman
25 Aug 1827 Noah Grim & Mary Johnson. Bondsman, John Johnson
28 Aug 1827 William Albert & Eliza Ann Brown. Bondsman, Michael Albert
29 Aug 1827 George Lock & Winifred Wilcox, daughter of Timothy Wilcox, the bondsman
5 Sep 1827 Samuel Renner & Elizabeth Hemelwright. Bondsmen, William Mcelwee & John Marker
7 Sep 1827 Joseph Dunn & Lucy Stimmel. Bondsman, Thomas Hancher
11 Sep 1827 Joseph Kerby & Lydia Chapman. Bondsman, Philip Berlin
17 Sep 1827 Elijah Minnix & Rachael Dyer. Bondsman, Hugh C. Dyer
18 Sep 1827 John Stellins & Mary Ann Garrison, daughter of Moses Garrison, the bondsman
19 Sep 1827 William Spurr & Mary Bush, daughter of William Bush, the bondsman
19 Sep 1827 Andrew Campbell & Polly Brown. No bondsman
22 Sep 1827 Lester Puller & Sarah Friedley, widow & relict of Henry Friedly. Bondsman, Edward Moore
24 Sep 1827 Edwin Moore & Eliza Friedly, stepdaughter of Lester Puller, the bondsman
24 Sep 1827 John Boswell & Catharine Brown. Bondsman, Moses W. Brown
26 Sep 1827 Battack Witherrow & Ann Marial Earhart. Bondsman, Robert Shepherd
26 Sep 1827 Edward Owens & Nancy Dyer widow & relict of James Dyer deceased. Bondsman Robert Shepherd

1 Oct 1827 Thomas Clark & Mary Hancher. Bondsman, James W. Hancher

2 Oct 1827 Philip C. Spengler & Margaret E. Richards. Bondsman, J. R. Richards

3 Oct 1827 George W. Murray & Catharine Dooley, widow & relict of James Dooley decd. Bondsman, Willis Day

3 Oct 1827 William White & Ann M. Kercheval. Bondsman, A. T. F. Stephens

8 Oct 1827 James Stillings & Laney Fisher. Bondsmen, James Cather & Lewis Fisher

9 Oct 1827 Abraham Clyne & Mary (Mercy?) Mckee. Bondsman, James Mckee

13 Oct 1827 James Puller & Sally Tillett, widow & relict of John Tillett decd. Bondsman, Joseph Palmer

15 Oct 1827 Abraham Shull & Maria F. Massie. Bondsman, George B. Ash

17 Oct 1827 William T. W. Taliaferro & Frances B. Harrison. Bondsman, David Timberlake Jnr

18 Oct 1827 John G. Senseney & Mary P. Kline. Bondsman, Anthony Kline

20 Oct 1827 John Feltner & Harriet Fleming, daughter of Archibald Fleming, the bondsman

27 Oct 1827 George Lemley & Ann Carver. Bondsman, Daniel Carver

27 Oct 1827 Jesse Orendorf & Mary Ann Cooper. Bondsman, Abraham Cooper

31 Oct 1827 David Groves, ward of Richard M. S. Timberlake, & Susan Reigle, daughter of Joseph Rigal, the bondsman

1 Nov 1827 Isaac Dawson & Aurelia Moore. Bondsmen, Killis Hord & Alfred P. Moore

3 Nov 1827 George St. Mire (probably Santmyer) & Elizabeth Cordell. Bondsman, William Walters

5 Nov 1827 James Lloyd & Susan Langham. Bondsman, James Smallwood

5 Nov 1827 Barnett Smallwood & Tabitha Blake, ward of the above bound Barnet Smallwood. Bondsman, James Smallwood

10 Nov 1827 Mason Oliver & Louisa Steel. Bondsman, Mandley Oliver

13 Nov 1827 Uriel Wright & Sarah G. Tuley. Bondsman, Philip B. Streit

20 Nov 1827 Enoch Triplett & Olivia Moore. Bondsman, Edwin Moore

27 Nov 1827 George Douglass & Sarah Ross. Bondsman, John Ross

28 Nov 1827 William Boxwell & Catharine Parsons. Bondsman, Cornelius Vincent

27 Nov 1827 John Hollingworth & Sally B. Green. Bondsman, Ebin Milton

3 Dec 1827 David Likens & Margaret K. Louthan. Bondsman, William Louthan

3 Dec 1827 Abraham Skillman & Delilah Alexander. Bondsman, John B. Taylor

4 Dec 1827 Robert Clark & Nancy Thompsn, daughter of John Thompson, the bondsman

10 Dec 1827 Edward Mires & Elizabeth Griffin. Bondsman, Joseph W. Kean

12 Dec 1827 Joseph Steidley & Elvira Rowland. Bondsman, Solomon Steidley

22 Dec 1827 William McDonald & Maria Simpson, widow & relict of James Simpson deceased. Bondsman, Mandley Oliver

23 Dec 1827 Stephen Whittlesey & Nancy Lyons. Bondsman, William Groves

24 Dec 1827 Jacob Miley & Susan Smith, daughter of James Smith, the bondsman

25 Dec 1827 Farland Fuller & Mary Chapman. Bondsman, John Taylor

26 Dec 1827 George Pearson & Elizabeth Britton. Bondsman, James Lynn

26 Dec 1827 Adam Hart & Elizabeth Williams, daughter of William Williams, the bondsman

26 Dec 1837 Joseph C. Bartlett & Nancy S. Brown. Bondsman, John Q. Berry

29 Dec 1827 John Coe & Louisa Fenton. Bondswman, John Carter

31 Dec 1827 Richard H. McEndree & Harrit Craig, ward of said Richard H. McEndree. Bondsman, Hiram W. Taylor

1 Jan 1828 Wilson Turner & Emily Jane Romine. Bondsman, Addison Romine

9 Jan 1828 Martin Smith & Lucy Yates. Bondsman, Jabez Carter

7 Jan 1828 Thomas Castleman & Martha P. Taylor, widow & relict of Bushrod Taylor deceased. Bondsman, Treadwell Smith

12 Jan 1828 Joseph Lockmiller & Delilah Bruner. Bondsman, Joseph Johnson

Marriage Bonds No. 15 1828-1831

15 Jan 1828 George Wigginton & Anna Hottel. Bondsman, John Wigginton

19 Jan 1828 William Perry & Lucy N. Walls. Bondsman, Thomas Weekly

21 Jan 1828 John Martin & Jane Wood, daughter of Alexander Wood. Bondsman, Geo. S. Lane

22 Jan 1828 James Doran & Mary Royston, daughter of Peter Royston, the bondsman

23 Jan 1828 George L. Dunn & Sally Lock, daughter of William Lock, the bondsman

23 Jan 1828 John C. Armistead & Ann S. Harrison. Bondsman, Robert L. Armstead

24 Jan 1828 Jacob Barley & Rebecca Thomas. Bondsman, William Thomas

1 Feb 1828 Manley Elgin & Evelina Garrison. Bondsman, Robert S. McKay

7 Feb 1828 William Vincent & Susan Ashdell. Bondsman, Wm D. Holliday

7 Feb 1828 Jacob Newcomer & Elizabeth McLeed. Bondsman, Michael Smith

12 Feb 1828 Daniel Maloney & Caroline McDonald, daughter of Daniel McDonald, the bondsman

14 Feb 1828 Robert McKay & Nancy A. McKay, daughter of Jacob McKay, the bondsman

16 Feb 1828 William Beadle & Harriet Madden. Bondsman, Samuel Madden

20 Feb 1828 George Moreland & Sally Marple. Bondsman, Enoch Marple

21 Feb 1828 John P. Ridings & Rebecca Stone, daughter of Philip Stone, the bondsman

23 Feb 1828 Jacob Lawyer & Mary Ware, daughter of James Ware, the bondsman

25 Feb 1828 Alexander S. Brown & Nancy Murphey. Bondsman, James A. Beall

25 Feb 1828 Goren White & Rachael Leonard. Bondsman, Alexander S. Brown

26 Feb 1828 Abraham Crim & Maria Throckmorton, daughter of William Lock, the bondsman

26 Feb 1828 Benjamin Bowser & Mary Pickerell. Bondsman, John H. Pickerell
1 Mar 1828 Asa Rozenburger & Mary Oats, widow of John Oats. Bondsman, Nathan Kearns
3 Mar 1828 Martin Brill & Agnes Orndorff, daughter of Samuel Orndorff, the bondsman
3 Mar 1828 Jacob V. Tabb & Susan Whittington. Bondsman, Solomon R. Jackson
3 Mar 1828 William Carpenter & Elizabeth Flynn. Bondsman, Hedgmon Triplett
6 Mar 1828 Henry Franks & Julian Franks. Bondsman, George ORear
7 Mar 1828 Joseph Smith & Mary Ann Sumption. Bondsman, James Conn
10 Mar 1828 Michael Shull & Margaret Wilson, daughter of William Wilson, the bondsman
15 Mar 1828 Parkinson D. Shepherd & Eliza Ann Gant, daughter of John Gant, the bondsman
17 Mar 1828 Thomas Short & Sidney Leach. Bondsman, William Leach
18 Mar 1828 Albert Lake & Mary Wilcox, daughter of Timothy Wilcox, the bondsman
18 Mar 1828 Jacob Larew & Prudence Marple, daughter of David Marple, the bondsman
19 Mar 1828 James G. Bryce (Boyce?) & Sarah Y. Funston. Bondsman, Edward H. Fry
24 Mar 1828 Isaac Heck & Susan S. Clark, daughter of Reuben Clark
24 Mar 1828 Bushrod McCormick & Emily R. Seevers. Bondsman, Charles Butler
31 Mar 1828 William Holliday & Eliza Wilson. Bondsman, John Snyder
31 Mar 1828 James E. Norris & Ann Maria Anderson. Bondsman, Bushrod Taylor
1 Apr 1828 John Zeiler & Barbara Berkhammer. Bondsman, John Dick
7 Apr 1828 James H. Cooke & Eliza Wykoff, daughter of Cornelius Wykoff, the bondsman
10 Apr 1828 Samuel D. Vance & Mary Elizabeth Vance. Bondsman, J. M. Glass
14 Apr 1828 George M. Singhass & Susan Arnold, daughter of William Arnold, the bondsman
17 Apr 1828 Jacob Showalter & Elizabeth Myers. Bondsman, Frederick Houser
22 Apr 1828 Thomas Ashby & Elizabeth Slisher. Bondsman, Thomas Carnell

22 Apr 1828 John Braithwaite & Susan Farmer, daughter of John Farmer, the bondsman

1 May 1828 John Nessmith & Susan Hurford. Bondsman, Isaac Hollingsworth

5 May 1828 Patrick Smith & Sarah Lupton. Bondsman, James Rankin

6 May 1828 Ferdinand Stone & Mary Pidgeon. Bondsman, George Payne

12 May 1828 Jacob Crim & Eliza Lock, daughter of William Lock, the bondsman

13 May 1828 Benjamin James & Mary McKinsey. Bondsman, Leroy Newcomb

14 May 1828 James McBride & Elizabeth McDonald. Bondsman, Eli Smith

22 May 1828 Haines McKay & Sally McKay, daughter of John McKay, the bondsman

22 May 1828 Philip Swann & Nancy Ash. Bondsman, George B. Ash

23 May 1828 Archibald Hook & Luvanna Anderson, daughter of John Anderson. Bondsmen, Thomas Hook & Jno Anderson

26 May 1828 Daniel D. Carlile & Mary Drake. Bondsman, Lawyer Drake

26 May 1828 Winterton Murphey & Mary Cook. Bondsman, James Bowen

26 May 1828 George Wheatley & Catherine P. Taylor. Bondsman, James Bowen

2 Jun 1828 James D. Carter & Charlotte Hammick, widow & relict of James Hammick decd. Bondsman, Vincent Settle

17 Jun 1828 James C. Kennan & Mary Wilson, widow & relict of Benjamin Wilson decd. Bondsman, Samuel Hefflebower

21 Jun 1828 Jacob Johnson & Mary Martin, free persons of colour. Bondsman, Joseph Chargo

23 Jun 1828 Gersham Drake & Mary Carver. Bondsman, George Carver

26 Jul 1828 John J. Bucher & Sarah Brill, daughter of Henry Brill

30 Jul 1828 WIlliam Phillips & Evelina Bearinger, daughter of Jacob Bearinger, the bondsman

31 Jul 1828 Monroe C. Garton & Susan Jane Barker. Bondsman, Joseph H. Miller

6 Aug 1828 Conrad Shuler & Mary Green, daughter of William Green, the bondsman

13 Aug 1828 Thomas Lake & Emily Cole, daughter of Isaac Cole, the bondsman

15 Aug 1828 Patrick McKewan & Margaret McCaulley, daughter of William McCaulley, the bondsman

28 Aug 1828 George Louthan & Phebe Carter, daughter of James Carter, the bondsman

30 Aug 1828 James Morrison & Catharine Marker, duaghter of John Marker, the bondsman

1 Sep 1828 Alfred Smallwood & Milly Downing. Bondsman, Elzey Smallwood

2 Sep 1828 William Johnston & Elizabeth Ann Osborn, ward of George Osborn, the bondsman

8 Sep 1828 William W. Holmes & Eliza Ann Shambaugh. Bondsman, John Shambaugh

8 Sep 1828 Henry Houghon & Abigail Holmes. Bondsman, William W. Holmes

8 Sep 1828 Felix Meetze & Jane Bowen, daughter of William Bourn, the bondsman

9 Sep 1828 Charles H. Clark & Sarah M. Gibson. Bondsman, Marsh L. Gordon

12 Sep 1828 Smith Conner & Hannah Kendale. Bondsman, Elijah Leach

16 Sep 1828 Burrows Britten & Sarah Ann Lucinda Thacker. Bondsman, Jonah Britten

16 Sep 1828 James Bell & Nancy Huff. Bondsman, Hiram Murphy

22 Sep 1828 William Chrlsman & Mary Stanley, daughter of Archelaus Stanley, the bondsman

22 Sep 1828 Joseph W. Hackney & Deborah Morgan. Bondsman, Valentine Payton

11 Oct 1828 Abner Babb & Anna Dehaven. Bondsman, James Robinson

11 Oct 1828 Aquilla Whitacre & Rachael Kerns, daughter of Nathan Kerns, the bondsman

11 Oct 1828 James Riely & Cloe Elizabeth Compton. Bondsman, George D. Harrison

13 Oct 1828 Joseph S. Ritenour & Harriet Russell, daughter of John Russell, the bondsman

14 Oct 1828 John A. Foreman & Mary Clowser. Bondsman, Joseph Clowser

18 Oct 1828 Martin Feltner & Mary Fleming. Bondsman, Joseph Fleming

23 Oct 1828 Samuel Parke & Elizabeth Ann McKee, daughter of Joseph McKee, the bondsman

27 Oct 1828 Samuel Seelock & Nancy McCashland. Bondsman, William Swart

27 Oct 1828 John Ritter & Deborah Campbell, daughter of John S. Campbell, the bondsman

30 Oct 1828 Robert Hendron & Mary Ann Glasscock. Bondsman, Hiram Glasscock

1 Nov 1828 Harrison Thompson & Maria Faidley. Bondsman, Lester Puller

10 Nov 1828 George Widmire & Mary Ann Grove, daughter of John Grove, the bondsman

10 Nov 1828 Edwin B. Ridings & Susana Painter, daughter of Robert Painter, the bondsman

11 Nov 1828 Joseph Pitman & Eleanor Amanda Williams. Bondsman, Jared I. Williams

15 Nov 1828 John Puller & Elizabeth Taylor. Bondsman, James William

25 Nov 1828 John I. Higgins & Martha C. Heterick, daughter of Robert Heterick, the bondsman

28 Nov 1828 William Sumption & Rebeckah Utterback. Bondsman, Alexander Finnell

29 Nov 1828 Alexander Pomeroy & Elizabeth Fletcher. Bondsman, William Beaty

1 Dec 1828 George Davis & Elizabeth Moore, widow & relict of James Moore deceased. Bondsman, John Scroggin

1 Dec 1828 Elijah Lambden & Louisa Cadwallader, daughter of John Cadwallader, the bondsman

2 Dec 1828 John Lawyer & Eleanor H. Kearfott, daughter of William Kearfott

4 Dec 1828 John Moyers & Rebecca Pritchard, widow & relict of John Pritchard deceased. Bondsman, Jacob Shambaugh

8 Dec 1828 Jonah Baldwin & Maria Nancy Curl, daughter of James Curl, the bondsman

8 Dec 1828 Peter Sperry Jr. & Juliat Taylor, daughter of Jesse Taylor, the bondsman

8 Dec 1828 Solomon S. Harmon & Evalina Harriet Mauck. Bondsman, Michael Mauk

10 Dec 1828 James M. Huston & Lavinia McCandless. Bondsman, Robert P. McCandless

15 Dec 1828 Jacob Rhodes & Patsy L. Beazley. Bondsman, William Beazley

15 Dec 1828 Elisha M. Dutton & Catharine Alley. Bondsman, Henry Hoffman

16 Dec 1828 Lewis McQuaid & Susan Oats. Bondsman, John Fletcher
16 Dec 1828 David W. Barton & Frances L. Jones. Bondsman, Thomas A. Tidball
18 Dec 1828 Gabriel Nevel & Elizabeth Debell. Bondsman, Nicholas Kern
20 Dec 1828 John Hunnins & Mary McFarland, stepdaughter of Frederick Maury
22 Dec 1828 Thomas Rogers & Lucinda Light. Bondsman, Reuben Kile
22 Dec 1828 John W. Snapp & Elizabeth Shaver. Bondsman, Paul Anderson
24 Dec 1828 Smith Brown & Seatta Grubs. Bondsman, Thompson H. Richards
24 Dec 1828 Jacob Shreck & Polly Bare. Bondsman, Frederick Bare
24 Dec 1828 Perrin Washington & Hannah F. Whiting. Bondsman, Treadwell Smith
24 Dec 1828 William Ford & Harriet McDaniel. Bondsman, Alexander Churchill
26 Dec 1828 Henry Clemmons & Susan Umpenhour. Bondsman, Michal Price
29 Dec 1828 Edward Castleman & Lucinda A. Compton, widow & relict of Alexander Compton deceased. Bondsman, Isaac McCormick
30 Dec 1828 Augustus Jones & Margaret Mumaw. Bondsman, John Mumaw
30 Dec 1828 James Fisher & Susan Webber. Bondsman, James McKenny
1 Jan 1829 Rees Hill & Louisa Abbott. Bondsman, Thomas A. Tidball
5 Jan 1829 Thomas C. Miller & Cassandar J. McKay. Bondsman, Washington McKay
5 Jan 1829 Jacob Good & Lucy Wigginton. Bondsman, James Wigginton
8 Jan 1829 John Smith & Mary D. Mitchell. Bondsman, Samuel Davis
12 Jan 1829 James Florence & Emily Fish. Bondsman, Henry Fish
12 Jan 1829 Steward Self & Ann Silvers. Bondsman, James Way
14 Jan 1829 Robert Ewing & Mary White. Bondsman, James White
15 Jan 1829 George W. Baker & Emily Susan Streit. Bondsman, James P. Riely
19 Jan 1829 Joseph Fisher & Catharine Grove. Bondsman, Henry Grove

19 Jan 1829 Peter Umpenhour & Polly Neff. Bondsman, Samuel Eckes

21 Jan 1829 John Guthridge & Elizabeth H. Smith. Bondsman, Newton Headley

30 Jan 1829 Edward B. Muse & Eliza Scrivener. Bondsman, Jonathan Lovett

2 Feb 1829 David Timberlake & Elizabeth Mason, daughter of Seth Mason, the bondsman

2 Feb 1829 William E. Ball & Catharan Canavan. Bondsman, Edward B. Jacobs

2 Feb 1829 Joseph Mahaney & Francis Whykoff. Bondsman, James H. Cooke

7 Feb 1829 George Knight & Rebeccah Pagget, daughter of Edward Pagett

7 Feb 1829 Enos Spaid & Elizabeth Bruner. Bondsman, Abner Dunlap

9 Feb 1829 John Dick & Margaret Puller, daughter of Lester Puller, the bondsman

16 Feb 1829 John Harmon & Elizabeth Cryder. Bondsman, William Hewitt

18 Feb 1829 Joseph Arthur & Hetty Z. Barton. Bondsman, Richard W. Barton

24 Feb 1829 Michael Mauk & Juliet Wilson, daughter of William Wilson, the bondsman

26 Feb 1829 John Millburn & Mary Strickling. Bondsman, William Shutts

2 Mar 1829 John Dehaven, son of Jonathan Dehaven, & Jane Daniels. Bondsman, father of groom

2 Mar 1829 Reuben Rowzee & Sarah Reynolds. Bondsman, Reuben Kile

2 Mar 1829 John Tipton & Asenath Harrison. Bondsman, Isaac Harrison

2 Mar 1829 Levi Reed & Phebeann Lewis. Bondsman, John Reed

7 Mar 1829 Jacob Moyers & Polly Yates, stepdaughter of William Hutton, the bondsman

9 Mar 1829 John Cleavenger & Mary Brown. Bondsman, James Carter

9 Mar 1829 Mason H. Tapp & ELizabeth Woodard. Bondsman, John Hurford

17 Mar 1829 William P. Rales & Susannah H. Ozbourne. Bondsman, Seth Mason

19 Mar 1829 Joseph Eaton & Mary Carr, widow of William Carr. Bondsman, John Eaton

24 Mar 1829 John Chapman Jnr. & Elizabeth Payne. Bondsman, Joseph Payne

24 Mar 1829 Andrew Kiger & Polly Rutherford, widow & relict of John Rutherford deceased. Bondsman, Peter Kremer

25 Mar 1829 John Shutz & Ann Light. Bondsman, Peter Ashton

31 Mar 1829 John Dunlap & ELiza McKee, daughter of Bartholomew Mckee, the bondsman

6 Apr 1829 Joseph Renner & Martha Larrick, daughter of Henry Larrick, the bondsman

6 Apr 1829 Austin Smith & Biddy Fitzsimmons. William H. Triplett, the bondsman

6 Apr 1829 William Trenary & Cynthia Nevill. Bondsman, Hirom Nevill

6 Apr 1829 William Corder & Margaret Cox. Bondsman, Hamilton Cox

8 Apr 1829 James A. Beall & Nancy Cook, daughter of William Cook Esq. Bondsman, Alexander L. Brown

9 Apr 1829 William L. Chipley & Emily L. Bowen, daughter of Phineas Bowen. Bondsman, Jas. P. Riely

13 Apr 1829 Henry Martin & Mary Ann Hoover, daughter of Philip Hoover, the bondsman

18 Apr 1829 James V. King & Lydia White. Bondsman, John Canter

20 Apr 1829 John Lewis Jr. & Elizabeth Lewis, daughter of Jacob Lewis, the bondsman

21 Apr 1829 Lorenzo McLeod & Anna Bell Tilden. Bondsman, John B. Tilden Jr.

28 Apr 1829 Isaac F. Hite & Maria Louisa Davison. Bondsman, John B. D. Smith

4 May 1829 Benjamin Warden & Lucinda Vannort. Bondsman, Isaac W. Baker

13 May 1829 Rinear Probasco & Margaret Mills. Bondsman, William Johnston

13 May 1829 Andrew Mason & Margaret Shane, stepdaughter of Reason Mason, the bondsman

16 May 1829 James Castleman & Emaline M. Castelman, daughter of Wm Castleman Jr. Bondsman, Province McCormick

23 May 1829 James Dowell & Matilda Daniel. Bondsman, Joseph Barker

25 May John Thompson & Edeth Foley. Bondsman, John Foley

25 May 1829 Adam Albert, son of Michael Albert, & Catharine Rinker, daughtr of Jacob Rinker. Fathers are bondsmen

30 May 1829 John Kearns & Sarah Giffin. Bondsman, John Giffin

30 May 1829 Joseph Martin & Catharine Gill. Bondsman, William H. Grove

1 Jun 1829 Jonathan Keller & Nancy Shrack. Bondsman, Jacob Shrack

2 Jun 1829 Thomas Trimble & Rachel Smith. Bondsman, Jacob R. Nicklin

15 Jun 1829 Noah Frasher & Mary Taylor. Bondsman, James Taylor

24 Jun 1829 James McCormick & Ann W. Nichols. Bondsman, Isaac McCormick

25 Jun 1829 Leonard Cooper & Sarah Cooper, daughter of Abraham Cooper, the bondsman

25 Jun 1829 Joseph Vincent & Eliza Spicknall, daughter of Clement Spicknall, the bondsman

27 Jun 1828 (sic) Jefferson M. Board & Eliza H. John, daughter of Thomas John, the bondsman

1 Jul 1829 Thomas Cornwell, son of William Cornwell, & Harriet Cole. Bondsman, father of groom

4 Jul 1829 George Reno & Mary Shanks, widow of ------ Shanks decd. Bondsman, McFarlin Puller

16 Jul 1829 Lewis H. Catlett & Eliza Ann Kerfott, daughter of William G. Kerfott, the bondsman

18 Jul 1829 John Zombro & Lucinda Hawkins. Bondsman, Robert Smith

27 Jul 1829 William Marquess & Elizabeth Phillips. Bondsman, Isaac Phillips

27 Jul 1829 Henry Keller & Mary Catlett. Bondsman, Richard Hatton

29 Jul 1829 James McDonald & Sarah Dowland, widow & relict of Edward Dowland deceased. Bondsman, Charles Cunningham

3 Aug 1829 George B. Ash & Elizabeth Hand. Bondsman, John W. Grove

3 Aug 1829 Abraham Burgess & Sarah McCleave. Bondsman, James W. Burgess

3 Aug 1829 Paul Anderson & Mariah Garven, daughter of James Garvin, the bondsman

4 Aug 1829 Joseph Thomas & Jemima Murphey. Bondsman, H. M. Murphey

11 Aug 1829 Lewis P. Hornaday & Ruth Peirson. Bondsman, George Swhier Jr.

19 Aug 1829 Azariah Rigal & Icy Cornwell, daughter of William Cornwell, the bondsman

19 Aug 1829 Israel Coborn & Catharine Carper. Bondsman, John Carper

21 Aug 1829 Andrew Pitman & Margaret Lefeaver, widow of Thomas Lefeaver decd. Bondsman, Hector Bell

24 Aug 1829 Francis G. Miley & Mariah Ashby. Bondsman, John B. Murphey

27 Aug 1829 Robert B. Jones & Sarah Chapman, daughter of Joseph Chapman, the bondsman

31 Aug 1829 Mahlon Demory & Elizabeth Matthews, daughter of Richard Matthews, the bondsman

1 Sep 1829 Peter Nossett, son of William Nossett, & Mary Ann Aldridge, daughter of John Aldridge. Fathers are bondsmen

5 Sep 1829 Clement W. Billingsly & Jane Smallwood. Bondsman, Alfred Lefevos (Lefevre?)

14 Sep 1829 John Chapman & Mary Carper, daughter of Frederick Carper, the bondsman

16 Sep 1829 Abner Hanshaw & Lacy Ann Martin (Mastin?). Bondsman, Barton Hanshaw

18 Sep 1829 Richard B. Haxall (Haxald?) & Lucy E. Thompson. Bondsman, David W. Barton

25 Sep 1829 Samuel Kean & Hannah Smith, widow & relict of James Smith. Bondsman, Bennet Russell

28 Sep 1829 Robert P. Page & Susan G. Randolph. Bondsman, John E. Page

15 Oct 1829 Fenton Thomas Adams & Mary M. Pine (Price?). Bondsman, Lewis A. Smith

23 Oct 1829 French Thompson & Nancy Ramey, daughter of Isaac Ramey

24 Oct 1829 John C. Hubert & Emily E. Brill, daughter of Michael Briel

24 Oct 1829 George Conner, son of Thomas Conner, & Sarah Smedley. Bondsman, father of groom

26 Oct 1829 Robert W. Christy & Sarah Carver. Bondsman, Daniel Carver

27 Oct 1829 Lampkin Lacey & Matilda Smallwood. Bondsman, Ellzey Smallwood

28 Oct 1829 James H. Darlington & Mary S. McLeod. Bondsman, Edmund Shackelford
28 Oct 1829 Presley Thompson & Jaquelina Dowell. Bondsman, Reuben Kile
2 Nov 1829 Samuel Milslagle & Joanna Glaze. Bondsman, Sampson Glaize
2 Nov 1829 Joseph Clutter & Susanna Albin. Bondsman, George Smith
2 Nov 1829 William G. Kerfott & Sarah K. Alexander. Bondsman, John Alexander
3 Nov 1829 Samuel Berlin & Elizabeth Rodgers. Bondsman, James G. Bryce
4 Nov 1829 John Taylor & Polly Crider, daughter of John Crider, the bondsman
9 Nov 1829 George W. Garrison & Lucinda Murphy, daughter of Finley Murphy
7 Nov 1829 William Lawyer & Sarah Ann Mitchell. Bondsman, James H. Sowers
11 Nov 1829 Samuel Ashwood & Sally Clevinger. Bondsman, Peter Good
13 Nov 1829 Joseph Carter & Elizabeth Jennings, daughter of Daniel Jennings, the bondsman
27 Nov 1829 James Harris & Christena Sirbaugh. Bondsman, Jacob Sirbaugh
28 Nov 1829 Thomas I. Kneedle & Mary I. Hesser. Bondsman, Samuel L. Hesser
5 Nov 1829 William Willingham & Matilda Allender, daughter of Jacob Allender, the bondsman
14 Dec 1829 Joseph M. Nicklin & Mary N. Lane. Bondsman, Lewis Glover
14 Dec 1829 Tarlton Carr & Parmelia I. Ash. Bondsman, George B. Ash
15 Dec 1829 Jacob S. Danner & Mary Sophia Miller. Bondsman, Jacob Senseney
19 Dec 1829 Joseph Keeding & Eliza Danner. Bondsman, Anderton Brown
26 Dec 1829 Robert Athey & Louisa Smith, daughter of James Smith, the bondsman
29 Dec 1829 John R. Haddox & Linna G. Compton. Bondsman, William C. Compton
29 Dec 1829 Isaac G. Bowles & Nancy Gill. Bondsman, James P. Riely
29 Dec 1829 Eleazer C. Hutchinson & Lucy B. Randolph. Bondsman, Daniel ?Gold

30 Dec 1829 Amos Johnson & Eliza Grinnell. Bondsman, William Drury

1 Jan 1830 Robert P. Benn & Ann C. Benson. Bondsman, Joseph Palmer

2 Jan 1830 Philip Gordon & Mary Gordon, daughter of Francis Gordon, the bondsman

4 Jan 1830 James T. Monroe & Eliza Monroe. Bondsman, John Monroe

6 Jan 1830 John Despanet & Catharine Cooper. Bondsman, Abraham Cooper

6 Jan 1830 William Waln & Mary Heironimus, daughter of Henry Heironimus, the bondsman

12 Jan 1830 Sanford Gilpin & Catharine Butt. Bondsman, John McCormick

12 Jan 1830 John Jenkins & Mary Lowry, daughter of George Lowrey, the bondsman

12 Jan 1830 William Cain & Nancy Cain, daughter of Marcus Cain, the bondsman

18 Jan 1830 James Keller & Mary A. Ritter, daughter of Henry Ritter, the bondsman

18 Jan 1830 Elias Dorsey & Ann Canniford. Bondsman, Henry Canniford

21 Jan 1830 James Orndorff & Mahala Orndorff, daughter of David Orndorff, the bondsman

27 Jan 1830 Adam Boise & Susan Epfler (Effler?). Bondsman, A. W. Green

30 Jan 1830 Andrew Fleming & Mary Fleming. Bondsman, James W. Conn

4 Feb 1830 John B. Ambrouse & Julia Ann Green, daughter of William Green, the bondsman

6 Feb 1830 George Albert, son of Michael Albert, & Eliza Raynolds, daughter of Nicholas Raynolds. Fathers are bondsmen

15 Feb 1830 John Johnston & Elizabeth Dalby. Bondsman, Israel Dalby

16 Feb 1830 Morgan Johnston & Rose Ann Shackelford. Bondsman, Buckner Ashby

16 Feb 1830 Strother Franks & Eliza Douglass. Bondsman, Henry Franks

16 Feb 1830 Cornelias Simpson & Margaret Jones, ward of Dolly Jones. Bondsman, Bennet Russell

17 Feb 1830 Samuel Shriver & Elizabeth Crigler, ward of John Alexander, the bondsman

18 Feb 1830 Thomas Knight & Elizabeth E. Dick, daughter of Henry Dick, the bondsman

22 Feb 1830 Thomas Drake & Eliza Ann Bulger. Bondsman, Paul Pierce

22 Feb 1830 Lewis Luttrell & Elizabeth Dick, daughter of Peter Dick, the bondsman

23 Feb 1830 Abraham Brill & Catharine Orndorff, daughter of Jonathan Orndorff, the bondsman

24 Feb 1830 William Taylor & Francis Arnold, daughter of William Arnold. Bondsman, John B. Campbell

25 Feb 1830 Archibald Dick & Francis Luttrell. Bondsman, Lewis Luttrell

2 Mar 1830 Thomas W. Hand & Mary E. Rickets, daughter of John Ricketts, the bondsman

2 Mar 1830 Bernard Withers & Lucinda Churchill. Bondsman, Alexander Churchill

No Date. Thomas Anderson & Sarah Haymaker, widow of Adam Haymaker. Bondsman, George W. Grim

8 Mar 1830 Nelson R. Stanford, stepson of Thos Crawford, & Elizabeth Bond. Bondsman, Thomas Crawford

8 Mar 1830 George Anderson & Nancy Stanford, stepdaughter of Thomas Crawford, the bondsman

15 Mar 1830 Moses Rily & Mary Osborn. Bondsman, David Osborn

16 Mar 1830 William Stricklin & Elizabeth Braithwaite. Bondsman, Samuel Walker

20 Mar 1830 John Lodor & Rebecca G. Hite. Bondsman, Wm Simpson

20 Mar 1830 William Newell & Rosena Switzer. Bondsman, Martin Funkhouser

22 Mar 1830 Henry Nagly & Mary Taylor. Bondsman, Patrick ?Moland

24 Mar 1830 Lewis Glover & Elizabeth E. ?Keahey. Bondsman, Cyrus McCormick

24 Mar 1830 James Reed & Martha Patty. Bondsman, William Reed

30 Mar 1830 Jesse P. Frye & Christena Snapp. Bondsman, Henry Snapp

1 Apr 1830 Alfred Moore & Lucinda Crawford. Bondsman, Samuel Crawford

1 Apr 1830 Wiliam S. Curlett & Susan Q. Elliott, daughter of Benjamin Elliott, the bondsman

3 Apr 1830 Isaac Trout & Araminta L. Pagett. Bondsman, Washington F. Pagett
5 Apr 1830 William Catlett & Charlotte Catlett. Bondsman, Landen Jolly
5 Apr 1830 Enoch Strother & Elizabeth Ferguson. Bondsman, Washington Ferguson
5 Apr 1830 Joseph Stephens & Mary H. Ritenour. Bondsman, George Ritenour
6 Apr 1830 Benjamin Brill & Ann Orndorff, daughter of Jonathan Orndorff, the bondsman
9 Apr 1830 Nicholas Noel & Nancy Kerns, daughter of Nathan Kerns, the bondsman
15 Apr 1830 Aaron H. Griffith & Mary P. Hollingsworth, daughter of Isaac Hollingsworth, the bondsman
15 Apr 1830 Knight G. Smith & Emily R. Thomas. Bondsman, James P. Riely
16 Apr 1830 William Feehner & Francis Oliver. Bondsman, John Rust
17 Apr 1830 William Holliday & Eliza Lee. Bondsman, William Bailey
20 Apr 1830 James F. Brown & Darkey Lewis, daughter of Jacob Lewis, the bondsman
21 Apr 1830 Lewis Fisher & Hannah Smoke, widow of Henry Smoke. Bondsman, Samuel Fish
21 Apr 1830 Lewis Lupton & Rachael Ann Mahaney. Bondsman, George M. Adams
23 Apr 1830 Robert C. Randolph & Lucy N. Wellford. Bondsman, James P. Riely
24 Apr 1830 Cyrus W. Murry & Sarah Morehead. Bondsman, Benjm M. Massie
26 Apr 1830 Albert Turner & Betsy C. Nelson. Bondsman, John G. Turner
27 Apr 1830 James Gamble & Charity Bailey. Bondsman, David Bailey
28 Apr 1830 Benjamin Scanland & Elizabeth Ann Tapp. Bondsman, John Kidwell
29 Apr 1830 Enos Spaid & Rosanna Stipe. Bondsman, John L. Anderson
3 May 1830 Philip Stickley & Rebecca Shull. Bondsman, Jonathan Shull
4 May 1830 Jacob Lewis & Elizabeth Vance. Bondsman, Henry Sullivan
10 May 1830 Jacob Doup & Sarah Ann Pugh. Bondsman, William Dillon
15 May 1830 David Pugh & Mary Kennaford. Bondsman, Jacob Cooper

22 May 1830 William Brauner & Elizabeth Knight, daughter of Thomas Knight, the bondsman

24 May 1830 Strother G. Humston & Elizabeth Ann Ford. Bondsman, James Ford

24 May 1830 Samuel Orndorff & Elizabeth Vance, daughter of Andrew Vance, the bondsman

26 May 1830 Jacob May & Polly Naville, daughter of Henry Navill, the bondsman

26 May 1830 Joshua Baldwin & Lucinda Patterson. Bondsman, George Folk

27 May 1830 Charles Sexton & Susannah Blakemore, widow of Thomas Blakemore. Bondsman, Marcus D. Baker

8 Jun 1830 James Tanquary & Maria Rust. Bondsman, Nathan Rust

10 Jun 1830 Robert L. Randolph & Mary B. Magill. Bondsman, James P. Riely

12 Jun 1830 William Cannington & Emily Gordon, daughter of Francis Gordon, the bondsman

15 Jun 1830 Herbert Hiner & Hannah Higgins, widow of William Higgins deceased. Bondsman, Achilles Willey

16 Jun 1830 Charles W. Castleman & Sarah E. Taylor. Bondsman, William W. King

17 Jun 1830 James Christy & Elizabeth Watson. Bondsman, Jas. P. Riely

23 Jun 1830 Jacob Lutz & Helena Smith. Bondsman, Samuel Rogers

1 Jul 1830 James H. Moore & Margaret Gray, daughter of Hannamus Gray. Bondsman, Levi Brannam

12 Jul 1830 William Harding & Mary Stonestreet. Bondsman, Joseph Stonestreet

15 Jul 1830 William Richardson & Elizabeth Ann Millar. Bondsman, James P. Riely

15 Jul 1830 Henry Brobeck & Mahala Hottle, daughter of David Hottle, the bondsman

17 Jul 1830 George Lowry & Sarah Cline. Bondsman, Leroy Newcomb/Newcum

19 Jul 1830 James Shumate & Ann Susan Rust, daughter of John Rust

21 Jul 1830 Thomas Grubbs & Frances Royston. Bondsman, Jacob Anderson

9 Aug 1830 Charles Hotsinpiller & Amelia S. Pitman. Bondsman, Jos. S. Ritenour

2 Aug 1830 Ephraim C. Slack & Harriet Isaacs. Bondsman, Josiah Murray

18 Aug 1830 Timothy Willcox Jnr. & Catharine Hughs. Bondsman, Charles Hughs

19 Aug 1830 Alfred Carper & Sarah Welch. Bondsman, Jacob Carper

19 Aug 1830 Charles Ruby & Margaret Gaw, ward of Wm. Denny, the bondsman

25 Aug 1830 Matthew Boyas & Juliet Epler, daughter of Peter Epler, the bondsman

28 Aug 1830 William Ross & Sophia Stickley. Bondsman, Simon Stickel

30 Aug 1830 Nimrod A. Davison & Mazy Larrick, daughter of George Larrick, the bondsman

6 Sep 1830 William Deahl & Ann Hefflebower. Bondsman, David Deahl

6 Sep 1830 Richard M. Sydnor & Mary Ann Brent. Bondsman, John G. Brent

8 Sep 1830 Isaac Pugh & ELizabeth McFarlan. Bondsman, Peter Sperry

9 Sep 1830 Thomas Phillips & Clarissa H. Baker. Bondsman, Robt Lockhart

13 Sep 1830 Joseph Carter & Catharine Reed. Bondsman, James Reed

20 Sep 1830 Benjamin Kidd & Hannah Rees, daughter of Jacob Rees, the bondsman

7 Oct 1830 Jos McDaniel & Margaret Millhorn. Bondsman, Michael H. Reed

11 Oct 1830 Elijah Weekley & Delilah Butler, widow of Robert Butler. Bondsman, George Brown

13 Oct 1830 Benoni Wheat & Rachel Ann Chapman, daughter of William Chapman, the bondsman

19 Oct 1830 Jonathan Fisher & Frances Dutton, daughter of William Dutton

25 Oct 1830 William C. Kerfoot & Eliza Ann Sowers. Bondsman, John Kerfoot

26 Nov 1830 Lewis Ambrouse & Elizabeth Hawkins, daughter of John Hawkins, the bondsman

28 Oct 1830 John Dehaven & Athalia Dehaven. Bondsman, James Robinson

28 Oct 1830 William Ott & Eliza Hartman. Bondsman, George Hay Lee

4 Nov 1830 Robert Worthington & Catharine Helm. Bondsman, John R. Cooke

7 Nov 1830 Benjamin Thompson & Juliet A. Drake. Bondsman, Gersham Drake

8 Nov 1830 John T. Cowgill & Rebecca McKee, daughter of Joseph McKee, the bondsman

8 Nov 1830 William C. Lauck & Eliza I. Sowers. Bondsman, Hector Bell

13 Nov 1830 Elias Collins & Rebecca Robinson. Bondsman, John Collins

18 Nov 1830 Elias E. Compton & Sarah T. Burgess. Bopndsman, Abraham Burgess

22 Nov 1830 Cornelius Hoff & Jane Fleming, daughter of Archibald Fleming, the bondsman

26 Nov 1830 James H. Sowers & Elizabeth Catlett. Bondsman, Thomas A. Tidball

4 Dec 1830 Buckner Ashby & Sophia G. Baker. Bondsman, William Baker

8 Dec 1830 Joseph White & Elizabeth Nelson. Bondsman, Moses Nelson

8 Dec 1830 Philip Berry & Nancy Gilbert. Bondsman, Saml Simpson

17 Dec 1830 William Fox & Jane Daniel. Bondsman, Jonathan Smith

19 Dec 1830 Jacob Brown & Eleaner McDonald, daughter of James McDonald, the bondsman

20 Dec 1830 James Night & Nancy Boxwell. Bondsman, Harison Knight

20 Dec 1830 Asa Larrick & Rebecca Hottle, daughter of David Hottle, the bondsman

21 Dec 1830 James P. Riely & Catharan M. Brent. Bondsman, Thomas Allen Tidball

22 Dec 1830 Cornelius Shewler & Harriet Kerns, daughter of Jacob Kerns, the bondsman

22 Dec 1830 Henry Collins & Susanna Mason, daughter of Bingly Mason, the bondsman

22 Dec 1830 Thomas Young & Elizabeth Way. Bondsman, John I. Monroe

22 Dec 1830 William Trowbridge & Lydia Watson, daughter of William Watson, the bondsman

23 Dec 1830 William S. Rodgers & Elizabeth Rodes, ward of Samuel Rogers

23 Dec 1830 William H. Coontz & Christena Afflick. Bondsman, Alexander Nulton

24 Dec 1830 Isaac Berlin & Mildred Oliver. Bondsman, John Rust

27 Dec 1830 William Little & Eliza Stump, daughter of Benjamin Stump. Bondsman, James Moss

28 Dec 1830 Jacob Oats & Virlinda Robinson, daughter of John T. Robinson, the bondsman

29 Dec 1830 John Stickley Mary Oatley (Ottsy?). Bondsman, Abdiel Davis

31 Dec 1830 Saml S. Kline & Ann C. Wolfe. Bondsman, James T. White

4 Jan 1831 Carter Williamson & Ann Elizabeth Hoover, upwards of 21 years of age. Bondsman, John F. Wall

5 Jan 1831 Nathaniel Albin & Catharine Peirce, daughter of Joseph Peirce, the bondsman

6 Jan 1831 Richard R. Phelps & Asberry Ana Tilden. Bondsman, John W. Wells

10 Jan 1831 James R. Ewan & Elizabeth Ann Widows, dauaghter of Robert Widows, the bondsman

11 Jan 1831 David Boise & Sarah L. Morris. Bondsman, John Dowell

18 Jan 1831 Joseph Corson & Catharine Carter. Bondsman, Joseph Carter

31 Jan 1831 Michael Fisar & Mary Connelly. Bondsman, George S. Lane

31 Jan 1831 Achilles Willey & Eliza Myers. Bondsman, Abraham Burges

4 Feb 1831 Moses Nelson & Elizabeth Ewan. Bondsman, Robert Ewing

5 Feb 1831 Andrew Milburn & Sarah Stricklyn, daughter of John Stricklyn. Bondsman, John Shutts

7 Jan 1831 John Saunders & Charlotte Glasscock. Bondsman, Kemp Glasscock

14 Feb 1831 Baylys W. Barrow & Nancy Myers, upward of 21 years of age. Bondsman, Thomas Barrow

15 Feb 1831 James Violet & Lucinda White, daughter of Isaac White, the bondsman

18 Feb 1831 Joseph Heck & Emily White, daughter of William White, the bondsman

24 Feb 1831 Henry Baker & Mary Ann Bywaters. Bondsman, William Bywaters

7 Mar 1831 Isaac N. Kline & Ana Snider, daughter of George Snider, who signs in German

12 Mar 1831 John Gardner & Rosanna Krouse, daughter of John Krouse. Bondsman, Robert Clark

14 Mar 1831 George H. Harper & Ann Probasco, upwards of 21 years of age. Bondsman, Henry Larrick

14 Mar 1831 John Jenkins & Emily Susan Evans, widow of Harvey Evans. Bondsman, William Jenkins

15 Mar 1831 David Hollingsworth & Eleanor Hollingsworth, daughter of Isaac Hollingsworth

17 Mar 1831 Isaac Baker & Elizabeth Kenny. Bondsman, John Kenny

22 Mar 1831 Timothy Willcox Senr. & Mary Curry, widow & relict of Thomas Curry decd. Bondsman, Jonathan Adams

23 Mar 1831 John Jinkins & Frances Smith, daughter of George Smith, the bondsman

23 Mar 1831 John H. Lewis & Mary Ann Yakeley. Bondsman, George Yakeley

24 Mar 1831 Thomas F. Bryarly & Mary Lupton. Bondsman, Enoch Fenton

25 Mar 1831 Bailey R. Glasscock & Lucy A. Kerfott, daughter of John Kerfoot

29 Mar 1831 Barney Pitcock & Eliza Spencer. Bondsman, Peter Good

2 Apr 1831 Philip Loyer? & Elizabeth Wear, daughter of James Ware, the bondsman

4 Apr 1831 Phillip Puller & Elizabeth Magruder, widow of Ninion Magruder deceased. Bondsman, John Strother

11 Apr 1831 George Taylor & Eliza Ann Colvin. Bondsman, Thomas Colvin

13 Apr 1831 Jonathan W. Adams & Ann Maria Hamilton. Bondsman, Robert P. McCandless

2 May 1831 Gottlieb Bodenhofer & Elizabeth Blum, his ward. Bondsman, John Smith Davison

2 May 1831 William Denny & Lana G. Jordan. Bondsman, Alexander Finnell

4 May 1831 Benjamin W. Jefferson & Lucy Ellen Sample Silver, daughter of Francis Silver, the bondsman

14 May 1831 Mahlon Lovett & Mary B. Muse. Bondsman, Martin B. Muse

14 May 1831 Henry Orndorf & Maria Boucher. Her age attested by Moses Boucher. Bondsman, Jonathan Orndorf

17 May 1831 Isaac Walker & Mariah S. Hale (Wall?). Bondsman, Thos Seevers

25 May 1831 John Cryder & Rebecca McFarland. Bondsman, Levin McFarland

6 Jun 1831 Baalis Davis & Eliza Timberlake, daughter of David Timberlake, the bondsman

9 Jun 1831 Alexander Clark & Caroline McKewan, upwards of 21 years of age. Bondsman, George Folk

13 Jun 1831 Charleton Slone & Mary Hoff, daughter of Elizabeth Hoff, the bondsman

22 Jun 1831 George Switzer & Elizabeth M. Allamong, daughter of William Allemong

23 Jun 1831 Alfred Cable & Sarah Barr. Bondsman, Eli Crupper

4 Jul 1831 Lawrence Turner & Jane W. Tobin. Bondsman, Laurence Cartright

11 Jul 1831 George F. Calmes & Lucy Ann Bonn. Bondsman, Meredith Helm

18 Jul 1831 John McCauley & Arthelia Allen. Bondsman, William Lane

19 Jul 1831 Moses Showalter & Susan Snyder. Bondsman, Josiah Massie

25 Jul 1831 Benjamin E. Cornwell & Nancy Grant. Bondsman, William Leach

25 Jul 1831 Anthony Rosenburger & Nancy Heffloebower, widow of Daniel Heffloebower. Bondsman, George Hefflebower Jnr., who signs in German

27 Jul 1831 David Grove & Mary Bickley, daughter of Elizabeth Bickley, the bondsman

30 Jul 1831 Thomas Cornell & Phebe Ann Tomlin. Bondsman, Thomas Ashby

2 Aug 1831 Robert Beatty & Jane Crouse. Bondsman, Robertson Way

6 Aug 1831 William G. Haines & Jane Smith, daughter of Michel Smith, the bondsman

6 Aug 1831 William Brown & Emily Baker. Bondsman, Henry Baker

11 Aug 1831 John Ready & Elizabeth McCauley, daughter of John McCauley, the bondsman

12 Aug 1831 John Holland & Rose Anna Puffinburger, daughter of John Puffinburger, the bondsman

16 Aug 1831 Solomon P. Spangler & Lucinda Tanquary, daughter of Walter Tanquary, the bondsman

21 Aug 1831 Charles Beam & Lucy Ann Hottle, daughter of Andrew Hottle, the bondsman

6 Sep 1831 John K. Triplett & Rachel Anderson. Bondsman, Jonathan Anderson

12 Sep 1831 Thomas A. Jackson & Maria Shull. Bondsman, Elijah Shull

15 Sep 1831 William H. Morrow & Mary Jane Murry, daughter of Cyrus W. Murry, the bondsman

20 Sep 1831 Robert Breedlove & Elizabeth Mark. Bondsman, Moses Showatter

27 Sep 1831 Isaac Dick & Mary Light, daughter of Henry Light, the bondsman

28 Sep 1831 Reubin S. Long & Elizabeth R. Miller. Bondsman, Joseph H. Miller

no date Burkley Tumblin & Lewiza Murphy, his ward. Bondsman, Alfred P. Moore

5 Oct 1831 William S. Thompson & Isabella Wilson (Neilson?). Bondsman, Joseph Miller

5 Oct 1831 Edmond Stanbrough & Susanna Person. Bondsman, George Person

8 Oct 1831 David Brown & Elizabeth Bowen. Bondsman, Augustine Holtzman

13 Oct 1831 Hiram Murphy & Grace F. Mitchell. Bondsman, Henry Smith

13 Oct 1831 John S. Crawford & Sarah A. Mitchell. Bondsman, Henry Smith

14 Oct 1831 William Kerr & Isabella Castleman. Bondsman, Thomas A. Tidball

17 Oct 1831 Jeremiah Marple & Nancy M. Johnston, daughter of Amos Johnston, the bondsman

17 Oct 1831 Nathaniel D. Parran & Anne E. Williams, Bondsman, Wright Gatewood

17 Oct 1831 George Carver & Ann Drake. Bondsman, Gersham Drake

18 Oct 1831 Abraham Barrow & Mahaley Larrick. Bondsman, Joseph Larrick

21 Oct 1831 Abram Emmart & Jane Vance, daughter of Andrew Vance, the bondsman

22 Oct 1831 Amos Marker & Margaret Brill, daughter of Henry Brill, the bondsman

24 Oct 1831 Elijah Hodgson & Eliza Hays. Bondsman, William Jinkins

29 Oct 1831 George Strother & Sarah Ferguson, daughter of John D. Ferguson, the bondsman

29 Oct 1831 Fairfax Washington & Emely Whiting. Bondsman, Herbert Washington

7 Nov 1831 James Holland & Mary Puffinburger. Bondsman, John Williams

9 Nov 1831 Lawrence Cartwright & Lucinda Tobin, daughter of Isaac Tobin, the bondsman

12 Nov 1831 Noah Racey & Salomy Orndorf. Bondsman, Moses Russell

14 Nov 1831 James M. Glass & Sarah Elizabeth Glass. Bondsman, Joseph G. Gray
15 Nov 1831 Daniel Sowers & Louisa C. Sowers, daughter of Fielding L. Sowers, the bondsman
16 Nov 1831 John Pierce & Elizabeth Louthan. Bondsman, George Louthan
16 Nov 1831 John Edwards & Mary Ann Brown, widow of Francis C. Brown. Bondsman, John Monroe
19 Nov 1831 Lewis Kearns & Hannah McDonald. Bondsman, Moses McDonald
21 Nov 1831 Samuel Lanham & Mary Gibbs, daughter of William Gibbs, the bondsman
23 Nov 1831 Samuel Cunningham & Elizabeth Hollis. Bondsman, John Smoke
28 Nov 1831 George Washington Brown & Rosanna Howard, upwards of 21 years of age. Bondsman, James Howard
1 Dec 1831 George Streit & Mary Manor, daughter of David Manor, the bondsman
2 Dec 1831 Isaac Piper & Margaret C. Stephens, daughter of Catharine Stephens, the bondsman
5 Dec 1831 Joseph Johnston & Matilda Greenway, daughter of James Greenway, the bondsman
6 Dec 1831 Matthias Ritter & Nancy Archer, daughter of William Archer
7 Dec 1831 Sampson B. Clark, son of Abner Clark, & Mary Null, daughter of David Null. Parents are bondsmen
7 Dec 1831 Joseph Larrick & Mary Gyer, widow of Ishmael Gyer. Bondsman, John Wright

Marriage Bonds No. 16 1831-1834
8 Dec 1831 Jacob Enders & Rebecca W. Blakemore. Bondsman, Province McCormick
19 Dec 1831 Eli Conner & Margaret John. Bondsman, Ashford John
22 Dec 1831 Jonathan Parsons & Mary Ann Carter. Bondsman, Arthur W. Carter
24 Dec 1831 John Patterson & Abigail Carr, widow of Richard Carr. Bondsman, Henry P. Ward
27 Dec 1831 John Sirbaugh & Elizabeth Hensell. Bondsman, Joseph Files

28 Dec 1831 Frederick Krider & Sarah Marpole. Bondsman, John C. Lemly

29 Dec 1831 Isaiah Young & Joannah M. Lyons. Bondsman, James Lyons

3 Jan 1832 Benjamin Kent & Betsy Stonestreat. Bondsman, Saml Stonestreat

6 Jan 1832 Edward Jones & Martha Henry. Bondsman, Adam Henry

6 Jan 1832 Daniel Grim & Sarah Watson. Bondsman, Hannah Watson

9 Jan 1832 Vance Bradford & Elizabeth A. Marpole, daughter of Jane Marpole. Signed, Jane (X) Bradford

14 Jan 1832 Benjamin Collins & Rebecca Ann Watson. Bondsman, John Watson

17 Jan 1832 Bennett D. Mattox & Mary Ann T. Horn. Bondsman, William Fox

24 Jan 1832 John Helpbringer & Tamson Wolfe. Bondsman, William Wolfe

25 Jan 1832 William Bowman & Phebe S. Parker. Bondsman, Joseph B. Parker

31 Jan 1832 Charles Bales & Elizabeth Fish, daughter of Robert Fish, the bondsman

6 Feb 1832 John Davison & Sarah Stevens. Bondsman, Archibard Dunlap

20 Feb 1832 Daniel W. Sowers & Mary E. Kerfott, daughter of John Kerfoot, the bondsman

20 Feb 1832 David Davis & Eleanor Darlinton. Bondsman, Richard Flower

22 Feb 1832 Samuel McDonald & Susanah Evans. Bondsman, Josiah McDonald

27 Feb 1832 John S. Ewing & Elizabeth Owens. Bondsman, Rudolph T. C. Boude

1 Mar 1832 Henry Crumley & Balindy Rodgers. Bondsman, Israel Dalbey

3 Mar 1832 Zachariah Carpenter & Catharine Bowen, widow of Meredith Bowen decd. Bondsman, Philip Carper

3 Mar 1832 Hiram A. Blanchard & Amanda Jane Stevens, daughter of Martin Stevens. Bondsman, Brian M. Stephens

5 Mar 1832 Samuel Vance & Hannah Orndorff, daughter of Samuel Orndorff, the bondsman

5 Mar 1832 Alfred Carper & Eliza Seifert. Bondsman, Jacob Keller

5 Mar 1832 Jonathan Jenkins & Eliza Bean. Bondsman, Mordecai Bean

7 Mar 1832 Alfred Shutts & Mary Eaton, daughter of John Eaton, the bondsman

7 Mar 1832 John Marshall & Betsy Green. Bondsman, Alfred Green

7 Mar 1832 Alfred Green & Jane Dowdell. Bondsman, William Hearle

8 Mar 1832 Watson Carter & Hannah Marvin. Bondsman, William Marven

10 Mar 1832 Hiram Gibbins & Mary Shreak. Bondsman, George D. Harrison

12 Mar 1832 William Bourn & Mildred Jane Hathaway. Bondsman, John Bourn

12 Mar 1832 William Baldwin & Ann Samsell. Bondsman, Edward Myers

13 Mar 1832 Rudolph Hammock & Nancy Foley. Bondsman, John Foley

13 Mar 1832 Thomas Leach & Rebecca Kendle. Bondsman, John Ford

20 Mar 1832 William Gardener & Mary Shiner. Bondsman, Stephen Ritter

28 Mar 1832 Michael Lawyer & Maria Baer, daughter of Frederick Baer, the bondsman

2 Apr 1832 Andrew Clendening & Elizabeth McDonald. Bondsman, Jacob R. Nicklin

3 Apr 1832 James W. Ash & Jane Lang. Bondsman, George Bell

3 Apr 1832 George H. Lewis & Susanna Yeakley. Bondsman, George Yeackley

10 Apr 1832 Benjamin Marpole & Rebecca Clark. Bondsman, Joseph Marple

14 Apr 1832 James Carpenter & Ann H. Lewis. Bondsman, Jacob Lewis

23 Apr 1832 Paul Peirce & Margaret Clevinger, daughter of John Clevinger

25 Apr 1832 Thompson McDonald & Hariet Macatee. Bondsman, Edward Gilbert

25 Apr 1832 John L. Campbell & Elizabeth Beckley. Bondsman, William R. Tapp

26 Apr 1832 William Stokes & Sarah Pitcock, daughter of John Pitcock. Bondsman, Philip A. Boucher made his mark being disabled in the right hand

30 Apr 1832 George Swhier Jr & Henrietta Richards, stepdaughter of Abraham Watson, the bondsman

30 Apr 1832 Michael Umpenour & Jane McElevene. Bondsman, Henry Clemmons

8 May 1832 Richard Smithey & Martha J. Gardner. Bondsman, Levi Henshaw

8 May 1832 Joseph B. Lacey & Jemima D. Richards. Bondsman, James R. Richards

16 May 1832 Joseph A. Williamson & Mary Mann Page. Bondsman, John Page Jr.

19 May 1832 John Criner, son of Elizabeth Griffy, & Darcus Cooley. Bondsman, Elizabeth Griffy

21 May 1832 Jacob Whetsel & Hannah Setser. Bondsman, Mical Yew

22 May 1832 Wesley McKay & Frances E. Garrison. Bondsman, Joseph McKay

28 May 1832 James M. Hall & Alcy Stephens. Bondsman, Greenbury Stephens

28 May 1832 William Reed Campbell & Eliza Ball Cartmell. Bondsman, Y. K. Cartmell

29 May 1832 Van E. Vanmeter & Mary V. Sowers. Bondsman, E. P. Hunter

2 Jun 1832 George Frailey & Elizabeth Linder. Bondsman, Christian Hull

4 Jun 1832 Barton Hanshaw & Thuza A. E. Minser. Bondsman, Franklin Huggins

6 Jun 1832 James Newman & Elmira Rowzee. Bondsman, John Latham

6 Jun 1832 John Day & Vina Anne Kline. Bondsman, Samuel Campbell

12 Jun 1832 John Wilson & Mary Raynolds, daughter of Thomas Raynolds, the bondsman

12 Jun 1832 Benjamin R. Lacy & Catharine Lindsey. Bondsman, James M. Lindsey

13 Jun 1832 Jonathan Hoover & Mary Ann Hiett, daughter of Thomas Hiett, the bondsman

14 Jun 1832 Samuel Pickrell & Eliza Moore. Bondsman, Balis Mackdonell

4 Jul 1832 Hierome Romine & Susan Carpenter. Bondsman, Thomas Trussell

2 Aug 1832 Samuel Swatts & Mary Ann Corson, daughter of Joseph Corson, the bondsman

6 Aug 1832 Casper Rogers & Eliza Ann Brown, daughter of Adam Brown decd. Bondsman, Robert Brown

6 Aug 1832 Harrison C. Brown & Emaline Romine. Bondsman, Dennis OConner

9 Aug 1832 Nathan Kerns & Catharine Noel. Bondsman, Nicholas Noel

11 Aug 1832 Jacob Vanmetre Jr. & Emily E. L. Ship. Bondsman, Bushrod Taylor
15 Aug 1832 Granville Chewining & Mary Ann Hainey. Bondsman, Moses W. Brown
16 Aug 1832 Abraham Williamson & Marenda Jane Ohaver. Bondsman, Adam Strosnider
23 Aug 1832 Spencer Riley & Elizabeth Conner. Bondsman, Thomas North
24 Aug 1832 Thomas Ashby & Amanda Wright. Bondsman, Wm Graham
28 Aug 1832 James McDonald & Frances Ann Simpson. Bondsman, John Churchill
1 Sep 1832 Jacob Sirbaugh & Elizabeth Oats. Bondsman, Lewis McQuaid
4 Sep 1832 James Cross & Sarah Ann G. Earle, ward of Seth Mason, the bondsman
1 Sep 1832 William S. Anderson & Ann M. Gibbons. Bondsman, George Aulick
12 Sep 1832 John Foley & Sarah Ann Housar, daughter of Frederick H. Houser, the bondsman
19 Sep 1832 Henry Grant & Frances Stokes. Bondsman, Abraham Breedlove
19 Sep 1832 Thomas Dann & Elizabeth Pugh, widow of Jesse Pugh decd. Bondsman, Leml Bent
21 Sep 1832 William Carper & Lucy Carper, daughter of William Carper, the bondsman
24 Sep 1832 Warner Nelson & Susan Anderson. Bondsman, Sydnor B. Anderson
24 Sep 1832 Joseph Carpenter & Liddy M. Keller, daughter of Peter Keller, the bondsman
25 Sep 1832 William Pyle & Ann Wayde, daughter of Thomas Wade, the bondsman
27 Sep 1832 Henry Weaver & Rachel Chapman. Bondsman, Joshua Chapman
1 Oct 1832 William (Wm. B.?) Talbott & Frances McGruder. Bondsman, Francis Magruder
2 Oct 1832 Addison Broy & Catherine Martin. Bondsman, Beryman Jones
2 Oct 1832 Beryman Jones & Sarah Andrews. Bondsman, Addison Broy
10 Oct 1832 John McDowell & Sidney O. Glass. Bondsman, James M. Glass
13 Oct 1832 Elias D. Bell & Elizabeth Correll. Bondsman, Nicholas Kern
13 Oct 1832 Robert Campbell & Maria Muckey, daughter of Catharine Muckey, the bondsman

15 Oct 1832 John Morgan & Meggy T. Little, daughter of Robert H. Little, the bondsman

17 Oct 1832 George H. Sickafoose & Elizabeth Brett (Butt?), daughter of Margaret McCormick

22 Oct 1832 Wilberforce Lyle & Susan D. Matthews. Bondsman, Thomas Allen Tidball

23 Oct 1832 Joseph Painter & Emily McKay, daughter of John McKay, the bondsman

24 Oct 1832 William H. Luckett & Lucy Ann Lefevre. Bondsman, Griffin Grant

24 Oct 1832 Henry Light & Sarah Dick, daughter of Peter Dick, the bondsman

22 Oct 1832 Lewis Fisher & Rachael Williams, daughter of William Williams, the bondsman

30 Oct 1832 Alexander W. Albin & Mary Ewan, daughter of Thomas Ewan, the bondsman

5 Nov 1832 John Watson & Rebecca ?Putty or Putts (ink blot). Bondsman, Jonas Ridgway

6 Nov 1832 Robert Brown & Barbara B. Cather. Bondsman, David Z. Brown

10 Nov 1832 Samuel J. Hackley & Susan Heutchins. Bondsman, Benjamin Smith

12 Nov 1832 John W. Byrd & Mary F. Page. Bondsman, John Page Jr.

12 Nov 1832 Thomas H. Crow & Frances Amelia Shepherd. Bondsman, E. C. Breedin

13 Nov 1832 William Green & Elizabeth Evans. Bondsman, William Pepper

15 Nov 1832 William Fletcher & Mary Utter. Bondsman, Thomas North

17 Nov 1832 Sydnor Edmonds & Margaret B. Edmonds. Bondsman, K. C. Hicks

21 Nov 1832 John Henry Arnold, son of Jesse Arnold, & Eliza Everheart, daughter of Margaret Everheart. Bondsmen, Jesse Arnold & Margaret Everheart

22 Nov 1832 Joseph Richard & Mary Magdaline, daughter of Joseph Frye, the bondsman

23 Nov 1832 Jarrod Mills & Jane Gill. Bondsman, Robertson Way

28 Nov 1832 Willson I. Sypher & Frances M. Hardesty. Bondsmen, William Dooley & Robert Morris

28 Nov 1832 John Swatts & Caroline Green, daughter of William Green, the bondsman

3 Dec 1832 Amos Spengler & Margaret Stewart. Bondsman, Philip Stockslager

5 Dec 1832 John Wood & Cassandra H. Brown. Bondsman, R. B. Ashby

10 Dec 1832 Philip A. Bucher & Hannah Dutton. Bondsman, William Dutton

10 Dec 1832 Amos A. Bonham & Eliza Ann McCormick. Bondsman, Albert McCormick

12 Dec 1832 William Tapp & Juliann Rowland, daughter of Martin Rowland, the bondsman

14 Dec 1832 Samuel Beatty & Hannah Johnston. Bondsman, Thomas Elsea

15 Dec 1832 Samuel Stipe & Lucy Drake. Bondsman, Gersham Drake

17 Dec 1832 Francis J. Ash & Mary Ann Way, daughter of Robertson Way, the bondsman

17 Dec 1832 Thomas Glass & Catharine Wood. Bondsman, Thomas Allen Tidball

17 Dec 1832 Peter Taylor, upwards of 20 years of age, & Malinda Nelson, upwards of 21 years of age. Bondsman, Patrick Moreland

22 Dec 1832 Edward Hines & Sarah Kerns, daughter of Adam Kerns, the bondsman

22 Dec 1832 Richard Waggoner & Mary P. Gains. Bondsman, Otway McCormick

24 Dec 1832 Thomas L. Humphrey & Delitha Riely. Bondsman, Moses Riley

24 Dec 1832 Henry Clink & Susan Everheart, daughter of Margaret Everheart, the bondsman

25 Dec 1832 John W. Ewan & Sarah Ann Abbott. Bondsman, William Hening

27 Dec 1832 Samuel Grubbs & Hannah Royston. Bondsman, Matthew Royston

3 Jan 1833 Samuel Stonestreat & Mary Ann Watkins. Bondsman, John Beavers

4 Jan 1833 George Smedley & Mahaly Burn, widow of John Burn decd. Bondsman, Felix H. Thornton

5 Jan 1833 Philip Earhart & Phebe Drake, widow of John Drake dec. Bondsman, Lewis A. Smith

10 Jan 1833 William N. Thompson & Elizabeth Glass. Bondsman, James V. Glass

15 Jan 1833 William Shores & Hannah Watson. Bondsman, Moses Stickel

17 Jan 1833 Matthew Rust & Comfort M. Marshall. Bondsman, John B. Rust

19 Jan 1833 George Knight & Elizabeth Henning. Bondsman, William Hening
21 Jan 1833 James Boggs & Rachel Ambrose, daughter of John Ambrose, the bondsman, who signs in German
21 Jan 1833 John M. Clark & Sarah V. Gilkeson, daughter of John Gilkeson, the bondsman
22 Jan 1833 John W. Sowers & Mary Emily Mitchell. Bondsman, James Sowers
23 Jan 1833 Joseph Cline & Eliza C. Pool. Bondsman, Daniel Snyder
23 Jan 1833 John Spengler & Margaret Russell. Bondsman, John Russell
23 Jan 1833 William M. Wilson & Mary Elizabeth Snapp. Bondsman, John Snapp
1 Feb 1833 John Ship & Juliet Castleman, widow of William Castleman dec & daughter of Henry Beatty, the bondsman
9 Feb 1833 Charles W. Andrews & Sarah W. Page. Bondsman, John E. Page
11 Feb 1833 Henry Barnes/Bruner & Mary Ann Matthews. Bondsman, Squire E. Matthews
19 Feb 1833 Samuel Campbell & Mary Moulden. Bondsman, John Wright
22 Feb 1833 Richard S. Calvert & Mahaly Garrett, daughter of Jacob Garrett, the bondsman
25 Feb 1833 Jacob Showalter & Arabella Abel. Bondsman, Charles Hulet
26 Feb 1833 Zachariah Kern & Sarah A. Hamilton, daughter of William Hamilton, the bondsman
28 Feb 1833 George Linawever & Rachel Fry. Bondsman, Daniel Kline
4 Mar 1833 Moses Bucher & Lydia Vanhorn. Bondsman, Matthas Rutter
4 Mar 1833 William Spencer & Mary I. Gantze. Bondsman, Solomon Herman
4 Mar 1833 Isaac Canby/Canter & Susan I. McCauley. Bondsman, Isaac White
5 Mar 1833 John Light & Rachelanne Kerr. Bondsman, William D. Kerr
7 Mar 1833 Nathaniel Cartmell & Sarah E. Lupton. Bondsman, Nathaniel C. Lupton
9 Mar 1833 Mason Orem & Mary Ann Hoff. Bondsman, Joseph Hoff

11 Mar 1833 Harley Greenwood & Frances Davis. Bondsman, David Timberlake, Jr.
12 Mar 1833 Gary Davis & Elizabeth Blake. Bondsman, Alfred P. Moore
13 Mar 1833 Joseph Hancher & Rebecca Tanquary. Bondsman, William Kerr
14 Mar 1833 Nathan Roberts & Elizabeth Sidebottom. Bondsman, Richard Sidebottom
16 Mar 1833 Augustin Holtzman & Mary Louisa Brown. Bondsman, Arthur W. Carter
18 Mar 1833 Nathan Bean & Rachel Jenkins. Bondsman, Jacob Jenkins
18 Mar 1833 John W. Moorisson & Jane Johnston. Bondsman, George Johnston
18 Mar 1833 James Violett & Matilda Gardner, daughter of George Gardner, the bondsman
19 Mar 1833 Presley N. Helm & Ann Elizabeth Blakemore. Bondsman, Chas McCormick
22 Mar 1833 William J. Clark & Frances E. Waln. Bondsman, Jesse Waln
23 Mar 1833 William Perry & Mary Ann Kern. Bondsman, Solomon Kern
23 Mar 1833 Solomon Taylor & Emeline Little. Bondsman, John Dowell
26 Mar 1833 Overton F. Heironimus & Maria Taylor. Bondsman, Thomas Colvin
27 Mar 1833 Carr W. Bayliss & Sarah Brent. Bondsman, Henry Navell
28 Mar 1833 Jacob Frye & Catharine Moss. Bondsman, Presley Moss
30 Mar 1833 George Mauzy & Margaret Fout. Bondsman, Henry Fout
30 Mar 1833 Martin Fries & Betsy Ann Fulkeson, daughter of John Fulkerson
1 Apr 1833 Archibald M. Simpson & Mary Barley. Bondsman, John Barley
2 Apr 1833 Thomas Wilson & Lydia Jackson. Bondsman, George Fyst
5 Apr 1833 Franklin Barrow & Barbary Ann Steel, daughter of Adam Steel, the bondsman
8 Apr 1833 Alexander Swany & Elizabeth Rummonds, daughter of Thomas Rummonds, the bondsman
16 Apr 1833 Joshua Gore & Majery D. Lockhart. Bondsman, Robert V. Lockhart

18 Apr 1833 Thomas Middleton & Susannah Dailey. Bondsman, Matthias Rutter
20 Apr 1833 Edward Fletcher & Hannah Scott. Bondsman, Evan Thatcher
22 Apr 1833 Emanuel Garmong & Rebecca Shipe. Bondsman, Isaac Shipe
27 Apr 1833 Levi Kile & Mary Jane Rogers, daughter of Thomas Rogers, the bondsman
4 May 1833 George McLeod & Adelaid Shackleford. Bondsman, Edmund Shackelford
6 May 1833 John Currey & Mary Ann Taylor, upward of 21 years of age, daughter of Catharine Taylor, the bondsman
6 May 1833 Henry Grove & Phoebe Mercer. Bondsman, Abraham Grove
6 May 1833 James Jones & Eliza Noland. Bondsman, William W. Holmes
8 May 1833 Edward C. McDonald & Francis H. Singleton. Bondsman, Robert C. Kercheval
8 May 1833 Robert C. Kercheval & Judith T. Singleton. Bondsman, Edward C. McDonald
20 May 1833 David N. Anderson & Margaret A. Holmes. Bondsman, Danl C. Clemmens
27 May 1833 Abraham Johnson & Mary Ann McCormick. Bondsman, WIlliam O. Bond
11 Jun 1833 Thomas John & Nancy White. Bondsman, Thornton Leach
13 Jun 1833 Robert M. Campbell & Rebecca A. Lockhart. Bondsman, Charles H. Clark
15 Jun 1833 Joshua Hudson & Catharine Brent, stepdaughter of Henry Navell
25 Jun 1833 Daniel C. Clemmons & Mary L. Holmes. Bondsman, John S. Hockinsmith
26 Jun 1833 Moses P. Watson & Lucinda McLaughlin. Bondsman, William Berry
9 Jul 1833 Abraham Shoe & Thursay Bateman, widow of John Bateman. Bondsman, Edwin Hart
16 Jul 1833 Philip Cissil & Lucinda Hardesty. Bondsman, Hezekiah Trenary
29 Jul 1833 Mager Anders & Isabell Perry. Bondsman, Caleb H. Perry
2 Aug 1833 Lemuel Stillions & Jane Garrison, daughter of Moses Garrison, the bondsman
6 Aug 1833 Squire Garmong & Louisa Mitchell. Bondsman, Maria Mitchell

8 Aug 1833 Thomas Riely & Margaret Kern, daughter of George Kern, the bondsman
10 Aug 1833 Jonas Janney Jr. & Ruth Davis. Bondsman, Gabriel H. Davis
12 Aug 1833 James Rogers & Rachel Parlett. Bondsman, John Parlett
16 Aug 1833 Benjamin Fravel & Elizabeth Abent, daughter of Jacob Abent
21 Aug 1833 William Kerns & Harriet Ann Michael. Bondsman, Jacob Kerns
22 Aug 1833 Toliver R. Owens & Mary Hass. Bondsman, John Ewing
2 Sep 1833 Singleton Trenary & Lydia Ritter. Bondsman, Stephen Ritter
2 Sep 1833 John Slane & Harriett Murphy, daughter of Thomas Murphy, the bondsman
7 Sep 1833 Thomas Graves & Lydia Ann Adams, daughter of William Adams, the bondsman
7 Sep 1833 Asa Fisher & Frances R. Williams. Bondsman, Benoni Wheat
9 Sep 1833 John Paynter & Elizabeth Leach. Bondsman, Thomas H. Crow
9 Sep 1833 Henry Noel & Lydia Farmer, daughter of John Farmer, the bondsman
10 Sep 1833 Chaplin S. Hedges & Mary R. Lee. Bondsman, Thomas Allen Tidball
10 Sep 1833 Garland T. Wheatly & Sarah Ann Taylor. Bondsman, James Bowen
11 Sep 1833 Jacob Henshaw & Hannah Chapman. Bondsman, Hiram Hancher
12 Sep 1833 Leonard Gordon Rowland & Naomi Hill. Bondsman, William Rowland
12 Sep 1833 Joshua Whitacre & Ann Nesmith. Bondsman, Jonas Whitacre
14 Sep 1833 James H. Neville & Mary Ann Price. Bondsman, Alexander Vance
16 Sep 1833 John B. Petty & Sarah H. Mitchell, stepdaughter of Alexander Finnell, the bondsman
16 Sep 1833 Thomas J. Duncan & Elizabeth B. Bywaters. Bondsman, Robert C. Bywaters
18 Sep 1833 Joseph Miller & Susan Jane Lemley, daughter of John Lemley, the bondsman
19 Sep 1833 William Green & Eliza Riely. Bondsman, Joseph Palmer
1 Oct 1833 Andrew W. Shane & Rebecca Dehaven, daughter of Job Dehaven

8 Oct 1833 James H. Burgess & Harriet Ann Beall, daughter of Eli Beall, the bondsman

14 Oct 1833 William B. Minser & Catharine Streit. Bondsman, George Streit

15 Oct 1833 William D. Gilkeson & Mary E. Baker. Bondsman, Daniel D. Clark

15 Oct 1833 James W. Mason & Martha Cook. Bondsman, Giles Cook

16 Oct 1833 John Q. Berry & Ann Collins. Bondsman, George Simpson

16 Oct 1833 John Lloyd & Mary Bowling. Bondsman, Samuel Lloyd

17 Oct 1833 Henry G. Walter & Hannah Hass. Bondsman, Toliver R. Owens

19 Oct 1833 Alexander Marshall & Emily Jane Conrad. Bondsman, Matthew Garban

19 Oct 1833 Robert Davison & Catharine May. Bondsman, James Foster

22 Oct 1833 Abraham V. Evans & Mary Eliza Rowland, daughter of Samuel Rowland, the bondsman

23 Oct 1833 John Stephens & Leah Belford. Bondsman, Archibald Stephens

28 Oct 1833 Joseph S. Baker & Mary Kenney. Bondsman, William Brown

29 Oct 1833 Thomas Stewart & Elizabeth Orem. Bondsman, Aaron E. Orem

5 Nov 1833 John Jinkins & Eliza Ann Hodgson, daughter of Robert Hodgson, the bondsman

11 Nov 1833 Abraham S. Rhodes & Ann R. Brinker. Bondsman, Jacob Senseney Jr.

12 Nov 1833 John Wilson & Juliet Ann Smallwood. Bondsman, John Dowell

13 Nov 1833 William Peters & Sarah Marks, daughter of Henry Marks, the bondsman

13 Nov 1833 Thomas Jackson & Catharine Campbell. Bondsman, Smith Taylor

18 Nov 1833 John C. Bonham & Sarah Jane Kerfott, daughter of John Kerfoot, the bondsman

20 Nov 1833 John Taylor & Margaret Ann Singhass, daughter of Geo. M. Singhass, the bondsman

26 Nov 1833 Henry Edwards & Mary Ann Chism, daughter of James Chism, the bondsman

28 Nov 1833 Joshua Kerns & Eliza Oats. Bondsman, Washington Whitacre

2 Dec 1833 Joseph Leith & Mary Mckee. Bondsman, David L. Mckee.
9 Dec 1833 William Cool & Catharine Shane. Bondsman, John Smith
9 Dec 1833 Napoleon B. Balthrope & Elizabeth Marshall. Bondsman, John Marshall
10 Dec 1833 Thomas Edwards & Eliza Trenary. Bondsman, William Carper
10 Dec 1833 William McDaniel & Gennette Collings. Bondsman, Baalis McDaniel
12 Dec 1833 Reuben Elliott & Mildred Triplett. Bondsman, N. B. Triplett
14 Dec 1833 Howard Thornton & A. C. Norris. Bondsman, J. C. R. Taylor
16 Dec 1833 Henry Sweitzer & Eve Grove. Bondsman, John Grove
19 Dec 1833 Thomas Lake & Mary Amanda Wrose, daughter of Thomas Wrose, the bondsman
20 Dec 1833 Charles Sumption & Susan Perry. Bondsman, Caleb H. Pearry
20 Dec 1833 John R. Feegan & Mary Elizabeth White. Bondsman, John Y. White
21 Dec 1833 William R. Haynie & Margaret F. Davis. Bondsman, Baalis Davis
23 Dec 1833 Martin B. Muse & Hannah Anderson. Bondsman, Robert V. Lockhart
23 Dec 1833 Andrew Kidd & Nancy Whittington. Bondsman, Joseph Whittington
28 Dec 1833 Samuel Edmonds & Sidney Dowell. Bondsman, Carr Chapman
30 Dec 1833 George Allender & Mary Allender, daughter of Jacob Allender, the bondsman
1 Jan 1834 Thomas G. Gordon & Frances C. Meagill. Bondsman, John S. Magill
3 Jan 1834 William Strother & Catharine Tewalt. Bondsman, Jacob R. Snapp
6 Jan 1834 Henry Ritter & Margaret Bare, daughter of Frederick Bare, the bondsman
7 Jan 1834 Edward Jenkins & Celia A. Myers. Bondsman, Joseph Myers
8 Jan 1834 Joshua Chapman & Rachel Messer. Bondsman, John Mark
9 Jan 1834 John Miller & Julia Ann Bishop. Bondsman, John V. Brown
10 Jan 1834 Joseph Drake & Harriett Bulger. Bondsman, Thos Drake

13 Jan 1834 John Robinson & Sarah Conrad. Bondsman, James W. V. Conrad
15 Jan 1834 James Shires & Elizabeth Garrett. Bondsman, Alexander C. Mills
15 Jan 1834 Alexander C. Mills & Matilda Garrett. Bondsman, James Shires
15 Jan 1834 Daniel Curl & Harriet Hackney. Bondsman, William Kerr
17 Jan 1834 Henry N. Griggsby & Harriet I. Knight. Bondsman, George Knight
20 Jan 1834 Hamilton Gibbins, son of Jacob Gibbins, & Magdaline Bechley, daughter of Magdalene Bechley (Beckley?)
23 Jan 1834 Samuel Byers & Susan Snyder. Bondsman, Robert Gill
29 Jan 1834 Whiting Hamilton & Ann Blake. Bondsman, Samuel Lloyd
29 Jan 1834 Moses Stickley & Mahaley Blake. Bondsman, Samuel Lloyd
29 Jan 1834 Jacob Mytinger & Evelina Watson. Bondsman, James H. Carson
29 Jan 1834 George W. Milton & Ann M. Haynie. Bondsman, Thomas W. Raynolds
15 Feb 1834 David Sirbaugh & Catharine Shuler. Bondsman, Cornelius Shuler
17 Feb 1834 Daniel Bouzer & Sarah Jane Richards. Bondsman, Abraham Watson
17 Feb 1834 John W. Page & Emily Smith. Bondsman, Thomas A. Tidball
22 Feb 1834 Joseph Light & Priscilla Robinson. Bondsman, Jonathan Dehaven
24 Feb 1834 Samuel Hopkins & Lavina E. Joliffe. Bondsman, John M. Brome
24 Feb 1834 David Hayward & Elizabeth H. Newcom. Bondsman, Jacob Newcom
27 Feb 1834 Anderton Brown & Martha J. Burgess. Bondsman, Andrew K. Smith
3 Mar 1834 William Lynn & Catharine Setzer. Bondsman, Philip Setzer
3 Mar 1834 David Clevenger & Hannah Brown. Bondsman, Asa Clevenger
5 Mar 1834 Martin Hott & Eleanor Barrett. Bondsman, George Streit
15 Mar 1834 John Lewis & Margaret Young. Bondsman, Mathew Rutter
17 Mar 1834 George W. Somerville & Elizabeth Laing. Bondsman, John Laing

22 Mar 1834 George Dorsey & Susan C. Keeler. Bondsman, Middleton Keeler
22 Mar 1834 David Haltaman & Ann G. Barnhard, daughter of John Bernhard, the bondsman
29 Mar 1834 Noah L. Gordon & Elizabeth Ann Peake. Bondsman, William Oscar Peake
29 Mar 1834 John Whittington & Rachel L. Gibbins. Bondsman, Jacob Gibbens
29 Mar 1834 William Gibbons & Catharine Beatty. Bondsman, Jacob Gibbens
31 Mar 1834 Sanford Gilpen & Mary E. Cartwright, daughter of Henry Cartwright, the bondsman
31 Mar 1834 Nicholas J. B. Morgan & Mary Elizabeth Phelps. Bondsman, Elisha P. Phelps
31 Mar 1834 John Butter & Elizabeth Hutsler. Bondsman, John Hutslor
2 Apr 1834 Thomas Roach & Elizabeth Benton, daughter of Levi Burton, the bondsman
4 Apr 1834 Thornton Flinn & Eliza Johnston. Bondsman, William Willey
7 Apr 1834 James B. Steidley & Rachel Reese, daughter of Jacob Rees, the bondsman
8 Apr 1834 Elisha Barrow & Alla L. Steele, daughter of James Steele, the bondsman
10 Apr 1834 Jacob Shade & Reanah Triplett. Bondsman, John Triplett
10 Apr 1834 John Wilcox & Maria Rankin. Bondsman, John Locksimon
15 Apr 1834 William Violett & Sarah Ann Gardiner, daughter of George Gardiner, the bondsman
22 Apr 1834 Joseph Marple & Mary Jones, daughter of Jonathan Jones, the bondsman
28 Apr 1834 Aaron Largent & Mary Catharine Hieronimus, daughter of Henry Hieronimus, the bondsman
30 Apr 1834 Richard Jackson & Mary Ann Brown, daughter of John Brown, the bondsman
12 May 1834 William Ritenour & Jane Margaret Hening, daughter of David Hening, the bondsman
12 May 1834 John Patterson & Harriet Russell. Bondsman, Williamm G. Everhart
13 May 1834 James W. Phillips & Eveline M. Windle. Bondsman, Daniel Gold

14 May 1834 William Thompson & Sarah McClunn. Bondsman, Joshua Osburn

14 May 1834 Abner Bond & Mary Beal. Bondsman, Joshua Osburn

15 May 1834 Joseph Ross & Sarah Jones, widow of Robert Jones. Bondsman, John Mayers

22? May 1834 Samuel Royen (Royer?) & Lydia Horner. Bondsman, Richard Flower

24 May 1834 James Watters & Sarah Suttle. Bondsman, Jeremiah Lee

2 Jun 1834 Samuel Bower & Catharine Dehaven. Bondsman, John Scrogin

2 Jun 1834 Henry D. Bartlett & Caroline N. Davis. Bondsman, John Gilkeson

3 Jun 1834 Joseph McGovern & Agnes M. Grotts. Bondsman, James M. Hulet

11 Jun 1834 Joseph Tewalt & Leah Vance, daughter of Andrew Vance. Bondsmen, Abraham Tewalt & Andrew Vance

12 Jun 1834 Isaac Shipe & Jane Dowell. Bondsman, Thomas Jones

15 Jun 1834 William Cather & Eliza G. Cather. Bondsman, James Cather

28 Jun 1834 Samuel McDonald & Eliza Saintmyers. Bondsman, Simpson Allison

3 Jul 1834 Amos H. McKay & Mary Jane Tanquary. Bondsman, Abagail Tanquary

29 Jul 1834 Thomas Watson & Nancy Franklin. Bondsman, Moses Franklin

29 Jul 1834 Benjamin Crampton & Elizabeth Jackson. Bondsman, Jacob Mesmer

2 Aug 1834 George Foster & Elizabeth Fries, daughter of David Fries, the bondsman

4 Aug 1834 Jacob A. Marker & Elizabeth Johnston. Bondsman, John Marker

4 Aug 1834 William Mason & Malinda Butler. Bondsman, Aaron E. Orem

12 Aug 1834 James M. Babb & Hannah Smith, daughter of John S. Smith, the bondsman

13 Aug 1834 John W. Whissen & Susan Berry. Bondsman, John M. Elliott

13 Aug 1834 John Marshall & Jane A. Wyatt. Bondsman, Harrison L. Wiatt

14 Aug 1834 Isaac H. Elliott & Rhoda Ann Cooper, upward of 21 years of age. Bondsman, Joseph Cooper

14 Aug 1834 Alfred Shores & Deanna Marts. Bondsman, John Marts
18 Aug 1834 John Glasscock & Mary Ann Leach. Bondsman, B. F. Bradford
22 Aug 1834 James Silver & Eliza Painter. Bondsman, Jesse Haines
25 Aug 1834 William Luttrill & Christiana Berkhemer. Bondsman, William Catlett
1 Sep 1834 Augustine Ball & Susan Richardson. Bondsman, Tilman Shumate
1 Sep 1834 Edward B. Jacobs & Mary Ann Shumate. Bondsman, Tilman Shumate
9 Sep 1834 Edward Jones & Sarah Strawbridge. Bondsman, Levi Shane
11 Sep 1834 William Yates & Mary Willey. Bondsman, William Willey
13 Sep 1834 Joshua Antrem & Permelia Stephens. Bondsman, Brian M. Stephens
16 Sep 1834 Peter Glasscock & Sidney Catlett. Bondsman, Jesse C. Bolen

Marriage Bonds No. 17 1834-1838
24 Sep 1834 Patrick McKeown & Mary Curray. Bondsman, Timothy Willcox
24 Sep 1834 John H. Dick & Mary Maria Herronimus. Bondsman, John C. Heironimus
27 Sep 1834 Henry Swann & Margaret Lupton. Bondsman, Thomas Allen Tidball
29 Sep 1834 Enoch C. Breedin & Lucy P. Singleton. Bondsman, Geo. W. Seevers
6 Oct 1834 George R. Hotzenpiller & Sophia M. Beatty. Bondsman, William Hening
7 Oct 1834 Amos Anderson & Eliza Albin, stepdaughter of George Smith
7 Oct 1834 Jacob Wright & Susan Mason, daughter of Andrew Mason, the bondsman
8 Oct 1834 Benjamin F. Brown & Miranda Lewis, daughter of John Lewis, the bondsman
11 Oct 1834 Robert Denny & Eliza Piper, daughter of Abraham Piper, the bondsman
15 Oct 1834 William Willey & Mary Catharine Houser, daughter of Frederick Houser, the bondsman
18 Oct 1834 Mark Bird & Sarah C. M. Hite. Bondsman, Walker M. Hite
18 Oct 1834 Isaac Bohrer & Rachel Jane Adams. Bondsman, Asa J. Adams

22 Oct 1834 George Barley & Julia Ann Specknale, daughter of Clement Spicknale, the bondsman
29 Oct 1834 John Stover & Catharine Susan Grim. Bondsman, George W. Grim.
3 Nov 1834 Jacob Hite & Mary Walters. Bondsman, Lawrence Walters
3 Nov 1834 Michael Stump & Harriet Whissen. Bondsman, Jacob Whetsell
3 Nov 1834 William H. Gooding & Martha Ellen Morgan, daughter of Richard Morgan, the bondsman
4 Nov 1834 Michael Bowser & Margaret Atty. Bondsman, Elisha Dutton
8 Nov 1834 George W. Black & Elizabeth Stipe, daughter of David Stipe, the bondsman
10 Nov 1834 Robert A. Colston & Matilda Gantt. Bondsman, John Gant
11 Nov 1834 Joseph Frye & Sarah Williams. Bondsman, Samuel Williams
18 Nov 1834 George Barr & Alecy Shacklet. Bondsman, Eli Crupper
25 Nov 1834 John Anderson & Mary M. Babb. Bondsman, Robert Brannon
1 Dec 1834 George W. Groves & Emily Morrison. Bondsman, John B. Earle
2 Dec 1834 William G. Russell & Sarah Catharine Wolfe. Bondsman, Jas M. Hulet
2 Dec 1834 Franklin Little & Mary Jane Bowen, daughter of Phineas Bown, the bondsman
2 Dec 1834 William Devoe & Elizabeth F. Rust, daughter of Peter Rust, the bondsman
4 Dec 1834 Thomas C. Ogden & Mary Miller. Bondsman, William H. Miller
4 Dec 1834 Henry Smith & Deborah L. Mitchell. Bondsman, Hiram Murphey
6 Dec 1834 John Smith & Maria Keiter. Bondsman, Benjamin Keiter
10 Dec 1834 Richard Cranswick & Catharine Owens. Bondsman, Simon Rees
16 Dec 1834 Benjamin Morgan & Martha Ann Castleman. Bondsman, James M. Hulet
17 Dec 1834 Philip Williams Jr. & Mary L. L. Dunbar. Bondsman, Francis L. Smith
20 Dec 1834 John D. Ferguson & Emily A. Green, daughter of James Green, the bondsman

20 Dec 1834 John W. Piper & Harriet OBoyle. Bondsman, George Piper

22 Dec 1834 Ezekial Barton & Susanna Whitacre. Bondsman, Jonas Whitacre

23 Dec 1834 William Ambrouse & Julia Ann Lock, daughter of William Lock, the bondsman

29 Dec 1834 John M. Piper & Martha Duncan. Bondsman, J. L. Feely

30 Dec 1834 Silas Bailey & Sarah Trotter. Bondsman, William Trotter

30 Dec 1834 John W. Hall & Ceatta White. Bondsman, Judge White

3 Jan 1835 Stephen J. Lindsey & Elizabeth H. Lindsey. Bondsman, Joseph B. Lindsey

5 Jan 1835 John Taylor & Sarah Cooper. Bondsman, Joseph Cooper

5 Jan 1835 David Keeler & Ann Fitzsimmons. Bondsman, John Anders

5 Jan 1835 George Milhorn & Mary Ann Helpbringer. Bondsman, John Helpbringer

6 Jan 1835 Bryan H. Henry & Sarah Ann Allen. Bondsman, James R. Richards

6 Jan 1835 Elisha Snapp & Druzilla Fry, daughter of Joseph Fry, the bondsman

12 Jan 1835 Elias Athey & Emily Ritter, daughter of Henry Ritter, the bondsman

14 Jan 1835 John Racey & Lucy Ellen Lyons, daughter of James Lyons, the bondsman

15 Jan 1835 Joseph A. Brown & Mary Ann Bartlet. Bondsman, Thomas D. Bartlett

28 Jan 1835 Amos Pitman & Sarah Barr, daughter of Samuel Barr, the bondsman

28 Jan 1835 John R. Hooper & Emily Settle. Bondsman, John Churchill

29 Jan 1835 John Enders & Mary Flemister. Bondsman, James M. Hulet

2 Feb 1835 Moncure Robinson & Charlotte B. R. Taylor. Bondsman, John C. R. Taylor

2 Feb 1835 Charles D. Shambaugh & Mary Jane Shambaugh. Bondsman, Jonas H. Shambaugh

2 Feb 1835 George Smith & Elleanor McKee, daughter of Bartholomew McKee, the bondsman

3 Feb 1835 Bennett Wood & Mary Feltner. Bondsman, Martin Feltner

11 Feb 1835 Edward J. Davison & Eleanor C. Baldwin. Bondsman, Isaac W. Baldwin

16 Feb 1835 Peter Keller & Eliza Ritter, daughter of Henry Ritter, the bondsman
17 Feb 1835 Henry Lloyd & Sarah Downing, daughter of Benjamin Downing, the bondsman
19 Feb 1835 Philip A. Hite & Mary A. Wilson, Bondsman, Thomas J. Wilson
20 Feb 1835 Thomas L. Way & Sarah M. Brown. Bondsman, Isaac N. Brown
21 Feb 1835 Solomon Pitman & Sarah G. Longacre. Bondsman, James H. Longacre
24 Feb 1835 James M. Richards & Lydia Ann Hollingsworth, daughter of Isaac Hollingsworth, the bondsman
24 Feb 1835 Edward Stonestreet & Lucretia Watkins, widow of William Watkins. Bondsman, William Hummer
24 Feb 1835 William Hummer (Haun) & Julian Huff, upwards of 21. Bondsman, Edward Stonestreet
25 Feb 1835 Edward B. Snapp & Elizabeth Dutton, daughter of William Dutton, the bondsman
26 Feb 1835 John Rosenburger & Catharine Ann Richards, daughter of Isaac Richards, the bondsman
28 Feb 1835 Amos Kidwell & Rachel Frederick. Bondsman, Samuel Stump
3 Mar 1835 Frederick W. Maurer & Elizabeth Huff. Bondsman, Jacob Lambert
9 Mar 1835 Robert Conner & Sarah McDaniel. Bondsman, Baalis McDaniel
10 Mar 1835 Isaac Tewault & Lucy Renner, daughter of Peter Renner, the bondsman
11 Mar 1835 Joseph Piper & Evelina C. Poole. Bondsman, W. G. Watson
13 Mar 1835 Richard Dement & Harriet S. Corbin. Bondsman, Allen Williams. No signature for groom
14 Mar 1835 Amos Lafollet & Maria Racey. Bondsman, William Lafollet
17 Mar 1835 Gabriel H. Davis & Mary McWhorter. Bondsman, Joseph B. Hackney
25 Mar 1835 John Sprout & Mary Ann Steward. Bondsman, John Callen
26 Mar 1835 Isaac Renner & Mary Larrick. Bondsman, Henry Larrick
31 Mar 1835 Washington F. Pagett & Margaret I. Barrow. Bondsman, Baylis Barrow

3 Apr 1835 Horace P. Smith & Susan T. Kerney. Bondsman, Lewis Glover

7 Apr 1835 Lawrence Wallers & Elizabeth Barnhart. Bondsman, Jacob Hite

7 Apr 1835 David Samsell & Margaret Ann Piper. Bondsman, John E. Samsel

8 Apr 1835 Thomas Clark & Martha Dehaven, daughter of West Dehaven, the bondsman

8 Apr 1835 Samuel Walker & Elizabeth Wilson. Bondsman, Henry B. Streit

13 Apr 1835 William Wigginton & Elizabeth Clouser. Bondsman, Joseph Clouser

16 Apr 1835 John T. Tabler & Elizabeth Ann Bowen. Bondsman, Phineas Bowen

16 Apr 1835 Levi Garrison & Jane Ross. Bondsman, William Ross

18 Apr 1835 James Dailey & Margaret Everett, granddaughter of Andrew Mason, the bondsman

22 Apr 1835 William M. Jackson & Mary A. Hopkins. Bondsman, Joseph S. Carson

23 Apr 1835 Adam Lawyer & Elizabeth Brady Kerfott. Bondsman, William Kearfott

25 Apr 1835 Joseph McCarty & Mary Strider, daughter of Henry Strider, the bondsman

2 May 1835 Jacob McKevor & Rachel Orndorff. Bondsman, John Orndorff

6 May 1835 William D. Kerr & Mary E. Davis. Bondsman, John Gilkeson

11 May 1835 James Stickley & Matilda Shull. Bondsman, Elijah Shull

13 May 1835 Jacob Rodgers & Nancy Louthan. Bondsman, David Likens

14 May 1835 John Willingham & Nancy Hess (widow). Bondsman, Ovid Willingham

14 May 1835 James Mitchell & Charlotte Ship. Bondsman, Ewell Baker

16 May 1835 James E. B. Rose & Martha Walter. Bondsman, William A. Rose

13 May 1835 Frederick Barrow & Sarah A. McClunn. Bondsman, John E. McClunn

28 May 1835 Archibald Lyon & Mary Mckee, daughter of Joseph Mckee, the bondsman

2 Jun 1835 James Carroll & Mary Ann Shoe, daughter of Abraham Shoe, the bondsman

2 Jun 1835 Samuel Garven & Melinda Johnson, his ward. Bondsman, John Johnson

3 Jun 1835 Addison Williams & Eliza Hart, daughter of Adam Hart, the bondsman

8 Jun 1835 Daniel Hupp & Sarah Walter. Bondsman, Henry G. Cartwright

13 Jun 1835 Amos Coulter & Sarah Ann Rowland. Bondsman, Saml Rowland

15 Jun 1835 John Addison & Sarah D. Lockhart. Bondsman, Robert V. Lockhart

20 Jun 1835 George R. Daniel & Lucinda Robertson. Bondsman, William Fox

23 Jun 1835 Kimble G. Hicks & Amanda F. Shackelford. Bondsman, Townsend W. Thomas

23 Jun 1835 Baalis McDaniel & Eliza Collins. Bondsman, John Churchill

23 Jun 1835 John Miller & Sarah Grove. Bondsman, John Crockwell Sr

24 Jun 1835 Thomas Butterfield & Catharine Briton. Bondsman, Samuel Cunningham

24 Jun 1835 Jesse J. Pugh & Elizabeth Larrick, daughter of Frederick Larrick, the bondsman

29 Jun 1835 George McFarland & Sarah Ann Jennings, daughter of Daniel Jennings, the bondsman

2 Jul 1835 Philip Carper & Susan Loyer. Bondsman, John Carper

4 Jul 1835 Henry Grant & Arthelinda Patton. Bondsman, David Patton

11 Jul 1835 Adam Peacemaker & Delilah Kerns. Bondsman, Jacob Heironimus

28 Jul 1835 Simon K. Burkholder & Rebecca Chrisman. Bondsman, Simon Kratzer

29 Jul 1835 George K. Boyer & Catherine Mourey, daughter of Frederick R. Moury, the bondsman

10 Aug 1835 John C. Gregg & Lucy A. Boston. Bondsman, George Boston

17 Aug 1835 John Greenhulgh & Alice Ridings, daughter of John Ridings, the bondsman

18 Aug 1835 Israel Dolby & Eliza Ogden. Bondsman, Joseph Dalbey

22 Aug 1835 Ephraim Snapp & Barbara Lemly. Bondsman, John C. Lemley

24 Aug 1835 James Gibbs & Mary Jane Starkey. Bondsman, Benjamin Starkey

25 Aug 1835 Adam W. Osborn & Maria N. Baldwin, widow of Jonah Baldwin decd. Bondsman, Daniel Curl

27 Aug 1835 John Hummer & Mary Ann Goss, daughter of Martin Goss, the bondsman

29 Aug 1835 Aquilla Osborn & Sibby Cornwell, widow of Robert Cornwell. Bondsman, Moses Riley

8 Sep 1835 Isaac Shinhoge & Margaret Streight. Bondsman, William Mincer

12 Sep 1835 William Shiner & Elizabeth Rutter. Bondsman, William G. Kerfott

14 Sep 1835 Joseph Johnston & Nancy Dunlap. Bondsman, Archibald Dunlap

15 Sep 1835 Nicholas Sampsell & Margaret A. Gibson. Bondsman, William H. Grove

21 Sep 1835 James Schultz & Louisa Jane Anderson. Bondsman, Benjamin Tanquary

23 Sep 1835 William Keller & Judith Bear, daughter of Frederick Bear, the bondsman

26 Sep 1835 George May & Mary Jones. Bondsman, Michael H. Reed

28 Sep 1835 James Dainty & Rebecca Albin, daughter of Andrew Albin, the bondsman

30 Sep 1835 James Smith & Martha A. Carver, daughter of Elisha Carver, the bondsman

30 Sep 1835 Samuel S. Yeakle & Mary J. Payne, daughter of George Payne, the bondsman

30 Sep 1835 Henry Brown & Ellen S. Wood. Bondsman, Johnson Furr

5 Oct 1835 John Eaton & Anna Owens. Bondsman, Joseph Eaton

10 Oct 1835 James Denges & Elizabeth Bradford. Bondsman, Abraham Tipple

10 Oct 1835 John L. Clark & Phebe Dehaven, daughter of Job Dehaven, the bondsman

12 Oct 1835 George Kremer Jr. & Rebecca Pelter, daughter of James Pelter, the bondsman

14 Oct 1835 David Lewis & Harriet Eagle. Bondsman, William Dooley

19 Oct 1835 William Lynn Jr. & Mary Ann Streit. Bondsman, George Streit

20 Oct 1835 Watson Perry & Rebecca Shambaugh. Bondsman, Jonas H. Shambaugh

21 Oct 1835 Daniel Dehaven & Mary Ann Light, daughter of Frederick Light, the bondsman

21 Oct 1835 William R. Johnson & Sarah A. Baker, daughter of Thomas Baker, the bondsman

27 Oct 1835 Addison Johnston & Mildred McClunn, daughter of Sarah McClunn, the bondsman

27 Oct 1835 Mager Steel & Eliza Kern, daughter of Adam Kern, the bondsman

27 Oct 1835 Ephraim Fenton & Mary A. Dooley. Bondsman, Robert Morris

29 Oct 1835 Robert L. Baker & Julia A. Baker, daughter of Henry W. Baker, the bondsman

31 Oct 1835 Adam Ritter & Nancy Albin, daughter of William Albin, the bondsman

2 Nov 1835 Michael H. Hite & Lucy E. Hamilton, daughter of William Hamilton, the bondsman

2 Nov 1835 George Swhier & Mary Shreck. Bondsman, James M. Hulet

5 Nov 1835 John B. Davis & Ann Hening, daughter of David Hening, the bondsman

6 Nov 1835 Frederick Heironimus & Maria Hutchinson, daughter of Jesse Hutchinson, the bondsman

7 Nov 1835 Benjamin F. Baker & Elizabeth Russell. Bondsman, James Russell

16 Nov 1835 Jacob Fries & Rebecca Mincer, daughter of John Minser, the bondsman

17 Nov 1835 Joseph Trowbridge & Lovinia Light, daughter of Henry Light, the bondsman

19 Nov 1835 Thomas Carter & Ann W. Page. Bondsman, Thomas F. Nelson

23 Nov 1835 James Russell & Margaret Ann Keckley. Bondsman, Benjamin Keckley

24 Nov 1835 Cornelius Jackson & Lucy Pitcock. Bondsman, William Stokes

26 Nov 1835 Jacob Mendenhall & Mary Ritter. Bondsman, David W. Barton

28 Nov 1835 Robert Frazier & Catharine Widdows, daughter of Robert Widdows, the bondsman

28 Nov 1835 Robert Widdows & Ellen Ewan, niece of Israel Ewan, the bondsman

7 Dec 1835 Edward B. Ridings & Eliza Barrow. Bondsman, George Ridings

8 Dec 1835 John Jenkins & Susan C. Anderson. Bondsman, Harrison Anderson

9 Dec 1835 James W. Harris & Catherine E. Kerney. Bondsman, James R. Richards

14 Dec 1835 Alexander Wood & Martha L. Doughty. Bondsman, William Doughty

16 Dec 1835 Benjamin T. Berkeley & Rebecca Ann Chinowith, daughter of John Chenowith, the bondsman

19 Dec 1835 John Shivers & Margaret Oats, daughter of Jacob Oats, the bondsman

21 Dec 1835 Robert Florence & Nancy Keller. Bondsman, John Richardson

23 Dec 1835 William Walters & Sarah Ann Keller, daughter of Peter Keller, the bondsman

24 Dec 1835 James M. Pine & Susan Brown, daughter of James Brown, the bondsman

25 Dec 1835 Josiah Tidball & Lucy G. Page. Bondsman, Thomas Allen Tidball

29 Dec 1835 Patrick Howard & Jane Cather. Bondsman, James Cather

30 Dec 1835 Franklin Shepherd & Susanna Oats, daughter of Jacob Oats, the bondsman

2 Jan 1836 George Swatz & Sarah Ann Klotz, daughter of Isaac Klotz, the bondsman

9 Jan 1836 Robert Smith & Elizabeth Vincent. Bondsman, John Vincent

14 Jan 1835 John Strickling & Debrah Shuler. Bondsman, William Shuler

15 Jan 1836 Griffin S. Taylor & Catharine Swatz. Bondsman, Edward Tigner

16 Jan 1836 George W. Hammond & Sarah A. Taylor. Bondsman, Bushrod Taylor

19 Jan 1836 Laban Wilson & Ann Painter. Bondsman, John Painter

22 Jan 1836 James Castleman & Catharine Shepherd. Bondsman, Champ Shepherd

25 Jan 1836 Thornton P. Pendleton & Emily J. Richardson, daughter of John Richardson, the bondsman

25 Jan 1836 Philip L. C. Burwell & Susan A. Lee. Bondsman, Francis B. Whiting

30 Jan 1836 Presley Ramey & Elizabeth M. Hammock. Bondsman, John Hammock

30 Jan 1836 Asa J. Adams & Mary Ann Dick. Bondsman, Peter Dick

2 Feb 1836 Charles H. Green & Rebecca H. Lane. Bondsman, Morgan Johnston

2 Feb 1836 Newman M. Jacobs & Julia A. Harris. Bondsman, Morgan Johnston

9 Feb 1836 Hiram Craig & Dicanda Dent Dick, daughter of Henry Dick, the bondsman

11 Feb 1836 John Scroggins & Mary Ann Figgins. Bondsman, Thomas Lake

11 Feb 1836 Solomon Jones & Sarah Ann Randell, daughter of Catharine Randell

13 Feb 1836 James Whittaker & Mary Stickle. Bondsman, Joseph Stickle

14 Feb 1836 Alfred Willey & Sarah Foley, widow of John Foley. Bondsman, William Yates

16 Feb 1836 John Snapp & Elizabeth Wilson, daughter of William Wilson, the bondsman

22 Feb 1836 Turner Kendall & Nancy Pritchett. Bondsman, Barnet Pritchet

23 Feb 1836 Ephraim Watson & Selina Eliza Lock, daughter of John Lock, the bondsman

23 Feb 1836 Elijah Shull & Harriet Johnston. Bondsman, Addison A. Johnston

26 Feb 1836 Obed Willingham & Mary Lanham. Bondsman, John Willingham

29 Feb 1836 Philip M. Earhart & Leana Graham. Bondsman, Jacob Shoop

1 Mar 1836 George W. Rutter & Amanda M. Hesser. Bondsman, Thomas J. Kneedler

2 Mar 1836 Truman Collins & Jane Smith, daughter of Eli Smith, the bondsman

2 Mar 1836 George Marpole & Livina Mckee. Bondsman, Enoch Marpole

9 Mar 1836 George W. Legg & Eliza Doughty. Bondsman, William S. Anderson

14 Mar 1836 John W. Owen & Cecilia Burwell, widow of Edwin B. Burwell. Bondsman, Samuel L. Hesser

14 Mar 1836 Lewis P. Kountz & Mary M. Miller. Bondsmen, Arthur F. Grim & Jas M. Hulet

18 Mar 1836 Thomas Shumate & Mary E. Knight. Bondsman, George Knight

19 Mar 1836 Elijah Cooper & Mary Hotzenpiller. Bondsman, William Langley

19 Mar 1836 William Anderson & Rachel Carter. Bondsman, James M. Hulet

21 Mar 1836 Martin Pool & Nancy Johnson. Bondsman, John Johnson

22 Mar 1836 Henry Hodson & Jane Jones. Bondsman, Joshua Lupton

22 Mar 1836 John M. Magson & Frances Dooley. Bondsman, Robert Long

24 Mar 1836 James Weaver & Ann Simmers. Bondsman, Stephen Jenkins

n. d. Peter Stotler & Elizabeth Bohrer, daughter of Isaac Bohrer, the bondsman

4 Apr 1836 John Chrisman & Lucinda Carter. Bondsman, Arthur W. Carter

11 Apr 1836 John Scanden & Elizabeth Clark. Bondsman, Thomas Morrison

13 Apr 1836 Robert H. Mckay & Eveline M. Massie, daughter of Josiah Massie, the bondsman

18 Apr 1836 Casper Nott & Mary A. Taylor. Bondsman, Nathan Haines

27 Apr 1836 Joseph McIntosh & Caroline Baker. Bondsman, Henry B. Streit

2 May 1836 John Ohaver & Jane Garrett. Bondsman, Timothy Ohaver

10 May 1836 Meredith Darlington & Rachel Ann Swatz, daughter of George Swatz, the bondsman

10 May 1836 Greenberry Milburn & Nancy Grove. Bondsmen, Henry Grove & James Milburn

10 May 1836 Isaac Frye & Catharine Wymer. Bondsman, Thomas Ewing

14 Jun 1836 James Chapman & Sarah A. Hooper. Bondsman, Charles Conrad

14 Jun 1836 Philip L. Kerns & Barbara Horner. Bondsman, Nathan L. McDonald

25 Jun 1836 George W. Shroads & Margaret Coats, daughter of James Coats, the bondsman

2 Jul 1836 George Tiler & Mary Ann Bohrer, daughter of Isaac Bohrer, the bondsman

6 Aug 1836 James K. Carter & Amelia B. Chrisman. Bondsman, Thomas A. Tidball

27 Aug 1836 Henry N. Heironimus & Peggy Ann Shivers. Bondsman, Thomas Shivers

30 Aug 1836 Green Underwood & Cecilia A. B. Legg. Bondsman, Henry G. Daniels

3 Sep 1836 Tilman Shumate & Eliza Brown. Bondsman, Thomas A. Tidball

6 Sep 1836 Henry Lloyd & Eliza Ann Craig. Bondsman, Hiram W. Taylor

7 Sep 1836 Joseph Fisher & Isabella Rinker, daughter of Casper Rinker, the bondsman

7 Sep 1836 John Smallwood & Eliza Hall, daughter of Robert Hall, the bondsman

15 Sep 1836 James McCormick & Elizabeth Ann Jones. Bondsman, John S. Owens

21 Sep 1836 Thomas Allen & Jane D. George. Bondsman, Thomas A. Tidball

21 Sep 1836 John Lewis & Sarah Ann Rachel Wolfe, daughter of Peter Wolfe, the bondsman

24 Sep 1836 Barton McKee & Elizabeth Grove. Bondsman, Henry Grove

27 Sep 1836 James M. Bowling & Margaret A. Petter. Bondsman, James Hoy

1 Oct 1836 Joseph B. Hackney & Rebecca Jane Kerr, daughter of Wm Kerr, the bondsman

8 Oct 1836 James Evans & Martha Ann Mckee, daughter of Robert Mckee, the bondsman

12 Oct 1836 Francis A. Stipe & Catharine Iden. Bondsman, Jonathan Iden

12 Oct 1836 Isaac Brill & Sarah Williams. Bondsman, Benjamin Williams

12 Oct 1836 Alexander G. Afflick & Ann Elizabeth Hoover. Bondsman, Henry Hamaker

17 Oct 1836 Martin Frees & Mary Ann Parlett. Bondsman, John Parlett

18 Oct 1836 Bryan M. Stephens Jnr & Julia Ann M. Ernest. Bondsman, Bryan M. Stephens Sr

19 Oct 1836 Joseph Sherrard & Sydney Ann Flower, daughter of Richard Flower, the bondsman

18 Oct 1836 David W. Wilson & Elizabeth H. Carr. Bondsman, Hugh H. Carr

24 Oct 1836 Anthony M. Cline & Emily B. Muse. Bondsman, Edward R. Muse

25 Oct 1836 Simon Stickel & Amelia Ashby, daughter of John Ashby, the bondsman

5 Nov 1836 William H. Keim & Lucy Jane Randolph. Bondsman, William L. Bent

7 Nov 1836 William Brown & Catharine Newman. Bondsman, Joseph Clark

7 Nov 1836 Joseph S. Jackson & Mary D. Lupton. Bondsman, Nathan Lupton

8 Nov 1836 William Collins & Mary Ann Marple, daughter of Morgan H. Marple, the bondsman

9 Nov 1836 James Duvall & Lydia R. Russell. Bondsman, Julius C. Waddle

12 Nov 1836 David Hook & Tacey Marpole, both upwards of 21 years of age. Bondsman, Enoc Marpole

30 Nov 1836 James Smith & Catharine Bear, daughter of Frederick Bear, the bondsman

10 Dec 1836 Isaac White & Mary Larrick, daughter of Frederick Larrick, the bondsman

10 Dec 1836 William Racy & Elizabeth Tewalt. Bondsman, John Vance

12 Dec 1836 Henry Nagley & Hannah I. Bunecutter. Bondsman, Christopher Bunecutter

12 Dec 1836 Daniel Carver & Catharine M. Newham. Bondsman, Henry Stoat

12 Dec 1836 James Shepherd & Elizabeth Dillon, widow of Wm Dillon. Bondsman, William Kern

14 Dec 1836 John C. Emitt & Catharine Mytinger. Bondsman, James R. Brooking

23 Dec 1836 George Fraley & Deborah Stephens. Bondsman, John Stephens

30 Dec 1836 William Gibbons & Barbara Rhodes. Bondsman, David Rhodes

10 Jan 1837 Willoughby M. McCormick & Ann Elizabeth Grove. Bondsman, William O. Bond

11 Jan 1837 Benjamin Frye & Harriet Snapp, daughter of William A. Wilson, the bondsman

16 Jan 1837 Jonathan Hiett & Margaret Mckee, daughter of Joseph Mckee, the bondsman

25 Jan 1837 Harman Oats & Ruth Kerns, daughter of Nathan Kerns, the bondsman

6 Feb 1837 John Mainer & Nancy Gardner. Bondsman, John P. Gardner

16 Feb 1837 John Stephens & Eliza Fraly. Bondsman, David W. Burton

29 Feb 1837 William Jonas Shrimp & Mahala Jane Smithy. Bondsman, Richard Smithey

4 Mar 1837 John Milhorn & Elizabeth Hodson. Bondsman, Robert Hodgson

11 Mar 1837 Philip Hartley & Helen Clevinger, daughter of Elizabeth Clevinger, the bondsman

13 Apr 1837 George Cooper & Mary Louthan. Bondsman, William R. Louthan

15 Apr 1837 Ezra Cadwalader & Maria McGueriom?. Bondsman, Alexander Affleck

27 Apr 1837 Gabriel Chisam & Lucy Newman. Bondsman, Thomas Newman

1 May 1837 Elliot W. Sturman & Rutta Jane Long, daughter of John Long, the bondsman

1 May 1837 John B. D. Smith & Elizabeth M. Peyton. Bondsman, Peyton Randolph

4 May 1837 R. B. Green & P. E. L. Hite. Bondsman, Hugh H. Hite

11 May 1837 Bartholomew H. Mckee & Elizabeth Evans. Bondsman, John Evans

16 May 1837 Otho W. Heiskell & Susan Mary Gibson, daughter of James Gibson. Bondsmen, Charles H. Clark & R. B. Holliday

5 Jun 1837 John Grim Jr. & Nancy Johnston. Bondsman, James Christy

6 Jun 1837 Francis C. Millhorn & Emily Anderson. Bondsman, Martin B. Muse

13 Jun 1837 John Yakle & Eliza Jane Krider. Bondsman, Frederick S. Shrock

16 Jun 1837 John Callan & Hannah C. Ridgway, widow of Richard Ridgway. Bondsman, Thomas A. Tidball

3 Jul 1837 Samuel Merchant & Mary Allemong. Bondsman, John Beagant

5 Aug 1837 James Britten & Sarah Hart. Bondsman, Casper Rogers

15 Aug 1837 Elias A. Hibbard & Maria Taylor, widow of the late James Taylor. Bondsman, William Snyder

16 Aug 1837 Edward Emanuel Noun & Elizabeth Shiner. Bondsman, John Shiner

22 Aug 1837 Zebulon H. Perrill & Rebecca C. Bywaters. Bondsman, Robert C. Bywaters

2 Sep 1837 Joel Barrett & Sarah Streit. Bondsman, John Hott

4 Sep 1837 Dennis S. Clower (Clouer?) & Nancy Michael. Bondsman, William Kerns

4 Sep 1837 Robert Christy & Sarah Pool. Bondsman, John Nisewanger

9 Sep 1837 Addison Turner & Harriet Orndorf. Bondsman, Phineas Orndorff

9 Sep 1837 John Ogden & Matilda Roe, daughter of Alexander Roe, the bondsman

11 Sep 1837 Peter F. Ridings & Mary Jane Larrick, daughter of Jacob Larrick, the bondsman

11 Sep 1837 Robert Winslow & Mary McClunn. Bondsman, Addison Johnston

13 Sep 1837 John S. Heist & Caroline F. Grant, daughter of John Grant, the bondsman

20 Sep 1837 Benjamin R. Barr & Julia Ann Lynn. Bondsman, Stephen Bell

22 Sep 1837 Theodore W. Simpson & Mary C. Stephenson. Bondsman, George H. Tate

10 Oct 1837 Jonah Nichols & Sarah Jane Orr. Bondsman, Jacob Nichols
18 Oct 1837 Joseph Wisecarver & Margaret Morrison. Bondsman, Thomas Morrison
23 Oct 1837 Michael Casler & Evalina M. Heironimus. Bondsman, Jacob P. Heironimus
26 Oct 1837 James Bowles & Mary Louisa Smith, daughter of Jonathan Smith, the bondsman
28 Oct 1837 Benjamin Webber & Martha Montgomery. Bondsman, Peter Ashton
28 Oct 1837 William B. Thompson & Catharine M. Stribling. Bondsman, James I. Miller
28 Oct 1837 James I. Miller & Ann T. Stribling. Bondsman, Wm B. Thompson
7 Nov 1837 William Shuler & Rachel Whitacre. Bondsman, John Johnson
12 Nov 1837 John Ramey & Mary Ann Marker, daughter of John Marker, the bondsman
23 Nov 1837 John Frenger & Mary Richard, daughter of Jacob Richard, the bondsman
28 Nov 1837 George Keller & Mary Garrett, daughter of Jacob Garrett, the bondsman
12 Dec 1837 William Shull & Sarah Johnson. Bondsman, Addison Johnson
12 Dec 1837 Isaac L. Vanhorn & Elizabeth Ann McDonald. Bondsman, William Kee (McKee)
12 Dec 1837 George M. Griffin & Jane White. Bondsman, Isaac White
18 Dec 1837 George Guard & Emily Sophia Shryock, daughter of Frederick S. Shryock, the bondsman
19 Dec 1837 Charles Barnes & Francis Ann Jorden. Bondsman, William Denny
26 Dec 1837 John Reed & Loy Ellen Douglass. Bondsman, William Grove
30 Dec 1837 Samuel Dooly & Mrs. Mary Baker. Bondsman, James B. Taylor
1 Jan 1838 John Kiter & Emily Coe. Bondsman, William Coe
3 Jan 1838 John Hummer & Alce Albin. Bondsman, Andrew Albin
4 Jan 1838 William Loy & Susanna Brown. Bondsman, William Campbell
8 Jan 1838 Jacob Wolfe & Jane Sprout. Bondsman, John Markwood
10 Jan 1838 Christopher Funk & Eliza Arnold. Bondsman, John Lupton

15 Jan 1838 William J. Rowland & Hannah S. Hackney. Bondsman, Aaron H. Hackney

20 Jan 1838 Thomas Clevenger & Catharine Osburn, daughter of George Osburn, the bondsman

14 Feb 1838 Leroy G. March & Regina Maria Bush. Bondsman, William Bush

19 Feb 1838 Edward Morrison & Elizabeth Ann Rinker, daughter of William Rinker, the bondsman

23 Feb 1838 Adam Shade & Louisa Jolly who was raised by John Shade, the bondsman

3 Mar 1838 John Van Cleave & Martha Marvin. Bondsman, Watson Carter

19 Mar 1838 Asa Anderson & Mary Marple, daughter of Enoch Marple, the bondsman

19 Mar 1838 John Stuart & Elizabeth Jane McCarty. Bondsman, John Markwood Jr.

26 Mar 1838 Robert Stephenson & Courtney Ann Rinker, daughter of Caspar Rinker

26 Mar 1838 Simon Thompson, free negro man, & Mary Wormley, free negro girl. Bondsman, John Thompson, free negro man

30 Mar 1838 Russell Jenkins & Isabella Cubbage. Bondsman, G. G. Grove

7 Apr 1838 Josiah Burton & Elizabeth Jane Flowers. Bondsman, Phillip L. Kearns

18 Apr 1838 John Noel & Phebe Whitacre. Bondsman, Aquilla Whitacre

21 Apr 1838 James Crawford & Mary Royer. Bondsman, Isaac Adams

21 Apr 1838 William Millison & Sarah Giffin, daughter of John Giffin, the bondsman

7 May 1838 John Lawrence & Harriet Seevers. Bondsman, Frederick Houser

19 May 1838 William Barton & Sarah Jane Mayhew, daughter of Tilman Mayhew, the bondsman

24 May 1838 William Owen & Elizabeth Wilson. Bondsman, Taliver R. Owens

30 May 1838 Thomas Croft & Julia Ann Hood. Bondsman, Joseph Parker

2 Jun 1838 Abner Straderman & Lucy Bly. Bondsman, John Hemmelright

4 Jun 1838 James W. Offutt & Sarah I. Shepherd. Bondsman, Charles L. Shepherd

30 Jun 1838 Simon Showalter, son of Valentine Showalter, & Ann Maria Sargent. Bondsman, Valentine Showalter

2 Jul 1838 Joseph H. Brown & Elizabeth Font, daughter of Henry Font, the bondsman

21 Jul 1838 Thomas C. Ogden & Mary Whisson. Bondsman, John Whisson

23 Jul 1838 James Albin & Elizabeth Carper, daughter of John Carper, the bondsman

1 Aug 1838 James Jones & Catharine Ritter. Bondsman, William Shiner

2 Aug 1838 John W. Clevenger & Dorothy Owens. Bondsman, John S. Ewing

15 Aug 1838 Henry Haverstick & Susan C. K. M. Polk. Bondsman, Lewis Eichelberger

15 Aug 1838 Joseph Winpiglar & Mary Ann Franklin, daughter of Moses Franklin, the bondsman

22 Aug 1838 Andrew H. Heironemus & Rebecca Weir, daughter of James Weir, the bondsman

3 Sep 1838 John Hook & Rebecca Ann Keiter. Bondsman, Thomas Hook

3 Sep 1838 Jonas Trenary & Ibby Leach. Bondsman, George Kendrick

5 Sep 1838 John Williams, a free negro man, & Amy Ann Brady, a free mulatto woman. Bondsman, William Briscoe, a free negro

8 Sep 1838 George Dent & Eliza Johnston. Bondsman, David Johnston

10 Sep 1838 Samuel Silver, injured in his right hand, & Ellen Bell. Bondsman, Zepheniah Silver

11 Sep 1838 Thomas S. Sangster & Martha Ann Chipley. Bondsman, James Chipley

12 Sep 1838 Amos Murray, a free negro, & Mary Ann King, a free negro. Bondsman, Harrison Murry, a free negro

Marriage Bonds No. 18 1838-1843

17 Sep 1838 Daniel C. Lovett & Emeline G. Lockhart. Bondsman, Mahlon S. Lovett

21 Sep 1838 Moses Hodge & Eliza W. Lind. Bondsman, James H. Longacre

27 Sep 1838 George W. Johnston & Mary Elizabeth Franklin. Bondsman, James D. Franklin

15 Oct 1838 Peirce Moore & Mahala I. Welsh. Bondsman, Alfred Carper

18 Oct 1838 William Thompson & Mary Sparrow, widow of John Sparrow decd. Bondsman, John Fletcher

22 Oct 1838 John C. Porter & Ann Eliza Bush. Bondsman, Archibald C. Bush

29 Oct 1838 Samuel McDougle & Mary Eveland. Bondsman, John Eveland

30 Oct 1838 Alexander McD. Davison & Matilda M. Hite. Bondsmen, Hugh H. Hite & C. B. Hite

3 Nov 1838 Thomas R. Allen & Dianna Snapp. Bondsman, Joseph Kean

14 Nov 1838 George W. Snider & Elizabeth Anderson. Bondsman, Edward R. Muse

16 Nov 1838 William H. Brown & Elizabeth Ann Fuller. Bondsman, Joshua Lupton

19 Nov 1838 Amos Payne & Mary F. Davis. Bondsman, David Davis

19 Nov 1838 James Turner & Judith Fry. Bondsman, James Bean

19 Nov 1838 Silas Simmons & Ceatte Larrick, daughter of George Larrick, the bondsman

26 Nov 1838 Lewis M. Forsyth & Julia Ann Bush, daughter of William Bush, the bondsman

28 Nov 1838 John W. Grim & Elizabeth A. Touchstone. Bondsman, George Kremer Jr.

6 Dec 1838 Lewis Dick & Octavia Owen Carter. Bondsman, John Carter

8 Dec 1838 John Washington Bagent & Isabella Ann Ware, daughter of James Ware, the bondsman

8 Dec 1838 Lewis S. Emett & Mary Evelina Wells, daughter of Richard Wells, the bondsman

17 Dec 1838 Elijah Smith & Sarah Luttrell. Bondsman, Robert Luttrell

17 Dec 1838 Smith Carpenter & Susan Anderson. Bondsman, Jonathan Lovett

21 (20?) Dec 1838 Robert W. Reed & Maria A. McLeod. Bondsman, George A. V. Reed

21 (20?) Dec 1838 Addison B. Riely & Ann R. Rea. Bondsman, James P. Riely

21 (20?) Dec 1838 Daniel Gano & Elizabeth A. Grove. Bondsman, William S. Grove

24 Dec 1838 Francis Whittington & Mary Catharine Anderson, daughter of Jacob Anderson, the bondsman

26 Dec 1838 Enos Leonard & Margaret Crider. Bondsman, Alexander Marks
26 Dec 1838 Madison H. Pascal & Sarah Crider. Bondsman, John Taleyr
28 Dec 1838 Enoch Whitacre & Susanna Kerns. Bondsman, Jonas Whitacre
5 Jan 1839 George H. Keller & Margaret Smith. Bondsman, James Smith
17 Jan 1839 Jacob W. Grafflin & Elizabeth Carnegy. Bondsman, James A. Hooper
23 Jan 1839 John McVicar & Catharine Thatcher, daughter of Evan Thatcher, the bondsman
28 Jan 1839 Mitchell Taylor, a free man, & Rachel Monmouth, a free woman. Bondsman, Abraham Coleman
30 Jan 1839 Jonas Kerns & Eliza Ann Whitacre. Bondsman, Enoch Whitaker
4 Feb 1839 Jacob Hutslar & Julia Butler. Bondsman, John Carter
4 Feb 1839 Thomas Hollis & Sarah Ann Bowers. Bondsman, Harrison Bowers
9 Feb 1839 William W. Jasper & Mary Jane Kile, daughter of Reuben Kile, the bondsman
11 Feb 1839 Peter Hinkins & Mary Ann Marker. Bondsman, Geo. A. Marker
12 Feb 1839 Samuel Towers & Cornelia F. VonReisen, ward of Charles H. Clark, the bondsman
13 Feb 1839 James Anderson & Ellen Marpole. Bondsman, David Hook
19 Feb 1839 Samuel Appold & Susan C. VonReesen, ward of Charles H. Clark
19 Feb 1839 John Hoff & Mary Shultz. Bondsman, Thomas A. Tidball
22 Feb 1839 John Shade & Othey Strowbridge. Bondsman, Isaac Strowbridge
23 Feb 1839 Samuel Stipe & Eliza Devoe, daughter of David Devoe, the bondsman
23 Feb 1839 Samuel Sperry & Ann E. Rhodes. Bondsman, Abraham H. Rhodes
25 Feb 1839 John H. Marker & Mary Ann Mager. Bondsman, James M. Morrison
4 Mar 1839 Joseph W. Cade & Angelina W. Rodgers. Bondsman, Reuben Kile
7 Mar 1839 Stephen D. Timberlake & Francis A. Timberlake. Bondsman, Richard M. Timberlake

12 Mar 1839 Amos Brill & Evelina Kerin, daughter of Ann Kerin, the bondsman

12 Mar 1839 Lewis Fleet & Susan Ritter. Bondsman, James Keller

14 Mar 1839 Jonathan Iden Jnr & Mary Waggener. Bondsman, Alfred Jolly

18 Mar 1839 Michael Freeze & Catharine Frieze, daughter of Jacob Freeze, the bondsman

23 Mar 1839 Willis Crane & Mary Ann Rinehart, daughter of David Rinehart, the bondsman

30 Mar 1839 Peter Spiker & Isabella Magonen. Bondsman, Ezra Cadwallader

6 Apr 1839 Atwell Shull & Louisa Hooper. Bondsman, John Shull

9 Apr 1839 John P. Bently & Emily Caroline Lauck. Bondsman, Lewis Eichelberger

24 Apr 1839 James Peery & Catharine Keckley. Bondsman, Ireson Peery

11 May 1839 John Jones & Sarah Ann Nicholson, widow of Thomas Nicholson decd. Bondsman, Henry Mitcham

18 May 1839 Solomon Glaze & Elizabeth Friez. Bondsman, George Friez

10 Jun 1839 Samuel Grove & Nancy Higins, daughter of John Higins, the bondsman

10 Jun 1839 John Holt & Rachel Friez. Bondsman, William Davison

19 Jun 1839 Mordecai Bean & Eliza Larrick, daughter of Henry Larrick, the bondsman

24 Jun 1839 Austin Bean & Harriet Hooper. Bondsman, Harriet Lewis (mother of the said Austin Bean an illigitimate child)

11 Jul 1839 James Carter & Rebecca Light. Bondsman, Isaac Dick

16 Jul 1839 Lemuel Crum & Nancy Mack, daughter of Henry Mark (Mack?), the bondsman

3 Aug 1839 James Hott & Susan Streit. Bondsman, Joel Barrett

7 Aug 1839 David S. Spesard & Martha Ann Kline, daughter of Anthony Kline, the bondsman

10 Aug 1839 Jacob Criser, who signs in German, & Sidney Ann Striker, daughter of Henry Striker, the bondsman

29 Aug 1839 Toliver Owens & Charlotte Walters. Bondsman, Laurence Walters

31 Aug 1839 Hiram Trotter & Lydia Maria Allemong, daughter of William Allemong. Bondsman, Lewis Allemong
2 Sep 1839 John H. Keim & Martha E. Randolph. Bondsman, Benj.? W. Jones. (Bond says John P. Jones)
2 Sep 1839 Charles B. Rust & Mary Ann Ashby. Bondsman, John H. Ash
3 Sep 1839 Bazil Catlett & Elizabeth Littrell. Bondsman, Stephen Miller
4 Sep 1839 Jacob A. Bucher & Elizabeth Lemley. Bondsman, John C. Lemley
5 Sep 1839 George W. Shacklett & Lucinda Morris. Bondsman, Albert A. Ashby
9 Sep 1839 Phineas Orndorff & Harriet S. Bucher. Bondsman, Samuel Bucher
10 Sep 1839 Adam Tait & Elizabeth Wright. Bondsman, Richard W. Barton
16 Sep 1839 John G. Rinker & Rebecca Long, daughter of Jane Long. Bondsmen, William Rinker & Jane Long
17 Sep 1839 James D. Musgrove & Mary L. Ellzy. Bondsman, Abraham Stickley
18 Sep 1839 Isaac B. Cole & Martha Green. Bondsman, John S. Green
21 Sep 1839. John J. Shepherd & Susan C. Shreck. Bondsmen, Willoughby Sheppard & Jacob Shreck
24 Sep 1839 John W. Miller & Jane Fitzhugh. Bondsman, Henry Grove
1 Oct 1839 Thomas L. Blakemore & Eliza C. Richards. Bondsman, George C. Blakemore
1 Oct 1839 Charles Kaufman & Eveline Corsch. Bondsmen, John Messner & Charles W. Gibbons
9 Oct 1839 Lewis Cole & Mary Bradford. Bondsman, Vance Bradford
9 Oct 1839 Henry H. Shepherd & Adeline H. Muir. Bondsman, Daniel Gold
10 Oct 1839 William Cole & Evelina Guard. Bondsman, George Guard
11 Oct 1839 Henry Stotlar & Susyan Hinkle. Bondsman, Adam Hinckle, Junr.
14 Oct 1839 Samuel Fries & Sarah Jane Rinker. Bondsman, William Rinker
21 Oct 1839 James T. Taylor & Martha E. Carson. Bondsman, James H. Carson

21 Oct 1839 William H. Lupton & Catharine N. Snapp, daughter of John Snapp, the bondsman
23 Oct 1839 Wilson L. Taylor & Catharine Taylor, daughter of David Miller, the bondsman
24 Oct 1839 John Blackwell & Mary Reason, widow of James Reason. Bondsman, Thomas Morrison
26 Oct 1839 John Riggle & Sarah Jenkins. Bondsman, John Rutter
5 Nov 1839 Harrison Faulconer & Maria Edmondson. Bondsman, James B. Simmons
7 Nov 1839 William Cochran & Jane C. Morrison. Bondsman, Thomas Morrison
9 Nov 1839 George Kerns Senr & Lydia Trowbridge. Bondsman, Beltzhuel Trowbridge
11 Nov 1839 William D. Kerr & Rebecca A. Berkeley. Bondsman, James G. Ficklen
13 Nov 1839 Willoughby H. Sheppard & Sarah Shuck. Bondsman, Jacob Shuck
13 Nov 1839 James Boyles & Margaret Pritchard. Bondsman, James Keenan
13 Nov 1839 Jonathan Gourley & Selina Danley, daughter of Hosea Danley, the bondsman
19 Nov 1839 Isaac Lupton & Catharine Oats, duaghter of Jacob Oats, the bondsman
28 Nov 1839 Jacob Clink & Rebecca Ross. Bondsman, Harison Gordon
5 Dec 1839 Daniel O. Brown & Jane Eton, daughter of Elizabeth Eaton, the bondsman
5 Dec 1839 Thomas Barron Jnr & Isabell Steel. Bondsman, Thomas Barron Sr
7 Dec 1839 Mordecai Strosnider & Rachel Brill. Bondsman, Joseph Brill
9 Dec 1839 Addison A. Johnston & Mary Elizabeth Rust. Bondsman, Samuel Rust
10 Dec 1839 John OFerrall & Jane L. Lovett. Bondsman, Thomas B. Campbell
12 Dec 1839 John Corban & Maria Millburn. Bondsman, Andrew Millburn
12 Dec 1839 Jacob Rinehart & Tamzon H. Scott. Bondsman, Peter Hott
13 Dec 1839 William Graham, a free mulatto man, & Sarah Strange, slave of George Fyst, the bondsman
19 Dec 1839 Abraham Everhart & Eliza Jones. Bondsman, Robert Long

21 Dec 1839 James Bean & Gueliemly? Fossett. Bondsman, Mary Enders
24 Dec 1839 Christopher Johnston, a free negro man, & Frances Fletcher, a free mulatto girl. Bondsman, James Fletcher
24 Dec 1839 Benjamin Stine & Adaline Aby. Bondsman, John Harrison
13 Jan 1840 Samuel Dobbins & Mary Edwards. Bondsman, Frederick Carper
14 Jan 1840 Craven Coe & Sarah Miller, daughter of Ephraim Miller. Bondsman, John Smith
15 Jan 1840 Jacob Shrimp & Susan Henshaw. Bondsman, John J. Henshaw
29 Jan 1840 Benjamin P. Ashby & Mary Ann Keller, daughter of Jacob Keller, the bondsman
31 Jan 1840 Meredith Bowen & Sarah H. Grove. Bondsman, Henry Grove
30 Jan 1840 Jonathan Richard Bowen & Mary Hoover. Bondsman, James Keenan
3 Feb 1840 Hanson Gordon & Mary Ann Barley. Bondsman, Peter Barley
5 Feb 1840 Levi Crabill & Priscilla M. Chrisman, daughter of Isaac Chrisman, the bondsman
8 Feb 1840 Samuel Boucher & Mary Pear. Bondsman, Phineas Orndorff
12 Feb 1840 Nimrod Korn & Eliza Bently. Bondsman, Edward Hines
17 Feb 1840 Henry Snapp & Margaret Ann Frye, daughter of Joseph Frye, the bondsman
24 Feb 1840 Daniel C. Shambaugh & Mary Ann Kline. Bondsman, Daniel Kline
24 Feb 1840 John Horn & Maria Howard. Bondsman, Eusebius D. Howard
26 Feb 1840 Joseph E. Barton & Nancy Barton. Bondsman, David Devoe
7 Mar 1840 Henry Horner & Ann Flower. Bondsman, James B. Taylor
7 Mar 1840 Harrison Cooper & Alcinda Whissen. Bondsman, John Whissen
10 Mar 1840 George William Gantz & Elizabeth Ann Parsons. Bondsman, Mason Chiles
17 Mar 1840 William Sonner & Harriett Taylor. Bondsmen, Joseph M. Dosh & John Taylor
18 Mar 1840 William Hodson & Elizabeth Milhorn. Bondsman, John Milhorn

19 Mar 1840 Frederick Carper Jr. & Emily Dicks, granddaughter of Henry Dicks, the bondsman

24 Mar 1840 Samuel I. C. Davenport & Emily S. Orrick. Bondsman, Robert B. Holliday

30 Mar 1840 James Smith & Ann Elizabeth Ward, daughter of Joel Ward decd. Bondsman, Lucius T. Kerfoot

31 Mar 1840 Landon Iden Jolley & Eleaner Littenell. Bondsman, Fielding Luttnell

31 Mar 1840 David N. Davis & Ann E. McBee. Bondsman, William T. McBee

4 Apr 1840 Isaac S. Keener & Asberina Pangle, daughter of Jacob Pangle, the bondsman

8 Apr 1840 John Smoot & Elizabeth Jones. Bondsman, Berryman Jones

14 Apr 1840 John Sherman & Hannah Mumaw, daughter of Margaret Mumaw, the bondsman

16 Apr 1840 John F. Jackson & Mary E. Grim. Bondsman, John Grim

23 Apr 1840 John S. Reynoldson & Louisiana M. Pagett. Bondsman, Washington F. Pagett

27 Apr 1840 John Carper & Susan Heck. Bondsman, Samuel H. Clark

11 May 1840 John P. Minnix & Margaret Pitman. Bondsman, George B. McLeod

11 May 1840 John M. Gough & Mary Ann Bowman. Bondsman, Joseph P. Mahaney

14 May 1840 Ludovicus Heinzalmann & Elizabeth Nesmith. Bondsman, Daniel Hinckle

16 May 1840 Alexander Carpenter & Catharine Bowen. Bondsman, Zachariah Carpenter

21 May 1840 George S. Williams & Mary Ann Mendenhall. Bondsman, Jacob Mendenhall

30 May 1840 Charles Rinehart & Mary Oats. Bondsman, Jacob Oats

1 Jun 1840 William G. Eggleston & Frances S. Muse. Bondsman, Edward R. Muse

3 Jun 1840 David Adams & Cassandra Light. Bondsman, Frederick Light

4 Jun 1840 Charles Lobb & Jane W. Dailey. Bondsman, Robert W. Wood

8 Jun 1840 Henry Orndorf & June Ohaver. Bondsman, Abraham Garrett

16 Jun 1840 Henry Stipe & Ann T. Reed, widow. Bondsman, John Carper

23 Jun 1840 Christy Sine & Nancy Murphy, daughter of Thomas Murphy, the bondsman
29 Jun 1840 William G. Barton & Rebecca Campbell. Bondsman, John M. Rutter
9 Jul 1840 Thomas Wood & Julia Ann Martin. Bondsman, Bennet Carlin
17 Jul 1840 Philip L. Kearns & Mary Ann Light. Bondsman, Henry Light
21 Jul 1840 Robert Miller & Margaret Marple. Bondsman, George Marple
25 Jul 1840 John W. Steel & Philoma Kern, daughter of Adam Kern, the bondsman
1 AUg 1840 Christopher Parish & Emily Parish. Bondsman, Thomas Murphy Jr.
3 Aug 1840 James Wm. Timberlake & Jane Mason. Bondsman, Seth Mason
3 Aug 1840 George W. Grubbs & Maria Clevenger. Bondsman, Colin Leach
8 Aug 1840 Thomas Montgomery & Mahala Proctor, an illegitimate child. Bondsman, John Hanshaw
19 Aug 1840 William Carper & Jane Carpenter. Bondsman, Philip Carper
31 Aug 1840 Andrew J. O'Bannon & Emily F. Brent. Bondsman, Charles J. Brent
31 Aug 1840 George Brown & Sarah Ann Rinehart, daughter of David Rinehart. Bondsmen, Charles Fox & David Rinehart
31 Aug 1840 Robert S. Walker & Mary S. Kiger, daughter of Augustin Kiger, the bondsman
5 Sep 1840 David L. McKee & Mahalah Fletcher, daughter of James Fletcher, the bondsman
5 Sep 1840 John Baker & Sarah McQuade. Bondsman, John Gander, who signs in German
10 Sep 1840 John N. Strother & Nancy Affleck. Bondsman, Alexander Affleck
28 Sep 1840 John Clevenger & Sarah Albin. Bondsman, William Albin
30 Sep 1840 William J. Reed & Mary E. Nicklin, daughter of Jacob R. Nicklin, the bondsman
1 Oct 1840 Lewis L. Lefevre & Ann Keeler. Bondsman, Alexander Marks
2 Oct 1840 Christopher Rivers & Mildred B. Widdows. Bondsman, Robert Widdows

5 Oct 1840 James Calderhead & Catherine Elizabeth Allemong. Bondsman, Lewis Allemong.

21 Oct 1840 Stephen Miller & Ann Krider. Bondsman, William Denny

22 Oct 1840 Lancelot Whitlock & Catharine Jane Parish, daughter of Joseph Parish, the bondsman

22 Oct 1840 Gilbert Ovelton & Mary Grey. Bondsman, George H. Smith

28 Oct 1840 Alfred Collins & Jane Clark, daughter of William Clark, the bondsman

28 Oct 1840 Ephraim Painter & Eliza Myers. Bondsman, George Mummaw

28 Oct 1840 James Grant, a free negro, & Sarah Marshall, a free woman. Bondsman, Robert Latham

2 Nov 1840 Michael Armbrist & Margaret Ann Crawford, daughter of William Crawford, the bondsman

6 Nov 1840 Thomas J. Miller & Sarah Catharine Russell. Bondsman, James A. Russell

9 Nov 1840 Joseph Braithwaite & Ann Elizabeth Dyer. Bondsman, John Everett

9 Nov 1840 Jesse Calvert & Thersa Wood. Bondsman, Isaac Wood

28 Nov 1840 James L. Clark & Nancy F. Pelter. Bondsman, George Pelter

28 Nov 1840 Solomon Webber & Susan Shepherd. Bondsman, Benjamin Webber

1 Dec 1840 Elias Overall & Frances C. Raynolds, widow of George Raynolds. Bondsman, Michael Copenhaver

2 Dec 1840 John Mead & Ann Nichols. Bondsman, Jacob Nichols

2 Dec 1840 John Lewis & Rebecca Carpenter, daughter of James Carpenter, the bondsman

3 Dec 1840 William Marck & Lavinia March. Bondsman, Leroy G. March

9 Dec 1840 Isaac Watson & Ann E. Pangle. Bondsman, Jacob Pangle

9 Dec 1840 John M. Larrick & Margaret Guyer. Bondsman, Joseph Larrick

9 Dec 1840 Thomas I. H. Wilcox & Elizabeth Jane Elliott. Bondsman, William Elliott

11 Dec 1840 Evan Rogers & Louisa C. Franks. Bondsman, Robert Pugh Jr.

15 Dec 1840 James W. Beetley & Theresa M. Laurens. Bondsman, Martin Laurens

16 Dec 1840 John S. Magill & Mary Ann Glass. Bondsman, David W. Barton

19 Dec 1840 George Gordon & Harriet Barley, upwards of 21 years of age. Bondsman, Peter Barley

19 Dec 1840 Abraham D. Cooper & Jane Cockerell. Bondsman, John Lupton

23 Dec 1840 Amos Shepherd & Elizabeth Ann Dunn, upwards of 21 years of age. Bondsman, William Dunn

24 Dec 1840 William Carper & Catharine M. Newcome, daughter of Elisha Newcome, the bondsman

29 Dec 1840 Charles Green & Nancy Brannen. Bondsman, Robert Brannan

2 Jan 1841 William R. Sollars & Jane Capper, daughter of Michael Capper

4 Jan 1841 James Douglass & Eliza Deck, upwards of 21 years of age. Bondsman, John Vincent

4 Jan 1841 Henson W. Wilburn & Lucinda E. McEndree, daughter of Nimrod McEndree, the bondsman

16 Jan 1841 William B. Harris & Lucy M. Berkeley. Bondsman, William D. Holliday

18 Jan 1841 Lewis Armistead & Sarah Ann Briscoe, daughter of William Briscoe, the bondsman

19 Jan 1841 John H. McIlwee & Catharine Ann Orndorff, daughter of Joseph Orndorff, the bondsman

20 Jan 1841 Joseph D. Davis & Julia A. Muse. Bondsman, Martin B. Muse

22 Jan 1841 Joseph D. Hamilton & Nancy J. Touchstone. Bondsman, William Touchstone

23 Jan 1841 Samuel Bumgarener & Rachel Frye. Bondsman, Lewis Eichelberger

25 Jan 1841 Hamilton L. Gibson & Rebecca Guard. Bondsman, George Guard

26 Jan 1841 William Bailey & Mary Ann Swhier. Bondsman, Peter Hott

26 Jan 1841 Samuel Webber & Maria Dailey. Bondsman, Solomon Webber

26 Jan 1841 George A. Bowen & Frances E. Brent, daughter of George Brent, the bondsman

30 Jan 1840 (sic) James Carper & Lucy E. Hite. Bondsman, Zacharias Kern

4 Feb 1841 Richard Jackson & Isabella Ruston, free negroes. Bondsman, James Murry, free negro

6 Feb 1841 Henry Sprinkel & Mary Morrison. Bondsman, John Coe

10 Feb 1841 Joseph Montgomery & Susan J. Murray. Bondsman, John Hanshaw

17 Feb 1841 Charles B. Bayly & Matilda Russell. Bondsman, Henry Richards

17 Feb 1841 William E. Hammock & Barbery Ann Sperry. Bondsman, William B. Walter

17 Feb 1841 Harrison Ryan & Sarah McFarland. Bondsman, Levin McFarland

19 Feb 1841 James Catlett & Mary Brewer. Bondsman, Bazil Catlett

22 Feb 1841 Samuel H. Clark & Delila E. Peters, upwards of 21 years of age. Bondsman, Abraham Tippell

25 Feb 1841 Abraham S. Cooper & Elizabeth A. Hemmelright. Bondsman, Henry Brill

27 Feb 1841 Abraham Hull & Martha W. Reynolds. Bondsman, Reuben Rouzee

2 Mar 1841 Henry Wisecarver Jr. & Rachel Ann Richard, daughter of Isaac Richard, the bondsman

8 Mar 1841 Thomas M. Morrison & Marinda Lupton. Bondsman, Jonah J. Lupton

8 Mar 1841 William Grove & Elizabeth Snapp. Bondsman, Thomas M. Morison

15 Mar 1841 Harrison Orndorff & Hannah Garrett. Bondsman, Abraham Garrett

17 Mar 1841 John W. Rogers & Mary Jane Raynolds. Bondsman, Jacob S. Danner

1 Apr 1841 William Rutter & Mary Lawyer. Bondsman, Christian Singhass

6 Apr 1841 James Z. Smith & Catharine Bowles. Bondsman, Jonathan Smith

20 Apr 1841 Henry B. Huntsberry & Lucy G. Duvall. Bondsman, Isaac Huntsberry

26 Apr 1841 John Carpenter & Elizabeth Patton. Bondsman, William Carper

5 May 1841 James H. Griffith & Jane R. Lupton. Bondsman, John M. Lupton

24 May 1841 Samuel Mendenhall & Mary Whittington. Bondsman, Andrew Redd

27 May 1841 James M. Mowrey & Rosetta Spencer. Bondsman, Bennett Pitcock

27 May 1841 Washington McKee & ?Debrah Popkins. Bondsman, Cravin Popkins

31 May 1841 Addison P. Orme & Anna R. Wilcox. Bondsman, William E. Wilcox

9 Jun 1841 John W. Heterick & Sarah M. Grant, daughter of Stewart Grant, the bondsman

10 Jun 1841 Anthony W. Littler & Mary E. Russell. Bondsman, Isaac Russell

24 Jul 1841 John A. Noakes & Mary Jane James. Bondsman, George Taylor

26 Jul 1841 Morgan A. Anderson & Susan Cooley, daughter of Joseph Cooley, the bondsman

3 Apg 1841 Andrew J. Brown & Margaret J. Gadisly. Bondsman, Thomas Montgomery

9 Aug 1841 Samuel Ransom, a free negro man, & Louisa McKay, a free mulatto woman. Bondsman, Robert Gill

14 Aug 1841 Philip Bohrer & Elizabeth Hutchinson, daughter of Jesse Hutchinson, the bondsman

14 Aug 1841 Anthony Bell, a free negro man, & Nancy Norman, a free black woman. Bondsman, John Norman, a free negro man

23 Aug 1841 John J. Brown & Mary Ann Polk. Bondsman, William C. Worthington

28 Aug 1841 John H. Ellner & Hannah Ferrell, daughter of Mordecai Farrell, the bondsman

1 Sep 1841 William Light & Maria Magalis, daughter of Godfrey Mirheles (sic), the bondsman

6 Sep 1841 John Kline & Eliza Gibbons. Bondsman, David Rhodes

6 Sep 1841 Luman S. Allen & Alvernon? H. Green. Bondsman, Thomas Phillips

15 Sep 1841 Robert B. Lewis & Mary Jane White, daughter of Jacob White, the bondsman

22 Sep 1841 Daniel OLeary & Harriet Bean, widow of Austin Bean. Bondsman, David Lewis

9 Oct 1841 Wallace Batt & Winnifred Lucas, free negroes. Bondsman, Thomas Lucas

11 Oct 1841 Alexander J. Watkins & Louisa Anderson, sister of John L. Anderson, the bondsman

16 Oct 1841 John W. Cooley & Mary Leech. Bondsman, Jonas Trenary

19 Oct 1841 Lewis M. Lauck & Emily Hannin?. Bondsman, George Aulick

26 Oct 1841 George W. Deems & Scotia Anna Sperry, daughter of Peter G. Sperry, the bondsman

27 Oct 1841 Hamilton Braithwaite & Mary Ann Everett. Bondsman, John Everett

27 Oct 1841 Edwin Triplett & Elizabeth Pool. Bondsman, Joseph Pool

27 Oct 1841 John W. Whissen & Sarah Elizabeth Clouser. Bondsman, Henry Clouser

8 Nov 1841 Vance W. Lemley & Lydia A. Gibson. Bondsman, Hamilton L. Gibson

11 Nov 1841 Nathan White & Fredericka Macky. Bondsman, Joseph N. Chiswell

13 Nov 1841 Jacob Larrick & Harriet Good, daughter of Felix Good, the bondsman

13 Nov 1841 Lewis Newland & Margaret Ann Fleet. Bondsman, Lewis Fleet

16 Nov 1841 Matthew Smith & Margaret Spangler. Bondsman, Thomas B. Campbell

17 Nov 1841 Robert Pugh & Jane Giffin. Bondsman, James Giffin

17 Nov 1841 Washington Kerns & Elizabeth Everett, daughter of John Everett. Bondsmen, Elisha Kerns & John Everett

17 Nov 1841 John W. Brown & Margaret Manuel. Bondsman, Thornton Manuel

23 Nov 1841 Jesse Boyd & Margaret Litrell. Bondsman, Bazil Catlett

26 Nov 1841 George Gray & Mary Nesmith, daughter of Jesse Nesmith, the bondsman

4 Dec 1841 William Howard & Adelaide Cather. Bondsman, James Cather

15 Dec 1841 Joseph Galino & Mary Hogan. Bondsman, Robert Long

20 Dec 1841 Michael Duffey & Susan Ann Fout. Bondsman, Henry Fout

20 Dec 1841 Joseph Stanley & Sarah Matilda Hart. Bondsman, William Hart

21 Dec 1841 John B. Hawthorn & Ellen Kiger. Bondsman, Isaac Kiger

22 Dec 1841 Christian C. Ambrose & Martha A. Cook. Bondsman, Henry Crum

23 Dec 1841 Alfred Pitcock & Mary Renner. Bondsman, Barnett Pitcock

23 Dec 1841 Thomas C. Briarly & Susan Glass. Bondsman, Robert J. Glass

29 Dec 1841 William Hart & Sarah ?Seiver. Bondsman, Robert Turner

1 Jan 1842 Thomas Edwards & Eliza Thompson. Bondsman, Robert Clark

4 Jan 1842 William B. Wilson & Julia Ann Furr. Bondsman, Moses D. Wilson

10 Jan 1842 Benoni Swingle & Susan Anna Henderson. Bondsman, Armistead Mason Henderson

10 Jan 1842 William H. Thompson & Sarah Zieler. Bondsman, Peter W. Zieler

12 Jan 1841 (sic) Frederick Ritter & Sarah Smith. Bondsman, George H. Keller

13 Jan 1842 James Renner & Mary Pitcock. Bondsman, Isaac Orndorff

13 Jan 1842 Henry Leisure & Elizabeth Eaton. Bondsman, John Shultz

14 Jan 1842 Henry P. Richard & Margaret Rozenberger. Bondsman, William Rosenberger

15 Jan 1842 James Howard & Lucinda Coyle, widow of Joseph Coyle. Bondsman, William Wright

17 Jan 1842 Joseph Keller & Salome M. Pitman, upwards of 21 years of age. Bondsman, Philip Pitman

18 Jan 1842 William C. Overall & Selina W. Joliffe. Bondsman, Washington G. Singleton

19 Jan 1842 Elijah Williams & Sarah B. Wigginton, upwards of 21. Bondsman, John Whisson

22 Jan 1842 William G. Butler & Rachael R. Barnes. Bondsman, Joseph Barnes

7 Feb 1842 William J. Clark & Lydia E. Hiatt. Bondsman, Andrew Hiatt

7 Feb 1842 David Watson & Catharine Pelter. Bondsman, George Pelter

7 Feb 1842 Jacob Kelknir & Nancy Keller. Bondsman, Peter Keller

8 Feb 1842 Patrick Brady & Alcinda Vaughan, daughter of Dolly Vaughan, the bondsman

11 Feb 1842 Simon H. Lauck & Elizabeth Ann Piper. Bondsman, David Bucher

15 Feb 1842 Peter Evans & Catharine Randall. Bondsman, George Fries

17 Feb 1842 Aaron H. Hackney & Sarah H. Heterick. Bondsman, Robt. M. Heterick

18 Feb 1842 Samuel Kerfoot & Eliza Carson. Bondsman, Jared W. Carson

21 Feb 1842 Patrick McDermott & Mary Ann Waller. Bondsman, Patrick Brady

22 Feb 1842 Elijah Cochran & Elizabeth Lamp, upwards of 21. Bondsman, John Lamp

28 Feb 1842 William D. Lee & Hannaretta Haas. Bondsman, Henry G. Walters

7 Mar 1842 John Lamp & Maria Jane White. Bondsman, Jesse White

14 Mar 1842 John M. Perry, son of Laura Perry, & Maria Ann Clevinger, daughter of Elizabeth Clevinger. Mothers are bondsmen

15 Mar 1842 John Duckwall & Rebecca J. Smith. Bondsman, Jonathan Smith

26 Mar 1842 Charles Shammock & Evelina Cain. Bondsman, William Peterson

29 Mar 1842 Solomon Bishop & Lucinda Owens. Bondsman, Toliver R. Owens

2 Apr 1842 William J. Myers & Elizabeth Ann Allen. Bondsman, George W. Allen

7 Apr 1842 A. J. Grubb & Phebe G. Taylor. Bondsman, Hiram W. Taylor

12 Apr 1842 Henry W. Baker & Rachel A. M. Swingle. Bondsman, Benoni Swingle

14 Apr 1842 Lewis V. Shearer & Margaret Ann Bush. Bondsman, Andrew M. L. Bush

18 Apr 1842 William Gardner & Ragina Rozenberger. Bondsman, William Rozenberger

20 Apr 1842 Jonathan J. Howard & Charlotte Ruble. Bondsman, David Davis

28 Apr 1842 Daniel A. Magruder & Margaret G. Osborn. Bondsman, George Osborn

3 May 1842 James Giffin & Eliza J. Kackley. Bondsman, H. T. Kackley

9 May 1842 John Lineburgh & Priscilla Orndorff. Bondsman, John Ramey

11 May 1842 John Cullers & Julia Ann May. Bondsman, Andrew Hobson

12 May 1842 William Fore (Fott) & Mahala J. Moore. Bondsman, William H. Miller

14 May 1842 Isaac Orndorff & Margaret Lee. Bondsman, William Desponet

23 May 1842 Andrew Roberts & Sarah Nelson. Bondsman, James Nelson

30 May 1842 Jacob Hilliard & Phebe Elliott. Bondsman, Nicholas Windle

3 Jun 1842 Joseph Edward Mowbray & Margaret Bocky. Bondsman, John Bobky

14 Jun 1842 George Purtlebaugh & Jane Long. Bondsman, George Randall

14 Jun 1842 Joseph Clark & Mary Darlinton. Bondsman, Meredith Darlington

15 Jun 1842 William Carpenter & Lydia Frances Gause. Bondsman, William Eddie

22 Jun 1842 Abner Gray & Nancy Bishop. Bondsman, John Grim

25 Jun 1842 Henry Hoover & Susan Carpenter. Bondsman, William Carpenter

1 Jul 1842 James Dailey & Nancy Ann Switzer. Bondsman, John W. Unger

17 Jul 1842 James Fuller & Elen Arnold. Bondsman, Jesse Arnold

1 Aug 1842 William H. Childs & Martha Lukens. Bondsman, Benjamin Shultz

11 Aug 1842 Edward Bulger & Catharine Renner, daughter of Peter Renner, the bondsman

13 Aug 1842 Andrew J. Marpole & Delilah Mitcham, daughter of Henry Mitcham. Bondsman, John Chrisman

15 Aug 1842 Robert B. Hackney & Susan Sibert. Bondsman, James W. Seibert

24 Aug 1842 John J. Crawford & Mahala J. Purtlebaugh, daughter of George Purtlebaugh. Bondsmen, William Crawford & George Purtlebaugh

26 Aug 1842 Edward Furgason & Ruth Harry, daughter of David Harry, the bondsman

26 Aug 1842 John Miller & Mary Jane Himmelwright, daughter of John Himmelwright, the bondsman

27 Aug 1842 William Fletcher & Rebeca Stipe. Bondsman, Uriah Fletcher

1 Sep 1842 Joseph T. Albin & Margaret Brent. Bondsman, George W. Brent

5 Sep 1842 Archibald Showalter & Mary Ann Day. Bondsman, Joseph Kline

5 Sep 1842 John Knage & Susan Odell. Bondsman, Henry Hosey

7 Sep 1842 Israel R. Anderson & Margaret Ellen Anderson, daughter of James Anderson, the bondsman

8 Sep 1842 Elijah Marker & Rachel Snapp, daughter of Henry Snapp, the bondsman

12 Sep 1842 Samuel Wingfield & Rebecca Rinehart. Bondsman, John Rinehart

15 Sep 1842 Alfred C. Jackson & Susan G. Osborne, daughter of George Osborn, the bondsman

15 Sep 1842 John K. Ball & Eliza Jane Jackson, upwards of 21 years of age. Bondsman, Alfred C. Jackson

20 Sep 1842 George R. Long & Harriet A. Richards. Bondsman, Thomas A. Tidball

20 Sep 1842 John Brandeburg & Henrietta M. Holtzman. Bondsman, Charles W. Gibbins

22 Sep 1842 Hanson French, a free man of color, & Sarah Spencer, a free woman of color. Bondsman, George H. Smith, a free man of color

29 Sep 1842 Peyton R. Mitchell & Frances C. Jackson. Bondsman, Solomon R. Jackson

8 Oct 1842 Daniel Denvar & Ann Brent. Bondsman, Hugh Raynolds

11 Oct 1842 Peter Taylor & Catherine Parlett. Bondsman, Patrick Moreland

15 Oct 1842 Peter ?Summers & Hannah Chapman. Bondsman, William Sumer

17 Oct 1842 David J. Miller & Mary Ellen Parkins. Bondsman, Alfred Parkins

29 Oct 1842 Isaac Stillman, a free mulatto man, & Charity Humbard, a free black girl. No bondsman

31 Oct 1842 John L. Anderson & Margaret Grove. Bondsman, Michael Capper

2 Nov 1842 Francis S. Mendenhall & Sarah Touchstone. Bondsman, Benjamin Touchstone

7 Nov 1842 William Gardiner & Nancy Cornwell. Bondsman, Thomas Cornwell

7 Nov 1842 Isaac H. Steer & Margaret Davis. Bondsman, David Davison

14 Nov 1842 Richard M. Slonaker & Elizabeth M. Davison. Bondsman, Daniel Davison

22 Nov 1842 A. P. Fitch & Mary G. Hartman. Bondsman, Lewis P. Hartman

22 Nov 1842 Isaiah Beans & Ann Hawkins (Hankins?). Bondsman, John F. Beans

24 Nov 1842 James Gilkeson & Sydney E. Parkins. Bondsman, William D. Gilkeson

12 Dec 1842 Joseph G. Heskett & Angeline Orr. Bondsman, Jacob Nicols

12 Dec 1842 Joseph F. Davis & Harriet A. Brown. Bondsman, David Z. Brown

12 Dec 1842 David Rhodes & Jane M. Cooper. Bondsman, Abraham Rhodes

13 Dec 1842 John W. Light & Rebecca Ann Jones, upwards of 21 years of age. Bondsman, Joshua Jones

3 Jan 1843 Asa H. Loy & Phebe Ruble. Bondsman, David Z. Brown

9 Jan 1843 Michael Farley & Hannah Aulebaugh. Bondsman, James Alobaugh

10 Jan 1843 John H. Hoover & Adaline Krider. Bondsman, John B. Krider

11 Jan 1843 George Petty & Emily S. Poland. Bondsman, Leonard Myers

24 Jan 1843 William Stimmel & Elizabeth Ann Brown. Bondsman, Benjamin F. Brown

1 Feb 1843 Cornelius J. Wykoff & Hannah Mowry, daughter of John R. Mowry, the bondsman

6 Feb 1843 James A. Piper & Ann E. Marks, daughter of Alexander Marks, the bondsman

8 Feb 1843 Benjamin Benner & Rachel Albin. Bondsman, Jackson Albin

11 Feb 1843 John H. Brill & Sarah Ann Millhorn. Bondsman, James Milhorn

13 Feb 1843 Elijah Rudolph & Catharine Snapp. Bondsman, Benjamin Fry

20 Feb 1843 Isaac Milton Hollingsworth & Mary C. Pritchard. Bondsman, Stephen Pritchard

20 Feb 1843 George W. Brent & Harriet Ebbert. Bondsman, William Ebbert

22 Feb 1843 John H. Snapp & Amanda E. Snapp. Bondsman, Benjamin Fry

27 Feb 1843 Henry C. Anderson & Elizabeth B. Aby. Bondsman, John S. Gryer

4 Mar 1843 Burr P. Williams & Mary Ann Lamp. Bondsman, John Lamp

6 Mar 1843 Ephraim Kern & Mary Eliza Hamilton. Bondsman, Zacharias Kern

14 Mar 1843 John Trenary & Sarah Jane Drake. Bondsman, James H. Drake

14 Mar 1843 George H. Ash & Evelina M. Massie. Bondsman, Benjamin M. Massie

15 Mar 1843 Levi Scrivener & Jane Coe. Bondsman, John Giffin Jr.

21 Mar 1843 Landon Racy & Rachel Tewalt. Bondsman, William Racy

27 Mar 1843 Josiah Frise & Margaret Ellen Boyd. Bondsman, John Boyd

29 Mar 1843 Frederick W. Carper & Marian Ritenour. Bondsman, Daniel B. Ritenour.

30 Mar 1843 William Dehaven & Sarah Light. Bondsman, Henry D. Dehaven

1 Apr 1843 Samuel McLunn & Mary Jane Poole. upwards of 21 years of age. Bondsman, Robert Christy

4 Apr 1843 Thomas Heflin & Mary M. Finch. Bondsman, Henry J. McDaniel

6 Apr 1843 Edmund H. Ridings & Louisa C. Orndorf. Bondsmen, Edwin B. Ridings & John W. Orndorff

19 Apr 1843 Thornton L. W. Boxwell & Elizabeth Bishop. Bondsmen, Robert Boxwell & Solomon Bishop

6 May 1843 George W. Everhart & Elizabeth Jane Williams. Bondsman, John Williams

12 May 1843 William Roe & Basheba Catlett. Bondsman, William Catlett

15 May 1843 Killion Shrout & Margaret Ann Pope. Bondsman, Conrad Pope. Shrout & Pope sign in German

15 May 1843 James B. Carter & Martha T. Haines. Bondsman, Aquilla J. Haines

22 May 1843 Barnett Lewis & Eliza M. Clark, daughter of Rubin Clark

24 May 1843 William Owens & Joanna Hardy. Bondsmen, James Nelson & Samuel Royer

25 May 1843 George S. Parlett & Catherine Furr. Bondsman, Isaac Furr

30 May 1843 Nimrod D. Keneaster & Mary A. Hawk, daughter of Michael Hawk, the bondsman

6 Jun 1843 Joseph H. Clower & Eliza Pingley. Bondsman, John R. Mowrey

11 Jun 1843 William Croner & Patsy Catlett, daughter of William Catlett, the bondsman

28 Jun 1843 Colin Leach & Nancy Reed. Bondsman, Thomas A. Tidball

29 Jun 1843 Henry Himmelwright & Hannah Jane Brill, daughter of Joseph Brill, the bondsman

29 Jun 1843 John W. Beagent & Sarah Ann Heironimus. Bondsman, Mary Heironimus.

13 Jul 1843 Thomas J. Crawford & Sarah Jane Brown, daughter of Mary Brown, the bondsman

15 Jul 1843 Isaac D. Hopewell & Mary Jane Myers, daughter of Joseph S. Miers, the bondsman

29 Jul 1843 Peter Rubbel & Eliza Ann Loy. Bondsman, Conrad Loy

5 Aug 1843 Benjamin McKee & Elizabeth Stipe. Bondsman, Samuel Giffin

12 Aug 1843 Jacob F. Hott & Jane Streit. Bondsman, Joel Barrett

25 Aug 1843 Benjamin Hoffman & Rebecca Shaffer. Bondsman, John B. Campbell

29 Aug 1843 John Hutslar & Mary A. Gibbons. Bondsman, Benjamin G. Manor

2 Sep 1843 Benjamin Keiter & Elizabeth Ann White. Bondsman, Jacob Keiter

4 Sep 1843 Robert H. McCleave & Sarah Ann Wilkeson. Bondsman, Thomas A. Tidball

13 Sep 1843 Jacob Cooper & Sarah Ann Richards, daughter of Jacob Richards, the bondsman

14 Sep 1843 George B. McCann & Mary M. Thatcher. Bondsman, Evan Thatcher

27 Sep 1843 Mordecai E. White & Margaret E. Hensell, daughter of Joseph Hensell, the bondsman

2 Oct 1843 Robert W. Daily & Rebecca H. Taylor. Bondsman, William B. Taylor

3 Oct 1843 Jeremiah G. Smith & Elizabeth Jane Furr, daughter of Newton Furr, the bondsman

4 Oct 1843 Lewis F. Wilson & Mary E. Chamberlin. Bondsman, William H. Streit

10 Oct 1843 Jacob King & Jarisia Ann Bazell. Bondsman, John Coe

18 Oct 1843 George Pine & Mary Lindsey. Bondsman, George Swhier

25 Oct 1843 Harrison Marpole & Barbara C. Loy. Bondsman, John Loy

27 Oct 1843 Andrew Bean & Mary A. W. Lind. Bondsman, Charles T. Lind

2 Nov 1843 James A. Marsteller & Harriet Langley. Bondsman, J. L. Langley

15 Nov 1843 John H. Stephens & Ann Pagett. Bondsman, George Fyst

20 Nov 1843 Jacob White & Elizabeth White, daughter of Isaac White, the bondsman

20 Nov 1843 William H. Weaver & Marenda Kern. Bondsman, Mager Steel

27 Nov 1843 Thomas E. Shambaugh & Barbara Ann Larrick. Bondsman, Charles D. Shambaugh

2 Dec 1843 John C. Edwards & Harriet C. Baker. Bondsman, George Baker
4 Dec 1843 James Owens & Catharine Mincer, upwards of 21 years of age. Bondsman, John Hott
5 Dec 1843 Marshall Anderson & Eliza Anderson. Bondsman, Daniel Anderson
11 Dec 1843 Henry W. Snapp & Juliet B. Frye. Bondsman, Henry Snapp
11 Dec 1843 John M. Holmes & Levinia J. Anderson. Bondsman, William S. Anderson
11 Dec 1843 Jefferson Ramey & Margaret Kern. Bondsman, Timothy Kerin
12 Dec 1843 James Sherman & Angelina Newcomb, daughter of Elisha Newcomb, the bondsman
13 Dec 1843 William Luttrell & Lucy Ann Bear. Bondsman, William Keller
15 Dec 1843 Augustus Bohrer & Amy Engle. Bondsman, William D. Engle
18 Dec 1843 Charles F. Parker & Ann Maria Walter. Bondsman, William B. Walter

Marriage Bonds No. 19 1843-1847
-- Dec 1843 Daniel Jefferson Murphey & Nancy Scrivener. Bondsman, David H. Hupp (date torn)
26 Dec 1843 Samuel McLun & Mary Jane Pool. Bondsman, Mathew W. Royston
-- Dec 1843 Alexander Wilson & Caroline Reason. Bondsman, Henry Wisecarver (date torn)
30 Dec 1843 James Ware & Elizabeth Collins. Bondsman, Daniel Collins
1 Jan 1844 Barack B. Fisher & Rebecca Anderson, ward of George W. Snider, the bondsman
2 Jan 1844 Lorenzo Oats & Sarah Grove. Bondsman, Daniel Oates
8 Jan 1844 John Wright & Sarah Kercheval. Bondsman, Joseph Tidball
9 Jan 1844 Levi Sherman & Mary C. Renner. Bondsman, James R. Duncan
11 Jan 1844 Thomas Cornwell & Mary Gardner. Bondsman, John M. Rutter

13 Jan 1844 Thomas Mills & Mary Ann Carter. Bondsman, James D. Merryman

16 Jan 1844 James Gardiner & Margaret Ann Violett. Bondsman, Thomas Cornwell

16 Jan 1844 Bazileial Tyson & Ursuley Catlett. Bondsman, John Catlett

27 Jan 1844 Davis Farmer & Jemima McKee. Bondsman, Isaiah Anderson

31 Jan 1844 Isaiah Anderson & Margaret Lafollet. Bondsman, Michael Capper

31 Jan 1844 William Mauzy & Mercy Whitacre. Bondsman, Wilson Whitacre

1 Feb 1844 James McGalis & Ellen E. Dooley. Bondsman, John M. Magson

9 Feb 1844 Thomas Drake & Mary S. Nicholson. Bondsman, Joseph Neill

12 Feb 1844 Isaac L. Frye & Mary M. L. Frye. Bondsman, Benjamin Frye

15 Feb 1844 Daniel Collins & Eliza Heironimus. Bondsman, Camallias H. Heironimus

15 Feb 1844 William H. Sherer & Barbara Ann Singhass, daughter of Christian Singhass, the bondsman

22 Feb 1844 John Hardy & Maria M. Fletcher, daughter of John Fletcher, the bondsman

26 Feb 1844 Henry Stine & Julia Ann Glaize, daughter of Solomon Glays, the bondsman

29 Feb 1844 Alfred Rutter & Jane Childs. Bondsman, William Henry Chiles

6 Mar 1844 Isaac Rhodes & Elizabeth Dinges. Bondsman, Jacob Senseny

9 Mar 1844 William P. Branson & Delilah Highley. Bondsman, Joseph E. Payne

15 Mar 1844 Joseph Keckley & Mary Ann Fishel. Bondsman, Samuel Orndorff

16 Mar 1844 James W. Stephenson & Sarah Fawcett. Bondsman, Josiah Massie

21 Mar 1844 Elijah H. Perry & Mary Jones, upwards of 21 years of age. Bondsman, John W. Milhorn

2 Apr 1844 David Connally & Sarah Ann Coats. Bondsman, John McUlboon

4 Apr 1844 George Griggs, free negro, & Catherine Brown. Bondsman, Robert C. Berkeley

8 Apr 1844 Franklin Grubb & Ann Maria Rector. Bondsman, James Howard

15 Apr 1844 John Peters & Elizabeth Miller, daughter of David Miller, the bondsman

16 Apr 1844 Abraham Sherea & Mary Howard. Bondsman, James Cather

17 Apr 1844 William Ettenger Jr. & Mary C. Nulton, daughter of Abraham Nulton, the bondsman

8 May 1844 Isaac M. Reager & Athanasia Edmonson. Bondsman, W. H. Edmonson

21 May 1844 William J. Reed & Sarah Jane Eddy. Bondsman, William Eddy

24 May 1844 James Lewis & Juliet Ann Clark, daughter of Rueben Clark, the bondsman

27 May 1844 Joseph Keller & Catharine Windle. Bondsman, Harrison Windell

28 May 1844 James M. Barber & Emily E. Ash. Bondsman, John H. Ash

3 Jun 1844 Simon Johnson & Lucinda Hamilton. Bondsman, John Johnson

11 Jun 1844 Michael Kaufmann & Sarah Bishop. Bondsman, Jacob Creiser

20 Jan 1844 David Pingley & Catherine Shambaugh. Bondsman, Daniel Shambaugh

26 Jun 1844 John Y. Parlett & Mary Ann Fries, daughter of David Fries, the bondsman

13 Jul 1844 John Pifer & Alcinda E. Nolen. Bondsman, John Nolen

19 Jul 1844 Michael C. Dolan & Mary M. Bageant, daughter of William Bageant, the bondsman

27 Jul 1844 George Whitacre & Jane Dehaven, daughter of Isaac Dehaven, the bondsman

31 Jul 1844 Seth S. Devoe & Mary Emmons. Bondsman, William Cain

5 Aug 1844 Daniel May & Harriett Dowell, stepdaughter of Isaac Shipe, the bondsman

8 Aug 1844 Jonathan Simmons & Nancy Murphy, upwards of 21 years of age. Bondsman, Aaron Simmons

12 Aug 1844 Christian O. Glassford & Catharine Ann Buncutter, daughter of Christopher Buncutter, the bondsman

13 Aug 1844 Charles Grubbs & Elizabeth Clevenger. Bondsman, James Chism

13 Aug 1844 Avery Stipe & Ann I. Redd. Bondsman, Alexander W. Albin

19 Aug 1844 John Stimmel & Elizabeth Sumption. Bondsman, Jacob Sumption

28 Aug 1844 Aaron Sirbaugh & Emily Kerns. Bondsman, Thomas Kerns

29 Aug 1844 James Webb, a free negro man, & Maria Wells, a free negro woman, daughter of Alfred Wells, the bondsman

30 Aug 1844 Jeremiah Shade & Octavia Brown, daughter of Wesley Brown, the bondsman

2 Sep 1844 Eli Owens & Juliet Touchstone. Bondsman, Henry Grim

4 Sep 1844 Abner Hodgson & Rebecca A. Lupton. Bondsman, Nathaniel C. Lupton

10 Sep 1844 John Wilson & Elizabeth Catharine Fiser, daughter of Mary Fiser, the bondsman

10 Sep 1844 Alfred Ritter & Hannah Dailey, upwards of 21 years old. Bondsman, Absolom Dailey

17 Sep 1844 Reuben Marker & Margaret Ann Newland. Bondsman, Joseph B. Parker

17 Sep 1844 William L. Hollis & Hannah Conrad, sister of Charles M. Conrad, the bondsman

23 Sep 1844 Daniel Hartsock & Emily S. Nelson. Bondsman, James H. Nelson

23 Sep 1844 James H. Nelson & Elizabeth E. Stevens. Bondsman, Daniel Hartsock

30 Sep 1844 George Kremer Jnr & Virginia C. Anderson. Bondsman, John Anderson

7 Oct 1844 Jonathan Oats & Elizabeth Oats. Bondsman, Jacob Oats

8 Oct 1844 Daniel J. Martin & Nancy C. Switzer, daughter of Jacob Switzer, the bondsman

8 Oct 1844 William F. Marker & Margaret Larrick, daughter of Henry Larrick, the bondsman

17 Oct 1844 Thomas Ferrell & Lavenia Vincent. Bondsman, Strawberry Chapman

17 Oct 1844 John Ridings & Elizabeth A. Barton. Bondsman, David Barton

19 Oct 1844 Nicholas Unger & Sarah Bohrer, daughter of Isaac Bohrer, the bondsman

29 Oct 1844 Benjamin Dailey & Margaret Jane Stephens. Bondsman, Thomas B. Harvey

29 Oct 1844 Arthur Dorsey & Rhody Brown. Bondsman, James Mack

30 Oct 1844 Joseph McDonald & Mary Ann Sirbaugh. Bondsman, Aaron Sirbaugh

31 Oct 1844 John Dickinson & Emily J. Nulton, daughter of Abraham Nulton, the bondsman

2 Nov 1844 Robert Johnson, a free negro, & Nancy Greyson, a free negro. Bondsman, William D. Gilkeson

4 Nov 1844 Joseph Henning & Jane M. Marple. Bondsman, Vance P. Bradford

12 Nov 1844 Jacob Fisher & Sarah Tewalt, upwards of 21 years of age. Bondsman, Abner Strawderman

12 Nov 1844 John Racey & Mary Ann Orndorff, daughter of Benjamin Orndorff, the bondsman

13 Nov 1844 John Bocky & Harriet Hubbard, daughter of Robert Hubbard, the bondsman

14 Nov 1844 John L. Green & Margaret Ann Cole. Bondsman, Isaac B. Cole

18 Nov 1844 William H. Edmondson & Sarah J. Gibbons. Bondsman, William J. Gibbons

18 Nov 1844 Barnet Pitcock & Mary Williams. Bondsman, Samuel Williams Jr.

20 Nov 1844 John Capper & Rebecca Good. Bondsman, Felix Good

27 Nov 1844 Westly Knight & Mary Ann Jenkins, daughter of Adam Jenkins, the bondsman

29 Nov 1844 Luster Riely & Sidney Haney. Bondsnam, Leroy Newcomb

29 Nov 1844 Joshua Jones & Mary Martha Campbell. Bondsman, Peter Light

5 Dec 1844 James McNabb & Margaret Ann Eagle. Bondsman, Joseph Kean

5 Dec 1844 James Mason & Margaret Jane Rutter, upwards of 21 years of age. Bondsman, Frederick Rutter

6 Dec 1844 Jefferson Largent & Sarah Jane Noel, stepdaughter of Abram Peasmaker, the bondsman

9 Dec 1844 James Pangle & Eliza Rinker. Bondsman, Casper Rinker

9 Dec 1844 Thomas Trussell & Emily Jane Gibson, upwards of 21 years of age. Bondsman, Hamilton L. Gibson

14 Dec 1844 Isaac Dehaven & Harriet Ann Christy. Bondsman, Elizabeth Christy

16 Dec 1844 Alexander W. Albin & Elizabeth Whissen. Bondsman, John Whissen

16 Dec 1844 Alfred Williams & Elizabeth Frye. Bondsman, Eli J. Frye

20 Dec 1844 John Cather & Jane Russell. Bondsman, Henry Richards
23 Dec 1844 William L. Dehaven & Sarah C. Smoke. Bondsman, Hiram Adams
3 Jan 1845 Jose Mountz & Rebecca C. George. Bondsman, Thomas Allen
4 Jan 1845 Eli J. Frye & Leah Finley, daughter of Archibald Findley, the bondsman
8 Jan 1845 William Dunn & Milly Jane Bonen, upwards of 21 years, stepdaughter of Zachariah Carpenter, the bondsman
10 Jan 1845 George H. Griffin & Frances Rector. Bondsman, Nelson Rector
14 Jan 1845 Fielding R. Jones & Sarah A. Bowen, daughter of John G. Bowen. Bondsmen, Mary Jones & John G. Bowen
21 Jan 1845 Jared D. Merryman & Catherine S. Singhass, daughter of Samuel Singhass, the bondsman
21 Jan 1845 Joseph W. Keeler & Ann R. Chiles. Bondsman, Griffin Chiles
23 Jan 1845 William McCleves & Mary E. White. Bondsman, William Brill
28 Jan 1845 Charles F. Swartz & Mary F. Conway. Bondsman, Hugh Conway
29 Jan 1845 David Robinson & Hannah E. Cather. Bondsman, Patrick Howard
7 Feb 1845 Joseph T. Dehaven & Rebecca Roe. Bondsman, Robert Roe
7 Feb 1845 John Oats & Rebecca Fout. Bondsman, Henry Fout
10 Feb 1845 Hiram Carper & Sarah Carper. Bondsman, John Carper
11 Feb 1845 Absalom Dailey & Margaret Grove. Bondsman, John Grove
11 Feb 1845 John W. Hyatt & Rachel Ann Clark. Bondsman, William Clark
17 Feb 1845 Edwin S. Baker & Martha A. Wood. Bondsman, Mordecai Purcell
20 Feb 1845 Frederick Eichholtz & Martha Ellen Bowen. Bondsman, Middleton M. Bowen
22 Feb 1845 John H. Buncutter & Mary Jane Brannon. Bondsman, Andrew F. Hytt
25 Feb 1845 Asberry Whitacre & Evelina McKee, daughter of Robert McKee, the bondsman
3 Mar 1845 Michael Anderson & Isabella Lockhart. Bondsman, Robert V. Lockhart

3 Mar 1845 Samuel Alexander & Mary Ann Guyer. Bondsman, Jacob Larrick

2 May 1845 Michael E. Ritenour & Mary Jones. Bondsman, John Snapp

10 May 1845 John Larrick & Margaret Murphy, ward of Robert Hook, the bondsman

10 Mar 1845 George Y. Fries & Ann Streit. Bondsman, Jacob Hott

10 Mar 1845 William Cochran & Hannah A. Stokes. Bondsman, John W. Milhorn

13 Mar 1845 Benjamin McDonald & Ruth Whitacre. Bondsman, Wilson Whitacre

15 Mar 1845 Joseph A. Dyer & Hannah M. Jolley. Bondsman, James Dailey

15 Mar 1845 John M. Miller & Elizabeth Pritchard. Bondsman, Robert J. Glass

17 Mar 1845 John Heironimus & Susan Mauzy. Bondsman, John Mauzy

27 Mar 1845 Patrick Conner & Emily Nevit. Bondsman, Samuel Noakes

31 Mar 1845 Daniel A. Kline & Martha Marker, daughter of George A. Marker, the bondsman

1 Apr 1845 George Furgeson & Mary C. Coe, daughter of Samuel Coe, the bondsman

4 Apr 1845 Thomas W. Ridings & Ann E. Anderson. Bondsman, Samuel Sperry

8 Apr 1845 Griffin Chiles & Ona Stipe. Bondsman, George Stipe

10 Apr 1845 John Beatty & Eliza Magalis, daughter of Godfrey Magalis (signature illegible), the bondsman

15 Apr 1845 Jacob Clouser & Mary Ann Cooper. Bondsman, Levi Cooper

19 Apr 1845 Joseph D. Rogers & Margaret Moyer. Bondsman, Joseph T. Fout

19 Apr 1845 John Moling & Margaret Clark. Bondsman, Jonathan M. Clark

21 Apr 1845 John Moss & Nancy Jones. Bondsman, Joseph P. Mahaney

22 Apr 1845 Henry Pitcock & Elizabeth Renner. Bondsman, Peter Renner

29 Apr 1845 George B. Stephens & Mary S. Ash. Bondsman, Alexander R. Newman

1 May 1845 Sydnor McDonald & Mary Jane Lockhart. Bondsman, Robert V. Lockhart

5 May 1845 Andrew M. Vanarsdale & Rachel Ann Dillon. Bondsman, Joseph B. Hackney

12 May 1845 James Lemley & Mary Ann Nisewanger, daughter of Lucinda Nisewanger, the bondsman

15 May 1845 Alonzo P. Ludden & Margaret C. Grove, daughter of John W. Grove, the bondsman

16 May 1845 Gerrard F. Mason & Isabella Stephenson. Bondsman, George W. Hammond

27 May 1845 Abraham Jones & Eliza Hodge. Bondsman, John Moss

4 Jun 1845 Zachariah M. Grim & Eliza June Beattey, daughter of William Beattey, the bondsman

4 Jun 1845 John W. Frazier & Elizabeth S. Moore, daughter of Strother Moore, the bondsman

6 Jun 1845 Solomon Bishop & Marcha G. Mitcham. Bondsman, Henry Mitcham

17 Jun 1845 William B. Moore & Catherine D. Turner. Bondsman, John W. Ewan

1 Jul 1845 Augustus J. Turner & Catherine M. Abbey. Bondsman, Jacob S. Niswander

19 Jul 1845 William Dick & Mary Ann Taylor. Bondsman, Edward Taylor (free negroes)

21 Jul 1845 James H. Bonwell & Sarah Brown, daughter of Michael Brown, the bondsman

25 Jul 1845 David Kerns & Angeline B. Allemong. Bondsman, Casper Allemong

29 Jul 1845 Nathaniel B. Triplett & Mary Steel. Bondsman, Paul P. Anderson

20 Jul 1845 Jacob Cutwait & Jane Sibert, widow of Michael Sibert. Bondsman, Nimrod McEndree

30 Jul 1845 George Taylor & Mary Ann Marcus. Bondsman, John Curry

31 Jul 1845 Isaac H. Hay & Ann M. Baldwin. Bondsman, Robert T. Baldwin

18 Aug 1845 Walter B. Grubb & Mary Elizabeth Stephens, daughter of George Stephens, the bondsman

19 Aug 1845 Raymond S. Davis & Elizabeth D. Swift. Bondsman, James P. Riely

21 Aug 1845 Jonas Chamberlain & Elizabeth Danner. Bondsman, Lewis T. Moore

27 Aug 1845 Thomas Matthews & Susan Willey. Bondsman, William Willey

30 Aug 1845 James Slonaker & Martha Ann McKee, daughter of William McKee, the bondsman
1 Sep 1845 Nathaniel B. Cooper & Rebecca M. Linneberger. Bondsman, William Linneberger
1 Sep 1845 Isaac Lambert & Pemelia Larrick. Bondsman, Jacob Larrick
8 Sep 1845 Philip S. Crabill & Elizabeth Ann Rosenberger. Bondsman, William Rosenberger
9 Sep 1845 William Adams & Barbara Ann Shane, daughter of John Shane. Bondsmen, Peter Adams & John Shane
13 Sep 1845 William Offord & Eliza Ann Bohrer, daughter of Isaac Bohrer, the bondsman
17 Sep 1845 Peter Shively & Elizabeth Webber. Bondsman, Daniel Shively
18 Sep 1845 Jonathan Smith & Hannah Crebbs. Bondsman, James Bowles
20 Sep 1845 John R. Mauzy & Susan Kerns. Bondsman, Nathan Kerns
29 Sep 1845 Amos Fisher & Sarah Oran. Bondsman, Caspar Curry
8 Oct 1845 Steward J. Brannon & Mary A. Carper, daughter of John Carper, the bondsman
11 Oct 1845 George Fries & Mary Jane Boyd. Bondsman, Robert Boyd
13 Oct 1845 Benjamin Barrett & Margaret Friese, upwards of 21 years of age. Bondsman, John Hott
14 Oct 1845 James Hutslar & Emily Gibbons. Bondsman, James B. Simmons
14 Oct 1845 Morgan Cain & Mary Ann Hilliard. Bondsman, Jacob Hilliard
15 Oct 1845 James Moreland & Sarah Pennybaker. Bondsman, William Seemer
22 Oct 1845 John C. Richardson & Sarah Ann Baker. Bondsman, William D. Gilkeson
23 Oct 1845 Lewis Newlin & Sarah Lavinia Jones, daughter of Mary Jones, the bondsman
11 Nov 1845 James Swaltz & Lavinia Albin. Bondsman, Asa Clevinger
<u>12 Mar 1846</u> (sic) George R. Cruzen & Elizabeth J. Kernan, daughter of James Keener (Keenan?), the bondsman
27 Oct 1845 Joshua Lupton & Mary Ann Hodgson. Bondsman, Abner Hodgson
31 Oct 1845 Benjamin F. Light & Esther Dehaven. Bondsman, Joseph T. Dehaven

3 Nov 1845 Thomas W. Chapman & Mary C. Shy. Bondsman, Henry S. Wunder

14 Nov 1845 Thomas A. Kackley & Elizabeth Garrett, upwards of 20 years of age. Bondsman, Abraham Garrett

17 Nov 1845 Harrison McCormick & Mary Dehaven. Bondsman, Isaac Dehaven

27 Nov 1845 Samuel Hardy & Mary S. March, upwards of 21 years of age. Bondsman, Leroy G. March

29 Nov 1845 Samuel Davison & Martha Jane Hyatt, daughter of Andrew F. Hyatt, the bondsman

15 Dec 1845 John Cook & Mary Ann Sherrick. Bondsman, Philip Sherrick

15 Dec 1845 Joseph Dewalt & Lucinda Orndorff. Bondsman, Israel Orndorff

22 Dec 1845 William M. Taylor & Mary Jane Lloyd. Bondsman, James Lloyd

23 Dec 1845 William Kirby & Catherine B. James. Bondsman, David Deahl

29 Dec 1845 Elias Athey & Alcinda Rutter. Bondsman, Peter Kennerly

20 Jan 1846 John Adams & Susan E. Jones. Bondsman, Jesse Wright

27 Jan 1846 James W. Hensell & Isabella Day, upwards of 21. Bondsman, Philip A. Hite

27 Jan 1846 Joseph Tewalt & Mary S. White, daughter of Jesse C. White, the bondsman

5 Feb 1846 Geo W. Lemley & Susan Margaret Ritenour. Bondsman, William Ritenour

23 Feb 1846 Robert Eddy & Catherine L. Morgan. Bondsman, Richd H. Morgan

28 Feb 1846 Lewis Brisco, free negro, & Kitty Peterson, free negro. Bondsman, Charles Shumbock, free negro

9 Mar 1846 David S. Hook & Mary Ann Murphy. Bondsman, Jonathan Simmons

13 Mar 1846 Alfred Freeman & Sarah Jane Leach. Bondsman, James F. Leach

16 Mar 1846 George H. Keiter & Ann Fout. Bondsman, Joseph H. Brown

17 Mar 1846 John G. M. T. Reisler & Emelene L. Deval, daughter of Reason Deval, the bondsman

20 Mar 1846 William Orndorff & Margaret Ann Anderson, daughter of Daniel Anderson, the bondsman

21 Mar 1846 Robert V. Lockhart & Mary E. B. Hall. Bondsman, William L. Bent

24 Mar 1846 William Cather & Emily A. C. Smith. Bondsman, James Cather

25 Mar 1846 George Gardner & Parandis Newcome. Bondsman, Elisha Newcome

28 Mar 1846 William Fries & Mary Jane Fulkerson, daughter of John Fulkerson, the bondsman

30 Mar 1846 George Glaize & Harriet Rinker, daughter of Casper Rinker, the bondsman

31 Mar 1846 John W. Eaton, upward of 21 years of age, & Sarah Marpole. Bondsman, Enoc (Enos?) Marpole

4 Apr 1846 Joseph Kline & Mary Ann Schwartz. Bondsman, Joseph Schwartz

8 Apr 1846 Levi T. Grim & Mary Elizabeth Steel. Bondsman, Thomas W. Russell

25 Apr 1846 Vincent Barnes & Sarah A. Welsh. Bondsman, George W. Legg

29 Apr 1846 Atwell Miller & Sarah Jane Barnett. Bondsman, Reuben Elliott

29 Apr 1846 John Grimes & Elizabeth Jones. Bondsman, James W. Jones

30 Apr 1846 George Stephens & Ellen Widows. Bondsman, Joseph Kean

7 May 1846 Joseph F. Brown & Maria Virginia Singleton, daughter of Washington G. Singleton, the bondsman

16 May 1846 Benjamin Dix & Mary M. Right. Bondsman, George Y. Fries

23 May 1846 Michael Ring & Anna Malta (Matta?), upwards of 21 years of age. Bondsman, Michael Cuntz

25 May 1846 Peter E. Hening & Mary Lavinia Piper. Bondsman, Abraham Piper

27 May 1846 Henry Montgomery & Ellen E. Baker, daughter of Hillarius Baker, the bondsman

9 Jun 1846 Benjamin Marple & Isabella Amanda Triplett. Bondsman, John K. Triplett

17 Jun 1846 James Knight & Emily Susan Hillman, daughter of Simeon Hillman, the bondsman

23 Jun 1846 David Connally & Ellen Myers. Bondsman, Elias H. Hibbard

29 Jun 1846 John Dignan & Leannah McNamie. Bondsman, John Fagan

29 Jun 1846 J. Frederick Blessing & Emily June Grim, daughter of Jacob Grim, the bondsman

21 Jul 1846 George A. Grove & Frances Widdows. Bondsman, Robert Frazier

29 Jul 1846 John Markell & Mary Shepherd. Bondsman, William L. Bent

5 Aug 1846 John Irvin & Mary Ann Sangster. Bondsman, Thomas S. Sangster

10 Aug 1846 Joseph Mahew & Susan Long, widow of Abraham Long decd. Bondsman, Tilghman Mayhew

11 Aug 1846 Andrew Shane & Lanah Adams, daughter of Peter Adams, the bondsman

15 Aug 1846 William Unger & Susan Ann Braithwaite, daughter of William Braithwaite, the bondsman

19 Aug 1846 Lemuel McCauley & Jane Farmer. Bondsman, Peter Farmer

22 Aug 1846 John L. Beatty & Jane Brill, daughter of Henry Brill, the bondsman

10 Sep 1846 Joseph H. Kline & Priscilla Wilson, upwards of 21 years of age. Bondsman, Daniel Powers

14 Sep 1846 Robert Whittington & Mary Gordon. Bondsman, Elias Overall

19 Sep 1846 Thomas P. Marshall & Amanda C. Sperry, daughter of Thomas Sperry, the bondsman

19 Sep 1846 William Bowen & Sarah Ann Franks, daughter of Henry Franks, the bondsman

21 Sep 1846 James Cubbage & Elizabeth Ann Hoover. Bondsman, Jacob Hoover

7 Oct 1846 Jacob Parrott & Ametia Howard. Bondsman, William Dick (free negroes)

7 Oct 1846 Henry F. Shaull & Harriet Beatty. Bondsman, William Beattey

7 Oct 1846 Clark Cather & Margaret Ann Lupton, daughter of Jonah Lupton. Bondsmen, James Cather & Jonah Lupton

10 Oct 1846 Alfred Hutzler & Hannah Williams, daughter of John Williams, the bondsman

17 Oct 1846 Robert Bull & Susan C. Jackson. Bondsman, James R. Jackson

20 Oct 1846 Jacob Rinehart & Caroline M. White. Bondsman, Anthony M. Kline

27 Oct 1846 Elkanah Fawcett & Margaret Ann Funkhouser. Bondsman, Martin Funkhouser

4 Nov 1846 Henry E. Mauck & Sarah Jane Lapole, daughter of Sarah Lapole, the bondsman

16 Nov 1846 Jonah J. Lupton & Mary Elizabeth Tavener, daughter of Stacy J. Tavener, the bondsman

16 Nov 1846 John M. Horner & Elizabeth McCormick, daughter of Levi McCormick, the bondsman

16 Nov 1846 John McFarlan & Susannah Keller, daughter of Abraham Keller. Bondsmen, Levi McFarlan & Abraham Keller

19 Nov 1846 Milton M. Grandstaff & Emily J. A. Frye. Bondsman, William E. Fry

21 Nov 1846 Charles E. Shyrock & Rachel Ann Young, daughter of George Young, the bondsman

28 Nov 1846 Jacob Mantz (Montz?) & Catherine Snyder. Bondsman, Jacob Hoffman

19 Nov 1846 John K. Woods & Lucy J. Gilkeson. Bondsman, William D. Gilkeson

23 Nov 1846 Jonathan H. Haines & Mary Ann Fagan, daughter of John Fagan, the bondsman

23 Nov 1846 Strother M. Cornwell & Athlinda Hotzenpillar, daughter of John Hotzenpillar, the bondsman

23 Nov 1846 Philip Lineburg & Susan A. Perry. Bondsman, Nicholas Perry

28 Nov 1846 James McVeigh & Tacy Hart. Bondsman, Benjamin F. Jackson

3 Dec 1846 William Newcome & Nancy Gardner. Bondsman, Robert Clark

3 Dec 1846 Frederick J. Gore (Goss?) & Mary A. Collins, widow of John Y. Collins. Bondsman, John Beatty

21 Dec 1846 Jacob Mummau & Elizabeth Ann Swartz, daughter of Joseph Schwartz, the bondsman

24 Dec 1846 William H. Redd & Cornelia Brison, daughter of James Brison, the bondsman

25 Dec 1846 Frederick Barrow & Mary A. Smith, daughter of Lewis Smith, the bondsman

29 Dec 1846 Warner Lucas & Rebecca Kingery. Bondsman, Gabriel H. Henshaw

30 Dec 1846 William W. Donly & Mary E. Redd. Bondsman, Robert C. Miller

2 Jan 1847 David Cooper & Mary Crabill. Bondsman, Jacob Crabill

14 Jan 1847 Andrew Aldridge & Mary J. Green. Bondsman, John Shac. Green

18 Jan 1847 William H. Gold & Margaret Ann Wood. Bondsman, Edwin S. Baker

23 Jan 1847 Thomas M. Cardell & Elizabeth Dean. Bondsman, George Reed

26 Jan 1847 Isaac Fletcher & Elizabeth Yeider, daughter of John Yeider, the bondsman

1 Feb 1847 J. H. Gunnell & Virginia Widdows. Bondsman, Samuel McClung

4 Feb 1847 Edward McCormick & Mary E. Stribling. Bondsman, Thomas A. Tidball

5 Feb 1847 Demanuel Catlett & Fanny Kerns, daughter of Elisha Kerns, the bondsman

9 Feb 1847 George Johnson & Rachel Finley, daughter of Archibald Finley, the bondsman

11 Feb 1847 James Butter & Mary Jane Hodges. Bondsman, James B. Taylor

11 Feb 1847 Philip Williams & Mary Vance. Bondsman, James A. Russell

14 Feb 1847 Michael Miller & Elizabeth Snively, daughter of Christian Snively, the bondsman

23 Feb 1847 Alfred Carper & Julia Ann Ritter, daughter of Adam Ritter, the bondsman

2 Mar 1847 Josiah Jackson & Mary Haines, daughter of A. J. Hains, the bondsman

3 Mar 1847 Jacob R. Nicklin & Mary Wolfe. Bondsman, Thomas A. Tidball

13 Mar 1847 Patrick Howard & Joanna Margaret Glaize, daughter of Henry Glaize, the bondsman

13 Mar 1847 James Light & Mary H. Mason, daughter of James Mason, the bondsman

17 Mar 1847 Samuel M. Mullin & Henrietta W. Price. Bondsman, George E. Price

27 Mar 1847 William S. Hook & Sarah Ann Mauzey, daughter of John Mauzy, the bondsman

23 Mar 1847 Joseph S. Smoke & Deborah M. Bell. Bondsman, James Bell

27 Mar 1847 James M. Porter & Rachel Rinehart. Bondsman, Joshua Johnston

30 Mar 1847 David McKee & Priscilla Evans, upwards of 21 years of age. Bondsman, James Evans

5 Apr 1847 William Lockmiller & Dorothy Conner. Bondsman, Elijah Pifer

8 Apr 1847 Joseph Emmons & Evelina Clark. Bondsman, Seth Devoe

12 Apr 1847 Isaac N. Pangle & Mary Jane Minkey. Bondsman, Robert Campbell

13 Apr 1847 Samuel Barker & Margaret Stephens. Bondsman, Abner Peters

13 Apr 1847 William A. Mitcham & Sarah Cochran. Bondsman, William Cochran

13 Apr 1847 David Patton & Louisa Lang. Bondsman, James Ridings

20 Apr 1847 Benjamin T. Whitson & Eliza Huntsberry, daughter of Isaac Huntsberry, the bondsman

20 Apr 1847 William Mason & Elizabeth Kerns, widow of John Kerns dec. Bondsman, William H. Kerns

24 Apr 1847 Dorsey Dehaven & Harriet Dehaven. Bondsman, Abijah Dehaven

10 May 1847 John Hott & Lucinda Rowland. Bondsman, Saml Rowland

14 May 1847 John Catlett & Margaret June Puffenberger, daughter of Jacob Puffenberger, the bondsman

22 May 1847 Isaac H. Baldwin & Mary E. Keckley. Bondsman, Joseph Clouser

24 May 1847 John W. Smith & Elizabeth E. Clark. Bondsman, Barret Luis

31 May 1847 Jesse Ashton & Harriet Williams. Bondsman, William H. Williams

31 May 1847 Braxton D. Smith & ?Lavenia A. Bond, daughter of William O. Bond, the bondsman

31 May 1847 William O. Bond & Sarah S. Barns. Bondsman, James H. Barns

14 Jun 1847 John W. Rogers & Catherine Ann Heironimus. Bondsman, Camellus H. Heironimus

17 Jun 1847 Archibald A. Hodge & Elizabeth B. Holliday. Bondsman, Algernon R. Wood

19 Jun 1847 Daniel Pifer & Sarah E. Chapman. Bondsman, George Chapman

19 Jun 1847 Charles D. Shambaugh & Sarah Elizabeth Guyer. Bondsman, Thomas E. Shambaugh

28 Jun 1847 Sabastian Smith & Mary Ann Stephens, widow of Joseph Stephens deceased. Bondsman, Aubrey G. Jones

30 Jun 1847 Louis G. Rice & Margaret S. Conway, daughter of Hugh Conway, the bondsman

1 Jul 1847 John Kerr & Alley Ann Edmondson. Bondsman, David Rhodes, who signs in German

1 Jul 1847 Horace Washington & Martha Armistead, free persons of color. Bondsman, John B. Gilkeson

2 Jul 1847 Peter Shade & Unula (Ursula?) Place, daughter of John Place, the bondsman

27 Jul 1847 Lawrence Garrett & Mary Catherine Pear. Bondsman, Samuel Willis

5 Aug 1847 John Ambler & Anna M. Mason. Bondsman, William M. Ambler

23 Aug 1847 Lewis Tapp & Rachael Ann Albin, widow of Andrew Albin. Bondsman, Conrad ?Piper, who signs in German

26 Aug 1847 Caleb Tate & Sarah Barrett. Bondsman, Jonathan Barrett

30 Aug 1827 John H. Peters & Jane Hodgson, widow of John Hodgson decd. Bondsman, Cornelius T. Wolfe

31 Aug 1827 Lewis Carpenter & Annetta Whitacre, upwards of 21 years of age. Bondsman, Robert R. Whitacre

4 Sep 1847 Daniel McCauley & Martha Jane Milhorn. Bondsman, William Milhorn

13 Sep 1847 Samuel S. Kline & Martha Grim, daughter of John Grim, the bondsman

18 Sep 1847 Isaac N. Heiskell & Martha E. Muse, ward of Edward R. Muse, the bondsman

20 Sep 1847 Michael Fisher & Perlina Strawderman. Bondsman, Benjamin Strawderman

21 Sep 1847 Thomas Wilson & Margaret Deck. Bondsman, George Deck

23 Sep 1847 James E. Tyson & Harriet S. Jolliffe. Bondsman, E. C. Jolliffe

25 Sep 1847 Israel Orndorff & Sarah Pitman, widow of Amos Pitman. Bondsman, Samuel Barr

27 Sep 1847 George Deck & Elizabeth Keller, daughter of Jacob Keller, the bondsman

11 Oct 1847 Washington Chapman & Rachel Ann Pidgeon, daughter of Isaac E. Pidgeon, the bondsman

9 Oct 1847 James W. Thompson & Mary J. Howard, daughter of James M. Howard, the bondsman

12 Oct 1847 John William McCord & Mary Jane Gross, daughter of Wm Gross, the bondsman

15 Oct 1847 Jacob Richard & Harriet A. Williams. Bondsman, Benjamin Williams
19 Oct 1847 William Parker & Mary Burton. Bondsman, James Burton
21 Oct 1847 George E. Price & Mary Jane Beckham. Bondsman, John Frame
25 Oct 1847 John J. Honesty, a free negro, & Ruthellen Briscoe, a free negro woman. Bondsman, Lewis Briscoe, a free negro
25 Oct 1847 Harrison Robinson, free negro man, & Harriet Johnson, free negro woman. Bondsman, Thomas Robinson, free negro man
1 Nov 1847 Jacob Crawford & Louemma Hood. Bondsman, Thomas Crawford
4 Nov 1847 John Taylor & Eliza J. Glenn. Bondsman, John A. Noakes
10 Nov 1847 Henry R. Fry & Sarah E. Brill, daughter of Joseph Brill, the bondsman
13 Nov 1847 William Brown & Mary Thomas. Bondsman, James L. Johnson
13 Nov 1847 Washington McCormick & Emily J. Carter, daughter of Watson Carter, the bondsman
13 Nov 1847 Thornton Augustus McCloud & Jane A. Long, daughter of Joseph Long, the bondsman
13 Nov 1847 Robert B. Muse & Ruhamah Sibert. Bondsman, James W. Seibert
18 Nov 1847 William Larew & Rachel Ann Parlett. Bondsman, Peter Taylor
23 Nov 1847 John W. Pifer & Margret M. Ritenour. Bondsman, Elisha P. Ritenour
29 Nov 1847 Mahlon Gore & Sidney S. Cather, daughter of James Cather, the bondsman
30 Nov 1847 William Peasmaker & Rebecca Chiles. Bondsman, Jacob Peasmaker
1 Dec 1847 Frederick H. Glenn & Elizabeth F. Seiver. Bondsman, John H. Rutherford
6 Dec 1847 Benjamin Perry, upwards of 21 years of age, & Catherine Jenkins. Bondsman, Stephen Jenkins. John M. Perry made oath to groom's age
6 Dec 1847 John V. Eddy & Lucy Ann Welch. Bondsman, Vincen Barns
1 Dec 1847 Ezra Dehaven & Jane Whitacre. Bondsman, George Whitacre
8 Dec 1847 Henry Coe & Mary Ann Umphs. Bondsman, Joseph H. Umphs

10 Dec 1847 Joseph S. Saunders & Harriet S. Orndorff, daughter of Joseph Orndorff, the bondsman

15 Dec 1847 John Pingley & Mary Clouser, daughter of Henry Clouser, the bondsman

18 Dec 1847 Barak Dehaven & Albena Adams of age. Bondsman, William Campbell

20 Dec 1847 Charles W. Sherman & Martha Dennahoo. Bondsman, J. Philip Smith

Marriage Bonds No. 20; 1847-1850

Dec 1847 James H. McElwee & Catharine Larick, upwards of 21. Bondsman, John H. Larick (corner torn off)

24 Dec 1847 John Williams & Matilda A. Brisen. Bondsman, James F. Leach

4 Jan 1848 Henry Knisell & Elizabeth Ann Mahew, daughter of Matilda Mahew, the bondsman

4 Jan 1848 James M. Baldwin & Catherin Keckley. Bondsman, Isaac H. Baldwin

10 Jan 1848 James Kneisly & Sophia McLeod. Bondsman, John W. F. Allemong

10 Jan 1848 John B. McLeod, Newtown: To the Clerk of Fredk. Cty Court

Sir: This is to request you to issue license authorizing the marriage of my daughter Ann Sophia to Mr James Kneisely. It is inconvenient for me to attend in person and I hope this will be sufficient for the procurement of license. Respectfully yours John B. McLeod (Permission slip loose in Bond Book No. 20)

13 Jan 1848 Harvy Dehaven & Charity Bailey. Bondsman, David Bailey

15 Jan 1848 Evan Rogers & Rebecca A. Dent. Bondsman, James D. McCoole

18 Jan 1848 James W. Jones & Sarah C. Griffith. Bondsman, William Meracle

18 Jan 1848 Edward Ritter & Ana Ann R. Carper, daughter of Alphred Carper, the bondsman

22 Jan 1848 Alexander H. Brown & Catherine A. Grove. Bondsman, James Maxwell

23 Jan 1848 James M. Reed & Mary C. Miller, daughter of Robert C. Miller, the bondsman

26 Jan 1848 James McCracken & Amelia A. Pain, daughter of Travis Pain, the bondsman

3 Feb 1848 Lewis W. Hale & Mary E. Enrich (Emmich?). Bondsman, Joseph Long

4 Feb 1848 John Drake & Ann C. Lemley, daughter of Jacob Lemley, the bondsman

4 Feb 1848 Robert B. Fletcher & Rebecca Ann White. Bondsman, Jacob White

5 Feb 1848 James Lockhart & Mahaley Oates. Bondsman, Samuel Oates

8 Feb 1848 John W. Streit & Elizabeth Fries, both upward of twenty years of age. Bondsman, George Y. Fries

9 Feb 1848 William M. Jones & Ruth Jackson. Bondsman, David Robinson

12 Feb 1848 William Buck & Elizabeth Emily Aulabaugh, sister of Jas S. Aulabaugh, the bondsman

13 Feb 1848 Josiah Lockhart & Eliza Triplett. Bondsman, Philip Groves

21 Feb 1848 George A. V. Reed & Mary A. Baker. Bondsman, Henry C. Baker

23 Feb 1848 Jeremiah Triplett & Margaret Beemer. Bondsman, Alexandria Vance

28 Feb 1848 Jacob H. Snapp & Sabrina Miller. Bondsman, Jacob Miller

n. d. Henry L. Stephens & Rebecca Jane Fleet. Bondsman, Lewis Fleet

1 Mar 1848 Joseph Maphis & Thersa W. Swarts, daughter of James Swartz, the bondsman

4 Mar 1848 Samsen Bagent & Susanah Hart. Bondsman, William Hart

4 Mar 1848 Jackson Triplett & Lucenda Abril, daughter of James Abrell, the bondsman

4 Mar 1848 William R. Kline & Sarah Grim. Bondsman, John Grim

7 Mar 1848 William Orndoff & Harriett Pitcock. Bondsman, James Perry

11 Mar 1848 Zachariah Mumert & Catharine S. Bayliss. Bondsman, Benjamin Fry

11 Mar 1848 Joseph W. Jones & Sidney S. Beemer. Bondsman, John Coe

13 Mar 1848 Thomas T. More & Francis Cather. Bondsman, James Cather

13 Mar 1848 Charles Hawkins & Rebecca Light. Bondsman, William Light

14 Mar 1848 James R. Jackson & Revertah A. Smoke, daughter of John Smoke, the bondsman

22 Mar 1848 Bartholomew Giffin & Elizabeth Fletcher. Bondsman, Robert B. Fletcher

1 Apr 1848 Samuel Strobridge & Elizabeth Miller. Bondsman, John Shade

5 Apr 1848 Francis Bell, free negro, & Elizabeth Ferry, free negro woman. Bondsman, William Elliott

5 Apr 1848 George E. Stipes & Mary M. Rector. Bondsman, Henry P. Rector

10 Apr 1848 Samuel Barrow & Rebecca E. Cline. Bondsman, Simon Kline

29 Apr 1848 David Hix & Maria Parish, daughter of William Parish, the bondsman

29 Apr 1848 Patrick Moriarty? & Margaret Melvina Alexander. Bondsman, William P. Alexander

6 May 1848 Samuel S. Seabright & Hannah Dailey. Bondsman, Joseph P. Flemister

10 May 1848 John S. Woods & Amanda McCord, daughter of George McCord, the bondsman

10 May 1848 Joseph S. Cummins & Maria S. Jones. Bondsman, George Ezra Bosten

24 May 1848 William Cain & Ann R. Leapold. Bondsman, Isaac R. Janney

29 May 1848 Andrew I. Emmons & Rachel Edmundson, upwards of 20 years of age. Bondsman, David Rodes, who signs in German

10 Jun 1848 Levi Johnson & Margaret Briscoe. Bondsman, Lewis Armsted

11 Jun 1849 Franklin Crisman & Ann Ryne. Bondsman, Bushrod Buckley, who "made oath to certificate of father"

14 Jun 1848 William H. Kile & Nancy Kile. Bondsman, William Elliott

14 Jun 1848 Charles W. Hodson & Mary H. Orndorff. Bondsman, Israel Orndorff

3 Jul 1848 William Turner & Margaret C. E. Albin. Bondsman, Henry Horner

5 Jul 1848 John White & Delila Green. Bondsman, James Striker

17 Jul 1848 Amer Seal & Elizabeth Brown, daughter of Wesley Brown, the bondsman

17 Jul 1848 William T. Simmons & Mary C. Anderson. Bondsman, George W. Anderson

22 Jul 1848 Alexander Catlett & Nancy Literal. Bondsman, Daniel McKeever

26 Jul 1848 John Nausett & Sarah Miers. Bondsman, Anthony Funkhouser

27 Jul 1848 Robert J. Kurtz & Ellen J. Barr, daughter of Hugh Barr, the bondsman

8 Aug 1848 George R. Goran (Goforth?) & Asberina C. White. Bondsman, Guran L. White

23 Aug 1848 George W. Anderson & Margaret Custer. Bondsman, Randolph Custer

28 Aug 1848 Hiram Bowen & Sarah E. Harris, daughter of Gabriel C. Harris, the bondsman

30 Aug 1848 John W. Engle & Sarah Jane Largent, daughter of Thomas Largent, the bondsman

1 Sep 1848 Sanford Kerns & Susan C. Sirbaugh, daughter of Henry Sirbaugh, the bondsman

6 Sep 1848 John D. Carper & Margaret Elizabeth Mercer. Bondsman, Hugh Barr

20 Sep 1848 John R. Elbon & Margaret C. Kern, daughter of Adam Kern, the bondsman

20 Sep 1848 Isaac W. Crebs & Mary Purtlebaugh, daughter of George Purtlebaugh, the bondsman

19 Sep 1848 John Shockley & Ursula Catlett, daughter of John Catlett, the bondsman

3 Oct 1848 Jackson Reynard & Mary Ann Peters. Bondsman, Joel R. Rider

4 Oct 1848 Jacob Ambrose & Mary Caroline Touchstone. Bondsman, Benjamin Touchstone

5 Oct 1848 Isaac W. Smith & Amanda Crebbs. Bondsman, Jonathan Smith

5 Oct 1848 Newton W. Snyder & Alexina Stewart. Bondsman, William C. Clark

11 Oct 1848 Collin Leach & Mary N. Donenly. Bondsman, Thomas A. Tidball

19 Oct 1848 Elias Stewart & Rachel R. Williams. Bondsman, William W. Williams

19 Oct 1848 William W. Meade & Virginia W. Meade. Bondsman, N. B. Meade

24 Oct 1848 Harrison Baylis & Ann Jane Fiser. Bondsman, Mary Fiser

25 Oct 1848 Elisha Dawson & Mary Shade. Bondsman, Josiah Shade

27 Oct 1848 Timothey Buckley & Margaret J. Rasey. Bondsman, William Rasey

27 Oct 1848 Joseph Mahew & Catharine Pool, upwards of 21 years of age. Bondsman, David H. Johnson

30 Oct 1848 John Hamilton & Sarah Martin. Bondsman, Mager Steele

30 Oct 1848 John Grim & Elizabeth Alburn. Bondsman, Wm. G. Russell

2 Nov 1848 Jacob F. Emert & Margaret Ann Cather. Bondsman, Robert Harrison

3 Nov 1848 David W. Henning & Jane Lemley. Bondsman, Jacob Lemley

6 Nov 1848 Joseph R. Henning & Mary M. Rosenberger. Bondsman, James H. Drake

7 Nov 1848 Aquilla I. Householder & Ann E. Lovett. Bondsman, Edward R. Muse

13 Nov 1848 William H. Anderson & Eliza Clowser, daughter of Joseph Clowser, the bondsman

18 Nov 1848 Travis Payne & Eliza J. McKee. Bondsman, Jeremiah R. McKee

25 Nov 1848 John Alexander & Mahaley Pifer. Bondsman, John S. Sargent

28 Nov 1848 Adam R. Bowman & Elizabeth S. Holliday. Bondsman, Philip Smith

28 Nov 1848 Liles Grim & Nancy L. Carper. Bondsman, John Carper

28 Nov 1848 Samuel Franks & Lacy Jane Swatz. Bondsman, William Thornburgh

29 Nov 1848 Joseph Orndorff & Rebecca Orndorff. Bondsman, William Orndorff (no signature for William Orndorff)

5 Dec 1848 George W. Hawkins & Elizabeth Spilman. Bondsman, Joseph Spilman

6 Dec 1848 James M. Hite Jr. & Harriet G. Meade. Bondsman, Hugh H. Hite

6 Dec 1848 Christopher Elliott & Mary Jane Ritter. Bondsman, William Carper

6 Dec 1848 John Snider & Mary Ann Shuler, upwards of 21. Bondsman, James L. Taylor

10 Dec 1848 John Shuley & Susan Boon. Bondsman, Jacob Warfel

16 Dec 1848 James Moss & Ann C. Nauset, daughter of William Nosset, the bondsman

16 Dec 1848 James W. McClure & Ann E. Merchant, daughter of Hiram Merchant, the bondsman

18 Dec 1848 Daniel W. Brown & Margaret Jane Cooper. Bondsman, Joseph Cooper

18 Dec 1848 Malachi Pugh & Elizabeth Ann Baker. Bondsman, George W. Baker

19 Dec 1848 George Copenhaver & Margaret Ann Crebs. Bondsman, Thomas A. Tidball

19 Dec 1848 Philip Carper & Margaret Jane Rutter, daughter of John Rutter, the bondsman

23 Dec 1848 Harrison Snapp & Rebecca I. Clouser. Bondsman, Henry Clouser

30 Dec 1848 James B. Cooley & Elizabeth Laypole. Bondsman, Joseph Cooley

9 Jan 1849 John H. Beatty & Lyda Ann Kirby. Bondsman, Joseph Kirby

9 Jan 1849 Elisha F. Orndorff & Margaret C. McElwee, upwards of 20 yrs. old. Bondsman, John McClure

16 Dec 1849 George N. Sandmiers & Elizabeth Day. Bondsman, Thomas Chapman

18 Jan 1849 John H. Crebs & Maria Kitchen. Bondsman, James Bowles

22 Jan 1849 Charles W. Powers & Elizabeth F. Kline. Bondsman, James R. Kline

23 Jan 1849 David Carper & Matilda J. Hamilton. Bondsman, John R. Hamilton

24 Jan 1849 Jonathan Taylor, a free black man, & Elizabeth Mummoth, a free mulatto woman. Bondsman, Charles Briscoe

28 Jan 1849 John Strother, a free black man, & Jane Dickeson, a free black woman. Bondsman, George Kremer Senr.

31 Jan 1849 James Wm Haines & Georgianna Steward. Bondsman, William C. Clark

3 Feb 1849 George Washington Sargent & Evelina Smith, daughter of Lewis Smith, the bondsman

5 Feb 1849 James F. Shryock & Caroline Kerns, upwards of 21 years of age. Bondsman, Adam Dean

14 Feb 1849 Thomas J. Smith & Susan Clark, daughter of Robert Clark, the bondsman

26 Feb 1849 James G. Smith & Sarah Ann Mills. Bondsman, Harrison Bowers

1 Mar 1849 Joshua M. Anderson & Elizabeth Jackson. Bondsman, Samuel A. Jackson

19 Mar 1849 John W. Rhodes & Mary W. Hartley. Bondsman, Frederick R. Milton

24 Mar 1849 James M. Smith & Mary Cornwall. Bondsman, George Knight

26 Mar 1849 Jackson Albin & Rebecca Dean, daughter of William Dean, the bondsman

26 Mar 1849 James H. Redd & Martha Ellen Nisewanger. Bondsman, Abraham Nisewanger

29 Mar 1849 Ezra Cadwaleder & Catherine Ann Evans. Bondsman, John Cadwaleder

2 Apr 1849 James Milburn & Rebecca Williams. Bondsman, Daniel Dehaven, who made affirmation that both of the parties are over 21

19 Apr 1849 George F. Anderson & Alse Ritter. Bondsman, Adam Ritter

2 May 1849 Thomas Wieland & Christena Miley. Bondsman, F. W. Kohlhousen

3 May 1849 Peter Milburn, upwards of 21 years of age, and Sarah Jane Sirbaugh. Bondsman, Henry Sirbaugh

5 May 1849 James Lamp & Levina Dehaven, upwards of 21 years of age. Bondsman, Ezra Dehaven

10 May 1849 John Glen & Emily White. Bondsman, Joseph Glen

14 May 1849 John S. Sargent & Margaret H. Marker, daughter of George A. Marker, the bondsman

15 May 1849 William Taylor & Gertrude McGuire. Bondsman, George W. Hammond

15 May 1849 John W. Stribling & Ann McCormick. Bondsman, Edward McCormick

21 May 1849 Jacob Vincenheller & Mary Maxwell. Bondsman, John F. Baker

23 May 1849 John Williams, a free negro man, & Malinda Grant, a free negro woman. Bondsman, Stephen Williams

24 May 1849 John H. Rutherford & Camilla C. Baker. Bondsman, Josiah L. Baker

26 May 1849 William Hiett & Rhoda Ellen Campbell. Bondsman, Thomas W. Ashton

7 Jun 1849 Eli W. Swann & Barbara E. Bowling, daughter of Jeremiah Bowling, the bondsman

11 Jun 1849 Franklin Crisman & Ann Ryne. Bondsman, Bushrod Buckley

11 Jun 1849 Elijah Hainey & Elizabeth Grant. Bondsman, Abraham S. Burgess

20 Jun 1849 James White & Margaret Ann Jackson. Bondsman, Joseph S. Jackson

3 Jul 1849 Elijah Shively & Christianna Shade, daughter of Adam Shade, the bondsman

5 Jul 1849 Charles C. Boxwell & Eveline Touchstone. Bondsmen, James H. Griffith & Robert Boxwell

10 Jul 1849 James M. White & Rebecca Jane Lamp, upwards of 21 years of age. Bondsman, Joseph Tewalt

20 Jul 1849 George H. Ritter & Maria Stimmel. Bondsman, Jacob Ritter

26 Jul 1849 Augustus W. Howard, a free colored man, & Sarah J. Henderson, a free colored woman. Bondsman, William Martin

31 Jul 1849 Wesley Morrison & Julean Tayler, daughter of George Taylor, the bondsman

9 Aug 1849 Joseph Stotler & Sophia Shade, daughter of Adam Shade, the bondsman

13 Aug 1849 Jacob Crouse & Evalina Catlett, daughter of William Catlett, the bondsman

29 Aug 1849 Thomas Mackenzie & Elenora Isabella Brevitt. Bondsman, J. Milton Baker

29 Aug 1849 James A. Copenhaver & Hannah Penn, upwards of 21 years of age. Bondsman, Henry G. von Riesen

5 Sep 1849 John A. Gibson & Ann A. Kenan. Bondsman, George R. Cruzen

7 Sep 1849 William H. Heist & Rachel A. Nicklin, age 21. Bondsman, John S. Heist

8 Sep 1849 Henry Light & Elizabeth Everhart. Bondsman, Jonah H. Lupton

15 Sep 1849 George L. Chapman & Lydia E. Jones. Bondsman, James Jones

18 Sep 1849 Josiah L. Baker & Alcinda Osburn. Bondsman, Benjamin Bushnell

1 Oct 1849 John W. Grim & Ann V. Clark. Bondsman, Joseph Emmons

3 Oct 1849 William Castleman & Juliet V. Shepherd. Bondsman, John Murkel

8 Oct 1849 John C. Huntsberry & Anna Adams. Bondsman, John Adams

8 Oct 1849 John Bell & Mary Jane Chrisman, daughter of William Chrisman, the bondsman

8 Oct 1849 Daniel McCauley & Hannah Brant, daughter of Adam Brant, the bondsman

9 Oct 1849 John W. Bayles & Frances Brill, daughter of Henry Brill, the bondsman

10 Oct 1849 Andrew Vance & Hannah Orndorf, widow of Isaac Orndorf. Bondsman, John C. Lee

15 Oct 1849 Addison R. Carter & Lucy Gwynn Burwell. Bondsman, Thomas A. Tidball

17 Oct 1849 George Keller & Frances Albin, upwards of 21 years. Bondsman, Lewis Albin

20 Oct 1849 Charles L. P. Guyer & Ann E. Bradford, upwards of 21 years of age. Bondsman, James A. Dinges

25 Oct 1849 Isaac Stine & Catharine Glaise, daughter of Solomon Glaiz, the bondsman

25 Oct 1849 Fleming Jorden & Margaret Brown, both free colored persons. Bondsman, Augustus Howard

25 Oct 1849 James P. Gay & Mary A. Senseney, daughter of Jacob Senseney, the bondsman

31 Oct 1849 Hector D. McLean & Frances E. Wintersmith. Bondsman, Nelson Gallaher

12 Nov 1849 John H. Frasher & Hannah C. Montgomery, daughter of Robert Montgomery, the bondsman

12 Nov 1849 Daniel Wade & Elizabeth A. Spicknell. Bondsman, John H. Frasher

15 Nov 1849 Mitchel H. Miller & Sarah C. Williams. Bondsman, Philip Williams

15 Nov 1849 James T. T. Milton & Mary E. Carter, daughter of William A. Carter, the bondsman

17 Nov 1849 David McElwee & Catharine Hemelwright, daughter of John Hemelwright, the bondsman

20 Nov 1849 Samuel Stine & Margaret Garrett. Bondsman, Isaac Garrett

20 Nov 1849 Olivar H. Vaughan & Elizabeth Newcom, upwards of 21 years of age. Bondsman, Philip H. Boehm

21 Nov 1849 David Dick & Elizabeth Ritter, daughter of Adam Ritter, the bondsman

26 Nov 1849 John H. Larrick & Sarah E. Fisher. Bondsman, Joseph Fisher

26 Nov 1849 James Brown & Jane Lewis. Bondsman, Barret Lewis

25 Nov 1849 William Kimmel & Mary Susan McDonald. Bondsman, Thornton McDonald

27 Nov 1849 Hesekiah Emery & Mary Owens. Bondsman, Alfred Shets (this name is probably Sheetz)

1 Dec 1849 Samuel P. Hiett & Susan Dehaven. Bondsman, Isaac Dehaven

3 Dec 1849 Martin Shinholt & Elizabeth Kerns, daughter of Nathan Kerns, the bondsman

3 Dec 1849 Samuel Oates & Mary Jane Nole. Bondsman, Nathan Kerns

5 Dec 1849 John R. Evans & Margaret Milburn. Bondsman, John Mendenhall

6 Dec 1849 Wilson Kerns & Alcinda Grove, daughter of Abram Grove, the bondsman

10 Dec 1849 James W. Haycock & Eliza R. Howard. Bondsman, Henry Blacker

10 Dec 1849 Richard Payne & Sarah A. Scrivner. Bondsman, Vincent S. Scrivner

11 Dec 1849 George S. Bartlebaugh & Mary C. Loyn. Bondsman, George Bartlebaugh

11 Dec 1849 Morris E. Walker & Mary Jane McCormick. Bondsman, Levi McCormick

13 Dec 1849 John A. Crous & Rebecca H. Aulabaugh. Bondsman, Jass Aulabaugh. (James Allabaugh in bond)

15 Dec 1849 Joseph P. Richards & Nancy Caroline Rinker. Bondsman, Casper Rinker

15 Dec 1849 Simon Cooper & Eliza Williams. Bondsman, Jonah Lupton

17 Dec 1849 Hiram Roe & Elizabeth Saunders. Bondsman, William Saunders

17 Dec 1849 Malachi Pugh & Elizabeth E. Mauzy. Bondsman, John Creswell

19 Dec 1849 Charles Furr & Elizabeth Keller, upward of 21 years of age. Bondsman, Isaac Marvin

19 Dec 1849 James L. Taylor & July Ann Beatty. Bondsman, William Beatty.

20 Dec 1849 Charles Hardy & Elizabeth Hamilton, daughter of Robert Hamilton, the bondsman

27 Dec 1849 Hirom O. Jordan & Maria L. Jefferson, a slave of Margaret Swann. Bondsman, Oliver M. Brown

29 Dec 1849 John Tobin & Catharine Pickeral. Bondsman, Michal C. Correll (Connell?)

2 Jan 1850 Samuel G. Noakes & Ann E. Glenhomes. Bondsman, John W. Bryarly

5 Jan 1850 Samuel Williams & Sarah C. Pitcock, daughter of Barnet Pitcock, the bondsman

7 Jan 1850 John W. Ridigs & Maria E. Funkhouser, daughter of Anthony Funkhouser, the bondsman

7 Jan 1850 George T. Byrd, a free man of colour, & Caroline Johnson, a free person of colour. Bondsman, Levi Wells, a man of colour

9 Jan 1850 Benjamin B. Moore & Cecelia Tancill, daughter of James Tancill, the bondsman

14 Jan 1850 Joseph S. Wheat & Marrander Grove. Bondsman, James Maxwell

16 Jan 1850 Joseph Wood & Rebecca L. Sheperd. Bondsman, Peter Miller

16 Jan 1850 James H. Longacre & Sarah A. Brown. Bondsman, Martin C. Lupton

21 Jan 1850 John W. Shinholt & Catharine J. Parlett. Bondsman, Josiah Fries

22 Jan 1850 Aaron Kerns & Martha Jane Grove. Bondsman, Abraham Grove

23 Jan 1850 Jacob S. Lauck & Rebecca Borden, upward of 21 years of age. Bondsman, Jeremiah Triplett

4 Feb 1850 Henry Jinkins & Elizabeth C. Ritter, daughter of John Ritter, the bondsman

1 Feb 1850 Josia R. Lock & Ann R. Reed. Bondsman, Jacob Barley

12 Feb 1850 David I. Castleman & Rachel A. C. Allemong. Bondsman, John W. Allemong

14 Feb 1850 James H. Baker & Mary F. Calvert. Bondsman, George W. Graves

15 Feb 1850 Bernard A. Brison & Margaret Ann Eagleston. Bondsman, Daniel Metzger

16 Feb 1850 James Bell & Catharine Conrad. Bondsman, Charles M. Conrad

18 Feb 1850 James H. Dunn & Margaret Newcum, daughter of Leroy Newcum, the bondsman

21 Feb 1850 John H. Langley & Cornelia E. Lyder, daughter of Jacob Lyder, the bondsman

25 Feb 1850 Joseph Gordon & Martha A. Royer. Bondsman, David Davis

26 Feb 1850 Vincent S. Scrivener & Eliza Elliott, upward of 21 years of age. Bondsman, William Elliott Jnr.

26 Feb 1850 Samuel Fovre & Margaret Boggs, upward of 21 years of age. Bondsman, John Farver. Oath of Isaac Bushman to age of bride

2 Mar 1850 James Dehaven & Ann Maria Bailey. Bondsman, Jackson Dehaven

4 Mar 1850 Benjamin M. Massie & Lucy Ellen Newman, upwards of 21 years of age. Bondsman, Samuel Rust

7 Mar 1850 George A. Thruston & Elizabeth M. H. Tidball. Bondsman, Chas B. Thruston

16 Mar 1850 James H. Larew & Sarah Ann Hyatt, daughter of A. F. Hyatt, the bondsman

18 Mar 1850 Isaac T. Parlett & Esther Ann Boyd. Bondsman, Josiah Fries

19 Mar 1850 Lewis C. Albin & Caroline Wise, daughter of Michael Wise, the bondsman

22 Mar 1850 Lewis Fletcher & Martha Kerns. Bondsman, Elihu Kerns

28 Mar 1850 Lewis R. Smith & Elizabeth Brown. Bondsman, Isaac Wood

6 Apr 1850 John A. Smith & Mary F. Reedy. Bondsman, Jackson A. Bulger

8 Apr 1850 William S. Zirkle & Martha R. Miller. Bondsman, John W. Schulz

9 Apr 1850 James W. George & Sarah Jane Miller. Bondsman, John Pugh

11 Apr 1850 John C. Lee & Pamelia Antrim. Bondsman, William L. Bent

13 Apr 1850 Francis M. Cunningham & Mary C. Funkhouser. Bondsman, Martin Funkhouser

13 Apr 1850 Samuel S. Lockhart & Parcina Murphy. Bondsman, David S. Hook

16 Apr 1850 James B. McWhorter & Mary Jane Harrison. Bondsman, Robert Harrison

19 Apr 1850 Bazzel L. Dyer & Elizabeth Coe, daughter of James Coe, the bondsman

25 Apr 1850 Volentine Dyck & Mary Painter. Bondsman, William Seemer

29 Apr 1850 Frederick R. Milton & Anna M. Miller. Bondsman, Lewis T. Moore

30 Apr 1850 Robert Roe & Susan Sanders. Bondsman, Hiram Roe

2 May 1850 Lafayette ORoark & Frances Ann Barr. Bondsman, Hugh Barr

14 May 1850 Jacob P. Ridenour & Susan E. Tapp. Bondsman, Frederick W. Kohlhousen

20 May 1850 Joshua McCauley & Mary Peter. Bondsman, Alex Vance

22 May 1850 Henry Anquin & Mary Catharine Miller, upwards of 21 years of age. Bondsman, Richard Trumbath

22 May 1850 John Bone & Julia Ann Miller. Bondsman, Richard Trembath

3 Jun 1850 Martin R. Kaufman & Rachael C. Pitman. Bondsman, Philip Pitman

3 Jun 1850 David Boyse & Sarah Lowery. Bondsman, Levi Mahue

6 Jun 1850 Jonathan R. Bowen & Rebecca Jane Sloat. Bondsman, John Sloate

25 June 1850 John W. Tewalt & Margaretta A. Putz, daughter of John W. Putz, the bondsman

6 Jun 1850 Sigismund S. Neill & Catharine S. Baldwin. Bondsman, Thomas A. Tidball

15 Oct 1850 Joshua Tyson & Martha Nessmith. Bondsman, John H. Nessmith

INDEX

Abbey
 Catherine M. 265
Abbott, John 107,
 Louisa 189,
 Sarah Ann 211
Abel, Arabella 212
Abent, Elizabeth
 215, Jacob 215
Abernathy, John 90,
 Samuel 90, Susan
 90
Abrell, James 156,
 276, Joseph 156
Abriel, Joseph 25
Abril, Lucenda 276
Aby, Adaline 243,
 Elizabeth B. 255
Adams, Albena 275,
 Amos 68, Anna
 282, Asa J. 221,
 229, Daniel 23,
 David 244, Fenton
 Thomas 193,
 George M. 197,
 Hannah 12, Henry
 10, Hiram 173,
 263, Isaac 236,
 Jacob 31, John
 25, 108, 110, 139,
 267, 282, Jonathan
 202, Jonathan W.
 202, Joseph 2,
 60, 115, Lanah
 269, Leith 110,
 Lydia Ann 215,
 Mary 133, Nimrod
 177, Peter 126,
 266, 269, Phebe
 60, Rachel 31,
 163, Rachel Jane
 221, Rhoda 25,
 Sarah 33, Thomas
 103, 168, Thompson
 137, William 3,
 31, 35, 124, 142,

Adams (continued)
 215, 266
Adamson, Sarah 3
Addison, John 226
Adiddell, Elias 57
Affleck, Alexander
 233, 245, James
 156, Nancy 245
Afflick, Alexander
 G. 232, Christena
 200
Ager, Tabort 9
Agre, William 87
Aid, Catherine 78,
 Elizabeth 31,
 John 31
Airs, Ann 20,
 Judith 20
Alban, Jane 48,
 Robert 48
Albert, Adam 191,
 Elizabeth 42,
 Fanny 94, George
 84, 99, 121, 123,
 195, Maria 135,
 Michael 26, 118,
 166, 181, 191, 195,
 Susan 166, William
 42, 94, 135, 181
Albin, Alce 235,
 Alexander W. 210,
 260, 262, Andrew
 105, 149, 163, 177,
 227, 235, 273, Ann
 136, Elijah 91,
 Eliza 221,
 Elizabeth 104,
 105, Frances 283,
 Jackson 255, 281,
 James 82, 104,
 237, John 179,
 Joseph T. 253,
 Lavinia 266,
 Lewis 283, Lewis
 C. 286,

Albin (continued)
Margaret C. E.
277, Martha 177,
Nancy 228,
Nathaniel 201,
Rachael Ann 273,
Rachel 255,
Rebecca 78, 227,
Robert 78, 149,
Sarah 245, Susan
163, Susanna 194,
William 28, 228,
245
Alburn, Elizabeth
279
Aldridge, Andrew
271, John 193,
Mary Ann 193
Alemong, Catharine
38
Alexander, Alcinda
176, Delilah 183,
Eleanor 1,
Elizabeth 18,
James 148, John
73, 194, 195, 279,
Joseph 10,
Margaret Melvina
277, Morgan 1,
Samuel 264, Sarah
K. 194, William
82, 104, William
P. 277
Aliff, John 156
Allamong, Casper
123, Elizabeth M.
203
Allan, John 130
Allemong, Angeline
B. 265, Casper
129, 140, 265,
Catherine Elizabeth
246, Daniel 139,
Elizabeth 129,
John W. 285, John
W. F. 275, Lewis
241, 246, Lydia

Allemong (continued)
Maria 241, Mary
139, 140, 234,
Rachel A. C. 285,
William 77, 203,
241
Allen, Afsenesh 13,
Andrew 118,
Aquilla 153,
Arthelia 203,
David 79,
Elizabeth Ann
252, George 2,
76, George W.
252, Harrison
102, John 94,
Joseph 69, Luman
S. 249, Mary 76,
Moses 141,
Rebecca 178,
Richard 106,
Robert 100, 178,
Samuel 67, Sarah
Ann 223, Thomas
232, 263, Thomas
R. 238, William
129, Winney 59
Allender, George
217, Jacob 51,
194, 217, Mary
217, Matilda 194
Allensworth, Amanuel
21, Ann 5,
Butler 5, 21, 42,
44, Catherine 21,
Elizabeth 59,
Eveline 177,
Kitty 111, Louiza
V. 125, Mary 93,
Mary Ann 139,
Philip 5, 93, 125,
Reuben 39, 63,
Sally 39, Simon
21, 33, William
111
Alley, Catharine
188

Allison, Catharine 156, Martin 156, Simpson 220
Alloway, William 32
Alobaugh, James 255
Alseep, Nancy 72
Alverson, Becknell 128
Ambler, John 273, William M. 273
Ambrose, Christian C. 250, Jacob 278, John 42, 212, Rachel 212
Ambrouse, John B. 195, Lewis 199, William 223
Amick, Jacob 137, 170
Amis, Thomas 48
Amiss, Lewis 48, 59, 67
Ammick, Philip 6
Anders, John 223, Mager 214
Anderson, Amos 221, Ann 33, Ann E. 264, Ann Maria 185, Anna 69, Asa 236, Catharine 137, Charity 118, Daniel 130, 258, 267, Daniel` 116, David 39, 139, David N. 214, Dorcas 175, Eli 176, Eliakim 26, Elie 118, Eliza 258, Elizabeth 238, Ely 174, Emily 167, 174, 234, Fanny 160, George 196, George F. 281, George W. 277, 278, Hannah 105,

Anderson (continued) 158, 217, Harrison 228, Henry C. 255, Isaiah 259, Israel R. 253, Jacob 7, 17, 26, 124, 170, 175, 198, 238, James 58, 91, 145, 239, 253, Jane 26, 120, Jesse 39, 99, Jno. 55, John 11-13, 23, 70, 73, 124, 132, 186, 222, 261, John L. 197, 249, 254, Jonathan 203, Joseph 33, 48, 99, Joshua M. 280, Levinia J. 258, Lidy 59, Louisa 249, Louisa Jane 227, Luvanna 186, Lydia 10, Malinda 152, Margaret 49, 99, Margaret Ann 267, Margaret Ellen 253, Maria 174, Marshall 258, Mary 9, 96, 176, Mary C. 277, Mary Catharine 238, Mason 172, 180, Michael 263, Morgan A. 249, Nancy 7, Nathan 97, Nicholas 94, Paul 189, 192, Paul P. 265, Peggy 73, Polly 23, 55, 58, Rachel 203, Rebecca 258, Richard 13, Robert 110, 141, 149, Ruth 165, Sarah 26, 48,

290

Anderson (continued)
Susan 209, 238,
Susan C. 228,
Sydnor B. 209,
Tacy 170, Thomas 114, 116, 152, 170, 172, 176, 196, Virginia C. 261, William 29, 59, 62, 230,
William H. 279,
William S. 209, 230, 258
Andrews, Charles W. 212, Sarah 209
Angier, Martha B. 117
Anquin, Henry 287
Antram, Elizabeth 75, James 137, John 44, Joshua 75
Antrem, Joshua 221
Antrim, Edward 27, Grace 27, Pamelia 286
Appold, Samuel 239
Archer, James 82, Mary 22, Nancy 62, 205, William 92, 205
Archey, Ann 4, Elizabeth 4
Arisman, Jacob 90
Armbrist, Michael 246
Armistead, John C. 184, Lewis 247, Martha 273, Sarah 21
Armstead, Addison B. 57, Robert L. 184
Armsted, Lewis 277
Armstrong, Catharine 47, James 96, Rebecca 96
Arniss, Lewis 61

Arnold, Andrew 130, Elen 253, Eliza 235, Francis 196, Jane 149, Jesse 210, 253, John Henry 210, Mary 130, Nancy 3, Susan 185, William 149, 185, 196
Arrisman, George 99
Arterbourn, Jacob 37
Arthur, Joseph 190
Ash, Buckner 118, Elizabeth 108, Ellen 172, Emily E. 260, Francis 118, Francis J. 211, Frank 108, George 137, 172, George B. 182, 186, 192, 194, George H. 255, James W. 207, John H. 241, 260, Littleton 89, Mary 118, Mary S. 264, Nancy 2, 186, Parmelia I. 194
Ashby, Albert A. 241, Amelia 232, Benjamin P. 243, Buckner 153, 195, 200, Charlotte 153, Dorothy 64, Enoc R. 143, Enoch 64, George 114, 176, John 232, Kitty 52, Lewis 52, Lucy 50, Mariah 193, Mary 14, Mary Ann 241, Mary E. 143, Mildred 89, Milley 76,

Ashby (continued)
Philadelphia 153,
R. B. 211,
Rebecca 80, Rezin
138, 164, Robert
96, 153, Robt
108, Sibey 75,
Sidney 170,
Thomas 185,
203, 209, Thos
14, William 50,
William R. 119
Ashdell, Susan 184
Ashenhurst, John 25
Ashenhust, Margaret
14, Oliver 14,
William 14
Ashford, John 134
Ashton, Hester 33,
Jesse 272, Peter
131, 191, 235,
Thomas W. 281
Ashwood, John 33,
Samuel 194
Askins, Posey 74
Atchison, Elizabeth 41
Atherton, Jane 14
Athey, Elias 223,
267, Robert 194
Aton, Joahnah 43
Atty, Margaret 222
Atwell, Samuel 140
Atwood, Gilbert
127, Jane 167
Audedell, Elias 47,
Hannah 47
Audiddle, Ann 57
Aulabaugh, Elizabeth
Emily 276, Jas S.
276, Jass 284,
Rebecca H. 284
Aulebaugh, Hannah 255
Aulick, George 209, 250
Austin, Regina 152

Awbrey, Delilah 54,
Samuel 54
Ayrison, Frederick 160
Babb, Abner 4, 30,
187, Blanch 18,
Charlotte 18,
David 58, Delbora
158, Eliza Ann
94, Elizabeth 90,
Harriet 126,
Henry 58, Henry
M. 93, 126, Henry
Mercer 94, James
48, 90, 113, James
M. 220, James W.
93, Joseph 158,
Mary 77, 174,
Mary M. 222,
Peter 9, 17, 131,
Polly 113,
Robinson 122, 174,
Thomas 3, 4, 18, 55
Bachlor, Ann 30
Badger, William 49
Baer, Frederick
207, Maria 207
Bagaent, John 112
Bageant, Mary M.
260, William 98, 260
Bagent, Catharine
149, John
Washington 238,
Mary 112, Samsen 276
Bail, Thomas 62
Bailes, John 84,
Moses 102
Bailey, Adam 71, Ann
117, Ann Maria
286, Charity 197,
275 David 197,
275 Elizabeth 3,
John 50, Levina 167
Polly 18,

Bailey (continued)
Polly 18,
Priscilla 20,
Silas 223, Thomas 42, William 122, 140, 197, 247
Bails, Moses 87, Susan 87, Thomas 87
Baily, Jessee 125
Bains, Mary Ann 179
Baker, Andrew 121, Ann 141, Benjamin F. 228, Camilla C. 281, Caroline 231, Clarissa H. 199, Daniel 46, 56, Edwin S. 263, 271, Elizabeth Ann 280, Ellen E. 268, Emily 203, Ewell 225, Francis 8, 30, George 258, George W. 189, 280, Harriet C. 258, Henry 118, 201, 203, Henry C. 276, Henry F. 148, Henry W. 228, 252, Hilarius 140, Hillarius 268, Isaac 73, 80, 82, 202, Isaac W. 191, J. Milton 282, Jacob 10, 56, 80, 150, 171, James 109, 141, James H. 285, John 146, 148, 245, John F. 281, Joseph 18, 73, Joseph S. 216, Josiah L. 281, 282, Julia A. 228, Louisa 150, Marcus 119,

Baker (continued)
Marcus D. 198, Mary 80, 163, 235, Mary A. 276, Mary E. 216, Rebekah 56, Robert L. 228, Saml 36, Sarah A. 228, Sarah Ann 266, Sophia G. 200, Thomas 28, 163, 228, William 200
Baldwin, Ann M. 265, Catharine S. 287, Cornelius 29, 96, 133, Cyrus B. 96, David 42, Eleanor C. 223, Eliza 148, Isaac H. 272, 275, Isaac W. 223, James M. 275, Jonah 188, 227, Joshua 148, 158, 198, Margaret 101, Maria N. 227, Rees 30, Robert T. 159, 265, Thomas 38, William 95, 101, 207
Bales, Catherine 160, Charles 206, Edwin 110, Moses 156
Ball, Ann 78, Augustine 221, Druscilla 83, Elizabeth 43, Frances W. 83, George Lewis 116, James 127, John 3, 13, 52, John K. 254, John S. 57, Mildred 117, Phebe 9, William

293

Ball (continued)
103, 169, William
E. 190, William
P. 77
Ballinger, Elizabeth
65, Samuel 65
Balmain, Alexander
21
Balthis, Elizabeth
168, William 168
Balthrope, Napoleon
B. 217
Banbridge, Absalom
4
Banks, Edward 64,
72, Nancy 64
Bantelbaugh, Henry
126
Barber, James 7,
James M. 260,
William 136
Barchelbaugh, George
126, Rachel 126
Barden, James 67
Bare, Frederick
189, 217, Margaret
217, Polly 189
Barger, Mary 5, 6
Barker, John 13,
Joseph 191, Moses
72, Samuel 272,
Susan Jane 186
Barlay, Eve Maria
39, John 39
Barley, George 222,
Harriet 247,
Jacob 184, 285,
John 86, 213,
Mary 213, Mary
Ann 243, Peter
243, 247
Barly, Charlotte 86
Barnes, Charles
235, Edward 146,
Elizabeth 146,
Hannah 51, Henry
212, Joseph 251,

Barnes (continued)
Rachel R. 251,
Sarah 43, 139,
Vincent 268
Barnet, Benjamin N.
50
Barnett, Ambrose
23, Benjamin N.
42, Elizabeth N.
175, George 94,
Jane Helm 169,
John 7, 90, Lewis
2, Nancy 129,
Neill 169, Rachel
8, Sarah Jane 268
Barney, John 8
Barnham, Jeremiah
14, Martin 14
Barnhard, Ann G.
219
Barnhart, Elizabeth
225
Barns, Fanny 108,
James 74, James
H. 272, Joseph
153, Nancy 74,
Sarah S. 272,
Stephen 68,
Vincen 274
Baroff, Henry 85
Barr, Alecy 127,
Benjamin 110, 127,
Benjamin R. 234,
Catharine 49,
Elizabeth 59,
Ellen J. 278,
Frances Ann 286,
Francis 34,
Frederick 49,
George 222, Hugh
106, 278, 286,
James 100, John
160, Peter 59,
Samuel 223, 273,
Sarah 84, 160,
203, 223, William
129

Barret, Henson 68,
 Sidney 18
Barrett, Arthur 50,
 Benjamin 33, 44,
 160, 266, David
 69, Eleanor 218,
 Joel 234, 240,
 257, Jonathan
 273, Joseph 50,
 64, Lemson 20,
 Rebecca 160,
 Richard 126,
 Sarah 273
Barrick, Jacob 44,
 John 15
Barron, James 2,
 Thomas 242
Barrow, Abraham 90,
 95, 204, Baylis
 224, Baylys W.
 201, Eleaser 155,
 Eleazer 43, 180,
 Elezer 110,
 Elisha 219, Eliza
 228, Elizabeth 31,
 Franklin 213,
 Frederick 225,
 270, John 3, 40,
 123, Margaret I.
 224, Mary 83,
 Matilda 180, Mazy
 177, Nancy 115,
 Rebeccah 126,
 Samuel 277,
 Thomas 201,
 William 31, 78,
 83, 115
Barthlow, Joshua
 128
Bartlebaugh, George
 158, 284, George
 S. 284
Bartlet, Mary Ann
 223
Bartlett, Eliza
 141, Henry 16,
 22, 46, Henry D.

Bartlett (continued)
 220, Joseph C.
 183, Mary 169,
 Nancy 168,
 Sanford 169,
 Sarah 12, Thomas
 101, Thomas D.
 223, William 27,
 157, 168, William
 D. 141
Barton, Amy 136,
 Catherine 119,
 David 96, 261,
 David W. 189, 193,
 228, 247,
 Elizabeth 153,
 Elizabeth A. 261,
 Ezekial 223,
 Hetty Z. 190, Jas
 G. 109, Joseph E.
 243, Juliana S. P.
 135, Mary G. 109,
 Nancy 243,
 Richard W. 190,
 241, Robert R.
 135, Samuel 119,
 William 236,
 William G. 245
Bastian, Mary 77
Batchellor, Margart
 62
Bateman, John 214,
 Thursay 214
Bates, Barzillai 62
Batt, Wallace 249
Bauer, Adam 78
Baughman, John 160
Bauker, Abraham 88
Bayles, John W. 283
Baylis, Harrison
 278, Henrietta
 87, Jane 172,
 John E. 93, 178,
 Thomas B. 168,
 William 87, Wm 11
Bayliss, Carr W.
 213, Catharine S.

295

Bayliss (continued)
276, Helen 137,
Henry 137, John
E. 180
Bayly, Charles B.
248, Rachel 122
Bazell, Jarisia Ann
257, John C. 127
Bazle, Catharine
151
Bazzell, Elizabeth
164, Ezekiel 178,
John 164
Bazzle, John 151
Beadle, William 184
Beadles, Sally 34
Beagant, John 149,
160, 234
Beagent, John W.
256
Beagles, James 10
Beal, Mary 220
Beale, Margaret 68,
Mary 68
Beall, Allianor
160, Ann 174,
Eli 216, Ely
153, Harriet Ann
216, James A.
184, 191, Mazy
21, Sarah 116,
Thomas 116
Bealle, Marcy 18
Beals, Moses 160
Beam, Charles 203
Beamer, John 165
Bean, Andrew 257,
Austin 240, 249,
Eliza 206,
Elizabeth 170,
Harriet 149, 249,
Isaac 139, 155,
James 70, 124,
238, 243, Juliett
124, Margaret
110, Mary 19,
Mordecai 19, 206,

Bean (continued)
19, 206, 240,
Nathan 213, Sarah
70, 110, William
55, 125, 154
Beans, Isaiah 254,
John F. 254
Bear, Catharine
232, Frederick
227, 232, Judith
227, Lucy Ann 258
Beard, Christopher
53, Robert 62
Bearen, J.? 59
Bearinger, Evelina
186, Jacob 186
Beattey, Eliza June
265, John 31,
Lettice 31,
William 265, 269
Beatty, Catharine
219, Elizabeth
57, George 6,
Harriet 269,
Henry 3, 126, 170,
212, John 264,
270, Joh H. 280,
John L. 269,
Joshua 42,
July Ann 284,
Mary 125, Mary
Irvin 126, Robert
65, 203, Samuel
140, 211, Sophia
M. 221, William
117, 284
Beaty, David 4,
Esther 4, Frances
162, John 10,
140, Mary 153,
Robert 34, 153,
Sarah 177,
William 45, 162,
188
Beaver, John 94,
William 106
Beavers, Elizabeth

Beavers (continued)
9, John 38, 79,
211, Mary 38,
Moses 38, 50,
Robert 176,
Samuel 54
Beazley, Patsy L.
188, William 188
Becham, Mary 97
Bechley, Magdalene
218, Magdaline
218
Beck, Eli 156,
James 172, James
W. 179, Mary 179
Becker, John 56
Beckham, Mary Jane
274
Beckley, Charles
85, 113, 115,
Elizabeth 207,
Matilda 115
Beckner, Elizabeth
82
Beddow, George 59,
93
Bedingar, Lavina 81
Bedinger, Elizabeth
150, Eunice 175,
Eveline 165
Bedingr, Mary 165
Beeks, Elizabeth
130
Beeler, Peggy 29
Beemer, Benjamin
58, George 40,
John 124,
Margaret 276,
Sidney S. 276
Beeson, Edward L.
181, Edward S.
171, Richard 135
Beetley, James W.
247
Beevers, Robert 174
Belfield, John W.
101

Belford, David 73,
Leah 216
Bell, Anthony 29,
249, Deborah M.
271, Elias D.
209, Eliza 74,
146, Elizabeth
31, Ellen 237,
Ferguson 74, 128,
Francis 277,
Frederick 119,
George 1, 41, 169,
207, Hector 193,
200, James 177,
187, 271, 285,
Jane 17, John 1,
56, 118, 141, 146,
282, Mary 1,
Nancy 41, 166,
Rachel 170, Sally
D. 118, Squire
143, 164, 177,
Stephen 145,
234, Thomas 31,
80, William A.
178
Beller, Margaret
106
Belt, Elizabeth 110
Benegar, David 28,
Samuel 44
Benn, Gabriel 145,
Maria 117, Robert
75, 117, Robert P.
195, Tereza 117
Benner, Benjamin
255
Bennet, Robert 59
Bennett, Elizabeth
98, Emeline 171,
George 99, Henry
60, James 55, 59,
98, 150, 171
Benson, Ann C. 195,
Harriet 118,
Isabella 118,
William 118

Bent, Leml 115, 209, William L. 232, 268, 269, 286
Bently, Eliza 243, John P. 240
Benton, Abel 36, Elizabeth 219
Berkeley, Abraham 152, Benjamin T. 229, Lucy M. 247, Rebecca A. 242, Robert C. 259
Berkhammer, Barbara 185
Berkheimer, Catharine 171
Berkhemer, Christiana 221
Berkley, Reuben L. 126
Berlin, Catharine 97, Isaac 92, 200, Jacob 72, 97, 155, Philip 97, 181, Samuel 194
Bernhard, John 219
Berrll, Elizabeth 139
Berry 2, Ann 56, Benjamin 51, Enoch 56, F.? 51, George 68, John Q. 183, 216, Joseph 63, 68, 92, Lucy M. 161, Maria 96, Mary 51, Philip 200, Reuben 24, Samuel 24, Sarah 68, Susan 220, Thornly 29, Thos 13, William 214, Winifred 108
Berson, Saml 65
Bezant, Elizabeth 11

Bickley, Elizabeth 203, Mary 116, 203
Biddenger, Christopher 119, Sarah 119
Biggs, Thos 5
Billingsly, Clement W. 193
Bimple, Martin 172
Binegar, Nancy 33, Samuel 33
Binigar, Rosana 45
Binnegar, John 28, 45
Bird, Mark 221
Bishop, Baily 3, Brice 50, Elizabeth 50, 256, Hiram 159, Joshua 66, Julia Ann 217, Lloyd 50, Nancy 141, 253, Sarah 260, Solemon 149, Solomon 164, 252, 256, 265
Bixler, Abraham 69
Black, George 13, 119, George W. 222, Kitty 21
Blackburn, Thomas 28
Blackemore, Elizabeth 23
Blacker, Henry 284, Luke 78
Blackford, Peter 35, Prudence 35
Blackmore, Mary 56, Nathl 56, Rachel 56
Blackord, Catherine 108, Henry 108
Blackwell, John 242
Blake, Ann 218, Betsy 114,

Blake (continued)
 Elizabeth 213,
 John 40, Mahaley
 218, Tabitha 182
Blakemore, Ann 7,
 Ann Elizabeth 213,
 George 102, 176,
 George C. 241,
 John M. 140,
 Laurence Owen 3,
 Lucy 40, Marquis
 129, Marquis Q.
 94, Rebecca W.
 205, Susannah
 198, Thomas 151,
 171, 172, 198,
 Thomas L. 241,
 Thos 7
Blanchard, Hiram A. 206
Blany, Elizabeth 66, William 66
Blaylock, Thomas 11
Blessing, J. Frederick 269
Bligh, Sarah 47
Blue, Mary 149, 165
Blum, Elizabeth 202
Blundell, William 9
Bly, Lucy 236, Phebe 138, Rebecca 88
Board, Jefferson M. 192, William 123
Bobky, John 253
Bocky, John 262, Margaret 253
Bodenhofer, Gottlieb 202
Bodkin, Thomas 2
Boehm, Philip H. 283
Boggs, James 212, Margaret 286
Bohan, Elizabeth 124
Bohrer, Augustus

Bohrer (continued)
 258, Eliza Ann
 266, Elizabeth
 231, Isaac 221,
 231, 261, 266,
 Mary Ann 231,
 Philip 249,
 Sarah 261
Boice, John 163
Boise, Adam 195, David 201
Bolen, Jesse C. 221
Boles, Elizabeth 104, James 32, 56, John 104, 175, Sally 175
Bolin, Jno 64, William 64
Boling, William 176
Bollen, Edward 35
Bollinger, Stephen 34
Bolton, Catharine 85, Polly 86
Boman, Dolly 19
Bonard, Jane 6
Bond, Abner 220, Elizabeth 196, Elizabeth A. 47, George 10, Isaac 14, John 35, Lavenia A. 272, Mary 29, Stephen 10, William 14, 15, 47, William O. 177, 214, 233, 272
Bone, John 287
Bonecutter, Christopher 91, George 67, Harmon 91
Bonen, Milly Jane 263
Bonham, Aaron 6, 41, Amos A. 211, Catharine 4, David 55, Deborah

Bonham (continued)
14, Elizabeth 55,
John C. 216,
Lydia 10, Samuel
177, Smith 71
Bonifield, Arnold
170, William 62
Bonn, Lucy Ann 203
Bonsell, Joseph 60
Bonwell, James H.
265
Booker, Elizabeth
4, Jacob 4
Booling, Jno 50
Boon, Susan 279
Booram, William 30
Booth, Isaac 45,
53, 73, Lydia 14,
Ruth 24, Thomas
73
Borden, George 47,
Rebecca 285
Borders, Catharine
57, George 57,
Henry 54
Borer, Jacob 73
Bosten, George Ezra
277
Bosteyon, Sarah 131
Boston, George 226,
Lucy A. 226
Bostyan, Adam 77
Bostyon, Adam 155,
Elizabeth 170,
Fanny 155
Boswell, John 181
Boucher, Catharine
103, Elias 103,
Elizabeth 103,
Jacob 9, Maria
202, Moses 202,
Philip A. 207,
Rebecca 98,
Samuel 243
Boude, Rudolph T. C.
130, 206
Bougher, Elizabeth

Bougher (continued)
50, John 35,
Mary Magdalen 11,
Sarah 35,
Susannah 41
Boughman, Barbara
116
Boum, William 12
Bourn, John 207,
William 12, 187,
207
Bouzer, Daniel 218
Bover, Peter 171
Bowan, Thomas 92
Bowen, Catharine
206, 244, Charles
45, Elizabeth
204, Elizabeth Ann
225, Emily L.
191, George A.
247, Hiram 278,
Isaac 45, 60,
James 109, 186,
215, James H.
161, Jane 187,
John 29, 55,
John G. 263,
Jonathan R. 287,
Jonathan Richard
243, Martha Ellen
263, Mary Jane
222, Meredith
132, 206, 243,
Middleton M. 263,
Morten 135,
Phineas 60, 191,
225, Sarah A.
263, Thornton W.
168, William 269
Bower, Samuel 220
Bowers, Elizabeth
38, George 80,
Harrison 239, 280,
Henry 38, Jacob
38, 140, Sarah
80, Sarah Ann 239
Bowie, John 98,

300

Bowie (continued)
   John B. 93
Bowland, David 35
Bowlding, Jeremiah 66
Bowles, Bowles 172, Catharine 248, Isaac G. 194, James 235, 266, 280, John 138, 172, Peggy 138
Bowling, Alexander W. 174, Barbara E. 281, George 154, James M. 232, Jemimah 74, Jeremiah 119, 281, Mary 216
Bowman, Adam R. 279, Daniel 19, John 127, 151, John H. 162, Mary Ann 244, William 206
Bown, Phineas 222
Bowre, William 118
Bowser, Benjamin 185, Michael 222
Boxell, John 6, Robert 6, William 52
Boxwell, Charles C. 282, Nancy 200, Robert 256, 282, Thornton L. W. 256, William 183
Boyas, Matthew 199
Boyce, John 103, 104, Nancy 103, Robert 1
Boyd, Esther Ann 286, Hester 171, James 175, Jane 63, Jesse 250, John 26, 171, 255, Margaret Ellen 255, Mary Jane

Boyd (continued)
   266, Robert 63, 266
Boyer, George K. 226, Jacob 162
Boyers, Jacob 60
Boyles, James 242, John 58
Boyse, David 287
Brabham, Joseph 138, Martha 145
Bradford, Alexr 36, Ann E. 283, B. F. 221, Elizabeth 227, Henry 64, 66, 122, Jane 206, Mary 241, Sarah 57, Vance 206, 241, Vance P. 262, William 86
Brady, Amy Ann 237, Caleb 78, Hannah C. 165, John 6, 58, John W. 165, Patrick 251, 252
Bragg, Thos 116
Braithwait, Susannah 122, William 122
Braithwaite, Benjamin 166, Elizabeth 196, Hamilton 250, Helen 151, John 186, Joseph 246, Susan Ann 269, William 100, 151, 269
Brandeburg, John 254
Branham, Edward S. 97, George 102
Brannam, Levi 198
Brannan, Robert 247
Brannen, Nancy 247
Brannom, Hannah 15, John 15
Brannon, Margaret

Brannon (continued)
181, Mary Jane
263, Robert 222,
Steward J. 266
Branon, Elizabeth
17
Branor, William 122
Branson, Hannah 28,
Lionel 28, Robert
23, Sarah 72,
Unus 23, William
P. 155, 259
Brant, Adam 282,
Hannah 282
Brauner, William
198
Brayerly, Dalconame
117, Robert 117
Brecount, David 5,
Sarah 5
Breedin, E. C. 210,
Enoch C. 221
Breedlove, Abraham
133, 209, Charles
94, Robert 204
Breeze, James 166
Brelsford, Barnard
74, Bernard 79,
Rachael 74
Brenon, John 17
Brent, Ann 254,
Catharan M. 200,
Catharine 214,
Charles 13, 27,
53, Charles J.
245, Eliza 116,
Elizabeth 53,
Emily F. 245,
Enos 174, Frances
E. 247, George
247, George W.
253, 255, James
83, John G.
199, Margaret
253, Mary 27,
Mary Ann 199,
Rachel 174,

Brent (continued)
Sarah 213
Brenton, Alexander
152
Brett, Elizabeth
210
Brevitt, Elenora
Isabella 282
Brewer, James 122,
Mary 248
Briarly, David 101,
116, Hannah 148,
Hannah Cox 62,
James 148, Thomas
C. 251
Bridges, Dillon 20
Bridine, Henry 69
Briel, Henry 64,
Michael 193
Brient, Elizabeth
69, Robert 69
Brierly, Samuel 63
Briley, William 167
Brill, Abraham 196,
Amos 240,
Benjamin 197,
Catharine 72,
Catherine 123,
Elizabeth 64, 79,
Elizabth 140,
Emily E. 193,
Frances 283,
George 62, Hamon
61, Hannah Jane
256, Henry 9, 15,
72, 79, 107, 123,
129, 140, 157, 186,
204, 248, 269, 283,
Isaac 232, Jane
269, John 152,
John H. 255,
Joseph 151, 242,
256, 274,
Margaret 9, 204,
Martin 185,
Motalina 15,
Rachel 242, Sarah

Brill (continued) 186, Sarah E. 274, William 263
Brinker, Ann R. 216, George 21, 85, Rebecca 21
Brinon, John 17
Brisco, Lewis 267
Briscoe, Betsy 137, Charles 280, James 151, Lewis 274, Margaret 277, Ruthellen 274, Sarah Ann 247, William 98, 237, 247
Brisen, Matilda A. 275
Brison, Benjamin 140, Bernard A. 285, Cornelia 270, James 133, 270, Margaret 72, Samuel 72
Britain, Jemima 6, Joseph 6
Briton, Catharine 226
Britten, Burrows 187, James 234, Jonah 142, 187
Britton, Abigail 47, Elizabeth 149, 183, Jesse 21, 40, 47, 48, 68, Joseph 7, Mary 68, Wilson 7
Brobeck, Henry 198, John 124
Brome, John M. 218
Brooke, Ann A. 172, Elizabeth W. 171, Mary Page 151
Brookes, Margaret 132
Brookhaffer, Priscilla 22

Brookhover, Susanah 48
Brooking, James R. 233
Brookover, Richard 27
Brooks, James 164, Mary 30, William 46
Brotherton, John 158
Brown, Abraham 37, Adam 59, 208, Alexander H. 275, Alexander L. 191, Alexander S. 184, Anderton 194, 218, Andrew J. 249, Anne 159, Barbara 25, Benjamin F. 221, 255, Cassandra H. 211, Catharine 11, 181, Catherine 259, Daniel O. 242, Daniel W. 280, David 53, 204, David Z. 210, 254, 255, Eleanor 65, Eliza 231, Eliza Ann 181, 208, Elizabeth 80, 277, 286, Elizabeth Ann 255, Enos 168, Fanny 115, Francis C. 153, 205, George 22, 141, 159, 199, 245, George Washington 205, Hannah 2, 218, Harriet A. 254, Harrison C. 208, Henry 227, Isaac N. 224, Jacob 200, James 25, 34, 69, 229, 283, James F.

Brown (continued)
197, James S.
141, 161, Jane
145, Joel 80,
John 4, 59, 65,
119, 219, John J.
249, John V. 217,
John W. 250,
Joseph 6, 128,
Joseph A. 223,
Joseph F. 268,
Joseph H. 237,
267, Juliana 96,
Lydia 97,
Margaret 283,
Maria R. 146,
Martha 16, 57,
Mary 118, 190,
256, Mary Ann
205, 219, Mary
Louisa 213,
Michael 265,
Moses N. 159,
Moses W. 132, 181,
209, Nancy S.
183, Octavia 261,
Oliver M. 284,
Polly 32, 33, 181,
Rebecca 37, Rhody
261, Robert 208,
210, Sarah 17,
265, Sarah A.
285, Sarah Jane
256, Sarah M.
224, Sary 33,
Smith 189, Susan
229, Susanna
128, 235, Susannah
54, Thomas 76,
92, 93, 129,
Vencon 11, Wesley
261, 277, William
122, 178, 203, 216,
232, 274, William
H. 238
Brownfield, Thomas
3

Browning, Charles D.
166, Joseph 65
Brownley, Archibald
23, Emily 147,
Sally 85
Broy, Addison 209,
John 180
Bruce, Amos I. 112,
Eliza 155,
Elizabeth 77,
George 49, 54, 97,
James 21, 77, Jas
97, John 138,
154, Rachel 120
Bruin, Susannah 18
Bruler, James D. 43
Brumley, Lewis 111
Brunar, George 162,
Mary 162
Bruner, Barbara
139, Delilah 183,
Elizabeth 190,
Henry 136, Jacob
58, John 128,
160, Mary Ann 136
Bryan, Samuel 163,
180
Bryant, Joseph 88
Bryarley, David 167
Bryarly, Apphia
175, David 63,
101, 159, James
175, 180, John W.
284, Louisa M.
180, Lucy H. 162,
Richard 28, Richd
13, Robert 58,
101, Samuel 162,
180, Sarah 101,
Thomas F. 202
Bryce, James G.
185, 194
Bryson, Saml 65
Buchanan, Evelina H.
171
Bucher, David 251,
Elias 180,

Bucher (continued)
Harriet S. 241,
Jacob A. 241,
John J. 186, John
William 177,
Moses 212, Philip
A. 211, Philip P
23, Philip P. 30,
Rachel 180,
Samuel 241
Buck, Annie C. 155,
Charles 24,
Elizabeth 102,
Isaac N. 180,
Isabella 48, John
L. 155, Leticia
A. 140, Lettitia
173, Rebecca 119,
Thomas 36, 48,
119, 140, 155,
William 276,
William R 40
Bucklebough, George
60, Mary 60
Buckley, Abraham
37, 109, Bushrod
277, 281, Hannah
104, Jayne 37,
Job 3, John 58,
Sarah 109,
Timothey 278
Buckwalter, Anthony
125
Buff, Elizabeth
161, John 14
Buffington, Joshua
102
Bulger, Edward 76,
253, Eliza Ann
196, Harriett
217, Jackson A.
286, Reuben 138,
William 158
Bull, Isaac 46,
Robert 269
Bumgarener, Samuel
247

Buncutter, Catharine
Ann 260,
Christopher 260,
John H. 263
Bunecutter,
Christopher 233,
Hannah I. 233
Burchell, Jane 89,
John 89, 162
Burchill, Amelia
75, John 75
Burges, Abraham
201, Matilda 55
Burgess, Abraham
192, 200, Abraham
S. 281, Abram S.
179, James H.
216, James W.
192, John West
55, Martha J.
218, Sarah T.
200, West 98,
William S. 146
Burk, Abigail 20
Burke, Cornelius
54, Sarah 142,
Susannah 54,
Thomas 72
Burkhammer, Mary M.
159
Burkharmer, Rosina
30
Burkheimer,
Elizabeth 23,
Henry 30, Philip
23
Burkholder, Simon K.
226
Burn, John 211,
Mahaly 211
Burner, Jacob 56,
Margaret 114
Burnett, Lettice 16
Burns, Edward 119
Burrell, William
115
Burringer, Charles

Burringer (continued) R. 177
Burris, Bartleman 58, William 58
Burriss, Thos 10
Burroughs, Philip 39
Burtlebaugh, George 62
Burton, Benja 11, Benjamin 140, David W. 233, Gilbreath 20, James 274, Josiah 236, Levi 162, 219, Mary 274, Samuel 12, Sarah E. 162
Burwell, Cecilia 230, Edwin B. 176, 230, Eliza G. 120, Lucy Gwynn 283, Mary 115, Nathaniel 17, Philip 17, Philip L. C. 229, William 120
Buscart, John 32
Bush, Andrew 107, Andrew M. L. 252, Ann Eliza 238, Archibald C. 238, Elizabeth 1, Julia Ann 238, Margaret Ann 252, Mary 181, Philip 1, Regina Maria 236, Vance 6, 65, William 39, 42, 137, 181, 236, 238
Busher, Anna 40, John 40
Bushman, Isaac 286
Bushnell, Benjamin 282
Buskirk, Abraham Van

Buskirk (continued) 79, Margaret 79
Butcher, Jeremiah C. 113
Butler, Ales 129, Catharine 179, Charles 124, 185, Delilah 199, Elizabeth 39, Julia 239, Lawrence 83, Malinda 220, Mary 130, Robert 199, Susan 143, William G. 251
Butt, Catharine 195, James 178, Margaret 178, Sarah 97, William 97
Butter, Catharine 154, Jacob 103, James 271, Jane 140, John 219, Joseph 105, Mary 175, Mehely 134, Robert 66, Trimble 140
Butterfield, Ann 80, James 9, John 14, 80, Mary 80, Thomas 9, 226
Buzzard, David 150, Henry 157, Mary 125, Susannah 117
Byers, Samuel 218
Byland, James 40
Byrd, Francis 80, George T. 285, John W. 210, Mary 80
Bythenman, Dedrick 13
Bywaters, Elizabeth B. 215, Lucy 142, Mary Ann 201, 201, Rebecca C.

Bywaters (continued)
234   Robert C.
215, 234,   William
142, 201
Cable,   Alfred   203,
Jacob   77
Cackley,   Elizabeth
18,   John   18
Cade,   Joseph W.   239
Cadwalader,   Ezra
233
Cadwaleder,   Ezra
281,   John   281
Cadwallader,   Ezra
240,   John   72,
188,   Louisa   188
Cahill,   Grace   105,
Mary   149,   William
105, 149
Cahoon,   Daniel   5,
Mary   5, 9,   Robert
9,   Samuel   55
Cain,   Charles   24,
Elizabeth   150,
Evelina   252,   John
16,   Levi   150,
166,   Marcus   195,
Morgan   266,   Nancy
56, 195,   Peter
178,   William   75,
195, 260, 277
Calaman,   Mary   82,
Moses   82
Calbert,   Jesse   176
Calderhead,   James
246
Caldwell,   Joseph   2
Cale,   George   78
Cales,   Joseph   98
Calin,   Moses   120
Callan,   John   234
Callen,   James   138,
John   224
Callin,   Henny   120
Calmes,   George F.
203
Calvert,   Ann   30,

Calvert (continued)
Jesse   246,   John
142,   Mary F.   285,
Richard S.   212
Calvin,   Thomas   174
Camblyn,   David   81
Camerer,   Sarah   155
Camfell,   Thomas   54
Campbell,   Amy   80,
Andrew   181,
Catharine   216,
Deborah   188,
Eliza   180,
Elizabeth   22, 90,
Grisel   65,   Jane
22, 33, 117,   John
29, 46, 81, 92,
John B.   115, 196,
257,   John L.   207,
John S.   65, 105,
133, 188,   Margaret
151,   Maria   115,
Mary   137, 146,
Mary Martha   262,
Rebecca   156, 245,
Rhoda Ellen   281,
Robert   209, 272,
Robert M.   214,
Samuel   208, 212,
Sarah   81, 130,
Thomas   92,   Thomas
B.   242, 250,
William   25, 35,
44, 99, 117, 126,
135, 137, 156, 157,
180, 235, 275,
William Reed   208
Campill,   Thomas   54
Canavan,   Catharan
190,   Elizabeth
174
Canby,   Isaac   212
Cannavan,   Marian
120
Canniford,   Ann   195,
Henry   195
Cannington,   William

Cannington (continued) 198
Canter, John 129, 191
Capper, Alley 58, Charles 97, David 81, Jane 247, John 262, John Wingfield 81, Michael 103, 247, 254, 259, Sidney 169
Cardell, Thomas M. 271
Carell, Sarah 137
Carlile, Daniel D. 186, John D. 91, Mary 105
Carlin, Bennet 245
Carlyle, Charles 156, William 156
Carnagy, Catherine 79
Carnegy, Ann Susan 153, Elizabeth 239, Mary Ann 167, William 104
Carnell, Thomas 185
Carpenter, Alexander 244, George 13, James 146, 163, 207, 246, Jane 245, John 248, Joseph 209, Lewis 273, Mary 13, Mathew 118, Milly 34, Rebecca 246, Smith 238, Susan 208, 253, William 185, 253, Zachariah 206, 244, 263
Carper, Adam 172, Alfred 199, 206, 237, 271, Alphred 275, Ana Ann R.

Carper (continued) 275, Catharine 132, 193, David 280, Elizabeth 91, 159, 237, Eve 171, Frederick 11, 51, 115, 124, 159, 193, 243, 244, Frederick W. 256, Hiram 263, Jacob 156, 199, James 248, John 112, 193, 226, 237, 244, 263, 266, 279, John D. 278, Lucy 209, Margaret 115, 124, Mary 114, 193, Mary A. 266, Nancy L. 279, Philip 91, 114, 132, 164, 206, 226, 245, 280, Sarah 263, William 209, 217, 245, 247, 248, 279
Carr, Abigail 205, David S. 159, Elizabeth 34, 88, Elizabeth H. 232, Hugh H. 232, Jacob 115, James 103, Mary 190, Richard 205, Sarah 31, Tarlton 194, Thomas 31, 49, 88, 149, Walter 173, Watson 157, William 190
Carrell, Collin 40, William 34
Carroll, Dempsey 149, James 225, Jesse 27, John 153, Lemuel 134
Carson, Ann S. 146, Beatty 75, 143,

308

Carson (continued)
  Elisha W. 141,
  Eliza 252, James
  H. 218, 241, Jane
  Reddice 160,
  Jared W. 252,
  John 118, Joseph
  142, Joseph S.
  225, Martha E.
  241, Peggy 40,
  Rachel 136, Simon
  120, 146, 160,
  Susan 25, Thomas
  157
Carswell, John 10
Carter, Adam 155,
  Addison R. 283,
  Alexander 45,
  Alexander F. 163,
  Alfred 158, Ann
  88, 92, 93, 106,
  Arthur 18, Arthur
  W. 34, 38, 114,
  124, 140, 151, 154,
  205, 213, 231,
  Betsy 116,
  Catharine 201,
  Charles 83,
  Dale 4, 30,
  Daniel 22, Edmund
  149, Elam 106,
  Eliza 140,
  Elizabeth 114,
  149, Emily J.
  274, Ezekiel 22,
  87, 88, George
  Washington 91,
  Jabez 144, 162,
  183, James 48,
  53, 103, 104, 135,
  178, 187, 190, 240,
  James B. 256,
  James D. 186,
  James K. 231,
  John 67, 80,
  106, 109, 116, 120,
  126, 129, 175, 177,

Carter (continued)
  183, 238, Joseph
  19, 53, 60, 116,
  117, 130, 194, 199,
  201, Joseph W.
  148, 175, Jumima
  18, Leana 25,
  Levina 130,
  Lucinda 231,
  Lydia 117, 165,
  Margaret 124,
  Mary 123, Mary
  Ann 205, 259,
  Mary E. 283,
  Nancy 177,
  Octavia Owen 238,
  Phebe 187, Rachel
  16, 38, 230,
  Rebecah 104,
  Richard 104, 106,
  Ruth 135, Samuel
  112, Sarah 112,
  151, Sidney 148,
  Thomas 228,
  Watson 136, 207,
  236, 274, William
  A. 283
Cartmell, Catharine
  27, Edward 71,
  Eliza Ball 208,
  George 122, John
  27, 44, Joseph
  30, 73, Mordecai
  B. 180, Nathaniel
  70, 212, Parthemia
  71, Rachel 30,
  Sarah 73, Thomas
  30, 73, Y. K. 208
Cartmill, Martin
  78, 101, Mary
  101, Nathan 21,
  Parthenia 75,
  Regina 75, Rogina
  21
Cartright, Laurence
  203
Cartwright, Henry

Cartwright (continued) 219, Henry G. 226, Henry Gimlich 52, Lawrence 204, Mary E. 219
Carty, William 25
Carver, Ann 182, Daniel 182, 193, 233, Elisha 154, 174, 227, Elizabeth 175, Gasper 38, George 186, 204, Martha A. 227, Mary 186, Sarah 193, Valentine 4
Casler, Michael 235
Castelman, Emaline M. 191
Castleman, Alfred 171, Benjamin 31, Catharine 158, Charles W. 198, David 31, 82, David I. 285, Edward 189, George 89, Isabella 204, James 140, 147, 164, 176, 191, 229, John 46, 158, Juliet 212, Martha Ann 222, Mary 46, Sarah 156, Stephen 156, Thomas 69, 183, William 76, 158, 212, 282, Wm 191
Cather, Adelaide 250, Barbara B. 210, Clark 269, David 91, 95, 152, 164, Eliza G. 220, Francis 276, Hannah 95, Hannah

Cather (continued) E. 263, James 130, 182, 220, 229, 250, 260, 268, 269, 274, 276, Jane 7, 229, Jasper 7, 9, John 27, 263, Margaret Ann 279, Mary 9, Robert 95, Sidney S. 274, William 108, 220, 268
Catlet, Susannah 31
Catlett, Alexander 97, 277, Basheba 256, Bazil 241, 248, 250, Calmes 112, Charlotte 197, David 46, Demanuel 271, Dolitha 46, Edith 36, Elijah 111, Elizabeth 200, Evalina 282, Henrietta 44, Henry 112, 178, Isabella 178, James 36, 176, 248, John 41, 42, 44, 80, 94, 97, 164, 259, 272, 278, Lewis H. 192, Louisa 80, Lucy 112, Mary 192, Matilda 94, Mildred 179, Nancy 42, Nimrod 68, 76, Patsy 256, Patsy D. 97, Peter 1, 41, 94, Sidney 221, Thomas 76, Ursula 278, Ursuley 259, William 50, 89, 167, 170, 197, 221, 256, 282, Winifred

Catlett (continued) 41
Catterlin, Joseph 5, 33
Caudy, Mary 13
Cauthen, Dabney 146
Cave, John 87, Samuel 87
Cawood, Elizabeth 103, John 13, 103, Stephen 103
Caywood, Richard 127
Chamberlain, Jonas 265
Chamberlin, Jonas 28, Mary E. 257
Chambers, William 115
Chamblen, Ann 40
Chamblin, Catherine 86, George 33, 105, John 41, Thomas 40
Chamblyn, Thomas 106
Chamlyn, Thomas 89
Chandler, Jane 107, Martin B. 94, Rebecca Winston 94
Chapman, Abraham 87, Carr 217, Elie 121, Elizabeth 173, George 272, George L. 282, George W. B. 165, Greenberry 100, Hannah 215, 254, James 231, Jane 103, John 16, 22, 39, 190, 193, Joseph 193, Joshua 103, 209, 217, Lydia 181, Mary 183, Nathan 128, Rachel 209,

Chapman (continued) Rachel Ann 199, Sarah 77, 121, 193, Sarah E. 272, Strawberry 261, Thomas 18, 141, 280, Thomas W. 267, Washington 273, William 77, 91, 96, 144, 199
Chappelear, Capanara 47
Chappellear, Richard 47
Chargo, Joseph 186
Charles, Charles 61
Chastain, Lewis 35
Cheek, James 19, Katey 19, Nancey 19
Chennoweth, William 70
Chenoweth, Mary 70
Chenowith, Elieanor 176, Hannah 161, John 68, 161, 229
Chew, Coleby 107, Joseph 9, 25, Sarah 61, Sophia 107, Thomas 160, William 46
Chewining, Granville 209
Childs, Alex 21, Jane 259, William H. 253
Chiles, Ann R. 263, Griffin 147, 263, 264, Mason 150, 243, Rebecca 274, William Henry 259
Chilton, Stephen 40, 45
Chinn, Elizabeth 157, James 157
Chinowith, John

Chinowith (continued)
229, Rebecca Ann 229
Chipley, James 237, Martha Ann 237, Nancy 30, Salley B. 55, William L. 191
Chisam, Gabriel 233
Chishire, John 51
Chism, James 216, 260, Mary Ann 216
Chiswell, Joseph N. 250
Chopson, George 8
Chrisman, Abra 14, Abraham 14, Amelia B. 231, Elizabeth H. 136, George 124, Henrietta 66, Isaac 18, 63, 174, 243, Jane 174, John 231, 253, Joseph 174, Mary 180, Mary Ann 101, Mary Jane 282, Peter 8, 147, 180, Priscilla M. 243, Rebecca 226, William 187, 282
Chrismell, Martha 147
Chrismore, John 175
Christie, Agnes 43, Henry 143, James 144
Christy, Elizabeth 144, 262, Harriet Ann 262, Hugh 56, James 198, 234, Jane 121, Phebe 66, Rebecca 66, Robert 121, 234, 256, Robert W.

Christy (continued)
193, Samuel 142, Thomas 20
Chunn, Andrew 115, 116
Churchill, Alexander 189, 196, Armistead 150, Charles 176, Elizabeth 150, John 209, 223, 226, Lucinda 196
Churchwell, Martha 176
Churchwill, Maria 172
Cissil, Philip 214
Clabaugh, John 53, Nicholas 53
Clancy, William 1
Clare, Eliza 111, James 111, Jas 108
Clark, Abner 160, 161, 205, Alexander 202, Ann 29, Ann V. 282, Charles H. 187, 214, 234, 239, Daniel D. 216, Eliza M. 256, Elizabeth 178, 231, Elizabeth E. 272, Evelina 272, George 4, Henrietta M. 133, James L. 246, Jane 246, John 52, John L. 227, John M. 212, John S. 125, Jonathan M. 264, Joseph 232, 253, Joseph P 23, Juliet Ann 260, Louisa 113, Margaret 264, Mary 17, 160,

Clark (continued)
Mary Ann 153,
Olevia 113,
Rachael 88,
Rachel Ann
263, Rebecca 207,
Reuben 125, 153,
185, Robert 183,
201, 251, 270, 280,
Rubin 9, 256,
Rueben 260,
Sampson B. 205,
Samuel H. 244,
248, Sarah 151,
Septimus 64,
Susan 280, Susan
S. 185, Thomas
182, 225, William
127, 138, 151, 178,
179, 246, 263,
William C. 278,
280, William J.
213, 251
Clarke, Abner 61,
173, Betsey 48,
Elizabeth 49,
George 49, John
24, Mathew 11,
Reubin 38, Ruth
24, William 66
Claspill, Elizabeth
152, Robert R.
152
Clauser, Catharine
106
Clawson, Cornelius
167, Sarah 167
Clayton, Amos 25,
Eliza 150, Philip
1
Cleave, John Van
236
Cleavenger, John
190
Cleavinger, Ann 71
Clemens, William 33
Clemmans, William

Clemmans (continued)
18
Clemmens, Danl C.
214, Samuel 88
Clemmons, Daniel C.
214, Henry 189,
207
Clendenen, Sarah 29
Clendening, Andrew
143, 207, Margaret
143
Cleveland, Elijah
111, 130, Maria E.
168, Nancy 111
Clevender, Maholan
48
Clevenger, Adam 34,
Asa 218, David
218, Elizabeth
260, George 134,
Jacob 34, 109,
John 102, 245,
John W. 237,
Lydia 134,
Maria 245, Martin
B. 157, Nancy
102, Thomas 236,
William 149
Clevinger, Abraham
23, Achrah 82,
Asa 61, 266,
Chloe 22, David
73, Edith 42,
Elizabeth 233,
252, Geo 16,
Helen 233, Jacob
11, 61, John 42,
207, Johnnah 43,
Joseph 42, 43,
Lydia 17,
Margaret 207,
Maria Ann 252,
Mary 34, Ruth
61, Sally 194,
Sarah 26,
Theodotia 34,
William 22,

Clevinger (continued) 119, 166, Wm 26
Cline, Anthony M. 232, Hiram 89, 98, Joseph 212, Mary 140, Rebecca E. 277, Sarah 198
Clines, Henry 113
Clink, Henry 211, Jacob 242, John 174
Clipart, George 132
Clopton, Elizabeth W. 125, Louisa A. 135
Cloud, Daniel 28, 173, Edith 80, Euphemia 167, Isaac B. 173, John 99, Mordecai 138, Ruth 99, Susan 123, William 121
Clouser, Benjamin 159, Elizabeth 225, Henry 14, 139, 250, 275, 280, Jacob 264, Joseph 225, 272, Mary 275, Rebecca I. 280, Sarah 159, Sarah Elizabeth 250
Clow, Thomas 134
Clower, Dennis S. 234, Joseph H. 256
Clowser, Benjamin 161, Eliza 279, John 120, Joseph 179, 187, 279, Leah 120, Mary 187
Clutter, John 16, Joseph 105, 194
Clutz, Isaac 47

Clyne, Abraham 182, Jacob 56, James R. 179, Michael 144, Sarah 144
Coate, Elijah 9
Coates, Clara 34
Coats, Elijah 14, James 175, 231, Margaret 231, Sarah Ann 259, Thomas 34
Coborn, Israel 193
Coburn, George 133
Cochran, Elijah 252, Elizabeth 21, 93, James 92, 93, John 57, July Ann 108, June 7, Margaret 144, Mary 27, 177, Nancy 43, Polly 63, Robert 43, 63, 108, Sarah 161, 272, William 144, 161, 242, 264, 272
Cochrane, Agnes 13
Cockerell, Jane 247
Cockran, James 2, John 146, Sarah 27
Cockrell, Edy 116
Coe, Craven 243, Elizabeth 113, 164, 286, Emily 235, Henry 274, James 134, 161, 286, Jane 95, 255, John 183, 248, 257, 276, Mary C. 264, Samuel 149, 264, Thomas 95, Westley 128, Westly 113, William 164, 235
Coffee, Abram 171,

Coffee (continued)
  William 155
Coffman, Harman 22,
  William 11
Cogill, Adam 46,
  Hannah 46
Cohagin, Catharine 5
Cole, Charity 2,
  Daniel 2, 20,
  Elenor 79, Emily
  187, Harriet 192,
  Isaac 147, 187,
  Isaac B. 241, 262,
  Jane 35, John
  50, 73, 79, Lewis
  241, Margaret Ann
  262, Mary 73,
  128, Mary Ann
  147, Sarah 33,
  William 79, 241
Coleman, Abraham
  239, Peter 45,
  Phebe 45
Collin, William 65
Collings, Ann 140,
  Gennette 217
Collins, Alfred
  246, Andrew 170,
  Ann 216, Benjamin
  206, Brian 53,
  Daniel 258, 259,
  Elias 200, Eliza
  226, Elizabeth
  169, 258, Henry
  200, Jane 154,
  John 200, John Y.
  270, Leciney 23,
  Mary A. 270,
  Moses 154, Nancy
  53, Peggy 121,
  Truman 230,
  William 94, 232
Collis, Daniel 100
Colston, Lucy L. C.
  174, Robert A.
  222

Colum, Rachael 60
Colvill, Jane 55
Colville, James
  155, 165
Colvin, Eliza Ann
  202, Thomas 202,
  213
Compton, Alexander
  80, 83, 189, Cloe
  Elizabeth 187,
  Elias E. 200,
  James 3, 23, 35,
  Linna G. 194,
  Lucinda A. 189,
  Robert 173,
  William 61,
  William C. 194
Concklin, Mary 33
Congroves, Susanah
  46
Congrows, John 15
Conklin, David 53,
  Sally 53
Conklyn, David 33
Conn, Hezekiah 48,
  102, James 185,
  James W. 195
Connally, David
  259, 268
Connelly, Mary 201
Conner, Christian
  101, Dorothy 271,
  Eli 205,
  Elizabeth 209,
  George 193, James
  87, 119, Jenney
  25, John 65,
  Margaret 31, Mary
  48, 87, Patrick
  264, Robert 224,
  Severn 146, Smith
  187, Thomas 25,
  193
Connor, Catharine
  101
Conrad, Catharine
  285, Charles 231,

Conrad (continued)
Charles M. 261, 285, Daniel P. 170, Elizabeth 22, 96, Emily Jane 216, Frederick 2, 15, Fredk 3, Hannah 261, Isaac 112, 147, James W. V. 218, Levi 128, Nancy 128, Sarah 218, William 41
Conrod, Mary 51
Constable, Charles 107
Conway, Hugh 263, 272, Jas 22, Margaret S. 272, Mary F. 263, Rachel 22
Cook, Alexander 105, Eliza 122, Giles 216, John 267, Martha 216, Martha A. 250, Mary 186, Nancy 191, Samuel 88, William 85, 191
Cooke, James H. 185, 190, John R. 199, Lucy Esthen 165
Cooksey, Elias 124
Cool, William 217
Coolbee, James 35
Cooley, Darcus 208, James B. 280, John W. 249, Joseph 249, 280, Peter 22, 31, 75, 114, 160, Samuel 121, Sarah 160, Susan 249
Cooly, Peter 3, 16, 121, Samuel 108
Coontz, William H.

Coontz (continued)
200
Coontzman, Daniel 162
Cooper, Abraham 182, 192, 195, Abraham D. 247, Abraham S. 248, Alce 137, Catharine 95, 195, Charlotte 171, David 270, Elijah 230, Elizabeth 34, 94, 154, Geo 68, George 7, 233, Hanah 98, Harrison 243, Henry 129, Isaac 162, Jacob 83, 197, 257, Jane M. 255, John 34, 94, 105, 152, John W. 153, Joseph 220, 223, 280, Leah 146, Leonard 95, 192, Levi 264, Margaret Jane 280, Martin 45, Mary Ann 182, 264, Nathaniel B. 266, Rachel 129, 152, Rachell 16, Rebecca 83, Rhoda Ann 220, Robert 106, Sally 135, Samuel 60, Sarah 192, 223, Simon 284, Susanna 143, Tenah 105, Thomas 2, 24, 98, 137, 143, 154, 171, William 34, 132
Cope, John 50, 54, Joseph 50, 54, Joshua 69
Copeland, Isabella 149, Richard 29,

Copeland (continued)
  William 149
Copelin, Elizabeth
  41, Henry 41
Copenhaver, George
  280, Jacob 131,
  James A. 282,
  John 175, Michael
  246
Coppesy, Baldwin 21
Corban, John 242
Corbett, James 78,
  Jane Letitia 78,
  John 17, Saml
  53, William 72
Corbin, Harriet S.
  224, John R. T.
  115
Cordell, Elizabeth
  63, 182, Frances
  152, John 15,
  Mary 42, Matilda
  133, Sarah 9
Corder, Alice 133,
  Benjamin 14, 26,
  79, 89, Chrisjohn
  141, Elizabeth
  14, Eve 26,
  James 27, 168,
  Jesse 168,
  John 85, 160,
  Joseph 27, 51,
  Lucy 106, 120,
  Mary 106, Morgan
  104, Nancy 89,
  Phoebe 168, Polly
  79, Susannah 51,
  William 191
Coreson, Joseph 65
Cornelius, Elizabeth
  72, Isabella 83
Cornell, Thomas 203
Cornwall, George
  123, John 165,
  Mary 281, William
  165
Cornwell, Anne 1,

Cornwell (continued)
  Benjamin E. 203,
  Catharine Ann 167,
  Fielding 76, Icy
  193, Nancy 254,
  Robert 75, 227,
  Sibby 227,
  Strother M. 270,
  Thomas 192, 254,
  258, 259, William
  52, 167, 192, 193
Correll, Andrew 51,
  Elizabeth 209,
  Mary 107, Michal
  C. 284
Corsch, Eveline 241
Corsgill, Elizabeth
  132
Corson, Joseph 201,
  208, Mary Ann 208
Cotes, Edward 49,
  Maria 49
Cotrell, William 17
Cougil, John 70
Cougill, James 99,
  109, Nancy 109
Coulter, Amos 226,
  Corben 11, Joseph
  169
Courtney, Barnabas
  72, Elliner 126,
  Mary 72
Cowan, Nathaniel 17
Cowdery, Elizabeth
  64, Jonathan 64
Cowgill, George 68,
  80, Hannah 66,
  John T. 200
Cowles, James 140
Cox, Fewell 61,
  Hamilton 191,
  John 1, Margaret
  191, Samuel 142,
  William 136, 142,
  178
Coyle, Joseph 251,
  Lucinda 251

Crabb, Daniel 60,
   James 144, John
   M. 106, Samuel
   89, Vincent 16,
   23
Crabill, Jacob 270,
   Levi 243, Mary
   270, Philip S.
   266
Crafford, Reubin
   11, William 84
Craig, Eliza Ann
   231, Elizabeth
   107, Harrit 183,
   Hiram 230, Hugh
   21, Jane 131,
   John 21, 107, 121,
   Joseph 8, Josiah
   129, 131, Mary
   111, 129, Peggy
   121, Robert 74,
   100, Samuel 54,
   81, 86, 111,
   Susanna 100,
   107, Susannah 74,
   121, William 118
Cramer, Ambrose 69,
   Margaret Shannon
   69
Crampton, Ann 156,
   Benjamin 220,
   Jacob 18, John
   18, 91
Crane, Lewis 66,
   Willis 240
Cranswick, Richard
   222
Craps, John 139
Crawford, Ediah 20,
   Jacob 274, James
   93, 236, John 20,
   125, John J. 253,
   John S. 204,
   Lucinda 196,
   Margaret Ann 246,
   Martin 95, Samuel
   48, 175, 196,

Crawford (continued)
   Sydney Ann 175,
   Thomas 175, 196,
   274, Thomas J.
   256, Thos 196,
   William
   246, 253
Crebbs, Amanda 278,
   Hannah 266
Crebs, Conrad 6,
   170, Isaac W.
   278, John H. 280,
   Lucy 170,
   Margaret Ann 280
Creiser, Jacob 260
Creswell, Abraham
   70, John 284
Crider, Ann 180,
   John 17, 78, 114,
   194, Margaret
   239, Margaret Ann
   114, Polly 194,
   Sarah 239
Crigler, Benjamin
   150, Catherine
   150, Elizabeth
   195, Lewis 104
Crim, Abraham 184,
   Jacob 186,
   Richard 181
Criner, John 208
Criser, Jacob 240
Crisman, Franklin
   277, 281
Crissmore, Anthony
   120, Elizabeth
   120
Crist, Jacob 21
Crizer, Jacob 145,
   148
Crizzor, Jacob 59
Crocket, Sarah 67
Crockett, Robert 41
Crockwell, George M.
   163, John 226
Crofford, Reuben 60
Croft, Thomas 236

Cromley, Aaron 14
Croner, William 256
Cronnen, Will 12, William 34
Crook, John 53
Crosen, Dorcas 77
Croson, Barnet 68, Dorcas 68, Zeheniah 68
Cross, Gabriel 28, James 209, Nicholas 85, Robert 28
Crouch, John D. 176
Crous, John A. 284
Crouse, Christiana 163, Elizabeth 109, Jacob 282, Jane 203, John 84, Michael 128, Susan 109
Crow, Elizabeth 179, John 76, 100, 178, Martha 100, 178, Thomas H. 210, 215, Wm 122
Crum, Abraham 152, 158, Anthony 9, 12, Barbara 91, Betsy 42, Catherine 125, Christian 13, 42, 64, 72, 79, 97, Christiana 72, Daniel 139, Elizabeth 89, Henry 89, 91, 125, 168, 250, John 91, 125, 158, Lemuel 240, Margaret 9, Mary 13, 152, Peter 179, Rachel 97, Rosanna 64
Crumley, Elizabeth 135, Henry 178,

Crumley (continued) 206, James 103, John 135, Mary 66, Sarah 27
Crumly, John 87, Stephen 66, Thomas 27
Crumm, Mary 79
Crummy, George 29
Crumpton, Jacob 9
Crupper, Eli 155, 203, 222, Elizabeth 111, John 77, 111, 115, Malinda 115, Phebe 77, Robert 131, 170
Cruzen, George R. 266, 282
Cryder, Abraham 29, Elizabeth 141, 190, George 173, Jacob 74, 117, John 6, 74, 102, 141, 202, Martin 35, Philip 25, Sarah 74
Crysor, Jacob 21
Cubbage, Isabella 236, James 269
Cullen, James 113
Cullers, John 252
Culver, John 121
Cumings, George 14
Cummings, John 99
Cummins, Joseph S. 277
Cumpton, James 23
Cuningham, John 12, 17, Nicholas 12
Cunningham, Charles 106, 129, 192, Elizabeth 69, Francis M. 286, John 69, Samuel 205, 226, Thomas 34, Thos 8

Cuntz, Michael 268
Curl, Daniel 218, 227, David 169, James 101, 188, John 102, Letitia 101, Margery 169, Maria Nancy 188
Curlet, Frances 8, Rachel 4
Curlett, Elizabeth 4, Rebecca 13, Wiliam S. 196
Curray, Mary 221
Currey, John 214
Curry, Caspar 266, Jane 91, John 265, Mary 202, Matthew 129, Thomas 78, 91, 202
Curtes, Henry 43, Jesse 43, Nancy 43
Curtis, Susannah 148
Cusick, David 65, Elizabeth 6
Custer, Elizabeth 40, Margaret 278, Randolph 278, Saml 40
Cutwait, Jacob 265
Cyder, Conrod 47
Cyfret, Catharine 40, Elizabeth 34, George 34, 40
Cypher, George 170, Rachel 170
Cyphert, Andrew 34, Freny 12, Philip 81, Sarah 16
Cyphret, Sarah 16
Dailey, Absalom 263, Absolom 261, Benjamin 261, Elizabeth 16, Hannah 261, 277, James 109, 137,

Dailey (continued) 172, 225, 253, 264, Jane W. 244, John 122, Joseph 29, Leah 29, Maria 247, Rachel 172, Samuel 114, 157, Sarah 157, Susannah 214
Daily, Dennis 136, Robert W. 257
Daingerfield, Elizabeth Frances 97, Henry 7, Lawrence Lewis 176, Mary B. 101, William 101
Dainty, James 227
Dalbay, Susannah 91
Dalbey, Israel 206, Joseph 91, 118, 226
Dalby, Elizabeth 195, Hannah 109, Israel 195, John 109, 144, Joseph 171
Daley, Elizabeth 114, William 53
Dalley, John 131, Mary 131
Daniel, Benjamin 109, Eliza 167, George R. 226, James 61, Jane 200, Matilda 191
Daniels, Henry G. 231, Jane 190
Danks, John 9
Danley, Hosea 83, 242, Selina 242
Dann, Thomas 88, 209, Thos 23
Danner, David S. 124, 145, Davis S. 135, Eliza 194, Elizabeth 97, 265,

Danner (continued)
  Jacob 12, Jacob
  S. 194, 248, Mary
  J. 135
Dansey, Lewis 114,
  132
Darkey, Uris 164
Darlington, James H.
  194, John 57,
  Maria L. 158,
  Meredith 23, 41,
  69, 231, 253,
  Sarah 57
Darlinton, David
  41, Eleanor 206,
  Mary 253
Darr, Ann 43,
  George 43, John
  60
Dasis, Polly 46
Daugherty, John 17,
  39, Susanna 17
Davenport, Benjamin
  69, Edrian 113,
  John 113,
  Samuel I. C. 244
Davidson, James 71,
  Mary 71
Davis, Abdiel 201,
  Abraham 14,
  Baalis 115, 202,
  217, Baylis 23,
  Benja. 59,
  Benjamin 68,
  Caroline N. 220,
  Catharine 14,
  Catharine M. 180,
  Daniel 20, David
  92, 206, 238, 252,
  285, David N.
  244, David T. 64,
  133, Deborah 149,
  Eli 110,
  Elizabeth 12, 16,
  22, 109,
  Frances 213,
  Francis 30,

Davis (continued)
  Gabriel 23, 30,
  Gabriel H. 106,
  215, 224, Gary
  12, 61, 213,
  George 13, 188,
  Hanah 50, Hannah
  33, Henry 20,
  Humphrey 105,
  James 89, 90, 113,
  114, 149, James H.
  42, Jane 68, Jas
  50, 109, John 44,
  65, 99, John B.
  228, Joseph D.
  247, Joseph F.
  254, Lydia 33,
  Margaret 59, 254,
  Margaret F. 217,
  Maria 138, Mary
  13, 16, 52, 102,
  Mary E. 225, Mary
  F. 238, Nelly
  83, Phebe 83, 89,
  Presley 131,
  Rachel 113,
  Raymond S. 265,
  Ruth 215, Sally
  89, Samuel 33,
  153, 189, Samuel
  H. 174, Sarah
  48, 89, 99, 106,
  167, 176, Stephen
  49, 81, Thomas
  37, William
  13, 16, 22, 87
Davison, Alexander
  McD. 238, Daniel
  49, 254, Davod
  254, Edward J.
  223, Elizabeth
  134, Elizabeth M.
  254, James 49,
  112, 126, Jane
  100, John 206,
  John S. 173, John
  Smith 177, 202,

Davison (continued)
  Maria Louisa 191,
  Nimrod A. 199,
  Robert 216,
  Samuel 119, 267,
  Susanah 100,
  Thomas P. 134,
  William 29, 80,
  133, 240
Dawalt, Abraham 88
Dawson, Amelia Lee
  36, Benj. 43,
  Benjamin 36,
  Elisha 278,
  George 7, 35, 79,
  177, Isaac 182,
  James 31, John
  45, Martha 7,
  Mary 156, Mary
  Ann 79, Sarah 35
Day, Catherine 145,
  David 53, Deborah
  53, Eleanor 180,
  Elizabeth 23, 99,
  138, 280, Isabella
  175, 267, James
  99, 132, 140, 168,
  Jeremiah 23, John
  79, 106, 208, Mary
  99, 151, Mary Ann
  253, Nancy 132,
  Samuel 138, 145,
  151, 167, 175,
  Thomas 76, 112,
  165, Willis 96,
  137, 139, 182
Deadrick, Philip
  55, Thomas 97
Deahl, David 199,
  267, William 199
Deal, Ann 71, 88,
  93, Anna 55,
  Catharine 24,
  Conrad 24, 71,
  Elizabeth 71, Eve
  93, George 37,
  James 128, Mary

Deal (continued)
  55
Deale, Polly 50
Dean, Adam 280,
  Ann 91, Barbara
  91, Elie 139,
  Elizabeth 33, 271,
  Jonathan 131, 140,
  Polly 120,
  Rebecca 281,
  William 39, 281
Deane, William 120
Dearmont, Margaret
  18, Michael 123,
  177, Peter 18
Debell, Ann 179,
  Elizabeth 189,
  Jeremiah 179,
  Lucidney 179
Deck, Eliza 247,
  George 273,
  Margaret 273
Decker, Henry 3,
  Lydia 3
Deems, George W.
  250
Dehaven, Abigail
  162, Abijah 272,
  Ann 110, Anna
  187, Athalia 199,
  Barak 275,
  Catharine 220,
  Daniel 227, 281,
  Dorsey 272,
  Drusilla 127,
  Esther 266, Ezra
  274, 281, Hannah
  45, Harriet 272,
  Harvy 275, Henry
  D. 127, 137, 256,
  Isaac 45, 66, 105,
  260, 262, 267, 284,
  Jackson 286,
  James 286, Jane
  260, Job 162,
  215, 227, John
  66, 190, 199,

Dehaven (continued)
  Jonathan 190, 218,
  Joseph T. 263,
  266, Lavina 281,
  Martha 225, Mary
  267, Phebe 227,
  Rebecca 215,
  Susan 284,
  Susannah 130,
  West 225,
  Westley 115,
  William 13, 97,
  130, 256, William
  L. 263, Wm 179
Delong, Jacob 71,
  John 58, 179,
  Margaret 120
Dement, Richard 224
Demoff, Nancy 150,
  Throckmorton 150
Demory, Mahlon 193
Deneal, John E. 171
Denges, James 227
Denis, Frederick 90
Denn, Elizabeth 96
Dennahoo, Martha 275
Denney, David 36
Denny, David 113,
  John 110, 129,
  138, Mary 36,
  Robert 221,
  William 58, 131,
  135, 139, 202, 235,
  246, Wm 199
Dent, Cassandra A.
  155, Delilah 148,
  George 237,
  Rebecca A. 275,
  Thomas 148, 155
Denton, Isaac 71
Denvar, Daniel 254
Denver, Danel 96,
  Patrick 117
Denvers, Patrick
  104, Rosa 104
Deshon, James 121

Despanet, John 195
Desponet, William 252
Deval, Emelene L.
  267, Reason 267
Devalt, Abraham
  104, Eleanor 104
Devo, David 4, 84,
  Sarah 4
Devoe, David 121,
  153, 179, 239, 243,
  Eliza 239,
  Evelina 179, John
  121, Samuel 97,
  Sarah 121, Seth
  272, Seth S. 260,
  William 222
Dewalt, Elizabeth
  8, Joseph 267
Dewaney, James 81
Dewnie, Elizabeth 103
Dews, John 104,
  Thomas 111
Dial, Thomas 104
Dick, Archibald
  196, Barbara 76,
  Benjamin J. E.
  167, Catherine
  108, Christena
  123, David 283,
  Dicanda Dent 230,
  Elinor 134,
  Elizabeth 98, 196,
  Elizabeth E. 195,
  George 8, Henry
  139, 162, 195, 230,
  Hieronimus 98,
  136, Isaac 204,
  240, Jacob 54,
  John 88, 103, 123,
  129, 185, 190,
  John H. 221,
  Lewis 238,
  Margaret 93, Mary
  30, 148, Mary Ann
  139, 229, Mary D.

Dick (continued)
162, Nancy 83,
Nicholas 107,
Peter 11, 30, 69,
76, 93, 107, 134,
144, 148, 157, 196,
210, 229, Sarah
210, Thomas 83,
William 265, 269
Dickay, Joseph 8
Dickeson, Jane 280
Dickinson, John 262
Dickison, John 81
Dicks, Emily 244,
Henry 244,
Hieronimus 159,
Stephen 114
Dickson, Nancy 81
Dier, Sarah 50
Dignan, John 268
Dillon, Daniel 5,
Elizabeth 233,
James 84, Joel
140, John 43, 55,
84, Lydia 55,
Mary 43, Rachel
Ann 265, William
152, 170, 172, 197,
Wm 233
Dimmett, Beal 8,
Belinda 8,
Ezekiel 8
Dingas, Georges 80,
Mary 87
Dinges, Elizabeth
259, James A. 283
Ditton, John 55,
Lydia 55
Dix, Benjamin 268
Dixon, Benjamin
159, John 39,
Martha 39,
Mildred 1, Samuel
2, William 9
Dobbins, Samuel 243
Dobbyns, Jesse 107
Dobyns, Frederick

Dobyns (continued)
56
Dodd, William 133
Dolan, Michael C.
260
Dolby, Israel 226,
Jane 172, John
92, 172, Rebecca
92
Donaldson, Mary 49,
Rachel B. 145,
Rebecca 54, Sally
17
Donenly, Mary N.
278
Donly, William W.
270
Dooley, Catharine
182, Elizabeth
16, Elizabeth Ann
179, Ellen E.
259, Frances 230,
James 145, 182,
Mary A. 228,
William 55, 174,
179, 210, 227
Dooly, James 139,
Samuel 235
Doran, James 184,
Mary 93, Michael
46
Dores, William J.
102
Dorsey, Arthur 261,
Elias 195, George
219, Levin 2,
Thomas J. 165
Dosh, Joseph M. 243
Doster, Atheliah
47, John 13, 83,
Rody 66, William
32, 47, 58, 67, 77
Dotson, Margaret 12
Dotts, Basten 30
Dougherty, Richard
59
Doughty, Anna 31,

Doughty (continued)
  Daniel 31, 41,
  Eliza 230,
  Elizabeth 41,
  Martha L. 229,
  Thomas 26,
  William 229
Douglas, Ann 177
Douglass, Adam 31,
  Eliza 195, George
  183, James 152,
  247, John 33,
  Loy Ellen 235,
  Sally 107
Doup, Jacob 197
Dowall, Elijah 75,
  Mary 75
Dowdan, Luca 115
Dowdell, Jane 207
Dowell, Delilah 85,
  Elijah 91, 98,
  Elizabeth 107,
  Harriett 260,
  Isaac 30, James
  191, Jane 39,
  220, Jaquelina
  194, Jesse 25,
  John 83, 98, 112,
  124, 137, 201, 213,
  216, Mary 98,
  Nancy 158,
  Ollaver 22,
  Richard 169,
  Sarah 124, Sidney
  217, Thomas 39,
  William 75
Dower, Sarah 136
Dowland, Edward
  192, Sarah 192
Dowlins, Isabella
  74
Downing, Benjamin
  224, Elen 92,
  James 92, 138,
  Milly 187, Sarah
  224
Doyle, Henry 152,

Doyle (continued)
  Peter H. 152
Drake, Ann 204,
  Edward 12,
  Elizabeth 16, 124,
  Francis 45, 164,
  Gersham 45, 98,
  148, 164, 186, 199,
  204, 211, Gershom
  16, 170, Hannah
  164, James 161,
  James H. 255, 279,
  John 88, 131, 211,
  276, Joseph 217,
  Juliet A. 199,
  Lawyer 186, Lucy
  211, Mary 186,
  Phebe 211, Phoebe
  148, Samuel 86,
  96, Sarah 86,
  176, Sarah Jane
  255, Susan 170,
  Thomas 196, 259,
  Thos 217
Draper, Edward 27,
  Joseph 42, Thomas
  27
Drew, Dolphin 81,
  128, Washington
  59
Drish, Elizabeth
  164, Horation 164
Driver, John W. 30,
  John Windsor 6
Drowning, Benjamin
  86
Drum, Lydia 70
Drumm, John 10,
  Margaret 10
Drury, William 195
Ducker, James 11,
  John 100, Lydia
  100, Mary 8, 88,
  William 88
Duckwall, John 252
Dudley, Henry 138,
  Joseph 141

Dudly, Henry 14
Duff, Alice 30,
  Peter 30, 163,
  Thomas 53
Duffey, Alley 99,
  Anna 117, Bernard
  99, Levi 99, 120,
  Michael 250
Dugan, Catharine 80
Duke, Alexander 81,
  Mark 124, Thomas
  120, 122, 153,
  Thomas H. 119,
  William 59
Dulany, William H.
  74
Duly, Daniel 62
Dunbar, Grace 41,
  Mary L. L. 222,
  Robert 62
Duncan, Elizabeth
  112, Elliner 127,
  James R. 258,
  John 127, Martha
  223, Mary 174,
  Patrick 47, 112,
  Thomas J. 215
Dunken, Patrick 131
Dunlap, Abner 190,
  Archibald 227,
  Archibard 206,
  Elizabeth 16,
  John 191, Nancy
  227
Dunn, Eliza 171,
  Elizabeth 47,
  Elizabeth Ann 247,
  George L. 184,
  James H. 285,
  Joseph 181,
  Robert 36, 171,
  Thomas 4, 36, 141,
  William 166, 247,
  263
Dunovan, Isaac 28
Dutton, Elisha 222,
  Elisha M. 188,

Dutton (continued)
  Elizabeth 224,
  Frances 199,
  Francis 14,
  Hannah 211,
  William 57, 199,
  211, 224
Dutts, George 114
Duty, Catharine 179
Duval, Rebecca 104
Duvall, James 232,
  Lucy G. 248,
  Rezin 165
Dyck, Volentine 286
Dyer, Ann Elizabeth
  246, Bazzel L.
  286, Elizabeth
  64, Hugh C. 135,
  162, 181, Hugh
  Carter 177,
  Israel 128,
  James 164, 166,
  181, John 64, 98,
  Joseph A. 264,
  Juliet 162,
  Margaret 98,
  Nancy 181,
  Rachael 181
Dyson, Aquila 18,
  Aquilla 82, 110,
  Elizabeth 112,
  Jane B. 82, John
  B 84, Joseph
  110, 112, 130,
  Mary 110
Eagan, Thomas 2
Eagle, Daniel 135,
  Harriet 227,
  Margaret Ann 262
Eagleston, Margaret
  Ann 285
Eamigh, Philip 6
Earhart, Ann Mariah
  181, Catherine
  166, Elizabeth
  175, George 26,
  Katy 82, Mary 82,

Earhart (continued)
  Philip 211,
  Philip M. 230,
  Susanah 61,
  Susannah 84
Earheart, John 127, 164, Lydia 30, Nancy 164, Philip 30, Sarah 127
Earl, Mary 116
Earle, Esaias 43, 171, Ezias 116, John B. 123, 222, Matilda B. 171, Sarah Ann G. 209
Eaton, Elizabeth 242, 251, Henry 154, John 190, 207, 227, John W. 268, Joseph 60, 190, 227, Mary 207, Thomas 156
Eavenson, Mary 131
Ebbert, Harriet 255, William 255
Eberman, Geo. A. 88
Ebler, Peter 95
Eckes, Samuel 190
Eddie, William 253
Eddy, Elizabeth 72, James 5, John 72, 93, John V. 274, Mary 93, Robert 267, Samuel 104, Sarah Jane 260, William 129, 260
Edenburgh, Jacob 9
Edinborough, Jacob 19
Edmonds, Benjamin 8, Margaret 109, Margaret B. 210, Samuel 217, Sydnor 210
Edmondson, Alley Ann 10, 100, 273 Eleanor 100, Maria 242, William H. 262
Edmonson, Athanasia 260, W. H. 260
Edmonston, Archd 10
Edmundson, Rachel 277
Edwards, Gideon 43, 84, Henry 216, Hezekiah 56, Ignatius 53, John 205, John C. 258, Joseph B. 162, Mary 243, Sarah 56, Thomas 126, 217, 251
Eggleston, William G. 244
Eichelberger, Lewis 237, 240, 247
Eichholtz, Frederick 263
Ejan, Mary 46
Elbon, John R. 278, Reubin 21
Elgin, Manley 184
Elkins, Elizabeth 96, 102, James 5, 44, Lucy 102, Mary 156
Elles, Rachel 59
Ellet, Elizabeth 118
Elliot, William 85
Elliott, Abraham 80, Benjamin 27, 146, 196, Christopher 279, Eliza 285, Elizabeth 126, Elizabeth Jane 246, Isaac H. 220, John 95, John M. 162, 220, Phebe 252, Reuben 19, 126, 217, 268,

Elliott (continued)
Susan Q. 196,
William 118, 143,
174, 246, 277, 285
Ellis, Ann 82,
Eleanor 7, Elijah
102, Elisha 58,
Ezer 54, 82,
Jonathan 22,
Leonard 77, Lewis
117, Liddy 53,
Margaret 42, Mary
67, Morris 32,
53, 82, 105, Sarah
53, 58, Susanna
105, Thomas 42
Ellner, John H. 249
Ellsea, Rachel 141,
Samuel 158,
Thomas 136
Ellzy, Mary L. 241
Elsa, Isaac R. 134,
John 134
Elsea, Isaac R.
160, Thomas 211
Elsey, John 24,
Moses 141
Elzea, Samuel 98
Elzey, Darcas 49,
Elizabeth 33, 90,
Hannah 44, Isaac
49, 55, John 33,
49, 82, Rebekah
49, William 23
Emert, Jacob F. 279
Emery, Hesekiah 284
Emett, Lewis S. 238
Emitt, John C. 233
Emmart, Abram 204
Emmett, John 1
Emmonds, Susannah 2
Emmons 5, Aaron
146, Andrew I.
277, Bertheny
180, Elias 46,
Elisha 8, 35,
Hester 75,

Emmons (continued)
Joel 60, 75,
Joseph 272, 282,
Mary 260, Thomas
46
Emmory, Polly 49
Enders, Jacob 205,
John 223, Mary
243
Engle, Amy 258,
John W. 278,
Joseph 11,
William D. 258
Enrich, Mary E. 276
Ensley, Elizabeth
145, William 48,
145, 166
Eo, Catharine 92
Epfler, Susan 195
Epler, Juliet 199,
Peter 133, 199,
Sarah 133
Ernest, Julia Ann M.
232
Ervine, William 129
Eskridge, William
176
Eton, Jane 242
Ettenger, William
260
Evans, Abraham V.
216, Catherine Ann
281, David 172,
Delilah 104,
Elizabeth 210,
234, Emily Susan
201, Harvey 160,
James 126, 232,
271, John 234,
John R. 284,
Lydia 30,
Margaret 8, 110,
Nathan 88, Peggy
24, Peter 251,
Priscilla 271,
Robert 151, Sarah
26, Susanah 206,

Evans (continued)
  Thomas 13,
  William 104, 119
Eveins, Mary 17
Eveland, John 238,
  Mary 238
Evens, Catherine
  125, Samuel 125
Everett, Elizabeth
  102, 250, John
  246, 250, Margaret
  225, Mary Ann 250
Everhart, Abraham
  242, Elizabeth
  115, 282, George
  135, 177, George
  W. 256, Henry
  141, Jacob 135,
  William 165,
  William G. 219
Everheart, Eliza
  210, Jacob 107,
  Margaret 210, 211,
  Michael 127, Mima
  127, Susan 211,
  William 164
Evert, John 122
Ewan, Elizabeth
  100, 201, Ellen
  228, Israel 228,
  James R. 201,
  John W. 211, 265,
  Mary 210, Thomas
  100, 210
Ewans, Sarah 133
Ewing, Debby 180,
  Elizabeth 130,
  Israel 58, 170,
  Jane 33, John
  215, John C. 171,
  John S. 206, 237,
  Margaret 180,
  Robert 180, 189,
  201, Thomas 20,
  33, 95, 130, 231,
  Trystram 2
Ewins, Thos 133

Fagan, Barnard 10,
  John 268, 270,
  Mary Ann 270,
  Sarah 169,
  William 107
Fagle, Daniel 149
Faidley, Henry 98,
  Maria 188
Fallert, William 8
Fallis, Job 28,
  Richard 43, 49
Fant, John L. 174
Farley, Michael 255
Farmer, Daicey 4,
  Davis 259, Jane
  17, 269, John 12,
  33, 67, 95, 186,
  215, Lydia 215,
  Mary 67, Peter
  269, Sarah 45,
  Susan 186, Thomas
  17, 45, Wm 4
Farnsworth, Jonathan
  176
Farquson, Jane 59
Farr, Cyrus 48
Farrell, Catharine
  31, David 150,
  163, Mordecai 249
Farris, Thomas 32
Farrow, George 71,
  Jacob 48, Nancy
  131
Farver, Catharine
  36, John 286
Fate, Wm. M. 32
Faughanden, John
  160
Faulconer, Harrison
  242
Fauntleroy, Wm Moore
  83
Fawcett, David 20,
  60, Elijah 131,
  Eliza 131,
  Elkanah 269, John
  29, 129, Joseph

Fawcett (continued)
32, 34, Lydia
129, Sarah 259
Fawson, Sarah 70
Featheringal, George
39
Featheringale,
Thomas 56
Featheringall,
Elizabeth 28,
John 28, Sarah
52
Featheringill, Nancy
39
Featherling, George
24, Polly 24
Feegan, John R. 217
Feehner, William
197
Feely, J. L. 223
Fegans, Elizabeth
174
Fegins, William 91
Feltner, John 182,
Martin 187, 223,
Mary 223
Felton, Lydia 16,
Thomas 16
Femster, James 94
Fenton, Benjamin
9, 80, 109,
Enoch 202,
Ephraim 40,
66, 228, Hannah
98, John 106,
Joseph 127,
Louisa 183,
Mary 108, Mildred
14, Ruth 106,
Sarah 9, 23,
Sydny 109
Ferguson, Abner 40,
Catherine 126,
David 43,
Elizabeth 197,
James S. 126,
John D. 204, 222,

Ferguson (continued)
Joshua 111, 126,
Josias 37,
Lucinda 158,
177, Mary 111,
157, Nancy 140,
Samuel 26,
Sarah 204,
Washington 197
Ferrell, Hannah
249, John 31,
Thomas 261
Ferril, David 121
Ferry, Elizabeth
277
Fetheringale, Hannah
27
Fetty, Thomas 162
Few, Samuel 120
Ficklen, James G.
242
Figg, Thomas 117
Figgins, Mary Ann
230, Sarah 169
File, Jacob 33
Files, Elizabeth
75, Joseph 143,
205
Finch, Mary M. 256,
Phebe 164
Findley, Archibald
263
Finley, Archibald
271, Leah 263,
Rachel 271,
Robert 150
Finnell, Alexander
143, 188, 202, 215,
Reuben 143
Fisar, Michael 201
Fiser, Ann Jane
278, Elizabeth
Catharine 261,
Mary 261, 278
Fish, Ana 178,
Elizabeth 206,
Emily 189, Henry

Fish (continued) 189, Mary 102, Matilda 160, Robert 102, 160, 178, 206, Samuel 197
Fishel, Mary Ann 259
Fisher, Amos 266, Asa 215, Barack B. 258, Barak 3, 10, 113, 115, Barick 19, Barrach 126, Barrick 108, Caroline 179, Catharine 10, Catherine 146, David 88, 179, Eleanor 3, Elias 178, Eliza 126, Elizabeth 3, 154, 166, Ellen 158, Esther 135, Frances 11, Jacob 262, James 189, John 71, Jonathan 199, Joseph 189, 231, 283, Laney 182, Leannah 14, Lewis 76, 182, 197, 210, Louisa 115, Luis 3, Michael 273, Rebecca 19, Robert 110, Sarah E. 283, Susana 3, Susanah 60, William 76
Fitch, A. P. 254
Fitsimons, Nicholas 31
Fitzhugh, Alexander 111, Jane 241
Fitzimmons, Nicholas 104

Fitzpatrick, John 58
Fitzsimmons, Ann 223, Biddy 191, John 96, Nicholas 66
Fitzsimons, Hugh 34
Flanigan, Charles 106
Flaugherty, James 3
Fleet, Catharine 92, Lewis 139, 240, 250, 276, Littleton 98, Margaret 98, Margaret Ann 250, Rebecca Jane 276
Fleming, Andrew 128, 195, Ann 106, Archibald 123, 144, 182, 200, Eliza 93, Elizabeth 134, 144, Harriet 182, Jane 115, 200, John 51, 84, 93, John W. 144, Joseph 187, Mary 187, 195, Sarah 123, Thomas 11, Thornton 41, William 106, 115, 134
Flemings, Archibald 86, Sarah 86
Flemister, Joseph P. 277, Mary 223
Fletcher, Edward 214, Elijah 97, Elizabeth 188, 277, Frances 243, Isaac 271, James 243, 245, John 189, 238, 259, Johnston 15, Lewis 286, Mahalah 245,

Fletcher (continued)
  Maria M. 259,
  Robert B. 276, 277,
  Thomas 158, Uriah 253, William 210, 253
Flin, Valentine 133
Flinn, Leucinda 116, Thornton 219, Volentine 116
Flore, John 150, 163, Mary 163, Sarah 150
Florence, James 189, Robert 229
Flower, Ann 243, John 91, Richard 108, 206, 220, 232, Sydney Ann 232
Flowers, Elizabeth Jane 236
Flynn, Austin 139, 146, Elizabeth 185, Valentine 138
Foley, Edeth 191, Isaac 12, Jacob 36, John 191, 207, 209, 230, Mary Ann 141, Nancy 207, Peggy 127, Polly 102, Rachel 103, Sarah 96, 102, 230, Selly 127, William 25
Folk, George 198, 202
Folke, Charles 17
Follet, Elizabeth 103, William 103
Follett, Ann 133, William 133
Font, Elizabeth 237, Henry 237

Foote, William Henry 150
Ford, Alexander 174, Elizabeth Ann 198, James 198, John 54, 207, John C. 153, Prudence 54, William 189
Fore, William 252
Foreman, Amos 32, John 112, John A. 187
Forguson, Samuel 40
Forman, Amos 48
Forsithe, Mary 41
Forster, James 162, 169, Sarah 162
Forsyth, Lewis M. 238
Forsythe, Abraham 132
Fossett, Gueliemly 243
Foster, Alfred Turner 143, Frances 142, George 220, James 216, John 8, 115, 148, 178, Jonathan 89, Nelson 160, 167, Robert 54, 57, 69, 70, 101, 110, 116, Samuel 129, Thomas 57, Vincent 83, William H. 166, 174
Foushee, William 148
Fout, Ann 267, Henry 213, 250, 263, Joseph T. 264, Margaret 213, Rebecca 263, Susan Ann 250

Fovre, Samuel 286
Fowler, James 164
Fox, Charles 245,
  William 200, 206,
  226
Foy, Mary 156
Frailey, George 208
Fraker, John 15,
  Michl 15
Fraley, George 233,
  William 147
Fraly, Eliza 233
Frame, John 274
Franck, Walter 167
Frank, Adam 109,
  Polly 74
Franklin, James 90,
  James D. 237,
  Mary Ann 237,
  Mary Elizabeth
  237, Moses 220,
  237, Nancy 220,
  Richard 158
Franks, Edward 171,
  Henry 130, 171,
  177, 185, 195, 269,
  James 163, Julian
  185, Kitty 130,
  Louisa C. 246,
  Nancy 171, Samuel
  279, Sarah Ann
  269, Strother
  195, William 44,
  76
Frasher, John H.
  283, Noah 192
Fravel, Benjamin
  215
Frazier, Amy 12,
  Hannah 59, John
  93, John W. 265,
  Robert 228, 269
Frear, Jacob 100
Fred, Rebecca 47
Frederick, Jacob
  84, John 30, 179,
  Rachal 84, Rachel

Frederick (continued)
  224
Freeman, Alfred
  267, Benjamin 26,
  Elizabeth 21,
  Mary 17, William
  21, Wm 17
Frees, Margaret 57,
  Martin 57, 232
Freestone, Daniel
  3, 5
Freeze, Catherine
  55, Daniel 64,
  Jacob 240, Martin
  55, Michael 240
Freize, Michael 44
French, Ann 165,
  Hanson 254,
  Hester 144,
  Polley 51, Walter
  144
Frenger, John 235
Fricklen, James G.
  142
Fridley, Henry 50
Friedley, Sarah 181
Friedly, Eliza 181,
  Henry 181
Fries, David 90,
  93, 98, 121, 150,
  220, 260,
  Elizabeth 220,
  276, George 251,
  266, George Y.
  264, 268, 276,
  Jacob 228, Josiah
  285, 286, Martin
  213, Mary Ann
  260, Michael 133,
  179, Samuel 241,
  William 268
Friese, Margaret
  266
Friez, Elizabeth
  240, George 240,
  Rachel 240
Frieze, Catharine

Frieze (continued)
179, 240, David
39, Mary 133
Frigg, Sarah 151,
Thomas 151
Frigger, James 107
Frise, Josiah 255
Froman, Hanah 48
Frost, Amos 69,
Elizabeth 114,
Hannah B. 69,
John 125, Sarah
132
Frumm, Catharine
26, William 26
Frure, Catherine 55
Fry, Anna 6,
Benjamin 6, 255,
276, Christopher
4, Daniel 28,
David 5, Druzilla
223, Edward H.
185, Elizabeth
166, George Michel
51, Henry R. 274,
Isaac 66, James
157, John 64, 76,
136, Joseph 75,
223, Judith 238,
Mary 4, 14,
Rachel 212,
Rebecca 166,
Rhoda 82, Sarah
5, William E. 270
Fryar, Sarah 14
Frye, Benjamin 10,
47, 104, 124, 233,
259, Eli J. 262,
263, Elizabeth
85, 104, 262,
Emily J. A. 270,
Isaac 104, 231,
Isaac L. 259,
Jacob 213, Jesse
P. 196, Joseph
4, 14, 210, 222,
243, Juliet B.

Frye (continued)
258, Margaret Ann
243, Mary 47,
Mary M. L. 259,
Nancy 179, Peter
179, Rachael 85,
Rachel 247, Sarah
104, Thomas 47
Fryer, Simeon 25
Fulcamore, Unitry
50
Fulk, Jacob 12,
Mary 12
Fulkerson, John
213, 268, Lewis
91, Mary Jane
268, William 102
Fulkeson, Betsy Ann
213, John 12,
Lewis 103
Fuller, Ann 70,
Daniel 88,
Elizabeth 8,
Elizabeth Ann 238,
Farland 183,
James 253
Funcke, John 114
Funk, Christopher
235, David 125,
John 6, Michael
20, Peter 40, 44,
Susan 179
Funkhouser, Anthony
278, 285, Margaret
Ann 269, Maria E.
285, Martin 196,
269, 286, Mary C.
286
Funston, Frances
156, Oliver 156,
Sarah Y. 185
Furgason, Edward
253
Furgeson, George
264
Furman, Agus T. 2
Furr, Catherine

334

Furr (continued) 256, Charles 284, Elizabeth Jane 257, Hannah 99, Isaac 256, Jesse 153, Johnson 227, Julia Ann 251, Newton 257, Thomas 46
Fussell, Charles 86
Fyst, George 147, 213, 242, 257
Gadisly, Margaret J. 249
Gainer, Mary 169
Gaines, Margaret 164
Gains, Absalom 16, Fanny 104, James 104, Mary P. 211
Galino, Joseph 250
Gallaher, Nelson 283
Gallennoe, Joseph 51
Galleno, Joseph 89
Gamble, James 197, Joseph 122
Games, John 144
Gander, David 156, Eve 58, George 102, Jacob 43, 47, 85, John 149, 245
Gannang, Christian 103
Gano, Daniel 238
Gant, Eliza Ann 185, John 110, 185, 222
Gantt, Matilda 222
Gantz, Catharine 36, George William 243, Jacob 93
Gantze, Mary I. 212
Garban, Matthew 216
Gard, John 70

Gardener, William 207
Gardiner, George 219, James 259, Mary 64, Sarah Ann 219, William 254
Gardner, Absalem 64, George 22, 36, 213, 268, Hatch Dent 178, Isaac R. 108, 143, 153, Jacob 71, James D. 112, James John 61, John 144, 201, John P. 233, Martha J. 208, Mary 258, Matilda 213, Nancy 36, 233, 270, Samuel 138, William 36, 252
Garman, Jacob 96, 104, Margaretta 104, Sophia 134
Garmong, Christian 55, Emanuel 214, Nancy 103, Squire 214, Susannah 55, William 102
Garner, Henry 11, Jeremiah 1, 44, Mary 11, Rhoda 144, Sampson 29, William 59, 74, Zachariah 145
Garnet, Elizabeth 57, Martin 57
Garnett, Ann 57, Martin 13, 57
Garrecht, Jacob 172
Garret, Henry 32, John 5, Luke 85
Garrett, Abraham 138, 244, 248, 267, Alfred 157, David

Garrett (continued)
85, Elizabeth
163, 218, 267,
George 84, Hannah
137, 248, Henry
90, Isaac 283,
Jacob 143, 212,
235, Jane 231,
John 180, Judith
90, Laurence 90,
Lawrence 273,
Leah 21, Luke
21, Mahaly 212,
Margaret 283,
Mary 21, 32, 143,
235, Matilda 218,
Nancy 84
Garrison, Ephraim
26, Evelina 184,
Frances E. 208,
George W. 194,
Jane 214, Levi
225, Mary Ann
181, Mildred 26,
Moses 181, 214,
Nancy 173,
Nehemiah 45,
Salley E. 172,
Thomas 34,
William 128, 173
Garton, Monroe C.
186
Garven, Mariah 192,
Samuel 225
Garvin, James 192
Gassaway, Polly 29,
Thos 13
Gatewood, Penelope
122, Wright 162,
204
Gauge, Sarah 126
Gaugh, Sarah 126
Gaunder, Mary 43,
Peter 43
Gaunt, Elizabeth
58, 73, Fanny 76,
John 56, 58,

Gaunt (continued)
Martin 73, 76, 81,
83, Mary 83,
Willis 81
Gause, Lydia Frances
253
Gaw, Margaret 199
Gawthrop, Isabella
63, Rachel 87
Gay, James P. 283
George, Elizabeth B.
158, James W.
286, Jane D. 232,
Joseph 138, Lewis
160, Rebecca C.
263, William 72,
158
Gerely, Ann 102,
John 102
Gerley, Ann 21,
John 21
Gibbens, Cornelius
123, Jacob 219
Gibbins, Charles W.
254, Hamilton
218, Hiram 207,
Jacob 54, 59, 218,
Rachel L. 219,
William 109
Gibbons, Ann M.
209, Charles W.
241, Eliza 249,
Emily 266, Jacob
108, 142, John
41, John L. 165,
Lydy 59, Mary A.
257, Sarah J.
262, Susannah
108, William 219,
233, William J.
262
Gibbs, James 226,
Mary 205, William
205
Gibson, Aaron 97,
Elizabeth 48,
Emily Jane 262,

Gibson (continued)
  Hamilton L. 247, 250, 262, James 234, John 101, 172, John A. 282, Jonathan 96, Lydia A. 250, Margaret A. 227, Sarah 102, Sarah M. 187, Susan Mary 234
Giffen, Kitty 141
Giffin, Anna 97, Bartholomew 277, James 164, 250, 252, Jane 96, 250, John 46, 192, 236, 255, Margaret 70, Samuel 144, 159, 257, Sarah 192, 236, William 70, 96, 97, 104, 141, 159
Gilbert, Edward 207, Edwd 114, Nancy 200, Youel 61
Gilham, Eliza 157, Ezekiel 97, Hannah 149, Levy Kerr 103, Lucy 166, Maria 180, Martha 119, 157, Mary 34, Peter 34, 155, William 35
Gilkeson, James 254, James D. 118, John 106, 212, 220, 225, John B. 273, Lucy J. 270, Nancy 81, Peggy 19, Polly 45, Sarah 81, Sarah V. 212, William 106,

Gilkeson (continued)
  106, William D. 216, 254, 262, 266, 270
Gilkison, Martha 100, Sarah 106
Gill, Cassandra 154, Catharine 192, Jane 210, John 154, Mordecai 59, Nancy 194, Nathaniel 135, Robert 218, 249, William F. 135
Gilles, John 18
Gilpen, Sanford 219
Gilpin, Edward 39, James 39, Sanford 195
Ginnis, John 6, John W. 6
Glaise, Catharine 283
Glaiz, Solomon 283
Glaize, George 268, Henry 137, 271, Joanna Margaret 271, Julia Ann 259, Sampson 194
Glascock, Joseph 71
Glass, Benjamin 129, Eliza W. 150, Elizabeth 211, J. M. 185, James M. 205, 209, James V. 178, 211, Joseph 100, Mary Ann 247, Robert 2, Robert D. 45, 84, Robert J. 251, 264, Ruth 20, Sarah 2, Sarah Elizabeth 205, Sidney O. 209, Susan 251, Thomas 211

Glasscock, Aaron B.
164, Asa 180,
Bailey R. 202,
Charlotte 201,
Eliza 140, French
F. 95, Gregory
95, Hiram 188,
Jesse 19, John
221, Kemp 201,
Kitty 180, Lydia
122, Mary 23,
Mary Ann 188,
Peter 221,
Rebeccah 109,
Sarah 95, Silas
140, Travis 57,
180, William 109
Glassford, Christian
O. 260
Glays, Solomon 259
Glaze, Joanna 194,
Simpson 155,
Solomon 170, 240
Glen, John 281,
Joseph 281,
Mathew 1
Glenhomes, Ann E.
284
Glenn, Eliza J.
274, Frances 85,
Frederick H. 274
Glover, Asher M.
106, Lewis 194,
196, 225
Gloyd, William 87
Goar, Tasie 15
Goasscock, William
122
Gobin, Hugh 59,
Jane 59
Gobins, Margaret 90
Godman, Asa 166,
Julius 135
Goff, Elizabeth 31,
Hannah 32, John
32, 74, Margaret
74, William 103

Goings, Bazell 169
Gold, Daniel 120,
178, 194, 219, 241,
James 133, Mary
154, William H.
271
Goldsberry, Benjamin
89
Goldsborough,
Lucretia Jane 163,
Robert 163
Good, Anna 117,
Elizabeth 58,
Felix 58, 67, 117,
142, 250, 262,
George 90,
Harriet 250,
Jacob 189,
Judith 19,
Margaret 67,
Peter 19, 194,
202, Rebecca
262, Sarah 103,
Thornton 177
Goodekunts, Margaret
17
Gooding, William H.
222
Goodnight, Betsy
42, Christopher
142, John 42
Goodrich, Joel 109
Goodycuntz, Mary 35
Goodykuns, George
35
Goodykuntz,
Catharine 49,
Daniel 49
Goose, George 11
Goran, George R.
278
Gorden, Arthur 8,
John 6
Gordon, Elizabeth
91, Emily 198,
Francis 5, 195,
198, George 247,

Gordon (continued)
  Hanson 243,
  Harison 242, John
  152, 173, John W.
  101, Joseph 46,
  285, Lydia 152,
  Marsh L. 187,
  Mary 195, 269,
  Matilda Ann
  101, Noah L. 219,
  Patrick 91,
  Philip 195,
  Thomas G. 217
Gore, Frederick J.
  270, Joshua 213,
  Mahlon 274
Gorley, Mary 21
Goss, Martin 112,
  227, Mary Ann 227
Gosset, William 29
Gossett, Abner 7,
  18, William 18,
  46
Gosson, William 53
Gough, John 149,
  John M. 244,
  William 48
Gourley, Jonathan
  242
Gourly, Thomas 143
Grady, Mary 13, 16,
  Michael 16
Graff, Sebastian
  109
Grafflin, Jacob W.
  239
Graham, Arthur 64,
  James 47, Jenny
  3, Leana 230,
  Patty 35, Rebecca
  58, Samuel 22,
  Thos 12, William
  168, 242, Wm 209
Grammer, John 135
Grandstaff, Milton
  M. 270
Grant, Caroline F.

Grant (continued)
  234, David 114,
  Elizabeth 281,
  Even 110, Griffin
  210, Henry 209,
  226, Isaac 81,
  James 246, John
  234, Malinda 281,
  Nancy 203, Sarah
  M. 249, Stewart
  249
Grantham, James
  152, 167
Grapes, Abraham 51,
  Barbara 51, David
  10, Sarah 69,
  Solomon 30
Grases, Catharine
  149
Graves, Charles 62,
  95, Elizabeth
  153, George W.
  285, Jacob 69,
  Jane 62, John
  14, 139, Joseph
  110, Mary 14, 31,
  95, Philip 31,
  Sarah 110,
  Susan 139, Thomas
  215, William 99
Gray, Abner 106,
  253, Agnes 78,
  Cyrus 11, Edward
  79, Elisha 115,
  George 250,
  Hammans 146,
  Hannamus 198,
  Hannoms 106,
  Hiram 139, Isaac
  169, James 78,
  81, 105, Jane 81,
  John 8, Joseph
  69, Joseph G.
  205, Joseph V.
  130, Margaret
  198, Rebecca 15,
  Robert 29, 150,

Gray (continued)
  Sarah 79, Susanna 62, Sussanah 69, Tacey 62, Thomas 14, 59, Willey Ann 59, William 33, 146, Zebedee 158
Grear, William 133
Green, A. W. 195, Alfred 207, Alvernon H. 249, Ann 2, Augustine 57, Austin 82, Betsy 207, Caroline 210, Charles 247, Charles H. 229, Delila 277, Elizabeth 89, 137, Emily A. 222, George 18, Hannah 98, James 23, 27, 55, 222, Jesse 136, John 33, 41, 89, 98, John L. 262, John S. 241, John Shac. 271, Julia Ann 195, Martha 241, Mary 82, 186, Mary J. 271, R. B. 234, Richard 137, Sally 27, Sally B. 183, William 53, 186, 195, 210, 215
Greenhulgh, John 226
Greenlee, David 135, Elizabeth 37
Greenway, James 205, Matilda 205
Greenwood, Harley 213
Greeny, Elizabeth 135
Greger, Charles L.

Greger (continued)
  P. 283
Gregg, John C. 226
Gregorey, Presley 112, Scinty 112
Gregory, John 103, Louisa 169, Susan 103
Grey, Mary 246
Greyson, Nancy 262
Grice, George 67, James 97
Grier, Sophia 136
Griffen, Rachel 44, Samuel 16
Griffin, Edward 44, Elizabeth 144, 183, George 24, 150, George H. 263, George M. 235, Levy 150
Griffis, William 15
Griffith, Aaron H. 197, Elijah 38, James H. 248, 282, John 143, 163, 169, Mary 2, 13, Priscilla 22, Samuel 38, 152, Sarah C. 275
Griffiths, David 22
Griffy, Elizabeth 208, John 98, Sarah 98
Grifiths, Ann Maria 21, David 21
Grigg, Mahlon S. 167
Griggs, Ann 71, George 259, James 177, Susanna 71
Griggsby, Dosie 19, Edmond N. 155, Elizabeth 180, Henry N. 218, Lucinda 144, Redmon 144

Grigsby, Edmund N. 147, Jesse 19, John 22, 23, 34, Nancy 54, Redmond 53, William 54
Grim, Arthur F. 230, Catharine Susan 222, Cetrin 108, Charles 106, Daniel 152, 206, Emily June 269, George 4, 13, George W. 196, 222, Henry 261, Jacob 269, John 106, 108, 121, 135, 151, 152, 176, 234, 244, 253, 273, 276, 279, John W. 238, 282, Julia Ann 135, Levi T. 268, Liles 279, Martha 273, Mary Ann 151, Mary E. 244, Noah 181, Sarah 106, 276, Simon 176, Zachariah M. 265
Grimes, Jane 23, John 268, Robert 51, Thomas 17, William 70, 157
Grinnell, Eliza 195
Grosman, Dorcas 77, Mary 24, Simon 24
Gross, Mary Jane 273, Wm 273
Grotts, Agnes M. 220
Grove, Abraham 62, 134, 174, 214, 285, Abram 284, Adam 11, 157, 173, Alcinda 284, Ann Elizabeth 233, Arianna 172,

Grove (continued) Catharine 62, 189, Catherine A. 275, Daniel 101, David 203, Elijah 131, Elizabeth 134, 232, Elizabeth A. 238, Eve 217, Fanny 143, G. G. 236, George A. 269, Henry 25, 161, 189, 214, 231, 232, 241, 243, Henry L. 171, Jacob 12, 143, 156, 169, 174, John 25, 134, 169, 172, 173, 178, 188, 217, 263, John W. 93, 173, 192, 265, Margaret 254, 263, Margaret C. 265, Marrander 285, Martha Jane 285, Mary 156, 157, Mary Ann 188, Nancy 231, Philip 61, Samuel 240, Sarah 12, 226, 258, Sarah H. 243, Sophia 161, William 235, 248, William H. 192, 227, William S. 238
Groves, Adam 117, Anna 16, Cathrene 129, David 32, 123, 182, Ezra 75, George W. 222, Henry 12, 104, 116, Isaac 116, Jacob 129, James 141, John 12, 41, 45, 54, Michael 4, Peggy 54, Peter 101,

Groves (continued)
Philip 276,
Ruth 75, Soloman 19, Susanah 45, William 117, 125, 183
Grubb, A. J. 252, Franklin 259, Walter B. 265
Grubbs, Charles 82, 260, Daniel 6, David 116, 123, Eleanor 157, Eli 7, Eliza 102, George W. 245, Humphrey 15, John 101, Justinian 60, Pailey 51, Rachel 123, Samuel 157, 211, Sarah 60, 101, Thomas 22, 60, 102, 107, 108, 122, 198, Thornburgh 153, Westley 123, William 29, 107
Gruber, Adam 116, John 160
Grubs, Anna 47, Daniel 14, 47, Elizabeth 6, Humphry 6, John 99, Samuel 140, 158, Seatta 189, Sidney 164, Virginia 136
Gryer, John S. 255
Guard, Evelina 241, George 235, 241, 247, Henry 147, 173, 180, John 83, Polly 179, Rebecca 247
Gumby, John 104
Gunnell, Catharine A. 171, J. H.

Gunnell (continued) 271
Gut, Peter 19
Guthridge, John 190
Guy, Hezekiah 65
Guyer, Charles L. P. 283, Elizabeth 272, Margaret 246, Mary Ann 264
Gyer, Ishmael 205, Mary 205
Haas, Hannaretta 252, John 95, 122
Habron, George 96, Matthew 88
Haburn, Mandly 88, Mary Ann 88
Hackley, Fanny 134, Jefferson 161, John 133, Samuel J. 210
Hackney, Aaron H. 236, 251, Hannah S. 236, Harriet 218, James 63, Joseph 152, Joseph B. 224, 232, 265, Joseph W. 187, Lydia 147, Robert B. 253
Haddock, John 50
Haddox, Enoch 51, 65, John 45, 51, John R. 194, William 45, 63
Hage, Mary 10
Hailton, Rachel 117
Haines, Abraham 165, Aquilla 170, 174, Aquilla I. 152, Aquilla J. 256, Elizabeth 170, Ellis 165, James Wm 280, Jesse 103, 117, 123, 221,

Haines (continued)
John 170,
Jonathan H. 270,
Martha T. 256,
Mary 271, Nathan
94, 231, Noah 49,
Rachel 165,
Thornton 160, 161,
165, Vincent 96,
William G. 203
Hainey, Elijah 281,
Jinny 28, Mary
Ann 209, Robert
165
Hains, A. J. 271
Hainy, Charles 122
Hair, Joseph 38
Haire, Joseph 172,
Mary Ann 172
Halbert, John 143,
Sarah 29, Thomas
38, 50
Hale, Elizabeth
Frances 155,
George 155, Lewis
W. 276, Mariah S.
202, Michael 67,
Samuel 77
Haley, Thomas 104
Hall, Benjamin 76,
Bennet 95,
Bennett 123, 125,
Edward 69, Elisha
I. 31, Eliza
231, Elizabeth
76, 95, 109, 177,
Hannah 45, 125,
146, Henry 122,
James 140, James
B 154, 156, James
M. 208, John W.
223, Joseph 66,
74, Marquis. D. F.
143, Mary E. B.
268, Nancy 66,
Priscilla 96,
Robert 231,

Hall (continued)
Sarah 156,
Susanna 74,
Thomas 96, 146,
William 140
Haller, Thomas 2
Halley, John 66
Haltaman, David 219
Halvey, Hugh 48
Ham, Peter 71
Hamaker, Henry 232
Hambaugh, Adam 94
Hamilton, Ann 163,
Ann Maria 202,
Elizabeth 284,
George 175, Henry
85, John 94, 163,
279, John R. 280,
Joseph D. 247,
Lucinda 260, Lucy
E. 228, Mary
143, Mary Eliza
255, Matilda J.
280, Robert 284,
Robert W. 109,
Sarah 94, Sarah
A. 212, Thomas
89, 143, 160,
Whiting 218,
William 116, 150,
212, 228
Hammack, Daniel S.
176, 179, Jacob
137, Samuel S.
166
Hammick, Charlotte
186, James 46,
186
Hammock, Ann 91,
Elizabeth M. 229,
John 229, Mary
Ann 179, Rudolph
207, William E.
248
Hammond, George W.
229, 265, 281,
James 25

Hampton, Joseph 59, 117, Margaret 66, Mary 117
Hamrel, Christian 36
Hamrick, James 107, John 73
Hamson, James 49, Mary 49
Hamway, Patrick 32, 33
Hanagan, Andrew 177
Hancher, Benjamin 87, David 54, 59, 64, Elizabeth 87, Hannah 118, Hiram 215, James W. 182, Jenny 53, John 135, Joseph 213, Lydia 46, Mary 182, Nicholas 118, Smith 150, Thomas 135, 181, William 45, 87, 132
Hancock, Elizabeth 127, George 126, John H. 126, Nancy D. 126
Hand, Elizabeth 192, Nancy 13, Thomas W. 196, William 42
Handle, Elizabeth 159, John 80, Nicholas 72, 92, 127, 159, 175, Rosanna 92, Sarah 72
Haney, Elizabeth 85, Robert 92, Sidney 262
Hangfield, Hannah 81
Hankins, Amos 30, Asa 29, 36,

Hankins (continued) Winney 67
Hannan, Elizabeth 56, John 56, Mathias 56
Hannin, Emily 250
Hannings, Mariann 61
Hannon, Mary 33
Hannum, Elizabeth 117, Margaret 141, Peter 170, Thomas 117, 141
Hannun, Ann 95, Thomas 95
Hansall, George 125
Hansbrough, Elijah 64, French 30, John 101
Hansecker, Thomas 52
Hansel, Catharine 123, George 94, 123, 154, Joseph 154, Susannah 94
Hansell, Barbarah 110, George 110, 116, 128, 143, 158, John 108, 115, 163, Margaret 128, Michael 163, Sarah 143
Hanshaw, Abner 193, Barton 193, 208, Hannah 77, John 245, 248, Nicholas 18, Sarah 45, Thomas 65, 77
Hanum, James 159
Harbert, George 88, John 96, Margaret 119
Hardacre, Benjamin 66
Harden, George 142, James G. 96, Susanna 142

Hardesty, Frances M.
210, Lucinda 214,
Richd 114
Hardgrove, Pollard
43
Hardin, George 160,
Nancy 160,
Richard 142
Harding, Nancy 64,
William 198
Hardy, Charles 284,
Joanna 256, John
259, Samuel 96,
267
Harfeldt, John 90
Hargrave, Elizabeth
155, William 155
Harkins, Daniel 34,
Diana 34, John
155
Harman, Geprge 22,
Jacob 16, Mathias
18, Peggy 18
Harmon, John 190,
Simon 171,
Solomon S. 188
Harper, Elizabeth
107, George H.
201, Joel T. 140,
John 149, Mark
17, 44, 69, Mary
7, Rachel 104,
Thos 7, William
16
Harrel, Anna 85,
Christian 36,
Mary 85
Harrell, Catherine
127, Lettice 54,
Nathan 54, Simon
112, William 89,
100
Harris, Benjamin
114, 141, Gabriel
143, Gabriel C.
278, Henry 147,
James 82, 194,

Harris (continued)
James W. 228,
Jane I. 141, John
33, 155, Julia A.
229, Lucinda B.
147, Rebecca 9,
Rebecca B. 114,
Sarah E. 278,
Sutton I. 166,
William B. 247
Harrison, Ann S.
184, Asaneth 190,
Benjamin 110,
Frances 38,
Frances B. 182,
George 44, George
D. 187, 207,
Isaac 112, 126,
160, 169, 190,
Jane 44, John
88, 243, Lydy
112, Mary Jane
286, Nancy 169,
Robert 155, 279,
286, Saml 112,
Sarah 160
Harry, David 89,
93, 253, James
97, Nancy 89,
Rachel 16, Ruth
253
Harsh, Joseph 14
Harsha, James 23
Harshe, Thomas 14
Hart, Adam 139,
183, 226,
Alexander 68, Ann
89, 111, Catharine
71, Daniel 35,
Edwin 214, Eliza
226, James 63,
Samuel 12, 89,
Sarah 234, Sarah
Matilda 250,
Susanah 276, Tacy
270, Vance 111,
William 250, 251,

Hartley, Mary W. 280, Philip 233
Hartman, Eliza 199, Lewis P. 254, Mary G. 254, Peter 170
Hartsock, Daniel 261
Harvey, Gideon 131, Rachel Cassandra 60, Thomas B. 261, William 60
Harvy, Thomas B. 147, 176
Hass, Conrad 122, 151, Eve Ann 122, Hannah 216, Mary 215, Peggy 151
Hastings, Elizabeth 162, Joel 123, 125, John 150, 162, Mary 90, 150, William 90
Hathaway, James 12, 87, Mildred Jane 207
Hatt, George 24, Peter 24
Hatton, Richard 192
Hauvermale, Elizabeth 24
Havely, William 45
Haverstick, Henry 237
Havey, Mary 75
Hawes, Susannah 38
Hawk, Mary A. 256, Michael 181, 256
Hawkes, Elijah 31
Hawkins, Ann 254, Charles 276, Elizabeth 199, George W. 279, John 96, 199, Lucinda 192, Simon 116

Hawley, James 81, Jeremiah 179, William 179
Hawthorn, John B. 250
Hawvermale, Rebeccah 24
Haxall, Richard B. 193
Hay, Isaac H. 265, James 120
Haycock, James W. 284
Hayes, David 49, Mary 166
Hayhurst, Cuthbert 14
Haymaker, Adam 11, 23, 196, Catharine 11, Hannah 173, Henry 61, 70, Michael 164, 173, Sarah 196
Haynes, John 115
Hayney, John 7
Haynie, Ann M. 218, John 52, Margaret 52, Maria 161, Robert 91, Sally B. 28, William R. 217
Hays, Eliza 204, Elizabeth 138, Ruth 99, Samuel 166
Hayward, David 218
Hazelwood, Mary 6, Robert 6
Headley, Newton 159, 190, Rebecca 116, William 65, 142, 169, Winneford 65
Headly, Lucinda 110, Newton 110, Polly 49, William 49

Heafer, John 27
Heaper, John 40
Hearle, William 207
Heberling, John 66
Heck, Isaac 132,
   133, 179, 185,
   Joseph 82, 201,
   Susan 244
Heckathorn,
   Christian 55
Heckerthorn, Daniel
   40
Heckethorn,
   Elizabeth 40
Hedges, Chaplin S.
   215, Edward 131,
   Elizabeth 64,
   John 64, Joseph
   64
Heel, John 152
Hefflebower, Ann
   199, George 203,
   Samuel 186
Heffloebower, Daniel
   203, Nancy 203
Heflebower, Daniel
   157
Heflin, Thomas 256
Heide, John 16
Heinzalmann,
   Ludovicus 244
Heinzman, Andrew
   142
Heironemus, Andrew
   H. 237
Heironimus, Andrew
   171, Camallias H.
   259, Camellus H.
   272, Catherine Ann
   272, Eliza 259,
   Evalina M. 235,
   Frederick 228,
   Henry 195, Henry
   N. 231, Jacob
   80, 226, Jacob P.
   235, John 264,
   John C. 221,

Heironimus
   (continued)
   221, Mary 195,
   256, Overton F.
   213, Sarah Ann
   256
Heiskell, Isaac 41,
   Isaac N. 273,
   John 42, 65, 111,
   163, Otho W. 234
Heist, John S. 234,
   282, William H.
   282
Helm, Ann Meredith
   89, Benjamin 99,
   120, Catharine
   199, Frances 70,
   Harriet S. 115,
   Helen M. 156,
   Mary Ann 62, Mary
   Gibbs 12,
   Meredith 15, 31,
   203, Peggy 31,
   Presley N. 213,
   Thomas 11, 15,
   William T. 151,
   171
Helpbringer, Dorothy
   61, Elizabeth
   152, John 206,
   223, Mary Ann
   223, Michael 61,
   77
Helpenstine, Henry
   18
Helphenstine, Peter
   4
Helphenston, William
   9
Helphinstine, Peter
   15
Helzel, Charles 8,
   12
Hemelwright,
   Catharine 283,
   Elizabeth 181,
   John 283

Hemmelright,
  Elizabeth A. 248,
  John 236
Henderson, Armistead
  Mason 251, Ruth
  2, Sarah 50,
  Sarah J. 282,
  Susan Anna 251,
  Uphamy 29,
  William 29, 50,
Hendly, Sarah 26
Hendren, Edward 90,
  John H. 56,
  Samuel O. 63,
  William D. 39
Hendrick, Job S.
  145
Hendricks, Job S.
  133
Hendron, Robert 188
Hendry, William 13,
  14
Hening, Ann 228,
  David 77, 129,
  219, 228, Isabella
  51, Jane Margaret
  219, John 89,
  151, Peter E.
  268, Robt 51,
  William 211, 212,
  221
Henning, David W.
  279, Elizabeth
  212, Joseph 262,
  Joseph R. 279,
  Lucy 129, Mary
  129, William 126
Henry, Aaron 20,
  Adam 206, Bryan
  H. 223, Elizabeth
  145, James 17,
  20, John 20, 26,
  114, 177, Martha
  206, Mary 111,
  Moses 11, Richard
  96, Susannah 26,
  William V. 178

Hensel, George 155
Hensell, Elizabeth
  205, James W.
  267, Joseph 257,
  Margaret E. 257,
  Mary 58
Henshaw, Gabriel H.
  270, Jacob 215,
  John J. 243, Levi
  208, Susan 243,
  Thomas 101,
  William D. 171
Henson, Thomas 83
Herbough, Hannah
  168
Herford, Maria 134
Herionimus, Andrew
  H. 237
Herman, Solomon 212
Heronimus, Mary 50
Herr, John 163
Herronimus, Mary
  Maria 221
Hesket, James 128
Heskett, Joseph G.
  254, Zedekiah 138
Hess, Abraham 90,
  167, Ann 10,
  Conrad 153, Nancy
  114, 225, Sarah
  90
Hesser, Amanda M.
  230, Elizabeth
  90, Emely 160,
  George 90, Mary
  I. 194, Samuel L.
  194, 230
Hessey, Edward 70
Hester, Solomon 118
Heterick, John W.
  249, Martha C.
  188, Robert 188,
  Robt. M. 251,
  Sarah H. 251
Heutchins, Susan
  210
Hewett, William 180

Hewitt, Daniel 160,
  Elizabth 160,
  William 190
Hiatt, Andrew 251,
  John 25, Lydia E.
  251
Hibbard, Elias A.
  234, Elias H. 268
Hickerson, John M.
  101
Hickerton, Daniel
  54, John 54
Hickey, David 5,
  27, Edward 35,
  Elizabeth 35
Hickle, Delilah 54,
  Elizabeth 69,
  George 69, Jacob
  98, Rebecca 98,
  Samuel 54, Tewalt
  31, 69
Hickman, Abraham
  116, Adam 15,
  Isaac 139, Jacob
  26, James 3,
  John 5, John
  Thomas 120,
  Lucretia 95,
  Margaret 22,
  Naomi 83, Peggy
  61, Rebecca B.
  138, William 42
Hickmon, Mary 15
Hicks, David 20,
  Elie 118, John
  84, 125, 138, K.
  C. 210, Kimble G.
  226, Levi 64,
  Lucy 20, Phebe
  125, Samuel 6,
  Sarah 128
Hieronimus, Andrew
  L. 159, Barbara
  10, Conrad 10,
  173, Henry 219,
  John 164, Mary
  Catharine 219

Hiett, Elizabeth
  180, John 138,
  Jonathan 233,
  Leonard 148, Mary
  Ann 208, Samuel
  P. 284, Thomas
  161, 180, 208,
  William 281
Higgins, Charles
  103, Elizabeth
  112, Hannah 198,
  James 100, 107,
  John I. 188,
  Thomas 100,
  William 103,
  198, Wm 112
High, Jacob 113
Highby, John 76,
  Nancy 76
Highley, Delilah
  259
Higins, John 240,
  Nancy 240
Hill, Adam 40,
  George 87, Naomi
  215, Rees 189,
  William 69
Hilliard, Jacob 49,
  252, 266, Mary Ann
  266
Hilling, Nathaniel
  26, William 80
Hillman, Emily Susan
  268, Simeon 268
Hills, William 11
Himelright, Henry
  166, John 143
Himmelwright, Henry
  256, John 253,
  Mary Jane 253
Hinckle, Adam 241,
  Daniel 244
Hiner, Herbert 198
Hines, Edward 211,
  243
Hingle, Adam 24,
  87, Betsy 87

Hinkins, Peter 239
Hinkle, Adam 122, 173, Mary 122, Sarah 173, Susyan 241
Hiskett, Abraham 125
Hite, Ann M. 173, C. B. 238, Hugh H. 234, 238, 279, Isaac 178, Isaac F. 191, Jacob 146, 222, 225, James M. 279, John 123, Joseph 27, Lucy E. 248, Mary Ann 128, Mary Eltinge 177, Mathias 128, Matilda M. 238, Michael H. 228, P. E. L. 234, Philip A. 224, 267, Rebecca G. 196, Sarah C. M. 221, Walker M. 221
Hittle, Lydia 114
Hix, David 277
Hobson, Andrew 252
Hockinsmith, John S. 214
Hockman, Benjamin 43
Hockstain, Jacob 60
Hodge, Archibald A. 272, Eliza 265, James 139, 142, 154, Mary 158, Moses 237, Robert 6, 158
Hodgen, Phebe 15
Hodges, John 119, Mary Jane 271
Hodgkins, William B. 161
Hodgson, Abner 24,

Hodgson (continued) 151, 261, 266, Delilah Ann 157, Elijah 204, Eliza Ann 216, Elizabeth 24, 151, Jane 97, 273, John 24, 28, 29, 68, 97, 273, Mary 68, Mary Ann 266, Nicholas 8, 22, Rebecca 25, Rob 124, Robert 9, 26, 29, 169, 170, 216, 233, Ruth 29
Hodson, Charles W. 277, Elizabeth 233, Henry 230, Margaret 124, William 243
Hoeman, Michael 79
Hoff, Cornelius 200, Elizabeth 203, Isaac 175, John 13, 239, Joseph 212, Lewis 65, Mary 203, Mary Ann 212, Morgan 17, Nancy 17
Hoffman, Benjamin 257, Henry 188, Jacob 34, 144, 270, Maria 166, Mary Ann 107, Sarah 48, William 180
Hog, Ann 2
Hogain, John 56
Hogan, Mary 250, Samuel 17, William 43
Hogans, Mary 2
Hoge, Arabella 67, Eliza 124, Hannah 91, Moses 55, Solomon 67,

Hoge (continued)
　William 11, 91,
　Wm 10
Hogland, James 51
Hoie, Barbara 4
Holbert, Hannah 50
Holden, Margaret 57
Holdenbary, William 18
Holdenby, Nancy 18
Holland, Archibald 12, 91, Deborah 12, Edward 27, Eleanor 159, James 204, John 132, 159, 203, Sarah 132
Hollandshead, Elizabeth 107, John 107, Thomas 93
Holleway, Thomas 64
Holliday, Elizabeth B. 272, Elizabeth S. 279, James W. 67, John 71, R. B. 234, Richard 91, 104, Richard John McKim 159, Robert B. 244, Sarah 91, William 185, 197, William D. 154, 176, 247, Wm D. 184
Hollingshead, Elizabeth 180, Richard 113
Hollingshedd, Polly 83
Hollingsworth, David 202, Eleanor 202, Eliza 137, Hannah 150, Hester 50, Isaac 98, 137, 186, 197, 202, 224, Isaac Milton 255, Jane 98, Joseph

Hollingsworth (continued) 29, Lydia Ann 224, Mary P. 197, Robert 50, Samuel 86, Thomas 82
Hollingworth, John 183
Hollis, Elizabeth 205, James I. 163, Thomas 239, William L. 261
Holloway, Daniel 37, Joseph 37, Mary 37
Holmes, Abigail 187, David 2, 3, 7, 114, Elizabeth 15, Hugh 15, John 44, John M. 258, Joseph 2, Margaret A. 214, Mary L. 214, Peggy 177, Polly 44, Sarah 14, 22, Will 14, William 29, William W. 187, 214
Holsclaw, Elias 78
Holt, George 8, John 240, Matilina 8
Holtsclaw, Elias 131
Holtzclaw, Henry 141
Holtzman, Augustin 213, Augustine 204, Henrietta M. 254
Holzenpeler, Benjamin 2
Homes, Alexander 34, John 177, Richard B. 164, Thomas 5
Honesty, John J.

Honesty (continued) 274
Honnold, John 24
Honnole, Jacob 24, John 24
Hood, Julia Ann 236, Louemma 274, Mary 24, Susanah 64, William 93
Hooe, Jane 50
Hook, Archibald 186, David 232, 239, David S. 267, 286, John 237, Robert 264, Samuel 137, Thomas 186, 237, William S. 271
Hooke, William 31, 37
Hooker, Hannah 46, Nancy 99, William 99
Hooper, Abraham 61, Elizabeth 61, Harriet 240, James A. 239, John 18, John R. 223, Louisa 240, Mary 51, Nicholas 141, Phebe 81, Samuel 51, Sarah A. 231
Hoover, Ann Elizabeth 201, 232, Elizabeth Ann 269, Henry 81, 253, Jacob 269, James 146, John 163, John H. 255, Jonathan 208, Mary 163, 243, Mary Ann 191, Philip 81, 191, Samuel 63
Hope, Christian 128, Emely 128,

Hope (continued) James T. 167
Hopewell, Isaac D. 256, William 153
Hopkins, John 138, Lucy Lyons 137, Mary A. 225, Samuel 218
Hopper, John 152, Joshua 169
Hoppermill, Christian 36
Horbaugh, Isaac 32
Hord, Killis 182
Horn, John 97, 243, Mary 16, Mary Ann T. 206
Hornaday, Lewis P. 193
Horner, Barbara 231, Henry 243, 277, John M. 270, Lydia 220
Horseman, David 44, 49, Elizabeth 44, Mary 49
Horton, Chloe 16, 22
Hosey, Henry 253
Hotsenpellar, Stephen 17
Hotsenpillar, Elizabth 129, Margaret 168
Hotsinbeller, Jacob 8
Hotsinpiller, Charles 198, Elizabeth 127, Joseph 127
Hotsinpillor, Christiana 4
Hotspiller, Jacob 52
Hott, Adam 31, Barbara 72, Catharine 31, 37,

Hott (continued)
　Conrad　60, 72,
　George　57, 60, 72,
　Henry　31, 37, 83,
　Jacob　264, Jacob
　F.　257,　James
　240,　John　57,
　103, 234, 258, 266,
　272,　Martha　31,
　Martin　218,
　Peter　31, 242,
　247,　Rebecca　103
Hottel, Anna　184
Hottle, Andrew 203,
　David　198, 200,
　Lucy Ann　203,
　Mahala　198,
　Rebecca　200
Hotzenpillar,
　Athlinda　270,
　Emelia 107,　John
　270, Martha　131
Hotzenpiller,
　Catharine　33, 156,
　George R.　221,
　Juliet　147,
　Margaret　135,
　Mary　230
Hotzenspillar, Mary
　88
Houghon, Henry　187
Housar, Sarah Ann
　209
House, George　120
Householder, Aquilla
　I.　279
Houseman, Elizabeth
　56, Martin　56
Houser, Frederick
　185, 221, 236,
　Frederick H.　209,
　Mary Catharine　221
Housman, Michael
　77, William　47
Housten, Jenny　34
Hove, Ann B.　55,
　Edward　55

Hover, John　167
Howard, Ametia 269,
　Ann 10,　Anthony
　96, 108, 130, 142,
　Augustus　283,
　Augustus W.　282,
　Charles 86,　Eliza
　R.　284,　Elizabeth
　96,　Eusebius D.
　243,　James　60,
　93, 128, 205, 251,
　259,　James M.
　273,　Jonathan J.
　252,　Margaret
　142,　Maria　243,
　Mary　260, Mary J.
　273,　Nancy　45,
　130,　Patrick　229,
　263, 271,　Rosanna
　205,　William　250
Howe, Elizabth 145,
　James　26,　John
　101, 145,　John C.
　121,　Mary　132
Howell, John　55,
　71, Lucresa　13
Hows, Charles　38
Howser, Frederick
　65, 175
Hoy, James　232
Hoye, Jane　175
Hoyle, Catha　13,
　Christian　16
Hubbard, Harriet
　262, Nancy　111,
　Robert　115, 262
Hubert, John C.　193
Huddle, George　33,
　Peggy　119
Hudson, Joshua　214
Huff, Elizabeth
　224, Julian　224,
　Mary 39,　Morgan
　39, Nancy　187
Huffman, Anthony
　101, Catharine 6,
　Henry 48,　Roden

353

Huffman (continued) 179
Huggins, Franklin 208, William 46, 107, 127, 132, 160
Hughes, Charles 133, Elenor 83, John 83, Mary 126, Thomas 83, William 126
Hughs, Abraham 143, Catharine 199, Charles 165, 199, Eliza 165, Frances Ann 166, Margaret 150, Nancy 143, William 150
Hulet, Charles 212, James M. 220, 222, 223, 228, 230, Jas M. 222, 230
Hull, Abraham 248, Betsy 62, Christian 88, 208, Eleanor 52, Mary 32
Humbard, Charity 254
Humble, Michael 2
Hummer, John 227, 235, Peter 33, William 224
Hummrickhouser, Barbara 8
Humphrey, Thomas L. 211
Humphries, John 2
Humpston, John 51
Humston, Jean 27, John 27, 72, 174, Strother G. 198
Hunnins, John 189
Hunsicker, Jacob 137, Peter 84
Hunsucker, Daniel 9, Margaret 9

Hunter, E. P. 208, Moses T. 92, Thomas 28
Huntsberry, Conrad 57, 91, 156, 178, Eliza 272, Elizabeth 178, Hannah 178, Henry 29, Henry B. 248, Isaac 136, 248, 272, John 173, John C. 282, Marine 156
Hupp, Daniel 226, David H. 258
Hurbough, Adam 67
Hurdle, Leonard 26
Hurford, Elizabeth 44, Isaac 108, Jesse 108, 122, John 41, 190, Joseph 44, Susan 186
Hurr, Mary 163
Hurry, James 49
Hurst, Fredk 22, James G. 171, Nathaniel 97, Peter 38, W. Fredk 18
Hurt, James 75
Huston, James M. 188
Hutchins, Francis 74, 79, Lucretia 51, Mary 79
Hutchinson, Eleazer C. 194, Elizabeth 249, Jesse 228, 249, Margaret 106, Maria 228
Hutchison, Jesse 102
Hutslar, Jacob 239, James 266, John 257
Hutsler, Catherine

Hutsler (continued)
70, Elizabeth
219, Jacob 70, 83
Hutslor, John 219
Hutton, William 18, 190
Hutzlar, Zadok 98
Hutzler, Alfred 269
Hyatt, A. F. 286, Andrew F. 267, John W. 263, Martha Jane 267, Sarah Ann 286
Hydenrich, Gregory 103
Hyland, Sarah 28
Hymes, Joseph 168
Hytt, Andrew F. 263
Iden, Catharine 232, Jonah 39, Jonathan 232, 240
Iles, Mary 2
Imswiler, Mary Ann 169
Intch, Henry R. 46
Ireland, James 52, 63, Jane 63, Leticia 82, Lucinda 83, Nancy 52, Thomas 26
Irvin, John 269
Irwin, Joseph 19, Samuel 42, William 29
Isaacs, Harriet 198
Isler, Abraham 123, Jacob 120
Ivins, Nancy 164
Jackson, Alfred C. 254, Ann 9, Ann Redman 87, Benjamin F. 270, Cornelius 228, Eliza 155, 180, Eliza Jane 254, Elizabeth 24, 220,

Jackson (continued)
280, Frances C. 254, Francis 68, George 163, Hannah 19, James 8, 10, 19, 90, Jame R. 269, 276, John 3, John F. 244, Joseph S. 232, 282, Josiah 271, Lydia 213, Margaret Ann 282, Nancy 132, Nathaniel 87, 98, Peggy 80, Richard 96, 219, 248, Ruth 80, 276, Samuel 166, Samuel A. 280, Solomon R. 111, 168, 185, 254, Susan 163, Susan C. 269, Thomas 63, 77, 132, 216, Thomas A. 203, William 88, 93, 114, William M. 225, Winifred 98
Jacob, John 139, 148
Jacobs, Baylor 93, Charity 26, Edward B. 190, 221, Francis 11, Jane 11, John 170, 171, Mary 60, Moses 23, Newman M. 229, Selonary W. 166, Thomas 166, William 2
James, Amelia 102, Benjamin 186, Catherine B. 267, Daniel 118, Henry 102, Lemuel 162, Mary Jane 249
Jameson, John 23

Jamieson, Sally 23
Jamison, Alexander 61, John 20
Janes, Matilda 131
Janney, Isaac R. 277, Jonas 215
Jarrett, Asbury 155
Jarvis, Washington 146
Jasper, William W. 239
Jay, David 5, Sarah 5
Jefferson, Benjamin W. 202, Maria L. 284
Jenkins, Abraham 92, Adam 262, Catherine 274, Edward 47, 112, 147, 217, Elizabeth 92, Flora 112, George 170, Hannah 22, Israel 44, Jacob 18, 20, 22, 33, 49, 213, John 22, 195, 201, 228, Jonathan 2, 206, Mary Ann 147, 262, Rachel 213, Rebecca 93, Russell 236, Sarah 242, Stephen 231, 274, Thomas 50, William 81, 201
Jennings, Daniel 152, 158, 164, 194, 226, Edward 5, Elizabeth 194, Isaac 17, Joanna 158, Joseph 152, Mary 5, Nancy 29, Rebecca 15, Samuel 164, Sarah

Jennings (continued) Ann 226
Jesper, Abraham 62, Mary 62
Jewell, Margaret 4, William 4, Wm 8
Jewett, Samuel 19
Jinkins, Adam 139, Belfield 108, Catherine 117, 124, Edward 117, 132, Henry 285, John 202, 216, Thomas 124, William 99, 132, 138, 204, Wm 124
Job, Charity 63, Elizabeth 106, Jacob 106, Martha 63
Jobe, John 98
John, Ashford 205, Eliza H. 192, Jesse 58, Margaret 205, Susannah 39, Thomas 192, 214
Johnson, Abraham 24, 214, Addison 235, Amos 24, 173, 195, Baldwin 14, 15, Caroline 285, David 139, David H. 279, Elizabeth 136, George 151, 271, George Reed 95, Harriet 119, 274, Humphrey R 19, Jacob 186, James L. 274, John 181, 225, 230, 235, 260, Joseph 114, 120, 183, Levi 277, Lewis 136, Mary 181, Melinda 225, Nancy 230,

Johnson (continued)
 Robert 262,
 Rosanna 95,
 Sally 17, Samuel 51, Sarah 235,
 Simon 260,
 Stephen 17, 146,
 Steven 121,
 Susanna 173,
 William 95,
 William R. 228
Johnsten, Synthia 56
Johnston, Adam 14,
 Addison 228, 234,
 Addison A. 230, 242, Amos 132, 168, 204, Atwell 82, Charles 75, Christopher 243, David 237, Eliza 219, 237,
 Elizabeth 24, 78, 132, 220, George 59, 115, 213,
 George W. 237,
 Hannah 12, 15, 165, 211, Harriet 230, Hugh 17,
 Jane 213, John 42, 77, 145, 165, 175, 195, John I. 147, Joseph 6, 176, 205, 227, Joshua 163, 173, 271, Mary 6, 25, 61, 77, 85, 107, 120, 122, Mima 81, Minty 89,
 Morgan 195, 229,
 Nancy 24, 70, 90, 129, 234, Nancy M. 204, Nimrod 90,
 Penelope 108,
 Polly 42,
 Rebecca 24,
 Robert 165,

Johnston (continued)
 Samuel 175,
 Sarah 176,
 Susanah 115,
 Susannah 120, 122,
 Sydny 120, Thomas 26, 38, 58,
 William 95, 114, 115, 187, 191
Joice, Mary 52
Joliffe, Elizabeth 16, John 70,
 Lavina E. 218,
 Selina W. 251
Jolley, Anna 166,
 Hannah M. 264,
 Landon Iden 244
Jolliffe, Amos 16, E. C. 273,
 Harriet S. 273,
 John 77, 89, 156, 180
Jolly, Alfred 240,
 Benjamin 40,
 Betsy 169,
 Catharine 40,
 Landen 166, 197,
 Landon 110,
 Louisa 236
Jones, Abraham 265,
 Alexander L. 120,
 Ann 114, Ann H. 73, Aubrey G. 272, Augustus 189, Barbara 4,
 Benj. W. 241,
 Benjamin 22, 59,
 Berryman 244,
 Beryman 209,
 Catharine 140,
 Catherine 90,
 Charles 133,
 Dolly 195, Edward 206, 221, Edward B. 38, 64, Elias 120, 171, Eliza 242, Elizabeth

Jones (continued)
138, 244, 268,
Elizabeth Ann 231,
Fielding R. 263,
Frances 64,
Frances L. 189,
Gabriel S. 148,
George 46,
Hubbard 22,
Israel 31, Jacob
31, 83, James 61,
107, 118, 143, 156,
214, 237, 282,
James W. 268, 275,
Jane 230, John
1, 2, 5, 37, 48,
51, 61, 63, 87, 90,
140, 240, John P.
241, Jonathan
134, 219, Joseph H
11, Joseph W.
276, Joshua 255,
262, Keziah 65,
Leah 172, Lewis
75, Lydia E. 282,
Margaret 195,
Maria S. 277,
Mary 110, 133,
219, 227, 259, 263,
264, 266, Nancy
51, 264, Nathan
45, 121, 172,
Polley 24, Polly
61, Rachel 82,
Rebecca 48,
Rebecca Ann 255,
Richd 113, Robert
136, 220, Robert
B. 193, Roger
128, Sally 116,
Sarah 220, Sarah
Lavinia 266,
Solomon 230,
Stephen 10, 65,
Susan E. 267,
Thomas 4, 173,
220, Tilbury 74,

Jones (continued)
William 7, 18, 46,
61, 73, William M.
139, 276, William
Mansfield 73,
Williamson P. 38,
Winney 41,
Winnyfred 47,
Zachariah 5, 114
Jonson, Stephen 95
Jordan, Charity 11,
Hirom O. 284,
Lana G. 202,
Thomas
114, 132, 165
Jorden, Fleming
283, Francis Ann
235
Jury, Abner 93,
Jesse 63
Justin, Joel I. 41
Kackley, Abraham
111, 139, Benjamin
103, Catharine
85, Catherine
111, Christena
103, Elias 78,
82, 176, Eliza 52,
Eliza J. 252,
George 78, H. T.
252, Isaac 28,
Jacob 36, 52,
171, Jonathan
110, 143, Margaret
Ann 171,
Margarett 88,
Polly 139,
Samuel 52, 85,
112, Thomas A.
267
Kackly, John 30
Kail, Mary 10,
Peter 10
Kain, Charles 50,
Henry 41, Humphry
45, James R. 155,
Molly 45

Kaler, Josiah 181
Kanara, Sarah 122
Kanester, John 98
Kannan, Polly 14
Kannon, Sarah 121, Susan 121
Karinge, George 100
Karns, William 116
Kaufman, Charles 241, Martin R. 287
Kaufmann, Michael 260
Kaufrey, John A. 104
Keach, John 11
Keahey, Elizabeth E. 196
Kean, Alsey 6, Ann 114, Elizabeth 124, James 178, 180, John 6, Joseph 238, 262, 268, Joseph W. 183, Marcus 180, Marquis 75, Nicholas 124, Richard 35, Samuel 193
Kearfoot, Margaret 128, William 109
Kearfott, Eleanor H. 188, William 188, 225
Kearnes, Edward 8
Kearns, Elisha 142, Jacob 81, 160, John 192, Lewis 205, Martha 81, Nathan 81, 185, Nathaniel 142, Philip L. 245, Phillip L. 236
Kecheval, Lydia 3
Keckley, Abraham 133, Benjamin 126, 228,

Keckley (continued) Catharine 240, Catherin 275, Elizabeth 133, Hanah 95, Jacob 120, John 95, Joseph 130, 259, Margaret Ann 228, Mary E. 272, Sarah 168
Kee, William 235
Keeding, Elizabeth 99, Joseph 194, Peter 99, 147
Keeler, Ann 245, David 223, Elizabeth 65, John 122, Joseph 157, Joseph W. 263, Jost 11, Middleton 219, Susan C. 219, William 96
Keen, Francis 135
Keenan, James 242, 243, Richard 171, Thomas 8, 64, 171
Keener, Isaac S. 244, James 266
Keeran, Eli 28, Sarah 28
Kehoe, Peter 2
Keim, John H. 241, William H. 232
Keiter, Benjamin 222, 257, George 70, George H. 267, Jacob 257, John 70, Maria 222, Rebecca Ann 237, Susannah 70
Kelknir, Jacob 251
Keller, Abraham 270, Eley 156, Elizabeth 273, 284, George 235, 283, George H.

Keller (continued)
239, 251, Henry
192, Jacob 34,
129, 156, 157, 206,
243, 273, James
195, 240, John
109, Jonathan
192, Joseph 251,
260, Liddy M.
209, Mary 8,
Mary Ann 243,
Nancy 229, 251,
Peter 57, 125,
209, 224, 229, 251,
Sarah Ann 229,
Susannah 270,
William 227, 258
Kelley, William 24,
25
Kello, John 81,
Polly 81
Kellor, Jane 42,
John 42
Kelly, John 29,
Mary 24, Nancy
74, 100
Kemp, Elizabeth 26,
Jesse 67, 116,
John 25, 26, 32,
William 25, 26
Kenan, Ann A. 282
Kendal, Betsy W. 29
Kendale, Hannah 187
Kendall, Elizabeth
5, George 24,
John 16, Ranson
53, Sarah 24,
Turner 230
Kendel, Shelton 10
Kendle, Rebecca
207, William 55
Kendrick, Benjamin
35, 93,
Christopher 128,
George 93, 237,
Hannah 85, 126,
Jacob 85, 116,

Kendrick (continued)
161, John 93,
110, 116, 169,
Mary 93,
Rebeccah 58,
Rebekah 85
Keneaster, John 80,
Nimrod D. 256
Kenester, Henry 96
Kennaford, Mary 197
Kennan, Alexander
90, Elizabeth 90,
James C. 186,
John 14, Thomas
90
Kennedy, Hugh 11,
William 12
Kenner, Winder H.
120
Kennerley, Thomas
153
Kennerly, Peter
267, Thomas 167
Kenney, Mary 216
Kennon, Fanny 118,
Jane L. 145
Kennor, Rebeccah
45, Thomas 45
Kenny, Elizabeth
202, John 202,
Joseph 43, 161
Kent, Benjamin 206
Kerby, James 65,
Joseph 181
Kercheval, Ann M.
182, Elijah 27,
53, Lewis C. 131,
Lucinda 131, Mary
C. 149, Robert C.
214, Samuel 149,
Sarah 258
Kerfoot, Catharine
116, Elizabeth
104, George L. 8,
167, John 167,
172, 199, 202, 206,
216, John B. 149,

Kerfoot (continued)
  Lucius T. 244,
  Samuel 252,
  William 104,
  172, William C.
  199
Kerfott, Eliza Ann
  192, Elizabeth
  Brady 225, Lucy
  A. 202, Mary E.
  206, Nancy 44,
  Sarah Jane 216,
  William G. 44,
  192, 194, 227
Kerin, Ann 240,
  Evelina 240,
  Timothy 258,
  William H. 232
Kern, Adam 71, 142,
  228, 245, 278,
  Anna 137, Eliza
  228, Ephraim 255,
  George 215, Henry
  34, Jacob 38,
  John 174, Marenda
  257, Margaret
  215, 258, Margaret
  C. 278, Mary
  150, Mary Ann
  213, Matilda
  142, Nicholas 51,
  137, 150, 189, 209,
  Nimrod 243,
  Philoma 245,
  Solomon 213,
  William 233,
  Zachariah 212,
  Zacharias 248, 255
Kernan, Elizabeth J.
  266
Kerney, Catherine E.
  228, Susan T. 225
Kerns, Aaron 285,
  Abner 176, Adam
  15, 211, Barry
  116, Caroline
  280, Daniel 47,

Kerns (continued)
  David 265,
  Delilah 226,
  Elihu 286, Elisha
  250, 271,
  Elizabeth 272,
  284, Emily 261,
  Fanny 271, George
  144, 242, Harriet
  200, Jacob 156,
  160, 200, 215,
  John 272, Jonas
  239, Joseph 67,
  Joshua 216,
  Margaret 100,
  Martha 286, Mary
  125, Nancy 116,
  197, Nathan 26,
  83, 105, 125, 162,
  176, 177, 187, 197,
  208, 233, 266, 284,
  Nicholas 100,
  Patrick 8, Philip
  L. 231, Rachael
  187, Rachel 149,
  Ruth 233, Sanford
  278, Sarah 162,
  211, Susan 266,
  Susanna 239,
  Thomas 261,
  Washington 250,
  William 215, 234,
  William H. 272,
  Wilson 284
Kerr, John 273,
  Mark 72,
  Rachelanne 212,
  Rebecca Jane 232,
  William 204, 213,
  218, William D.
  212, 225, 242, Wm
  232
Keyes, Charlotte
  11, George 75
Keys, Elizabeth 3,
  John 20
Kidd, Andrew 217,

Kidd (continued)
Benjamin 199,
James 171, Jane
69, Martha 87,
Olivia 44,
Richard 87
Kidwell, Amos 224,
John 197
Kigar, Augustine
128, Jacob 128
Kiger, Adam 47,
Andrew 191,
Augustin 245,
Eliza 144, Ellen
250, Emalina 150,
George 1, 150,
George N. 160,
George W. 82, 154,
171, Isaac 99,
250, Jacob 1,
Joseph W. 120,
143, 144, Mary S.
245, Patsy D. 120
Kilders, Joseph 166
Kile, Francis 118,
Isaac 156, James
77, John 139,
Levi 214, Mary
Jane 239, Nancy
277, Reuben 189,
190, 194, 239,
Sarah 77, 118,
Thomas 139,
William H. 277
Kiles, Reuben 75,
82
Killey, Winifred 29
Kime, David 165
Kimmel, William 283
Kindall, Zebidee 58
Kindle, Zebedee 55
Kindrick, Catherine
151, Samuel 151
King, Alena 100,
Aquilla 94, 113,
Benjamin 157, 168,
Elias 53, 113,

King (continued)
Jacob 257, James
V. 191, Louisa
104, Lucy 53,
Mary 113, Mary
Ann 237, Samuel
23, William 87,
William H. 30,
William W. 198
Kingery, Rebecca
270
Kingore, Amos 104,
Elizabeth 53,
John 115,
Margaret 166,
Mary 148,
Rhoda 162,
William 148, 162,
Winnifred 174, Wm
53
Kinlin, Mary Ann
166, Ransam 113,
William 21
Kinsler, John 74
Kirby, James 65,
John 40, 69,
Joseph 280, Lyda
Ann 280, William
267, Winneford 69
Kitchen, Joel 92,
Maria 280, Sally
92
Kiter, Esther 124,
George 124, Jacob
117, John 116,
124, 235
Klatz, Isaac 47
Klein, Jacob 11
Kline, Adam 12,
140, Anthony 182,
240, Anthony M.
269, Barbara 18,
Caroline 167,
Casper 12, 16,
Catharine 91,
Daniel 106, 133,
212, 243, Daniel

Kline (continued)
A. 264, Elizabeth 120, 133, Elizabeth F. 280, Fanny 165, Henry 79, Ingleheart 167, Isaac N. 201, Isabella 80, Jacob 18, 123, James R. 280, John 249, Joseph 253, 268, Joseph H. 269, Martha Ann 240, Mary Ann 243, Mary P. 182, Michael 91, 101, 120, 165, Philip 24, Saml S. 201, Samuel S. 139, 273, Simon 277, Susannah 12, 155, Vina Anne 208, William 80, William R. 276
Klotz, Isaac 229, Sarah Ann 229
Klyne, Daniel 152, Eve 63, Jacob 63, Mary Magdalene 11, Rebecca 171
Knage, John 253
Kneedle, Thomas I. 194
Kneedler, Thomas J. 230
Kneisly, James 275
Knight, Elizabeth 198, George 190, 212, 218, 230, 281, Harison 200, Harriet I. 218, James 178, 268, Margaret 45, Mary E. 230, Thomas 84, 195, 198, Westly 262,

Knight (continued)
William 45
Knip, Mary 139
Knipe, Barbary 49, Henry 49, Jacob 110
Knisell, Henry 275
Knister, John 16
Knox, Thomas F. 47
Koeler, John 99
Kohlhousen, F. W. 281, Frederick W. 286
Kountz, Lewis P. 230
Kramer, Conrad 78
Kratzer, Simon 226
Kreamer, Conrad 127
Kremble, Margaret 113
Kremer, Conrad 9, George 227, 238, 261, 280, Peter 191, Polly 169
Kreps, John 139
Krider, Adaline 255, Ann 246, Eliza Jane 234, Frederick 206, John B. 255
Krim, John 148
Krouse, John 201, Polly 155, Rosanna 201
Kuntz, Jacob 19
Kurtz, Adam 98, Nancy 38, Robert J. 278
Kuser, Barbara 2
Kyle, Frederick 48
Lacey, Johnston 61, Joseph B. 208, Lampkin 193
Lacy, Benjamin R. 208, Elizabeth 9
Ladley, Mary 106
Lafollet, Amos 224,

Lafollet (continued)
  Isaac 10,
  Margaret 259,
  William 224
Lafollett, George 46
Lahew, Spencer 42
Laing, Catharine 114, Elizabeth 218, James 114, John 218
Lair, Catharine 51, Conrad 40, Sophia 40
Lake, Albert 185, Baylis 140, James 57, Redman 70, Thomas 187, 217, 230, Willis 54
Lambden, Elijah 188
Lambert, Isaac 266, Jacob 224, Thomas 34
Lamkin, Hannah M 89
Lamp, Elizabeth 252, Goerge 28, James 281, John 94, 252, 255, Mary Ann 255, Rebecca Jane 282
Landacre, Giden 163, Gideon 137
Landakre, John 137
Landingham, Benjamin Van 33
Landrom, Thomas 114
Lane, Geo S. 184, George S. 96, 201, Martha 164, Mary N. 194, Rebecca H. 229, William 93, 143, 203
Lang, Benjamin 119, James 10, Jane 207, John 68, 157, 162, Jonathan 43, Joseph 147,

Lang (continued)
  Louisa 272, Nancy 157, Thomas 118, 162, William 175, William Simpson 21
Langham, Francis 52, Susan 182
Langley, Benja 13, Benjamin 21, 27, 47, 48, 141, 174, Curtis 21, Harriet 257, J. L. 257, Jeremiah 9, John H. 285, Joseph 13, William 21, 127, 131, 230, William C. 173
Lanham, Amasa 52, Barbara 96, Colmor 86, Dennis 42, Enos 99, George 167, Henry 42, 72, Jacob 85, Jeremiah 104, John 160, 170, Mary 104, 230, Samuel 72, 205, Susannah 42
Lantz, Henry 62
Lap, Philip 75
Lapole, Sarah 270, Sarah Jane 270
Larew, Jacob 185, James H. 286, William 274
Largen, Aaron 62
Largent, Aaron 58, 219, Jefferson 262, John 52, Lewis 52, Moses 57, Phebe 58, Sarah Jane 278, Thomas 278
Largin, Lewis 62
Larick, Catharine 275, John 113,

Larick (continued)
  John H. 275
Larrick, Asa 200,
  Barbara Ann 257,
  Casoer 105,
  Ceatte 238, Eliza
  240, Elizabeth
  141, 226,
  Frederick 67, 226,
  233, George 21,
  29, 87, 199, 238,
  Henry 141, 191,
  201, 224, 240,
  261, Isaac 68,
  Jacob 25, 56, 112,
  119, 234, 250, 264,
  266, John 264,
  John H. 283, John
  M. 246, Joseph
  113, 204, 205, 246,
  Mahaley 204,
  Margaret 261,
  Martha 191, Mary
  224, 233, Mary
  Jane 234, Mazy
  199, Pemelia 266
Larue, Jacob 15,
  John 19, John B.
  167, Phebe 11,
  Phoebe F. 167
Latham, John 86,
  124, 136, 143, 208,
  Robert 246
Latty, Agness 6,
  Joseph 6
Lauch, Simon 42
Lauck, Elizabeth
  60, Emily Caroline
  240, Jacob S.
  285, John 89,
  Lewis M. 250,
  Maria 142, Peter
  23, 112, 151,
  Saml 112, Simon
  60, Simon H. 251,
  William 108, 169,
  William C. 200

Laurence, Elizabeth
  100
Laurens, Martin
  247, Theresa M.
  247
Lautz, Maria 15
Lavael, Thomas 57
Law, John 158
Lawer, Elizabeth
  117, John 117
Lawflin, Elizabeth
  55
Lawrence, Edward
  119, John 109,
  236
Lawry, Moses 25
Laws, John 157,
  Shadric 86
Lawson, Theophiles
  116
Lawyer, Adam 15,
  225, Catharine
  12, Christena
  112, Elizabeth
  84, Jacob 84,
  184, John 12, 188,
  Margaret 15, 163,
  Mary 25, 248,
  Michael 207,
  Nancy 161,
  William 194
Lay, Conrad 83,
  George 118, John
  125, Michael 81,
  151, Sarah 151
Laypole, Elizabeth
  280
Leach, Benjamin 51,
  Charlotte 67,
  Colin 77, 245,
  256, Collin 278,
  Cresa 9, Dolly
  116, Elijah 36,
  187, Elisha 35,
  Elizabeth 215,
  Hannah 67, Ibby
  237, James 71,

Leach (continued)
James F. 267, 275, John 81, Joshua 90, Leroy 67, Margaret 153, Mary Ann 221, Rhoda 81, Samuel 120, Sarah Jane 267, Seniah 36, Sidney 185, Thomas 207, Thornton 214, Valentine 67, William 89, 142, 153, 185, 203
Leak, Bazil 10
Leapold, Ann R. 277
Leavael, Nancy 57, Thomas 57
Lecke, Basel 9
Leckhart, Andrew 25
Lee, Anna 12, Asa 112, Eliza 197, Elizabeth 36, George 94, George Hay 199, Jeremiah 220, John 7, 106, 116, 133, John C. 283, 286, Margaret 252, Mary R. 215, Nancy 94, Phebe 155, Richard 2, 90, Richard D. 148, Sarah Julinna Maria 98, Squire 174, 176, Susan A. 229, Theodorick 98, Thomas 106, 111, 117, William 174, William D. 252
Leech, Mary 249
Leepold, Lewis 160
Lefeaver, Margaret 193, Thomas 193
Lefever, Thomas 128
Lefevos, Alfred 193

Lefevre, Eliza S. 155, John 14, 145, 155, Lewis L. 245, Lucy Ann 210
Legg, Cecilia A. B. 231, George W. 230, 268
Lehew, Edia 38, Moses 28, Rebeccah 116, Spencer 38, 44, 116, William 22
Lehue, Moses 28
Leisure, Henry 251, Zephaniah 41
Leitch, Joshua 90
Leith, Joseph 217
Leizure, John 160, Nancy 146, Zepheniah 146
Lemley, Ann C. 276, Elizabeth 241, Geo W. 267, George 182, Jacob 87, 129, 276, 279, James 265, Jane 279, John 141, 172, 215, John C. 226, 241, Susan Jane 215, Vance W. 250
Lemly, Barbara 226, Catharine 141, Elizabeth 17, John C. 206, Sarah 154
Lemon, John R. 54, William 49
Lenox, John 62, Nancy 36, 62
Leonard, Elizabeth 146, Enos 239, Jeremiah 86, 110, Margaret 110, Mary 86, Rachael 184
Lessenger, James

Lessenger (continued) 148
Lett, Benjamin 82
Lewin, Samuel 159
Lewis, Abraham 81, 83, Ann H. 207, Barnett 256, Barret 283, Charity 77, Darkey 197, David 227, 249, Dilly 19, Eley 59, Elizabeth 73, 191, Elsae 59, Enoch 158, 175, Evan 20, 98, 139, Evin 158, 170, 177, Frederick 138, George H. 207, Harriet 240, Henry 4, 99, Jacob 83, 117, 191, 197, 207, James 260, Jane 283, Jemima 83, John 66, 146, 191, 218, 221, 232, 246, John H. 202, Joseph 137, Margaret 66, Mary 43, 117, Miranda 221, Phebeann 190, Polly 170, Rachel 81, 177, Robert B. 249, Samuel 43, 73, 85, Sarah 46, 127, Susan 175, Thomas 61, 119, Thos 59
Ley, Mary 83, Michel 118
Licks, Samuel 19
Light, Ann 191, Benjamin F. 266, Cassandra 244, Catharine 66, 144,

Light (continued) Elizabeth 137, 142, 144, 175, Frederick 30, 32, 137, 227, 244, Hannah 30, Henry 105, 175, 204, 210, 228, 245, 282, James 271, John 107, 142, 212, John W. 255, Joseph 218, Lovinia 228, Lucinda 189, Mary 179, 204, Mary Ann 227, 245, Peter 66, 262, Rebecca 240, 276, Sarah 256, William 249, 276
Likans, Jonas 7
Likens, Ann 40, David 149, 183, 225, Henry 40, 55, Mary 70, 149, Rebeca 70, Sarah 55
Likins, Elizabeth 123, James 99, Jonas 101, Leonard 135, Mary 123
Linar, Margaret 174
Linawever, George 212
Lind, Charles T. 257, Eliza W. 237, Mary A. W. 257
Linder, Elizabeth 208
Lindsay, Jacob 17, Thomas 65
Lindsey, Catharine 208, Edmond 1, Elizabeth H. 223, Jacob 1, 17,

Lindsey (continued)
  James 68, 92,
  James M. 208,
  John 68, Joseph B. 223, Lewis 152, 169, Mary 1, 257, Milly 112, Phebe 68, Samuel 17, Sarah 1, Stephen J. 223
Lineburg, Philip 270
Lineburgh, John 252
Lines, William 47
Linkheart, Barney 158, Susan 177, Thomas 158, 177
Linn, Anna Maria 60, Daniel 175, George 32, John 60, Mary 125
Linneberger, Rebecca M. 266, William 266
Lipscomb, John 66, John G. 122, Thomas 144
Literal, Nancy 277
Litrell, Margaret 250
Littenell, Eleaner 244
Little, Catherine 123, David 102, Emeline 213, Franklin 222, Jacob 81, James 45, Martin 133, Mary B. 164, Meggy T. 210, Robert H. 210, William 200
Littler, Ann 27, Anthony W. 249, Charles 118, Charles N. 159, Charles W. 150,

Littler (continued)
  Elijah 3, 32, 53,
  Eliza W. 150,
  Isaac 36, 56,
  John 27, 169,
  Joseph B. 83,
  Joshua 137,
  Lydia 21, Maria 118, Nathan 30,
  Rachel Ann 159,
  Rebecca 159, Saml 3
Littleton, Caron 38, Charles 38, John 36, 96, Margaret 35, Nancy 128, Thomas 62, 128, 135, William 35, 38, 54
Littlisher, Mary 8
Littlishr, John 8
Littrell, Elizabeth 241
Livingston, Sarah 2
Lloyd, Conrad 180, Eliza 162, Hannah 91, Henderson 168, Henry 123, 145, 150, 224, 231, James 176, 180, 182, 267, John 216, Joseph 91, Lucy 106, Mary Jane 267, Metilda 119, Salazy 151, Samuel 216, 218, Sarah 168, Thomas 62, 74, 91, William 114, Winny 119
Lloye, Samuel 151
Lobb, Charles 37, 244
Lock, Eliza 186, Elizabeth 72, George 25, 181,

Lock (continued)
  Harriet 163, John 74, 142, 230, Josia R. 285, Julia Ann 223, Patsy 142, Sally 184, Sarah 25, Selina Eliza 230, William 113, 142, 163, 184, 186, 223
Locke, George 72
Lockhart, Benjamin 131, Emeline G. 237, Isabella 263, James 276, Josiah 276, Majery D. 213, Mary Jane 264, Randal 178, Rebecca A. 214, Rebekah 49, Robert 49, 73, Robert V. 213, 217, 226, 263, 264, 268, Robt 199, Samuel S. 286, Sarah 73, Sarah D. 226
Lockheart, Elizabeth F. 162
Lockmiller, Joseph 183, William 271
Lockridge, George 13, Mary 13
Locksimon, John 219
Lodor, John 196
Lonas, Catharine 12
Long, Abraham 269, Conrad 113, 140, 168, 178, Elijah M. 168, Elizabeth 53, George R. 254, James 65, Jane 241, 253, Jane A. 274, Jas. 65, John 66, 233, Joseph 274, 276,

Long (continued)
  Mary 140, Mary E. 102, Nancy 65, Nimrod 7, 102, Rebecca 241, Reubin S. 204, Robert 129, 230, 242, 250, Rutta Jane 233, Sarah 113, Susan 269, Susanna 9, Thomas 9, 46
Longacre, Evelina 157, Hannah 46, James H. 224, 237, 285, John 14, Joseph 24, 29, 46, Joseph M. 142, Rebaca 22, Sarah G. 224
Longerbane, George 25, John 25
Longerbeen, George 130
Longerbone, Abraham 61, Catharine 61
Lonus, Henry 14
Lott, Lucinda 163
Louck, Philip 75
Loury, Frederick 163, Nancy 164, Robert 97
Louthan, Elizabeth 205, George 187, 205, Henry 104, John 124, 165, 167, 171, Lucy 89, Margaret K. 183, Mary 171, 233, Nancy 225, Walker 140, William 183, William R. 233
Louthen, Nancy 109
Love, Mary 32, Sarah 77, Tabitha 25

Lovell, Charles U. 102
Lovett, Ann E. 279, Daniel C. 237, Jane L. 242, Jonathan 173, 190, 238, Mahlon 202, Mahlon S. 237
Lowan, Jane 137
Lowery, Elizabeth 104, Frederick 179, Sarah 287, William 170
Lowrey, George 164, 195
Lowry, Catharine 104, Danl 104, Frederick 106, George 103, 198, Hannah 82, Hetty 106, Hetty Lou 113, John 76, Juliet 139, Mary 25, 195, Moses 25, 41, 82, Nancy 113, Polly 113, William 106
Lowthan, George 89
Loy, Andrew 108, 140, Asa H. 255, Barbara C. 257, Catharine 146, Conrad 73, 78, 91, 97, 155, 257, Eliza Ann 257, Elizabeth 91, Hannah 155, John 257, Michael 169, Peter 73, William 235
Loyd, Sally 114, Sarah 71, Stephen 71
Loye, Conrad 147, John 147
Loyer, Eve 115, Philip 202, Susan

Loyer (continued) 226
Loyn, Mary C. 284
Lucas, Henderson 157, Nancy 79, Thomas 79, 249, Warner 270, Winnifred 249
Luckett, Horace 135, William H. 210
Luckey, Elizabeth 77, James 77, Joseph 77
Lucky, James 72
Lucy 77
Ludden, Alonzo P. 265
Luis, Barret 272
Luke, Elizabeth 25, Peter 25
Lukens, Jesse 171, Joseph F. 152, Martha 253
Lukins, Joseph T. 131, Rachel 152
Lupton, David 110, Edah 115, Elizabeth 117, Hannah 13, Isaac 242, Jane R. 248, John 73, 156, 235, 247, John M. 248, Jonah 150, 269, 284, Jonah H. 282, Jonah J. 248, 270, Joshua 230, 238, 266, Lewis 197, Ludia 60, Margaret 221, Margaret Ann 269, Marinda 248, Martin C. 285, Mary 202, Mary D. 232, Nathan 232, Nathaniel C. 151,

Lupton (continued)
212, 261, Phebe
20, Rebecca A.
261, Sarah 163,
186, Sarah E.
212, Thomas C.
94, 163, William
38, William H.
242
Lutteral, Sarah 154
Lutterell, Elizabeth
173, Fielding
154, Robert 178
Luttnell, Fielding
244
Luttrell, Fielding
23, 155, 168, 173,
Francis 196, John
Luttrell 178,
Lewis 196, Nancy
168, Richard 156,
Robert 143, 238,
Sarah 238,
William 258
Luttrill, William
221
Lutz, Jacob 198
Lyder, Cornelia E.
285, Jacob 285
Lyle, Wilberforce
210
Lyles, John 2
Lynn, James 149,
183, Jane 65,
Julia Ann 234,
Martha 145,
William 218, 227
Lyon, Archibald
225, Richard 13
Lyons, Elizabeth
102, James 102,
126, 134, 153, 174,
206, 223, Joannah
M. 206, Lucy
Ellen 223, Mary
153, Nancy 183,
Sarah 126, Ury

Lyons (continued)
134
Lytleton, William
50
Macatee, Hariet 207
Macintire, John 165
Mack, James 261,
Nancy 240
Mackdonell, Balis
208
Mackenzie, Thomas
282
Mackewan, Thomas 25
Mackey, Eleanor
103, John 103,
John S. 126, Mary
104
Macky, Fredericka
250, John 154,
Robert 4, 11
Macmillan, Sarah 40
Macoughtry, James
55
Madden, Charlotte
92, Harriet 184,
Jacob 92, Jean
13, John 4,
Kitty 109, Mabra
13, 92, Mabray
109, Samuel 184,
William 110
Maddin, William 28
Magalis, Eliza 264,
Godfrey 264,
Maria 249
Magdaline, Mary 210
Mager, Mary Ann 239
Magill, Charles 62,
John S. 217, 247,
Mary B. 198
Magonen, Isabella
240
Magruder, Daniel A.
252, Elizabeth
202, Francis 209,
George A. 86,
Mary 178, Nimian

Magruder (continued) 71, Ninian 99, 102, 131, Ninion 202
Magson, John M. 230, 259
Mahamn, Margaret 95
Mahaney, Joseph 190, Joseph P. 244, 264, Rachael Ann 197
Mahany, Thomas 139
Mahew, Alexander 51, 55, Elizabeth Ann 275, Joseph 269, 279, Lloyd 168, Matilda 275, Nathan 168, William 88
Mahue, John 96, Levi 287
Mainer, Benjamin 157, John 233
Majors, Joseph 41
Malcolm, Harriet 159, Walter 159
Maley, Ann 48
Malin, Job 4, William 20
Mallen, Samuel 93
Maloney, Daniel 184
Malony, John 3, Martha 67, Mary 103, Sarah 67
Malta, Anna 268
Maltimore, Betsy 31
Malvin, Reubin 136
Manker, Jacob 41
Mann, Sarah 84, William 154
Manoliucks, William 10
Manor, Benjamin 103, Benjamin G. 257, David 205, Mary 205
Mantz, Jacob 270

Manuel, Margaret 250, Thornton 250
Maphis, Joseph 276
March, Ann 4, Elias 164, Henry 102, Lavinia 246, Leroy G. 236, 246, 267, Mary S. 267, Michael 4
Marck, Michael 2, William 246
Marcks, John 11
Marcus, Mary Ann 265, Peggy 9
Mark, Alexander 54, Elizabeth 204, Henry 15, 18, 240, John 217
Markell, John 269
Marker, Amos 204, Catharine 187, Elijah 253, George 8, George A. 239, 264, 281, Jacob A. 220, John 70, 180, 181, 187, 220, 235, John H. 239, Margaret H. 281, Martha 264, Mary Ann 235, 239, Reuben 261, William F. 261
Marks, Alexander 131, 175, 179, 239, 245, 255, Ann E. 255, Henry 173, 216, Mary 173, Polly 26, Sarah 216
Markwood, David 145, John 176, 235, 236
Marl, Hannah 34
Marles, Ann 28, Jacob 28
Marll, Jacob 34

Marlow, Henson 177
Marney, John 66
Marple, Ann 20,
  Anna 176, 180,
  Benjamin 149, 268,
  David 53, 185,
  Elizabeth 73,
  Enoc 176, Enoch
  20, 53, 62, 73, 77,
  98, 132, 149, 184,
  236, Ezekial 71,
  Ezekiel 8, 22, 51,
  70, George 71,
  245, Jane 22,
  Jane M. 262,
  Jeremiah 204,
  John 67, Joseph
  60, 62, 180, 207,
  219, Margaret
  245, Mary 178,
  236, Mary Ann
  232, Morgan H.
  232, Prudence
  185, Prudens 8,
  Sally 184, Sarah
  51, Thomas 70
Marpole, Andrew J.
  253, Benjamin
  147, 207, Betsy
  152, David 152,
  Elizabeth A. 206,
  Ellen 239, Enoc
  232, 268, Enoch
  230, Ezekiel 106,
  118, George 230,
  Hanah 106,
  Harrison 257,
  Jane 206, Mary
  147, Morgan H.
  124, Nancy 118,
  Rachel 175, Sarah
  206, 268, Tacey
  232, Thomas 166,
  Uriah 143, 175
Marques, William 4,
  Zachariah 113
Marquess, Fanny 19,

Marquess (continued)
  Isaac 9, 19, Kid
  54, William 192
Marquis, Elenor
  118, Elizabeth
  21, 127, Levi
  167, Mary 21,
  174, Samuel M.
  160, William 127
Marquiss, Kid 138
Marr, Hannah 11
Marrey, Frid 166
Marsh, Anna 26,
  Catharine 103,
  Clarissa 87,
  Edward 60, 72,
  Elizabeth 44,
  John 103, Mary
  129, Richard 26,
  44, 50, 87, 103,
  129, Sarah 50
Marshall, Alexander
  216, Comfort M.
  211, Eleanor 126,
  Elizabeth 217,
  James 23, 37,
  John 126, 207,
  217, 220, Martha
  107, Polly 23,
  Sarah 246, Thomas
  131, Thomas P.
  269, William 20,
  33, 35, 73, 107,
  108
Marsteller, James A.
  257
Marstin, Charlotte
  61
Martin, Catherine
  209, Charles 55,
  Conrad 58, Daniel
  J. 261, Elizabeth
  8, 59, 61, 81,
  Francis F. 61,
  Francis T. 59,
  Henry 58, 191,

Martin (continued)
Jacob 77, 101,
James 36, 90,
James Lee 4, Joel 59, John 66, 184, Joseph 192, Julia Ann 245, Lacy Ann 193, Margaret 7, 32, Mary 11, 28, 85, 115, 186, Mary Ann 169, Nancy 55, Rebecca 169, Sarah 279, Snoden 32, Thomas 33, 81, Ura 118, Vincent 98, William 8, 42, 90, 122, 282
Marts, Deanna 221, John 221
Marven, William 207
Marvin, Hannah 207, Isaac 284, Martha 236
Masefield, Letty 110
Mason, Andrew 102, 125, 142, 191, 221, 225, Anna M. 273, Armistead Thompson 84, Bingley 148, Bingly 200, Catharine 148, Elizabeth 108, 174, 190, George 161, Gerrard F. 265, Isabella 173, Jacob 46, James 175, 262, 271, James W. 216, Jane 142, 245, Jonathan 151, Mary H. 271, Mingly 100, Reason 191, Rebecca T. 174, Reson 148,

Mason (continued)
Rezin 28, 122, 125, Seth 190, 209, 245, Susan 221, Susanna 200, William 220, 272
Massie, Ann 27, Benjamin M. 255, 286, Benjm M. 197, Duncan T. 157, Evelina M. 255, Eveline M. 231, Josiah 203, 231, 259, Maria F. 182, Thomas 157, Thomas B. 170, Wilford P. 120, William 27
Mastin, Francis T. 67, John 61, Margaret 170, Samuel 130, Sarah T. 61
Mathany, Sarah 101, Thomas 101
Matheny, John 16
Mathew, William 111
Mathias, Elizabeth 99, John 99
Matson, Aaron 83, Benjamin 100, Enos 81
Mattex, Robert 55
Matthews, Cecelia 174, Elizabeth 193, Mary Ann 212, Richard 193, Squire 174, Squire E. 212, Susan D. 210, Thomas 265
Matthias, John 72
Mattox, Bennett D. 206
Mauch, George 144
Mauck, Ann 48, Barbara 157,

Mauck (continued)
  David 134,
  Evalina Harriet 188, Frederick 90, Henry E. 270, Jacob 117, 119, Maria 116, Mathias 2, Matthias 48, Michael 55, 95, 113, 116, 126, 157, Nancy 113, Polly 55, Rebecca 95
Mauk, Frederick 90, Louisa 166, Michael 166, 188, 190
Maumau, George 114
Maumaugh, Mary 114
Maurer, Frederick W. 224
Maury, Catharine 76, Frederick 76, 189
Mauzer, John 271
Mauzey, Sarah Ann 271
Mauzy, Elizabeth E. 284, George 213, John 264, 271, John R. 266, Susan 264, William 259
Mawk, Anthony 52
Maxwell, Betsy 53, James 275, 285, John 71, Mary 281, Parthenia 75, Wm 53
May, Catharine 216, Daniel 260, George 227, Jacob 198, John 134, 172, Julia Ann 252, Mary 134, Rosanna 8, Samuel 8, Susannah 172

Mayers, John 220
Mayhew, Sarah Jane 236, Tilghman 269, Tilman 132, 236
Mayhugh, Bryan 61, Eliza 150, Nathaniel 150, William 61
Maypole, Prudence 106
Mays, Joshua 136
McAlester, John 16
McAllister, John 126
McAnully, Elizabeth 8
McArter, Eli 37
McArty, Andrew 51, Peter 51
McAtee, Thomas 129
McAuley, Anna 41, Henry 41
Mcauly, John 41
McBean, Charles 160
McBee, Ann E. 244, William T. 244
McBride, James 21, 186, John 48
McCabe, Josiah 25, Margt 11, Mary 54, William 24
McCall, Nancy 10, Nathan 10
McCallum, Samuel 64
McCandless, Lavinia 188, Mary 154, Robert P. 188, 202
McCann, George B. 257
McCarden, Henry 18
McCartney, Joseph 158, Michael 57, Rachel 158
McCarty, Andrew 51, 124, Daniel 84, Elizabeth 85,

McCarty (continued)
Elizabeth Jane
236, Harry 131,
John 85, Joseph
13, 122, 145, 225,
Margaret 124,
Mary 122, Peter
116, Sarah 145
McCashland, Benjamin
140, Nancy 188
McCasland, Oliver
142
McCauley, Barnabus
31, Daniel 273,
282, Elizabeth
203, John 118,
203, Joshua 287,
Lemuel 269, Susan
I. 212
McCaulley, John
177, Margaret
187, William 187
McCaully, Daniel
55, John 81, 118,
William 24
McCawley, Joshua 23
McCleary, James 145
McCleave, Elizabeth
130, Margaret
165, Robert H.
257, Sarah 192
McCleland, David 78
McClenahan, Robert
44
McCleve, Robert 70
McCleves, William
263
McClintuck, Nancy
25, Samuel 25
McCloud, Nancy 59,
Thornton Augustus
274
McClun, Absalum B.
122, Thomas 3
McClung, Samuel 271
McClunn, Eliza 172,
John E. 225, Mary

McClunn (continued)
234, Mildred 228,
Sarah 220, 228,
Sarah A. 225
McClure, Hannah
136, James W.
279, John 136,
142, 280
McColle, John 166
McConnel, James 77
McConnell, Catharine
72, Daniel 72,
Dennis 72
McCool, Charity 88,
John 89, Martha
89
McCoole, Alivia 86,
Anna 41,
Catharine 41,
James 31, James
D. 275, John 41,
86, 108, 110, 113,
125, 135, 153, 154,
155, 157, Lewis
77, 79, Mary 29
McCord, Amanda 277,
George 158, 277,
John William 273,
Rebecca 158
McCormick, Albert
211, Ann 281,
Bushrod 185,
Chapline E. 152,
Chas 213, Cyrus
196, Dawson 121,
162, Edward 271,
281, Eli 131,
Eliza Ann 211,
Elizabeth 270,
Francis 173,
George 69, 161,
Hannah 173,
Harriet 131,
Harrison 267,
Isaac 161, 189,
192, James 192,
231, John

McCormick (continued)
178, 195, Levi
99, 270, 284,
Lourenna D. 181,
Marcus 181,
Margaret 161, 177,
210, Mary 121,
Mary Ann 214,
Mary Jane 284,
Otway 211,
Province 16, 162,
191, 205, Rachael
12, Samuel 66,
161, Washington
274, William 43,
66, 92, 177,
Willoughby M. 233
McCoun, John 33
McCoy, John 26, 64
McCracken, James
275, Thomas 9
McCrackin, James 75
McCrea, Charles 13,
68, 69, Isabella
69
McCue, Jesse 10
McCune, John 116,
Samuel 107
McDamith, Philip
111
McDaniel, Abraham
24, Baalis 217,
224, 226, Daniel
23, Enoch 24,
Harriet 189,
Henry J. 256,
John 143, Jos
199, Nancy 136,
Sarah 224,
Shelton 153,
William 136, 217
McDermott, Patrick
252
McDonald, Abraham
24, 74, Alexander
82, Allen 1, Ann
13, Archibald 82,

McDonald (continued)
Benjamin 264,
Caroline 184,
Charles 18,
Daniel 184,
Edward C. 214,
Eleaner 200,
Eleanor 14, 142,
Elizabeth 168,
186, 207,
Elizabeth Ann 235,
Gabriel 111,
Hannah 205, James
9, 16, 92, 165,
167, 192, 200, 209,
Jared 168, Jarred
173, Jenny 30,
John 51, 85,
Joseph 261,
Josiah 206, Julia
Ann 165, Mahala
167, Margaret
100, Mary 92,
Mary Susan 283,
Moses 66, 205,
Nathan L. 231,
Rachel 74,
Rebeccah 17,
Sally 173, Samuel
153, 206, 220,
Stephen 24,
Sydnor 264,
Thomas 30, 51,
178, Thompson 29,
207, Thornton
283, Thornton D.
180, William 158,
168, 183
McDougle, Samuel
238
McDowell, John 209
McDrum, Mary 1
McElaney, Harriet
92
McElevene, Jane 207
McElwain, William
181

McElwee, David 283, James H. 275, Margaret C. 280, William 181
McEndree, Lucinda E. 247, Nimrod 163, 247, 265, Richard H. 183
McEntire, Daniel 114
McFadden, Elizabeth 87, John 32, Robert 109, Roberty 87
McFaddin, John 66, Nancy 66, Robert 87
McFarlan, Elizabeth 199, John 270, Levi 270
McFarland, Elizabeth 15, Ezekiel 63, George 226, John 15, 76, 106, Joseph 22, Levin 202, 248, Mary 189, Nancy 106, Polly 144, Rebecca 202, Sarah 248, Thomas 5
McFarlene, Elizabeth 154, John 154
McFarlin, Hannah 63, James 92, John 63, Levin 175, Mary 175, Mary G. 71
McFarling, Charles 167, John 69, 92, Thomas 5
McFate, Wm 32
McFeeley, John 31
McFeely, Benjamin 60
McFerron, Milly 16
McFerson, Jesse 2

McGalis, James 259
McGarrety, Andrew 149
McGarrity, Andrew 166
McGinnis, John 6, 20, 22
McGoohen, Elizabeth 71
McGoughen, Mary 100
McGovern, Joseph 220
McGrogan, Mary 153
McGruder, Frances 209
McGueriom, Maria 233
McGuin, William 90
McGuinn, Nancy 153, Philip 153, William 109
McGuire, Edward 15, Gertrude 281, Mary 91, Philip 114
McGwinn, Philip 127
McIlwane, Susannah 32
McIlwee, John 148, John H. 247, Sarah 148
McIntire, Charles 54, Sarah 54, Thomas 30
McIntosh, Joseph 120, 155, 231
McKawan, Thomas 62
McKay, Abraham 156, Amos H. 220, Ann 19, Cassander J. 189, Emalia 64, Emily 210, George 157, Haines 186, Hannah 19, Jacob 75, 117, 136, 157, 172, 184, Jesse 67, Jobe 19,

McKay (continued)
  John 19, 137, 186, 210, Joseph 172, 208, Louisa 249, Mariam 169, Nancy A. 184, Otho 172, Rachel 120, Robert 111, 136, 184, Robert H. 231, Robert S. 184, Sally 186, Washington 189, Wesley 208
Mckee, Ann 37, 159, Bartholemew 40, Bartholomew 46, 191, 223, Bartholomew H. 234, Barton 232, Benjamin 257, David 271, David L. 217, 245, Eliza 191, Eliza J. 279, Elizabeth 27, 65, 98, 125, Elizabeth Ann 187, Elleanor 223, Evelina 263, James 182, Jane 8, Jasper 152, Jemima 259, Jeremiah R. 279, Jesse 65, John 98, 164, John Faguson 22, Joseph 169, 187, 200, 225, 233, Livina 230, Margaret 233, Martha Ann 232, 266, Mary 95, 182, 217, 225, Rebecca 200, Robert 7, 8, 27, 169, 232, 263, Sally 46, Sarah 176, Thomas 174,

Mckee (continued)
  Washington 249, William 133, 159, 176, 235, 266
McKeever, Daniel 277
McKenney, Oliver 119
McKenny, James 189
McKeown, Patrick 221
McKevor, Jacob 225
McKewan, Caroline 202, Patrick 187, Thomas 16, 29, 35, 37, 56, 59, 60
McKinsay, James 18
McKinsey, Mary 186
McKnight, Sarah 13, Uriah 160
McKnut, Massy 157
McKowan, Thomas 44
McKoy, Hatha 26, James 94, Moses 94, Rachel 94, Susanah 58
McLaughlin, Amos 43, Lucinda 214, Thomas 165
McLean, Hector D. 283, Mary 32, Thomas 32
McLeed, Elizabeth 184
McLeod, George 214, George B. 244, Henry 55, John B. 146, Lorenzo 191, Maria A. 238, Mary S. 194, Sophia 275, Thomas 160
McLun, Sa,ie; 258
McLunn, Samuel 256
McLurr, Jonathan 74
McMahan, Timothy 34
McMahon, Mary Ann

McMahon (continued) 63, Sarah 34, 63
McMan, Timothy 154
McMannus, Samuel 162, Susan 162
McMeeken, Samuel 29
McMeekin, John 41
McMillan, Hugh 32
McMorris, Ann 133, Anna 137, David 111, Elizabeth 111, James 174, 176, John 133
McMullan, Isabelle 97, Robert 97
McMullen, Alexander 76, Ester 76
McMurray, John 104, Martha 119, Peter 48, 119, 145
McNabb, James 262
McNally, James 22, Mary 79
McNamie, Leannah 268
McNeal, John 97
McNeale, John 50
McNease, Lydia 13
McNeely, Henry 96
McNeily, Jeremiah 127
McNelly, Amey 44, Ann 80, William 44, 179
McPhereson, Jane 97
McPherson, James 12, 161, Jane 75, Peter 36, Samuel 107, William 144
McQuade, Sarah 245
McQuaid, Lewis 189, 209
McUlboon, John 259
McVea, Eddy 31
McVeigh, Cintery 166, James 270
McVicar, John 239

McVicker, Catharine 97, Diana 170, Duncan 97, William 16, 170
McWhorter, Alexander 48, James B. 286, Jane 69, Mary 224, Robert 69, 125
Mead, John 246
Meade, David 102, Harriet G. 279, N. B. 278, Virginia W. 278, William W. 278
Meagill, Frances C. 217
Mecashland, Mary 110
Meem, Gilbert 4, 6, 17, 58
Meetze, Felix 187
Meldrume, Robert 110
Mellon, Elisha 104
Melon, Jacob 20, Jane 19, Mary 20
Mendenhall, Francis S. 254, Jacob 228, 244, John 284, Mary Ann 244, Samuel 121, 248
Meracle, William 275
Mercer, Ann 159, David 33, Dinah 16, Edward 3, 74, Elizabeth 81, Jesse 132, 137, Job 83, John 92, 168, Joseph 24, 71, Joshua 101, Lydia 71, 168, Margaret Elizabeth 278, Mary 18, 33, Moses 16, 33,

Mercer (continued)
Nathaniel 133,
Olivia 83,
Phoebe 214,
Robert 33,
William 24, 81,
101
Merchant, Ann E.
279, Dustus 113,
Hiram 279, Nancy
113, Samuel 234
Merryman, James D.
259, Jared D. 263
Mesmer, Jacob 132,
220
Mesmore, Catherine
78
Messen, Sidney 134
Messer, Calip 125,
Hannah 122, Job
72, Margaret 178,
Mary 101, Phoeby
125, Rachel 217
Messner, John 241
Metcalfe, Thomas
104
Metcath, Ruth 55
Metzger, Daniel 285
Meyers, Daniel 165
Mica, Charles 13
Michael, Harriet Ann
215, Nancy 234
Middleton, Delilah
106, John 144,
Pamillia 173,
Thomas 214,
William 16, 106,
173
Miers, Jacob 23,
John 76, Jonah
23, Joseph S.
256, Mary 23,
Sarah 278
Milbourn, John 70
Milburn, Andrew 37,
201, Elias 52,
Greenberry 231,

Milburn (continued)
James 231, 281,
Joseph 140,
Joseph Everett 88,
Margaret 284,
Peter 281,
Rebecca 37
Miles, John 68,
Josias 68, Nancy
68, William 14
Miley, Christena
281, Francis G.
193, Jacob 183
Milhorn, Elizabeth
243, George 223,
James 255, John
18, 157, 233, 243,
John W. 259, 264,
Martha Jane 273,
William 273
Millar, Daniel 19,
Elizabeth Ann 198,
John 49
Millburn, Andrew
242, John 190,
Maria 242
Miller, Abraham
136, 151, Adam
19, Alexander
123, 141, Anna M.
286, Atwell 268,
Betsey 119,
Casper 79, 155,
Catherine 145,
176, Christian
176, Daniel 24,
27, 152, David
168, 242, 260,
David J. 254,
Elizabeth 95, 155,
260, 277,
Elizabeth R. 204,
Ephraim 124, 243,
George 97, 162,
Henry 43, 49,
Jacob 20, 32, 112,
276, James 111,

Miller (continued)
James I. 235, James P. 115, John 87, 101, 217, 226, 253, John M. 264, John W. 241, Joseph 10, 204, 215, Joseph H. 186, 204, Julia Ann 287, Maria B. 123, Martha 32, Martha R. 286, Mary 79, 123, 222, Mary C. 275, Mary Catharine 287, Mary M. 230, Mary Sophia 194, Michael 271, Mitchel H. 283, Nancy 167, Nancy C. 141, Peter 62, 285, Philip 35, Rebecca 139, 152, Richard 32, Robert 245, Robert C. 175, 270, 275, Robert F. 165, Sabrina 276, Sarah 243, Sarah Jane 286, Stephen 18, 241, 246, Thomas C. 189, Thomas J. 246, William 154, 167, William H. 222, 252

Millhorn, Catherine 28, Francis C. 234, Henry 88, Margaret 92, 199, Sarah Ann 255

Millikin, Eliza 2, Jemima 2

Millison, William 236

Millner, Hannah 3, John 3

Mills, Alexander C. 218, Eli 4, Isaac D. 160, Jarrod 210, Margaret 191, Robert 80, Sarah Ann 280, Thomas 259

Millslagle, Jacob 13

Milslagle, Samuel 194

Milton, Alexander 42, 68, Alexander Ross 131, Ann 131, Ebin 137, 171, 176, 183, Elijah 68, Elizabeth S. 121, Florinda L. 162, Frederick R. 280, 286, George W. 218, James T. T. 283, John 176, Margaret 171, Richard 109

Mincer, Catharine 258, Rebecca 228, William 227

Minick, Gasper 2

Minicks, Catherine 18

Minkey, Mary Jane 272

Minnix, Elijah 181, John P. 244

Minoin, Hannah 121

Minor, William 70

Minser, John 129, 228, Julia 160, Lydia 157, Thuza A. E. 208, William B. 216

Minshall, Edward 27, Ellis 85,

Minshall (continued)
Lydia 27
Mires, Edward 183, Mary 93, Stephen 44
Mirheles, Godfrey 249
Mitcham, Delilah 253, Henry 240, 253, 265, Marcha G. 265, William A. 272
Mitchel, James 31
Mitchell, Carey 23, Catharine 143, Deborah L. 222, Frances 23, Frances E. 174, Grace F. 204, Henry 157, James 225, Jemima 35, John 143, Joseph 47, Louisa 214, Maria 214, Mary D. 189, Mary Emily 212, Orrato 161, Peyton R. 254, Sarah 76, Sarah A. 204, Sarah Ann 194, Sarah H. 215, Thomas 76, 88, William 174
Mock, Christinna 16, Geo 16, George 43
Moffett, John 10, 53, Martha 17, Walter 17
Moffitt, Ann 53, John 85, Robert 53
Moffott, Darcus 85
Moland, Patrick 196
Molding, Ann 90, Baptist 90
Moling, John 264, Nancy 166

Monmouth, Jacob 18, Rachel 239
Monroe, Eliza 195, Elizabeth 86, George 142, 143, 150, James T. 195, Jane 143, John 86, 89, 150, 165, 195, 205, John I. 200, Mary 142, Peggy 124, Robert 164, Sarah 111, Thomas 96
Monsy, James 79, Nicholas 79
Montgomery, Elizabeth 138, Hannah C. 283, Henry 268, Joseph 248, Martha 235, Matthew 101, Nancy 99, Robert 138, 145, 283, Sarah 115, Thomas 115, 245, 249
Moon, Henry 159
Mooney, Samuel 64
Moor, Presley 29
Moore, Alfred 175, 176, 196, Alfred P. 182, 204, 213, Anthony 43, 61, Aquilla P. 175, Aurelia 182, Benjamin B. 285, Delilah 127, Edward 181, Edwin 181, 183, Elijah 171, Elisha 37, Eliza 208, Elizabeth 177, 188, Elizabeth S. 265, Ezalpha 58, Fanny 86, Frances 43, George R. 141, Hannah 46, Jacob 15, James

Moore (continued) 120, 188, James G. 171, James H. 198, Jane 141, John 75, Joseph 95, 97, Lewis F. 166, Lewis T. 265, 286, Mahala J. 252, Margaret 176, Mariam 97, Olivia 183, Peirce 237, Polly 100, Rachael 13, Rebecca 166, Reuben 102, Solomon 126, Strother 161, 265, Therissa 175, Thomas 177, Thos 1, William B. 265
Moorisson, John W. 213
More, Thomas T. 276
Morehead, Joel 52, Sarah 197
Moreland, Augustus 96, George 184, James 266, John B. 151, Patrick 211, 254
Morford, John 12
Morgan 1, Abel 59, Benjamin 222, Catherine L. 267, Daniel 175, Deborah 187, Enoch 34, 37, Enock 60, Eusy 60, Evalina 147, George 34, John 3, 50, 51, 58, 119, 210, John R. 179, Joseph 26, Lettice 34, Lydia 29, Martha 87, Martha Ann

Morgan (continued) 124, Martha Ellen 222, Mary 40, 87, Nicholas J. B. 219, Noah 34, 37, Richard 222, Richd H. 267, Tho. 40, William 9, 97, 124
Morgen, John 64
Moriarty, Patrick 277
Morison, Thomas M. 248
Morley, John 5
Morris, Daniel 127, Frisby 115, Lucinda 241, Mahlon 115, Robert 179, 210, 228, Saml 17, Sarah 97, Sarah L. 201, Thomas 95, William 73, 108
Morrison, Edward 236, Elizabeth 178, Emily 222, James 30, 173, 187, James M. 239, Jane C. 242, Margaret 235, Mary 173, 248, Sarah 94, Thomas 231, 235, 242, Thomas M. 248, Wesley 282, William 94
Morrow, John 145, Peggy 10, William H. 203
Mosley, William 9
Moss, Catharine 213, James 200, 279, John 264, 265, Presley 213
Mott, Joseph 56,

Mott (continued)
  Tabitha 56
Moulden, George 89,
  Mary 212
Moulding, Elizabeth
  96
Mounts, Providence
  152
Mountz, Jose 263
Mourey, Catherine
  226
Moury, Frederick R.
  226
Mowbray, Joseph
  Edward 253
Mowrey, James M.
  249, John R. 256
Mowry, Frederick
  166, Hannah 255,
  Hiram 166, John
  R. 255, 256
Moyer, Margaret 264
Moyers, Jacob 99,
  190, John 188,
  Joshua 23,
  Michael 99
Muck, Susanna 97
Muckay, John 151
Muckelwee, David 97
Muckey, Catharine
  209, Maria 209
Muir, Adeline H.
  241
Mullen, Rebecca 136
Mullenecks, Henry
  44, Rebecca 44
Mullenix, Jacob 138
Mullennix, Nathan
  114
Mullin, Samuel M.
  271
Mullinix, Jacob 107
Mulloy, Thomas 33
Muma, Betsy 85,
  George 85
Mumaw, Hannah 244,
  John 189,

Mumaw (continued)
  Margaret 189, 244
Mumert, Zachariah
  276
Mumma, John 151
Mummau, George 103,
  Jacob 270
Mummaw, Catharine
  95, George 95,
  246
Mummoth, Elizabeth
  280
Murdock, George W.
  108
Murkel, John 282
Murphey, Daniel
  Jefferson 258, H.
  M. 192, Harrison
  170, Hiram 222,
  Jemima 192, John
  B. 193, Nancy
  184, Polly 59,
  Samuel 119, Susan
  170, Winterton
  186, Zachariah 16
Murphy, Ann H. 109,
  Daniel 17, 104,
  124, 167, Eleanor
  22, Finley 194,
  Harriett 215,
  Hiram 187, 204,
  Horatio 73,
  Isabella 31,
  James 175, Jane
  17, John 132,
  Josiah 163,
  Lewiza 204,
  Lucinda 194,
  Margaret 264,
  Mary 139, Mary
  Ann 267, Nancy
  245, 260, Parcina
  286, Patrick 31,
  Samuel 139, Tenly
  37, Thomas 61,
  215, 245, Thos
  37, Zachariah 13

Murray, Amos 237,
Cyrus W. 123,
Edward Jinkins
117, Geo 92,
George 115, 138,
George W. 182,
John 53, 56, 149,
Josiah 198, Mary
R. 102, Rachel
53, Richard 74,
Susan J. 248
Murry, Cyrus W.
197, 203, Harrison
237, James 248,
Jane 63, Mary
Jane 203
Muse, Edward B.
190, Edward R.
173, 232, 238, 244,
273, 279, Emily B.
232, Frances S.
244, Julia A.
247, Martha E.
273, Martin B.
202, 217, 234, 247,
Mary B. 202,
Nancy 173,
Robert B. 274,
Susannah 120, 122
Musgrove, James D.
241
Musselman, Michael
136
Mustin, James 172,
John 28, Nancy
Jones 172
Myers, Abraham 137,
Ann 38, Anna 57,
Barbara 112,
Catharine 78,
Catherine 154,
Celia A. 217,
Celia Ann 136,
Christiana 55,
Edward 207, Eliza
201, 246,
Elizabeth 23, 74,

Myers (continued)
90, 150, 185,
Ellen 268, Eve
76, George
134, Hannah 46,
Jacob 50, 145,
John 42, 48, 55,
76-78, 112, 121,
152, 154, 177,
Joseph 57, 114,
217, Joshua 6,
Leonard 173, 255,
Lydia 145, Martha
76, Mary 65, 78,
137, Mary Jane
256, Nancy 201,
Peter 46, 84,
Rebecca 152,
Samuel 128,
Sarah 48, Stena
121, Stephen 23,
Tabitha 180,
William 38,
William J. 252
Mylinger, Charles
143, Elizabeth
101, Isaac 72,
101
Myson, Bingledy 108
Mytinger, Catharine
233, Daniel 33,
58, 65, Elizabeth
58, Jacob 218,
Sarah 131
Nagley, Henry 233
Nagly, Henry 196
Naple, Henry 117
Nash, Alexander 94
Nauset, Ann C. 279
Nausett, John 278
Navel, Henry 124
Navell, Henry 115,
213, 214
Navill, Henry 198
Naville, Henry 174,
Polly 198
Neal, Francis 118,

Neal (continued)
  Joseph 84
Neale, Francis 111
Neel, John 74
Neff, Carter 93,
  Ezekial 111,
  Francis 16, 107,
  119, Jacob 113,
  James 80, John
  35, Polly 190
Negley, Henry 36
Negrier, Charles
  104
Neill, Abrm 7,
  Joseph 259, Lewis
  108, 119, 166,
  Sigismund S. 287,
  Thomas 11, 40, 77,
  Thos 29, Thos.
  68, William 93
Neilson, Isabella
  204, William 94
Nelson, Abraham 48,
  Betsy C. 197,
  Eleanor 20,
  Elizabeth 49, 200,
  Emily S. 261,
  James 70, 252,
  256, James H.
  261, John 49,
  Louisa 102,
  Malinda 211,
  Mann P. 176, Mary
  116, Mathias 57,
  Moses 200, 201,
  Polly 110, Robert
  136, Sarah 252,
  Thomas 108,
  Thomas F. 228,
  Warner 209
Nesmith, Ann 215,
  Elizabeth 244,
  Jesse 250, Joseph
  84, Mary 129,
  250, Rebecca 113,
  Sarah 119, Thomas
  113

Nessmith, John 186,
  John H. 287,
  Martha 287
Nevel, Gabriel 189
Nevell, Henry 112
Nevill, Cynthia
  191, Henry 159,
  Hirom 191, John
  159
Neville, Hiram 126,
  James H. 215
Nevit, Emily 264
Nevitt, Sarah 63
Newbank, Moses 48
Newbanks, Maria
  162, Moses 100,
  124, 162
Newbrough, John 42,
  Joshua 92, 93,
  William 167
Newby, William 43
Newcom, Elizabeth
  283, Elizabeth H.
  218, Jacob 218
Newcomb, Angelina
  258, Edward 179,
  Elisha 115, 258,
  Leroy 133, 171,
  186, 198, 262,
  Susanna 3
Newcome, Catharine
  M. 247, Elisha
  247, 268, Parandis
  268, William 270
Newcomer, Jacob 184
Newcomor, John 129
Newcum, Leroy 285,
  Margaret 285
Newell, Thomas W.
  143, William 83,
  196
Newham, Catharine M.
  233, Eliza 143,
  James 61, 75, 103,
  Mary 75, Westley
  T. 133
Newland, Jacob 67,

Newland (continued)
  John 2, 73, Lewis 250, Margaret Ann 261, Thornton 127
Newlin, Lewis 266
Newman, Alexander R. 164, 172, 264, Andrew 29, Ann 32, 147, Catesby 178, Catharine 232, Edmund 58, Elizabeth 58, James 32, 208, John 22, 96, 111, Lucy 233, Lucy Ellen 286, Mary Ann 153, Obediah 111, Thomas 233, Thos 147
Newton, William S. 154
Nicholas, John 38
Nicholls, Elizabeth 97, Saml 10
Nichols, Aner? 52, Ann 246, Ann W. 192, Henry 23, 52, Jacob 235, 246, Jonah 235
Nicholson, Mary S. 259, Sarah Ann 240, Thomas 240
Nicklin, Any 39, Jacob 87, Jacob R. 192, 207, 245, 271, Joseph 8, 39, Joseph M. 194, Mary 8, Mary E. 245, Rachel A. 282
Nickols, Jacob 136
Nicols, Jacob 254
Nighswanger, John 41
Night, James 200, Thomas 110
Nisewander, Abraham

Nisewander (continued)
  105, David 135, Mary 105, Peter 172
Nisewanger, Abraham 6, 281, John 1, 12, 134, 234, Lucinda 265, Lydia 6, Martha Ellen 281, Mary Ann 265
Niswander, Abraham 56, Jacob S. 265, Rhoda 71
Niswanger, Abraham 71, John 35, Mary 35, William 159
Nixon, Mary 16
Noakes, John A. 249, 274, Samuel 264, Samuel G. 284
Noblar, John 22
Noble, Emily L. I. W. 152, James 90, 92, John 19, 154, Noah 135, Ruth M. 154, William 92
Noel, Catharine 208, Elizabeth 174, Henry 215, John 90, 174, 177, 236, Nicholas 197, 208, Peggy 90, Sarah Jane 262
Nokes, Priscilla 21
Nolain, Pierce 40
Nolan, John 134
Noland, Amelia 67, Eliza 214, George 64, Hannah 156, Henry 105, Nancy 157, Obed 20,

Noland (continued)
  156, Pierce 67,
  Susannah 40
Noldin, John 5
Nole, Mary Jane 284
Nolen, Alcinda E.
  260, Henry 142,
  John 260, Joseph
  166, Milly Ann
  142
Nolls, Carr Bailey
  176
Norfolk, Thomas 82
Norman, Heney 26,
  John 249, Joseph
  29, Nancy 249,
  William 116,
  Wilson 26
Norris, A. C. 217,
  George H. 94,
  George Horten 57,
  James E. 185,
  Joseph 52, Liews
  8, Mary 52
North, Thomas 209,
  210
Northern, Betsy 19,
  Betty 19, Caty
  19, Elizabeth
  155, Jonathan 19,
  Mary E. 159,
  William 153, 159
Nosset, Joseph 54,
  76, 77, William
  54, 279
Nossett, Peter 193,
  William 193
Nott, Casper 231
Noun, Edward Emanuel
  234
Nowland, Mary 112,
  William 112
Null, Catharine
  106, David 205,
  Jacob 105, 106,
  122, Mary 205,
  Susannah 122

Nulton, Abraham
  260, 262,
  Alexander 200,
  Emily J. 262,
  John 128, Mary C.
  260
Nutt, Edward 27,
  73, 113, Elizabeth
  Ane 113, Ginny
  27, James 30,
  John 61, Mary 73
O Conner, John 147
O'Bannon, Andrew J.
  245
O'Conner, Dennis 87
O'Rear, Benjamin 90
Oare, Ann 6,
  Elizabeth 6
Oates, Daniel 258,
  Mahaley 276,
  Samuel 276, 284
Oatley, Mary 201
Oats, Catharine
  242, Eliza 216,
  Elizabeth 209,
  261, Harman 233,
  Jacob 73, 136,
  154, 200, 229, 242,
  244, 261, John
  100, 185, 263,
  Jonathan 261,
  Lorenzo 258,
  Margaret 229,
  Mary 100, 136,
  185, 244, Peter
  162, Susan 189,
  Susanna 229
OBoyle, Harriet
  223, James 153,
  Rhoda 153
OConner, Dennis 90,
  208, Jeremiah 46,
  78, John 160,
  161, Mary 46
Odell, Susan 253
OFerrall, John 242
Oferrell, Mary 88

Oferroll, Mary 88
Offord, William 266
Offutt, James W. 236, Nathl 114
Ogden, David 170, Eliza 226, John 234, Thomas C. 222, 237, Thomas L. 131
Ogelvee, George 5
Ogilvie, Margaret 35
Oglesbee, Isaiah 121, John 121
Oglesby, Eleanor 5, Elias 121, Isaiah 121, John 121
Ogleslbee, Isaiah 2
Oglevie, David 19
Oglisby, Aron 2
Oglisvie, Docia 8
Ohaver, John 88, 231, June 244, Marenda Jane 209, Timothy 104, 231
Oland, Anny 117
Oldacre, Henry 45, Isaac 123
OLeary, Daniel 249
Olever, Maria 99
Oliver, Daniel 138, Elie 120, Francis 197, James 123, Mandley 182, 183, Manley 179, Mason 123, 182, Matilda 123, Mildred 200, Nancy 8
Oller, Jacob 94, Peter 174
Olvie, Jane 64
Oran, Sarah 266
ORear, Benja 76, Benjamin 37, 128, Enoch 163, 170, George 130, 185, Jesse 90, 114,

ORear (continued) John 76, Louisa 170, Malinda 163, Nancy 76, Rebeccah 114, Susan 37
Orem, Aaron E. 216, 220, Elizabeth 216, Mason 212, William 169
Orendorf, Jesse 182
Orendorff, Sarah 179
Orenduph, John 144
Orier, Betsy 37, Jesse 37
Orme, Addison P. 249
Orndoff, William 276
Orndorf, Hannah 283, Harriet 234, Henry 202, 244, Isaac 283, John 88, 126, 130, Jonathan 202, Louisa C. 256, Mary 126, Mary Ann 161, Philip 92, Salomy 204, Samuel 161, William 130
Orndorff, Agnes 185, Ann 197, Benjamin 262, Catharine 196, Catharine Ann 247, David 195, Elisha F. 280, Hannah 78, 206, Harriet S. 275, Harrison 248, Isaac 179, 251, 252, Israel 267, 273, 277, James 195, Jesse 23, John 12, 142, 225, John W. 256,

Orndorff (continued)
Jonathan 116, 196, 197, Joseph 140, 247, 275, 279, Lucinda 267, Mahala 195, Mary Ann 262, Mary H. 277, Philip 12, Phineas 234, 241, 243, Priscilla 252, Rachel 142, 225, Rebecca 78, 151, 279, Samuel 38, 78, 151, 185, 198, 206, 259, William 34, 45, 267, 279
ORoark, Lafayette 286
Orr, Angeline 254, Martha 178, Mary 145, Sarah Jane 235, William 41
Orrick, Emily S. 244
Osborn, Acquilla 80, Adam W. 227, Aquilla 227, David 196, Elizabeth Ann 187, George 187, 252, 254, James 155, Margaret G. 252, Mary 196, Nancy 155, Richard 153
Osborne, Susan G. 254
Osbourn, James 10
Osbourne, Acquilla 73
Osburn, Abner 92, Alcinda 282, Catharine 236, Enos 156, George 236, Joshua 220
Osburne, David 62
Ott, William 199

Oubry, Henry 32, Mary 32
Ovelton, Gilbert 246
Overaker, Mary 1
Overall, Elias 246, 269, William C. 251
Overstake, Benjamin 6
Overton, Elizabeth 18
Owen, John W. 230, William 236
Owens, Anna 227, Catharine 222, Dorothy 237, Edward 181, Eli 261, Elizabeth 206, James 258, Jenny 24, John S. 231, Lucinda 252, Lucy 27, Mary 284, Nimrod 6, Scarlett 54, Taliver R. 236, Toliver 240, Toliver R. 215, 216, 252, William 256
Owgon, Martha 22
Ox, Daniel 36
Oysler, Polly 145
Ozbourne, Susannah H. 190
Pace, Sarah 58
Pack, Samuel C. 169
Page, Abby Byrd Nelson 138, Abinago 122, Ann W. 228, Elizabeth 17, Jane Byrd 94, John 102, 208, 210, John E. 193, 212, John W. 94, 218, Lucy G. 229, Mary Ann Mason

Page (continued)
128, Mary F. 210,
Mary Mann 208,
Mary W. 110,
Matthew 165,
Robert 94, Robert
P. 193, Sarah W.
108, 212, William
B. 108, 128,
William Byrd 110
Paget, Edmund 113,
Elizabeth 113
Pagett, Ann 257,
Araminta L. 197,
Catharine C. 153,
Edmund 153,
Edward 190,
Louisiana M. 244,
Washington F. 197,
224, 244
Pagget, Rebeccah
190
Paige, Thomas 5
Pain, Amelia A.
275, Travis 275
Painter, Abagail
80, Abraham 72,
Ann 229, Beula
171, Clarissa
179, Eliza 221,
Ephraim 246,
Isaac 19, 23, 33,
John 78, 102, 156,
229, Joseph 210,
Mahlon 179, Mary
286, Rachael 19,
Robert 102, 171,
188, Susana 188
Palmer, Daniel 168,
John 5, Joseph
182, 195, 215
Pangle, Ann E. 246,
Asherina 244,
Catharine 151,
David 90, 180,
Elizabeth 157,
Isaac N. 272,

Pangle (continued)
Jacob 95, 151,
244, 246, James
262, John 180,
Joseph 157, Vance
22
Pannill, Joseph 114
Panter, Mahlon 33
Parcel, Ruth 132
Parent, Hannah 74,
Samuel 65
Paricale, John 111
Parish, Catharine
Jane 246,
Christopher 245,
Emily 245, Joseph
73, 246, Maria
277, William 73,
112, 277
Parke, Samuel 187,
Uriah 145
Parker, Charles F.
258, Eliza 84,
John 3, Joseph
81, 236, Joseph B.
206, 261, Phebe S.
206, Rice 146,
Thomas 84,
William 165, 274
Parkins, Alfred
137, 254, David
12, Elizabeth 10,
Joseph 52, Mary
Ellen 254, Nathan
111, Susanah 52,
Sydney E. 254
Parkison, Nancy 41
Parlett, Catharine
J. 285, Catherine
254, David 178,
George S. 256,
Isaac T. 286,
John 93, 172, 215,
232, John Y. 260,
Joshua 82, Mary
Ann 232, Rachel
215, Rachel Ann

Parlett (continued)
274, Sarah 82
Parmer, Joseph 121
Parr, Henry 108
Parran, Nathaniel D. 204
Parrell, Ann 142, George 120, Jacob 16, John 99, Margaret 99
Parrish, William 73
Parrott, Catharine 115, Jacob 269, Joshua 115
Parsons, Catharine 183, Elizabeth Ann 243, Jonathan 205
Pascal, Madison H. 239
Paskell, Abraham 170, Cornelius 107
Pasmore, Joseph 100
Passmore, Joseph 9
Patch, Isaac 23, Jacob 74, 82, 84, Leah 82
Paton, Peggy 130
Patten, William 115
Patterson, John 205, 219, Lucinda 198
Patton, Arthelinda 226, Betsy 99, David 226, 272, Elizabeth 248, Jane 132, John 79, Martha 79
Patty, George 148, Martha 196, Mary 148
Paul, Henry 135
Paxson, Amos 5
Payne, Amos 238, Ann 65, Catharine 166, Elizabeth 190, George 186,

Payne (continued)
227, Isaac 77, 110, James 18, John 124, 141, Jonathan 98, Joseph 190, Joseph E. 259, Mary J. 227, Patty 98, Richard 284, Travis 279, William 56, 85
Paynter, John 215
Payton, Valentine 187
Peacemaker, Adam 226, Catharine 110
Peacock, Margaret 24
Peake, Elizabeth Ann 219, Henry 89, Oscar 151, William Oscar 219
Pear, Mary 243, Mary Catherine 273
Pearce, Catharine 25, James 130, Mary 13
Pearpoint, Evan 116
Pearry, Caleb H. 217
Pearse, Adam 119
Pearson, Alex 44, Anna 44, George 149, 183, James 161, Jemimah 161
Peasemaker, Jacob 128
Peasmaker, Abram 262, Adam 128, David 105, Jacob 105, 110, 274, William 274
Peaznaker, Philip 162
Peck, Ann 15, Benjamin 14, John

Peck (continued)
15, Joseph 32,
Saml 16, Samuel
C. 111
Peer, Philip 28
Peery, Ireson 240,
James 240
Peirce, Catharine
201, John 171,
Joseph 13, 66,
201, Paul 207
Peirson, Ruth 193
Pelter, Catharine
251, George 131,
246, 251, James
88, 227, Nancy
131, Nancy F.
246, Rebecca 227
Penabaker, Margaret
125, William 125
Pendergass, Vincent
48
Pendergast, Peter
152
Pendle, Edward 59
Pendleton, Thornton
P. 229
Pendor, Daniel 18
Penn, Hannah 282
Pennabaker, William
145
Pennybaker, Jacob
95, Joel 159,
Sarah 266,
William 167
Pepper, Arabella
75, William 210
Perkins, Eleanor 11
Perkizer, Michael
35, Polly 35
Perrill, Joseph 6,
Nancy 166, Ruth
6, Zebulon H. 234
Perry, Benjamin
274, Caleb H.
214, David 8,
Elijah H. 259,

Perry (continued)
Harriet 170,
Isabell 214,
James 276, John
7, John M. 252,
274, Joseph 46,
Laura 252,
Nicholas 124, 270,
Polly 108,
Richard 180,
Samuel 127,
Samuel W. 108,
154, Susan
217, Susan A.
270, Watson 227,
William 184, 213
Persley, Elizabeth
50, John 50
Person, George 204,
Susanna 204
Peter, Mary 287
Peters, Abner 152,
155, 169, 272,
Catharine 177,
Charles 132,
Delila E. 248,
Isaac 105, John
137, 260, John H.
273, Mary 58,
Mary Ann 278,
Peter 164, Sally
152, Sarah 105,
William 40, 216
Peterson, Easter
114, Elizabeth
10, John 10,
Kitty 267,
William 252
Petter, Margaret A.
232
Pettet, Mary B. 127
Pettit, George W.
127, Isaac H. 153
Petty, George 255,
John B. 215
Peyton, Elizabeth M.
233, Evan 147,

Peyton (continued)
J. 35, Jane 148,
John 37, 55, John
S. 166, Mary Howe
57, Valentine 87,
William 9, 148
Pflieger, Abraham T.
32
Phalen, Rebecca 149
Phelps, Elisha P.
219, Mary
Elizabeth 219,
Richard R. 201
Phetty, Philip 38
Philips, Catherine
10, 80, Isaac 59,
68, Jacob 26,
James 118,
Lucretia 68,
Philip 80
Phillips, Elizabeth
192, George 91,
Isaac 74, 192,
Israel 162, James
W. 219, Joshua
142, Sarah 102,
105, Thomas 162,
199, 249, William
102, 186
Phleager, Abraham
17, George 17
Phliegar, Michael
47
Picken, Margaret
53, Samuel 53
Pickeral, Catharine
284
Pickerel, Eliza
148, Jonathan 148
Pickerell, John H.
185, John Henson
111, Jonathan
133, Margaret Ann
133, Mary 185
Pickering, John 13,
34, 83, 115, Sarah
83, William 46,

Pickering (continued)
106, 108
Pickrell, James 84,
Samuel 208
Pickslar, Jacob 19,
Mary 19
Pidgeon, Isaac E.
273, Mary 186,
Rachel Ann 273
Pierce, Catharine
66, John 39, 109,
114, 205, Joseph
25, Michael 89,
179, Paul 196,
Rachel 142, Sarah
114
Pierpoint, Elizabeth
63, Joseph 63
Pifer, Daniel 272,
Elijah 271, John
260, John W. 274,
Mahaley 279
Pigeon, Isaac 113
Pilcher, Joshua 79
Pine, George 257,
Jacob 97, James
122, James M.
229, Mary M. 193,
Polly 18
Pingley, David 260,
Eliza 256, John
275
Pinkly, David 85
Piper, Abraham 86,
221, 268, Conrad
273, Elisha 123,
171, Eliza 221,
Elizabeth Ann 251,
George 223, Henry
37, Isaac 205,
Jacob 41, James
A. 255, John 69,
117, John M. 223,
John W. 223,
Jonathan 105,
Joseph 224,
Margaret Ann 225,

Piper (continued)
 Mary Lavinia 268,
 William 10
Pitcock, Alfred 250, Barnet 250, 262, 285, Barney 202, Bennett 249, David 166, Elizabeth 88, Harriett 276, Henry 264, John 57, 207, Lucy 228, Mary 251, Sarah 207, Sarah C. 285, Stephen 88
Pitman, Amelia S. 198, Amos 223, 273, Andrew 59, 72, 193, Elizabeth 72, John 64, 66, 101, 129, Joseph 188, Margaret 244, Philip 251, 287, Rachael C. 287, Salome M. 251, Sarah 273, Solomon 224
Place, Abraham 125, John 273, Mary 125, Unula 273
Plater, Thomas 171
Plum, Abraham 15
Plumb, Betsy 64, Casimer 35, Mary 35
Poe, John 47, 57
Poffenburger, George 106, John 122, 139, Sarah 139, Susannah 122
Poland, Emily C. 173, Emily S. 255, John 173
Polk, Mary Ann 249, Penelope Johnston 176, Susan C. K.

Polk (continued)
 M. 237
Pollard, Elijah 52, 82, 83, Joseph 35, Kitty T. 49, Nancy 109
Polock, Polly 41
Pomeroy, Alexander 188
Pool, Catharine 279, Eliza C. 212, Elizabeth 250, Joseph 24, 250, Martin 230, Mary Jane 258, Sarah 234, William 51
Poole, Elizabeth 37, Evelina C. 224, Glinda 65, John C. 83, Mary Jane 256, Peter 65, William 37
Pope, Conrad 256, Edmond 159, Eleanor 159, John W. 180, Margaret Ann 256
Popkins, Cravin 249, Debrah 249
Porter, Deborah 13, James M. 271, John C. 238
Postlethwait, Isaac 163
Poston, Samuel 14
Potts, Nathaniel 49, William 74
Powell, Alfred H. 37, 57, 114, Lucy 128, Lydia 27, Phebe 28, Robert 27
Powers, Aminy 22, Charles W. 280, Daniel 167, 269, Elizabeth 104,

Powers (continued)
  Frances 56, Jack 56, James 79, John 79
Poyles, Ann 63, 68, 76, Peggy 63, Polly 76, Sarah 68, William 63
Pratt, Ann 137
Preist, Lewis 80, Peter 65
Prepers, James 75
Price, Benjamin 19, Catharine 119, George 10, George E. 271, 274, Henrietta W. 271, John F. 64, Mary Ann 215, Michael 54, 177, Michal 189, Peter 119, Polly 24, Sarah 52, 100, William 58
Prichard, Elijah 52, Stephen 101
Priest, Peter 65
Prince, William 97
Printz, Henry 59, 127, Michael 52, Peter 161, 169
Pritchard, Elizabeth 145, 264, Howson 120, John 188, Margaret 242, Mary Ann 120, Mary C. 255, Rebecca 188, Stephen 255, Susan 133
Pritchet, Barnet 230
Pritchett, John 149, Nancy 230
Probasco, Ann 201, Christopher 103, 117, 129, George

Probasco (continued)
  40, Rinear 191
Proctor, Mahala 245
Puffenberger, Jacob 272, Margaret June 272
Puffinburger, John 203, Mary 204, Rose Anna 203
Pugh, Anna 95, Azariah 95, 109, David 165, 197, Eli 10, 59, 101, Elizabeth 209, Ellis 9, Hannaniah 57, Isaac 199, Jane 165, Jesse 10, 209, Jesse J. 226, John 53, 286, Joseph 13, Malachi 280, 284, Malin 61, 72, 90, Maria Jane 155, Mishael 24, Robert 13, 246, 250, Sarah 72, 109, Sarah Ann 197
Puller, Amos 123, Elizabeth 121, Fanny 130, James 182, Jane 128, John 188, Lester 121, 130, 181, 188, 190, Margaret 190, McFarlin 192, Nancy 167, Phillip 202
Pullin, George 12, Lester 128
Pully, Adam 43, 62
Pulse, Catherine 114, Elizabeth 113, George 107, 113
Pumphrey, John 143

Purcell, George 21,
    Mordecai 263
Purgelbaugh, George
    53, Margaret 53
Purkhiser, Elizabeth
    43, Samuel 43
Pursell, Hansford
    118
Purtlbaugh, Mary 62
Purtle, Nicholas 13
Purtlebaugh, Daniel
    150, Elizabeth
    15, George 253,
    278, Henry 142,
    Mahala J. 253,
    Mary 278
Purviance, James 11
Putty, Rebecca 210
Putz, John W. 287,
    Margaretta A. 287
Pyle, William 209
Quick, Laney 103,
    Martin 103, 124,
    Rachel 124
Race, Sarah 58
Racey, John 223,
    262, Maria 224,
    Noah 204, William
    78
Racy, John 78,
    Landon 255,
    William 233, 255
Radenour, Elizabeth
    7, John 7
Railsback, Thomas F.
    125
Raines, Richard
    128, Thomas 118
Rains, James 74
Rakestraw, Elizabeth
    62, John 62
Rales, William P.
    190
Ralph, John 119,
    Joseph 119
Ralston, John 27
Ramey, Abraham 27,

Ramey (continued)
    Asa 49, Caleb
    128, Catherine
    113, Daniel 149,
    Eady 79,
    Elizabeth 73,
    135, Frances 134,
    Isaac 35, 135,
    149, 163, 179, 193,
    Jefferson 258,
    Jesse 126, 128,
    John 27, 42, 63,
    134, 179, 235, 252,
    Lydia 27, Mary
    163, Nancy 193,
    Pressley 229,
    Samuel 27, Sarah
    128, 160, William
    79
Rams, Patrick 8
Ramsay, Mary 39
Ramsey, Abraham 151
Ramy, Isaac 18,
    John 27, 39, 52
Randall, Catharine
    251, George 167,
    168, 175, 253,
    Jane 168, John
    29, Robert P 88
Randell, Catharine
    230, George 181,
    Sarah Ann 230
Randle, Mary 10
Randolph, John 24,
    Lucy B. 194, Lucy
    Jane 232, Martha
    E. 241, Mary C.
    165, Nancy 123,
    Peyton 233,
    Philip G. 165,
    Robert C. 197,
    Robert L. 198,
    Susan G. 193,
    William B. 60
Randols, Richard
    179
Rankin, James 186,

Rankin (continued)
  Maria 219
Rannells, Samuel 19
Ransdell, John 136
Ransom, Samuel 249
Ransome, Charlotte 169
Rasey, Margaret J. 278, William 278
Rawyer, Sarah 91
Raynolds, Benedict 95, Betsy 23, Eliza 195, Frances C. 246, George 23, 147, 246, George H. 147, Hugh 254, John 139, Mary 208, Mary Jane 248, Nicholas 195, Thomas 117, 208, Thomas W. 130, 218
Rea, Allen 3, Ann R. 238, John 3, Joseph 3
Read, James 87, Samuel 39
Ready, John 203
Reager, Isaac M. 260, Michael 54
Reason, Caroline 258, James 242, Mary 242
Rector, Ann Maria 259, Frances 263, Henry P. 277, Mary M. 277, Nelson 263
Redd, Abner 100, Andrew 248, Ann I. 260, George 11, 78, 97, Hannah 163, James 150, 163, James H. 281, John 47, Mary E. 270,

Redd (continued)
  Meriam 97, Rachel 78, William H. 270
Redding, Delilah 101, Susannah 57
Reddon, Elizabeth 69
Redman, Augusta 156, Isaac 27, 39, James 26, John 64, Joseph 62, Margaret 71, Mary 62, Michael 71, Sally 62
Reed, Ann 15, 104, Ann R. 285, Ann T. 244, Casper 104, Catharine 199, Deborah 48, Elizabeth 174, Elizabeth Ann 178, Geo 41, 99, George 15, 48, 61, 103, 105, 169, 178, 271, George A. V. 238, 276, Jacob 125, James 41, 196, 199, James M. 275, Jeremiah 69, 109, John 5, 57, 81, 94, 161, 162, 168, 180, 190, 235, Levi 190, Margaret 25, 105, Martha 121, Michael H. 157, 199, 227, Nancy 146, 256, Rachael 26, Rachel 5, Rebecca 145, Robert W. 238, Thomas 6, 25, 26, 32, William 52, 121, 145, 172, 180, 196, William J.

Reed (continued)
245, 260
Reeder, Abel 21
Reedy, Mary F. 286
Rees, David 61,
157, Hannah 199,
Jacob 105, 121,
161, 199, 219,
Joseph 142, Lydia
105, Mary 9,
Rebecca 161,
Simon 222
Reese, Jacob 15,
Rachel 219
Regan, John 166,
Jonathan H. 166
Reid, George 46,
Hannah 48, James
40, John B. 117,
Nancy 40
Reigle, Jacob 165,
Susan 182
Reiley, Clarkey 20,
Geo 17, Hugh 20,
John 134
Reis, Rebecca 82
Reisler, John G. M.
T. 267
Relf, Eve 131,
Sarah 131
Relph, Catharine
58, Rosamond 67,
Thomas 58, 67
Remey, John 27
Remy, William 5
Renner, Catharine
253, Elizabeth
155, 264, Isaac
15, 155, 170, 224,
James 251, Joseph
191, Lucy 224,
Mary 250, Mary C.
258, Maudeline
57, Peter 116,
166, 224, 253, 264,
Samuel 181, Sarah
170

Reno, George 192
Respess, Machen C.
38
Retter, Stephen 86
Reveale, William 14
Reveil, William 75
Reverl, William 75
Reynard, Jackson
278, Peter 146
Reynolds, Catharine
168, Elizabeth
68, George 86,
Henry 96, Hugh
13, 168, John 3,
42, Martha W.
248, Sarah 190,
Stephen 9, Thomas
1, 104, William 9
Reynoldson, John S.
244
Rezin, Robert 63,
Sarah 63
Rhodes, Abraham 91,
255, Abraham H.
239, Abraham S.
216, Ann E. 239,
Barbara 233,
David 233, 249,
255, 273, Isaac
259, Isaac F.
173, Jacob 32,
69, 188, John
73, 145, John W.
280, Rehbecca 73,
Rhoda 145, Sarah
69, William 148
Rice, Andrew 30,
Edward 75,
Elizabeth 30,
George 92, Jacob
30, Louis G. 272,
Sara 17
Richard, Benjamin
119, Daniel 120,
123, Henry 34,
41, Henry P. 251,
Isaac 248, Jacob

Richard (continued)
235, 274, Joseph
210, Mary 235,
Rachel 34, Rachel
Ann 248
Richards, Alice Jane
170, Ann Jane
154, Benjamin 79,
109, Catharine
151, Catharine Ann
224, Eli 24,
Eliza C. 241,
Elizabeth 84,
Gershum 159,
Harriet A. 254,
Henrietta 207,
Henry 75, 78, 154,
248, 263, Isaac
168, 224, J. R.
182, Jacob 257,
James M. 224,
James R. 208, 223,
228, Jane 160,
Jemima D. 208,
John 19, 163,
Joseph P. 284,
Margaret E.
182, Martha 120,
Sarah 75, Sarah
Ann 257, Sarah
Jane 218,
Thompson 128,
Thompson H. 189
Richardson, Ann 27,
Edward 42, Emily
J. 229, Fanny
42, John 106,
229, John C. 266,
Marcus 136, Mary
3, Nancy 37,
Samuel 3, Susan
86, 221, William
86, 198
Rickets, Mary E.
196
Ricketts, John 159,
196

Ridd, Elizabeth 23
Riddle, Jeremiah 51
Ridenour, Christiana
89, Jacob P. 286,
Michael 89, Michl
53, Nancy 53
Rider, Joel R. 278
Ridgeway, Charity
95, John 25, 94,
Richard 176,
Sarah 94, Susanah
21, Tacy B. 180
Ridgway, Ann 167,
Clary 25,
Elizabeth 97,
Hannah C. 234,
Isaac 9, Jacob
144, Jonas 210,
Julia Ann 171,
Margaret 112,
Richard 95, 161,
234
Ridigs, John W. 285
Riding, Sarah E.
141
Ridings, Alice 226,
Edmund H. 256,
Edward B. 228,
Edwin 162, Edwin
B. 141, 188, 256,
George 228, James
147, 272, John
226, 261, John P.
180, 184, Peter F.
234, Thomas W.
264
Riely, Addison B.
238, Delitha 211,
Eliza 215,
Elizabeth Ann 177,
George 114, James
47, 154, 187,
James P. 177, 189,
194, 197, 198, 200,
238, 265, Jas. P.
191, 198, Luster
262, Martha 114,

Riely (continued)
  Mary 47, Thomas
  215
Riesen, Henry G. von
  282
Rigal, Azariah 193,
  Joseph 182
Rigden, James 114
Riggle, George 37,
  42, James 102,
  John 242, Joseph
  42, Nancy 102,
  Tiner 37
Right, Mary M. 268
Righter, John B.
  162
Rigway, Rebeccah
  113
Riley, Elisha 140,
  Franky 75, George
  78, 94, 164,
  Hannah 78, James
  47, 164, Jane 17,
  John 117, 130,
  Lewranny 94,
  Margaret 87,
  Matilda 162,
  Moses 211, 227,
  Partheany 167,
  Polly 26, Richard
  50, Spencer 209,
  Thomas 47,
  William 94
Rily, Moses 196
Rinehart, Abraham
  120, Charles 244,
  David 3, 240,
  245, Elizabeth
  173, Jacob 242,
  269, John 169,
  254, Mary 40,
  Mary Ann 240,
  Rachel 271,
  Rebecca 254,
  Sarah Ann 245
Rineheart, Sarah
  112

Ring, Michael 268
Rinker, Barbara
  181, Caspar 149,
  236, Casper 231,
  262, 268, 284,
  Catharine 191,
  Courtney Ann 236,
  Eliza 262,
  Elizabeth 138,
  Elizabeth Ann 236,
  Harriet 268,
  Isabella 231,
  Jacob 154, 168,
  181, 191, John G.
  241, Lamarian
  168, Nancy
  Caroline 284,
  Sarah 154, Sarah
  Jane 241, William
  100, 236, 241
Risler, George 120,
  John 109, 110,
  Sarah 110, Thomas
  113
Ritenour, Caty 28,
  Daniel 124, 162,
  Daniel B. 256,
  Elisha P. 274,
  Elizabeth 160,
  George 135, 160,
  197, Jos. S. 198,
  Joseph S. 187,
  Margret M. 274,
  Marian 256, Mary
  H. 197, Michael
  28, 81, 133,
  Michael E. 264,
  Polly 81, Sarah
  133, Susan 162,
  Susan Margaret
  267, William 172,
  219, 267
Ritter, Adam 228,
  271, 281, 283,
  Alfred 261, Alse
  281, Catharine
  237, Edward 275,

Ritter (continued)
  Eliza 224,
  Elizabeth 283,
  Elizabeth C. 285,
  Emily 223,
  Frederick 251,
  George H. 282,
  Henry 86, 195, 217, 223, 224,
  Jacob 157, 282,
  James 149, John 20, 188, 285,
  Julia Ann 271,
  Lydia 215,
  Margaret 171,
  Mary 228, Mary A. 195, Mary Jane 279, Matthias 205, Stephen 207, 215, Susan 240
Rivers, Christopher 245
Rizer, George 173
Roach, Catharine 157, James S. 163, Richard 1, Thomas 219, William 87
Roads, Jacob 71
Robenson, Wm 7
Roberts, Abraham 167, Andrew 252, James 44, Mary 167, Nathan 213, Philigathus 31, Priscilla 34, Sally 143
Robertson, James E. 177, Leonard 141, Lucinda 226, Mary 34, William M. 145
Robinson, Andrew 80, Anna 131, Archibald G. 127, Benjamin 110, Braxton 84,

Robinson (continued)
  Courtney 132,
  David 263, 276,
  Eliza 159, Garey 5, Gary 132, 159,
  Harrison 274,
  James 4, 30, 36, 110, 187, 199,
  Jane 30, John 7, 218, John C. 131, John T. 200, Katy 84,
  Lucinda 132, Mary 4, Moncure 223,
  Nancy 7,
  Priscilla 218,
  Rebecca 200,
  Susanna 4, Thomas 110, 134, 169, 274,
  Virlinda 200
Robison, Charles 22
Rockingbaugh, Jacob 172, Nancy 172
Rodes, David 133, 277, Elizabeth 159, 200, Henry 102, Henry S. 147, John 162, Lydia 162
Rodgers, Angelina W. 239, Balindy 206, Casper 105, Elizabeth 194, Hannah 127, Jacob 225, James 28, Robert 124, William S. 200, Zadok 90
Roe, Alexander 123, 234, Benjamin 113, Ebenezer 126, Hiram 284, 286, Matilda 234, Rebecca 263, Robert 263, 286, William 256
Roger, Daniel 48,

Roger (continued)
Rachel 48
Rogers, Agnes 20,
Ann 74, Casper
208, 234,
Catharine 20, 56,
62, Eleanor 62,
Esther B. 106,
Evan 36, 119, 246,
275, Even 109,
Fanny 49, Hannah
116, Isaac 155,
James 25, 87, 91,
170, 215, John
38, 119, 127, 139,
John W. 248, 272,
Joseph D. 264,
Levi 165, Mary
Jane 214, Owen
20, Rebecca
146, Rhoda 108,
Robert 18, 127,
Robert B. 139,
Samuel 38, 53, 69,
127, 132, 146, 198,
200, Sarah 139,
Sidney 36, Simon
21, Thomas 74,
75, 106, 189, 214,
William 49, 86,
146, 165, Zadock
180, Zedeck 52
Roland, Elizabeth
10, Gerold 32,
Sarah 32
Rolston, John 114,
Sarah 114
Romine, Abraham 26,
Addison 175, 183,
Eleanor 14,
Elijah 94, 130,
167, Ellener 123,
Emaline 208,
Emily Jane 183,
Esther 12, 62,
Hannah 26,
Henretta

Romine (continued)
118, Hierome 208,
Isaac 73, 76,
John 7, 8, 26, 43,
62, 126, Maria
126, Peter 14,
Rebeccah 123,
Reuben 94, 126
Ronimus, Andrew 38
Roper, George 16
Rose, James 23,
James E. B. 225,
John 27, Thomas
59, William A.
225
Rosebrough, John
160, Mary 160
Rosenberger,
Elizabeth Ann 266,
John 74, 117,
Mary M. 279,
William 251, 266
Rosenburger, Anthony
203, John 224
Rosinberger, John
76
Ross, Jane 225,
John 77, 100, 183,
Joseph 220, Mary
13, Rebecca 242,
Sarah 37, 183,
William 199, 225
Rosser, Nancy 54,
Nicholas 16, Thos
54
Rout, Rebeckah 65,
William 18
Rouzee, Reuben 248
Rowe, Rebecca 105
Rowland, Elizabeth
67, 110, Elvira
183, Juliann 211,
Leonard Gordon
215, Lucinda 272,
Martin 100, 151,
211, Mary 120,
Mary Eliza 216,

Rowland (continued)
Nancy 100,
Rebecca 67, Saml 226, 272, Samuel 60, 67, 110, 216, Sarah Ann 226, Thomas 10, William 215, William J. 236
Rowlands, Druscilla 7
Rowles, William 116
Rowzee, Elmira 208, Frances 175, Reuben 190
Rowzer, Edward 99, Frances 99
Rowzey, Mary 38, Reuben 38, William 17
Rowzy, Edward 127, Mary Ann 127
Roy, McCarty D. 145
Royen, Samuel 220
Royer, Ann 144, Martha A. 285, Mary 236, Samuel 256
Royston, Frances 198, Hannah 211, Mary 184, Mathew W. 258, Matthew 211, Peter 160, 184, Uriah 176
Roystone, Peter 33
Rozenberger, Isaac 172, Margaret 251, Ragina 252, William 252
Rozenburger, Asa 185, Margarot 154, Ragena 139, William 141
Rubb, Elieanor 38, John 38
Rubbel, Peter 257
Ruble, Abegail 142,

Ruble (continued)
Betsy 168,
Charlotte 252,
George 59, John 168, Phebe 255
Ruby, Charles 199
Rudolph, Elijah 255, George 4
Rummonds, Elizabeth 213, Thomas 213
Rush, Henry 145, 166, 174, Jane 23, Robert 52
Rusk, Ruth 52, Thomas M. 134, 167
Russall, David 107
Russell, Bennet 165, 193, 195, Elizabeth 228, Harriet 187, 219, Isaac 175, 249, James 12, 131, 228, James A. 246, 271, Jane 263, John 47, 164, 187, 212, Joseph 160, Lydia R. 232, Margaret 212, Mary 164, Mary E. 249, Matilda 248, Moses 30, 103, 130, 152, 204, Richard 69, Sarah Catharine 246, Thomas W. 268, William G. 222, Wm. G. 279
Rust, Ann 38, Ann Susan 198, Benedick 120, Benedict 77, Charles B. 241, Comfort M. 108, Elizabeth 110, Elizabeth F. 222, George 107,

Rust (continued)
  Hannah 70,
  Jeremiah 58, John 108, 156, 197, 198, 200, John B. 211, Letticia 77, Margaret 154, Maria 198, Marshall 156, Martha E. 156, Mary Elizabeth 242, Mathew 4, Matthew 77, 108, 110, 154, 211, Nancy 108, Nathan 198, Peter 38, 70, 110, 154, 222, Samuel 242, 286, Sarah 58, Thomas 89
Ruston, Isabella 248
Rutherford, Benjamin 11, 18, John 123, 191, John H. 274, 281, Polly 191
Rutter, Adam 105, Alcinda 267, Alfred 259, Catherine 115, Elizabeth 227, Frederick 262, George W. 230, Henry 63, 81, 115, 125, Jacob 109, John 20, 37, 52, 56, 104, 242, 280, John M. 245, 258, Lydia 99, Margaret 63, Margaret Jane 262, 280, Mary 14, Mathew 218, Matthas 212, Matthias 103, 214, Nancy 81, William 248

Ryan, Darby 38, Elizabeth 35, 154, George 140, Harrison 248, James 120, John 35, Laura 127, Mary Ann 158, Matilda 174, Polly 40, Priscilla 27, Samuel 140, 158, Sarah 38
Ryley, John 22
Ryne, Ann 277, 281
Saddler, Elizabeth 36, William 36
Sadler, Samuel 50
Sager, Jacob 55
Saintmyers, Eliza 220
Salyers, Reuben 120
Samp, Henry 94
Sample, Joseph 25, 145, 154, 169, Mary 154, Samuel 53, Susan 145
Sampsell, Nicholas 227
Sampson, Fanny 64, Joseph 64
Samsel, Elizabeth 37, John 37, John E. 225
Samsell, Ann 207, David 225, Henry 158, John 16
Sanders, Almon 10, Mary 113, Susan 286, William 171
Sandmiers, George N. 280
Sands, Anna 75, Catharine 39
Sandsberry, Milly 15, Verlinda 16, William 15
Sanford, John P 89,

Sanford (continued)
  Nancy 44
Sangster, Mary Ann
  269, Thomas S.
  237, 269
Sanks, John 107,
  Sarah 107,
  Zacharia 51
Sappington, John
  151
Sargeant, James 125
Sargent, Ann Maria
  236, George
  Washington 280,
  John S. 279, 281
Saunders, Dorotha
  124, Elizabeth
  181, 284, John 2,
  92, 129, 174, 201,
  Joseph S. 275,
  Phebe 89, Rhodie
  92, Sarah 121,
  William 284
Savage, George 23,
  47, Joseph 83,
  Mary E. 83, Sarah
  47
Saveley, Susanna 73
Saway, Nancy 38
Scaff, Elizabeth
  110, James 110
Scaggs, Sarah 87
Scanden, John 231
Scanland, Benjamin
  197
Scantz, Mary 116
Scarf, James 102,
  Jesse 68, Sarah
  112
Scarff, Ann B. 65,
  Eleanor 68,
  Elizabeth 56,
  James 56, Jane
  131, John 48, 65,
  68, 93, Mary 48,
  113, Nancy 154,
  Patty 16, Rebecca

Scarff (continued)
  93, William 113,
  123, 131, 154
Scell, Mary 17
Schaeffer, Danl 137
Schneider, George
  56
Schnider, Polly 56
Schofield, Henry 9
Schrack, George 108
Schreklingast,
  Daniel 9
Schultz, James 227
Schulz, John W. 286
Schwartz, Joseph
  268, 270, Mary Ann
  268
Scofiald, Harrison
  53
Scoggins, Turner 4
Scot, Jacob 5
Scott, Eleanor 126,
  Hannah 214, Isaac
  38, 79, 88, 132,
  Jacob 14, James
  15, 178, John
  168, Joseph 154,
  Joshua 132, Kitty
  14, Margaret 139,
  Mary 25, Moses
  62, 95, Nancy 25,
  Phebe 178, Polly
  79, Rachael 1,
  Samuel 126,
  Susanna 74,
  Tamzon H. 242
Scrivener, Elijah
  172, Eliza 190,
  Levi 255, Nancy
  118, 258, Vincent
  118, Vincent S.
  285
Scriviner, Benjamin
  139
Scrivner, Sarah A.
  284, Vincent S.
  284, William 113

Scrogan, Henrietta 130
Scrogans, Elizabeth 117
Scroggin, John 188, William 17
Scroggins, John 230
Scroghins, Polly 109
Scrogin, John 130, 220
Scrogins, Turner 138
Scrovins, William 48
Seabert, Adam 23, Christina 43, Jacob 43, Margaret 43, Rebecca 23
Seabright, Samuel S. 277
Seagle, Milly 8
Seagler, George 17
Seal, Amer 277, Caleb 25, 67, 68, Susanna 68
Seaver, Casper 11
Secrest, George 106, Henry 106
Secrist, Andrew 62, Elizabeth 67, George 6, 67, 71, Joseph 117, Mary 71
Seecrist, George 108, Sarah 108
Seelock, Samuel 188
Seemer, William 266, 286
Seever, Henry 36
Seevers, Casper 86, 123, Catherine 123, Emily R. 185, Geo. W. 221, George 40, Harriet 236,

Seevers (continued) Henry 159, James 139, Rebecca 138, Thos 202
Seibert, James W. 253, 274, Mary 28
Seifert, Eliza 206
Seile, James 72
Seilor, Peter 24
Seiver, Elizabeth F. 274, Sarah 251
Selby, Ralph 33
Self, Elizabeth 138, Fanny 98, Harris 102, John 82, 98, 138, Mary 118, Mishael 59, Nancy 82, Steward 189, William 82
Sellers, Baltzer 63
Senseney, Ann 147, Hannah 12, Jacob 194, 216, 283, John 22, 141, 147, John G. 182, Mary A. 283, Peter 12, 80
Senseny, Hanah 98, Jacob 162, 259, Peter 98
Sepenger, Lydia 119
Sergeant, Amos 133
Serrit, Ann 94
Setser, Hannah 208
Settle 11, Adam 79, Daniel 36, Elizabeth 79, Emily 223, Hugh 101, John 28, 45, 79, Larken 51, Lucinda 68, Margaret 79, Matilda 51, Strother 68, Tracy 45, Vincent 112, 186

Settlemire, Casper 71, Gasper 11, Mary 71, 78
Settlemyers, Huldah 160
Settlemyre, Elizabeth 56
Settles, John 69
Setzer, Catharine 218, Philip 97, 218
Severns, Edmund 90, 95, Hetty 95, Mary 90
Sevier, Caspar 53
Sewers, Casper 40
Sexsmith, Elizabeth 142, Matthew 142
Sexton, Charles 198, Gerrard 70, Joseph 27, 40, 103, 107, 139, Rachel 107, William C. 106
Seybold, Jesse 12
Shackelford, Amanda F. 226, Edmund 194, 214, Evelina O. 155, Joseph 34, 88, Nancy 88, Rose Ann 195, Samuel T. 155
Shackleford, Adelaid 214, Berthamia 55, Elizabeth 74, James 74, John 32, Joseph 55, Samuel 74
Shacklet, Alecy 222
Shacklett, George W. 241
Shade, Adam 236, 282, Christianna 282, Elizabeth 171, Jacob 128, 171, 181, 219, Jeremiah 261,

Shade (continued) John 236, 239, 277, Josiah 278, Mary 181, 278, Peter 79, 273, Sophia 282
Shades, Adam 87
Shadley, John 8
Shafer, John 119, 145
Shaffer, Rebecca 257
Shaffner, Barbara 155, Elizabeth 172, George 148, 155
Shalock, Nancy 140
Shambaugh, Abigal 119, Abraham 104, Benjamin 146, Catherine 260, Charles D. 223, 257, 272, Daniel 119, 260, Daniel C. 243, Eliza Ann 187, Hannah 6, Isaac 115, Jacob 177, 188, John 99, 165, 187, Jonas 174, Jonas H. 223, 227, Joseph 117, Margaret 6, 89, Mary Jane 223, Philip 6, 89, Rebecca 227, Thomas E. 257, 272
Shambeck, Jacob 91
Shambling, James 48
Shambough, Catharine 101, Daniel 101, Doratha 54, Jacob 83, John 58, 102, Joseph 101, Philip 54
Shammock, Charles 252

409

Shane, Andrew 269,
Andrew W. 215,
Barbara Ann 266,
Catharine 217,
John 148, 266,
Levi 221,
Margaret 191
Shank, Abraham 63,
Jona 43
Shanks, Mary 192
Shannon, Andrew A.
100, Nancy 45,
William 161
Shanon, John 29
Sharman, Jane 22,
John 22, Robert
144
Sharp, Spencer 3
Sharpless, Ann
Louisa 147
Shats, Daniel 151
Shaull, Henry F.
269
Shaver, Elizabeth
189, Jane 37,
John 146, Juliann
87, Martin 10
Shaw, Craven 114,
Oliver A. 172,
William 10
Shearer, Lewis V.
252, Philip 18
Shearman, Alice 35
Sheehon, William 30
Sheets, George 108
Sheetz, Elizabeth
52, George 52
Shehan, Hannah 122
Shehen, Elizabeth
122, William 122,
Wm 125
Shehin, Hannah 125
Shell, George 109,
Philip 172
Sheperd, Rebecca L.
285
Shephard, Elizabeth

Shephard (continued)
5, Richard 5
Shepheard, Thomas
120
Shepherd, Amanda F.
166, Amos 247,
Catharine 229,
Champ 229,
Charles L. 236,
David 81, Dolly
91, Emily 100,
Emily June 164,
Frances Amelia
210, Franklin
229, Hannah 51,
Henry H. 241,
Humphrey 150, 153,
James 233, John
J. 241, Jonah
126, Joseph
75, Juliet V.
282, Mariane 83,
Martha 76, 100,
125, Mary 269,
Moses 13,
Parkinson D.
185, Patsy 153,
Presley 51,
Rebecca 60,
Robert 166,
181, Sarah I.
236, Susan 246,
Thomas 60, 76, 88,
104, 161, William
100
Sheppard, Willoughby
241, Willoughby H.
242
Shepperd, Hannah 88
Sherea, Abraham 260
Sherer, William H.
259
Sherf, Elizabeth
128
Sherideen, Mary 172
Sherman, Charles W.
275, James 258,

Sherman (continued)
John 244, Levi 258
Sherran, James 86
Sherrard, Joseph 232, Sarah G. 84
Sherrick, Mary Ann 267, Philip 267
Sherriff, Benjamin 33
Shets, Alfred 284
Shewler, Cornelius 200
Shierly, Peter 158
Shiner, Elizabeth 234, Eve 11, George 142, John 63, 234, Mary 207, William 227, 237
Shinhoge, Isaac 227
Shinholt, John W. 285, Martin 284
Shinholtzer, Jacob 155
Shinholtzr, Peter 8
Ship, Charlotte 225, Edward G. 140, Eliza H. G. 140, Emily E. L. 209, Ewel 36, Ewill 36, Frances 178, James 122, John 178, 212, Lucy 36, Nancy 36
Shipe, Adam 132, Anne 96, Isaac 153, 214, 220, 260, Mary 17, 132, Robecca 112, 214, Rebeccah 95
Shipler, George 91, John 130, Martha 32, Mary 91, Susan 103
Shipman, Abigail 24

Shires, James 218
Shively, Daniel 266, Elijah 282, Jacob 74, 88, Peter 266
Shivers, John 229, Mary 54, Peggy Ann 231, Thomas 231
Shockey, Anna 178
Shockley, John 278
Shoe, Abraham 214, 225, Mary Ann 225
Shofner, Jacob 123
Shoop, Jacob 230
Shore, Thomas 48
Shores, Alfred 221, John 101, Sarah 84, 101, William 211
Short, Auny 28, George 28, James 12, 28, Thomas 39, 185
Shortness, Charles 179, Thomas 179
Showalter, Andrew 144, 157, Archibald 253, Catharine 157, Jacob 134, 136, 185, 212, Moses 203, Polly 134, Simon 236, Valentine 136, 236
Showalters, George 119
Showatter, Moses 204
Shrack, Jacob 192, Nancy 192
Shrade, Mary 72
Shreak, Mary 207
Shreck, Eliza 161, Jacob 189, 241, Mary 228, Susan C. 241

Shrimp, Jacob 243, William Jonas 233
Shriver, Samuel 195
Shroads, George W. 231
Shrock, Frederick S. 234
Shrode, Catharine 170
Shrout, Killion 256
Shryock, Emily Sophia 235, Frederick S. 235, James F. 280
Shuck, Jacob 242, Sarah 242
Shuler, Betsy 170, Catharine 218, Conrad 186, Cornelius 218, Debrah 229, Mary Ann 279, William 229, 235
Shuley, John 279
Shull, Abraham 10, 142, 149, 152, 156, 182, Anne Maria 61, Atwell 240, Catharine 149, Charlotte 107, Elijah 203, 225, 230, Henrietta 172, Henry 61, John 240, Jonathan 62, 197, Joseph 23, 38, 170, Joshua 107, 112, Kitty 112, Lewis 157, Maria 203, Mary 157, 163, Matilda 225, Michael 185, Polly 142, Rachel 156, Rebecca 152, 170, 197, Sarah 38, Thomas 163, William 235

Shultz, Benjamin 166, 253, Elizabeth 14, Jacob 25, John 251, Mary 239
Shumate, Elizabeth 159, James 198, Mary Ann 221, Thomas 230, Tilman 159, 221, 231, William 11
Shumbock, Charles 267
Shusher, Mary 73
Shut, George 131, 144, Mary Ann 131
Shuter, Mary 66
Shutt, Catharine 107, George 107
Shutts, Alfred 207, George 105, Henry 105, John 201, Peggy 105, William 190
Shutz, John 191, William 161
Shy, Mary C. 267
Shyrock, Charles E. 270
Sibert, Jane 265, Michael 265, Ruhamah 274, Susan 253
Sickafoose, George H. 210
Sickfort, George 165
Sidebottom, Elizabeth 213, Isaac 158, Joseph 66, Mary 164, Richard 213
Siders, Conrad 75, John 80, Kitty 75
Sigafuse, Jacob 79
Sigler, Mary 65

Silkwood, Solomon 48
Sill, Jane 18
Silver, Elizabeth 129, Francis 202, Gersham 156, Gershom 123, 129, James 13, 123, 129, 221, Lucy Ellen Sample 202, Rebeccah 123, Samuel 237, Sarah 143, Zepheniah 237
Silvers, Ann 189, George 112, Sarah 164, William 71
Simerall, Alexander 17
Simes, Margaret 66
Simington, William 132
Simmers, Ann 231
Simmons, Aaron 260, James B. 125, 242, 266, Jonathan 260, 267, Sarah 63, Silas 238, Susannah 9, William Powell 35, William T. 277
Simon, Abraham 78
Simonds, Barnett 134, Eleanor 134
Simons, James B. 159
Simpson, Alexander 150, Ann 60, Anne 79, Archibald M. 213, Cornelias 195, Elizabeth 116, Frances Ann 209, George 131, 158, 179, 216, James 3, 57, 87, 99, 183,

Simpson (continued) John 69, 99, 157, Lydy 112, Maria 183, Mary 19, Robert 117, Saml 200, Samuel 82, 141, Susannah 87, Theodore W. 234, William 60, Wm 196
Simrall, Alexander 17, James 58, William F. 45, William T 20
Simrell, Frances 6, James 6
Simson, John 19
Sinclair, James 97
Sine, Christy 245
Sines, Harmon 95
Singer, Joseph 28, Thomas 28
Singhase, Catherine 80, Christian 80
Singhass, Barbara Ann 259, Catherine S. 263, Christian 118, 248, 259, Geo. M. 216, George M. 185, Margaret Ann 216, Michael 86, Samuel 121, 263, Susan 118
Single, Nancy 96
Singleton, Elizabeth 77, Francis H. 214, James 43, Judith T. 214, Lucy P. 221, Maria Virginia 268, Washington G. 158, 251, 268
Sirbaugh, Aaron 261, Christena 194, David 218, Henry 278, 281,

Sirbaugh (continued)
  Jacob 194, 209,
  John 205, Mary
  Ann 261, Sarah
  Jane 281, Susan
  C. 278
Sivyers, George
  122, Mary 122
Skelding, John 1
Skelling, Margaret
  25
Skelton, Isaac 116
Skillman, Abraham
  183
Skinner, A. 107
Slack, Ann 179,
  Ephraim C. 198
Slagle, Eve 86,
  John 86
Slane, Jane 14,
  John 215, Thomas
  14
Slater, Edward 23,
  Water 41
Slighty, John 137
Slisher, Elizabeth
  185
Sloat, Rebecca Jane
  287
Sloate, John 287
Slonacker, Michael
  162
Slonaker,
  Christopher 172,
  James 266,
  Richard M. 254
Slone, Charleton
  203
Slonecker, Mary 162
Slonnaker, Christian
  73, Mary 73
Slownaker, George
  113
Sluser, Stuffle 38
Slusher, Frederick
  20, Fredk 6,
  Ingle 6, Savina

Slusher (continued)
  20
Slusser, Elisha 162
Smallwood, Alfred
  187, Ann 72,
  Barnett 182, Danl
  113, Delilah 170,
  Elijah 91, Elisha
  85, 124, 150,
  Ellzey 193, Elzey
  187, Griffin 127,
  Hanijah 137,
  Hebron 72, Israel
  155, James 35,
  71, 182, Jane
  193, John 231,
  Juliet Ann 216,
  Matilda 193,
  Vance 170
Smart, Joseph G.
  112, Mary 90,
  Thomas 90
Smedley, George
  211, Sarah 193
Smedly, Mary 84,
  William 84
Smilie, Alexander
  84
Smith, Alexander
  84, 119, Andrew
  44, Andrew K.
  218, Ann 11, 25,
  Anna 130, Arianne
  A. 154, Arthur
  5, Asy 66,
  Augustine 130,
  147, 164, Austin
  191, Barnett
  145, Bartholomew
  74, 169, Beady 6,
  Benjamin 107, 177,
  210, Bernard 175,
  Braxton D. 272,
  Casper 26,
  Catharine 31, 102,
  169, Charles 52,
  84, 96, Christian

414

Smith (continued)
148, 153,
Christopher 170,
177, Conrad 105,
Daniel 66, David
11, 43, 120, Dilly
59, Edmund 134,
Edward 1, 37, 176,
Eli 30, 186, 230,
Elijah 238,
Elisha 46, Eliza
176, Eliza B. 80,
Elizabeth 9, 21,
79, 130, 139, 144,
173, Elizabeth H.
190, Emily 218,
Emily A. C. 268,
Evelina 280,
Fannah 65,
Frances 202,
Francis L. 222,
George 8, 100,
108, 134, 136, 137,
140, 152, 164, 171,
194, 202, 221, 223,
George H. 246,
254, Hannah 108,
115, 193, 220,
Harriet B. 42,
Helena 198, Henry
204, 222, Horace
P. 225, Isaac
135, Isaac W.
278, J. Philip
275, Jabez 63, 95,
Jacob 135, 144,
James 9, 32, 82,
84, 117, 153, 183,
193, 194, 227,
232, 239, 244,
James G. 280,
James H. 159, 161,
James M. 281,
James Z. 248,
Jane 84, 203, 230,
Jaquelina H. 108,
Jeremiah 32,

Smith (continued)
Jeremiah G. 257,
Job 49, John 14,
28, 48, 62, 67, 79,
91, 109, 148, 155,
163, 166, 169, 170,
173, 189, 217, 222,
243, John A. 40,
45, 286, John B.
D. 191, 233, John
L. 118, John P.
109, John S. 163,
220, John W. 272,
Jonathan 3, 59,
98, 134, 200, 235,
248, 252, 266, 278,
Joseph 39, 43, 68,
79, 134, 146, 147,
185, Joseph D.
52, Judith 44,
Kidd 9, Kide 9,
Kirby 74, Knight
G. 197, Levi
121, Lewis 270,
280, Lewis A. 89,
109, 156, 193, 211,
Lewis R. 286,
Louisa 194,
Margaret 9, 128,
239, Maria 29,
Martin 37, 183,
Mary 1, 6, 32, 74,
105, 121, 140, 150,
155, Mary A. 270,
Mary Louisa 235,
Matthew 250,
Matthias 119,
Michael 59, 160,
184, Michel 203,
Milton 172, Molly
74, Patrick 150,
186, Philip 51,
138, 279, Rachael
29, Rachel 192,
Rebecca 52, 99,
Rebecca J. 252,
Robert 9, 27, 71,

Smith (continued)
115, 170, 192, 229,
Samuel 25, 98,
171, Sarah 1,
65-67, 140, 251,
Sebastian 272,
Sidney 126, 138,
Susan 183,
Suzannah 122,
Thomas 79, 117,
Thomas J. 280,
Timothy 98,
Treadwell 163,
183, 189, Tredwell
104, William 45,
110, 142, 146, 164,
168
Smithey, Richard
208, 233
Smithy, Mahala Jane
233
Smoke, Hannah 197,
Henry 137, 197,
John 154, 170,
205, 276, Joseph
S. 271, Revertah
A. 276, Sarah C.
263
Smoot, John 244,
Lewis 84, Walter
B. 181
Smoote, James 5
Smoots, Sarah 110
Snap, Elijah 136,
161, Magdalene
136, Rachel 136,
Sarah 171
Snapp, Adam 124,
Amanda E. 255,
Catharine 41, 56,
76, 255, Catharine
N. 242, Christena
105, 196, Dianna
238, Edward B.
224, Elijah 131,
136, Elisha 223,
Elizabeth 123,

Snapp (continued)
131, 248, Ephraim
226, George 41,
57, 69, Harriet
233, Harrison
280, Henry 196,
243, 253, 258,
Henry W. 258,
Jacob 56, 70, 123,
Jacob H. 276,
Jacob R. 217,
John 25, 89, 212,
230, 242, 264,
John H. 255, John
W. 189, Joseph
50, 76, 93, 136,
178, Laurence 56,
Leah 70, Madlin
93, Margaret 69,
Mary 25, Mary Ann
124, Mary
Elizabeth 212,
Rachel 253,
Samuel 105, 113,
Soloma 50
Snickers, Ed 1,
Mary 92, William
4
Snider, Ana 201,
George 201,
George W. 238,
258, Henry 32,
John 279, Mary
168
Snipe, Catharine
101
Snively, Christian
271, Elizabeth
271
Snodgrass, James 6
Snurr, Martin 169
Snyder, Catharine
162, Catherine
270, Conrad 69,
Daniel 212, Eli
A. 154, Elia
144, 169,

Snyder (continued)
  Elizabeth 13,
  Eve 90, George
  40, 162, Henry 9,
  13, Isabella 89,
  Jacob 63, 90, 98,
  99, 114, 147, 150,
  158, John 126,
  134, 136, 140, 144,
  145, 154, 185,
  John D. 167,
  Judith 69,
  Lydia 99, Mary
  9, 147, Newton W.
  278, Pernina 177,
  Philip 134,
  Samuel G. 89,
  Susan 203, 218,
  William 118, 234
Sole, Joseph 144
Sollars, William R.
  247
Somerville, George
  W. 218
Sommers, William
  109
Sommerville, George
  7, Will 15
Somsell, Catharine
  12
Sonanstone, Joseph
  53
Sonner, Philip 36,
  William 243
Sork, Matthias 15,
  Susanna 15
Southard, John 43,
  Peyton 145,
  Robert 37,
  Sebastian 37,
  William 43
Southward, John 61,
  Sarah 61
Sowers, Ann 42,
  Catharine 96,
  Catharine D. 167,
  Daniel 156, 205,

Sowers (continued)
  Daniel W. 206,
  Eliza Ann 199,
  Eliza I. 200,
  Fielding 85,
  Fielding L. 205,
  George K. 174,
  Jacob 42, 65,
  James 75, 212,
  James H. 194, 200,
  Jane 60, John
  60, 96, John C.
  41, 42, John W.
  212, Louisa C.
  205, Margaret 65,
  Mary 41, Mary V.
  208, Sarah 115,
  Sydney 111,
  William 124
Sowur, James H. 84
Spaid, Enos 190,
  197, John 75
Spangler, Joseph
  113, Margaret
  250, Solomon P.
  203
Sparks, Elijah 7
Sparrow, John 238,
  Mary 238
Spayth, Henry G.
  105
Spear, Peter 10
Spears, Nancy 64,
  Robert 64
Specknale, Julia Ann
  222
Speers, Hannah 22,
  Peter 22
Spence, James 95,
  John 39
Spencer, Eliza 202,
  Elizabeth 96,
  John 97, Miller
  36, Nicholas 134,
  Rachel 92,
  Richard 20,
  Rosetta 249,

Spencer (continued)
    Sarah 254,
    William 212
Spengler, Amos 211,
    John 212, Philip
    C. 182, Samuel
    166
Sperry, Amanda C.
    269, Ann 53,
    Barbery Ann 248,
    Elizabeth 144,
    Jacob 99, 118,
    Joseph 146, Mary
    118, Peggy 111,
    Peter 8, 111, 169,
    188, 199, Peter E.
    152, Peter G.
    250, Samuel 239,
    264, Scotia Anna
    250, Thomas 269
Spesard, David S.
    240
Spicknale, Clement
    222
Spicknall, Bazel
    115, Bazil 97,
    Clement 178, 192,
    Eliza 192,
    Elizabeth 60,
    John S. 97,
    Leonard 60
Spicknell, Elizabeth
    A. 283, Leonard
    110
Spiers, Peter 16
Spignall, Elizabeth
    116, John 116
Spikenall, Basil
    59, Clement 59
Spiker, Peter 240
Spillman, James
    102, Leah 149,
    Mary 102
Spilman, Catherine
    112, Elizabeth
    279, Jacob 112,
    138, Joseph 147,

Spilman (continued)
    149, 279, Magdalen
    138
Spinder, Mary 30,
    William 30
Spoon, Peter 61
Spore, Henry 73,
    John 73
Spots, Jacob 139,
    Joseph 175
Spotts, Jacob 151,
    Polly 156
Sprinkel, Henry 248
Sprint, Patrick 15
Sprout, Jane 235,
    John 224, Thomas
    19
Sproute, Margaret
    176
Spur, Mary 52
Spurr, John 52, 64,
    Richard 154,
    William 181
Spurrier, Arianna
    3, Elisha 3
St. Mire, George
    182
Stackhouse, James
    145
Stage, Ann 18,
    Elizabeth 55
Stallings, Abraham
    31, Hezekiah 39,
    Mary 77, Saml 37
Stallions, Thomas
    150
Stanbrough, Edmond
    204
Standford, James
    39, John 153,
    Margaret 17
Stanford, James 55,
    John 139, 156,
    Nancy 196, Nelson
    R. 196, Rebecca
    156, William 17
Stanley, Archelaus

Stanley (continued)
187, Joseph 250, Mary 187
Stark, Thomas H. 108
Starke, John 148
Starkey, Benjamin 226, Mary Jane 226
Starr, Henry 96
Stax, Reuben 133
Stear, James 60
Steavens, Celea 6, Joseph 6
Steel, Adam 97, 213, Barbary Ann 213, Catherine 47, Daniel 180, Florence 11, Isabell 242, Jane 91, John 10, 36, John W. 245, Joseph 129, Louisa 182, Mager 228, 257, Margaret 70, Mary 140, 265, Mary Elizabeth 268, Rachel 11, Sidney 140, Thomas 70, 112
Steele, Alla L. 219, Ann 10, Isabella I 87, James 219, John 64, Mager 279, Richard 8, Samuel 87
Steer, Grace 3, Isaac H. 254, Joseph 3, Mary Dinah 3
Steidley, James B. 219, Joseph 183, Solomon 183
Stellins, John 181
Step, Elizabeth 32,

Step (continued)
George 32
Stephens, A. T. F. 182, Alcy 208, Archibald 172, 216, Brian M. 140, 174, 206, 221, Bryan M. 118, 156, 232, Catharine 205, Deborah 233, Elennor 2, Elizabeth 68, 116, 169, George 153, 265, 268, George B. 264, Greenbury 208, Harriet 156, Henry 95, 155, 169, 170, Henry L. 276, John 57, 111, 150, 216, 233, John H. 257, Joseph 150, 197, 272, Margaret 272, Margaret C. 205, Margaret Jane 261, Mary 140, 155, Mary Ann 272, Mary Elizabeth 265, Permelia 221, Peter 52, 57, 68, 82, Polly 172, Rebecca H. 174, Rebeccah 23, Sarah 118, Tabitha 6
Stephenson, Elizabeth 27, Henry 110, Isabella 265, James W. 259, John 151, Mary C. 234, Robert 236, William 171, Wm 112
Sterlings, Hutcheson 16, Jane 16

Sterrett, Priscella
  92
Stevens, Amanda Jane
  206, Elizabeth E.
  261, John 128,
  Lewis 70, Martin
  206, Sarah 206
Steward, George 20,
  Georgianna 280,
  Mary Ann 224,
  Sarah 20, Thomas
  96
Stewart, Alexander
  29, Alexina 278,
  Elias 278, James
  42, 63, 107, John
  136, Margaret
  211, Mary 150,
  154, Moses 167,
  Phebe 99, Samuel
  150, Thomas 42,
  99, 216, William
  12, 33, 154
Stickel, Moses 211,
  Simon 199, 232
Stickle, George
  142, 146, Henry
  146, Joseph 230,
  Mary 230
Stickler, Abraham
  97
Stickles, Daniel
  153
Stickley, Abraham
  151, 241, Anna
  151, James 225,
  John 201, Joseph
  18, Moses 218,
  Philip 197,
  Sophia 199,
  Tobias 33
Stidley, Mary 84,
  Robert 19
Stidman, David 180
Stiele, James 155
Stiger, Henry 46
Stiggers, Mary 84,

Stiggers (continued)
  Nancy 84
Stigler, Catherine
  46, Elizabeth 73,
  John 46, 73
Stigley, Robert 19
Stillings, James
  182
Stillions, Lemuel
  214, Maria 142,
  Newman 142
Stillman, Isaac 254
Stimmel, John 260,
  Lucy 181, Maria
  282, William 255
Stine, Benjamin
  126, 243, Henry
  259, Isaac 283,
  Samuel 283
Stip, John 116
Stipe, Avery 260,
  Catherine 148,
  Christian 49, 89,
  David 222,
  Elizabeth 222,
  257, Francis A.
  232, George 35,
  40, 141, 264,
  Henry 125, 148,
  244, John 164,
  Mary 60, Nancy
  125, Ona 264,
  Rebeca 253,
  Rosanna 197,
  Samuel 211, 239,
  Selina 164
Stipes, George E.
  277
Stipp, John 62
Stoat, Henry 233
Stockslager, Philip
  211
Stoker, Vina 94
Stokes, Elizabeth
  108, Frances 209,
  Hannah 133,
  Hannah A. 264,

Stokes (continued)
John 103, Samuel 11, 133, William 207, 228
Stone, Catharine 51, Charity 78, Elizabeth 158, Ferdinand 186, Katey 18, Lewis 18, 78, 86, Margaret 78, Marshall 27, Mary 18, Mary C. 173, Peggy 108, Philip 72, 114, 173, 184, Rebecca 184, Susanna 15, Thomas 158, 172, 179
Stonebrook, Catharine 35
Stoner, Elizabeth 84
Stonestreat, Betsy 206, Saml 206, Samuel 211
Stonestreet, Edward 224, Elizabeth 111, George W. 181, Joseph 198, Mary 198
Stonesypher, Sally 176
Stotlar, Henry 241
Stotler, Joseph 282, Peter 231
Stover, John 222
Straderman, Abner 236
Strange, Sarah 242
Strattan, Seth 4
Stratton, Seth 4, 19
Strawbridge, Sarah 221
Strawderman, Abner 262, Benjamin

Strawderman (continued)
273, Perlina 273
Street, Elizabeth 170
Streight, Margaret 227
Streit, Ann 264, Catharine 216, Charles 55, Emily Susan 189, George 205, 216, 218, 227, Henry B. 225, 231, Jane 257, John W. 276, Mary Ann 227, Philip B. 182, Rosanna 11, Sarah 234, Susan 240, William H. 257
Stribling, Ann 108, Ann T. 235, Bushrod 122, Bushrod T. 121, Catharine M. 235, Francis 93, 108, 159, John 42, John W. 281, Margaret Perry 159, Mary 93, Mary E. 271, Sarah 42, Sigismund 141, Thomas 159
Stricker, Henry 62, John 134
Stricklin, Sarah 15, William 196
Strickling, Fanny 161, Henry 74, John 37, 229, Joseph 105, 125, 161, Mary 190
Stricklyn, John 201, Sarah 201
Strider, Henry 225, John 77, Mary

421

Strider (continued) 225
Striger, Sarah 47
Striker, Betsey 179, Henry 179, 240, James 277, Sidney Ann 240
Stringfellow, George 69
Strobridge, Samuel 277
Strodner, Adam 94
Strodurman, Christina 106
Strosnider, Adam 16, 209, Casper 16, Catharine 23, Isaac 87, Mordecai 242
Strother, Anthony 143, Charles 127, Delia 144, Elizabeth 126, Enoch 126, 144, 152, 197, George 204, James 3, 71, John 125, 202, 280, John N. 245, Mary 71, Susan 152, William 100, 217
Strowbridge, Isaac 239, Othey 239
Strowderman, Catherine 143
Strupe, William 39
Stuart, John 236, Susannah 42
Stubblefield, Beverely 92, John L. 64, Priscilla 92, William T. 104, 121
Stump, Abraham 89, Benjamin 200, Daniel 31, 78, David 94, Eliza

Stump (continued) 200, Elizabeth 63, 132, George 100, John 6, Joseph 31, 78, Lewis 6, 82, Mary 5, 121, 133, Michael 222, Samuel 224
Sturman, Elliot W. 233
Suddeth, Susanna 9
Sugars, Elizabeth 19
Sullivan, Henry 157, 175, 197, James 28, Lewis 151, Margaret 175, Sarah 157
Sumer, William 254
Summers, Peter 254, Thomas S. 95
Sumption, Charles 217, Charlotte 160, Elizabeth 260, Jacob 260, John 175, Mary Ann 185, Thomas 26, William 188
Supinger, Abraham 157
Suter, John 79, 120, William 66
Sutherland, Jane 145, John 68, 145
Sutor, John 28, Margery Forguson 28
Suttle, Sarah 220
Sutton, Richard 87
Suverby, Martin 75
Swallom, Elizabeth 96, Henry 112, 163, 164, Joseph 96
Swaltz, James 266
Swann, Eli W. 281,

Swann (continued)
  Henry 221,
  Margaret 284,
  Philip 186,
  William 144
Swany, Alexander 213
Swart, Mary 177,
  Notley 177,
  William 162, 177, 188
Swarts, Thersa W. 276
Swartz, Charles F. 263, Elizabeth Ann 270, James 276, John 111, 120, Mary 111, Phineas 10
Swatt, Elizabeth 99, John 99
Swatts, John 210, Samuel 208
Swattz, James 167
Swatz, Catharine 36, 229, Conrad 83, Elizabeth 120, George 125, 229, 231, Henry 138, John 129, Lacy Jane 279, Margaret 129, Rachel Ann 231
Swayne, Abner 28, Josiah 92, Lidia 28
Swearingen, Catharine S. 135, Elie 135, Isaac 70, John 47
Sweitzer, Henry 217, Jacob 173
Swhier, George 193, 207, 228, 257, Mary Ann 247
Swick, Phebe 146
Swiers, George 170

Swift, Elizabeth D. 265, Leroy W. 148, Richard 153
Swimley, Jacob 161, 177
Swingle, Benoni 251, 252, Rachel A. M. 252
Switz, Lewis 138
Switzer, Elizabeth 30, George 203, Jacob 30, 261, Lewis 74, Michael 11, Nancy Ann 253, Nancy C. 261, Rosena 196
Switzick, Jacob 155
Swope, John 55, Joseph 62, Mary 55
Sydnor, Ann 57, John 57, Mary Ellen 151, Richard M. 172, 199, Samuel 51, Samuel B. 116
Syfert, Philip 129
Sympson, James 87
Syphart, Polly 164
Sypher, Willson I. 210
Syphers, George 110, 117
Syphret, George 88, Nancy 88
Tabb, Jacob V. 185
Tabler, John T. 225
Taflinger, Philip 31
Taggart, Daniel 131
Tailor, Jesse 165
Tait, Adam 241, James 145, Wm 5
Taite, Polly 59
Talbott, Edward 96, Elenor 20, Eliza 96, Enoch 14,

Talbott (continued)
  Presly 27,
  William 20, 209
Taleyr, John 239
Taliaferro, William
  T. W. 182
Talor, John 96
Tambelin, Elizabeth
  61
Tancill, Cecilia
  285, James 285
Tanquary, Abagail
  220, Abraham 36,
  Benjamin 147, 166,
  227, James 48,
  91, 136, 163, 198,
  Lucinda 203, Mary
  Jane 220, Rachel
  177, Rebecca 213,
  Sarah 163, Walter
  126, 147, 177, 203,
  William 36
Tanquery, Walter 80
Tapp, Elizabeth
  113, Elizabeth Ann
  197, Frances 161,
  Lewis 113, 273,
  Mary 146, Mason
  H. 190, Samuel
  146, Susan E.
  286, William 211,
  William R. 207
Tarflinger,
  Catharine 64,
  Christopher 40,
  Jacob 18, 64
Tarr, Levi 110
Tate, Caleb 273,
  George H. 234,
  Joseph 87
Tatum, Ira 169
Tauquary, Walter
  179
Tavender, Unis 33
Tavener, Mary
  Elizabeth 270,
  Stacy J. 270

Tayler, Elizabeth
  171, Jesse 171,
  Julean 282
Taylor, Abraham 2,
  32, 54, Amos 14,
  Benjamin 16, 50,
  Bushrod 52, 117,
  121, 181, 183, 185,
  209, 229,
  Catharine 32, 96,
  101, 214, 242,
  Catharine G. 131,
  Catherine 32,
  Catherine P. 186,
  Charlotte B. R.
  223, Conrad 134,
  David 31, Eben
  42, Ebin 36,
  Edmund 1, Edward
  265, Elizabeth 4,
  49, 149, 152, 188,
  Elizabeth Ann 176,
  Emily B. 137,
  Frances A. 165,
  George 15, 32, 45,
  49, 202, 249, 265,
  282, Griffin 29,
  45, 79, 162,
  Griffin S. 229,
  Harriett 243,
  Henry 34, Hiram
  155, Hiram W.
  183, 231, 252, J.
  C. R. 217,
  Jacob 63, James
  59, 83, 111, 113,
  192, 234, James B.
  235, 243, 271,
  James L. 279, 284,
  James T. 241,
  Jesse 129, 135,
  176, 179, 188,
  John 8, 12, 15,
  26, 92, 149, 166,
  168, 183, 194, 216,
  223, 243, 274,
  John B. 183,

Taylor (continued)
John C. R. 223,
Jonathan 280,
Judith 140,
Juliat 188, Liddy
54, Louisa F.
176, Mandly 35,
49, 180, Manly
149, Maria 213,
234, Martha P.
183, Mary 79,
192, 196, Mary
A. 231, Mary Ann
172, 214, 265,
Mary Catherine
159, Mary
Margarett 23,
Mitchell 239,
Nicholas 69, 78,
101, Peter 211,
254, 274, Phebe G.
252, Polly 134,
Rachel 174,
Rawleigh 140,
Rebecca H. 257,
Richard 15,
Samuel 175, 176,
Sarah 14, 79, 83,
Sarah A. 229,
Sarah Ann 135,
215, Sarah E.
198, Smith 216,
Solomon 213,
Susan 180,
Susannah 129,
Thomas 144,
Walter 45,
Walters 24,
William 6,
16, 69, 92, 100,
114, 152, 173, 196,
281, William B.
257, William M.
267, Wilson L.
242
Teawalt, Abraham
138, Elizabeth

Teawalt (continued)
153, Peter 153
Tedford, John 54
Tellman, Jane 25
Temple, Jane 80
Templeman, Henry
51, John 24,
Nancy 24,
Nathaniel
144
Tennor, Polly 85
Tewalt, Abraham 87,
220, Catharine
217, Elizabeth
233, Henry 130,
John 72, John W.
287, Joseph 136,
220, 267, 282,
Leah 87, Rachel
255, Sarah 262
Tewault, Isaac 224,
John 163, Peter
9
Thacker, Isaac 72,
Sarah Ann Lucinda
187
Tharp, Elizabeth 42
Thatcher, Catharine
239, Evan 214,
239, 257, Mary
148, Mary M. 257,
Mildred I. 148,
Thomas 148
Thomas, Anne 10,
Darcus 15,
Elizabeth 25,
Emily R. 197,
George 21,
Grandison 132,
Hannah 10, Jacob
135, James 54,
John 13, Joseph
89, 133, 192,
Joshua H. 174,
177, Mary 54,
274, Mary W. 96,
Philip 55,

Thomas (continued)
  Phinehas 135,
  Rebecca 184,
  Sampson 25,
  Susannah 167,
  Townsend W. 155,
    226, William 132,
    161, 167, 184
Thomlin, Catharine
  11
Thompsn, Nancy 183
Thompson, Abel 56,
  107, Benjamin
  199, Eliza 251,
  Elizabeth 21, 38,
  41, French 193,
  Greenberry 170,
  Harrison 188,
  Jacob 13, James
  31, 47, 74, 151,
  James W. 273,
  John 38, 183, 191,
  236, Joseph 33,
  Lucinda 144, Lucy
  E. 193, Margaret
  47, 122, Mary 76,
  117, Mary Ann 62,
  Matilda 133,
  Milly 105,
  Presley 194,
  Robert 179,
  Samuel 21, 156,
  Sarah 97, 168,
  Scipio 137, Simon
  236, Susanna 151,
  William 97, 147,
  220, 238, William
  B. 235, William
  H. 251, William
  N. 211, William
  S. 204, Wm B.
  235
Thomson, Hannah 113
Thornaberry, Samuel
  77
Thornberg, Elizabeth
  32

Thornberry, Daniel
  12
Thornbrugh, Danl 32
Thornburg, William
  91
Thornburgh, John
  117, William 279
Thornton, Felix H.
  211, Francis 140,
  Howard 217
Thorp, Charles M.
  158
Throckmorton, Amelia
  96, Ann 12, John
  142, Maria 184,
  Robert 39, Thomas
  12, Warner 74
Thruston, Charles M.
  37, Chas B. 286,
  Elizabeth Mynn 7,
  Frances 3, George
  A. 286, Polly
  119, Sidney Ann
  37
Tibbs, Deseriah 133
Tidball, Alexander
  137, Alexander S.
  141, 175,
  Elizabeth M. H.
  286, Joseph 258,
  Josiah 229, T.
  Allen 92,
  Thomas 79, Thomas
  A. 77, 78, 102,
  189, 200, 204, 218,
  231, 232, 234, 239,
  254, 256, 257, 271,
  278, 280, 283, 287,
  Thomas Allen 100,
  104, 105, 112, 121,
  125, 131, 136, 140,
  148, 150, 154, 200,
  210, 211, 215, 221,
  229
Tiddon, John B. 61
Tidings, Julia Maria
  171

Tigner, Edward 120, 229, Polly 134, William 134
Tilden, Anna Bell 191, Asberry Ana 201, Cornelia 122, John B. 122, 191, Mary Ann Jane 99, Robert C. 84, 124
Tildon, Martha 61
Tiler, George 231
Tillett, John 182, Sally 182
Tilli, George 92
Tilly, Elizabeth 86, George 86
Tilman, George 36, 61, 138, Sarah 138
Timberlake, Alsey 141, David 13, 123, 157, 182, 190, 202, 213, Eliza 202, Elizabeth B. 152, Francis A. 239, Francis H. 177, James Wm. 245, Nancy 104, Richard M. 239, Richard M. L. 123, Richard M. S. 141, 182, Sarah 123, Stephen D. 239, Thomas 177, William 35, 109, 152
Timmens, Peter 64
Tinchman, Elizabeth 78
Tinson, William 132
Tippell, Abraham 248
Tipple, Abraham 227, Henry 63
Tipton, Jacob 170, John 190

Tobin, Isaac 204, Jane W. 203, John 284, Lucinda 204
Tole, Frederick 67
Tomblin, William 80
Tomlin, Peter 82, Phebe Ann 203
Touchstone, Benjamin 254, 278, Elizabeth 47, Elizabeth A. 238, Eveline 282, Juliet 261, Mary Caroline 278, Nancy J. 247, Rachel 83, Sampson 138, Sarah 254, William 47, 83, 247
Towers, Samuel 239
Townsend, Charlotte 99, George F. A. 110, 143, John 14, Sally 143
Tracy, Evrit 130
Tranary, Honor 69
Treige, Jane 57
Trembath, Richard 287
Tremble, Hannah 36
Trenary, Eliza 217, Hezekiah 159, 214, John 255, Jonas 237, 249, Manuel 164, Mary 107, Newton 167, Polly 73, Samuel 22, 69, 73, 92, Sarah Ann 153, Singleton 215, William 191
Trimble, Thomas 192
Triplet, James 8
Triplett, Danl M. 180, Edwin 250, Eliza 276,

Triplett (continued)
  Elizabeth 181,
  Enoch 183,
  Hedgmon 185,
  Isabella Amanda
  268, Jackson 276,
  Jane 132,
  Jeremiah 276, 285,
  John 133, 219,
  John K. 203, 268,
  Mary 158,
  Mildred 217, N.
  B. 217, Nathaniel
  B. 265, Nathl B.
  111, Reanah 219,
  William 132,
  William H. 191
Trisler, Catherine
  21, George 106,
  107, 121
Trotter, Catharine
  88, Hiram 241,
  Mary 46, Matthew
  88, Sarah 223,
  William 46, 76,
  223
Trout, David 128,
  Isaac 197, Jacob
  120, Mary 128,
  Rebecca 120
Trowbreidge, Jesse
  72
Trowbridge,
  Beltzhuel 242,
  David 16,
  Elizabeth 146,
  Joseph 228, Lydia
  242, William 200
Trumbath, Richard
  287
Trussel, Polly 137,
  William 73
Trussell, John 131,
  Thomas 208, 262,
  William 146
Tucker, Daniel 76,
  Hester 93, Nancy

Tucker (continued)
  39
Tuley, Belinda 127,
  Joseph 127, 135,
  Louzetta 157,
  Sarah G. 182,
  Thomas 127
Tumblin, Burkley
  204
Tupler, Jane S. 147
Turner, Addison
  234, Albert 197,
  Andrew 81,
  Augustus J. 265,
  Catherine D. 265,
  Clarissa 153,
  Edward 145,
  Elizabeth 130,
  Henry S. 137,
  Hezekiah 40, 45,
  James 178, 238,
  Jesse 173, John
  130, John G. 197,
  Lawrence 203,
  Mary 50, Mary Ann
  178, Nancy 124,
  Richard 9, 50, 54,
  Robert 80, 102,
  251, Samuel 115,
  Sarah 54, Susan
  40, 45, Thomas
  38, 158, William
  153, 277, Wilson
  183
Tuttle, Johnb 31
Tyler, Edmund 170,
  William 24
Tyson, Bazileial
  259, James E.
  273, Joshua 287
Ullery, Henry 75
Umbehouer, Abraham
  153
Umbenhower, John
  116
Umbenhuer, Rebecca
  160

Umpenhour, Peter
190, Susan 189
Umpenour, John 180,
Michael 207,
Umpenour 153
Umphs, Joseph H.
274, Mary Ann 274
Unbemhower, George
153
Underwood, Green
231, Joseph 80
Undrell, Deborah 4
Unger, John W. 253,
Nicholas 41, 261,
William 269
Usher, Susan 90
Utter, Mary 210,
William 133
Utterback, Rebeckah
188
Van Cleave, John
236
Van Landingham,
Benjamin 33
Vanacka, William H.
157
Vanarsdale, Andrew
M. 265
Vanaurt, John 27,
Peter 13
Vanbuskirk, Abraham
41, 50, Anna 41,
Elizabeth 50
Vance, Alex 287,
Alexander 105,
168, 215,
Alexandria 276,
Andrew 62, 66, 67,
198, 204, 220, 283,
Ann 29, Elizabeth
84, 197, 198,
James 20,
James D. 92, Jane
66, 204, Jas 19,
John 124, 233,
Leah 220, Mary
119, 271, Mary

Vance (continued)
Elizabeth 185,
Robert 21, Ruth
92, Saml 66,
Samuel 66, 206,
Samuel D. 185,
William 29, 93, 98
Vandel, John
Augustine 66
Vandiver, Jacob 74,
118
Vanhorn, Isaac L.
235, Ishmael 147,
John 39, 99,
Joseph 8, Lydia
212, Sarah Ann
176, William 74,
77, 103, William
H. 177
Vanhorne, William
92
Vanlandingham,
Lucinda 175,
William 28
Vanlangdinham,
Elizabeth 130,
George 130
Vanmeter, Catharine
93, Henry 93,
Van E. 208
Vanmetre, Jacob
209, William 145
Vannort, Isabella
146, Jacob 146,
Lucinda 191,
William 31
Vanort, Eleanor 14
Vanourt, Jacob 38
Vanskivers, David
160
Vaughan, Abraham
58, Alcinda 251,
Dolly 251, Oliver
H. 283, Stephen
51, 56, Thomas
56, Vincent 17,
58, 134

Vaughn, Elizabeth 133, Mary 138, Vincent 133, 138
Veach, Thomas 145
Venable, Catharine 70, John 132, Joseph 34, 66, 70, Margaret 124, Sarah 66
Venible, Elizabeth 119
Verta, Clarissa 144
Vickers, Charles 162, 167, Melinda 91, Tailiaferro 118, Thomas 91, 118
Victor, John 99, 122
Vincenheller, Jacob 281
Vincent, Catherine 131, Cornelius 39, 131, 147, 152, 183, Elizabeth 229, Jesse 79, John 165, 229, 247, Joseph 192, Lavenia 261, Sarah 147, William 155, 184
Violet, James 201
Violett, James 213, Margaret Ann 259, William 219
von Riesen, Henry G. 282, John 175, Juliet A. 175
VonReesen, Susan C. 239
VonReisen, Cornelia F. 239
Vowell, Samuel 10
Waddle, Julius C. 232
Wade, Daniel 63, 87, 283, Edward

Wade (continued) 46, Harrison 151, John 80, 145, Thomas 209
Waer, Mary 2
Waggener, Mary 240
Waggoner, Margaret 153, Richard 211
Waite, Maria A. 158, Obed 158
Walden, Elizabeth 15
Walker, Betsy 168, Isaac 202, James 16, Jeremiah G. 165, 175, Morris E. 284, Robert S. 245, Sally 48, Samuel 168, 196, 225, William 48
Wall, Ann 26, Catharine 94, George 94, John 29, John F. 201, Mariah S. 202, Mary 25, Richard 19, William 25, 26
Walleas, Nathaniel 11
Waller, Elijah 132, Mary Ann 252, Samuel 52, William 60
Wallers, Clara 60, Lawrence 225
Walls, James 121, Lucy N. 184, Mary 141
Waln, Elizabeth 178, Frances E. 213, Henry 98, Jesse 111, 166, 213, Joseph 134, Nancy 169, Samuel 98, Tacy 115, William 115, 195

Walter, Ann Maria
258, Henry G.
216, James 15,
John 52, 64,
Laurence 128,
Malinda 153,
Martha 225, Sarah
226, William 153,
William B. 180,
248, 258, William
L. 172, Zepheniah
K. 153
Walters, Charlotte
240, Elizabeth
107, Henry G.
252, John 2, 10,
107, John T. 82,
Laurence 240,
Lawrence 222,
Mary 222, Rebecca
82, Susannah 52,
Tobias 21, 32, 33,
48, Watt 107,
William 182, 229
Walton, John 127
Ward, Ann Elizabeth
244, Henry P.
177, 205, Joel
145, 244, Rachel
44, Sarah 33, 84,
Simeon 176, Thos
4
Warden, Ann 10,
Benjamin 191
Ware, Charles 50,
Isabella Ann 238,
Jacob 84, James
131, 141, 184, 202,
238, 258, Josiah
Wm. 178, Mary
184, Sarah E. T.
141
Warfel, Jacob 279
Warner, Godfrey 102
Warren, Nelly 145,
Preny 150,
William 52

Warrick, Robert 54
Washington, Amelia
Stith 176,
Fairfax 21, 204,
Frances 4, Henry
105, Herbert 204,
Horace 273,
Perrin 189,
Whiting 52
Wason, James 52
Wasson, Sarah 52
Waters, Walter 111
Watkins, Alexander
J. 249, Isham L.
108, Lucretia
224, Mary Ann
211, Nichs 17,
William 68, 224
Watson, Abraham 99,
207, 218, David
121, 251,
Elizabeth 99, 198,
Ephraim 230,
Evelian 218,
Francis 84,
Hannah 206, 211,
Henry 26, 99,
Isaac 157, 246,
James 16, 50, 85,
119, 179, John
55, 206, 210,
Joshua 99, 115,
Lurannah 26,
Lydia 200, Moses
62, 81, Moses P.
214, Priscilla
62, Rebecca Ann
206, Sarah 206,
Sinah 119,
Terissa 179,
Thomas 17, 167,
220, W. G. 224,
Walter 18, 50, 79,
154, William 119,
200
Watter, Sarah 128
Watters, Harriet

Watters (continued)
111, James 220
Wax, Henry 2,
Margaret 2
Waxwell, Margaret
72
Way, Abel 26,
Alice 26,
Elizabeth 200,
Fanny 166,
Frances 161,
James 128, 166,
177, 189, Mary
128, Mary Ann
211, Robertson
203, 210, 211,
Stephen 3, Thomas
L. 224
Wayde, Ann 209
Weakley, Catharine
53, William 53
Wear, Elizabeth 202
Weaver, Abraham 63,
Catharine 101,
104, Christian
117, David 99,
174, Elizabeth 7,
103, 125, 169,
Frances 7, Henry
108, 209, Jacob
79, 81, 86, 101,
103, 155, 160,
James 231, John
13, 15, 40, 89,
116, 125, 160, 169,
Leonard 6, 25,
Nancy 63, 79,
Polly 25, Rebecca
117, Thomas 83,
William 40,
William H. 257
Weavers, Rachell
165
Weavor, Elizabeth
18, Jacob 18
Webb, James 261
Webber, Benjamin

Webber (continued)
235, 246,
Elizabeth 266,
Samuel 247,
Solomon 246, 247,
Susan 189
Webster, Thomas F.
113
Weeden, Frances 171
Weekley, Elijah
142, 199
Weekly, Thomas 184
Weer, Isabella 61,
Joseph 2, 28, 61
Weir, James 237,
Rebecca 237
Welch, Dennis 98,
Lucy Ann 274,
Mary 135, Sarah
199, William 141
Welden, James 92,
Mary 92
Weldon, John B.
150, Samuel 43
Wellford, Lucy N.
197
Wells, Alfred 261,
John W. 201, Levi
285, Maria 261,
Mary Evelina 238,
Nancy 43, Richard
160, 168, 238
Welsh, Comfort 1,
Elizabeth 1, 100,
George 169, John
55, Mahala I.
237, Nancy 40,
Ruth 107, Sarah
A. 268, Thos 1
Wenkland, Elizabeth
6, Henry 6
Werr, Mary 28
Westbrook, William
85
Wetzel, Elizabeth
78, John 78, 88
Wetzell, Sarah 88

Wever, John 88,
 Mary 88
Whaley, James 76
Wharf, Ann 2
Wharton, Thomas 114
Wheat, Benoni 199,
 215, Joseph S.
 285
Wheately, John 103,
 Sarah 103
Wheatley, George
 186
Wheatly, Elizabeth
 140, Garland T.
 215
Wheeling, Catharine
 39
Whetsel, Christena
 124, Jacob 208,
 John 124
Whetsell, Jacob 222
Whetzel, Jacob 175
Whetzell, Charles
 112
Whissen, Alcinda
 243, Catharine
 70, Elizabeth
 262, Harriet 222,
 John 243, 262,
 John W. 220, 250,
 Joseph 50, 70, 82
Whissent, John 147,
 Joseph 88,
 Margaret 147
Whisson, John 237,
 251, Joseph 76,
 85, Mary 237
Whitacre, Annetta
 273, Aquilla 187,
 236, Asberry 263,
 Elisha 65, Eliza
 Ann 239,
 Elizabeth 10,
 Enoch 239, George
 125, 260, 274,
 Jane 274, Jonas
 125, 149, 215, 223,

Whitacre (continued)
 239, Joseph 54,
 Joshua 215,
 Letitia 177,
 Mercy 259, Nancy
 105, Phebe 236,
 Rachael 142,
 Rachel 164, 235,
 Robert R. 273,
 Ruth 164, 264,
 Susanna 223,
 Washington 216,
 Wilson 149, 259,
 264
Whitaker, Enoch
 239, Joshua 83,
 Sarah 83
White, Agnus 47,
 Asberina C. 278,
 Benjamin 174,
 Caroline M. 269,
 Catherine 32,
 Ceatta 223,
 Clemon 65, Daniel
 124, David 137,
 Edward 90,
 Elizabeth 86, 87,
 121, 175, 257,
 Elizabeth Ann 257,
 Emily 201, 281,
 Ezekiel 39,
 George 124, Goren
 184, Guran L.
 278, Hannah 176,
 Harriet 124,
 Henry 167, Isaac
 128, 148, 201, 212,
 233, 235, 257,
 Jacob 112, 174,
 249, 257, 276,
 James 156, 175,
 189, 282, James
 M. 282, James T.
 201, Jane 235,
 Jesse 70, 148,
 252, Jesse C.
 267, John 111,

White (continued)
129, 148, 163, 175, 277, John Y. 217, Jonathan 32, Joseph 9, 64, 123, 200, Judge 223, Kitty 109, Lucinda 201, Lydia 9, 191, Maria 33, Maria Jane 252, Mary 46, 123, 189, Mary E. 263, Mary Elizabeth 217, Mary Jane 249, Mary S. 267, Michael 86, 109, 115, 116, 151, Mordecai E. 257, Nancy 29, 93, 111, 214, Nathan 250, Phoebe 167, Rebecca Ann 276, Robert 21, Robert B. 148, Sarah 129, 137, 163, Susanna 144, Susannah 123, William 10, 11, 182, 201

Whitelock, William 99

Whiteman, Elizabeth 75, Henny 49, Jacob 75

Whiting, Emely 204, Frances 50, Francis B. 115, 229, Hannah 109, Hannah F. 189, Louisa 105

Whitlock, Lancelot 246

Whitloe, William G. 116

Whitson, Benjamin T. 272

Whittaker, Elizabeth 136, James 230

Whittingham, Joseph 108

Whittington, Elizabeth 109, Francis 238, James 161, John 219, Jonathan 34, Joseph 109, 217, Mary 248, Nancy 217, Robert 269, Susan 185, William 44, 161, 170

Whittlesey, Stephen 183

Whitzlar, Barbara 114, Susan 114

Wholihan, John 93, Margaret 93

Whollian, John 39, Mary 39

Whollihan, Elizabeth 150

Whykoff, Francis 190

Wiatt, Edward 117, Harrison L. 220

Wickersham, Abner 29, Catharine 36, Elizabeth 28, Enoch 64, Jonathan 113, Mary 32, Rebecca 4, William 4, 28, 32

Widdows, Catharine 228, Frances 269, Mildred B. 245, Robert 228, 245, Virginia 271

Widmire, George 188

Widows, Elizabeth Ann 201, Ellen 268, Robert 201

Wiear, Isaac 12

Wieland, Thomas 281
Wigginton, Elizabeth P. 117, George 184, James 124, 174, 189, Jane 144, John 184, Joseph 144, Lucy 189, Sarah B. 251, William 117, 225
Wilburn, Henson W. 247
Wilcox, Anna R. 249, Elizabeth 20, John 219, Mary 185, Thomas I. H. 246, Timothy 59, 181, 185, William E. 249, Winifred 181
Wildle, Samuel 161
Wiley, Cornelius 137, James 65, John 89, 138, Nancy 138, 139, Sarah 91, William 91
Wilfong, Barbara 33
Wilkerson, Malinda 150
Wilkeson, Lucinda 161, Sarah Ann 257
Wilkey, Frances 161, Mary Ann 132
Wilkin, Isabella Jane 161, Peggy 126, Rebecca 139, William 87, 161
Wilkins, Daniel 53
Wilkinson, Abel 98, 107, 112, John W. 161, 166
Wilkison, James 5, Job 5, John 5
Willcox, Timothy

Willcox (continued) 199, 202, 221
Willey, Achilles 198, 201, Alfred 230, Jacob 59, Mary 221, Susan 265, William 219, 221, 265 William 77, Jacob 142, James 188, Rebecca 168
Williamham, George 20, Milley 20
Williams, Addison 226, Alfred 262, Allen 156, 224, Ann E. 204, Anna 45, Barnett 3, Benjamin 67, 127, 232, 274, Burr P. 255, Catharine 35, 97, Daneil Webb 83, Daniel 73, 142, David 47, Delilah 164, Ebenezer 168, Edward 161, Eleanor 12, Eleanor Amanda 188, Eleanor E 7, Elias 69, Elijah 251, Eliza 284, Elizabeth 64, 165, 173, 183, Elizabeth Jane 256, Enoch 16, Frances C. 147, Frances R. 215, George 100, George S. 244, Hannah 137, 269, Harriet 272, Harriet A. 274, Isaac 164, Jackson 97, Jacob 37, 77, 86, James 60, 154, Jane Ann

Williams (continued)
Matilda 127, Jane E. 66, 70, 106, Jared 127, 130, Jared I. 188, Jared J. 165, Joel 127, John 76, 130, 147, 158, 165, 204, 237, 256, 269, 275, 281, Leroy P. 164, Letticia 70, Levi 37, Louisiana 162, Lucy 81, Margaret 3, Martha W. 165, Mary 94, 106, 262, Mary Carson 141, Minna 110, Nancy 166, Noah 111, Otho L. 159, Philip 173, 177, 222, 271, 283, Polly 89, 125, Rachael 168, 210, Rachel R. 278, Ralph 72, Rebecca 281, Robert 58, Samuel 222, 262, 285, Sarah 81, 152, 222, 232, Sarah C. 283, Sidney T. 159, Stephen 281, Susanna 158, Susannah 73, William 17, 92, 144, 166, 168, 180, 183, 210, William H. 272, William W. 278, Wm C 7
Williamson, Abraham 49, 209, Carter 201, Joseph A. 208, Margaret 56, Ralph 56, 171, Thomas 154

Willingham, John 20, 225, 230, Obed 230, Ovid 225, William 194
Willington, John 34, Nancy 34, Sarah 77
Willis, James 15, 44, 84, Nancy 39, Rachel 39, Samuel 273
Willy, Margaret 132, William 132
Wilson, Alexander 258, Alice 126, Aquila 100, Aquilla 109, Armistead 126, Benjamin 130, 186, David W. 232, Eliza 147, 185, Elizabeth 225, 230, 236, George 100, Hanah 20, Harriet 136, Isabella 204, Jacob 86, 100, James 46, 54, 62, Jeremiah 20, John 132, 208, 216, 261, Julian J. 148, Juliet 190, Laban 229, Lewis F. 257, Margaret 185, Mary 3, 46, 81, 186, Mary A. 224, Mary Ann 109, Mary K. 168, Milly 112, Moses D. 251, Nathl 37, Priscilla 269, Rebecca 43, Richard 33, 81, Robert 71, Russell 141, Ruth 86, Saml 27,

Wilson (continued)
Samuel 150, Sarah 37, Smith 78, Stacy 100, Stacy M. 85, Thomas 27, 75, 86, 169, 213, 273, Thomas J. 224, Thomas M. 109, William 33, 82, 136, 168, 185, 190, 230, William A. 168, 233, William B. 251, William M. 212
Wimer, John 2
Windell, Harrison 260
Windle, Ann 161, Catharine 260, Eveline M. 219, Nicholas 252, William 164
Windsor, Anna 78, Elizabeth 160, George 102, Ignatius 108, Jonathan 157, 160, Margarite 157, Mary 102, Sarah 158, Thomas 78, William 169
Wine, James 11
Wines, James 109
Winfield, Elijah 102, Lydia 102
Winfree, Christophr 122
Wingfield, John 58, Samuel 254, William 48
Winkfield, Elijah 103
Winkoop, Thomas 167
Winn, Kitty 61, Mary 82, Rachel 61
Winpiglar, Joseph

Winpiglar (continued) 237
Winslow, Robert 234
Wintersmith, Frances E. 283
Wirel, Samuel 126
Wiscent, Henry 130, John 130, Rachel 130
Wise, Caroline 286, Michael 286
Wisecarver, Abraham 47, Christena 103, George 33, Henry 70, 103, 248, 258, Joseph 47, 235
Wissinger, George 99
Wisson, Elizabeth 90, John 90
Withero, Martha 64
Witheroe, William 49
Witherrow, Battack 181, John 32
Withers, Bernard 196, Evalina 152, James 156, William 180
Withrow, John 31, 85, 89
Witon, Nancy 167
Wittington, Jean 34
Wittmore, Minty 119
Wizer, Hannah 12, John 96
Wolery, Barbara 158, Jacob 158
Wolfe, Ann C. 201, Cornelius T. 273, George 51, 67, 144, 168, Isaac 130, Jacob 235, Lewis 11, Mary 51, 271, Nancy 67, Peter 1, 25,

Wolfe (continued) 232, Sarah Ann Rachel 232, Sarah Catharine 222, Solomin 131, Stofel 51, Tamson 206, William 206
Wood, Alexander 118, 159, 161, 184, 229, Algernon R. 272, Bennett 100, 120, 223, Catharine 211, Comfort 109, Edy 67, Elizabeth 161, Ellen S. 227, Hannah 103, Isaac 118, 159, 167, 246, 286, James 1, Jane 184, Jesse 150, John 211, Joseph 285, Joshua 101, Lewis 67, 136, Margaret Ann 271, Martha A. 263, Mary 159, Polly 120, Rebeccah 118, Robert 1, Robert W. 244, Sarah 116, Stofley 134, Susan 129, Thersa 246, Thomas 245, William 109, 112, 180, William K. 137, Willm 5
Woodard, Elizabeth 190, James 164, Susan 164
Woodcock, John S. 63
Woodford, John 84
Woodrow, Abraham 44, Isaac 23
Woods, John K. 270, John S. 277

Woodward, Benedict 39, Lethea 39, Stephen 93
Woolford, John 170
Wormeley, Arianna I. 94, Susan B. 140
Wormley, James 57, Jane Bowles 57, John Cruges 57, Mary 91, 236, Mary B. 91
Worthington, Robert 199, William C. 249
Wright, Alsy 136, Amanda 209, David 37, Elizabeth 82, 132, 241, George 67, 85, 143, Hannah 139, Jacob 221, James 92, 126, 174, Jane 67, 132, Jesse 27, 267, John 67, 68, 102, 130, 132, 172, 205, 212, 258, Jotham 132, Jothan 146, Louisa 146, Nancy 85, Nathan 134, 139, Phebe 67, Philip 91, Rachall 62, Rachel 143, Reed 61, Sidney 101, Susannah 88, Uriel 182, William 12, 22, 82, 172, 251
Wroe, Benjamin 36, 52, 105, 138, Catherine 138, Jane 36, Original 19, Sally S.C. 52, Thomas 58, William 52
Wrose, Mary Amanda

Wrose (continued) 217, Thomas 217
Wunder, Henry S. 267
Wyatt, Jane A. 220
Wykoff, Catherine I. 146, Cornelius 146, 185, Cornelius J. 255, Eliza 185
Wymer, Catharine 231
Wyndham, Thomas C. 115
Wynn, Cassandra 59, Robert 82
Yakeley, George 174, 202, Mary Ann 202
Yakely, Catharine 100, Elizabeth 93, John 93, 100, 178
Yakle, John 234
Yander, Eve 58
Yates, Benjamin G. 119, Jane 138, Lucy 183, Polly 190, Sarah 102, William 221, 230
Yeackley, George 207
Yeager, Catherine 118
Yeakle, Samuel S. 227
Yeakley, Ann 137, John 137, Susanna 207
Yeats, John 111, Pheba 111
Yeider, Elizabeth 271, John 271
Yeo, Catherine 111, John 101, 133, 168
Yew, Mical 208
Yoe, Elizabth 129,

Yoe (continued) John 96, Joshua 99, Mary 111, 129, Peter 71
Youally, Nancy 24
Young, Ann 161, Anthony 86, 93, 141, 161, Archibald 34, Betsy 92, Dolly 29, George 179, 270, Henry 90, Hezekiah 20, Isaiah 206, Jane 93, John 50, Lucy 11, Margaret 141, 143, 218, Mary 135, Nathan 67, Polley 86, Rachel Ann 270, Samuel 68, 92, Thomas 200
Zeiler, Elizabeth 158, John 185, Peter 158
Ziagler, Jacob 65
Zidglur, Jacob 17
Zieler, Peter W. 251, Sarah 251
Ziler, Reuben 169
Zirkle, William S. 286
Zombro, John 192

439

www.ingramcontent.com/pod-product-compliance
Lightning Source LLC
Chambersburg PA
CBHW071223230426
43668CB00011B/1275